Blockchain and Digital Twin for Smart Hospitals

Blockchain and Digital Twin for Smart Hospitals

Edited by

Tuan Anh Nguyen

Institute for Tropical Technology, Vietnam Academy of Science and Technology, Hanoi, Vietnam

ELSEVIER

Elsevier
Radarweg 29, PO Box 211, 1000 AE Amsterdam, Netherlands
125 London Wall, London EC2Y 5AS, United Kingdom
50 Hampshire Street, 5th Floor, Cambridge, MA 02139, United States

ISBN: 978-0-443-34226-4

For Information on all Elsevier publications
visit our website at https://www.elsevier.com/books-and-journals

Publisher: Mara Conner
Acquisitions Editor: Craig Smith
Editorial Project Manager: Ashi Jain
Production Project Manager: Prem Kumar Kaliamoorthi
Cover Designer: Mark Rogers

Typeset by MPS Limited, Chennai, India

Contents

List of contributors

Abidemi Emmanuel Adeniyi
Department of Computer Science, College of Computing and Communication Studies, Bowen University, Iwo, Nigeria

Shruti Aggarwal
Department of Computer Science and Engineering, Thapar Institute of Engineering and Technology, Patiala, Punjab, India

Sayed Sayeed Ahmad
School of Engineering and Computing, De Montfort University, Dubai, United Arab Emirates

Clinton Ohis Aigbavboa
CIDB Centre of Excellence and Sustainable Human Settlement and Construction Research Centre, Faculty of Engineering and the Built Environment, University of Johannesburg, Johannesburg, South Africa

Sameer Ali
Australian National University, Canberra, ACT, Australia

Norah Alsaeed
Department of Computer Science, The Applied College, King Khalid University, Abha, Saudi Arabia

Fadi Al-Turjman
Artificial Intelligence, Software, and Information Systems Engineering Departments, Research Center for AI and IoT, AI and Robotics Institute, Near East University, Mersin, Turkey

Syed Anas Ansar
Department of Computer Applications, Babu Banarasi Das University, Lucknow, Uttar Pradesh, India

Chimay Anumba
College of Design, Construction and Planning, University of Florida, FL, United States

Swati Arya
Department of Computer Applications, Babu Banarasi Das University, Lucknow, Uttar Pradesh, India

Shafique Ahmad Awan
Department of CS&IT, Benazir Bhutto Shaheed University, Karachi, Sindh, Pakistan

Joseph Bamidele Awotunde
Department of Computer Science, Faculty of Communication and Information Sciences, University of Ilorin, Ilorin, Kwara State,Nigeria

Durgananda Lahari Bhamidipaty
Department of Biotechnology, Manipal Institute of Technology, Manipal, Karnataka, India

K.D.P. Bhamidipaty
Department of Radiology, GIMSR, Visakhapatnam, Andhra Pradesh, India

Veenadhari Bhamidipaty
Department of Computer Science and Engineering, Gitam Institute of Technology, Visakhapatnam, Andhra Pradesh, India

Rajesh Botchu
Department of Musculoskeletal Radiology, Royal Orthopedic Hospital, Birmingham, United Kingdom

Jun Cai
Network Intelligence and Innovation Laboratory (NI2L), Department of Electrical and Computer Engineering, Concordia University, Montreal QC, Canada

Marco Cascella
Anesthesia and Pain Medicine, Department of Medicine, Surgery and Dentistry "Scuola Medica Salernitana", University of Salerno, Baronissi, Italy

Jiayuan Chen
College of Computer Science and Technology, Nanjing University of Aeronautics and Astronautics, Nanjing, Jiangsu, P.R. China

Xuhang Chen
Brain Physics Lab, The University of Cambridge, Cambridge, United Kingdom

Fah Choy Chia
Department of Surveying, Universiti Tunku Abdul Rahman, Bandar Sungai Long, Selangor, Malaysia

Yanning Dai
AI Initiative, KAUST, Thuwal, Saudi Arabia

Manoj Kumar Dixit
Computer Science and Engineering, NIT, Jamshedpur, Jharkhand, India

David Ojimaojo Ebiloma
CIDB Centre of Excellence and Sustainable Human Settlement and Construction Research Centre, Faculty of Engineering and the Built Environment, University of Johannesburg, Johannesburg, South Africa

Peace Busola Falola
Department of Computer Sciences, Faculty of Pure and Applied Sciences, Precious Cornerstone University, Ibadan, Nigeria

Shuo Gao
School of Instrumentation and Optoelectronic Engineering, Beihang University, Beijing, P.R. China

Santosh Gore
Sai Info Solution, Nashik, Maharashtra, India

Hossein Hassani
Research Institute of Energy Management and Planning, University of Tehran, Tehran, Iran

Benjamin Irani
Digital Team, CARE Denmark, Copenhagen, Denmark

Avinash P. Jadhao
Department of Computer Science & Engineering, DRGIT&R, Amravati, Maharashtra, India

Ankush Jain
Computer Science and Engineering, Netaji Subhas University of Technology, Delhi, India

Garima Jain
Computer Science and Business Systems, Noida Institute of Engineering and Technology, Uttar Pradesh, India

Allah Rakhio Junejo
Government College University, Hyderabad, Sindh, Pakistan

Atul B. Kathole
Department of Computer Engineering, Dr. D. Y. Patil Institute of Technology, Pune, Maharashtra, India

Saroj Koul
OP Jindal Global University, Haryana, India

Dilip Kumar
Computer Science and Engineering, NIT, Jamshedpur, Jharkhand, India

Shabnam Kumari
Department of Computer Science, Faculty of Science and Humanities, SRM Institute of Science and Technology, Chennai, Tamil Nadu, India

Shalini Kumari
Chitkara University Institute of Engineering and Technology, Chitkara University, Punjab, India

Cong Li
School of Instrumentation and Optoelectronic Engineering, Beihang University, Beijing, P.R. China

Zhonghai Li
Department of Orthopedics, First Affiliated Hospital of Dalian Medical University, Dalian, Liaoning Province, P.R. China

Bilal Manzoor
Department of Building and Real Estate, The Hong Kong Polytechnic University, Hung Hom, Hong Kong, P.R. China

Amit Sanjiv Mirge
Information Technology Department, Pimpri Chinchwad College of Engineering, Pune, Maharashtra, India

Vinaytosh Mishra
Gulf Medical University, Ajman, United Arab Emeritus

Federica Monaco
Anesthesia and Pain Medicine, ASL Napoli 1, Napoli, Italy

Farrukh Nadeem
Department of Information Systems, Faculty of Computing and Information Technology, King Abdulaziz University, Jeddah, Saudi Arabia

Vincent Omollo Nyangaresi
Jaramogi Oginga Odinga University of Science & Technology, Bondo, Kenya; Department of Applied Electronics, Saveetha School of Engineering, SIMATS, Chennai, Tamilnadu, India

Samuel D. Okegbile
Network Intelligence and Innovation Laboratory (NI2L), Department of Electrical and Computer Engineering, Concordia University, Montreal QC, Canada; School of Computing, University of the Fraser Valley, Abbotsford, BC, Canada

Ornella Piazza
Anesthesia and Pain Medicine, ASL Napoli 1, Napoli, Italy

Chander Prabha
Chitkara University Institute of Engineering and Technology, Chitkara University, Punjab, India

Partha Pratim Ray
Department of Computer Applications, Sikkim University, Gangtok, Sikkim, India

Saharsadat Reihaninia
Digital Team, CARE Denmark, Copenhagen, Denmark

Amna Riaz
Department of Oral and Maxillofacial Surgery, De'Montmorency College of Dentistry Punjab Dental Hospital, Lahore, Pakistan

Richa
Department of Computer Science & Engineering, BIT Mesra, Ranchi, Jharkhand, India

Muhammad Malook Rind
Sindh Madressatul Islam University, Karachi, Sindh, Pakistan

Fayaz S.M
Department of Biotechnology, Manipal Institute of Technology, Manipal, Karnataka, India

Ramiz Salama
Artificial Intelligence, Software, and Information Systems Engineering Departments, Research Center for AI and IoT, AI and Robotics Institute, Near East University, Mersin, Turkey

Anwar Ali Sathio
Department of CS&IT, Benazir Bhutto Shaheed University, Karachi, Sindh, Pakistan; Sindh Madressatul Islam University, Karachi, Sindh, Pakistan

Tianze Sun
Department of Orthopedics, First Affiliated Hospital of Dalian Medical University, Dalian, Liaoning Province, P.R. China

Chenyu Tang
Cambridge Graphene Centre, The University of Cambridge, Cambridge, United Kingdom

Ivan W. Taylor
Policy Dynamics Inc., Ontario, Canada

Amit Kumar Tyagi
Department of Fashion Technology, National Institute of Fashion Technology, New Delhi, Delhi, India

Malgorzata Witkowska-Zimny
Department of Human Anatomy, Medical University of Warsaw, Warsaw, Poland

Changyan Yi
College of Computer Science and Technology, Nanjing University of Aeronautics and Astronautics, Nanjing, Jiangsu, P.R. China

About the editor

Tuan Anh Nguyen is a Senior Principal Research Scientist at the Institute for Tropical Technology, Vietnam Academy of Science and Technology, Hanoi, Vietnam. He received a BS in physics from Hanoi University in 1992, a BS in economics from Hanoi National Economics University in 1997, and a PhD in chemistry from the Paris Diderot University, France, in 2003. He was a Visiting Scientist at Seoul National University, South Korea, in 2004, and the University of Wollongong, Australia, in 2005. He then worked as Postdoctoral Research Associate and Research Scientist at Montana State University, United States, in 2006–09. In 2012 he was appointed as the Head of the Microanalysis Department at the Institute for Tropical Technology. His research areas of interest include smart sensors, smart networks, smart hospitals, smart cities, complexiverse, and digital twins. He has edited more than 73 books for Elsevier, 12 books for CRC Press, 1 book for Springer, 1 book for RSC, and 2 books for IGI Global. He is the Editor-in-Chief of *Kenkyu Journal of Nanotechnology & Nanoscience*.

Foreword

Healthcare as we know it is undergoing a rapid and profound transformation. The use of artificial intelligence (AI), the Internet of Things (IoT) and wearables, the power of big data and analytics for healthcare management and improvement, and robotics will streamline healthcare delivery efficiencies. This will create a vast amount of data and will transform medical devices into commodities, along with patient-level data and the associated analytics providing both revenue and precision learning for patient-centric care. Blockchain will be the underlying infrastructure for the digital healthcare world of the future, and combined with advances in digital twin technology, it has the potential to move to new immersive worlds for the provision of healthcare.

Technology demands new approaches to knowledge generation and sharing. The old-school model of slow university-based research published in traditional scientific journals needs disruption. New knowledge is being created at an exponential rate all around the globe. This innovative book has rapidly assembled research and innovation from 125 contributors from 21 countries: India, Pakistan, China, Nigeria, Canada, United Kingdom, Turkey, United States, Italy, Greece, Iran, Ireland, Malaysia, South Africa, Denmark, Saudi Arabia, UAE, Poland, Australia, Vietnam, and Kenya.

It's an exciting time to watch innovation unfolding across the world. The rapid "crowdsourcing" of new knowledge in *Blockchain and Digital Twin for Smart Hospitals* provides an exploration of the transformative convergence of cutting-edge technologies shaping the future of healthcare. The diverse chapters cover innovation on blockchain and digital twins from research institutes, in physical labs, in web labs, and healthcare institutions.

This book covers an analysis of the Internet of Medical Things (IoMT) architecture, trends, and challenges, laying the foundation for understanding the rapidly evolving digital landscape in healthcare. The initial chapters cover an introduction to blockchain technology and its applications in healthcare systems, as well as more specialized topics such as smart sensor networks, cyber-physical systems, and the impact of IoMT on healthcare stakeholders.

Contributors from across the globe provide insights on the utilization of blockchain for secure management of electronic health records, the integration of smart medical sensor networks, and the development of blockchain-based systems for healthcare digital twins. These chapters underscore the value of blockchain in ensuring data security, privacy, and efficient management of healthcare information.

This book also explores the application of smart healthcare systems, including the Internet of Things (IoT) for e-health, blockchain in clinical trials, and the advancement of electronic medical data protection through blockchain. Emerging technologies such as lab-on-chip devices, sustainable wireless sensor networks, and DNA computing for smart wireless sensor networks are examined for their potential to transform healthcare.

Digital twins are explored, including human body digital twins, the use of digital twins in brain surgery, and the enhancement of hospital operations through digital twin technology.

As we navigate the rapidly evolving world of digital health, this book will be a foundational resource for researchers, practitioners, and policymakers in building an understanding of how to harness the power of blockchain and digital twin technologies to improve healthcare. It is an opportunity to explore the innovative intersections of technology and healthcare that promise to redefine the future of medical science and patient care. I commend it to you.

Jane Thomason
Industry Associate, UCL Centre for Blockchain,
London, United Kingdom

CHAPTER

Introduction to smart hospital

1

Joseph Bamidele Awotunde
Department of Computer Science, Faculty of Communication and Information Sciences, University of Ilorin, Ilorin, Kwara State, Nigeria

1.1 Introduction

Global healthcare systems are about to undergo a revolutionary change due to a paradigm shift in digital technology from conventional healthcare to smart healthcare. Digital technologies are utilized in smart healthcare to integrate individuals, resources, and organizations, intelligently manage health environment demands, and facilitate easy health information navigation (Adeniyi et al., 2021). Smart healthcare integrates various stakeholders in the health system using emerging technologies such as artificial intelligence (AI), the Internet of Things (IoT), fog computing, cloud computing, blockchain, sensors, 5G technology (5G), and the Internet of Medical Things (IoMT) (Ajamu et al., 2023). Hospital 4.0 and 5.0 are original concepts that are now emerging, and these technologies are playing a significant part in their establishment (Mbunge et al., 2021). A new era of medical scenarios has begun with the introduction of 5G into smart healthcare systems. Recent advancements in smart healthcare, including 5G technology, edge computing, interconnected IoT devices, and data analytics, have enabled connected healthcare services for a happier and better life. The ongoing digital revolution is profoundly reshaping the healthcare industry, ushering in a new era characterized by Hospital 4.0 principles and the emergence of Hospital 5.0 (Mohanta et al., 2019).

Healthcare has undergone significant transformations over the years, evolving from Healthcare 1.0 to the more recent Hospital 5.0. Hospital 1.0, often referred to as the era of "paternalistic medicine," was characterized by a physician-centric approach (Gupta et al., 2019). In this phase, medical decisions were largely made by healthcare professionals, and patients played a passive role in their own care (Molina-Mula & Gallo-Estrada, 2020). The focus was on treating illnesses rather than preventing them, and information flow was limited between healthcare providers and patients (Oladipupo et al., 2023).

With the advent of Hospital 2.0, there was a notable shift toward patient empowerment and the utilization of technology (Castro et al., 2016). Electronic health records (EHRs) became prevalent, facilitating better information sharing among healthcare providers (Alexandre et al., 2024). Patients gained access to their medical records and started to participate more actively in their healthcare decision-making (Ebbers et al., 2024). Hospital 3.0 marked the integration of data analytics, personalized medicine, and the emphasis on preventive care (Brancato et al., 2024). This phase aimed to

Blockchain and Digital Twin for Smart Hospitals. DOI: https://doi.org/10.1016/B978-0-443-34226-4.00002-2

leverage Big Data to identify patterns and tailor treatments to individual patients, optimizing healthcare outcomes (Awotunde, Imoize, Jimoh, et al., 2023).

Hospital 4.0 brought about a more comprehensive integration of technology, including artificial intelligence, robotics, and the IoT (Akhtar et al., 2024). This phase focused on creating a connected healthcare ecosystem, where devices and systems could communicate seamlessly to enhance patient care (Rath et al., 2024). Telemedicine gained prominence, allowing remote consultations and monitoring (Awotunde et al., 2021). Hospital 5.0, the most recent evolution, emphasizes a holistic and human-centric approach (Carayannis et al., 2022). It acknowledges the importance of social determinants of health, patient experience, and community well-being. This phase aims to achieve optimal health outcomes by considering not only medical factors but also the broader socioeconomic and environmental influences on health (Kolossváry et al., 2023). Hospital 5.0 fosters collaboration among various stakeholders, including patients, healthcare providers, community organizations, and policymakers, to create a more inclusive and effective healthcare system (Gomathi et al., 2023).

In Hospital 4.0, smart sensors play a pivotal role in creating a connected and data-driven healthcare environment. These sensors, embedded in medical devices and wearable technologies, continuously collect real-time patient data, facilitating remote monitoring, personalized treatment plans, and preventive care. They contribute to the integration of AI and the IoT, enabling predictive analytics and early detection of health issues. In Healthcare 5.0, smart sensors take on an even more crucial role by extending beyond individual health monitoring to encompass broader aspects of community well-being and social determinants of health. These sensors aid in collecting data related to environmental factors, lifestyle choices, and community health trends, fostering a holistic and human-centric approach. By leveraging smart sensors, Hospital 5.0 aims to create a comprehensive understanding of health that goes beyond traditional medical data, fostering collaboration among diverse stakeholders for a more inclusive and community-focused healthcare system. Therefore this chapter endeavors to provide an extensive examination of the architecture and design choices associated with the integration of smart sensors in healthcare settings, particularly within the frameworks of Hospital 4.0 and the evolving paradigm of Hospital 5.0. As technological advancements continue to redefine healthcare delivery, the strategic deployment of smart sensors emerges as a pivotal factor in enhancing patient care, optimizing operational efficiency, and steering healthcare facilities toward intelligent and adaptive systems.

1.2 The paradigm shifts from Hospital 4.0 to Hospital 5.0 and significant proficiencies of smart sensors

Digital technologies and medical advancements are driving healthcare 4.0, transforming systems in countries like the United States, Germany, and the United Kingdom toward value-based, patient-centric services (Vijarania et al., 2023). Healthcare systems are being transformed toward a value-based approach, enhancing patient-centric services through smart care, connected care, and personalized medicine (Kumari et al., 2018). Hospital 4.0 brings industry 4.0 ideas and applications to the healthcare sector, allowing for real-time patient and provider personalization. Hence, Hospital 4.0 facilitates resilient performance in healthcare systems that is, their ability to adjust and deal with complexity. Adopted in Hospital 4.0, innovative digital technologies facilitate real-time customization of patient care, communication among stakeholders in the healthcare value chain, and the sharing of health-related information (Tortorella et al., 2020, 2021). They also collect data on patients, equipment, and materials, process and transform health data into information, and digitize and automate healthcare procedures (Aceto et al., 2020; Awotunde, Tripathy, et al., 2022). The healthcare delivery process is transformed into a cyber-physical system, integrating IoT, radio-frequency identification, smart wearable devices, intelligent sensors, and medical robots with cloud computing, Big Data, AI, and decision support techniques (Abikoye et al., 2021; Li & Carayon, 2021). The absence of emotive recognition and personalized health applications, coupled with the absence of emotive smart devices, necessitates the integration of intelligent sensors in Hospital 5.0 (Mbunge et al., 2022).

Around the world, sensors are being used to advance smart healthcare systems using AI, mobile devices, nanotechnology, transportation, and medical care. Since their introduction, sensor devices have greatly enhanced healthcare. A lot of sensors have been employed to record and convert medical data into electrical impulses that may be seen (Javaid et al., 2021). Sensory smart devices collect health data such as blood pressure, temperature, weight, heart rate, blood sugar level, stress level, and oxygen saturation rate and send them as electrical pulses for processing (An et al., 2017). Sensors are revolutionizing global health systems, particularly during the COVID-19 pandemic, enabling virtual care and transforming global healthcare delivery (Awotunde, Jimoh, AbdulRaheem, et al., 2022). With the ability to collect and interpret health data remotely, sensors have been successfully incorporated with smartphones, smart wearables, and the IoMT (Awotunde, Ogundokun, Adeniyi, et al., 2022). In the medical profession, sensors like biosensors are becoming more and more essential tools for tracking everyday activities, enhancing clinical diagnosis, and keeping an eye on biological molecules (Hatamie et al., 2020). Wearable sensors are utilized for remote patient monitoring in healthcare, with both flexible and nonflexible options available (Li et al., 2020).

Hospital 4.0 represents a paradigm shift in healthcare where digital technologies and data-driven approaches are integrated into the traditional hospital model. This phase emphasizes the use of EHRs, telemedicine, and interconnected medical devices to enhance efficiency, improve patient care, and streamline administrative processes. However, Hospital 5.0 marks a further evolution by placing a greater emphasis on personalized and patient-centric care. This paradigm shift involves leveraging advanced technologies such as AI, machine learning, and genomics to tailor medical treatments to individual patients. It aims to create a more holistic and collaborative healthcare ecosystem by integrating not only technological advancements but also patient preferences and social determinants of health into the decision-making process.

Smart sensors play a crucial role in both Hospital 4.0 and Hospital 5.0, offering significant proficiencies that contribute to the overall improvement of healthcare delivery. In Hospital 4.0, smart sensors are instrumental in monitoring patient vital signs in real time, automating data collection, and enhancing the accuracy of diagnostics. These sensors enable remote patient monitoring, providing healthcare professionals with valuable insights into patient health beyond the confines of traditional hospital settings. In Hospital 5.0, the proficiencies of smart sensors are expanded to include continuous health monitoring and the integration of wearable devices, allowing for a more comprehensive understanding of an individual's health. Additionally, these sensors contribute to the collection of Big Data, facilitating predictive analytics and personalized medicine by identifying patterns and trends that can guide healthcare decisions tailored to each patient's unique needs.

The evolution from Hospital 4.0 to Hospital 5.0 involves a significant enhancement in the capabilities and sophistication of smart sensors, enabling a more personalized, proactive, and interconnected healthcare ecosystem. Table 1.1 shows the types of smart sensors with examples used in Hospital 4.0 and Hospital 5.0.

In Healthcare 5.0, a variety of sensor technologies could be investigated to enhance and possibly provide more affordable delivery of medical services (Osama et al., 2023). Wearable flexible sensors, for example, are able to gather physiological data by intimately touching human skin (Maddikunta et al., 2022). The data is collected and sent in real time using wireless communication

Table 1.1 Types of smart sensors used in Hospital 4.0/5.0.

Types of smart sensors	Hospital 4.0	Hospital 5.0
Vital sign monitors	Traditional monitors for heart rate, blood pressure, and oxygen saturation.	Advanced wearables and implantable devices providing continuous health monitoring.
Remote patient monitoring	Basic remote monitoring devices for post-discharge care.	Sophisticated sensors tracking a broader range of health indicators in real time.
IoT-enabled medical devices	Smart infusion pumps, connected medical equipment.	Smart beds, intelligent garments, and advanced diagnostic tools connected through IoT.
Wearable health trackers	Basic fitness trackers and general health-aware wearables.	Advanced wearables continuously monitoring various health parameters.
AI-assisted diagnostic sensors	AI for image analysis and pattern recognition.	Integration of genomics, proteomics, and molecular sensors for precision diagnostics.
Blood glucose monitors	Automated glucose monitoring devices.	Advanced sensors providing real-time glucose monitoring and predictive analytics.
ECG (electrocardiogram) sensors	Traditional ECG monitors for cardiac activity.	Wearable ECG sensors offering continuous monitoring and early detection of anomalies.
Smart Inhalers	Inhalers with adherence monitoring capabilities.	IoT-enabled inhalers with real-time usage tracking and feedback mechanisms.
RFID-based asset tracking	RFID tags for tracking medical equipment.	Advanced RFID systems for tracking equipment, medications, and patient movement.
Smart prosthetics	Sensor-equipped prosthetics for basic feedback.	Prosthetics with advanced sensors providing more natural movements and feedback.
Temperature sensors	Traditional temperature monitoring devices.	Continuous temperature monitoring through wearable or implantable sensors.
Smart beds	Basic pressure-sensitive beds for patient comfort.	Intelligent beds with sensors adjusting support based on patient's needs and health.
Camera-based monitoring	Surveillance cameras for security purposes.	AI-enhanced cameras for patient monitoring, fall detection, and security.
Smart medication dispensers	Automated dispensers with basic tracking features.	Advanced dispensers with IoT connectivity, monitoring medication adherence in real time.
Gesture recognition sensors	Basic sensors for gesture-controlled interfaces.	Advanced sensors for hands-free interfaces, allowing healthcare professionals to interact with digital systems without physical contact.

technologies like Bluetooth and Wi-Fi for further analysis. Smart devices, including smart bands, vests, shoes, socks, smartphones, watches, clothes, disinfection tunnels, face masks, and helmets, can collect real-time body signals to monitor patient physiological signs. Smart sensory devices, including glucometers, smart watches, and blood pressure monitors, are widely used in healthcare to monitor chronic diseases like cardiovascular, asthma, cancer, and diabetes (Adeniyi et al., 2020). Smartphones offer immense opportunities for developing health applications that utilize sensors for collecting health data, patient proximity data, and emotive data for remote monitoring and virtual healthcare. Emerging digital technologies and sensors are revolutionizing connected healthcare, enabling remote monitoring and supporting patients with chronic conditions both in and out of health facilities (Awokola et al., 2023). Therefore biosensors have the potential to greatly improve disease prevention, prompt diagnosis, control, and treatment. The development of wearable biosensor prototypes is enhancing monitoring for various populations, including patients, athletes, premature infants, children, psychiatric patients, long-term care, the elderly, and those in impassable areas.

1.3 Emerging technologies and their applications in the Hospitals 4.0/5.0

Smart healthcare systems leverage emerging technologies to create more efficient, personalized, and interconnected healthcare experiences. One key component is the IoT, which involves the integration of smart devices and sensors into healthcare infrastructure (Pramanik et al., 2019). These devices can be embedded in wearables, medical equipment, and even within patients themselves to collect real-time data. This continuous stream of information enables remote patient monitoring, timely intervention, and the ability to predict health issues before they escalate (Shah et al., 2020). By connecting various elements in the healthcare ecosystem, smart healthcare systems enhance overall operational efficiency, patient engagement, and preventive care (Gardašević et al., 2020).

AI-based models are another pivotal technology in smart healthcare. AI-driven applications, such as machine learning algorithms and natural language processing, contribute to diagnostics, treatment planning, and predictive analytics (Ayoade et al., 2023). AI helps healthcare professionals analyze vast datasets quickly, identify patterns, and make more informed decisions. Virtual health assistants, powered by AI, provide patients with personalized health information, reminders for medication, and assistance in managing chronic conditions (Awotunde, Misra, et al., 2023). Additionally, AI facilitates predictive modeling for disease outbreaks and helps optimize resource allocation within healthcare organizations, making the healthcare system more responsive and adaptive.

Blockchain technology is gaining prominence in smart healthcare systems, offering secure and transparent solutions for data management. By providing a decentralized and tamper-resistant ledger, blockchain ensures the integrity and privacy of sensitive medical data. Patients can have more control over their health records, granting access to specific healthcare providers as needed. This not only enhances data security but also streamlines information exchange among different healthcare entities. The combination of IoT, AI, and blockchain in smart healthcare systems results in a comprehensive approach to healthcare that prioritizes efficiency, security, and individualized patient care.

1.3.1 Emerging technologies and their applications in the Hospital 4.0

Hospital 4.0, also known as Healthcare 4.0, is characterized by the integration of advanced technologies to enhance patient care, streamline operations, and improve overall healthcare outcomes (Haleem et al., 2022). One key emerging technology in Hospital 4.0 is the IoT. IoT-based devices, such as smart medical devices, wearable sensors, and connected patient monitoring systems, enable real-time data collection and remote patient monitoring (Ilangakoon et al., 2022). This facilitates proactive healthcare management, early detection of abnormalities, and personalized treatment plans.

Another significant technology in Hospital 4.0 is AI. AI applications, including machine learning algorithms and natural language processing, play a pivotal role in medical diagnostics, personalized medicine, and predictive analytics. These technologies enable healthcare professionals to analyze large datasets efficiently, identify patterns, and make more accurate diagnoses (Rehman et al., 2022). Additionally, robotic-assisted surgery and virtual reality (VR) for medical training are becoming integral components of Hospital 4.0, enhancing surgical precision and training effectiveness (Casas-Yrurzum et al., 2023). Together, these technologies contribute to a more interconnected, data-driven, and patient-centric healthcare ecosystem in Hospital 4.0. Fig. 1.1 shows the emerging technologies in Hospital 4.0.

Hospital 4.0 represents advanced stages of healthcare evolution, integrating cutting-edge technologies to enhance patient care, streamline operations, and improve overall efficiency. Here are some emerging technologies and their functions in Hospital 4.0:

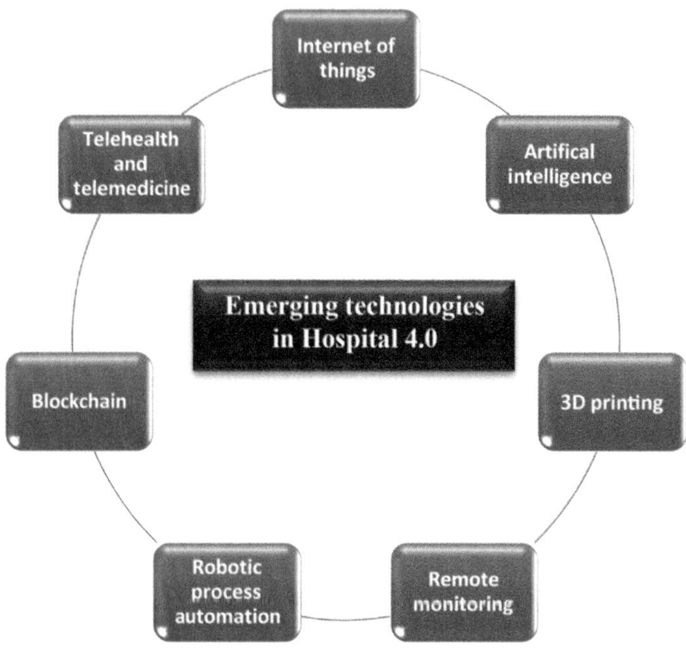

FIGURE 1.1

The emerging technologies in Hospital 4.0.

Internet of Things: IoT-based devices in Hospital 4.0 enable real-time monitoring of patients, equipment, and facilities (Awotunde, Folorunsho, et al., 2023). Wearable devices and sensors collect and transmit data, providing valuable insights into patient health and hospital operations. The IoT plays a crucial role in Hospital 4.0 by creating a connected and intelligent healthcare environment. IoT refers to the network of physical devices embedded with sensors, software, and other technologies that enable them to collect and exchange data (Awotunde, Bhoi, et al., 2022). In Hospital 4.0, IoT devices are extensively used to enhance patient care, streamline operations, and improve overall efficiency. These devices can be integrated into medical equipment, wearable devices, and patient monitoring systems, facilitating real-time data collection and communication (Putra et al., 2024).

The functions of IoT in Hospital 4.0 are diverse and impactful. Remote patient monitoring is a key application, allowing healthcare providers to track patients' vital signs and health metrics from a distance. This continuous monitoring enables early detection of anomalies and the ability to intervene promptly. IoT devices also contribute to the optimization of hospital operations, including asset tracking, inventory management, and maintenance scheduling. Smart medical devices, such as infusion pumps and imaging equipment, can communicate with each other and central systems to ensure proper functionality and timely maintenance (Ajagbe, Adigun, et al., 2022). Overall, the integration of IoT in Hospital 4.0 creates a more interconnected and data-driven healthcare ecosystem, leading to improved patient outcomes and operational efficiency.

Artificial intelligence and machine learning: AI and machine learning (ML) algorithms are used for diagnostic support, personalized treatment plans, and predictive analytics. They help analyze vast amounts of medical data to identify patterns, detect anomalies, and improve decision-making. AI and ML are transformative technologies in Hospital 4.0, revolutionizing various aspects of healthcare delivery, decision-making, and patient outcomes (Ajagbe, Awotunde, et al., 2022). AI refers to the simulation of human intelligence in machines, enabling them to perform tasks that typically require human cognitive functions, while ML is a subset of AI that focuses on the development of algorithms allowing machines to learn from data. In Hospital 4.0, AI and ML are applied to vast datasets generated in healthcare to extract valuable insights, improve diagnostics, and enhance treatment strategies (Alowais et al., 2023).

One critical function of AI and ML in Hospital 4.0 is in medical diagnostics. Advanced algorithms can analyze complex medical data, such as imaging and genetic information, to assist healthcare professionals in making more accurate and timely diagnoses (Awotunde, Folorunso, et al., 2022). AI-powered diagnostic tools can detect patterns and anomalies in medical images, aiding in the early identification of diseases. Additionally, predictive analytics, enabled by ML, allows healthcare providers to forecast patient outcomes and identify individuals at risk of certain conditions, facilitating proactive and preventive care (Rojek et al., 2024). Overall, the integration of AI and ML in Hospital 4.0 empowers healthcare professionals with data-driven insights, leading to more precise diagnoses, personalized treatment plans, and improved patient care.

Telehealth and telemedicine: The widespread adoption of telehealth technologies allows patients to consult with healthcare professionals remotely (Judijanto et al., 2024). This is particularly valuable for remote patient monitoring, follow-up consultations, and providing healthcare access to underserved areas. Telehealth and telemedicine are integral components of Hospital 4.0, leveraging digital communication technologies to provide remote healthcare services, consultations, and monitoring. Telehealth encompasses a broader spectrum of services, including remote patient monitoring, virtual consultations, and health-related education delivered through telecommunications technology. Telemedicine, on the other hand, specifically refers to the use of technology to provide clinical healthcare services remotely. In Hospital 4.0, both telehealth and telemedicine play crucial roles in enhancing access to healthcare, optimizing resource utilization, and improving patient outcomes (Judijanto et al., 2024).

The functions of telehealth and telemedicine in Hospital 4.0 are diverse. Virtual consultations enable patients to connect with healthcare providers from the comfort of their homes, reducing the need for physical visits to the hospital (Askari et al., 2024). Remote patient monitoring, facilitated by connected devices and wearables, allows healthcare professionals to track patients' vital signs and chronic conditions in real time, enabling early intervention and personalized care plans. Telehealth also promotes health education and awareness, empowering patients to actively participate in their own healthcare management (Gärtner, 2024). By leveraging these technologies, Hospital 4.0 not only extends the reach of healthcare services but also enhances patient engagement and overall healthcare efficiency.

Remote monitoring: Telehealth solutions facilitate remote consultations, allowing patients to access healthcare services from their homes. Remote monitoring tools keep track of patient vitals, reducing the need for frequent hospital visits (Awotunde, Imoize, Jimoh, et al., 2023). Remote monitoring is a critical aspect of Hospital 4.0, leveraging advanced technologies to monitor patients' health status and vital signs from a distance (Ndunagu et al., no date). This capability is made possible through the integration of IoT devices, wearable sensors, and other remote monitoring technologies. In Hospital 4.0, remote monitoring functions as a proactive and preventative healthcare approach, allowing healthcare providers to continuously track and analyze patient data without the need for frequent in-person visits.

One primary function of remote monitoring in Hospital 4.0 is the real-time tracking of patient vitals and health metrics. Wearable devices equipped with sensors can monitor parameters such as heart rate, blood pressure, glucose levels, and more. This continuous data collection enables early detection of abnormalities or changes in a patient's condition, prompting timely interventions and preventing potential health crises. Remote monitoring is particularly beneficial for managing chronic conditions, allowing healthcare professionals to personalize treatment plans based on the individual patient's data trends.

Remote monitoring also enhances patient engagement and empowers individuals to take an active role in their healthcare. Patients can receive personalized feedback, access their health data, and communicate with healthcare providers through digital platforms. This fosters a more patient-centric approach, promoting better adherence to treatment plans and improving overall health outcomes (Chibuike et al., 2024). In Hospital 4.0, the integration of remote monitoring technologies contributes to a more efficient and responsive healthcare system, emphasizing preventive care and personalized medicine.

Blockchain: Blockchain ensures secure and transparent management of patient records, billing, and supply chain. It enhances data integrity and interoperability and facilitates faster, more accurate transactions (Awotunde, Misra, & Pham, 2022). Blockchain technology is a foundational element in the evolution of Hospital 4.0, offering a decentralized and secure approach to managing health data. In Hospital 4.0, blockchain serves as a distributed ledger system that records and stores transactions across a network of computers (Mahajan et al., 2023). One primary function of blockchain in healthcare is to ensure the integrity and security of patient data. By using cryptographic techniques and decentralization, blockchain minimizes the risk of unauthorized access, tampering, or data breaches, enhancing the overall trustworthiness of health records.

Another crucial function of blockchain in Hospital 4.0 is the facilitation of interoperability and data exchange among different healthcare entities. Health records on the blockchain can be accessed and updated securely by authorized participants, such as healthcare providers, laboratories, and patients themselves. This creates a more seamless and efficient flow of information across the healthcare ecosystem, reducing administrative burdens, and improving the continuity of care. Patients can have greater control over their health data, granting permission for specific entities to access and contribute to their records and promoting transparency and data ownership (Awotunde, Misra, et al., 2022).

Blockchain also plays a significant role in supply chain management within healthcare. By utilizing blockchain for tracking and verifying the authenticity of pharmaceuticals and medical devices, Hospital 4.0 ensures the integrity of the entire supply chain. This helps prevent counterfeit drugs, enhances traceability, and ultimately contributes to patient safety. Overall, the integration of blockchain technology in Hospital 4.0 provides a secure, transparent, and interoperable framework for managing health data, fostering trust among stakeholders, and improving the overall efficiency of healthcare operations.

Big Data and Analytics: Advanced analytics tools process large datasets to extract valuable insights. Predictive analytics can help in early disease detection, resource optimization, and personalized medicine (Awotunde, Oluwabukonla, et al., 2022). Big Data and Analytics are pivotal components of Hospital 4.0, enabling healthcare providers to harness and analyze vast amounts of data for improved decision-making, personalized patient care, and operational efficiency. In Hospital 4.0, the healthcare industry generates massive datasets from various sources, including EHRs, medical imaging, and wearable devices (Awotunde, Jimoh, et al., 2022). Big Data refers to the ability to handle and process these large datasets, while Analytics involves extracting valuable insights from the data to inform healthcare practices.

One key function of Big Data and Analytics in Hospital 4.0 is predictive analytics for disease prevention and management (Wang et al., 2018). By analyzing historical and real-time data, healthcare professionals can identify patterns and trends, predict disease outbreaks, and assess the risk of individual patients developing specific conditions. This proactive approach allows for early intervention, personalized treatment plans, and better resource allocation within healthcare organizations.

Analytics in Hospital 4.0 also plays a crucial role in enhancing patient outcomes and operational efficiency. Healthcare providers can use advanced analytics to optimize treatment protocols, identify areas for improvement in clinical workflows, and reduce inefficiencies (Ronaghi, 2024). Additionally, patient data analytics contributes to the development of personalized medicine, tailoring treatment plans based on individual patient characteristics and responses (Nuryanto et al., 2024). This not only improves patient satisfaction but also leads to more effective and targeted healthcare interventions. Overall, the integration of Big Data and Analytics in Hospital 4.0 transforms healthcare delivery by leveraging data-driven insights for better decision-making, patient care, and organizational efficiency.

3D printing: 3D printing is used for creating patient-specific implants, prosthetics, and personalized medical devices. It enables cost-effective and customized solutions for patient care. 3D printing, also known as additive manufacturing, is emerging as a transformative technology in Hospital 4.0, offering innovative solutions in various aspects of healthcare. One crucial function of 3D printing in Hospital 4.0 is the production of personalized medical devices and implants. Using patient-specific data from medical imaging, 3D printing allows the fabrication of customized implants, prosthetics, and orthopedic devices tailored to the individual anatomy of patients. This not only improves the fit and functionality of the devices but also enhances patient outcomes and quality of life.

Another important application of 3D printing in Hospital 4.0 is in the creation of anatomical models for surgical planning and training. Surgeons can use 3D-printed models of a patient's anatomy to visualize complex procedures, practice techniques, and plan surgeries with greater precision. This hands-on approach improves surgical outcomes by allowing for a deeper understanding of the patient's unique anatomy, reducing the risk of complications, and optimizing the surgical approach.

3D printing also plays a role in pharmaceuticals by enabling the production of personalized medication with specific dosages and formulations. This allows for more precise drug delivery tailored to individual patient needs. The technology can be used to create complex drug structures that may not be achievable through traditional manufacturing methods. In Hospital 4.0, 3D printing thus contributes to advancements in patient-specific treatment strategies, surgical precision, and pharmaceutical innovation, showcasing its potential to revolutionize various aspects of healthcare.

Robotic process automation: Robotic process automation (RPA) automates repetitive administrative tasks such as billing, appointment scheduling, and data entry. This increases efficiency and allows healthcare professionals to focus more on patient care. RPA is a key technology in Hospital 4.0, offering automation solutions for routine, rule-based tasks to streamline administrative processes, enhance operational efficiency, and improve overall healthcare delivery. In Hospital 4.0, RPA can be applied to various administrative functions, such as billing, scheduling, and claims processing. By automating repetitive tasks, RPA reduces the workload on healthcare staff, minimizes errors, and accelerates the processing of administrative tasks, allowing healthcare professionals to focus more on patient care.

Another critical function of RPA in Hospital 4.0 is its role in data management and integration. RPA systems can seamlessly integrate with existing healthcare information systems, EHRs, and other data repositories. This ensures the smooth flow of information across different departments, preventing data silos and improving the accessibility and accuracy of patient information. RPA can assist in updating and maintaining patient records, reconciling data discrepancies, and facilitating efficient data exchanges between healthcare providers, contributing to a more cohesive and interconnected healthcare ecosystem.

In clinical settings, RPA can be applied to assist with routine medical tasks, such as medication dispensing, inventory management, and even aspects of patient care coordination. This not only enhances the precision and reliability of these processes but also frees up healthcare professionals to focus on more complex and patient-centric aspects of their roles. Overall, the integration of RPA in Hospital 4.0 optimizes administrative workflows, promotes data integration, and contributes to a more efficient and responsive healthcare system.

Robotic-assisted surgery: Robotic-assisted surgery is a cutting-edge technology in Hospital 4.0 that involves the use of robotic systems to enhance surgical procedures (Srivastava et al., 2024). One of the primary functions of robotic-assisted surgery in Hospital 4.0 is to improve the precision and dexterity of surgical interventions. Surgeons can control robotic arms equipped with specialized instruments, which offer a greater range of motion and enhanced maneuverability compared to traditional surgical techniques. This increased precision allows for minimally invasive procedures, reducing trauma to surrounding tissues, lowering the risk of complications, and facilitating faster recovery times for patients.

Another crucial function of robotic-assisted surgery in Hospital 4.0 is its ability to provide surgeons with enhanced visualization. High-definition cameras and 3D imaging systems integrated into robotic surgical platforms offer detailed and magnified views of the surgical site. This improved visualization allows surgeons to navigate complex anatomical structures with greater accuracy, leading to more successful outcomes in intricate procedures. The combination of precision and enhanced visualization contributes to advancements in various surgical specialties, including urology, gynecology, and orthopedics (AbdulRaheem et al., 2022; Jain et al., 2024).

Robotic-assisted surgery also supports tele-surgery, enabling skilled surgeons to perform procedures remotely. This has the potential to address geographical barriers, allowing patients in underserved areas to access specialized surgical expertise. The integration of robotic-assisted surgery in Hospital 4.0 exemplifies the commitment to advancing surgical capabilities, improving patient outcomes, and transforming the landscape of modern healthcare (Akhtar et al., 2024).

1.3.2 Emerging technologies and their applications in the Hospital 5.0

Hospital 5.0 represents the next evolution in healthcare, marked by the integration of cutting-edge technologies that aim to enhance patient care, streamline operations, and improve overall efficiency (Gomathi et al., 2023). One of the key emerging technologies in Hospital 5.0 is AI. AI is employed for tasks such as diagnostic imaging analysis, predictive analytics for patient outcomes, and personalized treatment plans (Falola et al., 2023). ML-based algorithms can analyze vast amounts of patient data to identify patterns and trends, aiding healthcare professionals in making more informed decisions. IoT technology, including wearable health monitors and smart medical equipment, is crucial in Hospital 5.0 for continuous monitoring of patient vital signs and transmitting real-time data to healthcare providers (Mishra & Singh, 2023). This facilitates remote patient monitoring and early detection of potential health issues, leading to proactive interventions and improved patient outcomes. Additionally, IoT helps in tracking medical equipment, optimizing inventory management, and ensuring the smooth functioning of hospital operations.

Digital twin technology is the main key in Hospital 5.0. Hospital digital twin would be the bridge between the real and virtual hospital. Hospital digital twin might also be the mirror that reflects the real hospital into the virtual hospital (Nguyen, 2023, 2024). Blockchain technology is also gaining prominence in Hospital 5.0, particularly for securing and managing patient data. By utilizing a decentralized and tamper-resistant ledger, blockchain ensures the integrity and confidentiality of EHRs. Patients have greater control over their data, and healthcare providers can access accurate and up-to-date information securely (Adeniyi et al., 2023). This not only enhances data security but also streamlines interoperability between different healthcare systems, fostering better collaboration among healthcare professionals. Telemedicine and virtual healthcare solutions are integral components of Hospital 5.0, especially in the context of remote patient care (Chhabra & Singh, 2024; Nguyen & Voznak, 2024). Advanced communication technologies enable virtual consultations, remote monitoring, and telehealth services, providing patients with more convenient access to healthcare. This not only reduces the burden on physical infrastructure but also improves healthcare accessibility for individuals in remote or underserved areas. Overall, the integration of these emerging technologies in Hospital 5.0 represents a transformative shift toward more efficient, personalized, and accessible healthcare (Fig. 1.2 and Fig. 1.3).

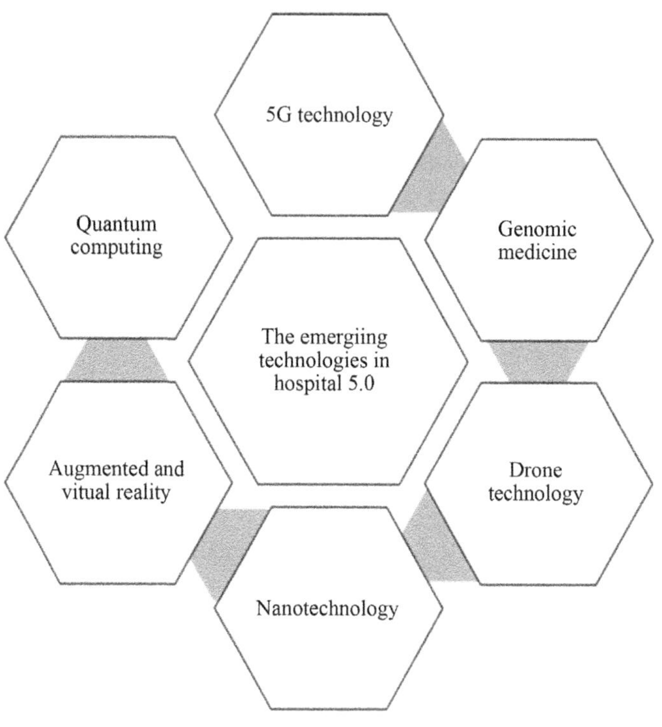

FIGURE 1.2

The emerging technologies in Hospital 5.0.

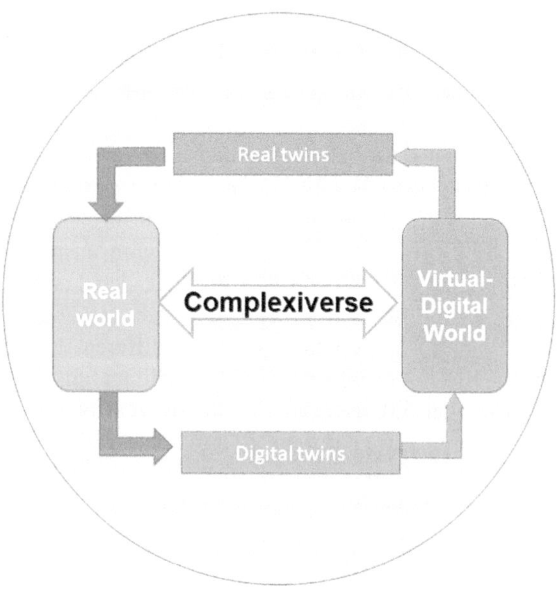

FIGURE 1.3

Digital twins, Real twins and Complexiverse (Nguyen, 2023, 2024).

5G technology: 5G networks can provide high-speed, low-latency connectivity, enabling real-time communication between medical devices and healthcare professionals (Ogundokun et al., 2023). This can enhance remote monitoring, telemedicine, and surgical procedures. In Hospital 5.0, one of the prominent emerging technologies is 5G technology, which represents the fifth generation of mobile networks. 5G brings about a significant leap in terms of connectivity, speed, and reliability compared to its predecessors. In the healthcare context, the implementation of 5G technology offers several transformative functions. One key aspect is the enhancement of real-time communication and data transfer within the hospital ecosystem. The high data transfer rates and low latency of 5G enable seamless transmission of large medical files, high-resolution imaging, and real-time monitoring, facilitating faster decision-making and improving overall patient care. Moreover, 5G technology plays a crucial role in enabling the IoMT (Awotunde, Oladipo, et al., 2022). With the increased number of connected devices and sensors, healthcare professionals can remotely monitor patients, track vital signs, and receive instant updates on their condition. This connectivity not only improves the efficiency of healthcare delivery but also opens avenues for remote patient monitoring and telemedicine, allowing healthcare services to extend beyond the hospital walls.

Another significant function of 5G in Hospital 5.0 is the support for augmented reality (AR) and VR applications. These technologies can be leveraged for medical training, surgical planning, and patient education. Surgeons can use AR to overlay important information during procedures, and VR can provide immersive training experiences for healthcare professionals (Desselle et al., 2020; Lungu et al., 2021). This not only enhances the skills of medical practitioners but also contributes to improved patient outcomes. Furthermore, the low latency of 5G technology is crucial for the development and implementation of robotic surgery systems. In Hospital 5.0, surgeons can utilize robotic-assisted systems with increased precision and control, facilitated by the minimal delay in communication between the surgeon's console and the robotic instruments (Morrison, 2024; Rus et al., 2023). This leads to more accurate surgeries and minimally invasive procedures, ultimately benefiting patient recovery and reducing hospitalization times. Overall, the integration of 5G technology in Hospital 5.0 brings about a paradigm shift in healthcare delivery, fostering innovation, efficiency, and improved patient care.

Drone technology: Drone technology is emerging as a transformative force in Hospital 5.0, offering unique capabilities that enhance various aspects of healthcare delivery. One of the primary functions of drones in healthcare is the efficient and rapid transportation of medical supplies and equipment. Drones can swiftly deliver critical items such as medications, blood samples, or even organs for transplant, overcoming traditional logistical challenges and reducing the time it takes to transport essential medical resources between facilities (Lammers et al., 2023). This ensures timely interventions and contributes to improved patient outcomes.

In Hospital 5.0, drones also play a vital role in emergency response and disaster management. They can be deployed to survey affected areas, assess the extent of damage, and deliver medical supplies to inaccessible or disaster-stricken regions. This capability is particularly crucial during natural disasters or public health emergencies, where quick and effective response is essential to save lives and mitigate the impact of the crisis. Moreover, drones enable the deployment of telemedicine services in remote or underserved areas (Emimi et al., 2023). Equipped with telehealth technologies, drones can serve as mobile healthcare units, allowing healthcare professionals to conduct virtual consultations, monitor patients, and deliver medical advice or prescriptions. This helps bridge the gap in healthcare accessibility, reaching populations that may face challenges in accessing traditional healthcare facilities. Additionally, drones can be employed for surveillance and monitoring within hospital premises. They can assist in enforcing safety protocols, ensuring compliance with hygiene standards, and monitoring patient flow. This contributes to the overall efficiency of hospital operations, enhances security, and helps in maintaining a safe and sanitized environment, especially in the context of infectious disease management. As Hospital 5.0 continues to evolve, the integration of drone technology promises to revolutionize healthcare delivery by addressing logistical challenges, improving accessibility, and enhancing emergency response capabilities (Olatunji et al., 2023).

Robotics and robotic surgery: Robotics in healthcare can assist in surgeries, rehabilitation, and patient care. Advanced robotic systems may perform minimally invasive procedures with precision, reducing recovery times and improving outcomes. Robotics and robotic surgery stand out as key emerging technologies in the evolution of Hospital 5.0, revolutionizing the landscape of healthcare delivery and patient care (Prerna et al., 2024). The integration of robotics into medical procedures offers unparalleled precision, dexterity, and control for surgeons, leading to improved surgical outcomes. In Hospital 5.0, robotic surgery systems enable minimally invasive procedures, reducing the need for large incisions and, consequently, minimizing patient trauma, pain, and recovery times. Robotic surgery systems in Hospital 5.0 are characterized by advanced features such as haptic feedback, allowing surgeons to feel the texture and resistance of tissues remotely (Anupama et al., 2024). This enhances the surgeon's ability to perform intricate procedures with greater accuracy. Additionally, robotics facilitates telepresence surgery, enabling experienced surgeons to perform surgeries from a remote location. This capability has the potential to address geographical barriers, allowing patients to access specialized surgical expertise regardless of their physical location.

The integration of robotics also contributes to the development of autonomous surgical procedures. In Hospital 5.0, intelligent robotic systems can perform certain routine and repetitive tasks with minimal human intervention (Koulaouzidis et al., 2023). This not only optimizes workflow within the hospital but also allows healthcare professionals to focus on more complex aspects of patient care. As technology advances, the potential for artificial intelligence and machine learning in conjunction with robotics holds promise for further enhancing surgical precision and adapting procedures based on real-time data. Moreover, robotics extends beyond the operating room in Hospital 5.0, with robotic-assisted devices aiding in rehabilitation and physical therapy. These devices can provide personalized and monitored rehabilitation exercises, promoting faster recovery for patients recovering from surgery or managing chronic conditions. As Hospital 5.0 continues to embrace robotics, the synergy between technology and healthcare promises to redefine the standards of surgical practice, patient outcomes, and rehabilitation processes (Gürce et al., 2023).

Virtual and augmented reality: VR and AR technologies can be used for medical training, patient education, and even remote surgeries. Healthcare 5.0 may leverage these technologies to enhance the patient experience and improve therapeutic interventions. Virtual and augmented reality (VR/AR) technologies are emerging as transformative tools in Hospital 5.0, offering innovative solutions for medical training, patient care, and healthcare system optimization (Mathkor et al., 2024). In the realm of medical training, VR provides immersive simulations that allow healthcare professionals to practice and refine their skills in a realistic and risk-free environment. Surgeons can use VR to simulate complex procedures, enhancing their proficiency and confidence before entering the operating room (Żydowicz et al., 2024). Additionally, VR facilitates collaborative training experiences, enabling interdisciplinary teams to train together regardless of their physical locations.

AR plays a crucial role in improving patient care within Hospital 5.0. AR overlays digital information onto the physical world, providing healthcare professionals with real-time, context-specific data during medical procedures. Surgeons can benefit from AR-assisted navigation systems that display critical information, such as patient anatomy or surgical plans, directly onto the surgical field (Seetohul et al., 2023). This enhances precision and reduces the risk of errors. AR can also be utilized in patient education, allowing healthcare providers to explain complex medical concepts to patients by visualizing information in an easily understandable manner. Furthermore, VR/AR technologies contribute to enhanced patient experiences and outcomes (Mai & Lee, 2023). In Hospital 5.0, VR can be employed for pain management, distraction therapy, and mental health interventions (el Mathari et al., 2024). Patients undergoing medical procedures or rehabilitation can use VR to immerse themselves in relaxing environments or engaging activities, alleviating stress and discomfort. AR applications can aid in preoperative planning, allowing patients to better understand their treatment plans and make informed decisions about their care. This patient-centric approach enhances communication between healthcare providers and patients, fostering a more collaborative and informed healthcare experience.

In the broader context of healthcare system optimization, VR/AR technologies are utilized for the design and planning of healthcare facilities. Architects and healthcare planners can use VR to create and simulate hospital environments, optimizing layouts for efficiency and patient well-being. Additionally, AR applications can assist in inventory management, allowing healthcare professionals to locate and track medical equipment and supplies within the hospital. As Hospital 5.0 continues to evolve, the integration of VR and AR technologies promises to elevate medical training, patient care, and overall healthcare system efficiency to unprecedented levels.

Genomics and personalized medicine: Advances in genomics enable a deeper understanding of an individual's genetic makeup. Healthcare 5.0 may involve tailoring treatment plans based on a person's unique genetic profile, optimizing drug effectiveness, and reducing adverse reactions. Genomics and personalized medicine represent groundbreaking technologies in the context of Hospital 5.0, ushering in a new era of precision healthcare tailored to an individual's genetic makeup (Azrour et al., 2024). The advancement of genomics allows for the comprehensive analysis of an individual's DNA, enabling healthcare professionals to understand the genetic basis of diseases and predict a patient's susceptibility to certain conditions (Awotunde, Adeniyi, et al., 2022). This information is invaluable in the development of personalized treatment plans, optimizing therapeutic interventions based on a patient's unique genetic profile.

In Hospital 5.0, genomics plays a pivotal role in disease prevention and early detection. Genetic testing can identify individuals at risk for hereditary diseases, allowing for proactive measures such as lifestyle modifications or targeted screening programs. Early detection through genomic screening enhances the potential for timely intervention and personalized preventive strategies, contributing to improved patient outcomes (Awotunde et al., 2020).

The integration of genomics in Hospital 5.0 also facilitates the development of targeted therapies. By analyzing the genetic mutations driving a particular disease, researchers can design medications that specifically target the underlying molecular mechanisms (Oselusi et al., 2024). This approach minimizes adverse effects and enhances treatment efficacy, as medications are tailored to the genetic characteristics of each patient. Personalized medicine, guided by genomics, transforms the treatment paradigm from a one-size-fits-all approach to a more precise and individualized model. Moreover, the use of genomics in Hospital 5.0 extends to pharmacogenomics, which involves analyzing how an individual's genetic makeup influences their response to drugs. This information helps healthcare providers prescribe medications that are most likely to be effective and well-tolerated by the patient, reducing the risk of adverse reactions and optimizing therapeutic outcomes. As genomics and personalized medicine continue to evolve, Hospital 5.0 is poised to deliver a new standard of care that is not only more effective but also tailored to the specific genetic makeup of each patient, leading to a truly personalized and precise healthcare experience (Abrahams & Downing, 2024; Casolino et al., 2024).

Nanomedicine: Nanotechnology can be applied to create nanoscale devices for drug delivery, imaging, and diagnostics. In Healthcare 5.0, nanomedicine may play a crucial role in targeted therapies and minimizing side effects. Nanomedicine and nanotechnology are emerging as transformative technologies in the context of Hospital 5.0, offering innovative solutions for diagnostics, drug delivery, and therapeutic interventions at the nanoscale (Wang et al., 2024). In Hospital 5.0, nanomedicine involves the manipulation and control of materials at the nanoscale to develop advanced medical applications. Nanoparticles, for example, can be engineered to carry drugs directly to target cells, allowing for more precise and efficient drug delivery (Elumalai et al., 2024). This targeted approach minimizes side effects and enhances the therapeutic efficacy of medications.

The use of nanotechnology in diagnostics is another key aspect of Hospital 5.0. Nanosensors and nanodevices can be designed to detect biomarkers associated with various diseases at an early stage, enabling prompt diagnosis and intervention. The high sensitivity and specificity of these nanoscale diagnostic tools contribute to more accurate and timely disease identification, improving the chances of successful treatment and patient outcomes. Nanomedicine also holds promise in imaging technologies within Hospital 5.0. Nanoparticles can be engineered to enhance contrast in medical imaging, providing clearer and more detailed images for diagnostic purposes (Gupta et al., 2024). This can be particularly beneficial in imaging techniques such as magnetic resonance imaging (MRI) and computed tomography (CT), where improved contrast can lead to better visualization of tissues and abnormalities (Nikpanah & Morgan, 2024; Zanon et al., 2024).

Furthermore, nanotechnology in Hospital 5.0 extends to regenerative medicine and tissue engineering. Nanomaterials can be utilized to design scaffolds that mimic the extracellular matrix, promoting the growth and regeneration of damaged tissues (Zanon et al., 2024). This approach has potential applications in the development of artificial organs, wound healing, and personalized tissue engineering, providing innovative solutions for patients with organ failure or tissue damage. As nanomedicine continues to advance, Hospital 5.0 is positioned to leverage these nanotechnological breakthroughs to enhance diagnostic accuracy, improve drug delivery, and revolutionize treatment modalities. The integration of nanotechnology into healthcare practices represents a paradigm shift toward more precise, targeted, and personalized approaches, ultimately leading to improved patient care and outcomes.

Quantum computing: Quantum computing has the potential to solve complex problems much faster than classical computers. In healthcare, this could accelerate drug discovery processes, optimize treatment plans, and advance our understanding of complex biological systems. Quantum computing is emerging as a revolutionary technology in the healthcare sector, holding significant potential for Hospital 5.0. Quantum computers leverage the principles of quantum mechanics to perform complex computations at speeds unattainable by classical computers (Mohanaprabhu et al., 2024). In Hospital 5.0, quantum computing can contribute to the advancement of medical research and drug discovery. Quantum algorithms can analyze vast datasets, simulate biological processes, and identify potential drug candidates with unprecedented speed and accuracy, significantly accelerating the pace of scientific discovery and innovation (Sharma, 2024).

One crucial application of quantum computing in Hospital 5.0 is in the field of genomics. The intricate analysis of genomic data involves complex computations that classical computers struggle to execute efficiently. Quantum computers can process and analyze genomic information more rapidly, leading to breakthroughs in understanding genetic factors influencing diseases, facilitating personalized medicine, and enabling healthcare professionals to tailor treatments to individual patients based on their unique genetic makeup (Pal et al., 2024). Quantum computing also has the potential to enhance optimization problems within healthcare systems. In Hospital 5.0, quantum algorithms can be employed for resource allocation, scheduling, and logistics optimization, improving the efficiency of hospital operations and reducing costs (Sadeghi & Mahmoudi, 2024). This optimization extends to healthcare supply chain management, ensuring the timely delivery of medical supplies, optimizing inventory, and enhancing overall healthcare system resilience.

Furthermore, quantum computing holds promise in solving complex problems related to medical imaging and diagnostics. Quantum algorithms can process and analyze vast amounts of imaging data with greater efficiency, leading to more accurate and timely diagnoses. This can contribute to early detection of diseases, improved treatment planning, and ultimately better patient outcomes. As quantum computing technology matures, its integration into Hospital 5.0 has the potential to revolutionize medical research, healthcare management, and diagnostic capabilities, ushering in a new era of computational power and transformative advancements in patient care.

1.4 Architecture and design choices for smart sensors in the Hospital 4.0/5.0

Considering Hospitals 4.0/5.0, smart sensors play a pivotal role in transforming healthcare by integrating advanced technologies into hospital environments to enhance patient care and operational efficiency (Ronaghi, 2024). The design and architecture choices for smart sensors in these settings prioritize real-time monitoring, data accuracy, and interoperability. The architecture and design choices for smart sensors in Hospitals 4.0/5.0 are driven by the need for advanced data collection, analysis, and integration to optimize patient care, operational efficiency, and resource utilization (Sukin et al., 2024). First, the sensors are designed with a focus on real-time monitoring to provide instant and continuous data on patient health and environmental conditions. This allows healthcare professionals to respond promptly to any critical situations, improving patient outcomes. The architecture incorporates high-frequency data transmission protocols and low-latency communication networks to ensure minimal delays in data acquisition and analysis (Daousis et al., 2024).

Secondly, data accuracy is a paramount consideration in the design of smart sensors for Hospitals 4.0 and 5.0. The architecture revolves around the concept of interconnectedness and data-driven decision-making. Smart sensors are strategically deployed throughout the hospital environment, including patient rooms, medical equipment, and infrastructure (Procopiou & Stavrou, 2024). These sensors leverage IoT technology to gather real-time data on various parameters such as patient vital signs, medication adherence, equipment performance, and environmental conditions (Ayesha & Komalavalli, 2024). The architecture is designed to accommodate a diverse range of sensor types and communication protocols, ensuring compatibility and interoperability across different devices and systems. These sensors employ advanced sensing technologies such as IoT-enabled devices, wearables, and medical-grade sensors to collect precise and reliable health-related information (Awotunde, Sisodia, et al., 2023). The architecture integrates data validation mechanisms, error correction algorithms, and secure data storage to maintain the integrity of the collected data, ensuring that healthcare professionals can trust the information for making informed decisions (Anikwe et al., 2022).

Interoperability is another key aspect of the design and architecture of smart sensors in modern hospitals. In the Hospitals 4.0/5.0 paradigm, various medical devices, EHRs, and other healthcare systems are interconnected (Mishra & Singh, 2023). Smart sensors are designed with standard communication protocols like Health Level Seven (HL7) or Fast Healthcare Interoperability Resources (FHIR), allowing seamless integration with existing hospital information systems (El-Sappagh et al., 2019). This interoperability enhances the overall connectivity of the healthcare ecosystem, enabling the exchange of data between different devices and systems, ultimately leading to more comprehensive patient care (Ruminski et al., 2016).

The design choices prioritize scalability and flexibility to adapt to evolving healthcare needs and technological advancements. Hospitals 4.0/5.0 embrace a modular approach to sensor deployment, allowing for easy expansion or reconfiguration of the sensor network as requirements change. The architecture supports plug-and-play integration of new sensors and devices, enabling seamless integration with existing infrastructure and minimizing disruption to hospital operations (Kusherdianti et al., 2023). Additionally, cloud-based platforms are commonly utilized to store and analyze the vast amount of sensor data efficiently, providing scalability and accessibility to healthcare providers (Awotunde, Imoize, Salako, et al., 2023).

Another crucial aspect of the architecture is data security and privacy. With the proliferation of connected devices and the increasing digitization of healthcare data, ensuring the confidentiality, integrity, and availability of sensitive information is paramount (Awotunde, Chakraborty, et al., 2022). Design choices include robust encryption algorithms, secure authentication mechanisms, and strict access control policies to safeguard patient data against unauthorized access, tampering, or data breaches. Compliance with industry regulations such as Health Insurance Portability and Accountability Act (HIPAA) and General Data Protection Regulation (GDPR) is a fundamental requirement to maintain patient trust and regulatory compliance (Naithani & Tiwari, 2023). Moreover, security and privacy are integral components of the design and architecture of smart sensors in Hospitals 4.0 and 5.0. Healthcare providers and patients use smart sensor technologies with robust encryption, authentication, and data transmission protocols to ensure patient confidentiality and maintain trust. The following are some of the architectural and design choices of Hospital 4.0 and 5.0 (Singh & Kaunert, 2024).

1.4.1 Interoperability and connectivity

Architecture: In Hospital 4.0, interoperability and connectivity are foundational principles in the architecture of smart sensors. The design prioritizes seamless communication and integration between diverse healthcare components, including smart sensors, medical devices, and information systems. To achieve this, the architecture adheres to standardized communication protocols such as HL7 and FHIR. These protocols enable a common language for data exchange, ensuring that smart sensors can efficiently share information with various elements of the healthcare infrastructure. The overarching goal is to create a cohesive and interoperable environment where data flows seamlessly, allowing for more effective collaboration and data-driven decision-making. In Hospital 5.0, the emphasis on interoperability and connectivity in smart sensor architecture evolves to meet the demands of a more advanced healthcare paradigm. The design continues to prioritize seamless communication but is enhanced by the incorporation of emerging technologies. Interconnected smart sensors in Hospital 5.0 contribute to a comprehensive IoT ecosystem, where devices collaborate efficiently. The architecture supports a unified network that enables smart sensors to interact not only with each other but also with AI algorithms, edge computing nodes, and other advanced systems. This interconnectedness ensures that data generated by smart sensors can be harnessed for real-time analytics, leading to more informed decision-making, personalized patient care, and optimized hospital operations.

Design choices: In the context of Hospital 4.0 and 5.0, interoperability and connectivity are critical design choices for smart sensors that contribute to the seamless integration and functioning of advanced healthcare systems. Interoperability refers to the ability of different smart sensors and devices to exchange and interpret data in a standardized manner. In Hospital 4.0, interoperability ensures that various sensors, such as patient monitoring devices, diagnostic tools, and inventory management systems, can communicate with each other effortlessly. This enables real-time data sharing and analysis, allowing healthcare professionals to make informed decisions swiftly. The transition to Hospital 5.0 further emphasizes interoperability by incorporating advanced technologies like the IoT and AI to create a more interconnected healthcare ecosystem. This interconnectedness enhances the overall efficiency of healthcare processes, from patient care to administrative tasks.

Connectivity, on the other hand, addresses the means by which smart sensors communicate with each other and with central systems. In Hospital 4.0, connectivity involves the use of robust networking protocols and secure communication channels to transmit data reliably. Hospital 5.0 builds on this foundation by adopting cutting-edge connectivity solutions, including 5G networks, edge computing, and decentralized architectures. These advancements ensure high-speed data transfer, low latency, and increased reliability, facilitating real-time monitoring and response. In both Hospital 4.0 and 5.0, the integration of interoperable and connected smart sensors is pivotal in creating a technologically advanced healthcare environment that improves patient outcomes, optimizes resource utilization, and enhances the overall quality of healthcare services. Choose communication protocols such as HL7, FHIR, or DICOM to enable interoperability. Employ middleware solutions that can translate data between different systems, allowing for a unified and standardized flow of information.

1.4.2 Data security and privacy

Architecture: Implement a secure and privacy-conscious architecture to protect sensitive patient data. This involves secure data transmission, encryption mechanisms, and access controls. The architecture framework for ensuring data security and privacy in Hospital 4.00 and 5.0 involves a multifaceted approach to create a robust and resilient system. First, a layered architecture model can be implemented to compartmentalize and secure different aspects of smart sensor data processing. This may include a sensor layer for data acquisition, a communication layer with encrypted protocols for secure transmission, and a centralized processing layer with intrusion detection and prevention systems. Each layer incorporates security measures such as firewalls, access controls, and regular security assessments to fortify the overall data ecosystem.

Additionally, a comprehensive identity and access management (IAM) system is crucial within this framework. Implementing IAM ensures that only authorized personnel can access and manipulate sensitive healthcare data generated by smart sensors. Role-based access controls, two-factor authentication, and audit logs are integral components of the IAM system. Furthermore, the architecture must adhere to international standards and regulatory requirements, such as HIPAA or GDPR, to ensure compliance and legal protection of patient data. This layered and identity-centric architecture framework establishes a solid foundation for data security and privacy in the advanced healthcare settings of Hospitals 4.0/5.0.

Design choices: In the context of Hospitals 4.0/5.0, where smart sensors play a pivotal role in healthcare systems, design choices for data security and privacy are paramount. First, encryption protocols are fundamental to safeguarding sensitive patient information collected by smart sensors. Implementing strong, end-to-end encryption ensures that data transmitted between sensors, devices, and central healthcare systems remains confidential and protected from unauthorized access. Additionally, adopting secure communication protocols, such as HTTPS, and employing robust authentication mechanisms can further fortify the integrity of data transmissions.

Second, incorporating privacy by design principles is crucial in the development of smart sensor technologies. This involves integrating privacy features at the core of the sensor systems, allowing for data minimization, anonymization, and user consent mechanisms. By limiting the collection of personally identifiable information and enabling patients to have control over their data, Hospital 4.0 and 5.0 can strike a balance between leveraging the benefits of smart sensors for healthcare optimization and respecting patient privacy. Furthermore, continuous monitoring, regular security audits, and updates to address emerging threats are essential components to ensure the ongoing resilience of the security infrastructure surrounding smart sensors in the evolving landscape of healthcare technology. Additionally, it is essential to use end-to-end encryption for sensor data transmission, implement robust authentication mechanisms, adhere to privacy regulations such as HIPAA, and consider edge computing for processing sensitive data closer to its source to minimize the risk of data breaches.

1.4.3 Scalability and flexibility

Architecture: Hospital 4.0 systems are designed to be scalable, allowing for the addition of new sensors and devices as needed. The architecture should be flexible enough to adapt to evolving technologies. The architecture design for scalability and flexibility in smart sensors within Hospital 4.0/5.0 revolves around a modular and scalable design to accommodate the dynamic nature of healthcare environments. Adopting a microservices architecture allows for the development and deployment of independent, loosely coupled modules, ensuring that each smart sensor component can be easily scaled up or down based on the evolving needs of the hospital. This modular approach enables seamless integration of new sensors and technologies, promoting flexibility and adaptability as healthcare systems evolve over time.

Furthermore, the use of cloud-based infrastructure plays a pivotal role in achieving scalability and flexibility. Cloud platforms provide the necessary computational resources on demand, allowing hospitals to scale their smart sensor networks based on the volume of data generated or the addition of new sensors. Cloud solutions also facilitate data sharing and interoperability among different hospital departments, ensuring a cohesive and unified approach to healthcare data management. Overall, the architecture framework for scalability and flexibility in Hospitals 4.0/5.0 embraces modular design principles and leverages cloud technologies to create an agile and adaptable ecosystem capable of meeting the ever-changing demands of modern healthcare.

Design choices: Determine modular and scalable sensor solutions that can be easily integrated into existing infrastructure. Consider cloud-based solutions that can scale based on demand and provide flexibility in sensor deployments. Design choices for scalability and flexibility in smart sensors within the context of Hospital 4.0 and 5.0 encompass several key considerations. First, the adoption of open standards and interoperable protocols is essential. Choosing standardized communication protocols and data formats ensures that smart sensors from different manufacturers can seamlessly integrate into the hospital's ecosystem. This interoperability fosters flexibility by allowing the hospital to select the most suitable sensors for specific use cases and easily replace or upgrade them without disrupting the entire system.

Second, leveraging cloud computing technologies is a strategic design choice for scalability and flexibility. Cloud-based solutions provide a scalable infrastructure that can dynamically adjust to varying workloads. Hospitals can efficiently scale their smart sensor networks by provisioning additional computing resources when needed, ensuring optimal performance during periods of high demand. Moreover, cloud platforms offer the flexibility to deploy and manage diverse applications, enabling hospitals to adapt and integrate emerging technologies, such as machine learning algorithms for predictive analytics, without the constraints of traditional on-premises infrastructure. These design choices collectively contribute to creating a scalable and flexible environment for smart sensors in the evolving landscape of Hospitals 4.0/5.0.

1.4.4 Edge computing and real-time analytics

Architecture: Hospital 5.0 emphasizes edge computing to process data closer to the source, enabling real-time analytics. This architecture reduces latency and allows for quicker decision-making. In Hospital 4.0/5.0, the architecture framework for edge computing and real-time analytics plays a crucial role in optimizing healthcare operations and enhancing patient care. In Hospital 4.0, the focus is on integrating advanced technologies like the IoT and smart sensors to gather real-time data from various medical devices, patient monitors, and other healthcare equipment. Edge computing is employed at the network periphery, allowing data processing and analytics to occur closer to the data source rather than relying solely on centralized cloud servers. This architecture minimizes latency and enables faster decision-making, crucial in time-sensitive healthcare scenarios.

Moving toward Hospital 5.0, the architecture framework evolves to further leverage AI and ML algorithms for advanced real-time analytics. Smart sensors embedded in medical devices and wearables continuously collect data, which is processed at the edge and then sent to the cloud for comprehensive analysis. This approach optimizes bandwidth usage and ensures that critical insights are generated promptly. Additionally, decentralized processing enhances data security and privacy compliance, addressing concerns in the healthcare industry. The combination of edge computing and real-time analytics in Hospital 5.0 establishes a resilient and responsive healthcare infrastructure, facilitating personalized patient care, proactive disease management, and overall operational efficiency.

Design choices: Deploy edge computing nodes strategically throughout the hospital to process sensor data locally. Implement real-time analytics algorithms that can provide actionable insights, enabling prompt responses to patient needs. In the design choices for edge computing and real-time analytics in Hospital 4.0, one key consideration is the selection of edge devices and gateways that efficiently manage the diverse array of smart sensors and IoT devices. These devices should be capable of processing and filtering data at the edge, reducing the volume of information transmitted to centralized systems. Additionally, the choice of communication protocols, such as MQTT or CoAP, is crucial for optimizing data transfer between sensors and edge devices. Furthermore, the deployment of edge analytics algorithms tailored to healthcare applications ensures that critical insights are derived locally, minimizing latency and enabling faster response times in patient care and operational management.

As Hospital 5.0 emerges, design choices evolve to accommodate more sophisticated AI and ML algorithms for real-time analytics. The selection of powerful edge computing resources capable of handling complex computational tasks becomes paramount. Implementing federated learning models allows collaborative training across distributed edge devices while maintaining data privacy and security. Moreover, hybrid architectures combining edge and cloud resources are adopted to harness the strengths of both, ensuring scalability, fault tolerance, and the ability to manage the increasing complexity of healthcare data. Design choices in Hospital 5.0 prioritize an adaptive and scalable infrastructure that integrates cutting-edge technologies, enabling healthcare systems to harness the full potential of smart sensors and real-time analytics for improved patient outcomes and operational efficiency.

1.4.5 AI and machine learning integration

Architecture: Hospital 5.0 leverages AI and ML for advanced data analysis, predictive analytics, and decision support. The integration of AI and machine learning into smart sensors for Hospital 4.0 and 5.0 involves a sophisticated architecture framework to optimize healthcare processes and enhance patient care. In Hospital 4.0, the architecture typically comprises interconnected sensors, edge computing devices, and a centralized cloud infrastructure. Smart sensors embedded in medical equipment collect real-time data, such as patient vitals, diagnostic images, and environmental conditions. This data is processed locally at the edge to reduce latency and enhance privacy before being transmitted to the cloud for further analysis. ML-based algorithms within the cloud analyze large datasets to identify patterns, predict patient outcomes, and optimize resource allocation. This framework enables predictive maintenance of medical equipment, personalized treatment plans, and efficient hospital operations.

As we move toward Hospital 5.0, the architecture becomes more intelligent and autonomous, with a focus on human-centric care. Advanced AI algorithms are embedded directly into the smart sensors, enabling real-time decision-making at the point of care. These intelligent sensors interact with each other and with the hospital's information systems, forming a cohesive and adaptive healthcare ecosystem. Edge computing capabilities are further enhanced, allowing for faster data processing and response times. The integration of AI in smart sensors for Hospital 5.0 not only improves diagnostic accuracy and treatment effectiveness but also fosters a patient-centered approach by tailoring healthcare experiences to individual needs. The architecture prioritizes seamless communication between devices, promotes interoperability, and leverages the full potential of AI to revolutionize healthcare delivery.

Design choices: Design the sensor architecture to support AI and ML algorithms. Integrate machine learning models that can analyze sensor data for predictive maintenance, early disease detection, and personalized patient care. Designing smart sensors for AI and ML-based integration in Hospitals 4.0/5.0 involves strategic choices to ensure efficiency, security, and scalability. In Hospital 4.0, the design choices revolve around creating a robust network of sensors with interoperability and standardization. Utilizing open standards for communication protocols ensures seamless integration with various devices and systems. Edge computing plays a pivotal role, enabling data preprocessing at the sensor level to reduce latency and prioritize critical information for transmission to the cloud. Emphasis is placed on data security and privacy through encryption and access control mechanisms. Machine learning algorithms are selected and optimized to run efficiently on edge devices, balancing computational load and accuracy.

In the transition to Hospital 5.0, design choices evolve to prioritize decentralized intelligence and real-time decision-making at the sensor level. Smart sensors are endowed with advanced AI capabilities, allowing them to autonomously analyze and respond to complex healthcare scenarios. The design emphasizes edge AI architectures that support distributed processing, minimizing the need for centralized cloud computing. These sensors are designed to adapt to dynamic healthcare environments, learning from real-time interactions and continuously improving their performance. Human-centric design principles are applied, ensuring that the integration of AI in smart sensors aligns with the goal of enhancing patient experiences and providing personalized, efficient healthcare services. The design choices for Hospital 5.0 focus on creating an intelligent and adaptive healthcare ecosystem that seamlessly integrates AI into the fabric of patient care.

1.4.6 Internet of Things ecosystem

Architecture: Hospital 5.0 relies on a comprehensive IoT ecosystem where sensors are part of a larger interconnected network of devices and systems. The architecture framework for IoT Ecosystem Integration in smart sensors for Hospitals 4.0/5.0 is a sophisticated and interconnected system designed to enhance healthcare services and efficiency. In Hospital 4.0, the integration revolves around the use of advanced sensors that collect real-time patient data, such as vital signs, movement, and environmental conditions. These smart sensors communicate through a robust network infrastructure, utilizing technologies like 5G for low-latency and high-throughput data transfer. The collected data is then processed by edge computing devices or sent to centralized cloud platforms for analysis. The integration extends to various hospital systems, including EHR, to provide a comprehensive view of patient health, streamline workflows, and enable predictive analytics for proactive healthcare management.

Hospital 5.0 builds upon the foundation of Hospital 4.0 with an emphasis on personalized and human-centric care. The IoT architecture framework evolves to incorporate more advanced artificial intelligence algorithms and machine learning models. Smart sensors become even more sophisticated, allowing for continuous monitoring and adaptation to individual patient needs. Integration extends beyond the hospital walls to include wearable devices and home-based monitoring solutions, fostering a seamless continuum of care. Interoperability standards play a crucial role in ensuring that devices and systems from different manufacturers can communicate effectively. Overall, the architecture framework for IoT Ecosystem Integration in Hospital 4.0 and 5.0 envisions a connected healthcare ecosystem that leverages data-driven insights, automation, and personalized care to improve patient outcomes and operational efficiency.

Design choices: Choose sensors that are IoT-enabled and can seamlessly integrate with other IoT devices. Implement a unified dashboard or control center that provides a holistic view of the entire hospital's IoT ecosystem. Design choices for IoT Ecosystem Integration in smart sensors for Hospital 4.0 and 5.0 are critical to ensure seamless connectivity, data accuracy, and efficient healthcare delivery. In Hospital 4.0, a key design choice involves selecting interoperable communication protocols and standards to enable seamless integration among various devices and systems. For instance, adopting standardized protocols like HL7 for data exchange between different healthcare applications and the use of FHIR for more modern and scalable data sharing are common choices. Additionally, the integration of edge computing is a strategic decision to process data closer to the source, reducing latency and enabling quicker responses for critical healthcare decisions.

In Hospital 5.0, design choices become more sophisticated, focusing on patient-centric and AI-driven healthcare. The selection of advanced machine learning algorithms for real-time data analysis and decision support becomes crucial. The integration of blockchain technology might be considered for securing and ensuring the integrity of patient data across the healthcare ecosystem. Wearable devices and home monitoring solutions require thoughtful design to ensure user-friendliness and continuous connectivity. Furthermore, privacy and security considerations drive the adoption of robust encryption mechanisms and authentication protocols to safeguard sensitive patient information. Ultimately, the design choices for IoT Ecosystem Integration in Hospital 4.0 and 5.0 aim to create a reliable, secure, and adaptable healthcare infrastructure that enhances patient care and operational efficiency.

1.4.7 Human-centric design

Architecture: Hospital 5.0 places a strong emphasis on human-centric design, ensuring that technology enhances the overall patient experience and healthcare delivery. The architecture framework for human-centric design in smart sensors for Hospitals 4.0/5.0 revolves around creating a seamless and responsive healthcare environment that prioritizes patient well-being and enhances overall hospital operations. In Hospital 4.0, the focus is on integrating the IoT and data analytics to develop interconnected smart sensors. These sensors collect real-time patient data, monitor vital signs, and communicate with other devices to provide a comprehensive understanding of the patient's health. The architecture emphasizes user-friendly interfaces and intuitive design to ensure healthcare professionals can easily interpret and respond to the data generated by these sensors. Furthermore, it incorporates machine learning algorithms to predict potential health issues and optimize resource allocation within the hospital.

As we move toward Hospital 5.0, the architecture evolves to a more adaptive and personalized approach. It incorporates advanced AI systems that analyze vast datasets to tailor healthcare solutions to individual patients. The human-centric design is extended to prioritize patient experience, with smart sensors incorporating feedback mechanisms to understand and respond to patient preferences. The architecture emphasizes ethical considerations, data security, and privacy to build trust in the use of technology. Additionally, it promotes collaboration among healthcare professionals, patients, and technology developers to ensure continuous refinement and improvement of the smart sensor systems, aligning with the principles of human-centric design in the evolving landscape of healthcare.

Design choices: Select sensors with user-friendly interfaces and consider patient feedback in the design process. Implement sensors that enhance patient comfort, automate routine tasks, and contribute to a more patient-centered care environment. Design choices for human-centric design in smart sensors for Hospitals 4.0/5.0 are pivotal in creating systems that prioritize user experience, enhance patient care, and streamline healthcare operations. In Hospital 4.0, design choices revolve around creating intuitive interfaces for smart sensors that are easily navigable by healthcare professionals. User-centric displays, ergonomic device shapes, and easily interpretable data visualization are essential to ensure efficient and accurate use of the sensor data. Integration of voice or gesture controls can further enhance accessibility, allowing healthcare providers to interact with the smart sensors without disrupting their workflow. Additionally, a focus on durability, hygiene, and ease of maintenance is crucial in the hospital setting, where devices must withstand frequent use and adhere to stringent cleanliness standards.

As the healthcare ecosystem progresses to Hospital 5.0, design choices become even more tailored to individual patient needs. Personalization and adaptability are key considerations, with smart sensors incorporating customizable settings to accommodate variations in patient preferences and comfort. The use of empathetic design principles ensures that the sensors contribute positively to the overall patient experience, acknowledging the potential stress and anxiety associated with healthcare settings. In Hospital 5.0, sensor design choices also emphasize the integration of real-time patient feedback mechanisms, allowing individuals to communicate their preferences and concerns directly to the healthcare system, fostering a more collaborative and patient-centric approach to healthcare delivery/in both Hospital 4.0 and 5.0, it is crucial to prioritize the selection of sensors that align with the hospital's specific needs, promote interoperability, ensure data security, and contribute to improved patient outcomes and operational efficiency. The design should be adaptive to technological advancements and scalable to accommodate future innovations in healthcare.

1.5 Conclusion

The chapter initiates with a contextualization of Hospitals 4.0/5.0, offering a nuanced understanding of the historical progression and the fundamental principles underpinning these transformative healthcare paradigms. Hospital 4.0, characterized by the integration of smart technologies, data analytics, and automation, lays the groundwork for Hospital 5.0, emphasizing the human-centric approach in healthcare delivery. The discussion navigates through the key features and implications of these paradigms, setting the stage for a detailed exploration of the role of smart sensors in shaping the healthcare landscape. An in-depth analysis of the architecture of smart sensor networks constitutes a significant portion of the chapter. The incorporation of IoT principles, edge computing, and cloud-based solutions is scrutinized to establish a robust foundation for intelligent healthcare systems. Emphasis is placed on the interoperability of sensors, enabling seamless communication between devices, and the efficient processing of data in real time. The discussion further delves into the selection of appropriate sensor types, communication protocols, and data processing techniques, acknowledging the significance of these design choices in ensuring the reliability, scalability, and security of smart sensor networks within healthcare environments. The concept of user-centric design takes center stage as the chapter progresses, recognizing the pivotal role of healthcare professionals and patients in the successful integration of smart sensors. The discussion encompasses human–machine interaction, user interfaces, and accessibility features, elucidating the importance of designing sensor systems that prioritize ease of use, seamless integration into existing workflows, and enhanced user experience. The chapter synthesizes a comprehensive exploration of the architecture and design choices associated with the integration of smart sensors in the context of Hospital 4.0 and 5.0. By blending theoretical frameworks with practical insights, the chapter serves as a valuable resource for researchers, healthcare practitioners, and decision-makers navigating the intricate landscape of intelligent healthcare integration. As the industry continues its trajectory toward digital transformation, the insights presented herein aim to inform strategic decision-making, foster innovation, and contribute to the realization of healthcare systems that are not only technologically advanced but also deeply human-centered.

References

AbdulRaheem, M., Awotunde, J. B., Chakraborty, C., Adeniyi, E. A., Oladipo, I. D., & Bhoi, A. K. (2022). *Security and privacy concerns in smart healthcare system. Implementation of smart healthcare systems using AI, IoT, and blockchain* (pp. 243–273). Nigeria: Elsevier. Available from https://www.sciencedirect.com/book/9780323919166, https://doi.org/10.1016/B978-0-323-91916-6.00002-3.

Abikoye, O. C., Bajeh, A. O., Awotunde, J. B., Ameen, A. O., Mojeed, H. A., Abdulraheem, M., Oladipo, I. D., & Salihu, S. A. (2021). *Application of internet of thing and cyber physical system in Industry 4.0 smart manufacturing. Advances in science, technology and innovation* (pp. 203–217). Nigeria: Springer Nature. Available from https://www.springer.com/series/15883, https://doi.org/10.1007/978-3-030-66222-6_14.

Abrahams, E., & Downing, G. J. (2024). *On the modern evolution of personalized medicine* (pp. 1–25). Elsevier BV. Available from https://doi.org/10.1016/b978-0-443-13963-5.00009-1.

Aceto, G., Persico, V., & Pescapé, A. (2020). Industry 4.0 and health: Internet of things, Big Data, and Cloud computing for Healthcare 4.0. *Journal of Industrial Information Integration, 18*, 100129. Available from https://doi.org/10.1016/j.jii.2020.100129.

Adeniyi, E. A., Awotunde, J. B., Ogundokun, R. O., Kolawole, P. O., Abiodun, M. K., & Adeniyi, A. A. (2020). Mobile health application and COVID-19: Opportunities and challenges. *Journal of Critical Reviews, 7*(15), 3481–3488.

Adeniyi, E. A., Ogundokun, R. O., & Awotunde, J. B. (2021). IoMT-based wearable body sensors network healthcare monitoring system. *Studies in Computational Intelligence, 933*, 103–121. Available from https://doi.org/10.1007/978-981-15-9897-5_6, http://www.springer.com/series/7092.

Adeniyi, J. K., Adeniyi, T. T., Awotunde, J. B., Abiodun, M. K., & Atanda, O. G. (2023). *Agrolend: A blockchain implementation approach of smart contract farming platform. International conference on science, engineering and business for sustainable development goals, SEB-SDG 2023*. Nigeria: Institute of Electrical and Electronics Engineers Inc. Available from http://ieeexplore.ieee.org/xpl/mostRecentIssue.jsp?punumber = 10124379, https://doi.org/10.1109/SEB-SDG57117.2023.10124467.

Ajagbe, S. A., Adigun, M. O., Awotunde, J. B., Oladosu, J. B., & Oguns, Y. J. (2022). *Internet of things enabled convolutional neural networks: Applications, techniques, challenges, and prospects IoT-enabled convolutional neural networks: Techniques and applications* (pp. 27–63). Nigeria: River Publishers, Nigeria River Publishers. Available from https://www.riverpublishers.com/book_details.php?book_id = 1012.

Ajagbe, S. A., Awotunde, J. B., Oladipupo, M. A., & Oye, O. E. (2022). Prediction and forecasting of coronavirus cases using artificial intelligence algorithm. *Machine learning for critical internet of medical things:*

Applications and use cases (pp. 31–54). Nigeria: Springer International Publishing. Available from https://link.springer.com/book/10.1007/978-3-030-80928-7, https://doi.org/10.1007/978-3-030-80928-7_2.

Ajamu, G. J., Awotunde, J. B., Jimoh, T. B., Adeniyi, E. A., Abiodun, K. M., Oladipo, I. D., & Abdulraheem, M. (2023). Online teaching sustainability and strategies during the COVID-19 epidemic. *The role of sustainability and artificial intelligence in education improvement* (pp. 106–132). Nigeria: CRC Press. Available from https://www.routledge.com/The-Role-of-Sustainability-and-Artificial-Intelligence-in-Education-Improvement/Rosak-Szyrocka-Zywiolek-Nayyar-Naved/p/book/9781032544649, https://doi.org/10.1201/9781003425779-6.

Akhtar, M. N., Haleem, A., & Javaid, M. (2024). Exploring the advent of Medical 4.0: A bibliometric analysis systematic review and technology adoption insights. *Informatics and Health, 1*(1), 16–28. Available from https://doi.org/10.1016/j.infoh.2023.10.001.

Alexandre, P. K., Monestime, J. P., & Alexandre, K. (2024). The impact of county-level factors on meaningful use of electronic health records (EHRs) among primary care providers. *PLoS One, 19*(1). Available from https://doi.org/10.1371/journal.pone.0295435, https://journals.plos.org//plosone/article?id = 10.1371/journal.pone.0295435.

Alowais, S. A., Alghamdi, S. S., Alsuhebany, N., Alqahtani, T., Alshaya, A. I., Almohareb, S. N., Aldairem, A., Alrashed, M., Bin Saleh, K., Badreldin, H. A., Al Yami, M. S., Al Harbi, S., & Albekairy, A. M. (2023). Revolutionizing healthcare: The role of artificial intelligence in clinical practice. *BMC Medical Education, 23*(1). Available from https://doi.org/10.1186/s12909-023-04698-z, https://bmcmededuc.biomedcentral.com/.

An, B. W., Shin, J. H., Kim, S. Y., Kim, J., Ji, S., Park, J., Lee, Y., Jang, J., Park, Y. G., Cho, E., Jo, S., & Park, J. U. (2017). Smart sensor systems for wearable electronic devices. *Polymers, 9*(8). Available from https://doi.org/10.3390/polym9080303, http://www.mdpi.com/2073-4360/9/8/303/pdf.

Anikwe, C. V., Nweke, H. F., Ikegwu, A. C., Egwuonwu, C. A., Onu, F. U., Alo, U. R., & Teh, Y. W. (2022). Mobile and wearable sensors for data-driven health monitoring system: State-of-the-art and future prospect. *Expert Systems with Applications, 202*.

Anupama, D., Kumar, A. R., & Sumathi, D. (2024). *Managing healthcare data using ML algorithms and society 5.0* (pp. 71–102). Springer Science and Business Media LLC. Available from https://doi.org/10.1007/978-981-99-8118-2_4.

Askari, S., Ghofrani, A., & Taherdoost, H. (2024). *Fintech-enabled telemedicine: Global healthcare advancement. Exploring Global FinTech Advancement and Applications* (pp. 313–330). Canada: IGI Global. Available from https://www.igi-global.com/book/exploring-global-fintech-advancement-applications/328773, https://doi.org/10.4018/979-8-3693-1561-3.ch012.

Awokola, A. J., Falola, B. P., Adeniyi, A. E., Abiodun, M. K., Madamidola, A. O., Awotunde, J. B., Olagunju, M., Atanda, O. G., & Omolehin, P. (2023). Development of an android-based reminder system for the Covid-19 management. *International conference on science, engineering and business for sustainable development goals, SEB-SDG 2023*. Nigeria: Institute of Electrical and Electronics Engineers Inc. Available from http://ieeexplore.ieee.org/xpl/mostRecentIssue.jsp?punumber = 10124379, https://doi.org/10.1109/SEB-SDG57117.2023.10124645.

Awotunde, J. B., Adeniyi, A. E., Ogundokun, R. O., Ajamu, G. J., & Adebayo, P. O. (2021). MIoT-based Big Data analytics architecture, opportunities and challenges for enhanced telemedicine systems. *Studies in Fuzziness and Soft Computing, 410*, 199–220. Available from https://doi.org/10.1007/978-3-030-70111-6_10. http://www.springer.com/sgw/cda/frontpage/0,11855,1-40356-69-1191779-0,00.html?changeHeader = true.

Awotunde, J. B., Adeniyi, E. A., Ajamu, G. J., Balogun, G. B., & Taofeek-Ibrahim, F. A. (2022). Explainable artificial intelligence in genomic sequence for healthcare systems prediction. *Studies in Computational Intelligence, 1021*, 417–437. Available from https://doi.org/10.1007/978-3-030-97929-4_19, http://www.springer.com/series/7092.

Awotunde, J. B., Ayo, F. E., Jimoh, R. G., Ogundokun, R. O., Matiluko, O. E., Oladipo, I. D., & Abdulraheem, M. (2020). Prediction and classification of diabetes mellitus using genomic data. *Intelligent IoT systems in personalized health care* (pp. 235–292). Nigeria: Elsevier. Available from https://www.elsevier.com/books/intelligent-iot-systems-in-personalized-health-care/sangaiah/978-0-12-821187-8, https://doi.org/10.1016/B978-0-12-821187-8.00009-5.

Awotunde, J. B., Bhoi, A. K., Jimoh, R. G., Ajagbe, S. A., Ayo, F. E., & Adebisi, O. A. (2022). Internet of things based enabled convolutional neural networks in healthcare. *IoT-enabled convolutional neural networks: Techniques and applications* (pp. 329–357). Nigeria: River Publishers. Available from https://www.riverpublishers.com/book_details.php?book_id = 1012.

Awotunde, J. B., Chakraborty, C., AbdulRaheem, M., Jimoh, R. G., Oladipo, I. D., & Bhoi, A. K. (2022). Internet of medical things for enhanced smart healthcare systems. *Implementation of smart healthcare systems using AI, IoT, and Blockchain* (pp. 1–28). Nigeria: Elsevier. Available from https://www.sciencedirect.com/book/9780323919166, https://doi.org/10.1016/B978-0-323-91916-6.00009-6.

Awotunde, J. B., Folorunsho, O., Mustapha, I. O., Olusanya, O. O., Akanbi, M. B., & Abiodun, K. M. (2023). An enhanced internet of things enabled type-2 fuzzy logic for healthcare system applications. *Studies in Fuzziness and Soft Computing*, *425*, 133–151. Available from https://doi.org/10.1007/978-3-031-26332-3_9, https://www.springer.com/series/2941.

Awotunde, J. B., Folorunso, S. O., Ajagbe, S. A., Garg, J., & Ajamu, G. J. (2022). AiIoMT: IoMT-based system-enabled artificial intelligence for enhanced smart healthcare systems. *Machine learning for critical internet of medical things: Applications and use cases* (pp. 229–254). Nigeria: Springer International Publishing. Available from https://link.springer.com/book/10.1007/978-3-030-80928-7, https://doi.org/10.1007/978-3-030-80928-7_10.

Awotunde, J. B., Imoize, A. L., Jimoh, R. G., Adeniyi, E. A., Abdulraheem, M., Oladipo, I. D., & Falola, P. B. (2023). AIoMT enabling real-time monitoring of healthcare systems security and privacy considerations. *Handbook of security and privacy of AI-enabled healthcare systems and internet of medical things* (pp. 97–133). Nigeria: CRC Press. Available from http://www.tandfebooks.com/doi/book/9781000963182, https://doi.org/10.1201/9781003370321-5.

Awotunde, J. B., Imoize, A. L., Salako, D. P., & Farhaoui, Y. (2023). An enhanced medical diagnosis system for malaria and typhoid fever using genetic neuro-fuzzy system. *Lecture Notes in Networks and Systems*, *635*, 173–183. Available from https://doi.org/10.1007/978-3-031-26254-8_25, https://www.springer.com/series/15179.

Awotunde, J. B., Jimoh, R. G., AbdulRaheem, M., Oladipo, I. D., Folorunso, S. O., & Ajamu, G. J. (2022). IoT-based wearable body sensor network for COVID-19 pandemic. *Studies in Systems, Decision and Control*, *378*, 253–275. Available from https://doi.org/10.1007/978-3-030-77302-1_14, http://www.springer.com/series/13304.

Awotunde, J. B., Jimoh, R. G., Ogundokun, R. O., Misra, S., & Abikoye, O. C. (2022). *Big Data analytics of IoT-based cloud system framework: Smart healthcare monitoring systems. Internet of things* (pp. 181–208). Nigeria: Springer Science and Business Media Deutschland GmbH. Available from http://www.springer.com/series/11636, https://doi.org/10.1007/978-3-030-80821-1_9.

Awotunde, J. B., Misra, S., Ajagbe, S. A., Ayo, F. E., & Gurjar, R. (2023). An IoT machine learning model-based real-time diagnostic and monitoring system. *Lecture Notes in Electrical Engineering*, *997*, 789–799. Available from https://doi.org/10.1007/978-981-99-0085-5_64, https://www.springer.com/series/7818.

Awotunde, J. B., Misra, S., Ayoade, O. B., Ogundokun, R. O., & Abiodun, M. K. (2022). Blockchain-based framework for secure medical information in internet of things system. *EAI/Springer innovations in communication and computing* (pp. 147–169). Nigeria: Springer Science and Business Media Deutschland GmbH. Available from springer.com/series/15427, https://doi.org/10.1007/978-3-030-89546-4_8.

Awotunde, J. B., Misra, S., & Pham, Q. T. (2022). A secure framework for internet of medical things security based system using lightweight cryptography enabled blockchain. *Communications in Computer and Information Science*, *1688*, 258–272. Available from https://doi.org/10.1007/978-981-19-8069-5_17, https://www.springer.com/series/7899.

Awotunde, J. B., Ogundokun, R. O., Adeniyi, A. E., Abiodun, M. K., Ayo, F. E., Ajamu, G. J., & Ogundokun, O. E. (2022). Cloud-IoMT-based wearable body sensors network for monitoring elderly patients during the COVID-19 pandemic. *Biomedical engineering applications for people with disabilities and the elderly in the COVID-19 pandemic and beyond* (pp. 33–48). Nigeria: Elsevier. Available from https://www.sciencedirect.com/book/9780323851749, https://doi.org/10.1016/B978-0-323-85174-9.00028-5.

Awotunde, J. B., Oladipo, I. D., AbdulRaheem, M., Balogun, G. B., & Tomori, A. R. (2022). An IoMT-based steganography model for securing medical information. *International Journal of Healthcare Technology and Management*, *19*(3-4), 218–236. Available from https://doi.org/10.1504/IJHTM.2022.10051371, http://www.inderscience.com/ijhtm.

Awotunde, J. B., Oluwabukonla, S., Chakraborty, C., Bhoi, A. K., & Ajamu, G. J. (2022). Application of artificial intelligence and Big Data for fighting COVID-19 pandemic. *International Series in Operations Research and Management Science*, *320*, 3–26. Available from https://doi.org/10.1007/978-3-030-87019-5_1, http://www.springer.com/series/6161.

Awotunde, J. B., Sisodia, D. S., Ayodele, P. A., Ogundokun, R. O., & Chouhan, V. S. (2023). Diagnosis expert system on breast cancer using fuzzy logic and clustering technique. *Lecture Notes in Networks and Systems*, *671*, 589–601. Available from https://doi.org/10.1007/978-3-031-31153-6_47, https://www.springer.com/series/15179.

Awotunde, J. B., Tripathy, H. K., & Bandyopadhyay, A. (2022). Hybrid particle swarm optimization with firefly based resource provisioning technique for data fusion fog-cloud computing platforms. *Fusion: Practice and Applications*, *8*(2), 25–32. Available from https://doi.org/10.54216/FPA.080203, http://www.americaspg.com/journals/show/3.

Ayesha, A., & Komalavalli, C. (2024). Smart ambulance: A comprehensive IoT and cloud-based system integrating fingerprint sensor with medical sensors for real-time patient vital signs monitoring. *International Journal of Intelligent Systems and Applications in Engineering*, *12*(2), 555–567. Available from https://ijisae.org/index.php/IJISAE/article/download/4299/2950.

Ayoade, O. B., Oladele, T. O., Imoize, A. L., Adeloye, J. A., Awotunde, J. B., Olorunyomi, S. O., Faboya, O. T., & Idowu, A. O. (2023). An ensemble models for the prediction of sickle cell disease from erythrocytes smears. *EAI Endorsed Transactions on Pervasive Health and Technology*, *9*. Available from https://doi.org/10.4108/eetpht.9.3913, https://publications.eai.eu/index.php/phat/article/view/3913/2520.

Azrour, M., Mabrouki, J., Guezzaz, A., Ahmad, S., Khan, S., & Benkirane, S. (2024). *IoT, machine learning and data analytics for smart healthcare*. *IoT, machine learning and data analytics for smart healthcare* (pp. 1–94). Morocco: CRC Press. Available from https://www.taylorfrancis.com/books/edit/10.1201/9781003430735/iot-machine-learning-data-analytics-smart-healthcare-mourade-azrour-jamal-mabrouki-azidine-guezzaz-said-benkirane-sultan-ahmad-shakir-khan?context = ubx&refId = 2dc240d9-421e-4607-ab85-ccc75e35e919, https://doi.org/10.1201/9781003430735.

Brancato, V., Esposito, G., Coppola, L., Cavaliere, C., Mirabelli, P., Scapicchio, C., Borgheresi, R., Neri, E., Salvatore, M., & Aiello, M. (2024). Standardizing digital biobanks: integrating imaging, genomic, and clinical data for precision medicine. *Journal of Translational Medicine*, *22*(1). Available from https://doi.org/10.1186/s12967-024-04891-8.

Carayannis, E. G., Dezi, L., Gregori, G., & Calo, E. (2022). Smart environments and techno-centric and human-centric innovations for industry and society 5.0: A quintuple helix innovation system view towards smart, sustainable, and inclusive solutions. *Journal of the Knowledge Economy*, *13*(2), 926–955. Available from https://doi.org/10.1007/s13132-021-00763-4, http://www.springer.com/economics/policy/journal/13132.

Casas-Yrurzum, S., Gimeno, J., Casanova-Salas, P., García-Pereira, I., García del Olmo, E., Salvador, A., Guijarro, R., Zaragoza, C., & Fernández, M. (2023). A new mixed reality tool for training in minimally invasive robotic-assisted surgery. *Health Information Science and Systems*, *11*(1). Available from https://doi.org/10.1007/s13755-023-00238-7.

Casolino, R., Beer, P. A., Chakravarty, D., Davis, M. B., Malapelle, U., Mazzarella, L., Normanno, N., Pauli, C., Subbiah, V., Turnbull, C., Westphalen, C. B., & Biankin, A. V. (2024). Interpreting and integrating genomic tests results in clinical cancer care: Overview and practical guidance. *CA Cancer Journal for Clinicians*, *74*(3), 264–285. Available from https://doi.org/10.3322/caac.21825, http://onlinelibrary.wiley.com/journal/10.3322/(ISSN)1542-4863.

Castro, E. M., Van Regenmortel, T., Vanhaecht, K., Sermeus, W., & Van Hecke, A. (2016). Patient empowerment, patient participation and patient-centeredness in hospital care: A concept analysis based on a literature review. *Patient Education and Counseling*, *99*(12), 1923–1939. Available from https://doi.org/10.1016/j.pec.2016.07.026, http://www.elsevier.com/locate/pateducou.

Chhabra, R., & Singh, S. (2024). *E-healthcare and society 5.0. Artificial intelligence and society 5.0: Issues, opportunities, and challenges* (pp. 133–142). India: CRC Press. Available from http://www.tandfebooks.com/doi/book/9781003825593, https://doi.org/10.1201/9781003397052-12.

Chibuike, M. C., Grobbelaar, S. S., & Botha, A. (2024). Overcoming challenges for improved patient-centric care: A scoping review of platform ecosystems in healthcare. *IEEE Access*, *12*, 14298–14313. Available from https://doi.org/10.1109/ACCESS.2024.3356860, http://ieeexplore.ieee.org/xpl/RecentIssue.jsp?punumber = 6287639.

Daousis, S., Peladarinos, N., Cheimaras, V., Papageorgas, P., Piromalis, D. D., & Munteanu, R. A. (2024). Overview of protocols and standards for wireless sensor networks in critical infrastructures. *Future Internet*, *16* (1). Available from https://doi.org/10.3390/fi16010033, http://www.mdpi.com/journal/futureinternet.

Desselle, M. R., Brown, R. A., James, A. R., Midwinter, M. J., Powell, S. K., & Woodruff, M. A. (2020). Augmented and virtual reality in surgery. *Computing in Science and Engineering*, *22*(3), 18–26. Available from https://doi.org/10.1109/MCSE.2020.2972822, http://ieeexplore.ieee.org/Xplore/home.jsp.

Ebbers, T., Takes, R. P., Smeele, L. E., Kool, R. B., van den Broek, G. B., & Dirven, R. (2024). The implementation of a multidisciplinary, electronic health record embedded care pathway to improve structured data recording and decrease electronic health record burden. *International Journal of Medical Informatics*, *184*. Available from https://doi.org/10.1016/j.ijmedinf.2024.105344, https://www.sciencedirect.com/science/journal/13865056.

El-Sappagh, S., Ali, F., Hendawi, A., Jang, J. H., & Kwak, K. S. (2019). A mobile health monitoring-and-treatment system based on integration of the SSN sensor ontology and the HL7 FHIR standard. *BMC Medical Informatics and Decision Making*, *19*(1). Available from https://doi.org/10.1186/s12911-019-0806-z, http://www.biomedcentral.com/bmcmedinformdecismak/.

Elumalai, K., Srinivasan, S., & Shanmugam, A. (2024). Review of the efficacy of nanoparticle-based drug delivery systems for cancer treatment. *Biomedical Technology*, *5*, 109–122. Available from https://doi.org/10.1016/j.bmt.2023.09.001.

Emimi, M., Khaleel, M., & Alkrash, A. (2023). The current opportunities and challenges in drone technology. *International Journal of Electrical Engineering. and Sustainability.*, 74–89.

Falola, P. B., Adeniyi, A. E., Madamidola, O. A., Awotunde, J. B., Olukiran, O. A., & Akinola, S. O. (2023). *Artificial intelligence in agriculture: The potential for efficiency and sustainability, with ethical considerations. Exploring ethical dimensions of environmental sustainability and use of AI* (pp. 307–329). Nigeria: IGI Global. Available from https://www.igi-global.com/book/exploring-ethical-dimensions-environmental-sustainability/325075, https://doi.org/10.4018/9798369308929.ch015.

Gardašević, G., Katzis, K., Bajić, D., & Berbakov, L. (2020). Emerging wireless sensor networks and internet of things technologies—foundations of smart healthcare. *Sensors*, *20*(13), 3619. Available from https://doi.org/10.3390/s20133619.

Gomathi, L., Mishra, A.K., & Tyagi, A.K. (2023). Industry 5.0 for Healthcare 5.0: Opportunities, challenges and future research possibilities. In *7th International conference on trends in electronics and informatics, ICOEI 2023 - Proceedings* (pp. 204–213). http://ieeexplore.ieee.org/xpl/mostRecentIssue.jsp?punumber = 10125569 https://doi.org/10.1109/ICOEI56765.2023.10125660.

Gupta, P. C., Sharma, N., Mishra, P., Rai, S., & Verma, T. (2024). *Role of gold nanoparticles for targeted drug delivery* (pp. 243–269). Springer Science and Business Media LLC. Available from https://doi.org/10.1007/978-981-99-7673-7_12.

Gupta, R., Tanwar, S., Tyagi, S., Kumar, N., Obaidat, M. S., & Sadoun, B. (2019). *HaBiTs: Blockchain-based telesurgery framework for healthcare 4.0. CITS 2019 - Proceeding of the 2019 international conference on computer, information and telecommunication systems*. India: Institute of Electrical and Electronics Engineers Inc. Available from http://ieeexplore.ieee.org/xpl/mostRecentIssue.jsp?punumber = 8850888, https://doi.org/10.1109/CITS.2019.8862127.

Gärtner, M. A. (2024). Telemedicine adoption in rural vs. urban areas: A detailed analysis of economic impact and accessibility in Germany. *Law and Economy*, *3*(1), 47–57. Available from https://doi.org/10.56397/le.2024.01.05.

Gürce, M. Y., Wang, Y., & Zheng, Y. (2023). *Artificial intelligence and collaborative robots in healthcare: The perspective of healthcare professionals. Transformation for sustainable business and management practices: Exploring the spectrum of industry 5.0* (pp. 309–325). Kuwait: Emerald Group Publishing Ltd. Available from https://www.emerald.com/insight/publication/doi/10.1108/9781802622775, https://doi.org/10.1108/978-1-80262-277-520231022.

Haleem, A., Javaid, M., Pratap Singh, R., & Suman, R. (2022). Medical 4.0 technologies for healthcare: Features, capabilities, and applications. *Internet of Things and Cyber-Physical Systems*, *2*, 12–30. Available from https://doi.org/10.1016/j.iotcps.2022.04.001, https://www.sciencedirect.com/science/journal/26673452.

Hatamie, A., Angizi, S., Kumar, S., Pandey, C. M., Simchi, A., Willander, M., & Malhotra, B. D. (2020). Textile based chemical and physical sensors for healthcare monitoring. *Journal of the Electrochemical Society*, *167*(3).

Ilangakoon, T. S., Weerabahu, S. K., Samaranayake, P., & Wickramarachchi, R. (2022). Adoption of Industry 4.0 and lean concepts in hospitals for healthcare operational performance improvement. *International Journal of Productivity and Performance Management*, *71*(6), 2188–2213. Available from https://doi.org/10.1108/IJPPM-12-2020-0654, http://www.emeraldinsight.com/info/journals/ijppm/ijppm.jsp.

Jain, Y., Lanjewar, R., & Shinde, R. K. (2024). Revolutionising breast surgery: A comprehensive review of robotic innovations in breast surgery and reconstruction. *Cureus*. Available from https://doi.org/10.7759/cureus.52695.

Javaid, M., Haleem, A., Rab, S., Pratap Singh, R., & Suman, R. (2021). Sensors for daily life: A review. *Sensors International*, *2*. Available from https://doi.org/10.1016/j.sintl.2021.100121, https://www.sciencedirect.com/science/journal/26663511.

Judijanto, L., Anurogo, D., Zani, B. N., Hasyim, D. M., & Ningsih, K. P. (2024). Implementation of telemedicine in health services: Challenges and opportunities. *Journal of World Future Medicine*, *2*(1), 37–50.

Kolossváry, E., Farkas, K., Karahan, O., Golledge, J., Schernthaner, G.-H., Karplus, T., Bernardo, J. J., Marschang, S., Abola, M. T., Heinzmann, M., Edmonds, M., & Catalano, M. (2023). The importance of socio-economic determinants of health in the care of patients with peripheral artery disease: A narrative review from VAS. *Vascular Medicine*, *28*(3), 241–253. Available from https://doi.org/10.1177/1358863x231169316.

Koulaouzidis, G., Charisopoulou, D., Bomba, P., Stachura, J., Gasior, P., Harpula, J., Zarifis, J., Marlicz, W., Hudziak, D., & Jadczyk, T. (2023). Robotic-assisted solutions for invasive cardiology, cardiac surgery and routine on-ward tasks: A narrative review. *Journal of Cardiovascular Development and Disease*, *10*(9), 399. Available from https://doi.org/10.3390/jcdd10090399.

Kumari, A., Tanwar, S., Tyagi, S., & Kumar, N. (2018). Fog computing for Healthcare 4.0 environment: Opportunities and challenges. *Computers & Electrical Engineering*, *72*, 1–13. Available from https://doi.org/10.1016/j.compeleceng.2018.08.015.

Kusherdianti, N., Ariswati, H. G., Wisana, I. D. G. H., Irianto, B. G., Triwiyanto., Setioningsih, E. D., Rahmawati, T., & Awotunde, J. B. (2023). Analysis of finite impulse response (FIR) filter to reduce motion artifacts of heart rate signal based on photoplethysmography. *Lecture Notes in Electrical Engineering*, *1008*, 657–680. Available from https://doi.org/10.1007/978-981-99-0248-4_42, https://www.springer.com/series/7818.

Lammers, D. T., Williams, J. M., Conner, J. R., Baird, E., Rokayak, O., McClellan, J. M., Bingham, J. R., Betzold, R., & Eckert, M. J. (2023). Airborne! UAV delivery of blood products and medical logistics for combat zones. *Transfusion*, *63*(3), S96. Available from https://doi.org/10.1111/trf.17329, http://onlinelibrary.wiley.com/journal/10.1111/(ISSN)1537-2995.

Li, J., & Carayon, P. (2021). Health Care 4.0: A vision for smart and connected health care. *IISE Transactions on Healthcare Systems Engineering*, *11*(3), 171–180. Available from https://doi.org/10.1080/24725579.2021.1884627, http://www.tandfonline.com/loi/uhse20.

Li, S., Ma, Z., Cao, Z., Pan, L., & Shi, Y. (2020). Advanced wearable microfluidic sensors for healthcare monitoring. *Small (Weinheim an der Bergstrasse, Germany)*, *16*(9). Available from https://doi.org/10.1002/smll.201903822.

Lungu, A. J., Swinkels, W., Claesen, L., Tu, P., Egger, J., & Chen, X. (2021). A review on the applications of virtual reality, augmented reality and mixed reality in surgical simulation: An extension to different kinds of surgery. *Expert Review of Medical Devices*, *18*(1), 47–62. Available from https://doi.org/10.1080/17434440.2021.1860750, http://www.tandfonline.com/loi/ierd20.

Maddikunta, P. K. R., Pham, Q. V., B, P., Deepa, N., Dev, K., Gadekallu, T. R., Ruby, R., & Liyanage, M. (2022). Industry 5.0: A survey on enabling technologies and potential applications. *Journal of Industrial Information Integration*, *26*. Available from https://doi.org/10.1016/j.jii.2021.100257, http://www.journals.elsevier.com/journal-of-industrial-information-integration.

Mahajan, H. B., Rashid, A. S., Junnarkar, A. A., Uke, N., Deshpande, S. D., Futane, P. R., Alkhayyat, A., & Alhayani, B. (2023). Integration of healthcare 4.0 and blockchain into secure cloud-based electronic health records systems. *Applied Nanoscience (Switzerland)*, *13*(3), 2329–2342. Available from https://doi.org/10.1007/s13204-021-02164-0, https://www.springer.com/journal/13204.

Mai, H. N., & Lee, D. H. (2023). Accuracy of augmented reality–assisted navigation in dental implant surgery: Systematic review and meta-analysis. *Journal of Medical Internet Research*, *25*(1).

el Mathari, S., Hoekman, A., Kharbanda, R. K., Sadeghi, A. H., de Lind van Wijngaarden, R., Götte, M., Klautz, R. J. M., & Kluin, J. (2024). Virtual reality for pain and anxiety management in cardiac surgery and interventional cardiology. *JACC: Advances*, *3*(2). Available from https://doi.org/10.1016/j.jacadv.2023.100814, https://www.sciencedirect.com/journal/jacc-advances.

Mathkor, D. M., Mathkor, N., Bassfar, Z., Bantun, F., Slama, P., Ahmad, F., & Haque, S. (2024). Multirole of the internet of medical things (IoMT) in biomedical systems for managing smart healthcare systems: An overview of current and future innovative trends. *Journal of Infection and Public Health*, *17*(4), 559–572. Available from https://doi.org/10.1016/j.jiph.2024.01.013, https://www.sciencedirect.com/science/journal/18760341.

Mbunge, E., Jiyane, S. 'esihle, & Muchemwa, B. (2022). Towards emotive sensory web in virtual health care: Trends, technologies, challenges and ethical issues. *Sensors International*, *3*, 100134. Available from https://doi.org/10.1016/j.sintl.2021.100134.

Mbunge, E., Muchemwa, B., Jiyane, S. 'esihle, & Batani, J. (2021). Sensors and healthcare 5.0: Transformative shift in virtual care through emerging digital health technologies. *Global Health Journal*, *5*(4), 169–177. Available from https://doi.org/10.1016/j.glohj.2021.11.008.

Mishra, P., & Singh, G. (2023). Internet of medical things healthcare for sustainable smart cities: Current status and future prospects. *Applied Sciences*, *13*(15), 8869. Available from https://doi.org/10.3390/app13158869.

Mohanaprabhu, D., Monish Kanna, S. P., Jayasuriya, J., Lakshmanaprakash, S., Abirami, A., & Tyagi, A. K. (2024). *Quantum computation, quantum information, and quantum key distribution*. *Automated secure computing for next-generation systems* (pp. 347–366). India: Wiley. Available from https://www.wiley.com/en-in/Automated + Secure + Computing + for + Next + Generation + Systems-p-9781394213924.

Mohanta, B., Das, P., & Patnaik, S. (2019). *Healthcare 5.0: A paradigm shift in digital healthcare system using artificial intelligence, IOT and 5G communication. Proceedings - 2019 International conference on applied machine learning, ICAML 2019* (pp. 191–196). India: Institute of Electrical and Electronics Engineers Inc. Available from http://ieeexplore.ieee.org/xpl/mostRecentIssue.jsp?punumber = 8967488, https://doi.org/10.1109/ICAML48257.2019.00044.

Molina-Mula, J., & Gallo-Estrada, J. (2020). Impact of nurse-patient relationship on quality of care and patient autonomy in decision-making. *International Journal of Environmental Research and Public Health, 17*(3), 835. Available from https://doi.org/10.3390/ijerph17030835.

Morrison,R. (2024). New medical device and therapeutic approvals in otolaryngology: State of the art review. **2022**.

Naithani, K., & Tiwari, S. (2023). *Deep learning for the intersection of ethics and privacy in healthcare. Machine learning algorithms using Scikit and TensorFlow environments* (pp. 154–191). India: IGI Global. Available from https://www.igi-global.com/book/machine-learning-algorithms-using-scikit/314217, https://doi.org/10.4018/978-1-6684-8531-6.ch008.

Ndunagu,J.N., Aderemi,E.H., Jimoh,R.G., & Awotunde, J.B. (no date). Time series: Predicting Nigerian food prices using ARIMA model and R-programming. In *2022 5th information technology for education and development (ITED)* (pp. 1–6). IEEE.

Nguyen, T. A (2023). Blockchain and digital twin for industry 4.0/5.0. *Kenkyu Journal of Nanotechnology & Nanoscience, 9*, 01–05.

Nguyen, T. A. (2024). Digital twin-based universe (complexiverse): Where real world and virtual/digital world are unified. *Kenkyu Journal of Nanotechnology & Nanoscience, 10*, 01–04.

Nguyen, H. S., & Voznak, M. (2024). A bibliometric analysis of technology in digital health: Exploring health metaverse and visualizing emerging healthcare management trends. *IEEE Access, 12*, 23887–23913. Available from https://doi.org/10.1109/ACCESS.2024.3363165, http://ieeexplore.ieee.org/xpl/RecentIssue.jsp?punumber = 6287639.

Nikpanah, M., & Morgan, D. E. (2024). Magnetic resonance imaging in the evaluation and management of acute pancreatitis: A review of current practices and future directions. *Clinical Imaging, 107*, 110086. Available from https://doi.org/10.1016/j.clinimag.2024.110086.

Nuryanto, U. W., Basrowi., & Quraysin, I. (2024). Big Data and IoT adoption in shaping organizational citizenship behavior: The role of innovation organizational predictor in the chemical manufacturing industry. *International Journal of Data and Network Science, 8*(1), 255–268. Available from https://doi.org/10.5267/j.ijdns.2023.9.026, http://www.growingscience.com/ijds/Vol8/ijdns_2023_174.pdf.

Ogundokun, R. O., Awotunde, J. B., Imoize, A. L., Li, C. T., Abdulahi, A. R. T., Adelodun, A. B., Sur, S. N., & Lee, C. C. (2023). Non-orthogonal multiple access enabled mobile edge computing in 6G communications: A systematic literature review. *Sustainability (Switzerland), 15*(9). Available from https://doi.org/10.3390/su15097315, http://www.mdpi.com/journal/sustainability/.

Oladipupo, E. T., Abikoye, O. C., Imoize, A. L., Awotunde, J. B., Chang, T. Y., Lee, C. C., & Do, D. T. (2023). An efficient authenticated elliptic curve cryptography scheme for multicore wireless sensor networks. *IEEE Access, 11*, 1306–1323. Available from https://doi.org/10.1109/ACCESS.2022.3233632, http://ieeexplore.ieee.org/xpl/RecentIssue.jsp?punumber = 6287639.

Olatunji, G., Isarinade, T. D., Emmanuel, K., Olatunji, D., & Aderinto, N. (2023). Exploring the transformative role of drone technology in advancing healthcare delivery in Africa; A perspective. *Annals of Medicine & Surgery, 85*(10), 5279–5284. Available from https://doi.org/10.1097/ms9.0000000000001221.

Osama, M., Ateya, A. A., Sayed, M. S., Hammad, M., Pławiak, P., Abd El-Latif, A. A., & Elsayed, R. A. (2023). Internet of medical things and healthcare 4.0: Trends, requirements, challenges, and research directions. *Sensors, 23*(17). Available from https://doi.org/10.3390/s23177435, http://www.mdpi.com/journal/sensors.

Oselusi, S. O., Dube, P., Odugbemi, A. I., Akinyede, K. A., Ilori, T. L., Egieyeh, E., Sibuyi, N. R., Meyer, M., Madiehe, A. M., Wyckoff, G. J., & Egieyeh, S. A. (2024). The role and potential of computer-aided drug discovery strategies in the discovery of novel antimicrobials. *Computers in Biology and Medicine, 169*. Available from https://doi.org/10.1016/j.compbiomed.2024.107927, https://www.sciencedirect.com/science/journal/00104825.

Pal, S., Bhattacharya, M., Lee, S. S., & Chakraborty, C. (2024). Quantum computing in the next-generation computational biology landscape: From protein folding to molecular dynamics. *Molecular Biotechnology, 66*(2), 163–178. Available from https://doi.org/10.1007/s12033-023-00765-4, https://www.springer.com/journal/12033.

Pramanik, P. K. D., Upadhyaya, B. K., Pal, S., & Pal, T. (2019). *Internet of things, smart sensors, and pervasive systems: Enabling connected and pervasive healthcare. Healthcare data analytics and management* (pp. 1–58). India: Elsevier. Available from https://www.sciencedirect.com/book/9780128153680, https://doi.org/10.1016/B978-0-12-815368-0.00001-4.

Prerna., Singh, P., & Singh, D. P. (2024). *Role of disruptive technologies in the smart healthcare sector of society 5.0. Artificial intelligence and society 5.0: Issues, opportunities, and challenges* (pp. 143–153). India: CRC Press. Available from http://www.tandfebooks.com/doi/book/9781003825593, https://doi.org/10.1201/9781003397052-13.

Procopiou, A., & Stavrou, E. (2024). *Privacy concerns in smart indoor environments in the internet of everything era: A smart university campus case study* (pp. 92–109). Springer Science and Business Media LLC. Available from https://doi.org/10.1007/978-3-031-51572-9_8.

Putra, K. T., Arrayyan, A. Z., Hayati, N., Firdaus., Damarjati, C., Bakar, A., & Chen, H. C. (2024). A review on the application of internet of medical things in wearable personal health monitoring: A cloud-edge artificial intelligence approach. *IEEE Access, 12*, 21437–21452. Available from https://doi.org/10.1109/ACCESS.2024.3358827, http://ieeexplore.ieee.org/xpl/RecentIssue.jsp?punumber = 6287639.

Rath, K. C., Khang, A., & Roy, D. (2024). *The role of internet of things (IoT) technology in Industry 4.0 economy* (pp. 1–28). Informa UK Limited. Available from https://doi.org/10.1201/9781003434269-1.

Rehman, A., Naz, S., & Razzak, I. (2022). Leveraging Big Data analytics in healthcare enhancement: Trends, challenges and opportunities. *Multimedia Systems, 28*(4), 1339–1371. Available from https://doi.org/10.1007/s00530-020-00736-8.

Rojek, I., Kotlarz, P., Kozielski, M., Jagodziński, M., & Królikowski, Z. (2024). Development of AI-based prediction of heart attack risk as an element of preventive medicine. *Electronics, 13*(2), 272. Available from https://doi.org/10.3390/electronics13020272.

Ronaghi, M. H. (2024). Toward a model for assessing smart hospital readiness within the Industry 4.0 paradigm. *Journal of Science and Technology Policy Management, 15*(2), 353–373. Available from https://doi.org/10.1108/JSTPM-09-2021-0130, http://www.emeraldinsight.com/loi/jstpm.

Ruminski, J., Bujnowski, A., Kocejko, T., Andrushevich, A., Biallas, M., & Kistler, R. (2016). The data exchange between smart glasses and healthcare information systems using the HL7 FHIR standard. *Proceedings - 2016 9th international conference on human system interactions HSI 2016* (pp. 525–531). Poland: Institute of Electrical and Electronics Engineers Inc. Available from https://doi.org/10.1109/HSI.2016.7529684.

Rus, G., Andras, I., Vaida, C., Crisan, N., Gherman, B., Radu, C., Tucan, P., Iakab, S., Al Hajjar, N., & Pisla, D. (2023). Artificial intelligence-based hazard detection in robotic-assisted single-incision oncologic surgery. *Cancers, 15*(13), 3387. Available from https://doi.org/10.3390/cancers15133387.

Sadeghi, M., & Mahmoudi, A. (2024). Synergy between blockchain technology and internet of medical things in healthcare: A way to sustainable society. *Information Sciences, 660*, 120049. Available from https://doi.org/10.1016/j.ins.2023.120049.

Seetohul, J., Shafiee, M., & Sirlantzis, K. (2023). Augmented reality (AR) for surgical robotic and autonomous systems: State of the art, challenges, and solutions. *Sensors, 23*(13), 6202. Available from https://doi.org/10.3390/s23136202.

Shah, J. L., Bhat, H. F., & Khan, A. I. (2020). *Integration of cloud and IoT for smart e-healthcare. Healthcare paradigms in the internet of things ecosystem* (pp. 101–136). India: Elsevier. Available from https://www.elsevier.com/books/healthcare-paradigms-in-the-internet-of-things-ecosystem/balas/978-0-12-819664-9, https://doi.org/10.1016/B978-0-12-819664-9.00006-5.

Sharma, P. (2024). Quantum computing in drug design: Enhancing precision and efficiency in pharmaceutical development. *Sage Science Review of Applied Machine Learning*, *7*(1), 1–9.

Singh, B., & Kaunert, C. (2024). Integration of cutting-edge technologies such as internet of things (IoT) and 5G in health monitoring systems: A comprehensive legal analysis and futuristic outcomes. *GLS Law Journal*, *6*(1), 13–20.

Srivastava, J. P., Kozak, D., Ranjan, V., Kumar, P., Kumar, R., & Tayal, S. (2024). Robotics in medical science. *Mechanical engineering in biomedical applications: Bio-3D printing, biofluid mechanics, implant design, biomaterials, computational biomechanics, tissue mechanics* (pp. 367–396). Wiley. Available from https://doi.org/10.1002/9781394175109.ch15.

Sukin, D. F., Fulin, T., & Uralkan, M. (2024). Building the smart hospital of the future with technology bets. *Management in Healthcare*, *8*(2), 144–155.

Tortorella, G. L., Fogliatto, F. S., Espôsto, K. F., Vergara, A. M. C., Vassolo, R., Mendoza, D. T., & Narayanamurthy, G. (2020). Effects of contingencies on healthcare 4.0 technologies adoption and barriers in emerging economies. *Technological Forecasting and Social Change*, *156*. Available from https://doi.org/10.1016/j.techfore.2020.120048, https://www.journals.elsevier.com/technological-forecasting-and-social-change.

Tortorella, G. L., Saurin, T. A., Fogliatto, F. S., Rosa, V. M., Tonetto, L. M., & Magrabi, F. (2021). *Technological Forecasting and Social Change*, *166*.

Vijarania, M., Gupta, S., Agrawal, A., Adigun, M. O., Ajagbe, S. A., & Awotunde, J. B. (2023). Energy efficient load-balancing mechanism in integrated IoT–Fog–Cloud environment. *Electronics (Switzerland)*, *12*(11). Available from https://doi.org/10.3390/electronics12112543, http://www.mdpi.com/journal/electronics.

Wang, Y., Kung, L. A., & Byrd, T. A. (2018). Big Data analytics: Understanding its capabilities and potential benefits for healthcare organizations. *Technological Forecasting and Social Change*, *126*, 3–13. Available from https://doi.org/10.1016/j.techfore.2015.12.019, https://www.journals.elsevier.com/technological-forecasting-and-social-change.

Wang, Z., Chen, J., Gao, R., Jiang, L., Zhang, G., & Zhao, Y. (2024). Shi, spatiotemporal manipulation metal–organic frameworks as oral drug delivery systems for precision medicine. *Coordination Chemistry Reviews*, *502*.

Zanon, C., Quaia, E., & Crimì, F. (2024). Introduction to special issue imaging in cancer diagnosis. *Tomography*, *10*(1), 101–104. Available from https://doi.org/10.3390/tomography10010009.

Żydowicz, W. M., Skokowski, J., Marano, L., & Polom, K. (2024). Current trends and beyond conventional approaches: Advancements in breast cancer surgery through three-dimensional imaging, virtual reality, augmented reality, and the emerging metaverse. *Journal of Clinical Medicine*, *13*(3), 915. Available from https://doi.org/10.3390/jcm13030915.

CHAPTER

Machine learning and AI for the smart healthcare

2

Ramiz Salama and Fadi Al-Turjman

Artificial Intelligence, Software, and Information Systems Engineering Departments, Research Center for AI and IoT, AI and Robotics Institute, Near East University, Mersin, Turkey

2.1 Introduction

Modern healthcare faces a new set of opportunities and difficulties because of the incorporation of cutting-edge technologies. Improved patient care, faster procedures, and better healthcare results are all possible with the emergence of smart healthcare, which is defined by the smooth integration of digital advances with conventional healthcare systems. However, this road of transformation is not without its problems. Chief among them are the complexities and vulnerabilities related to protecting the privacy and security of sensitive health data. Globally, as healthcare organizations shift to digitization, the amount of patient data created, analyzed, and exchanged has increased dramatically. The abundance of health data raises concerns about data breaches, unauthorized access, and the violation of individual privacy, even as it also holds great promise for individualized care and medical improvements. In the dynamic environment of smart healthcare, the need for strong solutions that go beyond traditional security measures is becoming more and more necessary to protect the confidentiality and integrity of patient data. In this setting, the idea of blockchain technology shows itself as a resilient and innovative light. Blockchain was first developed as the foundational technology for cryptocurrencies, but it has now expanded to provide a decentralized, impenetrable system with the ability to completely transform the healthcare industry. Blockchain, a distributed ledger technology, solves important issues facing healthcare systems by ensuring accountability, transparency, and immutability in the handling of sensitive health data. The goal of this study is to investigate how blockchain technology and the security and privacy requirements of smart healthcare can coexist. The main goal is to clarify how blockchain technology can be used to mitigate the vulnerabilities present in the current healthcare system. This introduction seeks to contextualize the significance of blockchain as a key solution to the many problems the healthcare industry faces by offering a broad review of the state of smart healthcare. By traversing the technical nuances and complexity that characterize this nexus of technology and healthcare, the research aims to delve into the nuances of blockchain deployment in smart healthcare. The goal of the study is to dissect the layers of innovation that support the revolutionary influence of blockchain technology in healthcare systems through a thorough analysis of consensus protocols, smart contract functionality, and cryptographic methods. The research goals are outlined in this introduction, along with the particular aspects of blockchain technology that will be examined. The study's purview includes

Blockchain and Digital Twin for Smart Hospitals. DOI: https://doi.org/10.1016/B978-0-443-34226-4.00003-4

investigating how blockchain technology can protect health information, promote interoperability, and support patient-centered care models. The introduction also highlights the research's wider significance in adding to the growing conversation about the morally sound and safe incorporation of technology in the hospital setting. This study sets out to explore the intricacies, difficulties, and possible resolutions that are at the intersection of blockchain technology, security, and privacy in the context of smart healthcare in the pages that follow. This research attempts to give useful insights for politicians, healthcare professionals, and technologists who are influencing the future of digital healthcare through a thorough examination of these interconnected themes (Adam & Mukhtar, 2024; Jiwani et al., 2023; Kavitha et al., 2023; Mala, 2023; Rahman et al., 2023). Additionally, it hopes to advance the academic knowledge of blockchain in the healthcare industry.

2.2 Quantity of previous publications

The investigation of blockchain applications in the healthcare field has attracted the interest of academics, researchers, and business professionals in equal measure. This section provides a thorough analysis of the body of research, providing a broad picture of how blockchain technology has developed in the healthcare industry as well as highlighting any knowledge gaps that demand more research. The field of smart healthcare has undergone a revolutionary transition, characterized by the integration of cutting-edge technological innovations into conventional healthcare models. In addition to streamlining healthcare procedures, the integration of Internet of Things (IoT) devices, telemedicine, and electronic health records (EHRs) has opened the door for a multitude of health data collection and interchange. The weaknesses and difficulties related to security and privacy are becoming more noticeable as healthcare becomes more data-driven and networked. Upon careful analysis, a growing corpus of research has been done on the application of blockchain technology as a possible solution to smart healthcare's security and privacy issues. This subject includes a wide range of study issues, from the actual applications of blockchain technology in healthcare settings to its basic concepts. Academic journals, conference proceedings, and business reports add to a plethora of information by presenting many viewpoints on how blockchain technology is changing healthcare environments. Key topics of investigation in the literature now in publication include the use of blockchain technology to secure health data, guarantee data integrity, and promote interoperability across various healthcare systems. Scholars have investigated the security characteristics of blockchain technology, the effectiveness of consensus protocols in upholding a decentralized ledger, and the use of smart contracts to automate medical procedures. Empirical research and case studies offer important insights into practical applications, showing the difficulties and triumphs of implementing blockchain in healthcare settings. There are still glaring gaps in the body of research, despite its abundance, which emphasizes the need for more study. The aforementioned gaps pertain to intricate facets such as the difficulties associated with scaling up large-scale healthcare networks, the legal and regulatory structures that oversee blockchain technology in the healthcare industry, and the socio-technical factors that impact healthcare stakeholders' adoption of this technology. To promote a fuller knowledge of the opportunities and problems related to blockchain deployment in smart healthcare, the review recognizes these gaps as opportunities for researchers to contribute to the expanding conversation. The literature's reflection on the development of smart healthcare emphasizes how dynamically technology and healthcare intertwine. It emphasizes how the healthcare sector is moving from traditional healthcare models to patient-centered, technologically enabled care delivery. The body of research also highlights how crucial cutting-edge security measures are to preserving the accuracy of medical records and fostering patient and healthcare provider confidence. This section summarizes the existing literature, which not only lays the groundwork for further research but also acts as a catalyst for finding gaps that advance the investigation (Ahmed et al., 2023; Al-Blihed et al., 2023; Deepa et al., 2023; Hassaballah et al., 2023; Raza et al., 2023). The integration of information from many sources paves the way for a thorough examination of blockchain technology's potential to strengthen security and privacy in the complex field of smart healthcare.

2.2.1 Analytical approach

The analytical approach is intended to methodically explore blockchain's potential in tackling the changing issues that healthcare organizations confront in protecting patient data and guaranteeing the privacy of health-related information.

2.2.1.1 Review of literature

The initial step of the process entails a thorough and methodical analysis of the body of research on blockchain applications in the medical field. To develop a basic grasp of the status of research in this field, a comprehensive review of academic papers, conference proceedings, and industry reports is done. The next steps of the research are informed by the important topics, knowledge gaps, and emerging trends that are found in the literature review.

2.2.1.2 Source selection

A careful selection of sources is made, drawing on knowledge gleaned from the literature study. These include credible conference proceedings, peer-reviewed academic journals, and industry publications that offer a range of viewpoints on the application of blockchain technology to smart healthcare. To guarantee that the most recent breakthroughs and developments in the subject are included, special attention is paid to recent publications.

2.2.1.3 Data collection methods

To capture the range and depth of insights, the research uses a mixed-methods approach to data collection, integrating qualitative and quantitative techniques. In-depth interviews with important stakeholders, such as medical professionals, IT specialists, and legislators, are used to collect qualitative data and understand their viewpoints on the opportunities and problems related to blockchain adoption in the healthcare industry. Quantitative data offers a strong basis for insights based on data because it is gathered via empirical research, case studies, and pertinent statistical data.

2.2.1.4 Technical analysis

An important part of the approach is a technical examination of blockchain protocols and how they are used in smart healthcare. This covers a thorough analysis of the cryptographic techniques used to protect health information, consensus methods that guarantee the accuracy of decentralized ledgers, and the use of smart contracts to automate medical procedures.

The technical analysis offers a detailed grasp of the underlying technologies influencing blockchain's effectiveness in medical environments.

2.2.1.5 Evaluation criteria

A set of criteria is defined to evaluate how well blockchain addresses security and privacy issues in smart healthcare. These standards cover things such as data security, openness, scalability, legal compliance, and the capacity to promote interoperability between various healthcare systems. The assessment criteria function as standards by which the study findings and results are evaluated, enabling a thorough and methodical examination.

2.2.2 Use-case analysis and case studies

A thorough analysis of actual case studies and use-case scenarios involving the application of blockchain technology in healthcare settings is incorporated into the methodology. These case studies provide useful insights into the difficulties encountered, strategies employed, and general implications of blockchain technology for privacy and security in various healthcare settings.

2.2.3 Moral points to remember

Since healthcare data is sensitive, ethical issues are a crucial component of the research approach. The study guarantees participant confidentiality and anonymity by adhering to ethical rules in data collecting. The analysis also incorporates ethical issues, highlighting how crucial it is to match medical technology improvements with moral standards. The research attempts to offer a solid and nuanced grasp of the role of blockchain in bolstering security and privacy within the ever-changing

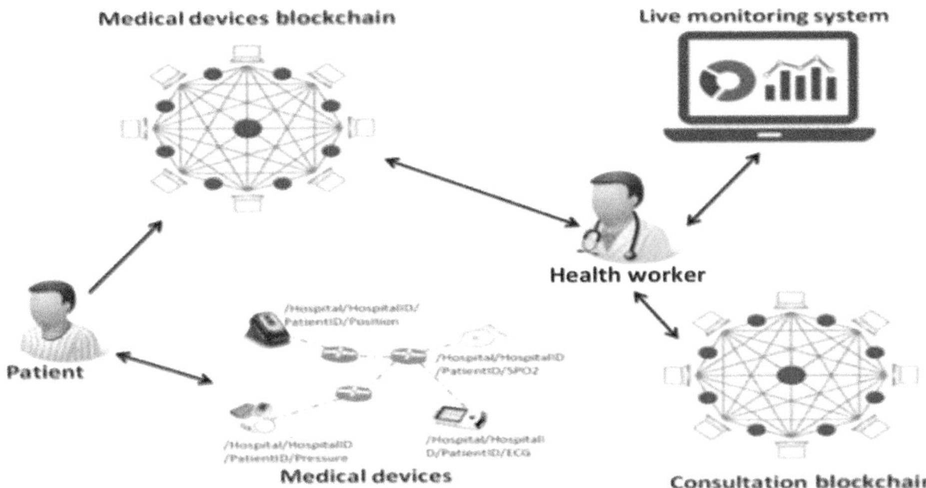

FIGURE 2.1

Medical devices blockchain.

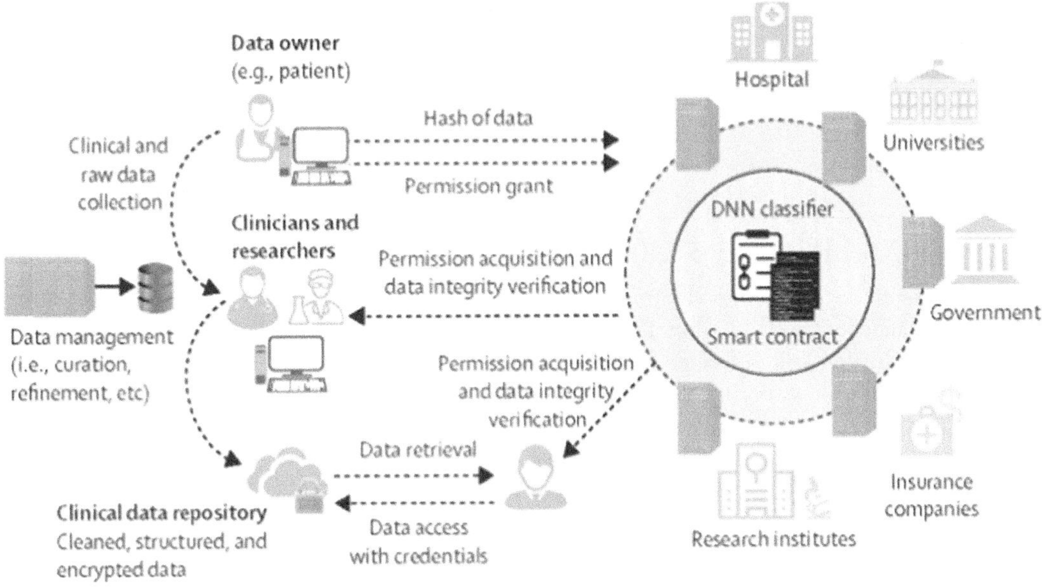

FIGURE 2.2

Clinical data repository.

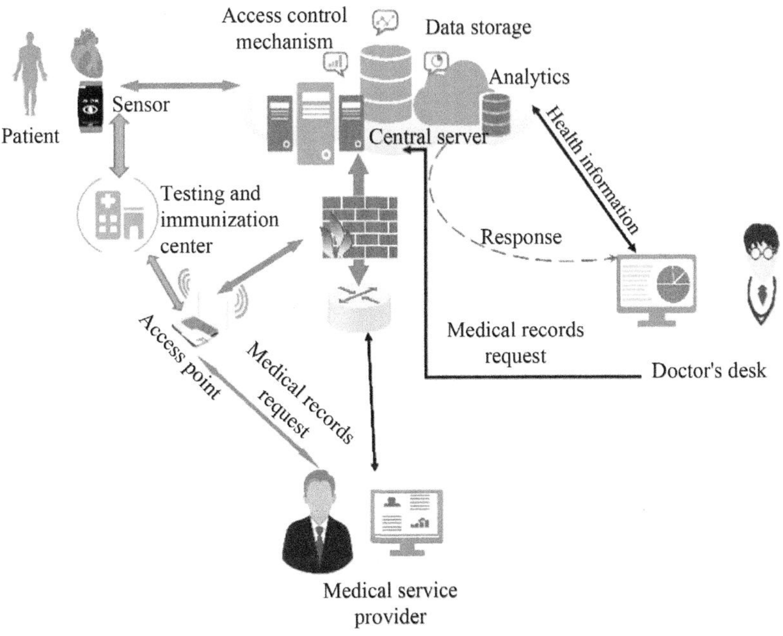

FIGURE 2.3

Medical service provider.

field of smart healthcare by utilizing this extensive methodology. The integration of several viewpoints is made possible by the multidimensional approach, which adds to a comprehensive analysis that explores the real-world applications of blockchain adoption in healthcare systems in addition to its theoretical underpinnings (Figs. 2.1–2.3).

2.3 Findings and discussion

This crucial section is the result of an extensive study approach and offers a wealth of information, perspectives, and empirical support for the use of blockchain technology in the field of smart healthcare. The results are presented in a way that is purposefully designed to cover a wide range of topics. Case studies, experimental findings, and in-depth analyses are all included to provide a comprehensive grasp of the transformational potential of blockchain technology (Hennebelle et al., 2023; Seng et al., 2023; Sharma & Sharma, 2024; Zafar et al., 2023).

2.3.1 Case studies and practical applications

The first part of the section examines case studies and actual applications of blockchain technology in smart healthcare settings. Every case study is examined in detail to reveal the nuances of the implementation procedure, the difficulties faced, and the observable advantages attained. Through improved interoperability and simplified health data administration, the case studies operate as models, providing insights into the real-world applications of blockchain adoption in various healthcare contexts.

2.3.2 Experimental results

The outcomes of the experimental analyses carried out as part of this research serve to supplement the case studies. These trials could involve blockchain solutions being tested in healthcare settings through real-world testing, prototyping, or simulations. A solid basis for evaluating blockchain's effectiveness in the context of smart healthcare is provided by the presentation and analysis of quantitative metrics pertaining to data security, transaction efficiency, and overall system performance.

2.3.3 Comparative analysis with existing literature

Using a comparative analysis with existing literature, the findings are carefully contextualized. This entails a critical analysis of the ways in which the findings concur with or differ from previously published studies. A thorough grasp of the changing environment is provided by the integration of knowledge from the literature review and current research findings, which highlights areas of convergence and divergence.

2.3.4 Interpretation of outcomes

The conversation in this part explores how outcomes should be interpreted rather than just presenting the facts. The complexities of blockchain's influence on data management, security, and privacy in smart health systems are examined, providing a detailed grasp of the underlying dynamics. To clarify the intricacies involved in the adoption of blockchain technology, interpretative frameworks that take into account both technological and socioeconomic elements are developed.

2.3.5 Implications for adoption

The conversation goes beyond summarizing the findings to consider the more general ramifications of the conclusions for the adoption of blockchain in smart healthcare. This entails investigating the problems that have been found, possible fixes, and the revolutionary effects of blockchain technology on healthcare ecosystems. The conversation foresees how blockchain use will spread, taking into account elements such as stakeholder acceptability, legal frameworks, and the scalability of blockchain solutions in actual healthcare infrastructures.

2.3.6 Future directions and recommendations

This part closes with a perspective that looks ahead, beyond the present. Based on the discussions and results, future directions for research are provided along with useful recommendations. This innovative strategy aids in guiding legislators, medical professionals, and IT entrepreneurs through the dynamic blockchain environment in smart healthcare.

Essentially, the Results and Discussion part is more than just a summary of the study's findings; it is a dynamic investigation and interpretive voyage that helps to close the gap between theoretical claims and real-world applications. This part provides a solid foundation for furthering our understanding of blockchain's function in bolstering security and privacy within the intricate web of smart healthcare through a thorough presentation of case studies, experimental results, and thoughtful discussion.

2.4 Conclusion

Because of this extensive research project, the findings, analyses, and insights are synthesized into a strong conclusion that not only captures the essence of the study but also advances the conversation about how blockchain technology can revolutionize security and privacy in smart healthcare systems. This conclusion acts as a compass, pointing researchers, legislators, and healthcare industry stakeholders in the direction of a more nuanced comprehension of the potential consequences and adoption paths of blockchain technology. *Key findings synopsis*: The conclusion starts with a brief but comprehensive synopsis of the major conclusions discovered during the investigation. These results cover a wide range of topics, including how well blockchain works to secure health data, promote interoperability, and support patient-centered care models. Case studies and experimental findings highlight the real-world uses and observable advantages, offering a basis for well-informed choices about the incorporation of blockchain technology into healthcare ecosystems. *Consequences for smart healthcare*: Examining the research's consequences, the conclusion analyzes how the results apply to the field as a whole. The discourse encompasses technological, operational, and socioeconomic aspects, tackling the recognized obstacles and shedding light on the possible advantages and revolutionary influence of blockchain implementation. Research findings are integrated into a story that highlights how blockchain technology has the ability to completely transform established healthcare systems and bring about a paradigm change toward the delivery of safe, open, and patient-centered care.

2.5 Suggestions for further research

Given the dynamic character of blockchain technology and healthcare systems, the conclusion goes beyond the scope of this study and offers a path forward for future investigation. The study's findings and gaps in the literature are addressed in the recommendations for further research. These suggestions can include investigating improved consensus methods, scaling strategies, and incorporating cutting-edge technologies that support blockchain in the healthcare setting. The end lays the groundwork for an ongoing and dynamic interaction with the blockchain's changing application in smart healthcare.

Significance of blockchain in smart healthcare: In highlighting the role that blockchain plays in smart healthcare, the conclusion also highlights how it has the ability to spur positive change in the sector. It explains how, in a time of digital innovation, the decentralized, tamper-resistant character of blockchain technology corresponds with the imperatives of data security and privacy. The end serves as a call to action for the sector to acknowledge blockchain as a fundamental tenet for establishing a safe, interoperable, and patient-centered healthcare data future—rather than just a new technology. *Impact and transformation on the industry*: The conclusion explores the wider implications for the industry, describing how the adoption of blockchain technology has the potential to completely alter the structure of healthcare institutions. It considers the potentially revolutionary path that healthcare organizations may pursue, highlighting the necessity of stakeholder cooperation to overcome obstacles and make use of blockchain's benefits. The promise of blockchain technology in smart healthcare extends beyond a simple technological change; it is a cultural revolution with the ability to fundamentally alter the way healthcare is delivered. Essentially, the conclusion is more than just a summary of the research findings—rather, it is a lighthouse that points the way ahead. The conclusion presents blockchain as a catalyst for a paradigm shift in the healthcare industry, in addition to a technology solution, through a thorough synthesis of the major results, consequences, and recommendations. The conclusion serves as a testament to the ongoing significance of blockchain in laying out the path toward a more secure, private, and patient-centric future in smart healthcare as the research baton moves from the areas of policymaking, healthcare practice, and further exploration.

References

Adam, M. A., & Mukhtar, A. (2024). Smart health solutions: The convergence of AI, machine learning, and deep learning for brain and heart care. *Revista Espanola de Documentacion Cientifica*, *18*(02), 238–268.

Ahmed, I., Chehri, A., & Jeon, G. (2023). Artificial intelligence and blockchain enabled smart healthcare system for monitoring and detection of COVID-19 in biomedical images. *IEEE/ACM Transactions on Computational Biology and Bioinformatics*.

Al-Blihed, N. S., Al-Mufadi, N. F., Al-Harbi, N. T., Al-Omari, I. A., & Al-Hagery, M. A. (2023). Blockchain and machine learning in the internet of things: A review of smart healthcare. *International Journal of Artificial Intelligence*, *12*(3), 995–1006.

Deepa, S., Sridhar, K. P., Baskar, S., Mythili, K. B., Reethika, A., & Hariharan, P. R. (2023). IoT-enabled smart healthcare data and health monitoring based machine learning algorithms. *Journal of Intelligent & Fuzzy Systems*, *44*(2), 2927–2941.

Hassaballah, M., Wazery, Y. M., Ibrahim, I. E., & Farag, A. (2023). Ecg heartbeat classification using machine learning and metaheuristic optimization for smart healthcare systems. *Bioengineering*, *10*(4), 429.

Hennebelle, A., Materwala, H., & Ismail, L. (2023). HealthEdge: A machine learning-based smart healthcare framework for prediction of type 2 diabetes in an integrated IoT, edge, and cloud computing system. *Procedia Computer Science*, *220*, 331–338.

Jiwani, N., Gupta, K., & Whig, P. (2023). *Machine learning approaches for analysis in smart healthcare informatics. Machine learning and artificial intelligence in healthcare systems* (pp. 129–154). CRC Press.

Kavitha, M., Roobini, S., Prasanth, A., & Sujaritha, M. (2023). *Systematic view and impact of artificial intelligence in smart healthcare systems, principles, challenges and applications. Machine learning and artificial intelligence in healthcare systems* (pp. 25–56). CRC Press.

Mala, D. J. (2023). *Machine learning-based intelligent assistant for smart healthcare. Machine learning and artificial intelligence in healthcare systems* (pp. 265–286). CRC Press.

Rahman, A., Hossain, M. S., Muhammad, G., Kundu, D., Debnath, T., Rahman, M., & Band, S. S. (2023). Federated learning-based AI approaches in smart healthcare: Concepts, taxonomies, challenges and open issues. *Cluster Computing*, *26*(4), 2271–2311.

Raza, A., Ali, M., Ehsan, M. K., & Sodhro, A. H. (2023). Spectrum evaluation in CR-based smart healthcare systems using optimizable tree machine learning approach. *Sensors*, *23*(17), 7456.

Seng, K. P., Ang, L. M., Peter, E., & Mmonyi, A. (2023). Machine learning and AI technologies for smart wearables. *Electronics*, *12*(7), 1509.

Sharma, A. K., & Sharma, R. (2024). Navigating the ethical landscape: Implementing machine learning in smart healthcare informatics. *Indian Journal of Community Health*, *36*(1), 149–152.

Zafar, I., Anwar, S., Yousaf, W., Nisa, F. U., Kausar, T., Ul Ain, Q., & Sharma, R. (2023). Reviewing methods of deep learning for intelligent healthcare systems in genomics and biomedicine. *Biomedical Signal Processing and Control*, *86*, 105263.

CHAPTER

Digital twin–based healthcare facilities management

3

Amit Kumar Tyagi[1] and Richa[2]

[1]*Department of Fashion Technology, National Institute of Fashion Technology, New Delhi, Delhi, India*

[2]*Department of Computer Science & Engineering, BIT Mesra, Ranchi, Jharkhand, India*

3.1 Introduction to digital twin technology, and smart healthcare services

In recent years, the convergence of advanced technologies has ushered in a new era of innovation in healthcare. Among these technologies, digital twin technology and smart healthcare services have emerged as key drivers in transforming the industry. Digital twin technology, originally popularized in manufacturing and industrial settings, involves creating a virtual replica or mirror image of physical objects, processes, or systems. In healthcare, this concept has been extended to create digital representations of medical facilities, equipment, and even individual patients. Digital twins in healthcare serve as dynamic, real-time models that capture and simulate the complexities of the physical environment. These virtual counterparts enable healthcare professionals to monitor, analyze, and optimize various aspects of patient care, facility management, and operational efficiency. The integration of digital twins in healthcare facilitates a more data-driven and proactive approach to decision-making (Bruynseels, Santoni de Sio, & van den Hoven, 2018).

This not only contributes to improved patient satisfaction but also aids in the recovery process. This chapter also addresses challenges related to data security, interoperability, and ethical issues in the implementation of digital twin technology in healthcare. Strategies to overcome these challenges are discussed, emphasizing the importance of collaboration between stakeholders, including healthcare professionals, technology vendors, and regulatory bodies. In summary, the adoption of digital twin technology in healthcare facilities management presents a paradigm shift in the way healthcare infrastructure is designed, operated, and optimized. The benefits of improved efficiency, predictive maintenance, and enhanced patient care make digital twins a promising avenue for advancing the capabilities of healthcare facilities in the modern era. The successful integration of digital twins in healthcare requires a holistic approach, considering technical, organizational, and ethical aspects to harness the full potential of this innovative technology (Hemamalini et al., 2024).

Smart healthcare services, use interconnected devices, data analytics, and artificial intelligence to enhance the overall quality and efficiency of healthcare delivery. These services encompass a range of applications, from remote patient monitoring and personalized treatment plans to predictive analytics for disease prevention. Smart healthcare aims to create a connected ecosystem where information flows seamlessly between patients, healthcare providers, and various healthcare

Blockchain and Digital Twin for Smart Hospitals. DOI: https://doi.org/10.1016/B978-0-443-34226-4.00004-6

systems. The convergence between digital twin technology and smart healthcare services is reshaping the healthcare landscape. Digital twins contribute to the development of intelligent, adaptive healthcare environments by providing real-time insights into patient conditions, resource utilization, and facility operations. This, in turn, enables the delivery of more personalized and efficient healthcare services. Note that this introduction sets the stage for a deeper exploration of the transformative impact of digital twin technology and smart healthcare services. As we discussed further about their applications, challenges, and potential, it becomes evident that the integration of these technologies has the power to revolutionize healthcare, providing improved patient outcomes, streamlined operations, and a more responsive and patient-centric healthcare system (Sharma et al., 2022).

3.1.1 Evolution and applications of digital twins in healthcare facilities

The evolution of digital twins in healthcare facilities has witnessed a remarkable journey, transforming the way medical environments are designed, managed, and optimized. Here is an overview of the evolution and applications of digital twins in healthcare facilities:

3.1.1.1 Early stage

Conceptualization and simulation (pre-2010s): The concept of digital twins initially gained traction in the manufacturing and aerospace industries. In healthcare, early applications focused on conceptualizing and simulating medical devices and processes in virtual environments. Limited by technology constraints, early digital twins had relatively simple representations.

3.1.1.2 Advent of IoT and advanced sensors (2010s)

The proliferation of Internet of Things (IoT) devices and advanced sensors provided the infrastructure for more detailed and real-time data collection. Digital twins evolved to incorporate real-time monitoring of medical equipment, patient vitals, and environmental conditions in healthcare facilities. Improved connectivity allowed for the creation of more sophisticated virtual replicas.

3.1.1.3 Integration with electronic health records and data analytics (mid-2010s)

Digital twins started to integrate with electronic health record (EHR) systems, enabling a comprehensive representation of patient data. Data analytics played an important role in deriving actionable insights from the large amount of information collected by digital twins. Applications expanded to predictive maintenance of medical equipment and optimization of facility workflows.

3.1.1.4 Personalized healthcare and patient experience (late 2010s–early 2020s)

Digital twins became instrumental in creating personalized healthcare environments and tailoring treatment plans and facility settings based on individual patient needs. Patient experience was enhanced through adaptive and patient-centric virtual environments. Applications extended to the simulation of medical procedures and training for healthcare professionals.

3.1.1.5 Advanced AI and machine learning integration (2020s–present)

The integration of advanced artificial intelligence (AI) and machine learning (ML) algorithms further enhanced the capabilities of digital twins. Predictive analytics became more sophisticated, allowing for the early detection of potential issues and the optimization of resource allocation.

Digital twins played an important role in the response to global health crises, providing insights into the spread of diseases and facilitating crisis management.

3.1.1.6 Future directions

Ethical issues and complete integration: Ongoing efforts focus on addressing ethical issues, data security, and interoperability challenges associated with digital twins in healthcare. Holistic integration involves collaboration among healthcare professionals, technology vendors, and regulatory bodies to ensure responsible and secure deployment.

In summary, the evolution of digital twins in healthcare facilities reflects a dynamic progression from conceptualization to sophisticated, data-driven applications. As technology continues to advance, Digital twins are poised to play an increasingly vital role in shaping the future of healthcare by fostering efficiency, personalization, and innovation in medical facilities management.

3.1.2 Digital twin technology: definition and concepts, components, characteristics, and capabilities

Digital twin technology involves creating a virtual representation or model of a physical object, system, or process. This digital counterpart mirrors the real-world entity, capturing its characteristics, behavior, and interactions. Digital twins enable real-time monitoring, analysis, and simulation, providing valuable insights for optimization and decision-making (Khajavi et al., 2019). Here are a few key concepts, which can be discussed as in Table 3.1.

Hence, digital twin technology, with its ability to bridge the physical and digital worlds, has transformative potential across various industries, including manufacturing, healthcare, and infrastructure management. Its continued evolution is expected to bring about further advancements in efficiency, innovation, and decision-making processes.

3.1.3 Adoption trends of digital twins in various industries of today's era

Adoption of digital twin technology has been gaining momentum across various industries, with organizations leveraging its capabilities to enhance efficiency, innovation, and decision-making. Here are some adoption trends in various industries:

3.1.3.1 Manufacturing

Manufacturers use digital twins to monitor equipment conditions in real time, predicting maintenance needs and minimizing downtime. Also, digital twins simulate manufacturing processes, allowing for optimization and efficiency improvements.

3.1.3.2 Healthcare

Digital twins of patients and healthcare facilities help optimize treatment plans, monitor patient health, and improve overall healthcare delivery. Simulation using digital twins assists in training healthcare professionals for complex medical procedures.

Table 3.1 Definition and concepts, components, and characteristics related to digital twin technologies.

Concept	Characteristics	Description
Components of digital twin technology	Physical entity	The tangible object, system, or process that exists in the physical world
	Sensors and IoT devices	Devices that collect real-time data about the physical entity, such as temperature, pressure, motion, etc.
	Connectivity	Networks and communication protocols facilitating the transfer of data between the physical entity and its digital twin
	Data processing and storage	Systems for processing and storing large amounts of data collected from sensors and devices
	Virtual model	The digital replica created using data integration, representing the physical entity in a virtual environment
	Analytics and algorithms	Tools and algorithms for analyzing data, deriving insights, and making predictions
	User interface	Interfaces for users to interact with and monitor the digital twin, often through dashboards and visualization tools
Characteristics of digital twin technology	Real-time monitoring	Provides continuous, real-time data about the status and performance of the physical entity
	Simulation and predictive analysis	Allows for the simulation of different scenarios and predictive analysis based on historical and real-time data
	Data integration	Integrates data from various sources, including sensors, IoT devices, and connected systems, to create a comprehensive virtual model
	Connectivity	Relies on robust connectivity to ensure seamless communication between the physical entity and its digital twin
	Adaptability	Capable of adapting to changes in the physical entity, allowing for dynamic updates and adjustments
Capabilities of digital twin technology	Optimization	Enables the optimization of processes, resource utilization, and performance based on real-time data
	Predictive maintenance	Predicts potential issues with the physical entity, allowing for proactive maintenance and reducing downtime
	Scenario analysis	Facilitates the simulation of different scenarios to assess the impact of changes and make informed decisions
	Personalization	Supports personalized experiences, such as adaptive environments or customized products/services
	Remote monitoring and control	Allows for remote monitoring and control of the physical entity, enhancing efficiency and responsiveness

3.1.3.3 Aerospace and defense

Digital twins of aircraft and defense systems enable real-time monitoring, leading to improved performance and reduced maintenance costs. Simulation and analysis support mission planning and risk assessment.

3.1.3.4 Energy and utilities

Digital twins aid in monitoring and managing energy infrastructure and optimizing the performance of power plants and distribution networks. Simulation helps optimize the placement and performance of renewable energy sources.

3.1.3.5 Smart cities

Digital twins assist in city planning by simulating infrastructure, traffic patterns, and energy usage, contributing to sustainable development. Simulation of emergency scenarios helps in planning for and responding to public safety incidents.

3.1.3.6 Automotive

Digital twins are used in the automotive industry for virtual prototyping, testing, and simulation of vehicle performance. Digital twins of vehicles contribute to the development and testing of connected and autonomous vehicle technologies.

3.1.3.7 Retail

Digital twins help optimize supply chain processes, from inventory management to distribution. Personalized shopping experiences are enhanced through digital twins that analyze customer preferences and behaviors.

3.1.3.8 Construction and real estate

Digital twins aid in the design, construction, and ongoing management of buildings, improving energy efficiency and maintenance. Also, cities and buildings utilize digital twins for smart infrastructure, including traffic management and building automation.

3.1.3.9 Telecommunications

Digital twins of telecommunications networks assist in optimizing performance, identifying bottlenecks, and planning for expansions. Also, Predictive analytics through digital twins help anticipate and prevent network failures.

3.1.3.10 Oil and gas

Digital twins enable real-time monitoring of equipment and facilities, enhancing safety and operational efficiency. Also, simulation aids in optimizing drilling processes, reducing costs and environmental impact.

Note that adoption trends may evolve over time as technology advances and industries continue to provide new applications for digital twin technology. Organizations are likely to increasingly embrace digital twins as they recognize the value of real-time insights, simulation capabilities, and data-driven decision-making across various sectors.

3.1.4 Benefits and disadvantages of implementing digital twins in healthcare facilities

This section will discuss a few benefits of implementing digital twins in healthcare facilities (Mihai et al., 2022), as follows:

Real-time monitoring: Digital twins enable continuous real-time monitoring of medical equipment, patient vitals, and facility conditions, allowing for proactive decision-making and quick response to changes.

Predictive maintenance: Anticipating equipment failures through predictive maintenance reduces downtime, ensures the availability of important assets, and minimizes disruptions to patient care.

Optimized resource utilization: Digital twins help healthcare facilities optimize the use of resources, including staff allocation, room utilization, and equipment availability, leading to improved operational efficiency.

Patient-centric environments: Personalized healthcare experiences are facilitated through adaptive environments and tailored treatment plans based on insights from digital twins, enhancing patient satisfaction and outcomes.

Efficient workflow management: Simulation capabilities allow for the testing and optimization of various workflows, streamlining processes, and enhancing overall efficiency in healthcare delivery.

Data-driven decision-making: Healthcare professionals can make informed decisions based on real-time and historical data, contributing to better patient care, resource allocation, and strategic planning.

Enhanced training and simulation: Digital twins support training for healthcare professionals by providing realistic simulations of medical procedures, contributing to improved skills and preparedness.

Remote patient monitoring: Digital twins enable remote monitoring of patients, allowing healthcare providers to extend care beyond the traditional healthcare setting and improving overall patient management (Fig. 3.1).

Improved crisis management: During health crises, digital twins provide insights into the spread of diseases and resource utilization and can aid in crisis management and decision-making.

Now some disadvantages and challenges of implementing digital twins in healthcare facilities are discussed as follows:

Data security and privacy issues: Digital twins involve the collection and storage of sensitive patient data, raising issues about data security, privacy, and compliance with healthcare regulations.

Interoperability issues: Integrating digital twin technology with existing healthcare systems and interoperability with diverse medical devices can be challenging and may require significant effort.

Initial implementation costs: The upfront costs associated with implementing digital twin technology, including infrastructure, sensors, and connectivity, can be substantial.

Complexity of implementation: Implementing digital twins in healthcare facilities may require specialized expertise and resources, and the complexity of the technology could pose challenges for some organizations.

Staff training and adoption: Healthcare professionals may require training to effectively use and interpret data from digital twins, and there may be resistance to adopting new technologies.

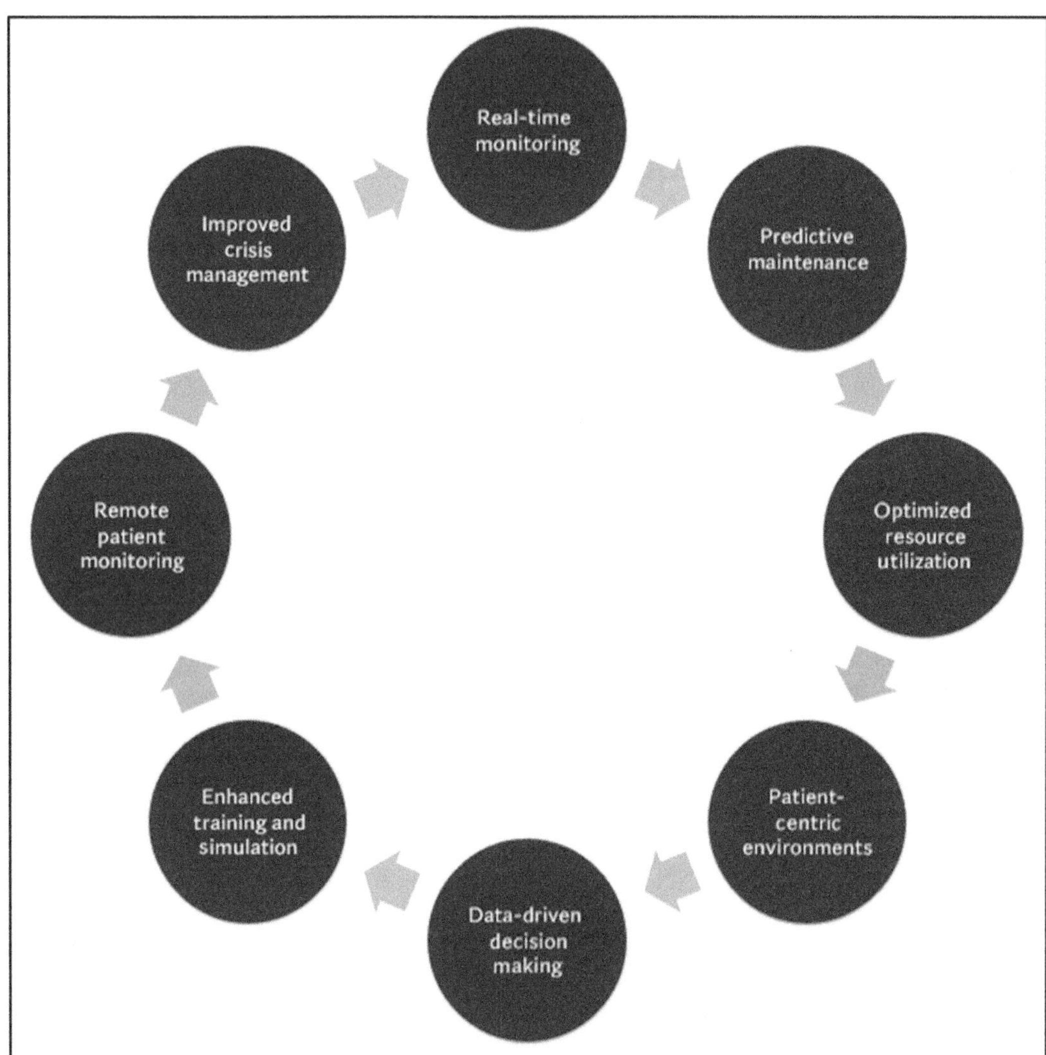

FIGURE 3.1

Benefits and disadvantages of implementing digital twins in healthcare facilities.

Regulatory compliance: Healthcare facilities must navigate and comply with regulatory frameworks that govern the use of technology in healthcare, adding a layer of complexity to the implementation process.

Technology maturity: The technology is still evolving, and healthcare facilities may face challenges related to the maturity of digital twin solutions and potential updates or changes (Fig. 3.2).

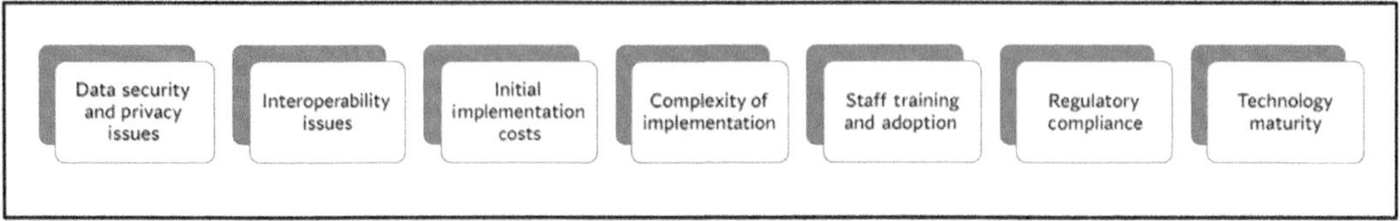

FIGURE 3.2

Disadvantages and challenges of implementing digital twins in healthcare facilities.

Note that despite these challenges, the benefits of implementing digital twins in healthcare facilities suggest that, with careful planning, consideration of ethical implications, and ongoing technological advancements, the positive impact on patient care and operational efficiency can be substantial.

3.2 Background work

Because they are vital to the delivery of healthcare, healthcare facilities need efficient facilities management systems. Regretfully, the existing paradigm for managing healthcare facilities (FM) is founded on the idea that "if it breaks, we fix it." This is because there is insufficient effective bidirectional coordination and real-time information updating to monitor, manage, and control important healthcare facilities. As a result, it is important to guarantee a preventive maintenance strategy (Madubuike & Anumba, 2021). The most complex facilities to design, build, and run in the architectural, engineering, and construction (AEC) sector are healthcare projects. The first step toward the efficient administration and upkeep of healthcare facilities would be to develop a digital twin (DT) using a methodical, transparent design that is validated using real-world use cases (Song & Li, 2022). The current models and frameworks for maintenance management have not investigated and assessed maintenance documentation as a whole concept. To achieve the DT maintenance management of hospital buildings in Nigeria, (Ebiloma, Aigbavboa, & Anumba, 2023) studied set out to highlight the importance of maintenance documentation for its adoption as one of the primary factors of efficient maintenance management. The software documentation idea was utilized to conceptualize this identified gap in maintenance management models for public hospital facilities in poor nations, after a theoretical assessment of previous works about documentation. Architecture, Engineering, Construction, and Facility Management (A/E/C/FM) firms are being compelled by changes in both domestic and international markets to produce more inventive and resilient operational building information models (BIMs). It is predicted that building information models, or BIMs, will evolve from static 3D models to digital twins that offer a fully digital depiction of the real asset or building they represent. The A/E/C/FM industry will be able to visualize, monitor, and optimize operational assets and processes to support better inspection and analysis for more effective facility operations and maintenance thanks to this metamorphosis into a dynamic digital twin (Harode, Thabet, & Dongre, 2023). As big data, cloud computing, and the IoT continue to advance, digital twins are being used in industry as a precision simulation tool from concept to implementation. Furthermore, simulation is crucial to the healthcare industry, particularly to studies on medical activity prediction, medical resource allocation, and medical pathway planning. A novel and effective method for delivering quicker, more accurate services for senior healthcare will be created by fusing digital twin technology with healthcare. Two major issues in the precision medicine era remain, though: how to monitor older people' personal health throughout their whole lifecycle and how to integrate the physical and virtual worlds of medicine to produce true smart healthcare (Liu et al., 2019). DT technologies are becoming more widely used in the AEC sector globally. This is because they have the potential to improve communication and collaboration between project stakeholders at every stage of the project lifecycle, from design to operation and maintenance (O&M) (Zhao et al., 2022). A survey is presented in (Machado & Berssaneti, 2023) that explores the field of technology sources still accounts for the majority of the digital twin articles in healthcare, which is a relatively recent development. The topic is mostly focused on the patient's digital twin group as well as the aspects, concerns, and/or policies subgroups related to precision medicine, even though the publication's keywords only reflect this on the group level. It is likely that digital twins in healthcare are emerging from their early stages. However, with all of the expertise gleaned from the manufacturing industry, digital twins in the hospital group and the device and facilities management subgroups are more advanced. A few publishing kinds are missing altogether, including the device and care subgroups and the whole body and hospital digital twins were not reported. The field of technology sources still accounts for the majority of the digital twin articles in healthcare, which is a relatively recent development. The topic is mostly focused on the patient's digital twin group as well as the aspects, concerns, and/or policies subgroups related to precision medicine, even though the publication's keywords only reflect this on the group level. It is likely that digital twins in healthcare are emerging from their early stages. However, with all of the expertise gleaned from the manufacturing industry, digital twins in the hospital group and the device and facilities management subgroups are more advanced. A few publishing kinds are missing altogether, including the device and care subgroups and the whole body and hospital digital twins were not reported (Yang et al., 2021).

3.3 Real-world case studies of digital twin application in healthcare facilities management

Several real-world case studies showcase the application of digital twin technology in healthcare facilities management (Augustine, 2020). Here are a few examples:

Cleveland Clinic—connected hospital rooms: The Cleveland Clinic implemented a digital twin system to create connected hospital rooms. These digital twins replicated patient rooms, monitoring patient conditions, adjusting environmental settings, and automating certain tasks. The system aimed to enhance patient experience, improve staff efficiency, and optimize resource utilization. Its Key Benefits are; Personalized patient care, improved operational efficiency, and proactive maintenance of medical equipment.

GE Healthcare and TMCx—patient care digital twin: GE Healthcare company collaborated with the Texas Medical Center's Innovation Institute (TMCx) to develop a digital twin solution for patient care. The digital twin incorporated patient data, treatment plans, and real-time monitoring to create a comprehensive virtual model of the patient's healthcare journey. This allowed for predictive analysis and personalized interventions. Its Key Benefits are: Enhanced patient outcomes, optimized treatment plans, and improved collaboration among healthcare providers.

Siemens Healthineers—smart hospital digital twin: Siemens Healthineers developed a smart hospital digital twin solution that integrated with medical devices, IT systems, and facility infrastructure. The digital twin simulated different scenarios, allowing for proactive planning, resource optimization, and predictive maintenance of medical equipment. Its Key Benefits are: Improved operational efficiency, predictive maintenance, and strategic planning for future healthcare needs.

Mayo Clinic—simulation for surgical planning: Mayo Clinic utilized digital twin technology to simulate surgical procedures and plan complex surgeries. The digital twin incorporated patient-specific anatomical data, enabling surgeons to visualize and plan surgeries in a virtual environment before the actual procedure. This approach enhanced precision and reduced risks. Its Key Benefits are: Improved surgical outcomes, enhanced preoperative planning, and reduced surgical complications.

University College London Hospitals (UCLH)—operating room optimization: UCLH implemented a digital twin system to optimize operating room efficiency. The digital twin incorporated real-time data on patient status, equipment utilization, and staff workflow. This allowed for dynamic scheduling, resource optimization, and improved communication among surgical teams. Its key benefits are as follows: increased operating room efficiency, reduced wait times, and improved communication among surgical teams.

These case studies demonstrate the diverse applications of digital twin technology in healthcare facilities management, ranging from patient care and surgical planning to operational efficiency and facility optimization. As the field continues to evolve, more healthcare institutions are likely to provide and implement digital twin solutions to enhance patient outcomes and streamline healthcare operations.

3.4 Open issues and challenges toward digital twin implementation for healthcare services

Despite the potential benefits, the implementation of digital twins in healthcare services comes with several open issues and challenges (Fuller et al., 2020; Jimenez, Jahankhani, & Kendzierskyj, 2019; Aloqaily, Bouachir, & Karray, 2023). Some of these challenges include the following:

Data security and privacy issues: Healthcare involves sensitive patient data, and ensuring the security and privacy of this information within the digital twin environment is a significant challenge. Unauthorized access or data breaches could have severe consequences.

Interoperability: Healthcare systems often use diverse and proprietary technologies. Achieving interoperability between these systems and ensuring seamless data exchange among them can be a complex and challenging task.

Regulatory compliance: Healthcare is subject to strict regulations and compliance standards. Adhering to these regulations while implementing digital twin technology requires careful consideration to avoid legal and ethical issues.

Integration with legacy systems: Many healthcare facilities still rely on legacy systems that may not be compatible with modern digital twin solutions. Integrating digital twins with existing infrastructure poses a significant technical challenge.

Ethical issues: Creating digital twins of patients raises ethical questions regarding informed consent, data ownership, and the responsible use of patient information. Striking a balance between innovation and ethical issues is important.

Data accuracy and reliability: The accuracy and reliability of data used to create and update digital twins are important. Inaccurate or outdated information may lead to incorrect insights and decisions, impacting patient care and operational efficiency.

Resource intensity: Developing and maintaining digital twin systems can be resource-intensive. Healthcare organizations may face challenges in terms of financial investment, skilled personnel, and ongoing support for these technologies.

User training and adoption: Healthcare professionals need to be trained on how to use and interpret data from digital twins effectively. Resistance to change and the need for additional training can slow down the adoption process.

Standardization: The lack of standardized protocols and frameworks for digital twins in healthcare can hinder collaboration and interoperability between different healthcare facilities and systems (Fig. 3.3).

Dynamic and evolving nature of healthcare: Healthcare is a dynamic field with evolving practices, technologies, and regulations. Ensuring that digital twins remain adaptable and scalable to meet changing healthcare needs is an ongoing challenge.

Patient trust and acceptance: Building trust among patients regarding the use of digital twin technology in their healthcare is essential. Ensuring transparency and effective communication about the benefits and safeguards is important.

Human–machine interaction: As digital twins become more integrated into healthcare decision-making, ensuring effective communication and collaboration between healthcare professionals and the digital twin systems is important.

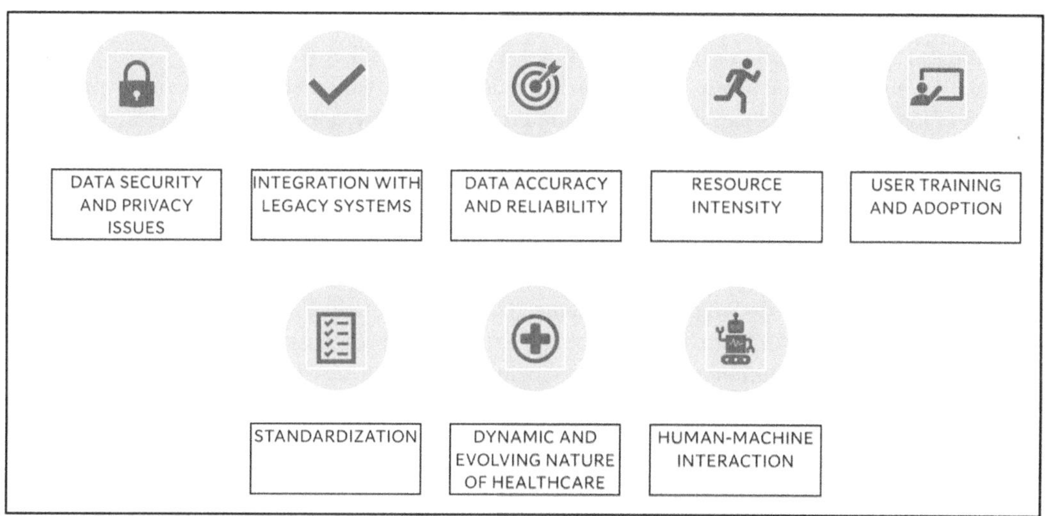

FIGURE 3.3

Open issues and challenges toward digital twin implementation.

Hence, addressing these challenges requires collaboration between healthcare providers, technology developers, regulatory bodies, and other stakeholders. By carefully navigating these issues, the healthcare industry can harness the full potential of digital twin technology to improve patient outcomes and optimize healthcare services.

3.5 Future innovations/opportunities toward digital twin implementation for healthcare services

The future of digital twin implementation in healthcare services holds exciting possibilities, with numerous innovations and opportunities on the horizon (Botín-Sanabria et al., 2022; Das et al., 2022; Rowan, 2024). Here are some key areas where we can expect advancements:

Personalized medicine and treatment planning: Digital twins can evolve to include more detailed and personalized patient models, incorporating genetic, lifestyle, and environmental factors. This can lead to highly individualized treatment plans, predicting responses to medications, and optimizing therapeutic interventions.

IoT integration for remote patient monitoring: Integrating digital twins with the IoT devices will enable continuous and real-time remote monitoring of patients. This can enhance preventive care, monitor chronic conditions, and provide early intervention based on the insights generated by the digital twin.

Augmented reality (AR) and virtual reality (VR) applications: AR and VR technologies can be integrated with digital twins to create immersive healthcare experiences. Surgeons, for example, could use AR to visualize digital twins during surgeries, improving precision and decision-making.

Advanced simulation for training and education: Digital twins will play an expanded role in medical training and education. Simulations can become more sophisticated, allowing healthcare professionals to practice and refine their skills in a risk-free virtual environment.

Predictive analytics for disease prevention: Future digital twins may use advanced predictive analytics to identify patterns and trends, enabling proactive disease prevention strategies. This could include early detection of potential health risks and lifestyle interventions.

Blockchain integration for data security: Integrating blockchain technology with digital twins can enhance data security and ensure the integrity of patient records. Blockchain's decentralized and tamper-resistant nature can provide a robust solution for protecting sensitive healthcare information.

Genomic digital twins for precision medicine: Digital twins could incorporate genomic data to create genomic digital twins, providing a comprehensive understanding of an individual's genetic makeup. This could revolutionize precision medicine by tailoring treatments based on genetic characteristics.

Human–machine collaboration in diagnosis and decision-making: Advanced AI algorithms and machine learning models integrated into digital twins can facilitate collaboration between healthcare professionals and intelligent systems. This collaboration can lead to more accurate diagnoses and treatment recommendations.

Collaborative healthcare ecosystems: Digital twins can be extended to create collaborative ecosystems, where data from different healthcare entities (hospitals, clinics, labs) can be securely shared. This can improve care coordination, enhance research capabilities, and contribute to population health management.

Continuous quality improvement and optimization: Digital twins will play an important role in continuous quality improvement in healthcare facilities. Real-time analytics and feedback loops can help optimize workflows, resource allocation, and overall operational efficiency.

Patient-generated health data integration: As patients increasingly contribute to their health data through wearables and other devices, digital twins can integrate this patient-generated health data for a more holistic view of an individual's health, fostering patient engagement and proactive healthcare.

Ethical and explainable AI in healthcare: Future digital twin implementations will prioritize ethical issues, ensuring transparency and explainability in AI-driven decision-making. This will be essential for gaining trust from both healthcare professionals and patients.

The future of digital twin implementation in healthcare services is dynamic, and ongoing research and technological advancements will shape its evolution. These opportunities present a vision of a healthcare system that is more personalized, efficient, and equipped to address the unique needs of individual patients.

3.6 Future opportunities toward digital twin implementation and emerging technologies for healthcare services

The future of digital twin implementation and emerging technologies in healthcare services holds numerous opportunities for innovation, efficiency, and improved patient outcomes. Here are some key future opportunities:

Integration with 5G technology: The widespread adoption of 5G technology will enhance connectivity and communication between devices in healthcare settings. Digital twins can use high-speed, low-latency networks to transmit real-time data, facilitating more responsive and efficient healthcare services.

Edge computing for real-time analytics: Edge computing can be integrated with digital twins to process data locally, reducing latency and enabling real-time analytics. This is particularly valuable for important applications such as remote patient monitoring and emergency response systems.

Artificial intelligence and machine learning advancements: Continued advancements in AI and machine learning will enhance the capabilities of digital twins. AI algorithms can analyze complex healthcare data, predict patient outcomes, and assist in treatment planning, contributing to more personalized and effective care.

Digital twins for population health management: Digital twins can be applied at a population level, creating models that represent diverse demographic groups. This approach can support population health management initiatives, allowing for targeted interventions and preventive strategies.

Blockchain for health data security: Blockchain technology can enhance the security and integrity of health data within digital twins. Decentralized and tamper-resistant ledgers can ensure that patient information is securely stored and accessed only by authorized parties.

Wearable technologies and Internet of Medical Things (IoMT): Wearable devices and IoMT can generate a wealth of real-time health data. Integrating this data into digital twins enables a more comprehensive and continuous monitoring of patients, promoting proactive healthcare interventions.

Quantum computing for complex simulations: The advent of quantum computing can significantly accelerate complex simulations within digital twins. This is particularly relevant for simulations involving intricate biological processes or drug discovery, leading to breakthroughs in healthcare research.

Extended reality (XR) for enhanced patient engagement: VR and AR can be integrated into digital twins to create immersive healthcare experiences. This can enhance patient engagement, facilitate virtual consultations, and improve patient education.

Digital twins for clinical trials and drug development: Digital twins can simulate and optimize clinical trial processes, contributing to more efficient and cost-effective drug development. This includes virtual testing of drug efficacy, prediction of patient responses, and identification of potential risks.

Human–machine collaboration in surgical procedures: Advanced robotics, coupled with digital twins, can enable more precise and minimally invasive surgical procedures. Surgeons can benefit from real-time data visualization and decision support, leading to improved surgical outcomes (Fig. 3.4).

Biometric data integration for behavioral health monitoring: Integrating biometric data, such as facial expressions and voice patterns, into digital twins can support behavioral health monitoring. This approach can aid in the early detection of mental health conditions and enhance personalized treatment plans.

Precision public health using geospatial data: Digital twins can incorporate geospatial data to enable precision public health initiatives. This includes mapping disease patterns, monitoring environmental factors, and optimizing healthcare resource allocation based on geographic needs.

Robotics and automation in healthcare operations: Robotics and automation, integrated with digital twins, can streamline healthcare operations. This includes automated inventory management, robotic-assisted surgeries, and autonomous delivery of medications within healthcare facilities.

Explainable AI for transparent decision-making: The development of explainable AI models ensures transparent decision-making processes within digital twins. This is important for gaining trust among healthcare professionals, patients, and regulatory authorities.

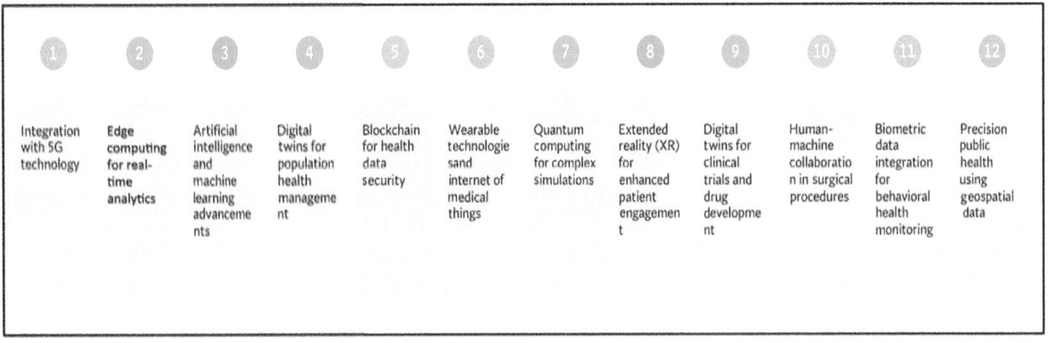

FIGURE 3.4

Opportunities toward Digital Twin Implementation.

Multidisciplinary collaboration platforms: Digital twins can serve as collaborative platforms that bring together healthcare professionals, researchers, and data scientists. This interdisciplinary approach fosters innovation, accelerates research, and improves healthcare delivery.

As these opportunities unfold, stakeholders in healthcare, technology, and research will need to collaborate to address challenges, ensure ethical issues, and maximize the potential of digital twin implementations and emerging technologies in healthcare services.

3.7 Implications for healthcare facilities management for next generation

The next generation of healthcare facilities management will be shaped by emerging technologies, changing patient expectations, and evolving healthcare delivery models (Tyagi, 2023; Sai & Tyagi, 2023; Gomathi, Mishra, & Tyagi, 2023; Menon, Prasad, & Soni, 2022; Nazeer et al., 2020). Here are several implications for healthcare facilities management in the next generation:

Digital transformation and smart facilities: The integration of digital twin technology, IoT devices, and smart sensors will transform healthcare facilities into intelligent and interconnected environments. This will enable real-time monitoring, predictive maintenance, and efficient resource utilization.

Telehealth and remote monitoring: The widespread adoption of telehealth services and remote patient monitoring will impact facility management. Healthcare facilities will need to support the infrastructure for virtual consultations and ensure the security and reliability of remote monitoring technologies.

Patient-centric environments: Healthcare facilities will be designed to provide patient-centric environments. Digital twins and IoT devices will enable adaptive spaces, personalized climate control, and customized patient experiences to enhance satisfaction and outcomes.

Robotics and automation: The use of robotics and automation in healthcare facilities will increase for tasks such as cleaning, logistics, and even assistance in surgeries. Facility managers will need to plan for the integration of robotic technologies into daily operations.

Data-driven decision-making: Facility managers will rely on data analytics and business intelligence tools to make informed decisions. This includes optimizing workflows, predicting equipment maintenance needs, and enhancing overall operational efficiency.

Energy efficiency and sustainability: Healthcare facilities will prioritize energy efficiency and sustainability. Digital twins can simulate and optimize energy usage, and facilities management will focus on implementing green technologies and practices to reduce environmental impact.

Security and privacy measures: With the increased use of digital technologies and interconnected systems, healthcare facilities must prioritize cybersecurity and patient data privacy. Robust security measures and compliance with regulatory standards will be essential.

Flexible and modular infrastructure: The design of healthcare facilities will incorporate flexible and modular infrastructure to accommodate changes in technology, healthcare delivery models, and unforeseen events. This adaptability will be important for long-term sustainability (Fig. 3.5).

Collaborative spaces for healthcare teams: The design of healthcare facilities will include collaborative spaces to facilitate teamwork among healthcare professionals. Digital twins can simulate and optimize the layout to enhance communication and collaboration.

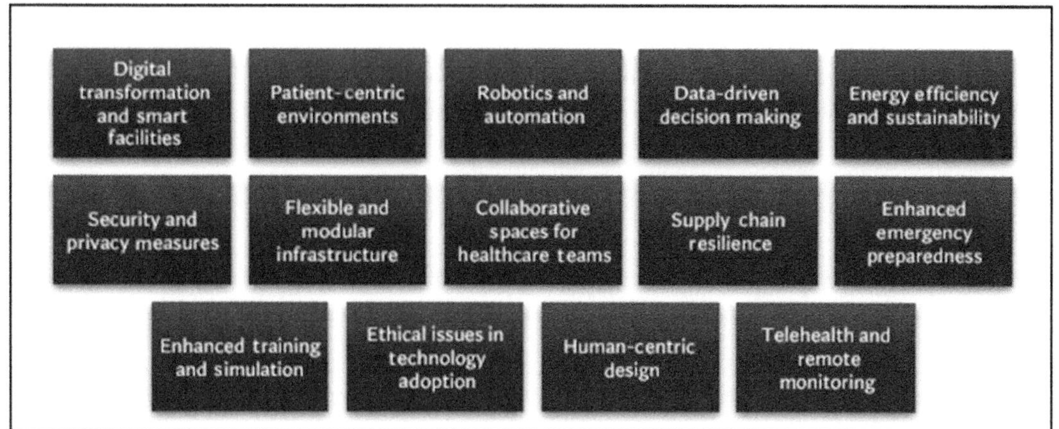

FIGURE 3.5

Implications for healthcare facilities management for next generation.

Supply chain resilience: Healthcare facilities will focus on building resilient and agile supply chains, especially in response to global disruptions. Digital twins can help simulate and optimize supply chain processes for improved reliability.

Enhanced emergency preparedness: Digital twins can simulate emergency scenarios, helping healthcare facilities enhance their preparedness and response capabilities. This includes optimizing evacuation plans, resource allocation, and communication strategies.

Enhanced training and simulation: Training programs for healthcare professionals will incorporate advanced simulations using digital twins. This will allow for realistic and immersive training experiences, improving the preparedness of healthcare teams.

Ethical issues in technology adoption: As healthcare facilities adopt advanced technologies, ethical issues will play an important role. Facility managers will need to ensure responsible and transparent use of technology, particularly in areas like AI, robotics, and patient data management.

Human-centric design: Healthcare facility design will prioritize human-centric elements to enhance the well-being of patients, visitors, and healthcare staff. This includes considerations for natural light, indoor air quality, and healing environments.

Hence, the next generation of healthcare facilities management will require a proactive approach to embracing technological advancements, ensuring regulatory compliance, and prioritizing patient-centered care. Facility managers will play an important role in navigating these changes and optimizing healthcare environments for improved patient outcomes and operational efficiency.

3.8 Conclusion

The application of digital twin technology in healthcare facilities management holds tremendous promise for revolutionizing the way healthcare environments are designed, operated, and optimized. The integration of virtual replicas of physical spaces, equipment, and processes enables healthcare providers to achieve unprecedented levels of efficiency, cost-effectiveness, and patient-centric care. Digital twins empower healthcare administrators with real-time data, allowing for proactive decision-making and predictive maintenance of important assets. The ability to simulate various scenarios aids in strategic planning, optimizing resource allocation, and improving overall workflow. This not only enhances operational efficiency but also contributes to better patient outcomes and experiences. Moreover, the personalized and adaptive capabilities of digital twins in healthcare settings create environments that cater to individual patient needs, fostering a more comfortable and conducive healing atmosphere. The positive impact on patient satisfaction and recovery outcomes highlights the potential for digital twins to elevate the quality of care provided. Despite these numerous advantages, challenges such as data security, interoperability, and ethical issues must be addressed for successful implementation. Collaborative efforts between healthcare professionals, technology vendors, and regulatory bodies are essential to ensure the responsible and secure deployment of digital twin technology in healthcare facilities. As we move forward, the continued exploration and refinement of digital twin applications in healthcare facilities management will likely lead to further innovations and improvements. The transformative potential of digital twins is poised to play an important role in shaping the future of healthcare, fostering a more efficient, patient-centered, and technologically advanced healthcare ecosystem. Embracing and overcoming the challenges will be important to unlocking the full potential of digital twin technology in revolutionizing healthcare facilities management.

References

Aloqaily, M., Bouachir, O., Karray, F. (2023). Digital twin for healthcare immersive services: Fundamentals, architectures, and open issues. *Digital Twin for Healthcare*, 39–71. Available from https://doi.org/10.1016/b978-0-32-399163-6.00008-1. Elsevier BV.

Augustine, P. (2020). The industry use cases for the Digital Twin idea. *Advances in Computers*, *117*, 79–105. Available from https://doi.org/10.1016/bs.adcom.2019.10.008, http://www.elsevier.com/wps/find/bookdescription.cws_home/705045/description#description.

Botín-Sanabria, D. M., Mihaita, A.-S., Peimbert-García, R. E., Ramírez-Moreno, M. A., Ramírez-Mendoza, R. A., & Lozoya-Santos, J. de J. (2022). Digital twin technology challenges and applications: A comprehensive review. *Remote Sensing*, *14*(6), 1335. Available from https://doi.org/10.3390/rs14061335.

Bruynseels, K., Santoni de Sio, F., & van den Hoven, J. (2018). Digital twins in health care: Ethical implications of an emerging engineering paradigm. *Frontiers in Genetics*, *9*. Available from https://doi.org/10.3389/fgene.2018.00031.

Das, C., Mumu, A. A., Ali, F., Sarker, S. K., Muyeen, S. M., Das, S. K., Das, P., Hasan, M., Tasneem, Z., Islam, M., Islam, R., Badal, F. R., Ahamed, H., & Abhi, S. H. (2022). Toward IoRT collaborative digital twin technology enabled future surgical sector: Technical innovations, opportunities and challenges. *IEEE Access*, *10*, 129079–129104. Available from https://doi.org/10.1109/access.2022.3227644.

Ebiloma, D. O., Aigbavboa, C. O., & Anumba, C. (2023). Towards digital twin maintenance management of health facilities in Nigeria: The need for maintenance documentation. *Buildings*, *13*(5), 1339. Available from https://doi.org/10.3390/buildings13051339.

Fuller, A., Fan, Z., Day, C., & Barlow, C. (2020). Digital twin: Enabling technologies, challenges and open research. *IEEE Access*, *8*, 108952–108971. Available from https://doi.org/10.1109/access.2020.2998358.

Gomathi, L., Mishra, A. K., & Tyagi, A. K. (2023). *Industry 5.0 for Healthcare 5.0: Opportunities, challenges and future research possibilities. 7th International conference on trends in electronics and informatics, ICOEI 2023 -*

Proceedings (pp. 204–213). India: Institute of Electrical and Electronics Engineers Inc. Available from http://doi.org/10.1109/ICOEI56765.2023.10125660, http://ieeexplore.ieee.org/xpl/mostRecentIssue.jsp?punumber = 10125569.

Harode, A., Thabet, W., & Dongre, P. (2023). A tool-based system architecture for a digital twin: A case study in a healthcare facility. *Journal of Information Technology in Construction*, *28*, 107–137. Available from https://doi.org/10.36680/j.itcon.2023.006.

Hemamalini, V., Armosh, F., & Tyagi, A. K. (2024). Digital Twin-Based Smart Healthcare Services for the Next Generation Society. In A. Sharma, N. Chanderwal, S. Tyagi, & P. Upadhyay (Eds.), *Future of AI in Medical Imaging* (pp. 247–277). IGI Global. Available from https://doi.org/10.4018/979-8-3693-2359-5.ch015.

Jimenez, J. I., Jahankhani, H., & Kendzierskyj, S. (2019). *Health care in the cyberspace: Medical cyber-physical system and digital twin challenges* (pp. 79–92). Springer Science and Business Media LLC. Available from http://doi.org/10.1007/978-3-030-18732-3_6.

Khajavi, S. H., Motlagh, N. H., Jaribion, A., Werner, L. C., & Holmstrom, J. (2019). Digital twin: Vision, benefits, boundaries, and creation for buildings. *IEEE Access*, *7*, 147406–147419. Available from https://doi.org/10.1109/access.2019.2946515.

Liu, Y., Zhang, L., Yang, Y., Zhou, L., Ren, L., Wang, F., Liu, R., Pang, Z., & Deen, M. J. (2019). A novel cloud-based framework for the elderly healthcare services using digital twin. *IEEE Access*, *7*, 49088–49101. Available from https://doi.org/10.1109/access.2019.2909828.

Machado, T. M., & Berssaneti, F. T. (2023). Literature review of digital twin in healthcare. *Heliyon*, *9*(9), e19390. Available from https://doi.org/10.1016/j.heliyon.2023.e19390.

Madubuike, O. C., & Anumba, C. J. (2021). *Digital twin application in healthcare facilities management. Computing in Civil Engineering 2021 - Selected papers from the ASCE international conference on Computing in Civil Engineering 2021* (pp. 366–373). United States: American Society of Civil Engineers (ASCE).

Menon, S. C., Prasad, S., & Soni, G. (2022). *Preserving privacy of patients with disabilities in the smart healthcare systems using multimedia systems, tools, and technologies for smart healthcare services* (pp. 191–205). India: IGI Global. Available from https://www.igi-global.com/book/using-multimedia-systems-tools-technologies/297080, https://doi.org/10.4018/978-1-6684-5741-2.ch012.

Mihai, S., Yaqoob, M., Hung, D. V., Davis, W., Towakel, P., Raza, M., Karamanoglu, M., Barn, B., Shetve, D., Prasad, R. V., Venkataraman, H., Trestian, R., & Nguyen, H. X. (2022). Digital twins: A survey on enabling technologies, challenges, trends and future prospects. *IEEE Communications Surveys & Tutorials*, *24*(4), 2255–2291. Available from https://doi.org/10.1109/comst.2022.3208773.

Nazeer, S. F., Ramachandra, T., Gunatilake, S., & Senaratne, S. (2020). Emerging sustainable facilities management practices in health-care sector. *Journal of Facilities Management*, *18*(1), 1–19. Available from https://doi.org/10.1108/jfm-10-2019-0056.

Rowan, N. J. (2024). Digital technologies to unlock safe and sustainable opportunities for medical device and healthcare sectors with a focus on the combined use of digital twin and extended reality applications: A review. *Science of The Total Environment*, *926*, 171672. Available from https://doi.org/10.1016/j.scitotenv.2024.171672.

Sai, D. Y., & Tyagi, A. K. (2023). *Introduction to smart healthcare: Healthcare digitization 6G-enabled IoT and AI for smart healthcare: Challenges, impact, and analysis* (pp. 1–22). India: CRC Press Available from:. Available from http://www.tandfebooks.com/doi/book/9781000895810.

Sharma, A., Kosasih, E., Zhang, J., Brintrup, A., & Calinescu, A. (2022). Digital twins: State of the art theory and practice, challenges, and open research questions. *Journal of Industrial Information Integration*, *30*, 100383. Available from https://doi.org/10.1016/j.jii.2022.100383.

Song, Y., & Li, Y. (2022). *Digital twin aided healthcare facility management: A case study of Shanghai Tongji Hospital 2-B. Construction Research Congress 2022: Computer applications, automation, and data analytics - Selected papers from Construction Research Congress 2022* (pp. 1145–1155). China: American Society of Civil Engineers (ASCE).

Tyagi, A. K. (2023). *Decentralized everything: Practical use of blockchain technology in future applications distributed computing to Blockchain: Architecture, technology, and applications* (pp. 19–38). India: Elsevier. Available from https://www.sciencedirect.com/book/9780323961462, https://doi.org/10.1016/B978-0-323-96146-2.00010-3.

Yang, D., Karimi, H. R., Kaynak, O., & Yin, S. (2021). Developments of digital twin technologies in industrial, smart city and healthcare sectors: a survey. *Complex Engineering Systems*, *1*(1). Available from https://doi.org/10.20517/ces.2021.06.

Zhao, J., Feng, H., Chen, Q., & Garcia de Soto, B. (2022). Developing a conceptual framework for the application of digital twin technologies to revamp building operation and maintenance processes. *Journal of Building Engineering*, *49*, 104028. Available from https://doi.org/10.1016/j.jobe.2022.104028.

CHAPTER

Role of digital twins and blockchain for the internet of medical things 4

Shalini Kumari and Chander Prabha

Chitkara University Institute of Engineering and Technology, Chitkara University, Punjab, India

4.1 Introduction

Healthcare 4.0 builds a learning healthcare system for data-driven decision-making and autonomous care. Industrial Internet of Things (IIoT), digital twins (DTs), machine learning (ML), and Big Data are used. Technological advancements in cyber-physical systems and high-performance computing (HPC) have made digital duplicates of products, processes, equipment, and systems affordable for industries. These reproductions are DTs, Multiphysics, multiscale, and probabilistic simulations that mimic real-world physical components. The emergence of innovative technologies such as cloud computing (CC), the Internet of Things (IoT), Big Data, and artificial intelligence (AI) has ushered in a new era of smart things. As a result, the increasing number of options is leading to the emergence of new ways in which system components can be interconnected, interact, and be controlled intelligently, thereby driving technological innovation. The innovative concept of DTs is a significant outcome of this technical progress (Zhou et al., 2020). Due to the availability of digital tools for data gathering and analytics, increased processing power, and reduced prices of cloud data storage, the barrier to creating DT is getting lower by the day. These tools offer various benefits. The use of DT in manufacturing for optimization and quality control (Schluse et al., 2018) allows for the creation and testing of virtual objects through the use of exploitative and destructive experiments that would not be allowed in the real world owing to ethical concerns, legal constraints, or high financial costs. A DT is a simulation of a complicated product that incorporates Multiphysics, multiscale, and probabilistic analysis to mimic its existence (Tao et al., 2019). DT is used in many areas, such as healthcare (Zhang et al., 2020), aerospace (Zhao et al., 2022), energy (Wang et al., 2021), and automobiles (Xie et al., 2022). DT technology is undergoing significant advancements in AI (Bharti et al., 2020), Big Data (Bazel et al., 2021), and other areas. DTs need periodic updates, limiting the data they may receive or provide when queried. Thus blockchain-based DT can model patient conditions and access particular services to facilitate care. In decentralized systems, adopting DT collaboration is still difficult due to the early stage of the DT paradigm.

Authentication: Decentralized systems may use DTs controlled by independent companies wanting to collaborate. The decentralized digital system needs secure and efficient technology for secure real-time data sharing and analysis across various participants.

Distributed ML: Large-scale input data from various users must be processed to anticipate decentralized system dangers accurately.

Blockchain and Digital Twin for Smart Hospitals. DOI: https://doi.org/10.1016/B978-0-443-34226-4.00005-8

Decentralized decision-making: Decentralization lacks global data, while centralization has single failure data. A decision-making consensus is needed.

Scalability and robustness: In decentralized systems, a system must support many DT representing items, devices, machines, nodes, people, workstations, and so on. The decentralized system must also manage various DTs and ensure robustness, especially with hacked nodes and malfunctioning cases.

4.2 Layers of DT framework

A multilayered approach is needed to implement a DT smart healthcare system, as indicated in Fig. 4.1, which includes technical and nontechnical factors. The four essential layers of DT smart healthcare system implementation are:

4.2.1 Device layer

The device layer includes physical devices that record and send data to the DT system. Consider wearable devices, medical imaging, patient-generated data (e.g., social media, fitness apps), and other patient data sources. The device layer depends on data quality and consistency in the DT system. Ensuring sensor data accuracy and dependability requires thorough calibration and noise filtering. A new calibration technique for wearable sensors uses machine learning and supervised learning algorithms to eliminate biases and drifts by analyzing sensor data and reference measurements from gold-standard devices. Proposes (Yu & Lee, 2022) a deep learning (DL) architecture for autonomous medical imaging equipment calibration, ensuring consistent data quality by addressing distortions and inconsistencies in uncalibrated images. For wearable sensor data, a hybrid approach combining the Kalman filter and wavelet transform provides robust noise filtering (Ahmadi-Assalemi et al., 2020). According to Yu & Lee (2022), adaptive filtering and DL-based image-denoising algorithms can reduce noise in medical images without affecting key information. It is useful for evaluating sensor technologies, calibration methodologies, and noise-filtering techniques. Highlights the significance of reference standards in medical imaging, promoting standardized protocols and phantoms for data accuracy and dependability, boosting value for clinical decision-making.

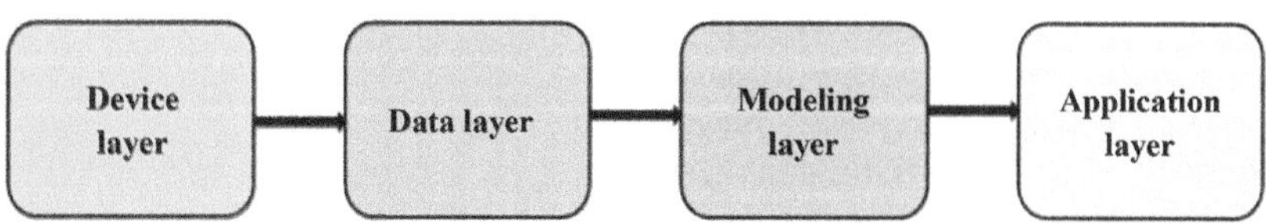

FIGURE 4.1

Layers of DT framework.

4.2.2 Data layer

The data layer accumulates, stores, and maintains patient data. This comprises electronic health records (EHRs), medical imaging, test reports, and other clinical data. The data layer transforms and cleans data to ensure quality and consistency. Additionally, the data layer combines data from various sources, including wearable devices and patient-generated data, to provide a complete health picture. DTs' Basic data processing techniques include cleaning, preprocessing, outlier detection, data imputation, and normalization to handle inconsistencies and mistakes (Liu, 2021). Transformation and feature engineering are crucial steps to analyze raw data, involving techniques like feature selection and dimensionality reduction. Integrating and fusing data from many sources, including EHRs, medical imaging, sensors, and patient-generated data, can provide a comprehensive perspective of a patient's health through approaches such as data alignment and merging. According to Korshunova and Shvetsova (2022), data warehouses, lakes, cloud storage, blockchain technology, and strong encryption methods offer secure and scalable centralized and decentralized storage solutions, ensuring patient privacy and data integrity. Layer 2 of the DT architecture includes complete orchestration, making the data layer crucial for the smooth functioning and efficacy of DT applications in smart healthcare systems.

4.2.3 Modeling layer

The modeling layer is crucial in DT architecture, developing and maintaining accurate patient models for behavior simulation and result prediction. Robust modeling techniques are essential for addressing healthcare system challenges such as nonlinear dynamics, data heterogeneity, and individual variations. To account for the complex interactions between physiological systems, nonlinear dynamics require modeling methods beyond linear paradigms (Sajedi, 2018). Effective feature engineering and integration strategies are necessary due to the heterogeneity of data sources, such as wearable sensors, medical imaging, and genomes (Tahir et al., 2020). Individual differences in treatment responses highlight the necessity for tailored-modeling approaches. ML approaches, including supervised and unsupervised learning, and DL algorithms like convolutional and recurrent neural networks, enable complicated dataset analysis for many healthcare applications. Agent-based modeling reveals complicated system dynamics by capturing emergent behaviors in unique contexts.

AI methods like explainable AI (XAI), generative adversarial networks (GANs), and federated learning enhance the modeling layer's adaptability. Several models, such as DeepMind's AlphaFold, IBM's Watson Oncology, and NVIDIA's Clara AI platform, demonstrate the practical use of these techniques for protein structure prediction, personalized cancer treatment plans, and AI-powered healthcare applications. In summary, the modeling layer encompasses several tools and procedures for healthcare systems, enabling personalized treatment, predictive healthcare, and virtual trials inside the DT framework.

4.2.4 Application layer

The application layer at Layer 4 of the DT in healthcare (DTH) architecture provides tools for analyzing and interpreting complicated datasets, bridging the gap between the system and healthcare providers. This layer relies on several data visualization approaches to give healthcare providers clear, concise, and actionable insights. Dashboards enable healthcare providers to monitor health trends and make educated decisions by providing a consolidated view of key metrics and indicators. Interactive 3D models and technologies like VR and AR enable realistic viewing of anatomical features, illness development, and treatment effects (Tahir et al., 2020). The DTH ecosystem provides visualizations through numerous methodologies, tools, and frameworks. Unity3D, Microsoft Azure DTs, Eclipse Ditto, and NVIDIA Clara AI platforms are crucial for creating immersive and informative user interfaces. These visualization techniques and technologies enable healthcare clinicians to gain actionable information, promoting seamless DTH system interactions and decision-making.

The four levels of DT smart healthcare are integrated to provide personalized medicine, predictive healthcare, enhanced diagnosis and treatment, virtual trials, and real-time monitoring and intervention. The advancement of DT technology will lead to more advanced and integrated systems that improve healthcare delivery and patient outcomes.

4.3 Related work

Due to its volatility and practical uses, DT formation has garnered too much interest. This section summarized a few recent and notable studies in the field. Also, this section discusses secure patient data sharing utilizing smart contracts with DT in healthcare.

The authors use DT technology to monitor patients and enhance outcomes, quality of life, and financial costs. According to this research, wearable sensors can detect health problems early and manage chronic illnesses. Assistive technology and real-time data can offer dynamic health care with low patient risk. Machine learning–based quick simulations for accurate crisis prediction are also proposed. Thus clinicians may plan intelligent control and emergency response using the patient's DT (Croatti et al., 2020). They conclude that DT can enable preventive healthcare for patients through trial-and-error simulations to evaluate therapy effects before administering them. This makes precision medicine cost-effective and offers patients individualized therapies.

They studied agent-based DT design and healthcare management. A case study shows how contextual DTs of a trauma victim alert hospital emergency medical staff with critical patient information. The authors of A Blockchain-based Secure Digital Twin Framework for Smart Healthy City suggest a three-layer framework: device, blockchain, and application. Their framework is applied to the COVID-19 pandemic and shown to apply to subsequent public health catastrophes. It showed a sequence diagram of how two DTs and a hospital may exchange public keys for infection notification. However, they do not prove encryption and other security protocols are needed to safeguard DT (EL Azzaoui et al., 2021).

By contrast, Liu et al. (2019) suggested a cloud-based healthcare DT architecture. Elderly individuals often avoid medical treatments due to apathy toward diseases, which is the motivation behind the project. The authors created a system with four components: physical items, virtual objects, cloud healthcare platforms, and healthcare data. While several key issues have been covered, no algorithm for predictive measurements has been provided. Using edge computing, the authors created a healthcare twin to treat heart illnesses. IoT devices will collect real-time data via smartphones, which will be stored in a central data storage after undergoing data fusion transformation. They created the twin with three structures: data source, AI-Inference Engine, and Multimodal Interaction and Smart Service.

Though data storage and security concerns remain unresolved, convolutional neural network (CNN) training is their primary motivation. A DT platform was proposed (Petrova-Antonova et al., 2020) to study behavioral changes in patients with confirmed cognitive impairments, specifically multiple sclerosis. One of the main features of this platform is data collection for the DT. Advanced analytical applications enable data collection, enrichment, analysis, and visualization, enabling knowledge creation and decision support. The authors want to gather patient data from several sources, including EHRs, open clinical databases, social media, and other external apps. However, they have not demonstrated actions to prevent data integrity and confidentiality breaches.

A risk assessment in the DT system (Rao & Mane, 2019) uses AI to improve liver disease decision-making. The authors employed their Random Forest (RDF) model and the cutting-edge explainable AI framework, Local Interpretable Model-Agnostic Explanations (LIME). Healthcare is a sensitive subject matter, they recommend using explainable AI. The authors gave sufficient algorithm information but did not address storage facilities or security (Kaushal et al., 2022; Kumar et al., 2022).

Peng et al. (2020) describe a completed hospital DT developed in China. The authors detail how the hospital twin was built using Continuous Lifecycle Integration. Real-time data is employed to simulate the hospital in virtual space. During construction, sensors were employed to gather real-time data from the healthcare facility. A DT enables remote operation of the entire system. Data access and encryption mechanisms are not revealed. No mention is made of how this massive data would be used to make reasonable decisions.

Barbiero et al. (2020) suggested a generative model architecture integrated with a graph-based description of pathophysiological circumstances. By utilizing synthetic data and augmented biological system states, their model can replicate complex clinical conditions that would be challenging to study. Numerous data models were utilized for structured data collection. In addition, they used graph neural networks for deep learning and predicted patient physiological changes. Various cardiovascular tissues were examined. DTs are not much without relevant information. Graph neural networks were utilized for DL to predict patient physiological state progression. A DT system was developed with AI to improve liver disease decision-making. The authors utilized their RDF model and the cutting-edge explainable AI package, LIME. They recommend using explainable AI to address the sensitive nature of healthcare. While the authors have supplied considerable information regarding the methods, they have not addressed storage facilities or security.

Recent important works in Healthcare DT include (Elayan et al., 2021). This work proposes and implements a system that benefits digital healthcare and operations. The intelligent healthcare system diagnoses cardiac abnormalities and identifies disease by classifying ECG heart rhythms using DT. DT integrates AI, data snalytics, IoT, VR/AR, and digital/physical objects. This interface offers real-time data analysis and status monitoring to prevent issues. It offers insights on risk management, cost reduction, and predicting future opportunities. Similar to prior efforts, they did not take any measures to protect the stored data.

4.4 Integration of digital twins

This section briefly overviews DTs, Healthcare DTs, and blockchain, including their elements. DT represents the anatomy of a digital asset in a digital realm, resembling physical occurrences. This complicated mechanism maintains digital-physical coherence and enhances cognitive awareness of the physical world. DT's main focus is the interaction between real and digital environments. The rapid development of information technologies such as radio-frequency identification (RFID) and IoT enables easy data collection from various physical phenomena (Ding & Jiang, 2018). DT has two categories according to its intended usage (Grieves & Vickers, 2017):

Digital twin for developing a product:

Although a tangible product has not yet been built, its representative DT has all the essential knowledge to develop it. DT predicts workflow and product behavior by analyzing past knowledge, current development status, work distribution, and product description. DTs can be implemented throughout hospital manufacture. This falls under Product Lifecycle Management (PLM) (Li et al., 2015) in healthcare.

Digital twin for an individual instance:

This DT may update its virtual state using real-time data from physical space using IoT sensors, recognizing tangible products or nonspatial phenomena. Imagine a car with sensors incorporated into all key parts. Therefore the DT would continuously receive vehicle data and assess its present state through vehicle health management (Ezhilarasu et al., 2019). The maintenance time, product longevity, and other characteristics can be remotely calculated to gain insight into the situation. Task performance, organ model creation, and physiological system study. Patient DTs need analytics and other service capabilities. Table 4.1 presents the qualities of DTs for an individual instance.

Table 4.1 DT qualities and their description.

No.	Quality	Description
1	Adaptability	It is the ability to absorb and incorporate adjustments to accommodate predict, expect, or stochastic changes if any to note. The virtual model must accommodate lifetime changes.
2	Extensibility	The DT must be expandable to track new parameters for best functioning and performance. This is crucial for a patient's DT as they cycle through health issues. New modules can be added to extend the DT's capabilities.
3	Modularity	Monitoring aspects of the individual can be virtualized and updated to improve care. Thus the patient DT has multiple interconnected modules divided into logical categories. Modules may represent physiological systems, conditions, and so on and can incorporate all patient-care data.
4	Connectivity	Analytic models differ from the DT in connectivity. Thus connectivity is the ability to feed data to systems, platforms, and services to operate the physical asset. Data sources with changes in preset categories, contexts, and conditions may update periodically. Data availability, bandwidth, and so on affect connectivity frequency.
5	Programmability	The patient DT can be used to collect data for trials to discover optimal health outcomes within confined bounds and situations. A DT instance can test and adapt treatment until it achieves the desired result. Since DTs can have several instances, failure of such tests does not harm the patient.
6	Flags	The DT can represent a physical system's conditions and states under restrictions. Data from the DT can be used to simulate and prevent patient conditions. Therefore the twin can receive settings that meet medical condition thresholds.

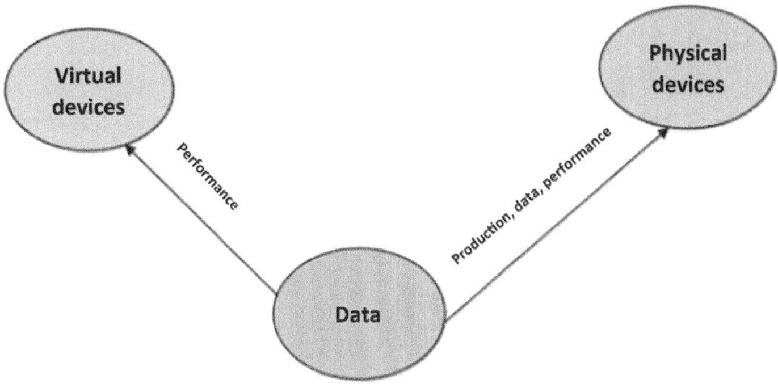

FIGURE 4.2

Main parts of digital twins.

The term "digital twin" refers to a method of combining the digital and physical realms. Machines, equipment, and robots in the warehouse, manufacturing, and process can be described in great depth using this. Improving data security and quality, lowering costs, and speeding up decision-making are some of the DTs' benefits in Industry 4.0. A DT is a one-to-one virtual representation of a physical object that shares its data, functions, and communication interfaces. Physical and virtual components, as well as the data that links them, make up DTs. Fig. 4.2 shows the above concept.

4.4.1 Combining blockchain, digital twins, and data analysis benefits

The main benefit is using DTs with blockchain technology for data storage and interaction. DTs can collaborate using blockchain technology by entering smart contracts. There are two possibilities for blockchain and DTs. DTs must be immutable, and blockchain is essential to their security. DT information might be stored in the blockchain instead of a database to confirm the data source. The necessity for DTs to interact makes blockchain–DT integration crucial. Thus blockchain technology relies on distributed ledgers and smart contracts. Thus DT should execute smart contracts. Also, ML can forecast and detect DT events. The five advantages of merging DTs, blockchain, and data analytics are as follows.

Ensuring the security of data: Since it would be extremely difficult, if not impossible, for hackers to compromise all DTs to access crucial data, the distributed nature of blockchain makes this task more difficult for them. In addition, the system is always safe and secure since any DT that acts suspiciously is immediately removed from the blockchain.

Data integrity: Blockchain guarantees data integrity using encryption and a rigorous verification method. It also brings much-needed transparency by allowing users to track their transactions.

Analytics of data in real time: Data analytics provides in-depth data analytics, whereas blockchain offers real-time transactions. When combined, these two technologies can provide real-time data analytics, which has the potential to simplify business operations and disrupt numerous industries.

Predictions: Data analytics can be applied to blockchain data to find important insights and hidden patterns.

Data sharing: By archiving information on a blockchain network, project teams can prevent rehashing previously used data or performing redundant data analytics. The method can also help with safe data transmission without the need for data cleansing every time.

While each has its advantages and disadvantages, data analytics and blockchain technology can work together to manage data quantity and quality more effectively. More use cases, such as data analytics, will be able to be investigated as blockchain technology develops and matures. However, the low storage costs of blockchain make it a good fit for data analytics. It will be interesting to see how these technologies evolve in reaction to current problems and show how they can alter data consumption and management.

4.4.2 Healthcare digital twin

The primary criterion for DT is that both virtual and physical qualities must always be consistent for the intended purpose. A patient-centric healthcare DT involves a virtual patient in a digital world that requires a large amount of data to represent the patient from a physical location. One aspect of patient data cannot provide a complete picture of a patient facing health risks. Patient data, including medicine, hospital, and management, is required. The human body is complicated and influenced by various factors such as environment, age, and social activities. Furthermore, the causes of an illness or comorbidity vary for each individual. By collecting all relevant patient data from birth to death, DT can accurately assess the current state and forecast future hazards through real-time data evaluation (Jouan & Hallot, 2020). The primary motive for patient-centric healthcare DT. In certain situations, such as remote patient observation, the DT provides critical data for responding to interrogations.

4.5 Blockchain

A blockchain is a distributed ledger that distributes block data to all peer nodes on the network. Replication across a dispersed network efficiently achieves immutability and nonreputability (Chowdhury et al., 2019). Blockchain has advanced technology by eliminating the need for third-party and central authority. Blockchain allows dispersed transactions across diverse organizations without a centralized infrastructure (Jiang et al., 2018). Blockchains store data append-only, with blocks added and linked using the Cryptographic Hash Function (Dagher et al., 2018). Blockchain could be the most effective solution for ensuring DTs' transparency, trust, and security. Fig. 4.3 illustrates DTs using blockchain to securely coordinate automotive design activities/processes. Smart contracts enable interactions between processes with separate DTs. This promotes transparency, uniqueness, and secure contact with DTs, achieving automobile design objectives. Maintaining consistency across nodes is challenging, but consensus methods rely on prior rule agreement and majority dominance. Blockchain can be generally categorized into two types:

Public blockchain: Anyone can create, validate, and write data on a public blockchain. Nodes in a public blockchain are not restricted, making it a permissionless blockchain (Alhadhrami et al.,

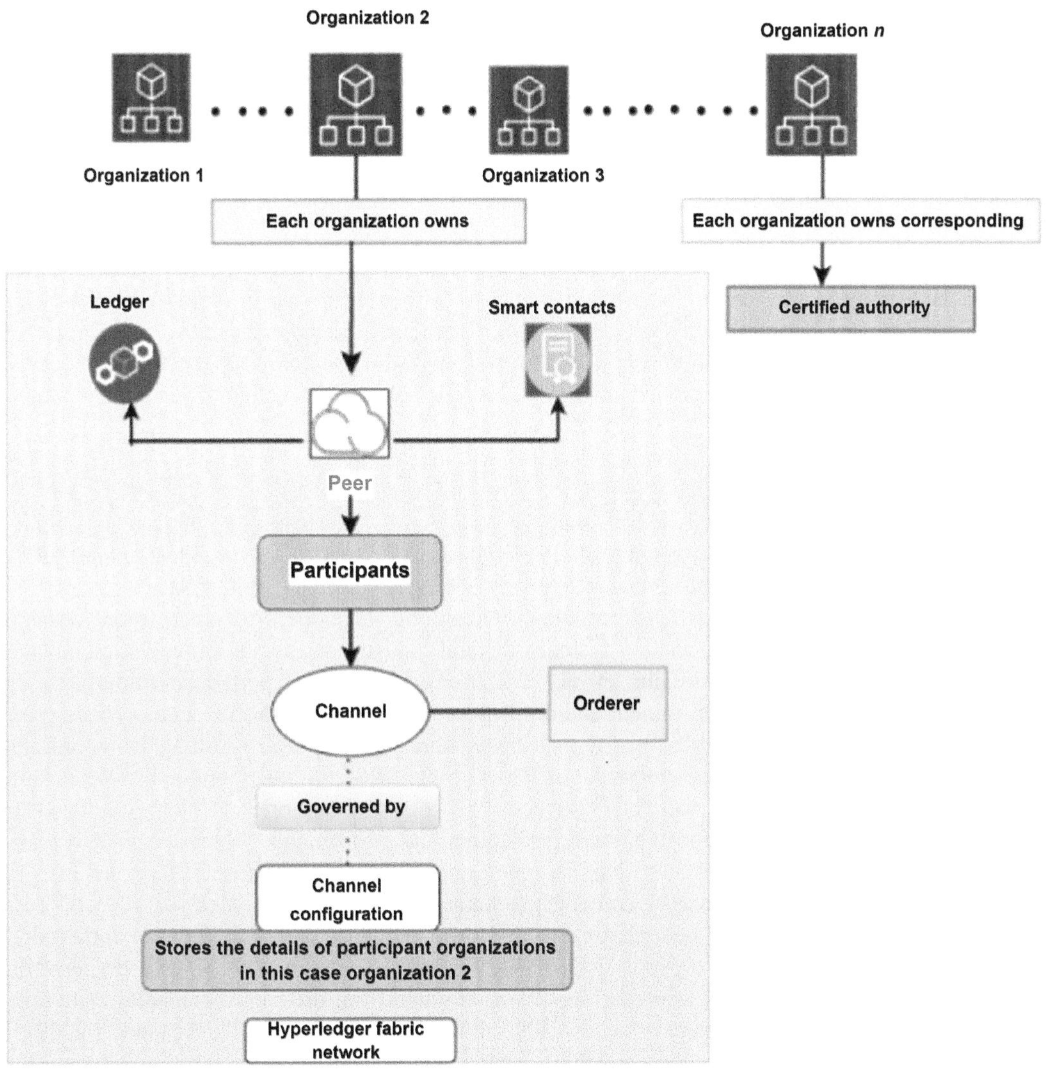

FIGURE 4.3

Hyperledger fabric parts.

2017). All transactions in a public blockchain are public, and participants are anonymous. Although very secure, propagation takes time, resulting in limited transaction throughput and high latency. Examples of public blockchain systems are Bitcoin (Squarepants, 2008), Ethereum (Buterin, 2014), and MedRec (Azaria et al., 2016), FHIRChain (Zhang et al., 2018).

Private blockchain: Private blockchains are permissioned, allowing only predefined entities to validate transactions. Blockchain technology provides sufficient security without affecting energy consumption. With fewer players in the block validation procedure, the synchronization of blocks over the dispersed network is quick. Data privacy and obscurity are sometimes necessary, such as in financial accounts and health records. The top private blockchain platforms include Hyperledger Fabric (Androulaki, 2018), Hyperledger Sawtooth, and Corda. Examples of private blockchain-based healthcare systems include HealthChain (Xu et al., 2019), ModelChain (Kuo & Ohno-Machado, 2018), Ancile, and MeDShare (Xia et al., 2017).

4.5.1 Smart contracts

A blockchain platform can execute smart contracts over distributed networks among distrusted entities. Real-life contractual constraints are converted into executable computer codes, integrated with digital assets, and executed autonomously without trusted authority. Since smart contracts operate in an immutable blockchain environment, their code must be vetted before deployment (Lautzenhiser, 2024).

4.5.1.1 Hyperledger fabric

Among the most popular permissioned blockchain technologies, Hyperledger Fabric boasts unique features and flexible deployment techniques. The Hyperledger Foundation, an open-source, global collaborative initiative of the Linux Foundation, produced Hyperledger Fabric (Nasir et al., 2018). The Hyperledger Foundation facilitates collaboration among developers to create more reliable, scalable, and efficient private blockchain systems. Several industry partners are involved in advancing the Hyperledger effort (Alotaibi et al., 2022). Out of all Hyperledger initiatives, the Hyperledger Fabric is the most prominent and developed. Hyperledger Fabric is an enterprise-grade permissioned distributed ledger platform that is open-source and trusted, resulting in identifiable users. Since Hyperledger Fabric is modular, it allows pluggable consensus protocols. When only one organization is involved, the network is operated by a trusted authority, reducing the need for Byzantine fault tolerance. This boosts system throughput and performance. Hyperledger Fabric has several key ideas. Further, a brief discussion is done to describe its components' functions. Fig. 4.3 shows the Hyperledger Fabric network components connected.

Organization: An entity must be a member of a group to connect to a Hyperledger Fabric blockchain network. Let us say that the people who buy and sell in a simple exchange business are from different companies. The people who run the system are also from different companies. The business sets up a user group so the network can easily see who uses the ledger (Sharma et al., 2019).

Certificate authority (CA): When something new is added to the blockchain network, the CA gives it a name that includes a private key, a public key, and a digital certificate. This way, the Hyperledger Fabric network can uniquely identify the new thing (Dabholkar & Saraswat, 2019). In Fig. 4.3, each company has its own CA. Other parts of the network can use the entity's public key. When an organization signs or endorses a transaction with its private key, there must be a way to ensure it is real. The Membership Service Provider (MSP) handles this. The MSP knows the entity's public key and all its public keys. It can check the signature or support to ensure it is real and uniquely identifies the entity and its certificate (Sukhwani et al., 2018). That way, each entity's permissions and access controls will be the ones that matter everywhere on the network.

Peer: A blockchain network has peer nodes. At least one peer is required for each organization to store ledgers and smart contracts (Jiang et al., 2020). Blockchain and smart contracts are essential for data storage and sharing, making peers the most crucial component. Fig. 4.3 shows peer-channel connection.

Endorser: The endorsing peer validates each transaction through a digitally signed response (Sukhwani et al., 2017). To validate, the endorsing peer must have smart contracts loaded. Verifying transactions requires endorsing peers, and an endorsement policy indicates the organization whose peers must digitally sign the transaction before committing it to the peer's ledger. An endorser reviews this process based on the policy.

Orderer: Orderers gather all network transactions and endorsements to form a block (Mukne et al., 2019). The blocks are then sent to all peer nodes in the network for validation, ensuring accurate ledger updates with the same order and state. Fig. 4.3 provides a clear grasp of the orderer node. System orderers can be single or numerous. Authorities or system admins specify the policy for orderer attributes.

Ledger: The blockchain ledger is a sequential, unchangeable record of block transactions. To ensure data replication across the network, each network component updates its own ledger when a new block is formed.

Channel: A network channel creates a private communication subdomain for businesses (Foschini et al., 2020). An organization can participate in several channels inside a network. Channel associates have autonomous control over configuration and rules for key elements such as participation, data availability, and endorsement policies. Channels effectively isolate entities for private communication and data access among members. Suppose a Hyperledger Fabric integrated system is used for financial transactions by four institutions. Two banks want to conduct a trade beyond the scope of the other two. Setting up a channel with these two banks will save time and money by eliminating the need for other banks to validate transactions and update their ledger. Our research does not cover the System Channel, which regulates orderer services.

Chaincode: Chaincode is Hyperledger Fabric's smart contract. Docker containers can be used to install smart contracts such as chaincodes on a peer. The chaincode must be installed to perform ledger activities. Chaincode produces key-value pairs that can be transmitted to the network and applied to all peers' ledgers (Honar Pajooh et al., 2021).

4.5.1.2 BigchainDB

BigchainDB has traits that are similar to both regular databases and blockchains. Due to MongoDB reliance, transaction size is limited. Any data can be saved in BigchainDB, although it is the most efficient way to store nonchanging data. The system is not recommended for large businesses as it only supports two transaction requests: "CREATE" and "TRANSFER."

CREATE transaction: Use the Create transaction to create a digital asset with additional metadata (Anggastya Diah Andita & Gusti Bagus Baskara Nugraha, 2022). The digital asset may have multiple owners. Encrypted raw data can be stored as an asset creation transaction in BigchainDB. A unique transaction ID will be assigned to each asset. Numerous built-in functions enable the construction and querying of stored data. The function "getTransaction" is primarily employed to retrieve assets or stored data. This function allows for data extraction against a transaction ID.

TRANSFER transaction: The transfer transaction only applies to another "CREATE" and "TRANSFER" transaction. BigchainDB's main purpose is to produce and transfer assets. Through a transfer procedure, an asset can be transferred to another owner or divided among multiple owners (Tian, 2017).

4.6 Analyzing requirements and threats

Complex systems have four emerging behaviors: predictable desirable, predictable unwanted, unpredictable desirable, and unpredictable undesirable. In DT, many obstacles may arise in real-time data perception in physical space and virtual analysis, processing, and decision-making. Threat modeling helps identify challenges and threats before implementing the system. Microsoft's well-established threat model, STRIDE (Shostack, 2014), was used to model various security risks.

Fraudulent identity: Spoofing is when an adversary adopts the identity of an authorized entity, such as a patient or sensor, to engage in illicit activity.

Data manipulation: An attacker may alter decisions to impair patients' health or hospital management processes, such as raising prescription dosage.

Repudiation: After modifying the data, the attacker can deny responsibility for their actions.

Disclosure of information: Leaks of restricted material, such as medical data of a prominent individual, might have serious consequences for their health security.

Denial of service (*DoS*): The system will struggle to complete its tasks.

Elevation of privilege: Access to higher amenities may give an attacker more privileges.

4.6.1 Misuse of system resources

Overusing system calculation power is unnecessary. Naive or malicious users may create repeated queries for minor objectives, straining the system's computing power. As the system interacts with multiple entities, data will be shared internally and externally. The lack of user privacy control poses several privacy hazards to the system. Table 4.2 shows the surgical procedure notation and semantics.

4.6.2 Examination needs in IoMT

Functional requirements (*Fr*): The system should always give all relevant data for creating a DT of an existing entity. A physician may generate a DT of a patient's heart. The system must offer forthcoming data on a patient's sensor, diagnosis, surgery, check-up, prescription, and other relevant heart data till that time. The system allows users to exchange their private data with entities under

Table 4.2 Surgical procedure notation and semantics.

Notations	Meaning
AV	Set of attribute value
ORF	Operating room factor
PD	Patient data
ST	Surgery team
STD	Surgery team data
SSF	Surgeon specific factor
TS	Set of timestamps

its jurisdiction, which should be verified. The system must verify consistent storage of dynamic data from IoT devices. Integrate the system with a private blockchain infrastructure to provide DT functionality and meet various security criteria for clinical transactions. Each entity will receive a unique ID to collect relevant data across the system.

Security requirements (*Sr*): The system should restrict access to data and participate in activities for authenticated and authorized users. It must be maintained and distributed securely to protect data integrity, authenticity, and confidentiality. The system should prevent DoS attacks, monitor resource consumption, and restrict service overuse.

Privacy requirements (*Pr*): Resolving privacy concerns requires consideration of privacy standards. The system must restrict transactions to user consent. Users require selective disclosure attribute privileges to pick which data to share.

4.7 Existing tools for DT framework

This section outlines the necessary tools for building a DT in healthcare, layer by layer. Additionally, it offers insights into end-to-end tools for the complete DT development process.

4.7.1 Layer for data acquisition and integration

Sensors from Fitbit, Apple Watch, and Garmin are crucial for collecting real-time health data, including heart rate, activity levels, and sleep habits. This data is useful for generating a tailored digital health portrayal of an individual. Wearable sensors provide continuous monitoring of DT, giving abundant and fast data for analysis and modeling. Acquiring extensive clinical data requires medical instruments such as Philips IntelliVue MX800 (Bracco & Backman, 2012) and GE Healthcare Vivid S6. Devices record vital signs, imaging data, and patient-specific measures.

Adding this data to the DT provides a complete picture of a patient's health. This layer ensures that the digital duplicate effectively reflects the patient's current condition. EHRs are essential for delivering healthcare history to patients. Solutions such as Epic electronic medical records (EMR), Cerner Millennium, and Allscripts TouchWorks manage patient data, medical history, and treatment plans. EHR data integration in the DT provides a comprehensive perspective of prior health records, enabling a more accurate representation of patient health over time.

Large-scale IoT platforms like Azure IoT Hub, AWS IoT Core, and Google Cloud IoT Core (Jacoby & Usländer, 2020) manage and process data from various sources. Platforms for managing enormous amounts of data from wearable sensors and medical devices are crucial. They enable safe data transmission and storage, enabling real-time integration into the DT. Effective data integration technologies, such as Informatica PowerCenter, IBM DataStage (Wrembel, 2023), and Talend Open Studio, are essential for integrating data from diverse sources. These solutions can combine DT data from wearable sensors, medical devices, and EHRs. They streamline data-to-insights, improving digital representation accuracy and dependability.

4.7.2 Simulation and model development

AnyLogic (Galli et al., 2019), Simulink, and COMSOL Multiphysics enable dynamic healthcare modeling and simulation. These tools are essential for constructing the DT architecture, representing complex systems, physiological processes, and medical interventions. TensorFlow, PyTorch, and sci-kit-learn are essential for improving DT capabilities. Integrating machine learning algorithms allows the DT to adapt to changing health data, offering predictive analytics and individualized treatment suggestions. TensorFlow and PyTorch provide flexible frameworks for tailoring advanced machine learning models to healthcare applications.

Advanced AI platforms like Google AI Platform, AWS AI Services, and Microsoft Azure AI enhance the DT. Platforms enable DT to analyze huge datasets, spot patterns, and gain valuable insights. Integrating AI enables the DT to comprehend complex medical data, aiding healthcare workers in decision-making and promoting tailored medicine. Platforms like NVIDIA DGX A100 and Google Cloud TPUs provide increased processing capabilities in HPC. These platforms support computationally heavy operations, including complicated simulations and large-scale data processing, improving DT performance and efficiency. The DT can conduct real-time simulations and analysis in healthcare scenarios by integrating HPC.

4.7.3 User interface and visualization

Use Unity (Madubuike & Anumba, 2023), Unreal Engine, and Blender (Pottier et al., 2023) to design realistic medical environments and architecture. These visually rich DT tools allow healthcare workers to investigate complex medical issues in 3D. Create realistic, dynamic visualizations with Unity and Unreal Engine to analyze complex healthcare data. HoloLens, Meta Quest 2, and HTC Vive Pro make the DT interactive. In these immersive systems, healthcare professionals can interact with virtual patient data, procedures, and environments. Create realistic virtual simulations with AR and VR to improve training, surgery planning, and medical education. Tableau, PowerBI, and Plotly help make complex healthcare data understandable. Healthcare professionals can study patient data in the DT using interactive visualization. Power BI and Tableau let customers build clear dashboards and reports with essential data. You need React, Angular, and Vue.js to make DT interfaces intuitive and responsive. Apps that navigate digital healthcare settings are easier to use with these frameworks. To provide the best user experience, healthcare apps use React, Angular, and Vue.js to develop dynamic, engaging user interfaces.

4.8 Existing end-to-end DT frameworks

ECLIPSE 3D: Eclipse 3D (Shah et al., 2022) is a sophisticated open-source platform for healthcare DTs customized for their needs. It builds intricate organ, tissue, medical device, and healthcare facility models. Its specialties include interactive physiological and medical devices, imaging surgery, and treatment plan simulations. 3D models with real-time data integration allow healthcare workers to see complex information easily through dashboards and visualizations. With Eclipse 3D, physicians may cooperate and train on shared 3D models. Medical procedures and surgery are taught in depth. Open-source platforms are cost-effective and accessible to healthcare institutions and academics. Developers can tailor their architecture to healthcare applications. Eclipse 3D supports many 3D formats, simplifying data integration and saving conversion costs. Augmented and virtual reality enhance education and patient interactions in Eclipse 3D. DT programs communicate and work together using standard frameworks.

Unity3D DT: Premier real-time 3D development platform Unity 3D (Leskovsky et al., 2020) optimizes healthcare construction. Virtual hospitals, gadgets, and human anatomy improve healthcare with new technologies: strong BIM, CAD, PLM, ERP, and IoT data unification. The link creates accurate, dynamic healthcare asset DTs. Deploy interactive DTs with real-time rendering, physics simulation, and scripting with the platform's intuitive interface and powerful capabilities. Unity's multiuser capabilities enable cross-device collaboration for students, researchers, patients, and practitioners. Visual scripting and real-time data visualization help specialists understand complex healthcare data, patient situations, treatment efficacy, and procedures. AR/VR from Unity aids healthcare practitioners' memory. Patient data helps Unity personalize treatment programs and approaches, increasing care and preventing issues.

4.9 Application areas for DT

In Precision Medicine, DTs play a significant role in creating virtual patient models by integrating genetic, biological, and environmental data. This technique provides customized treatment regimens, drug development, and health risk prediction. In addition, DTs are crucial for predictive diagnosis and disease monitoring, which uses real-time data from wearable sensors to track health and predict epidemics. In addition, Virtual Surgery and Surgery Planning can use DTs of organs and anatomical structures for preoperative planning, surgical simulation, and risk-free surgeon training. DTs optimize patient flow and resource allocation as part of hospital operations and resource management. They optimize staffing and equipment distribution to improve operational efficiency and reduce wait times by simulating patient flow and predicting resource needs. DTs aid in Predictive Maintenance of Medical Equipment by using real-time data to monitor performance, predict problems, and prevent downtime. Before physical construction, DTs of new medical facilities use virtual commissioning and training to anticipate potential difficulties and optimize layout.

DTs play a crucial role in Virtual Drug Testing and Safety Evaluation to eliminate animal testing and speed up drug research, generating virtual representations of organs and physiological systems. Furthermore, Personalized Drug Dosage Optimization utilizes patient DTs to predict pharmaceutical reactions, adjusting dosage for improved efficacy and fewer side effects. Virtual Clinical Trials using DTs enable speedier and more cost-effective testing of innovative medicines and medical equipment.

Finally, DTs aid in predicting and mitigating infectious disease outbreaks by modeling disease distribution among people in the Public Health and Disease Prevention domain. This assists public health workers in predicting and preventing outbreaks. To monitor and manage chronic diseases and environmental risks, DTs are used to identify persons at risk and enable early intervention. Moreover, DTs aid in creating personalized health interventions and behavioral change, supporting healthy behaviors at individual and population levels, and improving public health.

4.10 Constraints, obstacles, and future paths

This section presents important difficulties and possible solutions.

Optimized computing and expensive infrastructure: Large amounts of data make DT implementation in healthcare difficult. DTs need a lot of data to function efficiently, which may challenge storage, processing, and bandwidth. To solve this problem, efficient storage and computation solutions must be built to process massive datasets. Cloud computing makes digital transformation systems more productive and cost-effective by allowing resource adjustments and expansion. Edge computing, a promising technology, can process data locally, reducing data transport and latency. Creating and maintaining digital transformation infrastructure requires large processing, storage, and expertise investments. Cost may make digital technology integration and maintenance difficult for smaller healthcare providers or settings.

Security and privacy issues: Due to the sensitivity of healthcare data, DT incorporation into healthcare raises privacy concerns. Unauthorized disclosure can have serious consequences, requiring strong privacy safeguards. The use of blockchain technology to secure and protect data is being researched. Federation learning is a distributed method for training machine learning models that protects data while building global models. Data security and privacy are protected via differential privacy, multiparty differential privacy, homomorphic encryption, multiparty computation, and federated learning data and model poisoning detection. Due to model manipulation and structural vulnerabilities, the DT ecosystem is insecure.

Seamless incorporation into preexisting systems: Because of outmoded healthcare systems, integrating DT is tough. Older systems often lack standardized data formats, making data exchange with DTs difficult. Modern communication methods are incompatible with seamless integration, making real-time data and updates difficult to exchange. Large amounts of outdated medical equipment are still used, resulting in isolated data sets that limit historical and real-time data and DT use. The incompatibility of DTs with antiquated systems hinders healthcare delivery. Changing systems can be costly and disruptive. However, dependence on these systems limits the healthcare benefits of DTs.

Data collection and management: Current EHR designs are diverse and challenging to study, yet human decision trees require large datasets. Manual work or natural language processing is needed to extract information from disorganized formats. Due to the significant cost and time involved in hospital data collection, which relies heavily on blood testing and imaging equipment, data accuracy is problematic.

Development of intricate models: To simulate complex physiological systems or illnesses, one must understand the biological processes. Creating virtual representations of these systems involves healthcare and technical expertise.

Training and involvement from stakeholders: To successfully create and apply DT technologies in healthcare, stakeholders such as providers, patients, policymakers, and governments must be involved. Participation from stakeholders ensures DT tools suit real needs and are user-friendly. Successful deployment of DT technology requires education and training initiatives for healthcare professionals and patients. Healthcare personnel must understand and use DT data for individualized and effective care, while patients require training to access and analyze it.

4.11 Conclusion

Numerous developments aim to reduce health uncertainties. Many approaches, like AI and Big Data, are being employed without considering how to securely store and acquire enormous amounts of heterogeneous data from the real world. DT technology efficiently collects and analyzes data for insights. Data collected through many procedures requires secure storage and handling by a compact system to build a DT in healthcare. Modern healthcare emphasizes patient-centered treatment, which involves safe communication between parties. It requires secure patient data sharing and might be laborious. Automating a data-sharing mechanism with a patient DT can improve patient-care agency contact. This article offers a blockchain-secure patient DT for health data sharing. Patients have privacy and security over their medical records with Ethereum smart contracts. Secure DT data and instances using established computationally light cryptography. Use a permissioned blockchain to link our solution to healthcare systems for optimum privacy and security.

References

Ahmadi-Assalemi, G., Al-Khateeb, H., Maple, C., Epiphaniou, G., Alhaboby, Z. A., Alkaabi, S., & Alhaboby, D. (2020). *Digital twins for precision healthcare. Advanced sciences and technologies for security applications* (pp. 133–158). Cham: Springer International Publishing.

Androulaki, E. (2018). Hyperledger fabric: A distributed operating system for permissioned blockchains. In *2018 Proc. 13th EuroSys Conf* (pp. 1–15).

Alhadhrami, Z., Alghfeli, S., Alghfeli, M., Abedlla, J. A., & Shuaib, K. (2017). Introducing blockchains for healthcare. In *2017 International conference on electrical and computing technologies and applications,* ICECTA). IEEE.

Alotaibi, R., Alassafi, M., Bhuiyan, M. S. I., Raju, R. S., & Ferdous, M. S. (2022). A reinforcement-learning-based model for resilient load balancing in hyperledger fabric. *Processes (Basel, Switzerland), 10*(11), 2390. Available from https://doi.org/10.3390/pr10112390.

Anggastya Diah Andita, H., & Gusti Bagus Baskara Nugraha, I. (2022). A blockchain-based traceability system to achieve the quality objectives in the production process of a manufacturing industry. In *2022 International conference on information technology systems and innovation (ICITSI)*, IEEE.

Azaria, A., Ekblaw, A., Vieira, T., & Lippman, A. (2016). *MedRec: Using blockchain for medical data access and permission management. Proceedings - 2016 2nd International Conference on Open and Big Data, OBD 2016* (pp. 25–30). United States: Institute of Electrical and Electronics Engineers Inc.

Barbiero, P., Viñas Torné, R., & Lió, P. (2020). Graph representation forecasting of patient's medical conditions. *Towards a digital twin. bioRxiv*. Available from https://doi.org/10.1101/2020.09.19.20197764.

Bazel, M. A., Mohammed, F., & Ahmed, M. (2021). *Blockchain technology in healthcare big data management: Benefits, applications and challenges*. 2021 1st International conference on emerging smart technologies and applic*ations (eSmarTA)*. IEEE.

Bharti, U., Bajaj, D., Batra, H., Lalit, S., Lalit, S., & Gangwani, A. (2020). *Medbot: Conversational artificial intelligence powered chatbot for delivering tele-health after covid-19. Proceedings of the 5th International Conference on Communication and Electronics Systems, ICCES 2020* (pp. 870–875). India: Institute of Electrical and Electronics Engineers Inc., http://ieeexplore.ieee.org/xpl/mostRecentIssue.jsp?punumber = 9130794 doi: 10.1109/ICCES48766.2020.09137944.

Buterin, V. (2014). A next-generation smart contract and decentralized application platform ethereum foundation 3.

Bracco, D., & Backman, S. B. (2012). Philips monitors: Catch the wave!. *Can. Journal of Anesthesia/J. Canadien D'anesthésie*, *59*(3), 325–326.

Chowdhury, M. J. M., Ferdous, M. D. S., Biswas, K., Chowdhury, N., Kayes, A. S. M., Alazab, M., & Watters, P. (2019). A comparative analysis of distributed ledger technology platforms. *IEEE Access*, *7*, 167930–167943. Available from https://doi.org/10.1109/access.2019.2953729.

Croatti, A., Gabellini, M., Montagna, S., & Ricci, A. (2020). On the integration of agents and digital twins in healthcare. *Journal of Medical Systems*, *44*(9), 161. Available from https://doi.org/10.1007/s10916-020-01623-5.

Dabholkar, A., & Saraswat, V. (2019). Ripping the fabric: Attacks and mitigations on hyperledger fabric. In *Applications and techniques in information security*, (pp. 300–311). Singapore: Springer Singapore.

Dagher, G. G., Mohler, J., Milojkovic, M., & Marella, P. B. (2018). Ancile: Privacy-preserving framework for access control and interoperability of electronic health records using blockchain technology. *Sustainable Cities and Society*, *39*, 283–297. Available from https://doi.org/10.1016/j.scs.2018.02.014.

Ding, K., & Jiang, P. (2018). RFID-based production data analysis in an IoTenabled smart job-shop. *CAAJ. Autom. Sinica*, *5*(1), 128–138.

EL Azzaoui, A., Kim, T. W., Loia, V., & Park, J. H. (2021). *Blockchain-based secure digital twin framework for smart healthy city*, . *Lecture notes in electrical engineering* (Vol. 716, pp. 107–113). South Korea: Springer Science and Business Media Deutschland GmbH, http://www.springer.com/series/7818 doi: 10.1007/978-981-15-9309-3_15.

Elayan, H., Aloqaily, M., & Guizani, M. (2021). Digital twin for intelligent context-aware IoT healthcare systems. *IEEE Internet Things J*, *8*(23), 16749–16757.

Ezhilarasu, C. M., Skaf, Z., & Jennions, I. K. (2019). Understanding the role of a digital twin in integrated vehicle health management (IVHM). *Proc. IEEE Int. Conf. Syst*, 1484–1491.

Foschini, L., Gavagna, A., Martuscelli, G., & Montanari, R. (2020). *Hyperledger fabric blockchain: Chaincode performance analysis. IEEE International Conference on Communications*. Italy: Institute of Electrical and Electronics Engineers Inc., 10.1109/ICC40277.2020.9149080.

Galli, G., Patrone, C., Bellam, A. C., Annapareddy, N. R., & Revetria, R. (2019). Improving process using digital twin: A methodology for the automatic creation of models. *Proceedings of the World Congress Engineering Computer Science*, 396–400.

Grieves, M., & Vickers, J. (2017). Digital twin: Mitigating unpredictable, undesirable emergent behavior in complex systems. *Transdisciplinary Perspectives on Complex Systems*, 85–113.

Honar Pajooh, H., Rashid, M., Alam, F., & Demidenko, S. (2021). Hyperledger fabric blockchain for securing the edge Internet of Things. *Sensors*, *21*(2), 359. Available from https://doi.org/10.3390/s21020359.

Jacoby, M., & Usländer, T. (2020). Digital twin and internet of things- Current standards landscape. *Applied Science*, *10*(18).

Jiang, S., Cao, J., Wu, H., Yang, Y., Ma, M., & He. (2018). J. In *BlocHIE: A BLOCkchain-based platform for healthcare information exchange, international conference on smart computing (SMARTCOMP)*, IEEE.

Jiang, L., Chang, X., Liu, Y., Mišić, J., & Mišić, V. B. (2020). Performance analysis of hyperledger fabric platform: A hierarchical model approach, Peer Peer Netw. *Peer Peer Networking and. Applications*, *13*(3), 1014–1025.

Jouan, P., & Hallot, P. (2020). Digital twin: Research framework to support preventive conservation policies. *International Journal of Geo-Information*, *9*(4).

Kaushal, C., Islam, M. K., Singla, A., & Al Amin, M. (2022). An IoMT-based smart remote monitoring system for healthcare. In *IoT-Enabled Smart Healthcare Systems, Services and Applications*, Wiley. Available from https://doi.org/10.1002/9781119816829.ch8.

Korshunova, M. A., & Shvetsova, A. Y. (2022). 'Block chain technology in healthcare: A systematic review. *Technological Forecasting and Social Change*, *178*.

Kumar, S., Sharma, N., Kaur, A., & Kumar Kaushal, R. (2022). IoT enabled real-time pulse rate monitoring system. *ECS Transactions*, *107*(1), 8969–8977. Available from https://doi.org/10.1149/10701.8969ecst.

Kuo, T.-T., & Ohno-Machado, L. (2018). *ModelChain: Decentralized privacy preserving healthcare predictive modeling framework on private blockchain networks*.

Lautzenhiser, J.N. (2024). CoinDesk: Bitcoin, Ethereum, Crypto News and Price Data.

Leskovsky, R., Kucera, E., Haffner, O., & Rosinova, D. (2020). *Proposal of digital twin platform based on 3D rendering and IIoT principles using virtual/augmented reality. Proceedings of the 30th International Conference on Cybernetics and Informatics, K and I*. Slovakia: Institute of Electrical and Electronics Engineers Inc., http://ieeexplore.ieee.org/xpl/mostRecentIssue.jsp?punumber = 9034461 doi: 10.1109/KI48306.2020.9039804.

Li, J., Tao, F., Cheng, Y., & Zhao, L. (2015). Big data in product lifecycle management. *The International Journal of Advanced Manufacturing Technology*, *81*(1–4). Available from https://doi.org/10.1007/s00170-015-7151-x667–84.

Liu, H. (2021). Data cleaning and preprocessing for healthcare data analysis. *Transactions on Knowledge Discovery Data*, *15*(5), 1–39.

Liu, Y., Zhang, L., Yang, Y., Zhou, L., Ren, L., Wang, F., Liu, R., Pang, Z., & Deen, M. J. (2019). A novel cloud-based framework for the elderly healthcare services using digital twin. *IEEE Access*, *7*, 49088–49101. Available from https://doi.org/10.1109/access.2019.2909828.

Madubuike, O. C., & Anumba, C. J. (2023). Digital twin-based health care facilities management. *Journal of Computing Civil Engineering*, *37*(2).

Mukne, H., Pai, P., Raut, S., & Ambawade, D. (2019). *Land record management using hyperledger fabric and IPFS. 2019 10th International Conference on Computing, Communication and Networking Technologies, ICCCNT 2019*. India: Institute of Electrical and Electronics Engineers Inc. Available from http://ieeexplore.ieee.org/xpl/mostRecentIssue.jsp?punumber = 8932651, https://doi.org/10.1109/ICCCNT45670.2019.8944471.

Nasir, Q., Qasse, I. A., Abu Talib, M., & Nassif, A. B. (2018). Performance analysis of hyperledger fabric platforms. *Security and Communication Networks*, *2018*. Available from https://doi.org/10.1155/2018/3976093. Available from: https://www.hindawi.com/journals/scn/.

Peng, Y., Zhang, M., Yu, F., Xu, J., & Gao, S. (2020). Digital twin hospital buildings: An exemplary case study through continuous lifecycle integration. *Advances in Civil Engineering*, *2020*, 1–13. Available from https://doi.org/10.1155/2020/8846667.

Petrova-Antonova, D., Spasov, I., Krasteva, I., Manova, I., & Ilieva, S. (2020). *A digital twin platform for diagnostics and rehabilitation of multiple sclerosis. Computational science and its applications – ICCSA 2020* (pp. 503–518). Cham: Springer International Publishing.

Pottier, C., Petzing, J., Eghtedari, F., Lohse, N., & Kinnell, P. (2023). Developing digital twins of multi-camera metrology systems in blender. *Measurement Science and Technology*, *34*(7)075001. Available from https://doi.org/10.1088/1361-6501/acc59e.

Rao, D.J., Mane, S. (2019) Digital twin approach to clinical DSS with explainable AI. *arXiv [Cs.AI]*. http://arxiv.org/abs/1910.13520.

Sajedi, H. (2018). Applications of data hiding techniques in medical and healthcare systems: A survey. *Network Modeling Analysis Health Informatics Bioinformatics*, *7*(1).

Schluse, M., Priggemeyer, M., Atorf, L., & Rossmann, J. (2018). Experimentable digital twins—streamlining simulation-based systems engineering for Industry 4.0. *IEEE Transactions on Industrial Informatics*, *14*(4), 1722–17231. Available from https://doi.org/10.1109/tii.2018.2804917.

Shah, K., Prabhakar, T. V., Sarweshkumar, C. R., & Abhishek, S. V. (2022). Construction of a digital twin framework using free and open-source software programs. *IEEE Internet Computing*, *26*(5), 50–59.

Sharma, A., Agrawal, D., Schuhknecht, F. M., & Dittrich, J. (2019). *Blurring the lines between blockchains and database systems: The case of hyperledger fabric. Proceedings of the ACM SIGMOD international conference on management of data* (pp. 105–122). Germany: Association for Computing Machinery.

Shostack, A. (2014). *Threat modeling: Designing for security*. Hoboken, NJ, USA: Wiley.

Squarepants, S. (2008). Bitcoin: A peer-to-peer electronic cash system. *SSRN Electronic Journal*. Available from https://doi.org/10.2139/ssrn.3977007.

Sukhwani, H., Martínez, J. M., Chang, X., Trivedi, K. S., & Rindos, A. (2017). *Performance modeling of PBFT consensus process for permissioned blockchain network (hyperledger fabric). Proceedings of the IEEE symposium on reliable distributed systems* (pp. 253–255). United States: IEEE Computer Society. Available from http://doi.org/10.1109/SRDS.2017.36.

Sukhwani, H., Wang, N., Trivedi, K. S., & Rindos, A. (2018). *Performance modeling of hyperledger fabric (permissioned blockchain network). NCA 2018 - 2018 IEEE 17th International symposium on network computing and applications*. United States: Institute of Electrical and Electronics Engineers Inc., http://ieeexplore.ieee.org/xpl/mostRecentIssue.jsp?punumber = 8533540 doi: 10.1109/NCA.2018.8548070.

Tahir, A., Chen, F., Khan, H. U., Ming, Z., Ahmad, A., Nazir, S., & Shafiq, M. (2020). A systematic review on cloud storage mechanisms concerning E-healthcare systems. *Sensors (Basel, Switzerland)*, *20*(18). Available from https://doi.org/10.3390/s20185392.

Tao, F., Sui, F., Liu, A., Qi, Q., Zhang, M., Song, B., Guo, Z., Lu, S. C.-Y., & Nee, A. Y. C. (2019). Digital twin-driven product design framework. *International Journal of Production Research*, *57*(12), 3935–3953. Available from https://doi.org/10.1080/00207543.2018.1443229.

Tian, F. (2017). *A supply chain traceability system for food safety based on HACCP, blockchain & Internet of things. 14th International Conference on Services Systems and Services Management, ICSSSM 2017 - Proceedings*. Austria: Institute of Electrical and Electronics Engineers Inc.

Wang, F.-Y., Li, Y., Zhang, W., Bennett, G., & Chen, N. (2021). Digital twin and parallel intelligence based on location and transportation: A vision for new synergy between the IEEE CRFID and ITSS in cyberphysical social systems [Society News]. *IEEE Intelligent Transportation Systems Magazine*, *13*(1), 249–252. Available from https://doi.org/10.1109/mits.2020.3037573.

Wrembel, R. (2023). *Data integration revitalized: From data warehouse through data lake to data mesh* (14146, pp. 3–18). Springer Science and Business Media LLC. Available from http://doi.org/10.1007/978-3-031-39847-6_1.

Xia, Q., Sifah, E. B., Asamoah, K. O., Gao, J., Du, X., & Guizani, M. (2017). MeDShare: Trust-less medical data sharing among cloud service providers via blockchain. *IEEE Access: Practical Innovations. Open Solutions*, *5*, 14757–14767. Available from https://doi.org/10.1109/access.2017.2730843.

Xie, G., Yang, K., Xu, C., Li, R., & Hu, S. (2022). Digital twinning based adaptive development environment for automotive cyber-physical systems.". *IEEE Transactions on Industrial Informatics*, *18*(2), 1387–1396. Available from https://doi.org/10.1109/tii.2021.3064364.

Xu, J., Xue, K., Li, S., Tian, H., Hong, J., Hong, P., & Yu, N. (2019). Healthchain: A blockchain-based privacy preserving scheme for large-scale health data. *IEEE Internet of Things Journal*, *6*(5), 8770–8781. Available from https://doi.org/10.1109/jiot.2019.2923525.

Yu, H., & Lee, J. (2022). A deep learning-based framework for automatic calibration of medical imaging devices in digital twins. *J. Biomedical and Health Information*, *27*(1), 187–197.

Zhang, J., Lin Li, G. L., Da Fang, Y. T., & Huang, J. (2020). Cyber resilience in healthcare digital twin on lung cancer. *IEEE Access: Practical Innovations, Open Solutions*, *8*. Available from https://doi.org/10.1109/access.2020.3034324, 201900–201913.

Zhang, P., White, J., Schmidt, D. C., Lenz, G., & Rosenbloom, S. T. (2018). FHIRChain: Applying blockchain to securely and scalably share clinical data. *Computational and Structural Biotechnology Journal*, *16*, 267–278.

Zhao, L., Wang, C., Zhao, K., Tarchi, D., Wan, S., & Kumar, N. (2022). INTERLINK: A digital twin-assisted storage strategy for satellite-terrestrial networks. *IEEE Transactions on Aerospace and Electronic Systems*, *58*(5). Available from https://doi.org/10.1109/taes.2022.3169130, 3746–59.

Zhou, G., Zhang, C., Li, Z., Ding, K., & Wang, C. (2020). Knowledge-driven digital twin manufacturing cell towards intelligent manufacturing. *International Journal of Production Research*, *58*(4). Available from https://doi.org/10.1080/00207543.2019.1607978, 1034–51.

CHAPTER

Blockchain technology and neural networks for the Internet of Medical Things

Peace Busola Falola[1], Abidemi Emmanuel Adeniyi[2] and Joseph Bamidele Awotunde[3]

[1]Department of Computer Sciences, Faculty of Pure and Applied Sciences, Precious Cornerstone University, Ibadan, Nigeria [2]Department of Computer Science, College of Computing and Communication Studies, Bowen University, Iwo, Nigeria [3]Department of Computer Science, Faculty of Communication and Information Sciences, University of Ilorin, Ilorin, Kwara State, Nigeria

5.1 Introduction

A major development in patient care is the Internet of Medical Things (IoMT), which sprang from the larger Internet of Things (IoT) technology. Similar to IoT, IoMT enables connectivity between different devices, enabling communication by wired, wireless, or a combination of connections, contingent upon the infrastructure and devices that have been built (Bhushan et al., 2023). As smart cities expand, this interconnection becomes more and more important, boosting the demand for IoMT solutions. The financial ramifications are noteworthy: the adoption of IoMT is anticipated to save the healthcare sector roughly USD 300 billion, which represents a significant increase from the USD 28 billion in revenue recorded in 2017 and is projected to rise to USD 135 billion, drawing additional investors to this emerging field (Bhushan et al., 2023).

Healthcare and utilities expenditures have risen as the population has grown and new technologies have been used. IoMT offers more precise diagnosis, fewer problems, and lower treatment costs (Abbas et al., 2021). Here, with the increasing population and use of new technologies, healthcare and utility costs have risen. IoMT's features include more exact diagnoses, fewer complications, and reduced treatment costs (Abbas et al., 2021). This technology, along with a smartphone application, allows users to send their health details to doctors, which improves illness identification and monitoring while also preventing diseases (Abbas et al., 2021). IoMT enables precise data processing, quicker operations, and decreased waste, lowering the likelihood of mistakes dramatically. The IoT solution allows patient tracking in real time, which significantly reduces the need for actions and doctors (Abbas et al., 2021). IoMT in healthcare is used to monitor patient data collecting success using cloud servers. The cloud server's measuring and storage resources are utilized to measure the degree of intensity of a quantitative evaluation (Abbas et al., 2021). In IoMT data transmission, medical security concerns, notably data protection, arise from integrating, sharing, and transmitting data for processing by diverse devices (Abbas et al., 2021). In addition, there are legal and compliance difficulties since the accessibility or usage of data is inadequate in terms of transparency and data protection regulations (Abbas et al., 2021).

Blockchain and Digital Twin for Smart Hospitals. DOI: https://doi.org/10.1016/B978-0-443-34226-4.00006-X

Parallelly, the greater usage of IoT solutions in all sectors of everyday life, and the resultant technical developments, have made human body tests more precise (Ghubaish et al., 2021; Połap et al., 2020). However, integrating computing technology into healthcare presents hurdles, notably in safeguarding personal patient data against loss or destruction and ensuring that medical practitioners may access this data when necessary while barring unwanted access (Połap et al., 2020). The crucial nature of medical data demands cautious processing to avoid manipulation (Ellouze et al., 2020).

Despite these advancements, digitizing medical data alone does not ease diagnoses and treatment procedures; rather, it only boosts data accessibility (Ellouze et al., 2020). They propose the use of artificial intelligence (AI) to assist doctors, particularly within the IoMT framework, in which devices may share and process data remotely for specialized tests.

The discussion around IoMT also includes its security. IoMT, based on IoT principles, is naturally prone to cyber-attacks because of its heterogeneous nature, containing diverse devices, protocols, and operating systems (Bhushan et al., 2023). This vulnerability requires sophisticated security measures to secure the very valuable patient data within IoMT systems, which can be 50 times more costly than data in other industries (Bhushan et al., 2023). To protect against data breaches and cyber-attacks, several security methods are proposed, including symmetric and asymmetric key cryptography, as well as unique keyless approaches like token-based, biometric-based, proxy-based, and blockchain-based security (Bhushan et al., 2023).

The fast development of wearable and implanted sensors and wireless communication technology underscores the health sector's move to digitized and decentralized healthcare institutions for continuous and remote medical monitoring (Ellouze et al., 2020). With an expected 5.8 billion IoT devices by the end of 2020, a 20% increase from the previous year, IoMT devices are predicted to form 40% of the IoT market, demonstrating their vital role in lowering healthcare expenses, particularly for chronic illnesses and telemedicine (Ghubaish et al., 2021; Steger, 2020).

However, because of the possible impact on patient lives and privacy, IoMT system security remains a top priority. According to the 2020 CyberMDX research, over half of IoMT devices were vulnerable to vulnerabilities, emphasizing the critical need for comprehensive security measures to secure healthcare data throughout its lifespan (Ghubaish et al., 2021). The huge value of healthcare data on the black market underscores the need of putting security first to enable the effective installation and dependability of IoMT systems.

The primary contribution of this work is to perform the following:

- explain IoMT, its challenges, and its various application of it,
- discuss the integration of blockchain and neural network technologies in IoMT, and
- present potential future directions of blockchain and neural networks in IoMT.

5.2 Internet of Medical Things

The IoMT is described as the use of the basics, ideas, tools, techniques, and concepts of the well-known Internet approach, specifically for the medical and healthcare sectors and domains (Singh et al., 2020). The IoMT is a collection of medical equipment and software applications used to interconnect local and remote healthcare systems (Villanueva-Miranda et al., 2018). The IoMT is a subset of the IoT that links many medical devices, gathers knowledge or data from them, and sends and receives data in real time (Pradyumna et al., 2024). IoMT is vital for boosting the accuracy, dependability, and productivity of electronic devices in the healthcare sector (Pradyumna et al., 2024). IoMT has developed as a next-generation bio-analytical tool that converges network-connected biomedical equipment with applicable software applications to advance human health (Pradyumna et al., 2024). IoMT enables linkages between medical device infrastructures and applications that interact with a wide range of healthcare software platforms (Villanueva-Miranda et al., 2018). It required all efforts to create a realistic network of services so that accessible healthcare resources and diverse medical services may be integrated through the ultimate uses of Internet-based gadgets (Singh et al., 2020). The IoMT is playing an important role in the healthcare business by improving electronic device accuracy, consistency, and throughput (Villanueva-Miranda et al., 2018). The suggested IoMT ideas play critical roles when medical treatments need to be given in remote places. The implementation of IoMT principles and techniques has transformed healthcare, medical procedures, and services (Singh et al., 2020).

In an IoMT architecture, clinical sensors collect patients' physiological data and transfer it to a database store that can be accessed by authorized healthcare professionals (e.g., specialists, medical attendants, and physicians) (Jeyavel et al., 2021). An IoMT framework-based smart healthcare consists of many phases. The data will then be sent via the Internet to the component responsible for the prediction and analysis phase (Srivastava et al., 2022).

After obtaining the medical data, it may be analyzed using an appropriate AI-based data transformation and interpretation approach (Srivastava et al., 2022). In the event of a critical situation, physicians or other medical professionals can be contacted via clever AI-based applications on smartphones (Srivastava et al., 2022). Self-preventive actions can be used in less serious circumstances. The IoMT has altered the strategic perspective of healthcare organizations because it has the ability to uncover the key to lowering costs while increasing clinical efficiency (Jeyavel et al., 2021).

The IoMT may aid in the real-time monitoring of a patient's health as well as the assessment of therapy effectiveness. IoMT is a potential arrangement that does not require clinical resources and can assist minimize avoidable hospitalizations (Jeyavel et al., 2021). Around 60% of global healthcare institutions have already incorporated IoT technology, with an additional 27% expected to do so by 2021 (Jeyavel et al., 2021). When compared to conventional healthcare services, IoMT will reduce clinical expenses while increasing flexibility (Jeyavel et al., 2021). The recurrence of contact between patients and doctors/nurses can be decreased altogether utilizing IoMT, particularly during the pandemic (i.e., COVID-19) (Jeyavel et al., 2021). Adapting IoMT and associated technologies has fixed several problems using telemedicine, remote monitoring, sensors, robotics, and so on (Pradyumna et al., 2024).

5.2.1 Current challenges in IoMT (data security, privacy, interoperability)

Although IoMT provides dependable and effective healthcare services, it has significant drawbacks, such as data leakage (Jeyavel et al., 2021). Adopting IoMT technology for a large population is difficult owing to substantial data management, privacy, security, upgradability, and scalability (Pradyumna et al., 2024). Specifically, clinical sensors collect a patient's clinical data and send it to data servers via an open Internet route (Jeyavel et al., 2021). Vindictive clients may wiretap (or listen in) on personal information as it is being transmitted, resulting in data leaks. Traditional cryptographic approaches such as access control, identity authentication, and data encryption are often used to ensure security during wireless communication (Jeyavel et al., 2021). However, in the case of medical sensors, computational resource needs are not practical due to restricted memory space, processing capabilities, and energy capacity (Jeyavel et al., 2021). Some other challenges are outlined below:

Interoperability: One of the most significant impediments to IoMT deployment is a lack of healthcare interoperability standards (Shafiq et al., 2024). It is currently one of the most pressing challenges in the linked Internet of Industrial Things (IIoT), since industrial equipment are now capable of seamless communication, among other things (Subramaniam et al., 2023). Thus compatibility is essential. In the IoMT ecosystem, healthcare services are provided by a variety of organizations, including users, devices, and information sources (Shafiq et al., 2024). For example, remote patient monitoring necessitates the use of a range of personal health equipment, data processing algorithms, and communication protocols that include vital sign measurement, processing, and transmission (Shafiq et al., 2024). The acquired data is transformed into useful information and transmitted to the cloud server via the gateway node. Doctors and caregivers in healthcare can use the cloud to retrieve stored information remotely, decreasing data soils (Shafiq et al., 2024). This procedure sounds easy, yet interoperability is a key difficulty when implementing internetworking across many types of devices, information sources, and platforms (Shafiq et al., 2024). Without uniform healthcare standards, we cannot reap the benefits of smooth communication under the different demands of IoMT solutions (Shafiq et al., 2024). In this context, ANSI HL7 International established a series of standards that are of great interest in view of the growing needs of IoMT for various interoperability specifications, such as electronic health records, personal health records, medical document and resource exchange, structured product labeling, and representation of clinical summaries, medical recommendations, and clinical conditions (Shafiq et al., 2024).

Security and privacy of healthcare data: IoMT has altered the healthcare sector by connecting medical equipment and systems to enhance patient care and results (Ahmed et al., 2024). However, this interconnectedness poses security concerns, which must be addressed to secure individual patients' information, medical equipment, and the overall security of healthcare networks (Ahmed et al., 2024). IoMT services must handle the bring-your-own-device (BYOD) phenomenon, in which patients and clinicians utilize personal devices to access medical data stored in the cloud (Shafiq et al., 2024). On the one hand, BYOD policies enable crowdsourcing and cost-effective delivery of IoMT services (such as e-visits, telemedicine, and remote patient monitoring) (Shafiq et al., 2024). On the other hand, it poses significant problems to the security and privacy of medical data. One of the most significant challenges is the susceptibility of IoMT devices to cyber-attacks, such as illegal access, data breaches, and intentional manipulation (Ahmed et al., 2024). The security of protocols, bioinformatics, and health data has grown critical because of the potential severity of a healthcare system assault, notably the loss of control of life-sustaining equipment (Ahmed et al., 2024). Authentication, authorization, data confidentiality, availability, and integrity are among the most important security concerns in IoMT (Ahmed et al., 2024). As a result, we must implement rigorous security and privacy safeguards to prevent medical data available on the Internet from falling into the hands of hackers (Shafiq et al., 2024). In this context, numerous research issues have garnered attention, including but not limited to risk assessment, device security, session security, cloud security, data protection, and authentication (Shafiq et al., 2024).

5.2.2 Applications of IoMT in modern healthcare

5.2.2.1 Monitoring infectious diseases

IoMT technologies are becoming more diversified and widely used, making them ideal candidates for preventing, forecasting, and monitoring new infectious illnesses (Aman et al., 2021). IoMT as a health-monitoring system offers real-time surveillance using wearable health-monitoring devices, Wireless Body Area Networks (WBAN), AI, and cloud-based remote health testing. An early warning system can assist restrict the spread of infectious illnesses by utilizing IoMT functional components such as data collecting, storage, transmission, and analytics (Aman et al., 2021). End-user devices like mobile phones, tags, or health monitors collect sensor data, which is then transferred to a cloud platform for decision-making and analytics (Aman et al., 2021).

5.2.2.2 Treating orthopedic patients

The IoMT provides all feasible therapies to orthopedic patients in a variety of modes and procedures, including those involving bones, tendons, ligaments, joints, and muscles. Orthopedic patients are dealing with a number of critical and serious complications during this difficult COVID-19 period (Singh et al., 2020). The proposed IoMT concept provides solutions and treatments to these issues concerning orthopedic patients by combining advanced technology and intelligent machine learning-based approaches to provide fruitful proposals for orthopedic patient treatment, particularly in today's COVID-19 pandemic context (Singh et al., 2020).

5.2.2.3 Remote patient monitoring

Remote patient monitoring (RPM) is one of the most important applications for IoMT. Clinicians may now monitor patient health data in real time with AIoMT technology (Awotunde et al., 2023). Several IoMT uses for hospitalized patients were discovered, ranging from bed monitoring as described to more advanced applications, such as monitoring the sedation levels of patients in the surgery block (Monteiro et al., 2021). Patients who are accompanied by physicians yet require continuous monitoring of their vital signs, such as blood pressure and heart rate, frequently employ IoMT programs that offer follow-up throughout their everyday activities (Monteiro et al., 2021). RPM devices capture a variety of health data from patients, including vital signs, blood pressure, heart rate, and glucose levels, outside of regular clinical settings. This information is subsequently sent to healthcare practitioners in real time, allowing for continuous monitoring of patients with chronic diseases or those recuperating from surgery, minimizing the need for hospital visits and enabling early diagnosis of possible health risks. These programs also retain the acquired data in the cloud for future checks or analysis, and in the event of an irregularity, the tool can issue an alarm for the doctor to follow up (Monteiro et al., 2021).

5.2.2.4 Patients with respiratory diseases monitoring

This IoMT application is intended for individuals with chronic respiratory disorders who require oxygen cylinders (Monteiro et al., 2021). The solution aims to improve the quality of life for persons who have this requirement. Initially, this application was intended to be used in a personal context, following the patient during his or her daily activities; however, this IoMT application can also be used in hospitalizations because it can measure the amount of oxygen circulating through the patient's blood via IoT devices (Monteiro et al., 2021).

5.2.2.5 Wearable health devices

Wearable gadgets, including fitness trackers, smartwatches, and biosensors, are critical components of the IoMT ecosystem (Tamiziniyan & Keerthana, 2022). These gadgets track physical activity, heart rate, sleep patterns, and other factors, providing users and healthcare practitioners with vital information about their health and well-being (Tamiziniyan & Keerthana, 2022). Wearables can also notify users of possible health concerns, promoting proactive health management.

5.2.2.6 Elderly monitoring

With increased life expectancy, numerous IoMT applications for monitoring the elderly have evolved, ranging from blood pressure monitoring to daily activity tracking using digital image processing methods (Monteiro et al., 2021).

5.2.2.7 Detection of heart attacks

IoMT apps for detecting heart attacks employ a variety of wearable devices, such as smartwatches and smartphones, to monitor the patient, determine when an attack happens, and send a warning to the nearest hospital (Monteiro et al., 2021).

5.2.2.8 Smart implants

Smart implants, such as pacemakers or insulin pumps, are IoMT devices that are inserted into the body to replace, support, or improve a biological structure (Hassija et al., 2021; Shuvo et al., 2022). These devices can monitor and automatically alter their function based on the patient's current health data, therefore increasing the quality of life for those with chronic diseases (Hassija et al., 2021; Shuvo et al., 2022). Furthermore, they allow physicians to remotely monitor patients' status and device functionality.

5.2.2.9 Medication management

IoMT technologies are being utilized to create smart drug dispensers that remind patients when to take their medications and measure adherence (Ghozali, 2023). These devices are especially useful for older patients or those with chronic diseases that need complex prescription regimens, as they greatly reduce the likelihood of medication mistakes while increasing treatment results (Ghozali, 2023).

5.2.2.10 Connected inhalers and injection devices

Patients with asthma, diabetes, or other disorders that require inhalers or injections can use linked devices to measure consumption, check adherence, and even offer feedback on technique.

This information may be shared with healthcare practitioners to help tailor treatment approaches and enhance patient results.

5.2.2.11 Telehealth and virtual consultations

IoMT plays an important role in telehealth, allowing for virtual consultations with healthcare practitioners (Siddiqui, 2021). This is especially useful in rural or underdeveloped regions, where access to treatment may be restricted. Patients can obtain rapid medical advice, diagnosis, and treatment plans using video conferencing, messaging platforms, and digital examination tools without having to go physically (Siddiqui, 2021).

5.2.2.12 Hospital workflow and asset management

IoMT devices are useful for streamlining hospital processes and managing medical assets (Shelke, 2020). Real-time location systems (RTLS) can track medical equipment, lowering the amount of time employees spend looking for it (Overmann et al., 2021). Similarly, IoMT can monitor ambient factors in hospitals, such as temperature and humidity, which are essential for patient comfort and safety.

5.2.2.13 Data analytics and predictive analytics

The massive volumes of data acquired by IoMT devices can be used to provide insights into patient health trends, treatment results, and disease patterns (Wagan et al., 2022). Predictive analytics can identify individuals who are at risk of acquiring specific illnesses, allowing for preventative measures or early treatments that can lead to improved health outcomes and lower healthcare costs (Razzak et al., 2020).

5.2.2.14 Enhanced patient engagement and satisfaction

IoMT devices empower patients by allowing them to control their health data and actively engage in healthcare operations (Mishra & Singh, 2023). This leads to enhanced patient participation, satisfaction, and adherence to treatment programs, which all contribute to better health outcomes.

5.3 Blockchain technology in IoMT

Blockchain is the initial term given to the structural architecture of the Bitcoin cryptocurrency, which was suggested in 2008 and implemented in 2009 (Girardi et al., 2020). The original technology consists of a public and digital record held by a number of entities known as nodes, none of which are guaranteed to be reliable. Each transaction is recorded in a chain of connected blocks, which extends over time as new blocks are filled and added (Girardi et al., 2020). Each block includes a timestamp, a list of transactions, and the prior block's cryptographic hash, ensuring an intrinsic and accurate record of the chain's history (Girardi et al., 2020). One of the most significant benefits of this technology is its simplicity in resolving two of the most feared problems in the world of transactions: the "Byzantine generals" problem (ensuring that a message has been received and understood) and the "double spending" problem (A sends money digitally to B, but you cannot be certain that A will not reuse the same file to send the same money to C) (Girardi et al., 2020).

The safe transmission of blockchain technology may be attributed to three things. First, it has an immutable "ledger" that anybody may access and manage (Ktari et al., 2022). It guarantees that once a record is entered into the ledger, it cannot be changed. Furthermore, each transaction in the ledger must adhere to certain predetermined criteria (Ktari et al., 2022). Second, blockchain is a distributed system that works across various devices and computers (Ktari et al., 2022). Third, blockchain adheres to agreement norms and data exchange policies via a smart contract mechanism (Ktari et al., 2022).

The smart contract controls identities and defines rights to access various electronic medical reports (EMRs) stored on the blockchain. It means that clinicians can only access the EMRs to which they have permission (Ktari et al., 2022). In recent years, various blockchain initiatives have been launched in the healthcare business to manage EMR, pharmaceutical prescription, and clinical routes.

Blockchain has the ability to provide security and protection against losses and dangers, as well as assist preserve privacy. It is critical to emphasize that patients' data must be provided and received on time in blockchain-based IoMT applications, particularly in remote health-monitoring applications such as emergency healthcare, wireless capsule endoscopy, telemedicine systems, and elderly patient monitoring (Adavoudi Jolfaei et al., 2021). Patients' health data must be communicated and received quickly via these systems so that physicians, nurses, and medical personnel may monitor patients remotely and in real time, resulting in a correct and accurate diagnosis (Adavoudi Jolfaei et al., 2021).

5.3.1 Enhancing IoMT with blockchain

Blockchain technology has proven effective in current healthcare systems by improving user security and privacy (Awotunde, Misra, et al., 2022). The complexity and expense of healthcare systems can be decreased by implementing blockchain and improving medical record management (Awotunde, Misra, et al., 2022). This has proven effective in transactions involving medical records, data security, smart contacts, and insurance billing, as well as offering a distributed database of transactions. On the verification of users linked with healthcare data, the blockchain network conforms to the ideal of maximum secrecy, which aids in the security of medical information (Awotunde, Misra, et al., 2022). Healthcare professionals are increasingly adopting IoT to modernize the analysis and care processes. The Internet connects billions of sensors and devices (Ktari et al., 2022). RPM technology is now often used in patient therapy and care. However, these technologies offer major privacy and security vulnerabilities in terms of information transmission and data transaction logging (Ktari et al., 2022). These security and confidentiality issues with medical information might cause treatment delays and potentially risk the patient's life (Ktari et al., 2022). Blockchain technology may be used to protect the administration and analysis of sensitive medical data. Blockchain integration with IoMT might transform how healthcare data is maintained, shared, and secured. For example, blockchain-enabled IoMT devices may automatically log data entries into a secure, immutable ledger, allowing for safe and efficient data exchange among authorized healthcare practitioners, patients, and researchers. This connection can also help with the creation of smart contracts that automatically execute depending on predetermined criteria, such as giving medical data to certain researchers while maintaining patient permission and confidentiality.

Blockchain technology introduces smart contracts as a new method of engagement. They enable the automation of complicated multistep procedures. By merging IoT with blockchain, diverse patient data may be readily acquired from several nodes, allowing for real-time patient monitoring while keeping the data more secure (Ktari et al., 2022). Blockchain technology can help healthcare organizations save money and collaborate more effectively. This prevents hackers from keeping or modifying vital patient information. Blockchains offer strong, distributed systems with the capacity to connect with nodes in a dependable and auditable manner. Devices in the IoT ecosystem serve as interfaces with the physical world.

Furthermore, blockchain can improve supply chain management for medical equipment and medicines, increasing traceability from manufacturing to end-use and lowering the danger of counterfeit items entering the healthcare system. This degree of transparency and accountability can result in better healthcare results and more patient confidence in IoMT applications.

5.3.2 Advantages of blockchain for IoMT (security, transparency, and data integrity)

5.3.2.1 Security

Blockchain technology, a distributed ledger, has the potential to improve IoMT applications (Adavoudi Jolfaei et al., 2021). One of the main advantages of blockchain technology is its distributed design, which may alleviate a fundamental problem, namely the cloud's point of failure in IoMT applications (Adavoudi Jolfaei et al., 2021). Furthermore, blockchain technology has several advantages, including smart contracts, security through data access control, tamper-proof recordkeeping, transparency, trustless consensus, and open architecture (Adavoudi Jolfaei et al., 2021). Blockchain's major advantage for IoMT is its capacity to improve network security. In an environment where patient data breaches can have serious effects, blockchain's decentralized structure and cryptographic hash functions provide a strong protection mechanism. Unlike traditional centralized databases, which are profitable targets for hackers, blockchain distributes data over several nodes, making it extremely difficult for unauthorized parties to harm the network's integrity. Each transaction on a blockchain is encrypted and connected to the preceding transaction, creating a chain that assures any effort at data tampering would necessitate changing all subsequent entries in every copy of the ledger dispersed over the network. This degree of security is crucial for IoMT applications that rely on the confidentiality and integrity of health data, protecting sensitive patient information from cyber threats and unauthorized access.

5.3.2.2 Transparency

Data exchange across various medical devices and healthcare professionals plays a significant role in an IMoT network (Ktari et al., 2022). However, data fragmentation is a significant problem for safe data exchange. An information gap between healthcare providers connected to a single patient may result from data fragmentation (Ktari et al., 2022). The course of treatment may be hampered by inadequate information. Healthcare facilities can connect the many data repositories in the network and overcome data fragmentation with the usage of blockchain technology (Ktari et al., 2022). This promotes openness between physicians and patients and further guarantees the safe and secure exchange of private medical information (Ktari et al., 2022). Additionally, blockchain technology encourages organizations and healthcare practitioners to work together on qualitative research projects (Ktari et al., 2022). Blockchain offers a previously unheard-of degree of openness, which helps IoMT. Blockchain technology creates an unchangeable and transparent record of all data transfers by recording every transaction on a ledger that is available to all network users. This functionality is especially helpful in the IoMT for monitoring the provenance of medical equipment and guaranteeing the legitimacy of pharmaceuticals. Additionally, it promotes a trustworthy atmosphere in which patients are fully informed about who has access to their medical records and why. Transparency also helps with regulatory compliance, giving stakeholders and healthcare providers a permanent audit trail to prove compliance with data protection laws and regulations.

5.3.2.3 Data integrity

Companies in the pharmaceutical and healthcare sectors have already invested millions of dollars to attest to the efficacy of blockchain (Ktari et al., 2022). According to a recent report, the healthcare sector's blockchain market is expected to reach a valuation of $890.5 million by 2023 (Ktari et al., 2022). Blockchain is acknowledged as a useful instrument in the healthcare industry to prevent data breaches, improve the quality of medical information, and save expenses (Ktari et al., 2022). Blockchain technology is being tested in a few nations, including the United Kingdom and Australia, to handle medical information and transactions involving patients, healthcare providers, and insurance companies (Ktari et al., 2022). Conflicting data is automatically identified by a decentralized network of computers that maintains the blockchain and concurrently records every transaction (Ktari et al., 2022). Blockchain technology's fundamental component of data integrity provides a major benefit to the IoMT ecosystem. Because blockchain data is immutable, information stored on it cannot be changed or removed without the network's approval, maintaining the integrity and consistency of medical records across time. For patient records, clinical trials, and other medical data that need to be very accurate and reliable, this feature is essential. Blockchain can protect the integrity of real-time health data collected by IoMT devices, guaranteeing that the data is unchanged from the moment of collection to the end-user. Accurate diagnosis, treatment choices, and research are dependent on its integrity, which enhances patient outcomes and advances medical knowledge.

5.3.3 Challenges and limitations of implementing blockchain in IoMT

Using blockchain technology to improve data security, integrity, and interoperability inside the IoMT offers a viable way to transform healthcare. Blockchain technology presents a number of challenges to IoMT notwithstanding its advantages. These challenges include a lack of standards and regulations, scalability issues, firmware and hardware vulnerabilities, a lack of reliable authorities and data feeds, and issues with smart contracts that include call stack depth, timestamp dependence, and dependence on transaction order (Adavoudi Jolfaei et al., 2021). In blockchain-based systems, greater attention needs to be paid to the problems of scalability, adaptability, latency, cost difficulties, and energy usage. The challenges arise from the fact that blockchain technology is still in its infancy as well as the intricate needs of the healthcare industry. The following are the challenges and limitations associated with implementing blockchain in IoMT:

Scalability and performance: Scalability is one of the biggest obstacles to blockchain implementation in IoMT. Blockchain networks may experience sluggish transaction processing times and constrained throughput, particularly if they use Proof of Work (PoW) consensus processes (Lashkari & Musilek, 2021). In the IoMT applications, where real-time data gathering and processing from hundreds of medical devices is crucial, this turns into a crucial problem (Dwivedi et al., 2022). The present blockchain solutions' intrinsic latency and scalability issues may make it difficult for them to effectively manage massive amounts of healthcare data.

Interoperability and standards: A vast range of devices, data formats, and protocols define the healthcare ecosystem (Fatoum et al., 2021). A major difficulty is incorporating blockchain while achieving interoperability across these various systems (Fatoum et al., 2021). It is still challenging to seamlessly integrate blockchain technology across a variety of IoMT devices and healthcare systems given the absence of global standards for data sharing and device connection. To fully achieve the promise of blockchain in IoMT, worldwide standards must be developed and adopted.

Energy consumption: Blockchain networks are infamously energy-intensive, especially those based on PoW (Albers van der Linden, 2022). Concerns about sustainability and ethics arise from the environmental effects of this kind of energy use, particularly for healthcare institutions trying to lower their carbon footprints (Albers van der Linden, 2022). For IoMT applications, switching to other consensus mechanisms like Proof of Stake (PoS) or discovering energy-efficient blockchain solutions remains a difficulty, despite the fact that these models consume less energy.

Privacy and regulatory compliance: It is crucial to protect patient privacy while adhering to strict healthcare laws, such as the General Data Protection Regulation (GDPR) in the European Union or the Health Insurance Portability and Accountability Act (HIPAA) in the United States (Williamson & Prybutok, 2024). Requirements for privacy may clash with blockchain's open nature, which makes transactions available to every member of the network (Williamson & Prybutok, 2024). Furthermore, changing or removing data from a blockchain goes against the irreversible nature of blockchain technology and is required to comply with laws like the GDPR's "right to be forgotten." Managing these legal constraints and privacy considerations is a difficult task for blockchain deployment in IoMT.

Security concerns: Blockchain is not impervious to all cyber-attacks, even though decentralization and encryption improve security (Rahman & Jahankhani, 2021). Attacks may be possible on the interfaces connecting blockchain networks and IoMT devices (Rahman & Jahankhani, 2021). Furthermore, smart contracts—a vital part of many blockchain applications—may include flaws or vulnerabilities that might be used by hostile parties. IoMT blockchain installation security demands ongoing attention to detail and cutting-edge cybersecurity protocols.

Cost and complexity: There are substantial operational and financial costs associated with integrating blockchain technology into IoMT. Blockchain network creation, implementation, and upkeep necessitate large hardware, software, and knowledge expenditures. Healthcare providers and IoMT device makers face a steep learning curve due to the intricacy of blockchain technology. Healthcare firms must weigh the potential benefits of blockchain installations against their costs and complexity.

5.4 Neural networks in IoMT

AI-enabled IoMT-based systems are revolutionizing the healthcare industry lately, and their use may be profitable, particularly for the detection, prognosis, and management of various disease outbreaks (Awotunde, Folorunso, et al., 2022). In the healthcare sector, the use of AI-enabled IoT-based solutions can speed up illness monitoring and diagnosis while reducing the workload associated with medical procedures (Awotunde, Folorunso, et al., 2022). Modern AI is built around neural networks, which are changing data analysis and decision-making in the healthcare industry. These sophisticated algorithms imitate the structure and operations of the human brain, allowing robots to learn from data, spot trends, and anticipate outcomes. AI enables a computer or robot under computer control to carry out activities that are typically completed by humans using their intelligence. With the right data interpretation methods, a computer in a smart healthcare system may also track health metrics by utilizing wearable or implanted sensors on the subject's body (Srivastava et al., 2022). AI may be used to control and prevent diseases in real time while improving the user experience. Smart Healthcare System (SHS) handles the patient under observation's extremely private medical information (Srivastava et al., 2022). Thus one of the most important tasks in IoMT-based SHS is to provide necessary security measures. AI may also be utilized to provide security in the IoMT by identifying intermediary security assaults and network intrusions within the IoMT systems, as well as by utilizing an Internet of Medical Things Security Assessment Framework (IoMT-SAF) device to do web-based security evaluations (Srivastava et al., 2022).

In an emergency, AI can send an automated alarm to several parties, allowing them to take rapid action and perhaps save a life (Srivastava et al., 2022). As a result, doctors may simply maintain their patients' information and deliver off-hours medical treatments utilizing AI.

The use of neural networks in healthcare data analysis and decision-making is improving patient care, research, and operational efficiency. Machine learning is commonly used to aid in the decision-making process for health-related concerns (Sahoo et al., 2020). Machine learning algorithms may be used to easily classify and forecast diseases. The machine learning approach may be used in a variety of applications, including image segmentation, fraud detection, pattern identification, and illness prediction (Sahoo et al., 2020).

In today's society, the majority of individuals suffer from diabetes. The glucose factor in the blood is the primary cause of diabetes (Sahoo et al., 2020). Diabetes develops from fluctuations in blood glucose levels. Machine learning and deep learning, which employ concepts such as probability, statistics, and neural networks, play an important role in predicting diabetes. Deep learning is a subset of machine learning in which different layers of neural networks are used to determine illness categorization and prediction (Sahoo et al., 2020). Significant areas of neural networks in some critical areas are highlighted below:

Enhanced diagnostic accuracy: Neural networks have shown to be extremely useful for identifying illnesses with more precision and speed than previous approaches. Neural networks can detect tiny patterns and abnormalities in large datasets such as medical photographs, test findings, and patient histories that the human eye may miss (George et al., 2023). In radiology, for example, deep learning algorithms have demonstrated extraordinary effectiveness in diagnosing malignancies, fractures, and neurological problems from imaging images, lowering diagnostic mistakes, and increasing patient outcomes.

Predictive analytics for personalized medicine: Neural networks also excel in predicting disease progression and treatment results. By evaluating vast information, these algorithms can estimate the risk of illness onset, allowing preventative interventions to be implemented (Kanakaraddi et al., 2021). Furthermore, neural networks make customized medicine possible by predicting how specific patients will react to different treatments, allowing healthcare practitioners to adjust therapies to the patient's genetic composition, lifestyle, and other characteristics. This tailored method improves therapy efficacy while minimizing unwanted responses.

Streamlining clinical trials: Neural networks play an important role in improving clinical trial efficiency. These algorithms can identify the most promising therapy options and patient populations that are likely to benefit from them by assessing historical data and current trial outcomes (Husnain et al., 2023). This skill not only speeds the discovery of novel medications but also lowers the cost and duration of clinical trials, allowing patients to access revolutionary cures sooner.

Operational efficiency and resource allocation: Neural networks help healthcare managers improve operational efficiency and allocate resources more effectively. Forecasting patient admission rates, duration of stay, and resource requirements allows hospitals to more effectively coordinate employee planning, bed occupancy, and inventory control (Jaén, 2024). This predictive power enables healthcare institutions to enhance patient care, shorten wait times, and cut expenses.

5.4.1 Applications of neural networks in IoMT

Neural networks, with their capacity to learn from data and detect complicated patterns, are becoming increasingly important in the IoMT. This collaboration between neural networks and IoMT is driving advances in healthcare, notably in illness prediction and diagnosis, patient data analysis for individualized treatment strategies, and medical imaging. How neural networks are transforming healthcare delivery and patient management are highlighted below:

Disease prediction and diagnosis: Neural networks have demonstrated exceptional ability to predict and diagnose illnesses by evaluating data acquired from IoMT devices (Kakhi et al., 2022). These technologies, which range from wearable health monitors to embedded sensors, create massive volumes of health data that may be used to identify early indicators of disease. For example, neural networks may evaluate patterns in heart rate variability, breathing patterns, or blood glucose levels to forecast the start of illnesses like heart disease, asthma, or diabetes far sooner than traditional approaches. These early detection capabilities allow for proactive management of diseases, perhaps reducing disease development and improving patient outcomes.

Patient data analysis for personalized treatment plans: The use of neural networks in IoMT extends to the personalization of patient care via tailored treatment regimens. Neural networks can discover the most successful treatment procedures for specific patients by assessing real-time data obtained from various IoMT devices (Manickam et al., 2022). This study takes into account a variety of elements, including genetic information, lifestyle decisions, environmental influences, and real-time health data, to adapt therapies to each patient's distinct health profile. This technique not only increases therapeutic efficacy but also reduces the likelihood of adverse responses, resulting in dramatically improved patient care.

Image recognition and analysis for medical imaging: Neural networks are transforming medical imaging with their sophisticated picture identification and processing capabilities. Neural networks may identify anomalies such as cancers, fractures, or symptoms of neurological illnesses with high precision when processing pictures from CT scans, MRIs, and X-rays (Barhoom et al., 2023). These algorithms can detect small characteristics in pictures that human eyes may miss, making them an effective tool for radiologists and other medical practitioners to diagnose illnesses reliably and quickly. Furthermore, neural networks can follow changes in medical pictures over time, providing crucial insights into disease development or the efficacy of treatment regimens.

5.4.2 Challenges in integrating neural networks with IoMT

Incorporating neural networks with the IoMT provides a big step forward in healthcare technology, with potential advances in illness prediction, individualized therapy, and patient monitoring. Nevertheless, this incorporation is not without obstacles. The problems stem from technology limits, data concerns, ethical considerations, and regulatory compliance challenges. The following explores the key challenges in integrating neural networks with IoMT.

5.4.2.1 Data privacy and security

One of the most significant concerns is maintaining the privacy and security of patient data. IoMT devices continually gather sensitive health data, which neural networks use to make predictions or judgments (Manickam et al., 2022). Given the strict standards controlling patient data, such as HIPAA in the United States and GDPR in Europe, it is vital to protect sensitive data against unauthorized access or breaches. Implementing strong encryption technologies and safe data transfer protocols is critical yet difficult, considering the variety of devices and volume of data involved.

5.4.2.2 Data quality and availability

The quality and quantity of training data have a significant impact on neural networks' efficacy. Data from various devices and manufacturers might vary greatly in terms of accuracy, completeness, and format when used in IoMT. Ensuring that data is clean, consistent, and accurately labeled for training purposes is a major difficulty. Furthermore, the availability of big and diverse datasets is critical for training effective models, but privacy issues and data silos might limit access to this data.

5.4.2.3 Computational constraints

IoMT devices, particularly wearable and portable devices, sometimes have limited processing power and battery life, limiting the complexity of neural network models that may be implemented directly on them. While cloud computing provides a solution by offloading processing, it introduces latency and necessitates constant Internet access, which is not always available or desired for real-time applications.

5.4.2.4 Interoperability and standardization

A wide ecosystem of IoMT devices, each with its own unique software and hardware requirements, creates substantial interoperability issues. Integrating these devices into a unified system capable of collecting, transmitting, and analyzing data using neural networks necessitates the standardization of data formats, communication protocols, and APIs. Achieving this degree of consistency across manufacturers and healthcare providers is a difficult and continuous issue.

5.4.2.5 Scaling and deployment

Scaling neural network systems from pilot studies to general usage is necessary for successful deployment in a real-world healthcare context, which might expose challenges with data management, system integration, and user training. To ensure uptake and efficacy, healthcare practitioners must be effectively taught to use and comprehend neural network outputs.

5.5 Integrating blockchain technology and neural networks in IoMT

The combination of blockchain technology with neural networks has transformational potential for the IoMT, altering how healthcare data is maintained, shared, and used. This convergence of technology provides a distinct combination of security, transparency, and powerful analytical capabilities, encouraging an environment in which medical data may be safely shared and studied without jeopardizing patient privacy or data integrity.

The integration of AI and blockchain technology has the potential to disrupt several sectors, including healthcare systems (Falola et al., 2023). Telehealth, or the remote delivery of healthcare services, has grown in popularity in recent years (Falola et al., 2023). Telehealth systems that use AI and blockchain technology can improve efficiency, security, and accessibility while also increasing patient outcomes (Falola et al., 2023).

Blockchain technology, due to its decentralized nature, provides a secure and immutable ledger for transaction recording. In the context of IoMT, this means that all medical device data may be safely kept with a clear audit trail (Kumar & Tripathi, 2021). This intrinsic security feature addresses key data privacy and security concerns in healthcare by protecting sensitive patient data from unwanted access and alteration (Awotunde et al., 2021).

In contrast, neural networks bring advanced data analytic capabilities to the table. They can learn from massive volumes of data, detecting patterns and insights that may not be obvious to human analysts (Samek et al., 2021). When applied to the IoMT, neural networks can assess data from a variety of medical devices in real time, allowing for predictive analytics in patient care. This implies that possible health concerns may be discovered and handled ahead of time, resulting in better patient outcomes and fewer reactionary treatments.

The combination of blockchain with neural networks in the IoMT setting gives a strong framework for data integrity and intelligent analytics (Khan & AbaOud, 2023). The architectural framework of aims to leverage the strengths of both technologies to create a secure, decentralized, and intelligent healthcare ecosystem. Blockchain guarantees that the data supplied into neural networks is accurate and tamper-proof, hence increasing the dependability of the insights gained. Furthermore, the decentralized nature of blockchain allows for the sharing of these insights among many players in the healthcare ecosystem while maintaining data confidentiality and patient privacy.

This integration also creates new opportunities for individualized medication. By securely gathering and analyzing patient data from several sources, healthcare professionals may personalize therapies to each patients' particular requirements, enhancing efficacy and satisfaction (Ullah et al., 2023). Furthermore, the openness and immutability of blockchain may build confidence among patients by ensuring that their data is managed safely and ethically.

The combination of blockchain and neural networks in IoMT not only tackles data security and privacy concerns but also allows for advanced data analytics to enhance healthcare results.

5.5.1 Addressing the challenges of integration (computational requirements, data privacy, regulatory compliance)

The incorporation of cutting-edge technology into current systems presents a complex mix of issues, with computing needs, data protection, and regulatory compliance standing out as particularly major obstacles. Each of these problems, while separate, is intricately linked, impacting the overall effectiveness of technology integration initiatives.

Computational needs are frequently the first hurdle faced during the integration of new technology. As systems get more sophisticated and data-intensive, the need for processing power increases. This increased demand for processing power might put a strain on current infrastructure, prompting upgrades or the implementation of new computing paradigms such as cloud computing or edge computing. While these methods are successful, they involve new complications and considerations, such as cost, scalability, and the architectural redesign of systems to incorporate decentralized computing resources.

Data privacy is another crucial issue, particularly in industries that handle sensitive information, such as healthcare or banking. The combination of technologies such as AI and the IoT necessitates the gathering, storage, and analysis of massive volumes of data, presenting serious privacy issues (Chanal et al., 2021). Ensuring data confidentiality and integrity while allowing new technology functions necessitates strong encryption, safe data handling methods, and the use of privacy-preserving technologies like federated learning or homomorphic encryption (Chanal et al., 2021).

Regulatory compliance hampers integration attempts. As technology advances, regulatory frameworks frequently fail to keep up, resulting in an environment of complicated and even contradictory requirements that enterprises must negotiate. Compliance with these standards is not optional; it is a crucial necessity for maintaining confidence and safety in technology adoption. Organizations must thus keep current on applicable legislation, which may include data protection laws, industry-specific requirements, and international standards. Ensuring compliance necessitates a full grasp of both the law and spirit of these standards, which may be as difficult as it is important.

To address these difficulties, a holistic strategy is required, which includes infrastructure investment, a commitment to data protection, and a proactive approach to regulatory compliance. Solutions must be scalable, adaptable, and developed with both present and future requirements in mind. Furthermore, successful integration requires coordination among stakeholders, such as technology suppliers, regulatory authorities, and end users. Through such coordinated efforts, it is feasible to fully realize the promise of new technologies while minimizing the dangers involved with their implementation.

5.6 Conclusion and future directions

The incorporation of blockchain technology and neural networks into the IoMT offers a significant opportunity to transform healthcare by improving data security, efficiency, and tailored treatment. This architectural framework combines blockchain's security and transparency with neural networks' analytical capabilities to create a safe, decentralized, and intelligent healthcare environment. To fully exploit the promise of this integration, future approaches should focus on addressing hurdles in computing needs, data protection, and regulatory compliance. Technologists, researchers, and politicians must work together to manage these difficulties and ensure that advances in IoMT improve healthcare outcomes and patient care.

References

Abbas, A., Alroobaea, R., Krichen, M., Rubaiee, S., Vimal, S., & Almansour, F. M. (2021). Blockchain-assisted secured data management framework for health information analysis based on Internet of Medical Things. *Personal and Ubiquitous Computing*. Available from https://doi.org/10.1007/s00779-021-01583-8.

Adavoudi Jolfaei, A., Aghili, S. F., & Singelee, D. (2021). A survey on blockchain-based IoMT systems: Towards scalability. *in IEEE Access, vol. 9*, 148948–148975. Available from https://doi.org/10.1109/ACCESS.2021.3117662.

Ahmed, S. F., Alam, S. B., Afrin, S., Rafa, S. J., Rafa, N., & Gandomi, A. H. (2024). Insights into internet of medical things (IoMT): Data fusion, security issues and potential solutions. *Information Fusion*. Available from https://doi.org/10.1016/j.inffus.2023.102060.

Albers van der Linden, T. (2022). The flip side of the coin-The environmental footprint of blockchain-based NFT art. Master's thesis.

Aman, A. H. M., Hassan, W. H., Sameen, S., Attarbashi, Z. S., Alizadeh, M., & Latiff, L. A. (2021). IoMT amid COVID-19 pandemic: Application, architecture, technology, and security. *Journal of Network and Computer Applications, 174*. Available from https://doi.org/10.1016/j.jnca.2020.102886.

Awotunde, J. B., Imoize, A. L., Jimoh, R. G., Adeniyi, E. A., Abdulraheem, M., Oladipo, I. D., & Falola, P. B. (2023). *AIoMT enabling real-time monitoring of healthcare systems. In: Handbook of security and privacy of AI-enabled healthcare systems and Internet of Medical Things* (1st ed.). CRC Press. Available from https://doi.org/10.1201/9781003370321.

Awotunde, J. B., Jimoh, R. G., Folorunso, S. O., Adeniyi, E. A., Abiodun, K. M., & Banjo, O. O. (2021). *Privacy and security concerns in IoT-based healthcare systems. In the fusion of internet of things, artificial intelligence, and cloud computing in health care* (pp. 105–134). Cham: Springer International Publishing.

Awotunde, J. B., Folorunso, S. O., Ajagbe, S. A., Garg, J., & Ajamu, G. J. (2022). AiIoMT: IoMT-based system-enabled artificial intelligence for enhanced smart healthcare systems. In F. Al-Turjman, & A. Nayyar (Eds.), *Machine learning for critical internet of medical things*. Cham: Springer. Available from https://doi.org/10.1007/978-3-030-80928-7_10.

Awotunde, J. B., Misra, S., Ayoade, O. B., Ogundokun, R. O., & Abiodun, M. K. (2022). Blockchain-based framework for secure medical information in internet of things system. In S. Misra, & A. Kumar Tyagi (Eds.), *Blockchain applications in the smart era. EAI/Springer innovations in communication and computing*. Cham: Springer. Available from https://doi.org/10.1007/978-3-030-89546-4_8.

Barhoom, A., Jubair, M. R., & Abu-Naser, S. S. (2023). A survey of bone abnormalities detection using machine learning algorithms. AIP conference proceedings. *AIP Publishing*, 2808(1).

Bhushan, B., Kumar, A., Agarwal, A. K., Kumar, A., Bhattacharya, P., & Kumar, A. (2023). Towards a secure and sustainable internet of medical things (IoMT): Requirements, design challenges, security techniques, and future trends. *Sustainability*, *15*(7). Available from https://doi.org/10.3390/su15076177.

Chanal, P. M., Kakkasageri, M. S., & Manvi, S. K. S. (2021). Security and privacy in the internet of things: computational intelligent techniques-based approaches. *In recent trends in computational intelligence enabled research* (pp. 111–127). Academic Press.

Dwivedi, R., Mehrotra, D., & Chandra, S. (2022). Potential of internet of medical things (IoMT) applications in building a smart healthcare system: A systematic review. *Journal of Oral Biology and Craniofacial Research*, *12*(2), 302–318.

Ellouze, F., Fersi, G., & Jmaiel, M. (2020). Blockchain for internet of medical things: A technical review. In M. Jmaiel, M. Mokhtari, B. Abdulrazak, H. Aloulou, & S. Kallel (Eds.), The impact of digital technologies on public health in developed and developing countries. ICOST 2020. Lecture notes in computer science. Cham: Springer, 12157. Available from https://doi.org/10.1007/978-3-030-51517-1_22.

Falola, P. B., Awotunde, J. B., Adeniyi, A. E., Jimoh, R. G., Adebayo, A. O., Olatunji, E. K., & Imoize, A. L. (2023). Artificial intelligence and blockchain enabling data access authorization in telehealth systems. *Artificial Intelligence and Blockchain Technology in Modern Telehealth Systems.* Available from https://doi.org/10.1049/PBHE061E_ch5.

Fatoum, H., Hanna, S., Halamka, J. D., Sicker, D. C., Spangenberg, P., & Hashmi, S. K. (2021). Blockchain integration with digital technology and the future of health care ecosystems: systematic review. *Journal of Medical Internet Research*, *23*(11), e19846.

George, A. H., Shahul, A., & George, A. S. (2023). Artificial intelligence in medicine: A new way to diagnose and treat disease. *Partners Universal International Research Journal*, *2*(3), 246–259.

Ghozali, M. T. (2023). Implementation of the IoT-based technology on patient medication adherence: A comprehensive bibliometric and systematic review. *Journal of Information and Communication Technology*, *22*(4), 503–544. Available from https://doi.org/10.32890/jict2023.22.4.1.

Ghubaish, A., Salman, T., Zolanvari, M., Unal, D., Al-Ali, A., & Jain, R. (2021). Recent advances in the internet-of-medical-things (IoMT) systems security. *In IEEE Internet of Things Journal*, *8*(11), 8707–8718. Available from https://doi.org/10.1109/JIOT.2020.3045653.

Girardi, F., De Gennaro, G., Colizzi, L., & Convertini, N. (2020). Improving the healthcare effectiveness: The possible role of EHR, IoMT and blockchain. *Electronics*, *9*(6), 884. Available from https://doi.org/10.3390/electronics9060884.

Hassija, V., Chamola, V., Bajpai, B. C., & Zeadally, N. S. (2021). Security issues in implantable medical devices: Fact or fiction? *Sustainable Cities and Society*, *66*. Available from https://doi.org/10.1016/j.scs.2020.102552.

Husnain, A., Rasool, S., Saeed, A., & Hussain, H. K. (2023). Revolutionizing pharmaceutical research: Harnessing machine learning for a paradigm shift in drug discovery. *International Journal of Multidisciplinary Sciences and Arts*, *2*(2), 149–157.

Jaén, S. (2024). The decrease of ED patient boarding by implementing a stock management policy in hospital admissions. *Operations Research Perspectives*, 100298.

Jeyavel, J., Parameswaran, T., Mannan, J. M., & Hariharan, U. (2021). Security vulnerabilities and Intelligent solutions for IoMT systems. In D. J. Hemanth, J. Anitha, & G. A. Tsihrintzis (Eds.), *Internet of medical things. internet of things*. Cham: Springer. Available from https://doi.org/10.1007/978-3-030-63937-2_10.

Kakhi, K., Alizadehsani, R., Kabir, H. D., Khosravi, A., Nahavandi, S., & Acharya, U. R. (2022). The internet of medical things and artificial intelligence: trends, challenges, and opportunities. *Biocybernetics and Biomedical Engineering*, *42*(3), 749–771.

Kanakaraddi, S. G., Gull, K. C., Bali, J., Chikaraddi, A. K., & Giraddi, S. (2021). Disease prediction using data mining and machine learning techniques. *Advanced Prognostic Predictive Modelling in Healthcare Data Analytics*, 71–92.

Khan, M. F., & AbaOud, M. (2023). Blockchain-integrated security for real-time patient monitoring in the internet of medical things using federated learning. *IEEE Access*.

Ktari, J., Frikha, T., Ben Amor, N., Louraidh, L., Elmannai, H., & Hamdi, M. (2022). IoMT-based platform for E-health monitoring based on the blockchain. *Electronics*, *11*(15), 2314. Available from https://doi.org/10.3390/electronics11152314.

Kumar, R., & Tripathi, R. (2021). Towards design and implementation of security and privacy framework for internet of medical things (iomt) by leveraging blockchain and ipfs technology. *Journal of Supercomputing*, 1–40.

Lashkari, B., & Musilek, P. (2021). A comprehensive review of blockchain consensus mechanisms. *IEEE Access*, *9*, 43620–43652.

Manickam, P., Mariappan, S. A., Murugesan, S. M., Hansda, S., Kaushik, A., Shinde, R., & Thipperudraswamy, S. P. (2022). Artificial intelligence (AI) and internet of medical things (IoMT) assisted biomedical systems for intelligent healthcare. *Biosensors*, *12*(8), 562.

Mishra, P., & Singh, G. (2023). Internet of medical things healthcare for sustainable smart cities: current status and future prospects. *Applied Sciences*, *13*(15), 8869.

Monteiro, K., Silva, É., Remigio, É., Santos, G. L., & Endo, P. T. (2021). Internet of medical things (IoMT) applications in E-health systems context. In J. Alja'am, S. Al-Maadeed, & O. Halabi (Eds.), *Emerging technologies in biomedical engineering and sustainable telemedicine. Advances in science, technology & innovation*. Cham: Springer. Available from https://doi.org/10.1007/978-3-030-14647-4_1.

Overmann, K. M., Wu, D. T., Xu, C. T., Bindhu, S. S., & Barrick, L. (2021). Real-time locating systems to improve healthcare delivery: A systematic review. *Journal of the American Medical Informatics Association*, *28*(6), 1308–1317.

Połap, D., Srivastava, G., Jolfaei, A., & Parizi, R. M. (2020). Blockchain technology and neural networks for the Internet of Medical Things. In *IEEE INFOCOM 2020 - IEEE conference on computer communications workshops (INFOCOM WKSHPS)*, Toronto, ON, Canada (pp. 508–513). Available from https://doi.org/10.1109/INFOCOMWKSHPS50562.2020.9162735.

Pradyumna, G. R., Hegde, R. B., Bommegowda, K. B., Jan, T., & Naik, G. R. (2024). Empowering healthcare with IoMT: Evolution, machine learning integration, security, and interoperability challenges. *IEEE Access*, *12*, 20603–20623. Available from https://doi.org/10.1109/ACCESS.2024.3362239.

Rahman, M., & Jahankhani, H. (2021). Security vulnerabilities in existing security mechanisms for IoMT and potential solutions for mitigating cyber-attacks. *Information Security Technologies for Controlling Pandemics*, 307–334.

Razzak, M. I., Imran, M., & Xu, G. (2020). Big data analytics for preventive medicine. *Neural Computing and Applications*, *32*, 4417–4451.

Sahoo, A. K., Pradhan, C., & Das, H. (2020). Performance evaluation of different machine learning methods and deep-learning based convolutional neural network for health decision making. In M. Rout, J. Rout, & H. Das (Eds.), *Nature inspired computing for data science. studies in computational intelligence* (871). Cham: Springer. Available from https://doi.org/10.1007/978-3-030-33820-6_8.

Samek, W., Montavon, G., Lapuschkin, S., Anders, C. J., & Müller, K. R. (2021). Explaining deep neural networks and beyond: A review of methods and applications. *Proceedings of the IEEE*, *109*(3), 247–278.

Shafiq, M., Choi, J. G., Cheikhrouhou, O., & Hamam, H. (2024). Advances in IoMT for healthcare systems. *Sensors*, *24*(1). Available from https://doi.org/10.3390/s24010010.

Shelke, Y. (2020). IoMT and healthcare delivery in chronic diseases. *Advances in Telemedicine for Health Monitoring*, 239.

Shuvo, M. M. H., Titirsha, T., Amin, N., & Islam, S. K. (2022). Energy harvesting in implantable and wearable medical devices for enduring precision healthcare. *Energies*, *15*(20). Available from https://doi.org/10.3390/en15207495.

Siddiqui, M. F. (2021). IoMT potential impact in COVID-19: Combating a pandemic with innovation. In K. Raza (Ed.), *Computational intelligence methods in COVID-19: Surveillance, prevention, prediction and diagnosis. Studies in computational intelligence*. Singapore: Springer, 923. Available from https://doi.org/10.1007/978-981-15-8534-0_18.

Singh, R. P., Javaid, M., Haleem, A., Vaishya, R., & Shokat Ali. (2020). Internet of medical things (IoMT) for orthopaedic in COVID-19 pandemic: Roles, challenges, and applications. *Journal of Clinical Orthopaedics and Trauma*, *11*(4), 713–717. Available from https://doi.org/10.1016/j.jcot.2020.05.011.

Srivastava, J., Routray, S., Ahmad, S., & Waris, M. M. (2022). Internet of medical things (IoMT)-based smart healthcare system: Trends and progress. *Computational Intelligence and Neuroscience, Hindawi*. Available from https://doi.org/10.1155/2022/7218113.

Steger, A. (2020). *How the Internet of Medical Things is impacting healthcare* [Online]. <https://healthtechmagazine.net/article/2020/01/how-internet-medicalthings-impacting-healthcare-perfcon/>. Accessed 21.02.24.

Subramaniam, E. V. D., Srinivasan, K., Qaisar, S. M., & Pławiak, P. (2023). Interoperable IoMT approach for remote diagnosis with privacy-preservation perspective in edge systems. *Sensors*, *23*(17). Available from https://doi.org/10.3390/s23177474.

Tamiziniyan, G., & Keerthana, A. (2022). Future of healthcare: Biomedical Big Data analysis and IoMT. *The Internet of Medical Things (IoMT): Healthcare transformation*. Wiley. Available from https://doi.org/10.1002/9781119769200.ch13.

Ullah, M., Hamayun, S., Wahab, A., Khan, S. U., Rehman, M. U., Haq, Z. U., & Naeem, M. (2023). Smart technologies used as smart tools in the management of cardiovascular disease and their future perspective. *Current Problems in Cardiology*, *48*(11), 101922.

Villanueva-Miranda, I., Nazeran, H., & Martinek, R. (2018). A semantic interoperability approach to heterogeneous Internet of Medical Things (IoMT) platforms. In *2018 IEEE 20th international conference on e-health networking, applications and services (Healthcom)*, Ostrava, Czech Republic (pp. 1–5). Available from https://doi.org/10.1109/HealthCom.2018.8531103.

Wagan, S. A., Koo, J., Siddiqui, I. F., Attique, M., Shin, D. R., & Qureshi, N. M. F. (2022). Internet of medical things and trending converged technologies: A comprehensive review on real-time applications. *Journal of King Saud University-Computer and Information Sciences*, *34*(10), 9228–9251.

Williamson, S. M., & Prybutok, V. (2024). Balancing privacy and progress: A review of privacy challenges, systemic oversight, and patient perceptions in AI-driven healthcare. *Applied Sciences*, *14*(2), 675.

CHAPTER

Blockchain technology in AI-powered smart hospital

Shabnam Kumari[1], Amit Kumar Tyagi[2], Richa[3] and Sayed Sayeed Ahmad[4]

[1]Department of Computer Science, Faculty of Science and Humanities, SRM Institute of Science and Technology, Chennai, Tamil Nadu, India [2]Department of Fashion Technology, National Institute of Fashion Technology, New Delhi, Delhi, India [3]Department of Computer Science & Engineering, BIT Mesra, Ranchi, Jharkhand, India [4]School of Engineering and Computing, De Montfort University, Dubai, United Arab Emirates

6.1 Introduction to overview of smart hospitals and medical devices

In the ever-evolving landscape of healthcare, the concept of smart hospitals and the integration of advanced medical devices are at the forefront of a healthcare revolution. Smart hospitals represent a paradigm shift in the way healthcare is delivered, using cutting-edge technology to enhance patient care, streamline operations, and improve overall efficiency (Holzinger et al., 2015; Kwon et al., 2022; Tian et al., 2019). This overview provides an introduction to the key components and implications of smart hospitals and the role of innovative medical devices in shaping the future of healthcare.

Smart hospitals, often referred to as digitally integrated healthcare institutions, harness the power of emerging technologies such as the Internet of Things (IoT), artificial intelligence (AI), and blockchain, to create an environment where every aspect of healthcare is interconnected and intelligent. These hospitals aim to provide patient-centric care by seamlessly integrating data, processes, and devices to deliver timely, accurate, and personalized healthcare services.

One of the cornerstones of smart hospitals is the deployment of advanced medical devices. These devices, which range from wearables and remote monitoring tools to diagnostic equipment and surgical robots, play an important role in transforming patient care. They collect and transmit data in real time, enabling healthcare professionals to make informed decisions swiftly. Moreover, they empower patients to actively participate in their healthcare management and monitoring.

The key aspects that will be discussed in this overview include the following:

- *IoT integration*: Smart hospitals use IoT technology to connect medical devices, wearable gadgets, and even the hospital infrastructure itself. This interconnectivity facilitates the real-time monitoring of patients, equipment, and resources, ultimately improving operational efficiency.
- *Data and analytics*: The large amount of data generated by medical devices and hospital operations can be harnessed through AI and data analytics. This data-driven approach enables predictive diagnostics, personalized treatment plans, and efficient resource allocation.

Blockchain and Digital Twin for Smart Hospitals. DOI: https://doi.org/10.1016/B978-0-443-34226-4.00007-1

- *Patient-centric care*: Smart hospitals prioritize patient-centric care by empowering individuals with access to their health data and providing tools for self-monitoring. This approach fosters better patient engagement and adherence to treatment plans.
- *Enhanced diagnostics and treatment*: Innovative medical devices, such as AI-assisted diagnostic tools and robotic surgical systems, elevate the precision and effectiveness of medical procedures. They open new possibilities in diagnosis, treatment, and surgery.
- *Operational efficiency*: Smart hospitals optimize resource management, streamline administrative processes, and reduce operational costs. This efficiency leads to cost savings and enhanced healthcare delivery.
- *Issues and challenges*: While the concept of smart hospitals holds immense promise, there are challenges to overcome, including data security and privacy issues, interoperability issues, and regulatory compliance (Fig. 6.1).

As healthcare continues to evolve and embrace digital transformation, understanding the fundamental principles and implications of smart hospitals and the role of innovative medical devices is important for healthcare professionals, policymakers, and the general public. This overview will move toward these key aspects, shedding light on the transformative potential of smart hospitals and the advancements in medical technology that are reshaping the future of healthcare.

6.1.1 Convergence of AI, blockchain, and healthcare

In recent years, the healthcare industry has been witnessing a profound transformation through the convergence of three cutting-edge technologies: AI, blockchain, and healthcare. This convergence holds the promise of revolutionizing the way healthcare data is managed, patient care is delivered, and medical research is conducted (Bhatt et al., 2021; Lobo et al., 2020). Here, we discuss the key aspects and implications of this fusion.

- *Artificial intelligence in healthcare*: AI, driven by machine learning and deep learning algorithms, has proven to be a game-changer in healthcare. AI can analyze large volumes of medical data, from electronic health records to medical images, with remarkable speed and accuracy. It enables predictive diagnostics, personalized treatment plans, and even robotic surgeries. AI-driven chatbots and virtual assistants are enhancing patient engagement and

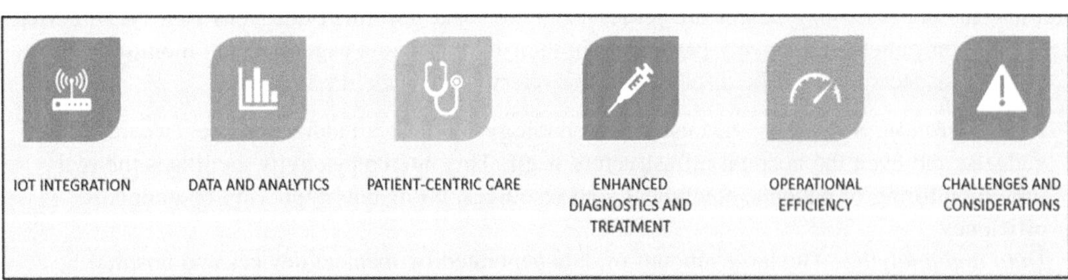

FIGURE 6.1

Key aspects.

facilitating telehealth services. Furthermore, AI can aid in drug discovery and clinical trial optimization, speeding up the development of new treatments.

- *Blockchain technology in healthcare*: Blockchain, originally designed for secure and transparent financial transactions, is now being adopted to address important issues in healthcare. It provides a secure, tamper-proof ledger for health data, ensuring that patient records are immutable, confidential, and interoperable. Patients can have greater control over their health information, granting access only to authorized parties. Supply chain management, drug traceability, and clinical trial data can also benefit from blockchain, reducing fraud and improving transparency.
- *Data security and privacy*: The convergence of AI and blockchain addresses some of the most pressing issues in healthcare, such as data security and privacy. While AI requires large amounts of sensitive patient data, blockchain ensures that this data is protected through decentralized and encrypted ledgers. This combination bolsters patient trust in the healthcare system.
- *Interoperability and data exchange*: Healthcare systems often struggle with interoperability, hindering the seamless sharing of patient information among different providers. Blockchain can create a unified, standardized system for sharing and accessing healthcare data, regardless of the source, improving care coordination and reducing redundancy.
- *Research and development*: AI and blockchain also hold immense potential in medical research and drug development. The fusion of these technologies can create secure, anonymized data-sharing networks that allow researchers to collaborate, access comprehensive datasets, and expedite discoveries.

The convergence of AI, blockchain, and healthcare represents an exciting frontier in the medical field (Fig. 6.2).

It has the potential to improve patient care, enhance data security, streamline healthcare processes, and accelerate medical research. As these technologies continue to mature and their integration becomes more widespread, the healthcare industry is poised for a significant transformation.

6.1.2 Blockchain in AI-powered medical devices in this smart era

In the age of smart healthcare, the convergence of blockchain and AI-powered medical devices presents a transformative opportunity to revolutionize patient care, data management, and overall healthcare efficiency. This synergy is poised to address important issues in healthcare, such as data security, patient privacy, interoperability, and data management (Krittanawong et al., 2022;

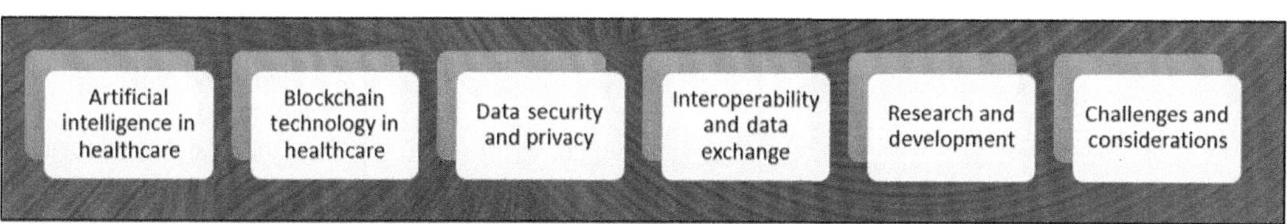

FIGURE 6.2

Key aspects: artificial intelligence, blockchain, and healthcare.

Kumar et al., 2022). Here, we move toward the implications of integrating blockchain technology with AI-powered medical devices in the smart healthcare era (refer Table 6.1).

1. *Data security and privacy:*
   a. *Secure data storage*: Blockchain provides a decentralized and tamper-proof ledger for storing medical data generated by AI-powered devices. This ensures the integrity and security of patient information, making it resistant to cyberattacks and data breaches.
   b. *Patient control*: Patients can have greater control over their health data, granting access to their records only to authorized individuals or entities. This empowers patients to actively manage their privacy.
2. *Data integrity and traceability*:
   a. Blockchain ensures the immutability of data recorded by medical devices, making it easier to trace the origin and changes to medical records. This feature is invaluable for maintaining an accurate and complete patient history.
3. *Interoperability and data exchange*:
   a. AI-powered medical devices can generate diverse data formats. Blockchain can serve as a standardized platform for data exchange, enhancing interoperability among different devices and healthcare systems.
   b. This interoperability streamlines data sharing among healthcare providers, improving care coordination and reducing redundancies in tests and procedures.
4. *Clinical trials and research*:
   a. AI and blockchain can collaborate to accelerate medical research and clinical trials. By securely sharing anonymized patient data through blockchain networks, researchers can access comprehensive datasets for innovative studies and drug development.
   b. Data from AI-powered devices, such as wearables and remote monitoring tools, can contribute to real-world evidence and enhance the efficacy of clinical trials.

Table 6.1 Blockchain in AI-powered medical devices in this smart era.

Blockchain in AI-powered medical devices in this smart era		
	Data security and privacy	Secure data storage
		Patient control
	Data integrity and traceability	Immutability of data
	Interoperability and data exchange	Diverse data formats
		Streamlines data
	Clinical trials and research	Collaborate to accelerate medical research
		Wearables and remote monitoring tools
	Supply chain management	Traceability and authenticity
	Enhanced diagnostic and treatment precision	Informed decisions and tailor treatments
	Challenges and issues:	Regulatory compliance
		Infrastructure investment

5. *Supply chain management*:
   a. Blockchain can be used to enhance the traceability and authenticity of medical devices and pharmaceuticals throughout the supply chain. This technology helps reduce counterfeit products, improve quality control, and ensure the safety of medical devices used in healthcare.
6. *Enhanced diagnostic and treatment precision*:
   a. AI-powered devices equipped with blockchain-enabled data can improve diagnostic accuracy and treatment precision. By accessing a patient's comprehensive medical history, physicians can make more informed decisions and tailor treatments to individual needs.

Issues and challenges:

- *Regulatory compliance*: Integrating blockchain in healthcare must adhere to regulatory standards, including data protection and privacy laws.
- *Infrastructure investment*: Implementing this technology requires investments in infrastructure, including blockchain networks, AI capabilities, and training for healthcare professionals.

Hence, the convergence of blockchain and AI-powered medical devices holds immense potential to improve patient outcomes, streamline healthcare operations, and strengthen data security in the smart healthcare era. While challenges exist, overcoming them through collaboration and innovation can lead to a more patient-centric, efficient, and secure healthcare system. As these technologies continue to evolve and mature, their integration will play an important role in shaping the future of healthcare.

6.2 Foundations of smart hospitals

6.2.1 The evolution of healthcare systems

Healthcare systems have undergone significant transformations throughout history, driven by technological advancements, changing societal needs, and evolving medical practices. The evolution of healthcare systems can be divided into several distinct eras, each characterized by its own set of challenges and innovations (Burstin et al., 2016; Lenz & Kuhn, 2004). Here, we provide an overview of the key stages in the evolution of healthcare systems.

- *Ancient and traditional medicine*: The earliest healthcare systems were rooted in traditional medicine, relying on natural remedies, herbs, and spiritual practices. Ancient civilizations, such as those in Egypt, Mesopotamia, and India, developed medical knowledge and surgical techniques. We use methods in this period like healing temples, shamans, and herbalists played important roles in healthcare delivery.
- *Premodern medicine*: The premodern era saw the emergence of formal medical practices, with the establishment of medical schools and the codification of medical knowledge. Key figures like Hippocrates in ancient Greece laid the foundations for rational medical thought. During this period, Hospitals, initially serving as hospices, began to appear in medieval Europe, primarily run by religious organizations.

- *Modern medicine and scientific revolution*: The scientific revolution and the Age of Enlightenment led to significant advances in medicine and the understanding of diseases. Innovations like the microscope, developed by Anton van Leeuwenhoek, allowed for the discovery of microorganisms, fundamentally changing medical practices. The development of the smallpox vaccine by Edward Jenner marked the beginning of immunization.
- *Industrialization and public health*: The industrial revolution brought about urbanization and the growth of cities, which necessitated public health reforms. Cholera and other epidemics prompted the establishment of public health departments and the improvement of sanitation and hygiene. Hospitals evolved into more organized institutions, with the training of physicians becoming increasingly formalized.
- *Post-World War II and the rise of universal healthcare*: In the mid-20th century, many countries, especially in Europe, implemented universal healthcare systems, aiming to provide healthcare services to all citizens. The development of antibiotics and vaccines, as well as advances in surgical techniques, significantly improved patient outcomes. Government involvement in healthcare became more pronounced, with the establishment of public healthcare systems in many nations.
- *Information age and digital healthcare*: The advent of the Information Age brought about the digitalization of healthcare systems, including electronic health records, telemedicine, and health informatics. Medical technology, such as MRI and CT scanners, robotic surgery, and wearable health devices, advanced diagnosis and treatment options. Genetic research and personalized medicine emerged, tailoring treatments to individual genetic profiles.
- *Healthcare in the smart era*: Presently, healthcare is entering the smart era, marked by the convergence of technologies like artificial intelligence, blockchain, and the IoT. Smart hospitals, remote patient monitoring, and AI-assisted diagnostics are enhancing patient care and operational efficiency. Emphasis is on patient-centric care, preventive medicine, and improving healthcare data security.

The evolution of healthcare systems is an ongoing and dynamic process. As the healthcare landscape continues to change, it is important for healthcare professionals, policymakers, and technologists to adapt to these shifts and address the emerging challenges and opportunities in healthcare delivery, making quality healthcare accessible and efficient for all.

6.2.2 Smart hospitals: a new paradigm

In the rapidly evolving landscape of healthcare, smart hospitals are emerging as a transformative and innovative approach to healthcare delivery. These institutions, equipped with cutting-edge technology, represent a new paradigm in patient care, hospital management, and the overall healthcare experience (Holzinger et al., 2015). This work discusses the concept of smart hospitals and the myriad ways in which they are revolutionizing healthcare.

- *Integration of advanced technologies*: Smart hospitals use a wide array of advanced technologies, including the IoT, AI, big data analytics, and blockchain, to create a seamlessly connected healthcare ecosystem. These technologies enable real-time data collection, analysis, and decision-making, improving patient care and streamlining operations.

- *Enhanced patient-centric care*: Smart hospitals prioritize patient-centric care. Patients can actively participate in their health management, access their medical records, and communicate with healthcare providers through digital platforms. Wearable devices and remote monitoring tools facilitate continuous health tracking and early intervention, promoting overall well-being.
- *Predictive diagnostics and treatment*: AI-powered systems in smart hospitals analyze large datasets, enabling predictive diagnostics and personalized treatment plans. Physicians can make data-driven decisions, leading to quicker interventions and improved patient outcomes.
- *Data security and privacy*: Data security and patient privacy are paramount in smart hospitals. Blockchain technology is often employed to ensure the integrity and confidentiality of medical records. Patients have greater control over their data, granting access only to authorized parties, thus increasing trust and mitigating data breaches.
- *Interoperability and efficiency*: Smart hospitals address the longstanding challenge of data interoperability. Different healthcare systems, devices, and platforms can seamlessly share and access patient data, reducing redundant tests, enhancing care coordination, and lowering costs.
- *Telemedicine and remote monitoring*: Telemedicine services allow for virtual consultations, extending healthcare access to remote or underserved areas. Remote monitoring tools keep patients connected to their healthcare providers, enabling early detection of health issues.
- *Sustainable and eco-friendly practices*: Smart hospitals often incorporate sustainable and eco-friendly practices, such as energy-efficient infrastructure, waste reduction, and the use of renewable energy sources. This not only benefits the environment but also reduces operational costs.
- *Research and development*: Smart hospitals actively contribute to medical research and development. Anonymized and secure data-sharing networks facilitate collaborative research, expediting the development of new treatments and therapies.
- *Issues and challenges*: While the concept of smart hospitals holds immense promise, it is not without challenges. Regulatory compliance, data standardization, and the need for substantial infrastructure investments are key considerations. Ensuring equitable access to these advanced healthcare technologies is also a priority.

In summary, smart hospitals are redefining healthcare delivery. They prioritize patient well-being, data security, and operational efficiency, ushering in a new era of healthcare. As we navigate the opportunities and challenges of this paradigm shift, it is imperative that users, including healthcare providers, policymakers, and technology developers, collaborate to ensure the responsible and effective implementation of smart hospitals, ultimately improving healthcare experiences and outcomes for all.

6.2.3 The role of AI and blockchain in smart hospitals

AI and blockchain are two innovative technologies that have the potential to transform the healthcare industry and play a significant role in the development of smart hospitals (Chamola et al., 2023; Haddad et al., 2022; Rajawat et al., 2022). Here is how AI and blockchain can contribute to the evolution of smart hospitals:

6.2.3.1 Role of AI in smart hospitals

Data Analysis and Insights: AI can analyze medical images, such as X-rays and MRIs, and help in diagnosing conditions with high accuracy. It can also assist in predicting disease risks based on patient data. Also, AI can process and analyze large amounts of patient data to provide insights into individual health and population health trends.

Patient care and monitoring: AI-powered devices can continuously monitor patients' important signs and alert healthcare providers to any anomalies, enabling proactive care. Also, AI can help create personalized treatment plans, taking into account a patient's medical history, genetics, and lifestyle factors.

Efficient healthcare operations: AI can optimize resource allocation, such as staff scheduling, room utilization, and inventory management, leading to cost savings and improved patient care. Also, AI can predict equipment failures, allowing for timely maintenance and reducing downtime.

Chatbots and virtual assistants: AI-driven chatbots and virtual assistants can provide immediate responses to patient queries, schedule appointments, and provide information on common health issues.

Drug discovery and development: AI algorithms can significantly accelerate drug discovery by analyzing large datasets, predicting potential drug candidates, and simulating their effects.

Telemedicine and telehealth: AI can enhance telemedicine by assisting with virtual diagnoses, prescribing medication, and providing postconsultation follow-up care.

6.2.3.2 Role of blockchain in smart hospitals

Data security and privacy: Blockchain provides a secure and tamper-proof ledger for patient records, ensuring the integrity and confidentiality of health data. Patients can control access to their medical information, sharing it securely with authorized healthcare providers when needed.

Interoperability: Blockchain can facilitate data exchange and interoperability among different healthcare systems, ensuring that patient information is easily accessible to authorized providers.

Supply chain management: Blockchain can be used to track the supply chain of pharmaceuticals and medical devices, ensuring transparency and preventing counterfeit products.

Clinical trials: Blockchain can be used to streamline and secure the process of conducting clinical trials, making data collection and sharing more efficient and trustworthy.

Smart contracts: Blockchain-based smart contracts can automate and secure various healthcare processes, including insurance claims, billing, and payments.

Credential verification: Healthcare professionals' qualifications and certifications can be stored on a blockchain, allowing for quick and secure verification.

Research data sharing: Researchers can securely and transparently share and access medical research data, accelerating the pace of medical discoveries.

Immutable audit trail: Blockchain records every transaction or change in data, providing a permanent and unchangeable audit trail, which is important for ensuring accountability and compliance in healthcare.

In smart hospitals, AI and blockchain can work in conjunction to enhance patient care, data security, and overall efficiency. While AI improves diagnosis, patient monitoring, and operational efficiency, blockchain ensures the secure and transparent management of health records and transactions. Together, these technologies can lead to more patient-centric, cost-effective, and secure healthcare systems.

6.3 Available medical devices in the AI-based smart era

In the AI-based smart era of healthcare, there are numerous medical devices and applications that incorporate artificial intelligence and machine learning to improve patient care, diagnosis, and treatment (Kang et al., 2018; Nasr et al., 2021). Here are some examples:

AI-enhanced diagnostic imaging:

- *AI-interpreted radiology*: AI algorithms can assist radiologists in interpreting X-rays, CT scans, and MRIs, helping to detect abnormalities and diseases.
- *AI in pathology*: AI is used to analyze tissue samples, aiding pathologists in cancer diagnosis and other diseases.

Wearable health devices:

- *Smartwatches and fitness trackers*: These devices can monitor heart rate, activity levels, and sleep patterns and can give insights into overall health.
- *Continuous glucose monitors (CGMs)*: For people with diabetes, CGMs track blood glucose levels continuously, providing real-time data and trends.
- *Smart ECG monitors*: These devices can record electrocardiograms and identify irregular heart rhythms.
- *Telemedicine platforms*: Telemedicine apps that incorporate AI can assist in diagnosing common illnesses, monitoring chronic conditions, and providing access to healthcare professionals remotely.
- *AI-powered chatbots*: Virtual health assistants and chatbots can provide information, schedule appointments, and even provide initial health assessments.
- *Medication management*: Smart Pill Dispensers: These devices help patients manage their medications by providing reminders and dispensing the right pills at the right time.
- *AI medication adherence apps*: AI-driven apps remind patients to take their medication and provide educational information (Table 6.2).

Disease management and risk prediction:

- AI algorithms can assess patient data to predict disease risks and assist in developing personalized care plans.
- *Remote patient monitoring*: Devices and platforms for remote monitoring of important signs and chronic conditions, which enable healthcare providers to track patients' health status in real time.
- *Surgical robots*: AI-assisted surgical robots help surgeons perform complex procedures with precision, minimizing human error.
- *Drug discovery*: AI is used to analyze large datasets, helping researchers identify potential drug candidates and predict their efficacy.

Table 6.2 Available medical devices in the AI-based smart era.

Available medical devices in the AI-based smart era		
	AI-enhanced diagnostic imaging	AI-interpreted radiology
		AI in pathology
	Wearable health devices	Smartwatches and fitness trackers
		Continuous glucose monitors
		Smart ECG monitors
		Telemedicine platforms
		AI-powered chatbots
		Medication management
		AI medication adherence apps
	Disease management and risk prediction	AI algorithms
		Remote patient monitoring
		Surgical robots
		Drug discovery
		Mental health apps
		Rehabilitation devices
		Health data analytics
		AI-assisted diabetic management
		AI-enhanced prosthetics and exoskeletons
		Voice assistants for healthcare

- *Mental health apps*: AI-based mental health apps provide cognitive-behavioral therapy, mood tracking, and crisis intervention services.
- *Rehabilitation devices*: AI-powered devices aid in physical therapy and rehabilitation, monitoring progress and providing personalized exercises.
- *Health data analytics*: AI and machine learning are used to analyze large healthcare datasets to improve patient care, optimize hospital operations, and identify trends and patterns.
- *AI-assisted diabetic management*: AI helps in the continuous monitoring and management of diabetes, providing insulin dose recommendations and predicting glucose trends.
- *AI-enhanced prosthetics and exoskeletons*: AI algorithms are used to enhance the functionality and control of prosthetic limbs and exoskeletons.
- *Voice assistants for healthcare*: Voice-activated devices are increasingly used to provide healthcare information, schedule appointments, and assist with medication reminders.

These examples demonstrate the integration of AI into various aspects of healthcare, from diagnosis to treatment, patient management, and even drug discovery. As technology continues to advance, we can expect even more innovative AI-based medical devices and applications to improve healthcare delivery and outcomes.

6.4 Blockchain technology in healthcare: uses, benefits, and limitations

Blockchain technology has the potential to revolutionize the healthcare industry by addressing key challenges related to data security, interoperability, and transparency (Abu-Elezz et al., 2020; Attaran, 2022). Here are some of the uses, benefits, and limitations of blockchain in healthcare:

Uses of blockchain in healthcare (refer Fig. 6.3):

Health data management:

- *Electronic health records (EHRs)*: Blockchain can securely store patient records, ensuring that data is tamper-proof and accessible to authorized healthcare providers.
- *Patient consent management*: Patients can control who has access to their health data and grant or revoke permissions through smart contracts.
- *Interoperability*: Blockchain can enable seamless data exchange between different healthcare organizations and systems, improving care coordination and reducing errors.

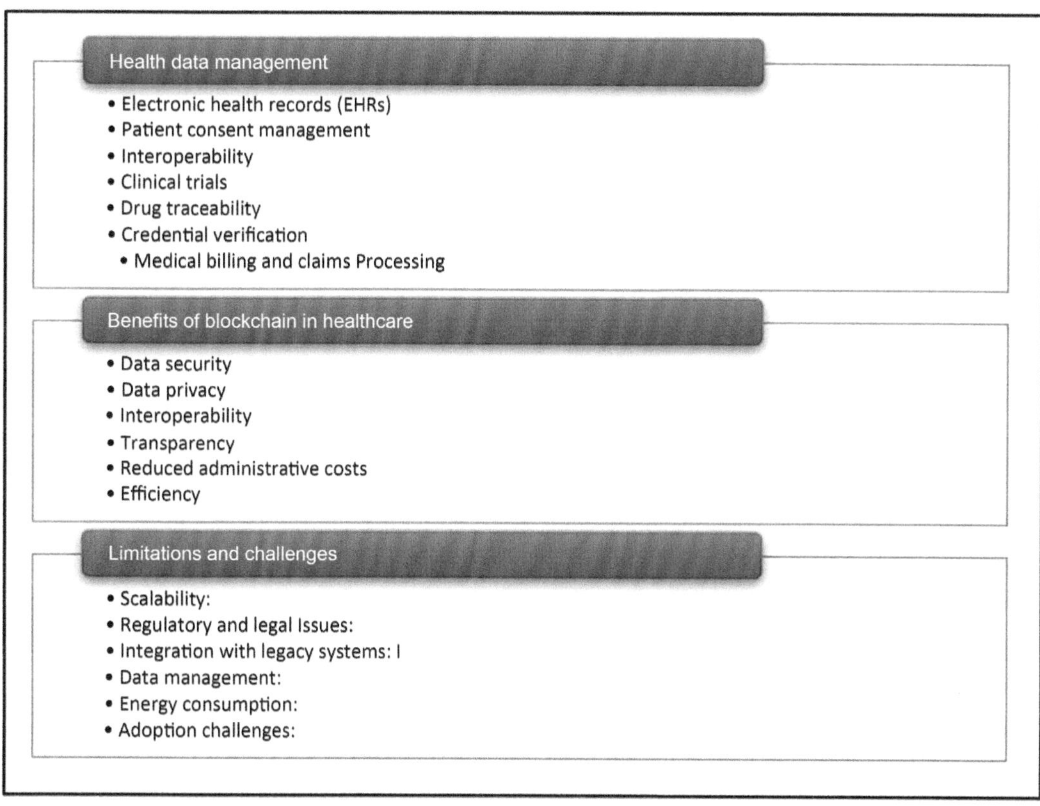

FIGURE 6.3

Blockchain technology in healthcare: uses, benefits, and limitations.

- *Clinical trials*: Blockchain can streamline the management of clinical trial data, ensuring the integrity and transparency of research results.
- *Drug traceability*: Blockchain can be used to track the supply chain of pharmaceuticals, reducing the risk of counterfeit drugs and ensuring quality control.
- *Credential verification*: Healthcare providers' qualifications and certifications can be stored on a blockchain, simplifying the verification process.
- *Medical billing and claims processing*: Smart contracts can automate and streamline the medical billing process, reducing administrative costs and errors.

Benefits of blockchain in healthcare:

- *Data security*: Blockchain's decentralized and immutable nature makes it highly secure, protecting patient data from breaches and unauthorized access.
- *Data privacy*: Patients have greater control over their health data, choosing who can access it and for what purpose, enhancing privacy.
- *Interoperability*: Blockchain can help standardize data formats and facilitate interoperability among different healthcare systems, improving care coordination.
- *Transparency*: The transparent and tamper-proof nature of blockchain enhances trust among users and ensures data integrity.
- *Reduced administrative costs*: Smart contracts can automate various administrative processes, reducing paperwork and costs associated with billing and claims processing.
- *Efficiency*: Streamlined data sharing and record-keeping processes can save time and improve the efficiency of healthcare operations.

Limitations and challenges:

- *Scalability*: Blockchain technology can be resource-intensive, making it challenging to scale for large healthcare networks, potentially leading to slower transaction processing.
- *Regulatory and legal issues*: Healthcare is heavily regulated, and blockchain implementation must comply with existing regulations, which can be complex and vary by region.
- *Integration with legacy systems*: Integrating blockchain with existing healthcare systems can be challenging and expensive, as many healthcare organizations rely on outdated technology.
- *Data management*: While blockchain secures data, it does not address data accuracy or quality, and erroneous data input can lead to inaccuracies on the chain.
- *Energy consumption*: Some blockchain networks, such as Bitcoins, are energy-intensive, which may not be sustainable in the long term for healthcare applications.
- *Adoption challenges*: Widespread adoption of blockchain in healthcare requires buy-in from healthcare providers, payers, and regulatory bodies, which can be slow to change.

Blockchain technology has the potential to address important issues in healthcare, particularly related to data security and interoperability. However, its successful implementation requires overcoming technical, regulatory, and adoption challenges to realize its full potential for improving healthcare delivery and patient outcomes.

6.5 Integration of AI and blockchain for smart medical devices and smart hospitals

The integration of AI and blockchain in smart medical devices and smart hospitals can significantly enhance healthcare by improving data security, interoperability, and the overall quality of patient care (Fatoum et al., 2021; Xie et al., 2021). Here is how these two technologies can be combined, as mentioned in Table 6.3.

Note that the integration of AI and blockchain in smart medical devices and smart hospitals can lead to a more efficient, secure, and patient-centric healthcare system. It ensures data privacy, interoperability, and transparent record-keeping while using AI's capabilities for data analysis, diagnostics, and personalized care. However, it is important to address the technical and regulatory challenges associated with these technologies to realize their full potential in healthcare.

Table 6.3 Convergence of AI and blockchain for smart medical devices and smart hospitals.

Types	Blockchain	AI
Secure health data management	Blockchain can be used to create a secure and tamper-proof ledger for storing patient data, electronic health records (EHRs), and other medical information. This ensures data integrity and enhances security.	AI algorithms can process and analyze the data stored on the blockchain, providing insights and supporting diagnosis and treatment decisions.
Interoperability	Blockchain can serve as a common platform for data exchange among different healthcare providers, ensuring that patient data is easily accessible and transferable.	AI can help standardize and process data from various sources, improving interoperability and enabling seamless information sharing among smart medical devices and healthcare systems.
Patient consent management	Patients can control access to their health data and grant or revoke permissions through smart contracts, ensuring data privacy and consent management.	AI can assist in monitoring and enforcing consent rules set by patients, ensuring that data is only accessed and used as authorized.
Remote patient monitoring	Patient data collected by smart medical devices can be securely stored on the blockchain, guaranteeing its integrity and privacy.	AI can analyze this data in real time to monitor patient health and provide early warnings and insights to healthcare providers.
Drug traceability	Blockchain can track the supply chain of pharmaceuticals and medical devices, ensuring quality control and authenticity.	AI can verify the authenticity of products and track any irregularities or recalls in real time.
Clinical trials	Blockchain can provide transparency and security for clinical trial data, ensuring the integrity of research results.	AI can assist in data analysis for clinical trials, speeding up the process and improving accuracy.
Smart contracts for billing and payments	Smart contracts can automate medical billing and claims processing, reducing administrative costs and errors.	AI can verify and process claims, ensuring accuracy and compliance with contract terms.
Research data sharing	Researchers can securely and transparently share and access medical research data, promoting collaboration and innovation.	AI can help researchers analyze and make sense of the large amount of data available for medical research.

6.6 AI-driven data analytics and blockchain implementation for smart healthcare services

AI-driven data analytics and blockchain implementation can significantly enhance smart healthcare services by improving data security, interoperability, and the overall quality of care (Golec et al., 2023). Here is a closer look at how these technologies can be applied in this context:

AI-driven data analytics in smart healthcare services:

- *Clinical decision support*: AI algorithms can analyze patient data, including EHRs and real-time sensor data, to assist healthcare providers in making more accurate and timely diagnoses and treatment decisions.
- *Predictive analytics*: AI can predict disease outbreaks, patient readmissions, and other important events, enabling healthcare organizations to take proactive measures and allocate resources more effectively.
- *Patient monitoring and personalization*: Smart healthcare devices, such as wearables, can continuously monitor patient data, and AI can analyze this data to provide real-time insights and personalized recommendations for patients to improve their health.
- *Drug discovery*: AI can sift through large datasets to identify potential drug candidates, significantly accelerating the drug discovery process and reducing costs.
- *Operational efficiency*: AI-driven analytics can optimize healthcare operations by managing resources, scheduling staff, and reducing wastage, ultimately leading to cost savings and better patient care.
- *Healthcare research*: Researchers can use AI-driven data analytics to uncover trends and insights from large datasets, advancing medical research and innovation.

Blockchain implementation in smart healthcare services:

- *Secure health data management*: Blockchain can serve as a secure and tamper-proof ledger for patient records, EHRs, and health data, ensuring data integrity and preventing unauthorized access.
- *Interoperability*: Blockchain can facilitate data exchange and interoperability among different healthcare providers and systems, improving care coordination and patient outcomes.
- *Patient consent management*: Smart contracts on the blockchain can enable patients to control and manage who has access to their health data, enhancing data privacy and consent management.
- *Drug traceability*: Blockchain can be used to track the supply chain of pharmaceuticals, ensuring authenticity, reducing the risk of counterfeit drugs, and improving drug safety.
- *Clinical trials*: Blockchain can provide transparency and security for clinical trial data, ensuring the integrity of research results and accelerating the development of new treatments.
- *Credential verification*: Healthcare professionals' qualifications and certifications can be securely stored on a blockchain, simplifying the verification process for both providers and patients.
- *Billing and claims processing*: Smart contracts can automate billing and claims processing, reducing administrative overhead and the risk of errors.
- *Research data sharing*: Researchers can securely and transparently share and access medical research data, promoting collaboration and speeding up the pace of medical discoveries.

Note that the combination of AI-driven data analytics and blockchain implementation in smart healthcare services can lead to a more efficient, secure, and patient-centric healthcare ecosystem. It ensures data privacy, interoperability, and transparent record-keeping while harnessing the power of AI to improve diagnostics, treatment, and patient care. However, it is essential to address regulatory, technical, and ethical issues when implementing these technologies in healthcare services to realize their full potential.

6.7 Blockchain-powered AI in medical devices for improved diagnostics and patient care

The integration of blockchain technology with AI in medical devices holds great promise for improving diagnostics and patient care in healthcare (Kumar et al., 2022; Wang et al., 2018). Here is how this combination can enhance the field (refer Fig. 6.4):

- *Secure and tamper-proof health data*: Blockchain provides a secure, decentralized ledger for storing and managing patient data, medical records, and diagnostic information. This ensures data integrity, eliminates unauthorized access, and guards against data breaches, thus enhancing patient privacy and trust.

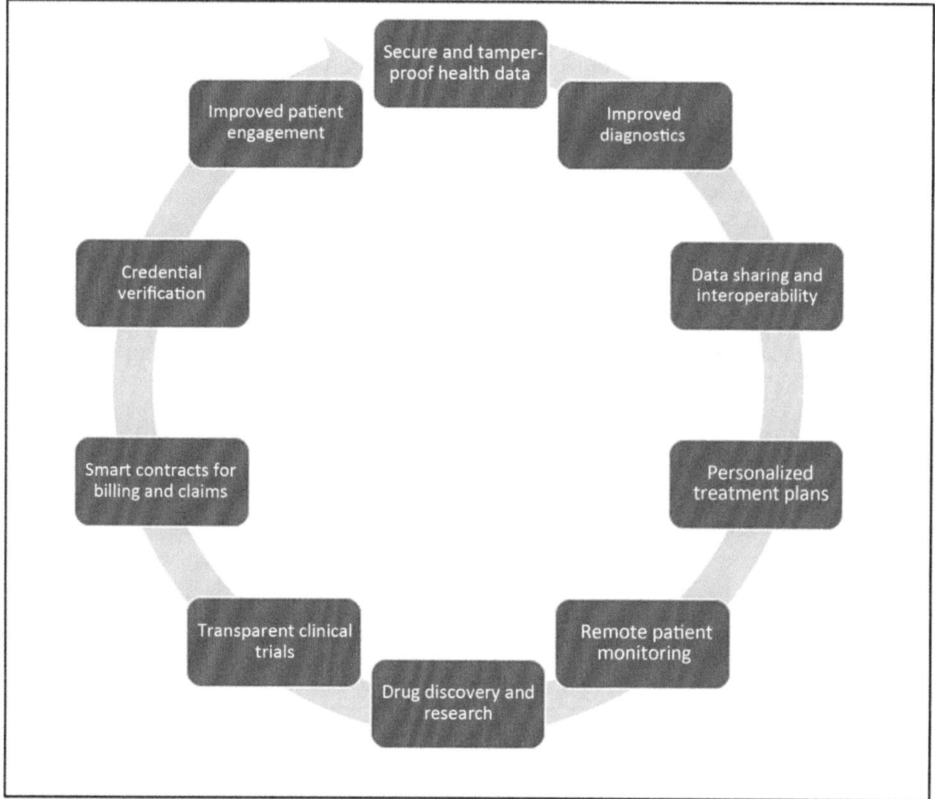

FIGURE 6.4

Blockchain-powered AI in medical devices.

- *Improved diagnostics*: AI algorithms can process and analyze medical data from various sources, such as medical images, patient records, and real-time monitoring data, to assist healthcare professionals in making more accurate and timely diagnoses. Machine learning models can detect patterns and anomalies, helping identify diseases and conditions early.
- *Data sharing and interoperability*: Blockchain can facilitate the secure and efficient exchange of medical data between healthcare providers, patients, and medical devices. It ensures data is easily accessible, traceable, and interoperable across different healthcare systems and devices.
- *Personalized treatment plans*: AI-driven medical devices can use patient data to generate personalized treatment plans and recommendations. These devices can take into account a patient's medical history, genetics, lifestyle, and real-time health data to create tailored care strategies.
- *Remote patient monitoring*: Securely storing real-time patient data on the blockchain ensures data integrity and enables healthcare providers to monitor patients remotely while maintaining data privacy. AI can analyze the continuous stream of data from medical devices and provide real-time insights, triggering alerts or interventions when necessary, thus improving patient care and reducing hospital readmissions.
- *Drug discovery and research*: AI can significantly expedite the drug discovery process by analyzing large datasets, identifying potential drug candidates, and simulating their effects. This can lead to the development of more effective and targeted medications.
- *Transparent clinical trials*: Clinical trial data can be securely stored on the blockchain, providing transparency, traceability, and data integrity. AI can be used to analyze this data to validate the effectiveness and safety of new treatments.
- *Smart contracts for billing and claims*: Smart contracts can automate billing, claims processing, and payment procedures, reducing administrative overhead and enhancing the accuracy and efficiency of financial transactions within the healthcare system.
- *Credential verification*: Healthcare professionals' qualifications and certifications can be securely stored on a blockchain, simplifying and speeding up the verification process.
- *Improved patient engagement*: AI-driven medical devices can provide patients with personalized insights, recommendations, and reminders, empowering individuals to take more proactive roles in their healthcare.

The combination of blockchain and AI in medical devices not only provides data security and privacy but also transforms healthcare by enhancing diagnostics, personalizing treatment, and improving patient care. This integration fosters a healthcare ecosystem that is more transparent, efficient, and patient-centric, ultimately leading to better outcomes and a higher quality of care. Nevertheless, challenges such as regulatory compliance, data standardization, and technology adoption should be addressed to fully unlock the potential of these technologies in healthcare.

6.8 Security and privacy issues in smart medical devices, hospitals, and smart healthcare

Security and privacy are important issues in the deployment of smart medical devices, hospitals, and healthcare systems. These issues can have serious consequences if not properly addressed

(Karunarathne et al., 2021; Nidhya et al., 2022). Here are some of the key challenges and potential threats:

Security issues:

- *Data breaches*: Unauthorized access to patient data, medical records, and sensitive information can lead to data breaches. This may result from weak network security, inadequate authentication, or unpatched software vulnerabilities.
- *Malware and ransomware*: Smart devices and healthcare systems are vulnerable to malware and ransomware attacks, which can compromise data integrity and availability. Ransomware can encrypt important data, making it inaccessible until a ransom is paid.
- *Device vulnerabilities*: Smart medical devices can have security vulnerabilities that hackers can exploit. For example, a connected infusion pump with a security flaw could be tampered with remotely, endangering patient safety.
- *Insider threats*: Malicious actions by healthcare employees or insiders can pose a significant security risk. Unauthorized access to patient data or other confidential information can be damaging.
- *IoT device security*: IoT devices in healthcare, such as wearables and remote monitoring devices, may lack robust security measures, making them susceptible to attacks.

Privacy ssues:

- *Data privacy*: The collection, storage, and sharing of health data need to be done with strict adherence to privacy regulations (e.g., HIPAA in the United States, GDPR in Europe) to protect patients' rights and privacy.
- *Patient consent*: Ensuring that patients provide informed consent for data collection, sharing, and treatment is essential. Consent management can be complex, especially with the proliferation of data sources in healthcare.
- *Deidentification*: Removing or protecting personally identifiable information (PII) is important in sharing and analyzing health data while preserving patient privacy. AI and blockchain technologies can assist in deidentification.
- *Data sharing*: Data sharing among healthcare providers, researchers, and organizations can be limited due to issues about patient privacy and regulatory compliance.
- *Cybersecurity awareness*: Many healthcare employees may not be adequately trained in cybersecurity, making them more susceptible to phishing attacks and unintentional data breaches.

To address these security and privacy issues, healthcare organizations and users must take a proactive approach. Here are some measures to consider:

- *Security audits and vulnerability assessments*: Regularly evaluate the security of medical devices, healthcare systems, and networks to identify and rectify vulnerabilities.
- *Encryption and authentication*: Use strong encryption for data in transit and at rest. Implement multifactor authentication to enhance access control.
- *Access control*: Enforce strict access control policies to limit data access to authorized personnel only.
- *Regular updates and patch management*: Keep software, operating systems, and devices up to date with the latest security patches.

- *Security awareness training*: Educate healthcare professionals and staff on cybersecurity best practices and how to identify and respond to potential threats.
- *Compliance and regulation*: Adhere to healthcare privacy regulations and maintain compliance with data protection laws.
- *Incident response plan*: Develop and regularly update an incident response plan to manage and mitigate security incidents effectively.
- *Privacy-preserving technologies*: Implement technologies such as blockchain and differential privacy to protect patient privacy while sharing data and conducting analysis.

Hence, balancing the benefits of smart healthcare with the associated security and privacy risks is an important challenge in the modern healthcare landscape. It requires ongoing vigilance, investment in cybersecurity, and a commitment to safeguarding patient data and privacy.

6.9 Challenges and recommended solutions for smart medical devices, hospitals, and smart healthcare

Implementing smart medical devices, hospitals, and smart healthcare systems comes with numerous challenges, but there are also practical solutions that can address these issues (Baker et al., 2017; Tian et al., 2019). Here are some key challenges and recommended solutions, as follows:

Challenges:

Interoperability: Smart devices and healthcare systems often use different standards and protocols, making data exchange and communication between devices and systems challenging. As a solution, we promote the development and adoption of interoperable standards and technologies, such as fast healthcare interoperability resources (FHIRs), to ensure seamless data exchange.

Security and privacy: Protecting patient data from breaches, unauthorized access, and cyberattacks is a top priority. As a solution, we Implement robust cybersecurity measures, including encryption, access controls, regular security audits, and employee training. Adhere to data protection regulations (e.g., HIPAA, GDPR).

Data integration: Smart healthcare systems generate large amounts of data that need to be efficiently collected, integrated, and analyzed for meaningful insights. As a solution, we Invest in data analytics tools and platforms that can handle the volume and variety of healthcare data, enabling better clinical decision support and research.

Regulatory compliance: Complying with healthcare regulations, including those specific to medical devices, can be complex and costly. As a solution, we keep abreast of regulatory changes, ensure devices and systems meet compliance standards, and involve legal and regulatory experts in the development and deployment process.

Cost and funding: Implementing smart healthcare systems can be expensive, and healthcare organizations may face budget constraints. As a solution, we discuss various funding options, including public–private partnerships, grants, and investments in health technology to support the development and implementation of smart healthcare solutions.

Adoption and resistance: Healthcare professionals may resist the adoption of new technologies and workflows due to unfamiliarity, skepticism, or issues about job displacement. As a solution, we involve healthcare staff in the decision-making process, provide comprehensive training, and demonstrate the benefits of smart healthcare solutions, such as improved patient outcomes and streamlined processes.

Technology integration: Integrating new technologies into existing healthcare systems and workflows can be challenging. As a solution, we plan for a phased implementation, assess the impact on existing systems, and ensure adequate support and training for healthcare staff.

Scalability: Ensuring that smart healthcare solutions can scale to meet the needs of growing patient populations is a long-term challenge. As a solution, we design systems with scalability in mind, consider cloud-based solutions, and continuously monitor and optimize performance.

Patient engagement: Engaging patients in their care and in using smart healthcare solutions can be challenging. As a solution, we develop patient-friendly interfaces, provide education and support, and provide incentives for patients to actively participate in their healthcare management.

Hence, addressing these challenges requires collaboration among healthcare organizations, technology providers, and regulatory bodies. A multidisciplinary approach that includes healthcare professionals, technologists, ethicists, and legal experts is essential to developing and implementing smart healthcare solutions successfully.

6.10 Future opportunities/emerging technologies toward AI and blockchain-based smart hospital and healthcare

The future of AI and blockchain in healthcare is promising, with emerging technologies providing new opportunities to create smarter, more efficient, and patient-centric healthcare systems (Singh et al., 2022; Tuli et al., 2020). Here are some future opportunities and emerging technologies in the context of AI and blockchain-based smart hospitals and healthcare, as mentioned in Table 6.4.

Hence, the convergence of AI and blockchain with emerging technologies holds great potential for transforming healthcare and creating smarter, more patient-centric systems. As these technologies mature and become more integrated into healthcare workflows, we can expect to see significant improvements in patient care, data security, and the overall healthcare experience.

6.10.1 Potential advancements in AI-powered medical devices

Advancements in AI-powered medical devices are poised to revolutionize healthcare by enhancing diagnostic accuracy, treatment effectiveness, and patient care. Here are some potential advancements in this field:

- *Enhanced diagnostic imaging*: AI algorithms can further improve the accuracy and speed of interpreting medical images, including X-rays, CT scans, MRIs, and mammograms, aiding radiologists in detecting and diagnosing conditions such as cancer, fractures, and neurological disorders.
- *Wearable health monitoring*: AI-powered wearables and smart sensors will provide continuous, real-time monitoring of important signs, chronic conditions, and fitness metrics, providing early warning systems and personalized health recommendations.

Table 6.4 Opportunities/emerging technologies toward AI and blockchain-based smart hospital and healthcare.

Emerging technologies	Opportunity	Applications
Edge computing	Edge computing allows for real-time data processing at or near the source, reducing latency and enabling faster decision-making.	Smart medical devices, IoT sensors, and AI algorithms can benefit from edge computing to provide rapid insights and immediate responses for important patient care.
5G technology	5G networks provide ultra-fast, low-latency connectivity, enabling seamless data exchange between devices and healthcare systems.	Telemedicine, remote monitoring, and the rapid transfer of large medical datasets benefit from 5 G technology, enhancing the efficiency of smart healthcare solutions.
Federated learning	Federated learning allows AI models to be trained across decentralized datasets while keeping data on local devices, preserving privacy.	Healthcare institutions can collaborate and improve AI models without sharing sensitive patient data, enabling more accurate diagnostics and treatment recommendations.
Explainable AI (XAI)	XAI technologies aim to make AI algorithms more interpretable and transparent, which is important in healthcare.	Patients and healthcare providers can have more confidence in AI-driven decisions when the reasoning behind those decisions is understandable, leading to better trust and adoption.
Quantum Computing	Quantum computing has the potential to solve complex healthcare problems and accelerate drug discovery through faster data analysis.	Quantum computing can perform sophisticated simulations and optimizations, which can lead to the discovery of novel treatments and therapies.
AI in genomics	AI can analyze and interpret genomic data quickly, enabling precision medicine and personalized treatment plans.	AI can identify genetic markers, assess disease risk, and recommend treatments based on an individual's genetic profile.
Decentralized identity (SSI)	Self-sovereign identity (SSI) solutions based on blockchain can give patients control over their healthcare data, enhancing privacy.	Patients can securely share their medical records and information with healthcare providers and researchers while maintaining ownership and control of their data.
Blockchain for drug traceability	Blockchain can be used to track pharmaceuticals throughout the supply chain, reducing the risk of counterfeit drugs and enhancing patient safety.	Patients and healthcare providers can verify the authenticity and quality of medications and medical devices.
3D printing and AI	AI can assist in designing and optimizing 3D-printed medical devices and prosthetics.	Customized implants, prosthetics, and medical models can be created with greater precision, enhancing patient care and outcomes.
AI-enhanced robotics	AI-powered robots can assist in surgery, patient care, and medication management.	Robotics can improve surgical precision, patient rehabilitation, and elderly care, particularly in smart hospitals and healthcare facilities.

- *Personalized treatment plans*: AI can analyze large amounts of patient data to generate highly individualized treatment plans. These plans consider a patient's medical history, genetics, lifestyle, and real-time health data to optimize care.

- *Remote patient monitoring*: AI-driven devices and platforms enable the remote monitoring of patients with chronic conditions, allowing healthcare providers to intervene proactively and reduce hospital readmissions.
- *Predictive analytics*: AI can predict disease outbreaks, patient readmissions, and other health-related events, assisting healthcare organizations in resource allocation and early intervention.
- *Surgical robotics*: AI-powered surgical robots can enhance the precision and efficiency of minimally invasive procedures, reducing human error and improving patient outcomes.
- *Voice and natural language processing*: AI-based voice assistants and natural language processing can improve patient engagement, streamline administrative tasks, and support clinical documentation.
- *AI-integrated EHR systems*: AI will be integrated into EHR systems to assist healthcare providers with data entry, clinical decision support, and predictive analytics for improved patient care.
- *AI in drug discovery*: AI algorithms will analyze large datasets to accelerate the drug discovery process, identifying potential drug candidates and predicting their efficacy and safety profiles.
- *AI-enhanced mental health apps*: AI-driven mental health apps will provide personalized cognitive-behavioral therapy, mood tracking, and crisis intervention services, increasing access to mental healthcare.
- *Neurological and cognitive monitoring*: AI-powered devices can monitor and analyze brain and cognitive functions for the early detection of neurological disorders, such as Alzheimer's disease and Parkinson's disease.
- *Proactive medication management*: AI will assist in the monitoring and management of chronic conditions, providing medication adherence reminders, dosage adjustments, and medication safety checks.
- *Genomic analysis*: AI can analyze genomic data to identify disease risks, tailor treatment plans to individual genetic profiles, and predict responses to specific therapies.
- *Wearable exoskeletons*: AI-enhanced exoskeletons can improve mobility and rehabilitation for individuals with mobility impairments, enabling greater independence and improved quality of life.
- *AI-enhanced dentistry*: AI algorithms can assist dentists in diagnosing oral health conditions, analyzing X-rays, and providing personalized oral care recommendations.

In summary, these advancements in AI-powered medical devices are set to transform healthcare, improving the accuracy of diagnosis, personalizing treatment plans, and enhancing patient care. As technology continues to evolve, we can expect to see even more innovative and impactful applications of AI in healthcare.

6.10.2 The transformative power of AI and blockchain in smart hospitals in near future

he transformative power of AI and blockchain in smart hospitals in the near future is expected to have a profound impact on healthcare delivery, patient outcomes, and operational efficiency. Here are some of the transformative changes and benefits that can be expected:

- *Enhanced diagnostics and treatment*: AI-driven diagnostic tools will significantly improve the accuracy and speed of disease identification, allowing for earlier intervention and more precise treatment plans; whereas, blockchain will secure patient data, ensuring that treatment history and diagnostic information are readily available to healthcare providers, enhancing patient care.

- *Predictive healthcare*: AI will enable predictive analytics to anticipate disease outbreaks, patient readmissions, and other health-related events, optimizing resource allocation and healthcare planning. Also, blockchain can provide transparent and tamper-proof records for public health monitoring and epidemiological studies.
- *Telemedicine and remote monitoring*: AI-powered telemedicine platforms will allow for virtual consultations, making healthcare more accessible and convenient, especially in rural or underserved areas. Remote patient monitoring with AI analytics will enable real-time health tracking, reducing the need for frequent in-person visits and enhancing care for chronic conditions.
- *Personalized medicine*: AI will analyze large datasets, including genomics, to create personalized treatment plans, considering an individual's genetics, medical history, lifestyle, and real-time health data. And blockchain will securely store and share patient genomic data, ensuring privacy and control over sensitive information.
- *Healthcare data security*: Blockchain will provide robust security and privacy measures for healthcare data, reducing the risk of data breaches and unauthorized access. AI will help identify and respond to security threats in real time, enhancing data protection.
- *Smart contracts for healthcare transactions*: Blockchain-based smart contracts will automate billing and claims processing, reducing administrative costs and errors in financial transactions. Patients, providers, and insurers can have more transparent, efficient interactions through smart contracts.
- *Drug discovery and clinical trials*: AI will accelerate drug discovery by analyzing extensive datasets, predicting potential drug candidates, and simulating their effects. Blockchain will ensure data integrity in clinical trials, making results more reliable and transparent.
- *Enhanced hospital operations*: AI-driven systems will optimize resource allocation, staff scheduling, and inventory management, leading to cost savings and improved patient care. Blockchain can improve supply chain management, reducing the risk of counterfeit pharmaceuticals and medical devices.
- *Patient empowerment*: AI-powered virtual assistants and health apps will provide patients with personalized insights, reminders, and recommendations, enabling them to actively engage in their healthcare. Blockchain will give patients control over their health data, allowing them to securely share it with healthcare providers and researchers as needed.
- *Research collaboration*: Researchers can securely and transparently share medical research data using blockchain, accelerating the pace of medical discoveries and fostering collaboration. AI will assist in analyzing large datasets, making it easier to identify trends and insights.

In summary, the integration of AI and blockchain in smart hospitals will ultimately lead to healthcare that is more patient-centric, secure, efficient, and accessible. Patients will benefit from more accurate diagnoses and personalized treatment, while healthcare providers will have the tools to optimize their operations and improve patient care. This transformative power is set to shape the future of healthcare in the coming years.

6.11 Conclusion

The fusion of artificial intelligence and blockchain technology in the context of smart hospitals represents a groundbreaking advancement in the healthcare industry. This powerful combination has the potential to revolutionize patient care, data security, and operational efficiency. As we conclude our exploration of AI-powered blockchain technology for smart hospitals, it is evident that the benefits provided by this integration are profound. Smart hospitals equipped with AI-driven predictive diagnostics and real-time patient monitoring can significantly improve patient outcomes by enabling early interventions. The integration of blockchain technology ensures that patient data remains secure, immutable, and readily accessible only to authorized personnel. The advantages of interoperability, reduced administrative overhead, and enhanced drug traceability further contribute to the transformation of healthcare delivery. However, the path to realizing these benefits is not without challenges. Regulatory hurdles, data interoperability issues, and substantial infrastructure investments pose significant barriers. Yet, the promise of improved patient care, data integrity, and cost efficiency makes the pursuit of AI-powered blockchain technology in smart hospitals a worthwhile endeavor. In summary, the convergence of AI and blockchain technology has the potential to redefine the healthcare landscape, creating a more patient-centric, efficient, and secure ecosystem. As we move forward, it is imperative that users, including healthcare providers, regulators, and technology developers, collaborate to overcome the obstacles and advance the adoption of this transformative approach. With continued research, innovation, and investment, the vision of smart hospitals powered by AI and blockchain can become a reality, ultimately enhancing the quality of healthcare and the overall well-being of patients worldwide.

References

Abu-Elezz, I., Hassan, A., Nazeemudeen, A., Househ, M., & Abd-Alrazaq, A. (2020). The benefits and threats of blockchain technology in healthcare: A scoping review. *International Journal of Medical Informatics, 142*104246.

Attaran, M. (2022). Blockchain technology in healthcare: Challenges and opportunities. *International Journal of Healthcare Management, 15*(1), 70–83.

Baker, S. B., Xiang, W., & Atkinson, I. (2017). Internet of things for smart healthcare: Technologies, challenges, and opportunities. *IEEE Access, 5*, 26521–26544.

Bhatt, P. C., Kumar, V., Lu, T.-C., & Daim, T. (2021). Technology convergence assessment: Case of blockchain within the IR 4.0 platform. *Technology in Society, 67*101709.

Burstin, H., Leatherman, S., & Goldmann, D. (2016). The evolution of healthcare quality measurement in the United States. *Journal of Internal Medicine, 279*(2), 154–159.

Chamola, V., Goyal, A., Sharma, P., Hassija, V., Binh, H. T. T., & Saxena, V. (2023). Artificial intelligence-assisted blockchain-based framework for smart and secure EMR management. *Neural Computing and Applications, 35*(31), 22959–22969.

Fatoum, H., Hanna, S., Halamka, J. D., Sicker, D. C., Spangenberg, P., & Hashmi, S. K. (2021). Blockchain integration with digital technology and the future of health care ecosystems: systematic review. *Journal of Medical Internet Research, 23*(11), e19846.

Golec, M., Gill, S. S., Golec, M., Xu, M., Ghosh, S. K., Kanhere, S. S., Rana, O., & Uhlig, S. (2023). BlockFaaS: Blockchain-enabled serverless computing framework for AI-driven IoT healthcare applications. *Journal of Grid Computing 21, no. 4*, 63.

Haddad, A., Habaebi, M. H., Islam, M. R., Hasbullah, N. F., & Zabidi, S. A. (2022). Systematic review on ai-blockchain based e-healthcare records management systems. *IEEE Access*, *10*, 94583–94615.

Holzinger, A., Röcker, C., & Ziefle, M. (2015). From smart health to smart hospitals. *Smart Health: Open Problems and Future Challenges*, 1–20.

Kang, M., Park, E., Cho, B. H., & Lee, K.-S. (2018). Recent patient health monitoring platforms incorporating internet of things-enabled smart devices. *International Neurourology Journal*, *22*(Suppl 2), S76.

Karunarathne, S. M., Saxena, N., & Khan, M. K. (2021). Security and privacy in IoT smart healthcare. *IEEE Internet Computing*, *25*(4), 37–48.

Krittanawong, C., Aydar, M., Hassan Virk, H. U., Kumar, A., Kaplin, S., Guimaraes, L., Wang, Z., & Halperin, J. L. (2022). Artificial intelligence-powered blockchains for cardiovascular medicine. *Canadian Journal of Cardiology*, *38*(2), 185–195.

Kumar, R., Arjunaditya., Singh, D., Srinivasan, K., & Hu, Y.-C. (2022). AI-powered blockchain technology for public health: A contemporary review, open challenges, and future research directions. *Healthcare*, *11* (1), 81.

Kwon, H., An, S., Lee, H.-Y., Cha, W. C., Kim, S., Cho, M., & Kong, H.-J. (2022). Review of smart hospital services in real healthcare environments. *Healthcare Informatics Research*, *28*(1), 3–15.

Lenz, R., & Kuhn, K. A. (2004). Towards a continuous evolution and adaptation of information systems in healthcare. *International Journal of Medical Informatics*, *73*(1), 75–89.

Lobo, V. B., Analin, J., Laban, R. M., & More, S. S. (2020). *Convergence of blockchain and artificial intelligence to decentralize healthcare systems. 2020 Fourth international conference on computing methodologies and communication (ICCMC)* (pp. 925–931). IEEE.

Nasr, M., Islam, M. M., Shehata, S., Karray, F., & Quintana, Y. (2021). Smart healthcare in the age of AI: recent advances, challenges, and future prospects. *IEEE Access*, *9*, 145248–145270.

Nidhya, R., Kumar, M., Maheswar, R., & Pavithra, D. (2022). Security and privacy issues in smart healthcare system using internet of things. *IoT-Enabled Smart Healthcare Systems, Services and Applications*, 63–85.

Rajawat, A. S., Bedi, P., Goyal, S. B., Shaw, R. N., Ghosh, A., & Aggarwal, S. (2022). Ai and blockchain for healthcare data security in smart cities. *AI and IoT for Smart City Applications*, 185–198.

Singh, S., Sharma, S. K., Mehrotra, P., Bhatt, P., & Kaurav, M. (2022). Blockchain technology for efficient data management in healthcare system: Opportunity, challenges and future perspectives. *Materials Today: Proceedings*, *62*, 5042–5046.

Tian, S., Yang, W., Le Grange, J. M., Wang, P., Huang, W., & Ye, Z. (2019). Smart healthcare: making medical care more intelligent. *Global Health Journal*, *3*(3), 62–65.

Tuli, S., Tuli, S., Wander, G., Wander, P., Gill, S. S., Dustdar, S., Sakellariou, R., & Rana, O. (2020). Next generation technologies for smart healthcare: Challenges, vision, model, trends and future directions. *Internet Technology Letters*, *3*(2), e145.

Wang, S., Wang, J., Wang, X., Qiu, T., Yuan, Y., Ouyang, L., Guo, Y., & Wang, F.-Y. (2018). Blockchain-powered parallel healthcare systems based on the ACP approach. *IEEE Transactions on Computational Social Systems*, *5*(4), 942–950.

Xie, Y., Lu, L., Gao, F., He, S.-jiang, Zhao, H.-juan, Fang, Y., Yang, J.-ming, An, Y., Ye, Z.-wei, & Dong, Z. (2021). Integration of artificial intelligence, blockchain, and wearable technology for chronic disease management: A new paradigm in smart healthcare. *Current Medical Science*, *41*, 1123–1133.

CHAPTER

Intelligent health care: applications of artificial intelligence and machine learning in computational medicine

7

Veenadhari Bhamidipaty[1], Durgananda Lahari Bhamidipaty[2], Fayaz S.M[2], K.D.P. Bhamidipaty[3] and Rajesh Botchu[4]

[1]Department of Computer Science and Engineering, Gitam Institute of Technology, Visakhapatnam, Andhra Pradesh, India [2]Department of Biotechnology, Manipal Institute of Technology, Manipal, Karnataka, India [3]Department of Radiology, GIMSR, Visakhapatnam, Andhra Pradesh, India [4]Department of Musculoskeletal Radiology, Royal Orthopedic Hospital, Birmingham, United Kingdom

7.1 Introduction

7.1.1 AI and ML's foundations in health/cancer care

Healthcare has seen a significant transformation thanks to artificial intelligence (AI) and machine learning (ML), which offer the ability to analyze massive datasets for purposes like classification, prediction, or drawing insightful conclusions. While ML focuses on statistical models trained on real-world data to predict outcomes, AI includes a variety of computer algorithms. From clinical decision-making tools to the analysis of electronic medical records (EMRs), these technologies are being incorporated into many facets of healthcare. AI's capacity to manage "Big Data," which is defined by volume, velocity, variety, authenticity, and value, is the foundation for its use in the healthcare industry.

Big Data analytics can boost research skills outside of typical clinical trial settings, which can lead to better medical outcomes. However, due to privacy concerns, there is still skepticism over successful adoption. Big Data analytics and ML have the potential to significantly enhance clinical decision-making procedures in intensive care units (ICUs), where enormous volumes of data are analyzed on a daily basis. Similarly, ML has demonstrated promise in identifying treatment prediction models and patient subgroup clustering in pediatric care related to long-term illnesses characterized by disease heterogeneity, such as nutrition in preterm infants or pediatric inflammatory bowel disease (IBD).

The advances in deep learning algorithms, exponential computing power, and availability of digital patient data like never before have led to a wave of interest and investment in artificial intelligence in healthcare. No radiology conference is complete without a substantial dedication to AI. Many radiology departments are keen to get involved but are unsure of where and how to begin. This short article provides a simple road map to aid departments to get involved with the technology, demystify key concepts, and pique an interest in the field. We have broken down the journey into seven steps: problem, team, data, kit, neural network, validation, and governance. Still, there

Blockchain and Digital Twin for Smart Hospitals. DOI: https://doi.org/10.1016/B978-0-443-34226-4.00008-3

are a lot of obstacles to overcome. Data quality is crucial because inaccurate outputs from low-quality inputs may have a negative impact on patient management. To ensure that these technologies are used fairly, ethical issues pertaining to openness and interpretability must also be taken into account during the development process. New developments such as ChatGPT demonstrate how ML technologies may communicate with users by offering dialog responses that are derived from large training datasets. Its application in arthroplasty, for example, shows its potential usefulness but also points out differences between the answers provided by ChatGPT and those found through traditional web searches. This suggests that more research is necessary before ChatGPT and other similar platforms are widely accepted as trustworthy resources for patients looking for online medical information.

Additionally, chatbots that can understand complicated lab results have the potential to completely change the field of laboratory medicine. However, before these apps can be consistently used, they must first undergo a thorough examination against accepted clinical practices. This emphasizes how crucial it is for therapists to be technically proficient as well as to be aware of the limitations of the AI systems in use today, which have the potential to spread false information, exhibit inconsistencies, and be incapable of reasoning in the same way as humans. Another area where the immutable spatial context may improve the accuracy of spatiotemporal mapping of real-world events and lead to smarter, healthier cities and regions is geospatial blockchain technology. To fully realize blockchain's potential in the health sector, however, interoperability, security, privacy, and sustainable business models continue to be major obstacles.

Overall, these results show that while AI/ML has great potential in a number of healthcare domains, its effective application depends on a number of challenges that must be overcome. These include ensuring that the input data is of high quality, upholding ethical standards during development, addressing security and privacy concerns, and encouraging interdisciplinary collaboration between clinicians and data scientists. Additionally, strong evaluation frameworks must be developed to confirm the validity and reliability of the outputs produced by AI/ML systems.

7.1.2 Explanation and synopsis of AI and ML

The goal of AI, a vast field in computer science, is to imitate human intellect in robots. Algorithms that allow computers to learn from data without being explicitly programmed for particular tasks are known as ML, a subset of AI. Deep learning is a sophisticated ML technique that analyses complicated patterns in data by building multilayered neural networks (deep neural networks). AI/ML has been incorporated into medicine in a variety of ways. Through pattern identification in clinical data, AI/ML in pediatric neurology can help with neuro-oncology imaging analysis and help diagnose disorders like autism or epilepsy. By predicting molecular activity or improving clinical trial design through increased efficiency and predictive capacities, ML has completely changed pharmaceutical research and development. The growth of drug development has also profited greatly from advances in computational techniques made possible by AI/ML technology. Through improved target protein identification during drug design procedures, these methods have shortened the time to market for novel medications and decreased associated costs. Similarly, clinical decision support systems and supervised and unsupervised ML techniques are used by musculoskeletal physiotherapy to improve patient care delivery. AI's capacity to improve prognostication accuracy through the analysis of digital pictures for the diagnosis of oral squamous cell carcinomas among other cancers has shown promise for applications in oncologic histopathology. AI-based solutions supporting laboratory diagnoses such as antimicrobial resistance profiling or public health outbreak monitoring, as demonstrated by the COVID-19 pandemic response efforts are beneficial to infectious disease management. One field where intelligent algorithms are being used more and more is medical imaging. From radiomics, which extracts a lot of features from image data to deep learning models, which can identify pathological findings sometimes better than human experts, these algorithms are being used more and more in this field. When biotechnology research focuses on global issues like food security or climate action, combining biological sciences with the potent computational methods provided by AI can result in creative solutions that effectively address these urgent problems and encourage sustainable practices across all involved industries. Even with these developments in genomics analysis and electronic health record mining for healthcare settings, privacy hazards and ethical problems around algorithmic transparency bias potential consequences when using ML-based systems still exist. In summary, comprehending the basic principles of CADD in conjunction with more recent paradigms such as explainable AI, which aims to provide transparency in model decisions, is essential for promoting responsible implementation and adoption in various life sciences domains, such as precision therapeutics and personalized medicine.

7.1.3 Significance of AI and ML in health/cancer care

In the healthcare industry, AI and ML have become game-changers because of their potential to improve medical research, therapy personalization, disease diagnostics, and patient care efficiency. While ML is a subset of AI that focuses on methods that allow computers to learn from data without being explicitly programmed, AI itself includes a variety of computational techniques that replicate human cognitive capabilities including learning and problem-solving. AI in dentistry has demonstrated potential for using convolutional neural networks (CNNs) or artificial neural networks (ANNs) for image processing in the diagnosis of oral disorders. These are capable of identifying minute details that humans are unable to notice, which enables the early detection of disorders like periodontal disease or dental caries. However, due to issues like algorithmic limitations requiring constant improvement, AI integration into routine practice remains limited despite its potential benefits, which include reduced observer fatigue and increased diagnostic accuracy. AI has a role in understanding complex biological processes in addition to diagnosis. For example, using high alanine aminotransferase levels as a surrogate marker for nonalcoholic fatty liver disease, Genome-Wide Association Study (GWAS) utilizing ML algorithms has revealed genetic regions related to the condition. This illustrates how AI can shed new light on the etiology of disease.

Moreover, compassion is a crucial element in providing high-quality healthcare. A comprehensive scoping assessment demonstrated how AI technologies could enhance therapeutic interactions through virtual health coaching platforms or improve sympathetic awareness among healthcare providers through simulation training to facilitate compassionate care. AI has made a substantial contribution to oncology research by finding biomarkers that indicate how quickly cancer will progress or how well a treatment will work. Research has demonstrated correlations between dysbiosis of the lower airway microbiota, identified through ML analyses, and the prognosis of lung cancer; likewise, activation of the β-catenin pathway, identified through bioinformatics, was associated with immune evasion in hepatocellular carcinoma, impacting the results of anti-PD-1 therapy. Furthermore, sophisticated analytics were used to assess futibatinib's effectiveness against

Fibroblast Growth Factor Receptor (FGFR)-aberrant tumors, highlighting the value of targeted therapy based on genomic profiling made possible by ML techniques. Another example of how ML provides useful predictive information regarding colorectal cancer survival outcomes is the assessment of macrophage polarization within tumor microenvironments through the use of multiplex immunofluorescence in conjunction with digital image analysis. Despite these achievements spanning fields from endodontics to oncology, there remain considerable gaps involving drug–food interactions altering direct oral anticoagulant levels where further ML-based research could provide vital insights. To successfully integrate these various applications, it will be necessary to address existing issues with data privacy, ethical issues with automated decision-making, inclusivity in datasets used for training algorithms, interdisciplinary collaboration between technologists and clinicians, cost-effectiveness evaluation before widespread adoption, and more.

7.1.4 Key concepts: supervised learning, unsupervised learning, reinforcement learning

AI has the potential to greatly advance precision medicine, help with diagnostic procedures, forecast patient outcomes, customize therapy regimens, and maximize operational efficiencies. An algorithm is trained using supervised learning on a labeled dataset with a known output variable.

Using this technique, models can generalize patterns discovered during training to predict results based on fresh input data. Unsupervised learning works with unlabeled datasets in which the model finds links or structures that are present in the data by nature. By contrast, reinforcement learning works by having an agent learn how to behave in a given environment by acting and then getting rewarded or penalized according to how well the action is performed.

Understanding how AI/ML systems modify their decision-making abilities over time in response to new information or changing situations is crucial for developing adaptive healthcare solutions.

These fundamental ideas are what make AI/ML systems so powerful.

7.1.5 Ethics in healthcare/cancer AI

Significant ethical questions that touch both technological innovation and clinical practice have been brought up by the introduction of AI into healthcare. Three general categories of ethical concerns are traceability issues referring to accountability, normative questions involving justice and societal implications, and epistemic challenges linked to the validity of the evidence. AI applications must individually guarantee patient autonomy by addressing data use in informed consent procedures. Given that they have the potential to change conventional treatment paradigms, interpersonal relations between patients and AI systems need to be carefully considered. The equitable distribution of AI benefits presents issues at the group or institutional levels, including the possibility of an increase in health disparities if inclusive management is not implemented. A crucial issue that comes up in the ethical discussion about healthcare AI is data stewardship. Strong regulatory frameworks that strike a balance between innovation and patient rights protection are necessary to preserve privacy and promote interoperability throughout health systems. Furthermore, it is imperative that algorithmic decision-making procedures be transparent to preserve stakeholder confidence, which includes regulators, patients, and physicians. Addressing potential biases in datasets used to train AI models is a further layer of work. This issue is made worse by subpar data or a lack of representation from varied communities, which can result in unjust clinical outcomes. Healthcare personnel need to be well-versed in AI ethics since their role is changing from providing direct treatment to interpreting and supervising technology-enhanced interventions. This change necessitates reevaluating professional competencies in addition to a creating curriculum that includes ethical issues unique to digital health technologies. Furthermore, before widespread adoption into real-world situations can happen, assuring safety in clinical applications necessitates thorough validation procedures beyond laboratory circumstances. Comprehending the enduring consequences of perspectives about sickness narratives molded by engagements with nonhuman therapeutic agents, like embodied AI, in the context of psychiatry or psychotherapy, is part of this. It takes proactive involvement from a variety of actors to navigate these complex ethical landscapes effectively: policymakers must set clear guidelines; developers must consider ethics from the outset of their work; clinicians must promote morally sound practices; and researchers must produce empirical data evaluating the ethical implications as well as the practicality of implementing AI in healthcare settings.

7.2 Data in computational medicine

7.2.1 Importance of data in healthcare

Data is essential to healthcare in many ways; it can be used for early disease identification, personalized therapy, patient care optimization, and overall improvement of health outcomes. CM refers to the use of computational techniques in these large datasets, which has become a fundamental component of contemporary healthcare systems. Many approaches have been used in the field of early warning score systems (EWSs) to create predictive algorithms using clinical data. Data-driven models are indispensable tools in various fields, including healthcare, finance, and environmental science. However, their effectiveness can often be limited by the specificity of the data they are trained on. This specificity arises from the unique combination of predictors and outcomes present in different settings or populations. For example, a predictive model for disease diagnosis trained on data from one hospital may not perform as well when applied to another hospital with different patient demographics or healthcare practices.

To address this challenge, researchers and practitioners have turned to standardized reporting frameworks such as transparent reporting of a multivariable prediction model for Individual Prognosis Or Diagnosis (TRIPOD). These frameworks provide guidelines for transparently reporting the development and validation of prediction models, facilitating better understanding, interpretation, and comparison of model performance across different studies and settings. By adhering to these reporting standards, researchers can enhance the credibility and reproducibility of their findings, thereby fostering trust in the predictive models they develop.

The acceptance and adoption of health information technology (IT) among healthcare professionals, particularly doctors, are pivotal factors in the successful integration of digital tools into clinical practice. Various theories and models have been developed to understand and predict the acceptance of technology in healthcare settings. One such prominent framework is the technology acceptance model (TAM), which has been extensively studied and applied in the context of health IT acceptance.

Holden and Karsh (2010) delved into the application of TAM in the healthcare domain, shedding light on its relevance and effectiveness in predicting doctors' acceptance of health IT systems. TAM posits that an individual's intention to use technology is influenced by two primary factors: perceived usefulness and perceived ease of use. Perceived usefulness refers to the belief that the technology will enhance performance or productivity, while perceived ease of use pertains to the perception of how easy it is to use the technology. According to TAM, these factors collectively determine an individual's attitude toward using the technology, which in turn influences their actual usage behavior.

In the context of healthcare, doctors' acceptance of health IT systems hinges on their perceptions of the technology's utility and usability in supporting clinical tasks and improving patient care. Perceived usefulness may be influenced by factors such as the system's ability to streamline workflows, access patient information efficiently, facilitate communication with colleagues, and enhance clinical decision-making. Meanwhile, perceived ease of use encompasses considerations such as the system's user interface design, navigation simplicity, training requirements, and technical support availability.

Holden and Karsh (2010) examination of TAM in healthcare settings likely revealed insights into the specific determinants of health IT acceptance among doctors. Their findings may have highlighted the importance of factors such as system functionality, interoperability with existing workflows, training adequacy, and organizational support in fostering favorable attitudes and intentions toward health IT adoption.

Understanding doctors' perceptions and attitudes toward health IT is crucial for designing and implementing effective strategies to promote technology acceptance and usage in clinical practice. By leveraging theoretical frameworks like TAM, healthcare organizations can identify key drivers of acceptance and address potential barriers to adoption, ultimately facilitating the successful integration of health IT systems into routine clinical workflows.

They contend that although a significant percentage of health IT adoption or acceptance can be well explained by TAM, there is still potential for improvement through context-specific modifications that make use of belief elicitation techniques. In their assessment of Big Data analytics in personalized medicine, Cirillo and Valencia (Cirillo et al., 2021) noted how automated tools for collecting and analyzing large-scale clinical and molecular datasets have a transformative effect on biomedical research. Their research highlights the breakthroughs in science that are needed to properly use Big Data for individualized care. Hassan's study (Hassan et al., 2022) concentrated on Big Data analytics in conjunction with genomics advancements as the main forces behind personalized medicine. They talk about ML algorithms designed for the analysis of genomic data while recognizing the difficulties that researchers currently confront as a result of the continually expanding datasets. The studies show that efficient use of computational techniques necessitates both technical know-how and careful attention to integrating various kinds and sources of medical information. This allows for more accurate diagnosis as well as customized treatment plans that take into account the particular biological profile of each patient.

7.2.2 Challenges and opportunities in healthcare data collection

The review of the literature reveals important obstacles and prospects in the gathering of healthcare data, especially in the field of computational medicine. As a comprehensive view from standard healthcare delivery sources such as electronic health records (EHRs), registries, patient-generated data, billing and claims data, mobile health apps, and wearable technology, real-world evidence (RWE) is becoming more and more valued at different stages of the drug approval process. In CM, deep learning technology shows promise as a means of deriving significant insights from intricate biomedical data. Deep learning offers end-to-end models that can handle high-dimensional, unstructured data without requiring extensive feature engineering or domain knowledge, offering an opportunity to outperform conventional statistical learning techniques. The Saudi Arabian scenario highlights systemic problems, including a lack of trained medical professionals and a low rate of acceptance of electronic health solutions, highlighting the difficulties some areas have implementing cutting-edge healthcare data systems. Through the use of digital health data, AI is revolutionizing healthcare by improving our understanding of diseases. Nevertheless, multimodal data integration and model interpretability problems are two real-world hurdles brought about by AI that are especially pertinent to the field of computational medicine. Studying the prevalence of attention-deficit hyperactivity disorder (ADHD) through administrative prevalence studies with RWE is crucial. This method drives therapeutic courses and service delivery, highlighting the need for effective data-collecting strategies in computational medicine. Notwithstanding apprehensions over the quality and consistency of real-world data (RWD), the COVID-19 pandemic underscored the pivotal function of RWE in product development, stressing the necessity of promptly adjusting to incorporate novel data into patient care. While Big Data analytics is revolutionizing the way hypertension is treated through comprehensive EHRs and other sources, it also raises questions about the degree of statistical rigor necessary for computational medicine to be used effectively. Personalized medicine has new opportunities thanks to agent-based computational medicine approaches that use simulation models to mimic individual behaviors in healthcare systems. But before they are deployed, they must be carefully assessed in comparison to real results. In CM, patient-generated health data (PGHD)—such as self-reports and biometric sensor outputs—becomes essential to oncology research and clinical treatment. However, PGHD confronts difficulties with EMR integration workflow redesign and evidential limits in comparison to patient-reported outcomes (PROs). Finally, qualitative research conducted in the Democratic Republic of the Congo has shown how primary care physician services affect integrated district health systems. It highlights the impromptu and unsupportive nature of these services, emphasizing the need for doctors to integrate professionally and their potential influence on treatment acceptability and patient financial accessibility.

7.2.3 Structured and unstructured data in healthcare

The advancement of computational medicine in the healthcare industry depends critically on the integration of both structured and unstructured data. Information that is well-organized, simple to search, and easily accessible in formats like spreadsheets or databases is referred to as structured data. Free text, photos, and any other nonstandardized format that calls for more intricate processing techniques are examples of unstructured data (Goh et al., 2021). Although they are excellent sources of health-related data, EHRs frequently combine these two categories of information. It takes a lot of work to normalize and standardize processes to use EHRs for clinical decision support systems, research projects, quality-improvement metrics, and patient care optimization. Apart from deriving valuable insights from the unstructured narratives present in clinical notes, a significant difficulty is guaranteeing interoperability across various health IT systems by using standardized terminology such as HL7 or Digital Imaging and Communications in Medicine (DICOM). For example, utilizing string comparisons and similarity matching based on Levenshtein distance, algorithms have been created to translate drug prescriptions into anatomical therapeutic chemical (ATC) classification codes; additional refinement is required to enhance accuracy. An AI algorithm's ability to predict sepsis earlier than doctors could do so manually using conventional methods shows how promising AI, particularly ML techniques applied to natural language processing (NLP), has been for early diagnosis and prediction purposes when interpreting unstructured clinical notes (Goh et al., 2021). Research shows that automation of quality assessment from EHRs, which is crucial for evaluating compliance with best practices, has good reliability when monitoring specific care procedures with codable data only. Underestimation is still a problem, though, because documentation from nonstructured sectors sometimes needs to be reviewed by hand, or because semistructured documentation can be handled using hybrid approaches that combine rule-based systems and NLP. Additionally, when combined with free-text report mining in addition to coded administrative data, administrative claim datasets using International Classification of Diseases (ICD) coding can be accurate instruments for identifying conditions like adult congenital heart diseases—offsetting sensitivity limitations when describing disease spectrums exclusively via ICD codes. While there have been advancements in automating core measure calculations directly from EHRs, an area that has historically been prone to errors during manual extraction, the heterogeneity across different EHR platforms suggests that more work needs to be done to develop fully integrated solutions that can accurately handle Substance Use Disorder (SUD) treatment records without relying on paper records. High-throughput phenotyping will ultimately require the widespread use of standardized vocabularies in conjunction with reliable informatics models that facilitate the execution of the storage discovery process across various institutional frameworks. This strategy emphasizes the need for policy-level actions targeted at promoting uniformity across healthcare system infrastructures, in addition to technical innovation.

7.2.4 Overview of EHRs

Since they offer a wealth of data for clinical treatment, research, and public health surveillance, EHRs are essential to computational medicine. A number of legislation and regulations that support the adoption and meaningful use of health informatics while defending patient rights have had an impact on the development of EHRs. These documents serve as platforms for sophisticated analytics that can raise the standard and effectiveness of healthcare in addition to serving as archives for patient data (Rosenbloom et al., 2019). Big Data analytics is an emerging topic in medicine that refers to the integration and analysis of enormous amounts of complex heterogeneous data, including genomic information, alongside biomedical data within EHRs. By providing more accurate diagnostics, prognostics, and therapies catered to the unique profiles of individual patients, this integration holds potential for personalized medicine interventions (Table 7.1). The full value proposition that EHRs offer is still not fully realized, despite these possible advantages. Significant obstacles include problems with privacy, security, interoperability between various systems, and user interface design that can lead to mistakes or burnout in clinicians (Rosenbloom et al., 2019). Furthermore, in light of technical developments like mobile health apps integrating with EHRs, it is necessary to update legal frameworks like the Health Insurance Portability and Accountability Act

Table 7.1 Example of electronic health records (EHRs).

Patient ID	Age	Gender	Diagnosis	Biomarker level	Treatment response
001	45	Male	Hypertension	mmHg	Positive
002	35	Female	Diabetes	dL	Controlled
003	50	Male	Cancer		In progress
004	28	Female	Cardiovascular disease	mmHg	Negative

(HIPAA) (Rosenbloom et al., 2019). Usability elements that fit clinical workflows are significant predictors of effective EMR adoption, particularly in mental health settings where extensive narrative recording is necessary. Similar to this, pediatric informatics uses EMRs that are in line with other social determinants, such as genetic characteristics or environmental effects, that have an impact on population health outcomes. This means that EMR designs must have integrated population health information models. Because end-user satisfaction alone cannot ensure safety or performance improvements, human factors engineering principles should be ingrained in the design process. Postimplementation comprehensive evaluations, including cost-effectiveness analyses, are necessary to ensure long-term, sustainable benefits. Through incentives or mandates, public policy plays a critical role in promoting innovation in EHR technologies and guaranteeing fair access for a variety of populations, regardless of socioeconomic status or level of digital literacy. This helps to popularize medical information among consumers on a large scale, which is in line with the larger objectives of achieving health equity in the digital age. Last but not least, usage trends currently show that chronic illness prevalence estimates derived from EHRs can yield results that are comparable to those of traditional national surveys, providing real-time alternatives to traditional surveillance methods and enabling more focused resource allocation for successful intervention prevention initiatives at local and regional levels.

7.3 Applications of AI in diagnostics

7.3.1 Early cancer (disease) detection using AI

The adoption of ML and AI in the healthcare industry has been gaining speed (Syed & Zoga, 2018; Kelly et al., 2022; van Leeuwen et al., 2022; Gore, 2020; Heo et al., 2021; Duong et al., 2019; Nensa et al., 2019; Hung et al., 2020; Putra et al., 2022; Duong et al., 2019). Across a range of medical specialties, including infectious diseases (Syed & Zoga, 2018), oncology (Nensa et al., 2019), cardiology, surgery (Hung et al., 2020), radiology (Putra et al., 2022), pediatrics (Duong et al., 2019), and even during public health emergencies like the COVID-19 pandemic (Duong et al., 2019), AI and ML applications in early disease detection within intelligent healthcare systems have demonstrated potential. AI-driven clinical decision support systems (CDSSs) have demonstrated potential in the field of infectious illnesses, particularly in the areas of diagnosis, categorization, outcome prediction, antibiotic treatment, and treating bacterial infections. Nevertheless, there are still issues because there are not enough assessments that go beyond performance metrics to consider the impact of clinical practice in the actual world (Syed & Zoga, 2018).

Deep learning, a subset of machine learning, has shown promise in the identification of breast cancer by effectively analyzing high-dimensional data through feature extraction from imaging modalities such as mammography or histopathological pictures. Before these tools can be incorporated into standard clinical decision-making procedures, external validation is still required for the technical correctness of deep learning (DL) models in the detection of breast cancer (Kelly et al., 2022). They discovered that typical deep learning models could accurately predict race across a variety of imaging modalities. This unexpected feature presents moral questions about possible biases that could appear when using this technology among different populations without fully comprehending how it might affect results or health disparities and outcomes (van Leeuwen et al., 2022). Within their study group, the inclusion of Social Determinants of Health (SDOH) characteristics significantly enhanced predictive usefulness, particularly for Black patients, but not for non-Black patients (Gore, 2020). Recent years have seen a major increase in the use of artificial intelligence in cardiac computed tomography, with applications spanning from image capture optimization to cardiac event prediction analytics (Heo et al., 2021). Similar to this, AI-CDS systems for identifying children at risk for particular diagnoses or deterioration could be beneficial for pediatric care (Duong et al., 2019). Before there can be widespread acceptance, Chua et al.'s work highlights the significance of overcoming obstacles including biased datasets and inadequate clinical validation (Nensa et al., 2019). According to Rogers et al.'s analysis, as AI techniques are increasingly incorporated into surgical procedures, doctors need to be aware of both their advantages and disadvantages (Hung et al., 2020). The integration of AI in radiology services, which are major cost drivers, has the potential to increase productivity while reducing costs. This can be achieved through the use of predictive analytics to optimize throughput, improve image quality, facilitate interpretation, prioritize worklists, improve reporting efficiency, and support population-level screening initiatives (Putra et al., 2022). It is possible to employ ML during the initial stages of COVID-19 identification and prognostic assessment. Despite having high rates of diagnostic accuracy based on findings from published literature, it is important to remember that further research is required to guarantee robustness before clinician-led judgments are replaced.

7.3.2 Image analysis in medical diagnostics (e.g., radiology and pathology)

Particularly in the area of image analysis, the incorporation of AI and ML into medical diagnostics has had a revolutionary effect. Multilayered neural networks, which define DL, a subset of ML, have made DL an effective tool for pattern detection in complicated datasets like medical pictures (Chan et al., 2020). AI systems have shown adept at picking up patterns in radiology that might be invisible to human sight. In tasks like lesion identification or classification, CNNs, a kind of deep neural network that is most frequently used to analyze visual images, have shown significant promise (Chan et al., 2020; Le et al., 2019), frequently surpassing conventional computer-aided detection systems. One area where AI has advanced significantly is breast imaging. A significant obstacle preventing additional advancement is the lack of large-scale, well-annotated datasets, which are required for building reliable models. Additionally, thorough testing in real-world settings is necessary for clinical application, in addition to evaluations incorporating feasibility and cost-effectiveness studies (Le et al., 2019). Additionally, explainable AI systems that offer interpretable decision-making procedures complying with laws such as the GDPR are becoming more and more necessary (Le et al., 2019). Clinicians must continue to play a crucial role in the development of intelligent healthcare systems that are enhanced by computational medicine applications like predictive analytics for the management of chronic diseases or recommendations for precision therapy. Enhancing diagnostic processes while preserving clinical practice's credibility can be achieved by combining human experience with technological precision.

In summary, research on the subject shows that AI methods, specifically DL, have significantly advanced the field of medical image analysis in a variety of specializations. Even though there are still obstacles in the form of data accessibility and model transparency, current developments point to a time when computational medicine-driven intelligent healthcare will be smoothly incorporated into standard clinical procedures.

7.3.3 AI-driven diagnostic tools

The paradigm of disease diagnosis, management, and patient care has changed as a result of the integration of AI and ML into the healthcare industry. AI-driven diagnostic tools have demonstrated a great deal of promise in terms of enhancing precision, effectiveness, and prognostication across a range of medical professions. Through real-time computer-aided detection systems during colonoscopy procedures, AI has been successfully implemented in gastroenterology to improve early detection rates for colorectal neoplasia. Since over 25% of colorectal neoplasms are missed during screening colonoscopies, such developments are imperative. Similar to this, ML algorithms have been used to analyze wearable device data to forecast ADHD and sleep issues in kids with respectable prediction performance. The use of AI goes beyond diagnosis; autonomous robotic surgery is another field in which it is extremely important. When compared to the manual procedure used by skilled surgeons, an improved autonomous strategy for laparoscopic soft tissue surgery showed higher consistency and accuracy (Saeidi et al., 2022). This suggests that surgical procedures, where accuracy is crucial, may become increasingly automated. AI is especially helpful in managing chronic illnesses because of its capacity to handle large volumes of data in an efficient manner. To predict exacerbations for patients with chronic obstructive pulmonary disease (COPD), for example, an acute exacerbation prediction system that combined wearable device data with ML performed exceptionally well. This could allow for earlier interventions that could enhance patient outcomes. Furthermore, AI-powered intelligent healthcare solutions allow for personalization. After regular use at home, a web-based upper limb home rehabilitation system that combined an ML model with wristwatch data significantly improved the function of stroke survivors (Chae et al., 2020). AI-driven technologies are not just for noninvasive uses; they can also be used for invasive diagnosis. By evaluating electronic health data or using machine learning models on medical imaging, AI opens up new possibilities for early identification of pancreatic cancer, a disease that is frequently detected late due to vague symptoms. The potential applications of AI techniques like deep learning and neural networks for the Internet of Medical Things (IoMT) are numerous and include diabetes control and cardiac monitoring. Moreover, biophysical signals and electronic technology are intimately merged in the developing field of cyber-physiochemical interfaces, which opens the door for the development of personal healthcare devices in the future. Due to inherent selection biases in retrospective research designs, which are frequently employed in the development of these systems, establishing robust verification through external validation using unbiased datasets remains crucial despite recent developments. Further research is also necessary due to interpretability concerns with deep learning models since understanding decision-making processes is essential for safety protocols and social acceptance. Last but not least, and perhaps most significantly, tailoring medical implants—like knee replacements—directly from CT scan data using machine learning techniques shows promise and saves time compared to more conventional customization methods, indicating broad applicability across various implantable device types.

In summary, the integration of artificial intelligence-driven diagnostic tools with intelligent health care is a revolutionary approach that can greatly improve computational medicine capabilities, impact clinical decision-making processes, and ultimately improve patient outcomes. However, the ethical implications of this integration must be carefully considered. Concerns about interpretability arise when using such cutting-edge technology in therapeutic settings.

7.3.4 Case studies and success stories

While the effectiveness of many commercially available AI-driven diagnostic tools is not well-supported by peer-reviewed research, there are instances of success. Innovative CADe/CADx methods powered by deep learning show promise in improving detection rates and reducing false positives in breast cancer screening programs. AI research in dentistry, specifically in dental radiography, is expanding rapidly, showing promise in applications from forensic odontology to caries diagnosis. Despite the current limitations, it is expected that future generations will address interpretability issues and seamlessly integrate into clinical workflows, serving as intelligent support for patient care.

7.4 AI and personalized medicine

7.4.1 Overview of personalized medicine

Personalized medicine's incorporation of AI and ML signifies a paradigm shift toward more sophisticated healthcare systems. Precision medicine is becoming more and more important, and this shift is highlighted by the volume and complexity of biomedical data growing. Beyond human skills, AI's ability to analyze large datasets presents previously unheard-of possibilities for prognostic predictions, personalized therapy recommendations, and illness diagnosis.

The use of computational medicine in genomics and clinical informatics integration for predictive Health care is one important area where AI has demonstrated great promise. Through the use of deep learning algorithms to multiomics datasets that include genomic, transcriptomic, and proteomic information, scientists have started to create models that can predict drug response and disease susceptibility with very high accuracy. For example, genome-wide gene expression profiles paired with chemotherapeutic drug sensitivity data have been used to discover molecular markers for targeted treatment in acute myeloid leukemia using deep neural networks.

Furthermore, CNNs, a kind of deep learning model created especially for processing pixelated input, are used in medical imaging diagnostics as an example of AI applications. Through automated image analysis, CNNs have shown useful in improving diagnostic accuracy in a variety of fields, including oncology and reproductive health. Notably, based on digital pathology pictures coupled with genomic biomarkers, these technologies provide potential not only in identifying diseases but also in forecasting patient outcomes. This is a tribute to the comprehensive approach made possible by AI-driven studies.

Despite these developments, issues still exist, most notably those related to interpretability (the "black-box" problem) and the morality of privacy and bias in training datasets. To solve these problems, Explainable AI (XAI) aims to provide fairness for a variety of populations while promoting trust between patients and clinicians by bringing transparency to decision-making processes.

Moreover, barriers to widespread clinical usage are interoperability problems and regulatory barriers. If the full promise of personalized treatment is to be realized through intelligent healthcare systems, then it is imperative that norms for data exchange be established while maneuvering through intricate regulatory environments. The combination of clinical informatics and medical genomics is a prime example of how interdisciplinary cooperation may spur innovation in the healthcare industry. Recent research demonstrating the range of bioinformatics applications from optimizing semen analysis to improving treatment techniques for children's diseases—all supported by ML techniques—it is evident that computational approaches have the ability to fundamentally alter the conventional paradigms that currently direct medical practice.

7.4.2 Genetic and genomic data in personalized medicine

A paradigm change from the conventional one-size-fits-all approach to healthcare toward individualized therapies based on patient genetic and genomic data is represented by personalized medicine. Leading this change are AI and ML technologies, which provide creative answers to challenging issues in a variety of medical research fields.

AI systems have demonstrated promise in cancer by enhancing diagnostic precision in image recognition tasks, like detecting malignant tumors from radiographic data. For early identification and intervention tactics that have a major influence on patient outcomes, this expertise is essential. Furthermore, by identifying patterns linked to the course of the disease and the effectiveness of treatment, deep learning algorithms applied to omics data types have advanced our understanding of cancer biology. Beyond cancer, AI has transformed drug discovery procedures by allowing for more efficient virtual screening of candidate compounds than as previously possible. Impeding the mainstream deployment of AI is the absence of defined standards for incorporating AI into clinical workflows. One noteworthy work used coupled whole-exome and RNA sequencing data from various tumor areas to investigate the evolution of genomic-transcriptome in lung cancer metastasis. Martínez-Ruiz and colleagues used machine learning methods that combined transcriptome and genomic data to find signals linked to the propensity for metastasis-seeding in primary tumors. This work is a perfect example of how merging disparate datasets might reveal new information about cancer biology and guide treatment choices.

7.4.3 AI applications in treatment optimization

A paradigm shift toward precision medicine, driven by the integration of AI and ML into healthcare, particularly in therapy optimization within computational medicine, has revolutionized oncology. AI holds vast potential to enhance cancer care by refining cancer diagnoses, tailoring treatment protocols based on individual genetic profiles, and discovering new anticancer drugs.

A subset of ML techniques known as DL, utilizing multilayered neural networks to extract patterns from extensive datasets like genetic data or histological images, has shown remarkable promise. Meanwhile, AI techniques effectively manage the complexity of large datasets, opening avenues for innovative drug discovery in oncology, notably for hepatocellular carcinoma (HCC). By leveraging large-scale genomic databases, AI algorithms can explore genomic pathways, identify novel therapeutic targets, or repurpose existing medications for new applications. The application of Data-Independent Acquisition Mass Spectrometry (DIA-Ms) exemplifies the synergy between AI and personalized medicine, offering highly reproducible retrospective analysis crucial for advancing cancer research projects.

7.4.4 Drug discovery and development with AI

AI algorithms significantly impact drug development processes by efficiently navigating large chemical libraries and predicting biological activity profiles. This efficiency reduces the time required to bring novel medications to market compared to traditional methods. However, challenges, including ethical, economic, and regulatory considerations, must be addressed alongside technological advancements to ensure fair access and protect patient privacy rights.

In summary, the incorporation of cutting-edge computational techniques, such as AI, into personalized medicine holds enormous potential. To reach its full capacity and enhance global patient care, careful consideration is necessary, addressing implementation challenges that range from technological constraints to societal implications.

7.5 Predictive analytics and disease prevention

7.5.1 Predictive modeling in healthcare

In the healthcare industry, predictive analytics employs sophisticated analytical methods to forecast future health developments. This synthesis explores various aspects, including disease prevention through AI, identifying at-risk populations, predictive modeling, and AI applications in public health.

7.5.2 Insights from TBI's epidemiology

The Lancet Neurology commission paper provides insights into traumatic brain injuries (TBIs), covering epidemiology, preventative tactics, clinical management, characterization techniques, outcome evaluations, and prognostication enhancements using novel biomarkers and quantitative imaging analyses. Although TBI is the specific focus, the broader discussion encompasses predictive modeling in healthcare.

7.5.3 Identification of at-risk populations

Effective disease prevention relies on identifying populations at risk. The article highlights specific risk factors for TBI, such as alcohol usage and age-related fragility, serving as opportunities for targeted preventative efforts. Predictive models offer potential assistance in tailoring interventions, considering treatment differences based on injury mechanisms.

7.5.4 AI-driven interventions for disease prevention

AI-driven solutions demonstrate the potential to improve healthcare decision-making. For instance, therapy strategies for TBI patients have been customized through automated analysis of intracranial pressure and blood pressure data. Predictive models in AI can contribute to more personalized and effective interventions.

7.5.5 Public health applications of AI

AI applications extend to public health, including extensive observational studies funded by programs like International Traumatic Brain Injury Research (TBIR). These initiatives utilize cooperative research efforts worldwide, combining AI with regulatory compliance and medical advancement through ML algorithms on federated databases without compromising patient privacy.

While the chosen article focuses on TBI, its content underscores the broader significance of predictive analytics in healthcare. The potential influence of these technologies extends beyond TBI treatment, encompassing improved patient outcomes through automated systems optimizing intensive care therapies, federated learning techniques transforming data-sharing procedures, and predictive models incorporating biomarkers and imaging data for increased accuracy.

7.6 AI and ML in treatment planning

7.6.1 Treatment recommendations based on patient data

In recent years, there has been a lot of interest in and development surrounding the integration of AI and ML into treatment planning across a range of medical domains. AI describes robots that can carry out tasks that normally require human intelligence, whereas ML is a subset in which algorithms identify patterns in data to forecast fresh data. Applications of AI in dentistry have demonstrated promise in enhancing patient care, treatment planning, diagnosis, and research. Through the automation of repetitive processes like image processing for diagnosis or treatment result prediction, these technologies offer increased efficiency. Moreover, by using predictive analytics based on unique patient data, they might support personalized therapy.

When it comes to recognizing cephalometric landmarks used in orthodontic diagnosis and treatment planning, AI systems have proven to be as reliable as human experts (Subramanian et al., 2022), indicating that their applicability may extend to clinical decision-making procedures. Similar to this, AI models built on neural networks have the ability to accurately forecast facial beauty after surgery or identify whether orthodontic extractions are necessary. Before these techniques may be completely incorporated into regular practice, there are still obstacles to overcome. Restrictions include problems with data availability and quality, which are necessary for building strong machine learning models, as well as moral challenges with privacy and autonomy. Workflow integration requires overcoming obstacles related to interoperability between various EHR systems. Notwithstanding these obstacles, using AI/ML approaches in healthcare contexts has definite advantages. By automating specific duties associated with patient care delivery methods that are guided by EHRs, for instance, intelligent systems can potentially alleviate the admin

Istrative loads placed on clinicians. This decrease may mitigate certain factors that lead to burnout among clinicians. Furthermore, developments in explainable AI are critical because they shed light on the decision-making processes of these systems, enhancing user confidence and guaranteeing ongoing supervision based on the principles of evidence-based medicine is upheld throughout their use in clinical settings. The application of AI/ML goes beyond diagnostic support; it also helps physiotherapists by supporting automated decision-making based on patient measurement data, improving service delivery throughout the domains of musculoskeletal medicine.

While talking about the use of this technology in healthcare settings, ethical issues must be ignored. The overarching principles guiding the responsible deployment of these technologies alongside ongoing innovations aimed at further improving system efficiencies without compromising care quality standards expected by both patients and professionals providing those services include protecting individual rights and promoting transparency about the use of personal health information.

7.6.2 Adaptive treatment planning with ML

A revolutionary strategy in personalized medicine, particularly in oncology, is adaptive therapy planning utilizing ML and AI (Saeidi et al., 2022). Through a critical analysis of six relevant papers, this synthesis will discuss how AI and ML help adaptive treatment planning. Enhancing image-based therapy planning has been demonstrated to be a promising outcome of integrating radiomics into oncologic patient care. Using data-characterization techniques, radiomics extracts a huge number of quantitative variables from medical pictures that may reveal illness characteristics that are not evident to the unaided eye. An algorithmic lifestyle optimization method was created by Eetemadi and Tagkopoulos to quickly identify individual-level effective lifestyle interventions. This idea goes beyond pharmaceutical treatments but is essential in adaptive treatment frameworks where nonpharmacological factors have a significant impact on outcomes. The last route toward precision medicine that has been investigated is autonomous robotic surgery. Improved autonomous strategies that enable operators to choose surgical plans carried out by robots autonomously—with implications on increasing consistency and patient outcomes through All of these studies show how AI/ML applications can be applied to a wide range of fields. For example, prognostic biomarker identification can guide therapeutic decisions, lifestyle intervention optimization can improve overall health management, drug tolerance predictions can prevent adverse effects, and robotics can improve surgical precision. Precise execution under motion constraints is critical during laparoscopic surgeries (Saeidi et al., 2022).

7.6.3 Surgical assistance and robotics

A major development in the medical industry is the incorporation of AI and ML into robotics, surgical support, and treatment planning. In a variety of specialties, such as dentistry, radiation therapy, cardiovascular diseases (Saeed et al., 2023), implant dentistry, radiotherapy, urooncology, general advancements in dentistry, glioblastoma diagnosis and care (Ibrahim et al., 2023), smart dental practices, and prostate cancer management, these technologies are being used more and more to improve precision, efficiency, consistency, and outcomes. By evaluating massive datasets using sophisticated algorithms that can spot patterns that are difficult for human clinicians to see, AI is being used in dentistry to increase diagnosis accuracy for conditions including caries detection and orthodontic assessments. This improves individualized treatment planning for improved patient outcomes in addition to supporting early intervention. Additionally, robotics is making strides in dentistry, providing enhanced precision for operations like implant placement. ML models that forecast important factors at every stage of the process have significantly improved radiation treatment planning, eliminating the need for trial-and-error techniques and guaranteeing consistently high-quality plans. Comparable developments are seen in radiotherapy, where deep learning methods support imaging analysis, resulting in more precise tumor delineation—a critical component of targeted treatments. Robotic-assisted surgeries have made cardiovascular interventions more safe and minimally invasive; in the meantime, AI algorithms have made it easier to identify diseases early and optimize treatment plans based on the risk profiles of specific patients (Saeed et al., 2023). Urooncology makes use of AI methods like ML, DL, and NNs, among others, to enhance the interpretation of imaging data, support nodal staging or grading schemes, and find appropriate therapies or biomarkers—often surpassing conventional techniques used by medical practitioners. Radiomics combined with genetics via radiogenomics offers an innovative approach that allows classification based on specific mutations enhancing both diagnostic capabilities as well as treatment personalization efforts through predictive modeling regarding postoperative complications or survival estimations (Ibrahim et al., 2023). This is especially useful for aggressive brain tumors like GBM, where timely diagnosis is critical due to its rapid progression rates. To improve overall management protocols and, consequently, patient quality-of-life aspects postintervention, prostate cancer management also makes use of AI's strengths, particularly in areas like image analysis that predict treatment responses and further contribute to stratified patient care. Despite these encouraging advancements, technical difficulties and ethical concerns about data privacy algorithm transparency continue to be urgent problems that call for cooperation among stakeholders, including healthcare providers to ensure that patients' confidence and consent processes are maintained throughout their healthcare journey using AI-augmented modalities, researchers, ethicists, and regulatory agencies must work together to ensure responsible development implementation within clinical settings. To sum up, the integration of AI/ML into medical practice, particularly in the surgical domain, has enormous potential to transform the planning, execution, monitoring, and evaluation of procedures. This will pave the way for more precise, efficient, and personalized forms of medicine that can greatly improve patient care outcomes.

7.6.4 AI applications in radiotherapy and chemotherapy

This constitutes a paradigm change toward more individualized, efficient, and potentially effective cancer care: the integration of AI and ML into treatment planning for chemotherapy and radiation (Avanzo et al., 2020; Nguyen et al., 2022). AI applications in various fields use computational models that can learn from data without explicit programming to optimize the diagnosis-treatment-follow-up chain from start to finish (Avanzo et al., 2020). When combined with deep learning algorithms, radiomics—a technique that extracts a great deal of information from radiographic medical images—has demonstrated promise in radiotherapy, especially for lung cancer. It can be used to predict treatment response, identify nodules, characterize malignancy, and even predict side effects like radiation-induced pneumonitis (Avanzo et al., 2020). Similar to this, artificial intelligence is advancing brachytherapy through innovations like intensity-modulated brachytherapy (IMBT), where high-density shielding designs enhance plan quality; deep learning techniques automating different workflow aspects; novel optimization algorithms for catheter placement; and additive manufacturing for custom applicators. By adding multiparametric quantitative data into oncologic workflows, from disease diagnosis to patient follow-up, radiomics integration could improve image-based planning for liver tumors treated with stereotactic body radiation (SBRT) and enable customized therapeutic approaches. Using AI technologies helps expedite processes while maintaining strict accuracy requirements due to the high dose per fraction regimens characteristic of SBRT, in addition to enhancing target delineation accuracy and organs-at-risk segmentation during SBRT planning phases. AI's impact goes beyond the initial phases of treatment. Deep learning techniques help with real-time adjustments during therapy delivery, whether it is external beam or brachytherapy, depending on anatomical changes identified by imaging modalities such as cone-beam CTs or MRI-linear accelerators. This flexibility is essential because it enables doctors to dynamically adjust strategies in response to changes or tumor responses. Furthermore, another area where AI applications have been investigated is result prediction following SBRT. Predictive analytics can be created by employing ML models to analyze past treatment data and associated results. This allows for the forecasting of individual patient responses, which can help with decision-making before therapeutic regimens are started. AI interventions are beneficial for radiation oncology quality assurance as well. Automated algorithms that have been trained on prior plan measurements can forecast whether new plans will satisfy necessary standards, decreasing the amount of manual labor involved in patient-specific quality assurance procedures while maintaining safety. Challenges such as algorithmic openness, interpretability, generalizability across many institutions, and due diligence addressing ethical considerations relating to data security and privacy concerns still exist despite these developments (Nguyen et al., 2022). Furthermore, before clinical implementation can be widely adopted, thorough validation studies and regulatory approvals are needed.

7.7 Natural language processing in healthcare/cancer care

7.7.1 Extracting insights from clinical notes and medical literature

The ability to extract useful information from unstructured clinical notes and medical literature has made NLP a game-changer in the healthcare industry. Free-text data is transformed into structured formats by NLP algorithms so that it can be subjected to large-scale computer analysis. Because most of the data created in EHRs is unstructured and therefore underutilized, this feature is essential. NLP has a wide range of applications in the healthcare industry, including text summarization, medical note classification, clinical entity recognition, information extraction, translation between medical languages, and other custom applications. DL-based methods, in particular, have made significant progress in clinical NLP by utilizing word embeddings like word2vec and complicated neural network topologies like recurrent neural networks. The domain-specific adaptation known as BioBERT is exemplified by Bidirectional Encoder Representations from Transformers (BERT), a pretrained language model, which has been refined on biomedical corpora, leading to notable gains in performance for various biomedical text-mining tasks, including named entity recognition and relation extraction. This emphasizes how crucial domain-specific training is to attaining high accuracy when working with a specific language that is unique to the biomedical field. Even with these developments, problems still exist. Data imbalance problems are common; a lot of machine learning models do not have strong evaluations against unbalanced datasets, which might distort prediction performance. Furthermore, methods for managing the linguistic subtleties unique to subfields such as metabolic pathway mining or radiation oncology—where nonstandard nomenclature and heavy jargon usage are common—are needed. When automatically extracting data from narratives using text-mining methods, traceability back to the original document sources is ensured by incorporating provenance metadata into the collected information. Additionally, innovations like BioBERT show how pretraining on domain-specific corpora improves algorithm comprehension of complex texts compared to generic models trained just on general-domain corpora. There is potential for text mining outside of conventional therapeutic contexts. Urban research uses NLP in a methodical manner to examine public health data and governance documents. This enhances city management by facilitating well-informed decision-making processes that arise from extensive textual analyses. Further highlighting efforts to harmonize outputs from commercial text-mining tools with leading clinical information model standards is the integration with semantic standards such as FHIR. This integration not only facilitates interoperability across disparate systems but also embeds critical metadata describing the generative processes behind FHIR instances obtained from clinical narratives. Future developments in the domains of ecology and evolutionary biology point to the unrealized potential for the application of computer techniques based on NLP, which could lead to improved data synthesis efficiency and the formalization of research bias analyses and knowledge gap detection.

7.7.2 Improving patient–doctor communication with NLP

A rapidly developing topic, the integration of NLP into patient–doctor communication has the potential to transform healthcare interactions through the improvement of understanding, improvement of diagnostic accuracy, and the personalization of patient care. NLP systems have the ability to analyze human language and derive insights and patterns that have practical applications in the medical field. To train nurses in communication skills. This application trained voice chatbots to appear as three-dimensional avatars by using Google Cloud's Dialog Flow as an NLP engine. Through interactions with these virtual patients (VPs), nursing students engaged in learning objectives-related scenarios, such as judging pain and demonstrating empathy. The research emphasized the significance of real-world learning settings led by VPs in raising confidence and self-efficacy before actual clinical assignments. The International Health Congress proceedings from IPLeiria offered insight into a range of health-related subjects, including the use of technology in healthcare settings. Though not directly, it highlights the increased interest in using technology to address health service concerns, even though it is not specifically focused on NLP. Fundamental themes emerge from the synthesis of these sources, including the necessity of providing healthcare professionals with adequate communication training, technological innovation intended to supplement established practices, and the possible influence of advanced analytics derived from natural language data on care quality. With the usage of VPs, interactive simulation-based learning is becoming more prevalent, and NLP is essential to producing realistic scenarios that closely resemble real-world discussions. In addition to providing practitioners with greater preparation, this approach offers countless practice opportunities without the added financial burden of standardized patient care. Moreover, the adoption of speech-based Human Activity Recognition (HAR) systems is a step in the right direction toward clinical documentation process automation. Automation of this kind might significantly lessen the administrative workload for medical professionals while also recording subtle features of patient-provider interactions that could be used to guide quality-improvement initiatives. These developments suggest a changing environment in which digital instruments with advanced NLP capabilities are essential components that aid in healthcare professional education as well as operational efficiency in clinical settings. However, issues with expectations management, technology constraints, content creation, and protecting privacy when using HAR systems based on verbal communications still exist. All things considered, using NLP in patient–doctor communication has potential, but it will need constant improvement in addition to strict testing procedures to prove its usefulness in a variety of healthcare settings.

7.7.3 Case studies on NLP applications in healthcare

A developing field at the intersection of linguistics, clinical practice, and AI is the application of NLP in healthcare. NLP systems are a subset of AI technologies that analyze language to identify patterns and insights that are significant. For example, using a variety of data sources including EHRs, mood rating scales, brain imaging data, new monitoring systems like smartphones or video recordings, and social media platforms, ML algorithms applied through NLP can predict or classify mental health illnesses. Systematic scoping assessments have assessed the integration of NLP into community-based primary health care, demonstrating its potential for disease management and surveillance as well as pointing out notable differences in reporting approaches. In many applications, neural networks have proven to be highly accurate; yet, worries about biases resulting from demographic characteristics like sex and ethnicity have been voiced. Regarding the assessment of psychometrics in psychosis research, particularly in relation to tracking paranoia using smartphone "selfies," there is data that supports criterion validity when controlling for variables such as location context while recording. However, because of possible generalized deficiencies across multiple cognitive domains, issues with test–retest reliability and divergent validity still exist. Additionally, the creation and improvement of taxonomies for behavior change interventions through the application of NLP techniques highlight the significance of both identifying the content of interventions and promoting international collaboration in the pursuit of more efficacious interventions targeted at enhancing global health outcomes. Surgeons can improve patient safety outcomes by using NLP in surgical process modeling to address workflow disruptions in the current information communication technology infrastructures used in operating rooms. This can be done from an operational perspective to help understand complex procedures. In addition to identifying clusters where mHealth research focuses on everything from lifestyle management clinical research to sensor-based device innovation, text-mining analysis has revealed trends indicating shifts from mobile phone usage terminology toward smartphone apps reflecting technological advancements over time. Comprehensive psychometric evaluations that take into account factors influencing reliability validity and mitigate biases arising from demographic differences are necessary to fully realize the potential offered by Big Data analytics enabled through ML/NLP methods. This will ensure equitable deployment across diverse populations and ultimately lead to personalized medicine approaches that are tailored according to individual needs and preferences, ultimately optimizing healthcare delivery models globally. In summary, although there is encouraging data demonstrating the effectiveness of use cases involving the application of ML/NLP techniques across a range of healthcare domain aspects, critical assessments concentrating on psychometric properties, such as test–retest reliability and divergent validity, must be conducted methodically to address the current barriers to the widespread clinical adoption of these novel tools.

7.8 Biotechnology and industrial biotechnology

7.8.1 Applications of artificial intelligence and machine learning in biochemical engineering

The amalgamation of AIML and Biochemical engineering can have a transmutive impact in handling complex biological systems and environmental challenges (Zhang et al., 2023). Advances in AI have rendered it conceivable for engineers to develop sophisticated algorithms that are capable of identifying patterns in enormous databases that are frequently inaccessible to human analysts. Artificial intelligence has been applied to environmental microbiology to optimize waste management, avoidance of pollution, and biochar synthesis. More efficient workflow controls and optimization approaches can result through machine learning models' capabilities to forecast outcomes based on an array of inputs, such as material characteristics or operational variables.

It is particularly pertinent to keep at heart for evaluating the complex relationships among environmental variables and microbial dynamics in fermentative biohydrogen production—a process in which machine learning holds promise in terms of boosting prediction accuracy. Another area of application is in personalized medicine, notably in the treatment of cancer, where machine learning algorithms incorporate clinical and genomic data to forecast the course of a patient's specific disease progression or how well a patient would respond to medication (Cho et al., 2023). These resources are extremely helpful to physicians when they are determining customized treatment programs. It is imperative to take into thought not just the technical viability but also the ethical ramifications of embedding artificial intelligence into biological systems. As we move closer to developing biologically-based computing entities that are more autonomous, concerns about control, autonomy, and unanticipated consequences begin to surface, much like those brought up by nonbiological AI.

7.8.2 Applications of artificial intelligence and machine learning in synthetic biology

DL, a subset of ML characterized by multilayered neural networks, has shown promise in predicting molecules with antibacterial activity. AI might identify biological features relevant to structural prediction. AI algorithms have been successfully employed in drug discovery protocols including peptide synthesis and ligand-based virtual screening to forecast toxicity or potential for drug repositioning. The significance of neural networks in the pharmaceutical pipeline at different stages. It implies workflows in synthetic biology that involve complex datasets could be transformed by employing comparable approaches. AI has the potential for intelligent behavior modeling with little assistance from humans, a concept that can be applied in numerous areas of medicine, including synthetic biology where automation is increasingly sought after for experimental design and hypothesis testing. The recent breakthroughs in medical AI systems could inform approaches within synthetic biology—particularly regarding digitized data management and predictive analytics based on omics datasets which are central resources within the field. Challenges associated with implementing ML models such as interpretability issues or dataset reliability concerns—areas equally pertinent when applying these methods within synthetic biology contexts like gene circuit design or metabolic pathway optimization. Radiomics' potential applications using neuroimaging techniques powered by machine learning algorithms; similarly, advanced imaging analysis could aid in cellular component identification crucial for tasks like chassis cell selection or organelle targeting within engineered organisms. Applications of deep learning in mammography concerning algorithmic performance optimization could lead to better processes for training models of complicated biological systems that are encountered in initiatives involving synthetic biology. Not only feasibility but also tangible benefits derived from integrating sophisticated computational models into biotechnological endeavors. Advancements made possible due to enhanced pattern recognition capabilities inherent within DL frameworks capable of handling vast amounts of heterogeneous data typical within life sciences research today.

7.8.3 Applications of artificial intelligence and machine learning in precision agriculture

The integration of AI and ML into precision agriculture is revolutionizing how we approach farming, offering solutions that are more efficient, sustainable, and productive (Liakos et al., 2018). AI-driven precision agriculture leverages high-performance computing and Big Data analytics to optimize crop management through yield prediction, disease detection, weed detection, quality assessment, and species recognition (Liakos et al., 2018), as well as livestock management by improving welfare assessments and production systems. In specialty crops specifically, AI applications have been instrumental in enhancing various aspects such as pest control strategies and optimizing resource use. Innovations in remote sensing technologies combined with computer vision enable real-time monitoring that facilitates immediate decision-making based on accurate field data. The digital transformation in livestock farming has seen the implementation of biometric techniques using AI for health assessment. This advancement reduces reliance on subjective visual inspections by professionals while increasing efficiency through noncontact methods that can monitor physiological parameters associated with animal welfare. Biological sciences have also benefited significantly from AI applications beyond traditional fields. In agriculture specifically, farmers are utilizing these technologies to reduce waste and increase output efficiently—shortening the time needed to bring products to market. Machine learning algorithms play a crucial role here; they intelligently analyze large-scale datasets leading to smart automation within agricultural systems. Furthermore, IoT technology integrated with ML is paving the way toward smarter microalgae farming—a practice essential for sustainable agriculture due to its requirement for precise environmental condition monitoring during cultivation stages. These advancements highlight how critical it is not only to develop effective models but also to ensure their deployment within commercial settings. Next-generation breeding strategies incorporate genomic-assisted breeding (GAB) and CRISPR/Cas genome editing systems along with high-throughput phenotyping approaches driven by AI/ML tools like prime editing or base editing. Such integrations aim at developing climate-resilient crops capable of meeting future global food demands under changing environmental conditions. Phenomics—the study of phenotypes on a large scale—is another area where AI's impact has been profound. Image analysis enhanced by machine learning helps manage vast amounts of phenotype data collected via noninvasive imaging techniques more effectively than ever before. Open-source devices powered by AI facilitate community-driven research efforts across different domains including plant science. DL, a subset of ML characterized by its ability to extract features autonomously from complex datasets without explicit programming, has shown promise in Systems Medicine (SM)—analogous areas could be explored within precision agriculture for predictive modeling-related tasks such as forecasting crop yields or identifying stress factors affecting plant growth. Finally, yet importantly, is the consideration given toward ensuring these technological advances deliver tangible clinical impacts while addressing interpretability issues—an aspect equally important when applying DL within SM contexts. As precision agriculture continues evolving toward complete digitalization or automation through next-generation multidisciplinary platforms integrating diverse tools including GABs alongside speed breeding methodologies supported by advanced computational resources—its potential seems boundless.

7.8.4 Applications of artificial intelligence and machine learning in structural bioinformatics

The integration of AI and ML into structural bioinformatics has revolutionized the field by enabling the analysis of complex biological data at an unprecedented scale and depth. This synthesis will focus on fundamental themes such as protein structure prediction, cancer diagnosis and prognosis through omics data analysis, drug design optimization using deep learning methods, miRNA tool development trends, geometric deep learning for RNA structure elucidation, AI's role in diabetes care management which indirectly relates to understanding disease mechanisms at a molecular level. One cornerstone application is the accurate prediction of protein structures. AlphaFold's neural network-based model demonstrates how incorporating physical knowledge about protein structure can lead to predictions with atomic accuracy even when no similar structures are known. This represents a significant leap forward in addressing the gap between known protein sequences and their corresponding structures. In oncology, deep learning techniques have been applied successfully across various domains including image recognition tasks in radiology, genomic analysis for cancer diagnosis (Tran et al., 2021), treatment selection, and even creating decision support tools integrating different omics data types (Tran et al., 2021). These approaches facilitate personalized medicine by allowing more precise predictions regarding disease progression and response to therapy. Drug design has also benefited greatly from AI advancements. Techniques like machine learning algorithms have improved virtual screening processes for lead identification while ensuring resource optimization during drug discovery phases (Patel et al., 2020). Moreover, there is growing interest in employing deep learning models that can predict ADME/T properties effectively without extensive experimental testing. The development trends within miRNA bioinformatics tools illustrate how classic machine learning methods remain valuable but are increasingly complemented by novel approaches such as those involving disease-associated analyses. Similarly important is geometric deep learning which has shown potential not only for predicting RNA structures but could also be applicable across diverse scientific disciplines beyond biology alone due to its reliance solely on atomic coordinates without necessitating domain-specific information inputs. While these applications demonstrate considerable progress brought about by AI/ML technologies within structural bioinformatics specifically—and biomedical research generally—there remain challenges related to the explainability of models as well as ethical considerations surrounding patient data privacy when utilizing these powerful computational tools. Nevertheless, it is clear that AI/ML methodologies hold transformative potential for advancing our understanding of complex biological systems at both macroscopic (e.g., clinical outcomes) and microscopic (e.g., molecular interactions) levels.

7.8.5 Applications of artificial intelligence and machine learning in comparative genomics

The integration of AI and ML into comparative genomics is revolutionizing our approach to understanding biological complexity across different species (Gupta et al., 2021). Comparative genomics involves comparing genomic features such as DNA sequences, gene structures, regulatory regions, and genomic architecture between different organisms to understand evolutionary relationships and functional biology. One fundamental application is in the area of oncology where deep learning algorithms have been employed for predictive modeling using omics data types like genomics, methylation patterns, transcriptomic data as well as histopathological images. These models help identify prognostic biomarkers that can be used for cancer diagnosis or predicting patient responses to treatments like immunotherapy. In drug discovery processes such as peptide synthesis or ligand-based virtual screening, AI has shown the potential to reduce time consumption while improving efficacy by analyzing complex datasets derived from high-throughput screenings (Gupta et al., 2021). This approach enables researchers to predict pharmacokinetic properties or potential off-target effects early in the development process. Deep learning techniques have also been applied successfully for integrative analysis combining histology with genomic data. Employing weakly supervised multimodal deep learning algorithms capable of fusing heterogeneous modalities like whole-slide images with molecular profile data across multiple cancer types has led not only to outcome predictions but also facilitated the identification of morphological correlates associated with patient prognosis at both disease-specific and individual levels. Furthermore, precision medicine leverages machine learning methods for multimodal data integration allowing detailed analyses leading toward personalized healthcare strategies. Machine learning's ability to handle large datasets facilitates broad analysis resulting in an enhanced understanding which could translate into better disease prediction models or therapeutic interventions tailored specifically for individual patients' genetic makeup. However significant challenges remain; one being explainability issues within deep learning models which hinder clinical translation due to its "black-box" nature. Another challenge includes assembling phenotypically rich datasets that are representative enough for model training purposes without introducing bias. Additionally, interoperability among diverse biomedical databases remains a technical hurdle impeding seamless multiomic integration necessary for comprehensive comparative analyses. Despite these challenges, advances continue at a pace evidenced by innovative approaches such as "digital biopsy" wherein traditional assessment methods may eventually be supplanted by AI-driven analyses offering more holistic insights into tumor biology thus potentially benefiting a larger cohort of patients.

7.8.6 Applications of artificial intelligence and machine learning in network biology

The integration of AI and ML within network biology represents a transformative approach toward understanding complex biological systems and disease mechanisms. Network biology involves the construction and analysis of biological networks that represent various interactions among genes, proteins, metabolites, or other molecular entities. AI and ML can process large-scale omics data to identify patterns, infer interactions, predict outcomes, and suggest novel hypotheses in these networks. Transfer learning has emerged as a powerful tool in network biology by leveraging pre-trained models on extensive datasets that can be fine-tuned for specific tasks with limited data availability. This is particularly beneficial for rare diseases or clinically inaccessible tissues where transcriptomic data may be scarce. For example, Geneformer—a context-aware attention-based deep learning model—demonstrates how transfer learning can enhance predictive accuracy across different tasks related to chromatin dynamics and gene regulation. Machine learning techniques like deep learning have been instrumental in studying complex cellular systems such as biological networks. They enable model generation that learns from vast datasets to make predictions about likely outcomes. Challenges at the intersection of ML and network biology include managing multidimensional datasets while extracting meaningful insights into disease biology or drug discovery. In cancer research specifically, AI methods integrated with network biology help elucidate multidrug resistance phenotypes by analyzing large "omics" databases through sophisticated algorithms capable of interpreting interconnected biological networks. These methodologies assist in identifying new drugs or predicting drug-target-system properties crucial for advancing diagnostics and treatment strategies. Systems biology approaches combined with machine learning technologies provide comprehensive insights into plant–pathogen interactions by integrating multiomics datasets. Similarly, phytopathology benefits from machine learning frameworks that dissect plant–pathogen interactions at molecular scales up to network scales. An innovative application is seen where biologically informed engineered features derived from network topology are used within machine learning models to predict cancer gene dependencies robustly; this also sheds light on tumor-specific coordinating mechanisms underlying these dependencies. Network-based analyses are not confined only to human diseases but extend their utility toward understanding complex disease biology more broadly through omics approaches integrated via systems-level perspectives provided by AI/ML techniques. Drug repurposing efforts during crises like COVID-19 have gained momentum through AI-driven network-based approaches which offer faster alternatives compared to traditional de novo drug development processes; these methods utilize proximity measures within interaction networks alongside advanced computational tools like graphic processing units for rapid identification of potential therapeutic candidates against emerging viral threats. Data integration using advances in machine learning facilitates alignment between heterogeneous biological data sources leading toward advancements in both pharmacogenomics and molecular (network) biology fields; it underscores the importance of neural architectures such as CNNs, recurrent neural networks (RNNs), and autoencoders applied across various stages including ligand–protein interaction prediction or compound property/activity prediction within drug discovery pipelines. Finally, predicting synergies between drugs using classification models based on collective effects observed on biological networks emphasizes the role played by complementary signaling pathways captured via ML-derived features—such as overlap distance between perturbed transcriptome profiles—in precision medicine applications.

7.8.7 Applications of artificial intelligence and machine learning in bioremediation optimization

The integration of AI and ML techniques into bioremediation processes represents a paradigm shift in environmental management strategies. Bioremediation optimization using AI/ML involves the enhancement of biological systems' capacity to degrade pollutants through intelligent prediction, monitoring, control, and design. Composting is an essential process within the broader scope of bioremediation where organic waste is converted into valuable compost. Mathematical modeling has been pivotal in simulating dynamic parameters involved in composting to optimize its efficiency. Potential improvements for composting models include phase changes, pH modifications, volume changes, and AI applications. This highlights how computational tools can be employed to refine existing biodegradation processes. Bioelectrochemical Systems (BESs), which utilize microbial metabolic activities for electricity production or consumption during metabolism assistance are complex mechanisms that benefit from AI-based methods such as ANNs and fuzzy logic among others (Li et al. 2023). Li et al. discussed how these algorithms could predict microbial communities' behavior thereby improving BES performance (Li et al., 2023), indicating a significant role for AI in optimizing microbe-mediated degradation pathways. ML can aid in determining optimal conditions for maximal pollutant breakdown by microbes. Artificial microbial consortia have been explored for their ability to produce environmentally friendly alternatives like medium-chain-length polyhydroxyalkanoates (mcl-PHAs). Genetic manipulations coupled with AI predictions could tailor nanoparticle persistence conducive to targeted drug delivery applications. The vast potential is held by integrating advanced computational methodologies within various facets of bioremediation optimization—from enhancing predictive accuracies about system performances under different conditions all the way to elucidating complex biochemical pathways at play during pollutant breakdown.

7.8.8 Applications of artificial intelligence and machine learning in waste management

The integration of AI and ML within waste management has been increasingly recognized as a transformative approach that can address the multifaceted challenges associated with waste processing, treatment, and resource recovery (Aydın Temel et al., 2023; Singh et al., 2023). These technologies offer innovative strategies for optimizing operations, predicting outcomes, enhancing decision-making processes, and ultimately contributing to more sustainable practices. In composting processes, ML algorithms such as ANNs, random forest (RF), adaptive-network-based fuzzy inference systems (ANFIS), support vector machines (SVMs), and deep neural networks (DNNs) have been applied to optimize process parameters and predict compost stability (Aydın Temel et al., 2023). However, it is noted that there is still underutilization of certain AI algorithms like genetic algorithm (GA) or particle swarm optimization (PSO) in parameter optimization (Aydın Temel et al., 2023). Biological wastewater treatment systems also benefit from AI/ML applications. Models like ANNs, fuzzy logic algorithms, RF, and long short-term memory networks have been employed for predictive control of effluent parameters including biological oxygen demand (BOD), chemical oxygen demand (COD), nutrient parameters, and solids content among others (Singh et al., 2023). Model performance indicators such as root mean squared error (RMSE) are commonly used for accuracy analysis in these studies (Singh et al., 2023). Microalgal wastewater treatment represents an area where AI/ML tools hold significant promise due to their potential to manage complex cultivation variables related to physiological conditions or illumination parameters. Commonly used MLAs include ANNs and

SVMs which facilitate large-scale microalgae cultivation by enabling accurate analysis of extensive datasets. Municipal solid waste management has seen the application of ML algorithms across various stages from waste generation prediction through collection and transportation up until final disposal. More than two decades' worth publications indicate a growing trend toward employing advanced technology solutions for sustainable environmental development in this domain. Heavy metal adsorption using modified biochar is another field where AI/ML approaches are being explored. They provide cost-effective means for optimizing adsorption variables thus improving efficiency in removing toxic heavy metals using biochar derived from biomass pyrolysis. Furthermore, Australia's efforts toward adopting AI techniques reflect how Solid Waste Management (SWM) problems can be addressed through technological innovation while aiming at improved economic and environmental outcomes along with social benefits. This includes better forecasting abilities regarding solid waste generation compared to traditional methods thereby supporting enhanced sustainability measures within SWM practices. The use cases extend beyond just operational aspects into design considerations too; robotic techniques based on AI have demonstrated capabilities in sorting reusable materials effectively thus contributing toward circular economy goals by maximizing resource utilization efficiently while minimizing wastage. Despite these advances, several challenges remain prevalent including issues related to data availability, selection reproducibility, and lack of real-world application evidence, among others. Addressing these gaps will be critical to ensuring the successful widespread adoption of intelligent technologies within global waste management frameworks moving forward.

7.8.9 Applications of artificial intelligence and machine learning in drug repurposing

The application of AI and ML in drug repurposing represents a paradigm shift in pharmaceutical development. Drug repurposing, also known as drug repositioning, involves identifying new therapeutic uses for existing drugs. This approach can significantly reduce the time and cost associated with traditional drug discovery processes. AI and ML algorithms have been integrated into various stages of the drug discovery pipeline including target identification, virtual screening, toxicity prediction, pharmacophore modeling, quantitative structure–activity relationship (QSAR), polypharmacology analysis, physiochemical property prediction, and notably drug repurposing (Vatansever et al., 2021). These technologies harness large datasets derived from genomics, proteomics, and clinical trial data among others to uncover novel associations between drugs and diseases that may not be readily apparent through conventional methods. In oncology specifically, AI has facilitated the elucidation of cancer biology mechanisms leading to more successful identification of repurposing opportunities by leveraging "omics" data alongside advanced computational strategies. Similarly in central nervous system diseases—where developing effective treatments is notoriously challenging—AI/ML approaches are being harnessed to improve success rates by aiding tasks such as blood–brain barrier permeability prediction. One significant advantage offered by AI/ML is their ability to analyze complex biological networks. For instance in Traditional Chinese Medicine—which typically employs multicomponent therapies—network pharmacology approaches enabled by AI help elucidate interactions between multiple compounds and biological pathways involved in disease treatment. Moreover, amidst urgent needs such as during the COVID-19 pandemic or other rapidly emerging health crises—the speed at which AI-driven methodologies can propose potential therapeutic candidates through structural biology insights or rapid screening against viral proteins becomes invaluable. However, it is important to note that while these tools offer tremendous promise they are not without limitations. Challenges include scarcity of high-quality clinical patient data integration issues across diverse datasets, interpretability concerns regarding ML models' decisions, and ethical considerations around algorithmic biases among others. Despite these challenges, advancements continue at pace; recent developments include improved algorithms capable of generating de novo designs for molecules with desired properties, better predictive models for absorption distribution metabolism excretion toxicity (ADMET) characteristics enhanced understanding synthetic accessibility routes using quantum mechanics-informed approaches, and so on. All these efforts contribute toward a more efficient rationalized approach toward discovering new applications for existing drugs thus potentially revolutionizing the personalized medicine landscape (Vatansever et al., 2021).

7.8.10 Applications of artificial intelligence and machine learning in clinical trial optimization

The integration of AI and ML into clinical trial optimization is a significant shift in drug development processes. AI can play a transformative role in patient recruitment, protocol design, site selection, monitoring, and data analysis by leveraging predictive analytics on vast datasets from EHRs, social media, and other sources. This approach accelerates recruitment and enhances diversity within trial populations.

In terms of protocol design, AI tools can analyze previous trial protocols alongside RWD to suggest optimal inclusion/exclusion criteria that minimize patient dropouts while ensuring safety and efficacy endpoints are met. These dynamic adjustments during trials could potentially reduce time to market for new drugs. Site selection has traditionally been based on investigator experience and historical performance, but ML models can predict site performance by considering factors such as patient population characteristics and logistical considerations. This results in better matching between trials' needs and sites' capabilities.

Monitoring during clinical trials is another area ripe for innovation through AI/ML applications. Risk-based monitoring strategies powered by these technologies allow for real-time detection of anomalies in data quality or participant safety issues. By focusing resources on high-risk areas identified through predictive models, sponsors can ensure regulatory compliance while optimizing monitoring efforts.

The application of ML techniques to analyze complex datasets generated during trials holds promise for uncovering novel insights that may lead to more personalized medicine approaches. Advanced analytics can detect patterns correlating genetic markers with treatment responses among subpopulations within trial participants, a process that would be unfeasible with human analysis alone due to the sheer volume and complexity of data.

To fully harness the benefits of AI/ML in clinical trials, it requires overcoming significant barriers including concerns over privacy/security with EHR usage, standardization across heterogeneous datasets, interpretability/transparency around decision-making algorithms, integration into existing workflows without disruption, and addressing regulatory expectations regarding validation/usefulness evidence supporting adoption decisions made based on outputs from computational tools/systems.

7.8.11 Applications of artificial intelligence and machine learning in stem cell research

The integration of AI and ML into stem cell research represents a transformative shift in regenerative medicine. AI's capacity to analyze large datasets with complex patterns has been leveraged across various domains within stem cell research, including diagnostics (Du-Harpur et al., 2020), therapeutic applications, bioink formulation for bioprinting (Muhsen et al., 2020), hematological disease diagnosis, aptamer-target binding prediction, cytometry data analysis (David et al., 2019), and pharmaceutical compound data exploitation in drug discovery processes. In diagnostic applications, AI algorithms have demonstrated proficiency comparable to human experts when classifying diseases such as age-related macular degeneration and diabetic macular edema using optical coherence tomography images or pediatric pneumonia using chest X-ray images (Yousif et al., 2022). This suggests that AI can play a pivotal role in expediting the diagnosis process where high-throughput screening is necessary. Stem cell-based therapies are at the forefront of regenerative medicine due to their potential for organ or tissue repair. Herein lies an opportunity for ML algorithms to predict outcomes based on patient-specific characteristics by analyzing clinical databases, potentially leading to more personalized treatment strategies that could improve clinical outcomes significantly. Bioink formulation is another area where ML has shown promise; it aids optimization processes by reducing iterative steps through real-time error detection during bioprinting—a technique crucial for creating physiologically relevant tissue architectures constituted with multiple cell types and heterogeneous spatial material properties (Muhsen et al., 2020). In hematology, ML methods have been applied successfully for image-recognition-based diagnoses utilizing cytometry data that profile the immune system at single-cell resolution with extensive protein markers. Such techniques facilitate high-dimensional data analysis that would be laborious if not impossible without computational assistance (David et al., 2019). Furthermore, structure-based methods like molecular docking simulations combined with ML approaches help predict aptamer-target interactions more accurately than traditional experimental procedures alone could achieve. This synergy between computational predictions and laboratory experiments accelerates aptamer selection while minimizing labor-intensive tasks associated with Systematic Evolution of Ligands by Exponential Enrichment (SELEX) processes traditionally used for identifying high-affinity ligands. Last, deep learning technologies have found application in exploiting large-scale compound datasets generated through High-Throughput Screening (HTS) technologies in industrial pharmaceutical research settings. These advancements showcase how AI can streamline drug discovery by predicting activity profiles against biological targets efficiently. Collectively these findings underscore the versatility of AI/ML methodologies across various aspects of stem cell research—from benchtop experimentation to bedside implementation—indicating their potential impact on accelerating discoveries while ensuring precision medicine practices become increasingly feasible.

7.8.12 Applications of artificial intelligence and machine learning in tissue engineering

AI and ML have rapidly advanced fields such as diagnostic radiology, dermatology, breast pathology (Yousif et al., 2022), ophthalmology, tissue staining transformation, respiratory medicine, plasma proteomics for organ aging assessment lymph node metastasis detection in breast cancer patients using deep learning algorithms compared to pathologist performance under time constraints (WTC) or without time constraints (WOTC). These advancements are now being explored within the domain of tissue engineering. Tissue engineering aims at developing biological substitutes that restore, maintain, or improve tissue function. AI/ML can significantly contribute by optimizing scaffold design through predictive modeling, improving material selection processes via data-driven analysis, enhancing bioprinting techniques through precision control systems, and tailoring personalized treatments based on patient-specific data. In cranioplasty treatment following decompressive craniectomy (DC), AI has been suggested as a tool to accelerate the design and manufacturing process for patient-specific cranial implants while reducing manual intervention. This approach could lead to more predictable clinical outcomes due to its ability to handle complex datasets efficiently and learn from previous cases for improved decision-making in implant fabrication. Machine learning applications are also pivotal in drug repurposing strategies where existing drugs are screened against new therapeutic targets. During the COVID-19 pandemic, ML methods facilitated rapid screening of potential drug candidates including traditional Chinese medicines which may offer novel therapies against emerging diseases like COVID-19.

The integration of AI/ML into tissue engineering is not without challenges; however, it offers several advantages:

- *Design optimization*: By analyzing vast amounts of biomaterial properties data alongside clinical outcomes databases using ML algorithms, optimal designs for scaffolds can be predicted that would best support cell growth and differentiation tailored toward specific tissues or organs.
- *Material selection*: Advanced computational models can predict how different materials will interact with biological systems thereby aiding in selecting suitable biomaterials for specific tissue engineering applications.
- *Personalization*: Utilizing patient-derived data such as genetic information or disease progression patterns enables the personalization of tissue-engineered products ensuring higher success rates postimplantation.
- *Process efficiency*: Automated systems powered by AI can streamline manufacturing processes making them faster and more cost-effective while maintaining high-quality standards necessary for medical-grade products.
- *Predictive analytics*: Predictive models built upon historical data enable forecasting potential complications associated with certain materials or designs thus allowing preemptive measures before they occur during clinical use.

- *Drug repurposing*: In scenarios requiring urgent medical interventions such as pandemics where vaccine development is time-consuming, ML provides an avenue for quick identification of existing drugs that might be effective against new pathogens offering immediate relief until long-term solutions become available. Overall, the level of evidence indicates a strong trend toward incorporating sophisticated computational tools into various stages ranging from product design all the way up through postmarket surveillance within the tissue engineering field indicating an ongoing paradigm shift toward more technologically driven approaches across the biomedical sciences spectrum.

7.8.13 Applications of artificial intelligence and machine learning in health informatics

The integration of AI and ML into health informatics represents a transformative shift in healthcare delivery and management. AI's capacity to emulate human cognitive functions extends across various data modalities within healthcare, including both structured and unstructured data. ML techniques such as SVMs, neural networks, DL, and NLP are instrumental in harnessing this data for improved patient outcomes (Tack, 2019). In musculoskeletal physiotherapy, AI applications have been explored for diagnostic imaging, patient measurement data interpretation, and CDSSs. Studies suggest that ML can perform at or above human accuracy levels in certain tasks within this domain. Similarly, digital pathology has witnessed significant advancements through whole-slide imaging combined with AI algorithms facilitating image-based diagnoses previously limited to other specialties like radiology. AI is also reshaping clinical workflows by augmenting decision-making processes with predictive models that leverage large integrated datasets. This approach holds promise for enhancing translational research outcomes while addressing privacy concerns associated with Big Data utilization in healthcare. In medical image analysis specifically, DL has demonstrated superior performance compared to conventional techniques for lesion detection or classification tasks—sometimes even outperforming radiologists—which suggests potential improvements in computer-aided diagnosis (CAD) systems' accuracy and efficiency. Diabetes care exemplifies an area where AI could revolutionize management strategies through targeted precision care built upon predictive modeling using principles of machine learning. Moreover, ultrasound diagnostics benefit from the implementation of AI technologies capable of automating complex pattern recognition tasks traditionally reliant on manual physician evaluation—potentially reducing operator-dependence errors inherent to ultrasound imaging practices. Public health stands to gain significantly from the application of AI coupled with Big Data analytics; however ethical considerations regarding professional employment implications must be addressed as these technologies become more pervasive within society at large. Breast pathology is another field where digitalization paired with advances in AI offers opportunities for enhanced detection rates as well as refined tumor classification methodologies critical for personalized treatment planning. Finally, cardiac electrophysiology has long utilized simple forms of AI but now faces new opportunities due to deep learning innovations enabling sophisticated electrocardiography analyses that may lead toward virtual heart simulations or noninvasive ablation therapies guided by robotics technology—a testament to how far-reaching the impact of AI might be across diverse aspects related to arrhythmia care alone.

7.8.14 Applications of artificial intelligence and machine learning in remote patient monitoring

The integration of AI and ML into remote patient monitoring (RPM) has been increasingly recognized as a transformative force across numerous medical specialties. In diabetes management, AI has facilitated predictive modeling for risk assessment and empowered patients through digital therapeutics for self-management, leading to improved glycemic control. Similarly, in anesthesia, AI technologies have shown the potential to enhance perioperative care through accurate risk prediction and operating room organization (Bellini et al., 2022). In nursing care settings, AI applications have focused primarily on tasks such as documentation processes while also supporting clinical decision-making. Despite the promise these technologies hold for improving efficiency and patient outcomes, there is a noted lack of extensive evidence regarding their effectiveness outside laboratory conditions (Seibert et al., 2021). Orthopedic surgery is another area where ML can significantly impact patient-specific payment models by analyzing Big Data to predict costs associated with procedures like lower extremity arthroplasty. Furthermore, advancements in mobile health technology allow RPM postsurgery to monitor therapy compliance using passive data collection methods such as range-of-motion tracking after total knee arthroplasty. Teledentistry benefits from AI by enabling remote screening and diagnosis which could shift focus from curative treatments toward preventive personalized dental care. This approach could potentially serve larger populations especially those residing in inaccessible areas. Pharmacological applications have seen fewer widespread implementations at the point-of-care despite existing validated algorithms for precision dosing due mainly to external validation requirements along with logistical challenges related to implementation. Cardiac imaging has leveraged AI not only for diagnostic support but also for generating individualized risk assessments beyond human cognition capabilities—facilitating tailored management plans based on real-time analysis incorporating multiple clinical variables. Environmental monitoring using remote sensing coupled with ML techniques offers significant contributions toward understanding air quality impacts on public health. Such approaches fill spatial gaps left by ground stations providing comprehensive datasets necessary for robust AQ modeling that informs health-related decisions at both individual and population levels. Last, ubiquitous computing advances within Smart Health Monitoring (SHM) frameworks are crucial given rising chronic disease rates alongside aging populations. While RPM via SHM was previously questioned before COVID-19 pandemic constraints highlighted its necessity; now it is becoming increasingly accepted within healthcare systems aiming toward CD management without continuous personal supervision. Challenges persist around architecture design security privacy network issues however prospects remain promising particularly concerning predictive analytics within healthcare empowering patients through data-driven insights provided by ML models developed specifically within SHM contexts. In summary, evidence suggests that while promising strides have been made regarding application scenarios involving AI/ML across different aspects of medicine further research reflecting specific perspectives objectives outcomes benefits remains essential particularly concerning technological societal discourse surrounding ethical legal implications associated with these technologies' usage (Table 7.2).

[Start] --> [Data Collection]

|

v

[Pre-processing] --> [Feature Extraction]

|

v

[Model Training] --> [Validation]

|

v

[Model Testing] --> [Performance Evaluation]

|

v

[Decision Making] --> [Clinical Integration]

|

v

[End]

Table 7.2 Emerging applications of AI/AL techniques.

Application area	AI/ML technique used	Examples of impact
Disease diagnosis	Deep learning, SVM, decision trees	Improved accuracy in diagnosing diseases like cancer
Drug discovery	Natural language processing, GANs	Accelerated drug development through analysis of biomedical data
Personalized medicine	Genetic algorithms, random forest	Tailoring treatment plans based on individual patient data
Image analysis	Convolutional neural networks	Enhanced medical imaging interpretation and diagnostics
Predictive analytics	Time series analysis, reinforcement learning	Early identification of potential health issues and risks
Electronic health records (EHRs)	Natural language processing	Efficient extraction of insights from unstructured clinical data
Telehealth	ML for remote monitoring	Remote monitoring of patients, predictive interventions for chronic conditions
Surgical assistance	Robotics, computer vision	Precision in surgical procedures, assistance in complex surgeries
Population health management	Clustering algorithms, predictive modeling	Identifying high-risk populations, optimizing public health strategies
Genomic medicine	Bioinformatics, genomic data mining	Identifying genetic markers, predicting disease susceptibility, and treatment responses
Wearable technology	ML for wearable data	Monitoring health metrics, detecting abnormalities through wearables
Virtual health assistants	Natural language processing, Chatbots	Providing personalized health information, medication reminders
Clinical trials optimization	Predictive modeling, randomized control trials	Identifying suitable candidates, optimizing trial designs and recruitment
Cybersecurity in healthcare	Anomaly detection, ML for network security	Protecting patient data, detecting and preventing cyber threats
Telemedicine diagnosis support	Pattern recognition, diagnostic algorithms	Assisting healthcare professionals in remote diagnosis
Healthcare fraud detection	Anomaly detection, pattern recognition	Identifying irregularities in billing and insurance claims
Behavioral health monitoring	Sentiment analysis, ML for behavioral patterns	Monitoring mental health through social media and electronic health records
Public health surveillance	Data mining, predictive analytics	Early detection of disease outbreaks, monitoring population health trends
Radiomics and radiogenomics	Radiomics feature extraction, genomic data integration	Extracting quantitative features from medical images, linking imaging characteristics with genomic data
Predictive maintenance for medical equipment	ML for predictive maintenance	Reducing downtime of medical equipment through predictive maintenance
Patient engagement and education	Recommender systems, personalized content delivery	Customizing health education materials, improving patient engagement
Drug adverse event detection	Text mining, signal detection algorithms	Identifying adverse drug reactions from electronic health records and biomedical literature

References

Avanzo, M., Stancanello, J., Pirrone, G., & Sartor, G. (2020). Radiomics and deep learning in lung cancer. *Strahlenther Onkology*, *196*(10), 879–887. Available from https://doi.org/10.1007/s00066-020-01625-9, Epub 2020 May 4. PMID: 32367456.

Aydın Temel, F., Cagcag Yolcu, O., & Turan, N. G. (2023). Artificial intelligence and machine learning approaches in composting process: A review. *Bioresource Technology*, *370*, 128539. Available from https://doi.org/10.1016/j.biortech.2022.128539, Epub 2023 Jan 3. PMID: 36608858.

Bellini, V., Valente, M., Gaddi, A. V., Pelosi, P., & Bignami, E. (2022). Artificial intelligence and telemedicine in anesthesia: Potential and problems. *Minerva Anestesiologica*, *88*(9), 729–734. Available from https://doi.org/10.23736/S0375-9393.21.16241-8, Epub 2022 Feb 14. PMID: 35164492.

Chae, S. H., Kim, Y., Lee, K. S., & Park, H. S. (2020). Development and clinical evaluation of a web-based upper limb home rehabilitation system using a smartwatch and machine learning model for chronic stroke survivors: Prospective comparative Study. *JMIR Mhealth Uhealth*, *8*(7), e17216. Available from https://doi.org/10.2196/17216, PMID: 32480361; PMCID: PMC7380903.

Chan, H. P., Samala, R. K., Hadjiiski, L. M., & Zhou, C. (2020). Deep learning in medical image analysis. *Advances in Experimental Medicine and Biology*, *1213*, 3–21. Available from https://doi.org/10.1007/978-3-030-33128-3_1, PMID: 32030660; PMCID: PMC7442218.

Cho, S. H., Jung, S., Park, J., Lee, S., Kim, Y., Lee, J., Fai Tsang, Y., & Kwon, E. E. (2023). Strategic use of crop residue biochars for removal of hazardous compounds in wastewater. *Bioresource Technology*, *387*, 129658. Available from https://doi.org/10.1016/j.biortech.2023.129658, Epub 2023 Aug 15. PMID: 37591466.

Cirillo, D., Núñez-Carpintero, I., & Valencia, A. (2021). Artificial intelligence in cancer research: Learning at different levels of data granularity. *Molecular Oncology*, *15*(4), 817–829. Available from https://doi.org/10.1002/1878-0261.12920, Epub 2021 Feb 20. PMID: 33533192; PMCID: PMC8024732.

David, L., Arús-Pous, J., Karlsson, J., Engkvist, O., Bjerrum, E. J., Kogej, T., Kriegl, J. M., Beck, B., & Chen, H. (2019). Applications of deep-learning in exploiting large-scale and heterogeneous compound data in industrial pharmaceutical research. *Frontiers in Pharmacology*, *10*, 1303. Available from https://doi.org/10.3389/fphar.2019.01303, PMID: 31749705; PMCID: PMC6848277.

Du-Harpur, X., Watt, F. M., Luscombe, N. M., & Lynch, M. D. (2020). What is AI? Applications of artificial intelligence to dermatology. *British Journal of Dermatology*, *183*(3), 423–430. Available from https://doi.org/10.1111/bjd.18880, Epub 2020 Mar 29. PMID: 31960407; PMCID: PMC7497072.

Duong, M. T., Rauschecker, A. M., Rudie, J. D., Chen, P. H., Cook, T. S., Bryan, R. N., & Mohan, S. (2019). Artificial intelligence for precision education in radiology. *British Journal of Radiology*, *92*(1103), 20190389. Available from https://doi.org/10.1259/bjr.20190389, Epub 2019 Jul 26. PMID: 31322909; PMCID: PMC6849670.

Goh, K. H., Wang, L., Yeow, A. Y. K., Poh, H., Li, K., Yeow, J. J. L., & Tan, G. Y. H. (2021). Artificial intelligence in sepsis early prediction and diagnosis using unstructured data in healthcare. *Nature Communications*, *12*(1), 711. Available from https://doi.org/10.1038/s41467-021-20910-4, PMID: 33514699; PMCID: PMC7846756.

Gore, J. C. (2020). Artificial intelligence in medical imaging. *Magnetic Resonance Imaging*, *68*, A1–A4. Available from https://doi.org/10.1016/j.mri.2019.12.006.

Gupta, R., Srivastava, D., Sahu, M., Tiwari, S., Ambasta, R. K., & Kumar, P. (2021). Artificial intelligence to deep learning: Machine intelligence approach for drug discovery. *Molecular Diversity*, *25*(3), 1315–1360. Available from https://doi.org/10.1007/s11030-021-10217-3, Epub 2021 Apr 12. PMID: 33844136; PMCID: PMC8040371.

Hassan, M., Awan, F. M., Naz, A., deAndrés-Galiana, E. J., Alvarez, O., Cernea, A., Fernández-Brillet, L., Fernández-Martínez, J. L., & Kloczkowski, A. (2022). Innovations in genomics and big data analytics for personalized medicine and health care: A review. *International Journal of Molecular Sciences*, *23*(9), 4645. Available from https://doi.org/10.3390/ijms23094645, PMID: 35563034; PMCID: PMC910478.

Heo, M. S., Kim, J. E., Hwang, J. J., Han, S. S., Kim, J. S., Yi, W. J., & Park, I. W. (2021). Artificial intelligence in oral and maxillofacial radiology: What is currently possible? *Dentomaxillofacial Radiology*, *50* (3), 20200375. Available from https://doi.org/10.1259/dmfr.20200375, Epub 2020 Nov 16. PMID: 33197209; PMCID: PMC7923066.

Holden, R. J., & Karsh, B.-T. (2010). The technology acceptance model: Its past and its future in health care. *Journal of Biomedical Informatics*, *43*(1), 159–172. Available from https://doi.org/10.1016/j.jbi.2009.07.002.

Hung, K., Montalvao, C., Tanaka, R., Kawai, T., & Bornstein, M. M. (2020). The use and performance of artificial intelligence applications in dental and maxillofacial radiology: A systematic review. *Dentomaxillofacial Radiology*, *49*(1), 20190107. Available from https://doi.org/10.1259/dmfr.20190107, Epub 2019 Aug 14. PMID: 31386555; PMCID: PMC6957072.

Ibrahim, M., Muhammad, Q., Zamarud, A., et al. (2023). Navigating glioblastoma diagnosis and care: Transformative pathway of artificial intelligence in integrative oncology. *Cureus*, *15*(8), e44214. Available from https://doi.org/10.7759/cureus.442141.

Kelly, B. S., Judge, C., Bollard, S. M., Clifford, S. M., Healy, G. M., Aziz, A., Mathur, P., Islam, S., Yeom, K. W., Lawlor, A., & Killeen, R. P. (2022). Radiology artificial intelligence: A systematic review and evaluation of methods (RAISE). *European Radiology*, *32*(11), 7998–8007. Available from https://doi.org/10.1007/s00330-022-08784-6, Epub 2022 Apr 14. Erratum in: Eur Radiol. 2022 May 20. PMID: 35420305; PMCID: PMC9668941.

Le, E. P. V., Wang, Y., Huang, Y., Hickman, S., & Gilbert, F. J. (2019). Artificial intelligence in breast imaging. *Clinical Radiology*, *74*(5), 357–366. Available from https://doi.org/10.1016/j.crad.2019.02.006, Epub 2019 Mar 18. PMID: 30898381.

Li, C., Guo, D., Dang, Y., Sun, D., & Li, P. (2023). Application of artificial intelligence-based methods in bioelectrochemical systems: Recent progress and future perspectives. *Journal of Environ Management*, *344*, 118502. Available from https://doi.org/10.1016/j.jenvman.2023.118502, Epub 2023 Jun 28. PMID: 37390578.

Liakos, K. G., Busato, P., Moshou, D., Pearson, S., & Bochtis, D. (2018). Machine learning in agriculture: A review. *Sensors (Basel)*, *18*(8), 2674. Available from https://doi.org/10.3390/s18082674, PMID: 30110960; PMCID: PMC6111295.

Muhsen, I. N., Shyr, D., Sung, A. D., & Hashmi, S. K. (2020). Machine learning applications in the diagnosis of benign and malignant hematological diseases. *Clinical Hematology International*, *3*(1), 13–20. Available from https://doi.org/10.2991/chi.k.201130.001, PMID: 34595462; PMCID: PMC8432325.

Nensa, F., Demircioglu, A., & Rischpler, C. (2019). Artificial intelligence in nuclear medicine. *Journal of Nuclear Medicine*, *60*(Suppl 2), 29S–37S. Available from https://doi.org/10.2967/jnumed.118.220590, PMID: 31481587.8.

Nguyen, D., Lin, M. H., Sher, D., Lu, W., Jia, X., & Jiang, S. (2022). Advances in automated treatment planning. *Seminars Radiation Oncology*, *32*(4), 343–350. Available from https://doi.org/10.1016/j.semradonc.2022.06.004, PMID: 36202437; PMCID: PMC9851906.Nlp.

Patel, L., Shukla, T., Huang, X., Ussery, D. W., & Wang, S. (2020). Machine learning methods in drug discovery. *Molecules*, *25*(22), 5277. Available from https://doi.org/10.3390/molecules25225277, PMID: 33198233; PMCID: PMC7696134.

Putra, R. H., Doi, C., Yoda, N., Astuti, E. R., & Sasaki, K. (2022). Current applications and development of artificial intelligence for digital dental radiography. *Dentomaxillofacial Radiology*, *51*(1), 20210197. Available from https://doi.org/10.1259/dmfr.20210197, Epub 2021 Jul 8. PMID: 34233515; PMCID: PMC8693331.

Rosenbloom, S. T., Smith, J. R. L., Bowen, R., Burns, J., Riplinger, L., & Payne, T. H. (2019). Updating HIPAA for the electronic medical record era. *Journal of the American Medical Informatics Association*, *26* (10), 1115–1119. Available from https://doi.org/10.1093/jamia/ocz090, PMID: 31386160; PMCID: PMC7647238.

Saeed, A., AlShafea, A., Bin Saeed, A., Nasser, M., & Ali, R. (2023). Robotics and artificial intelligence and their impact on the diagnosis and treatment of cardiovascular diseases. *Cureus*, *15*(7), e42252. Available from https://doi.org/10.7759/cureus.42252, PMID: 37605683; PMCID: PMC10440146.

Saeidi, H., Opfermann, J. D., Kam, M., Wei, S., Leonard, S., Hsieh, M. H., Kang, J. U., & Krieger, A. (2022). Autonomous robotic laparoscopic surgery for intestinal anastomosis. *Science Robotics*, *7*(62), eabj2908. Available from https://doi.org/10.1126/scirobotics.abj2908, Epub 2022 Jan 26. PMID: 35080901; PMCID: PMC8992572.

Seibert, K., Domhoff, D., Bruch, D., Schulte-Althoff, M., Fürstenau, D., Biessmann, F., & Wolf-Ostermann, K. (2021). Application Scenarios for Artificial Intelligence in Nursing Care: Rapid Review. *Journal of Medical Internet Research*, *23*(11), e26522. Available from https://doi.org/10.2196/26522, PMID: 34847057; PMCID.

Singh, N. K., Yadav, M., Singh, V., Padhiyar, H., Kumar, V., Bhatia, S. K., & Show, P. L. (2023). Artificial intelligence and machine learning-based monitoring and design of biological wastewater treatment systems. *Bioresource Technology*, *369*, 128486. Available from https://doi.org/10.1016/j.biortech.2022.128486, Epub 2022 Dec 14. PMID: 36528177.

Subramanian, A. K., Chen, Y., Almalki, A., Sivamurthy, G., & Kafle, D. (2022). Cephalometric analysis in orthodontics using artificial intelligence-A comprehensive review. *Biomed Research International*, *2022*, 1880113. Available from https://doi.org/10.1155/2022/1880113, PMID: 35757486; PMCID: PMC9225851.

Syed, A. B., & Zoga, A. C. (2018). Artificial intelligence in radiology: Current technology and future directions. *Seminars in Musculoskeletal Radiology*, *22*(5), 540–545. Available from https://doi.org/10.1055/s-0038-1673383, Epub 2018 Nov 6. PMID: 30399618.

Tack, C. (2019). Artificial intelligence and machine learning applications in musculoskeletal physiotherapy. *Musculoskeletal Science and Practice*, *39*, 164–169. Available from https://doi.org/10.1016/j.msksp.2018.11.012, Epub 2018 Nov 23. PMID: 30502096.

Tran, K. A., Kondrashova, O., Bradley, A., Williams, E. D., Pearson, J. V., & Waddell, N. (2021). Deep learning in cancer diagnosis, prognosis and treatment selection. *Genome Medicine*, *13*(1), 152. Available from https://doi.org/10.1186/s13073-021-00968-x, PMID: 34579788; PMCID: PMC8477474.

van Leeuwen, K. G., de Rooij, M., Schalekamp, S., van Ginneken, B., & Rutten, M. J. C. M. (2022). How does artificial intelligence in radiology improve efficiency and health outcomes? *Pediatric Radiology*, *52* (11), 2087–2093. Available from https://doi.org/10.1007/s00247-021-05114-8, Epub 2021 Jun 12. PMID: 34117522; PMCID: PMC9537124.

Vatansever, S., Schlessinger, A., Wacker, D., Kaniskan, H. Ü., Jin, J., Zhou, M. M., & Zhang, B. (2021). Artificial intelligence and machine learning-aided drug discovery in central nervous system diseases: State-of-the-arts and future directions. *Medicine Research Revolution*, *41*(3), 1427–1473. Available from https://doi.org/10.1002/med.21764, Epub 2020 Dec 9. PMID: 33295676; PMCID: PMC8043990.

Yousif, M., van Diest, P. J., Laurinavicius, A., Rimm, D., van der Laak, J., Madabhushi, A., Schnitt, S., & Pantanowitz, L. (2022). Artificial intelligence applied to breast pathology. *Virchows Archiv*, *480*(1), 191–209. Available from https://doi.org/10.1007/s00428-021-03213-3, Epub 2021 Nov 18. PMID: 34791536.1.

Zhang, J., Hu, Y., Wu, L., Zeng, Q., Hu, B., Luo, Z., & Wang, Y. (2023). Causal effect of gut microbiota on Gastroduodenal ulcer: A two-sample Mendelian randomization study. *Frontiers in Cellular and Infection Microbiology*, *13*, 1322537. Available from https://doi.org/10.3389/fcimb.2023.1322537, PMID: 38156322; PMCID:PMC10753992.2.

CHAPTER

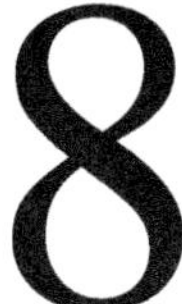

Intelligent machines with enhanced episodic memory for transformation of healthcare

Manoj Kumar Dixit[1], Garima Jain[2], Dilip Kumar[1] and Ankush Jain[3]

[1]Computer Science and Engineering, NIT, Jamshedpur, Jharkhand, India [2]Computer Science and Business Systems, Noida Institute of Engineering and Technology, Uttar Pradesh, India [3]Computer Science and Engineering, Netaji Subhas University of Technology, Delhi, India

8.1 Introduction

The integration of cutting-edge technologies has ushered in a new era in healthcare, commonly known as Healthcare 4.0 or 5.0. This transformative shift adopts a holistic strategy, utilizing state-of-the-art technologies to enhance patient care, streamline procedures, and optimize overall efficiency, transcending traditional healthcare paradigms. At the forefront of this groundbreaking evolution are Smart Hospitals and Smart Healthcare. A convergence of advanced technologies collaborates to redefine the patient experience, forming the core of the healthcare revolution. Intelligent machines driven by Artificial Intelligence (AI) have become crucial tools for personalized medicine, diagnosis, and treatment planning. By employing sophisticated algorithms and deep learning to analyze extensive datasets, these devices empower medical practitioners to make well-informed decisions, ultimately improving patient outcomes. The development of networked healthcare ecosystems is significantly propelled by the Internet of Things (IoT) and the Internet of Medical Things (IoMT). IoT and IoMT enhance remote patient monitoring, preventive care, and data-driven healthcare management. Examples include wearable devices that provide real-time monitoring of vital signs and intelligent medical equipment seamlessly transmitting data to centralized systems. The introduction of Robotics into medical procedures has revolutionized patient care, surgery, and rehabilitation. Robotic-assisted surgeries, for instance, enable accuracy and minimally invasive operations, leading to shortened recovery times and improved surgical outcomes. Additionally, robotic devices assist in repetitive tasks, allowing medical professionals to focus on more complex patient care issues. Moreover, these technologies not only converge at the level of individual devices but also form intelligent systems and platforms that facilitate interoperability, data exchange, and seamless communication. Smart Hospitals exemplify this interconnectedness, orchestrating the entire healthcare ecosystem with an emphasis on patient-centric care and operational efficiency. The combination of Intelligent Machines, AI, IoT, IoMT, and Robotics is propelling the healthcare sector into uncharted territories during this era of Smart Healthcare and Smart Hospitals. These technologies enhance healthcare delivery, making it more responsive, adaptable, and tailored to each patient's needs, ultimately raising the bar for the quality of patient care. We

Blockchain and Digital Twin for Smart Hospitals. DOI: https://doi.org/10.1016/B978-0-443-34226-4.00009-5

stand at the crossroads of Healthcare 4.0 and 5.0, witnessing a future where technology and innovation converge to create a healthier and more connected world.

In this paper, we aim to explore the advancements in computational modeling of episodic memory. We begin by providing an overview of episodic memory, drawing insights from biological and psychological theories. Subsequently, we delve into the latest technical progress in computational modeling techniques for episodic memory. Furthermore, we discuss the limitations of existing approaches and outline future directions to be explored in this field. Throughout the paper, we emphasize the integration of episodic memory modeling within the context of Industry 4.0, highlighting its potential to revolutionize human-computer interactions and advance the capabilities of intelligent machines.

Computational modeling of EM requires a deep understanding of a human's EM to illustrate the technical objectives achieved by modeling. Since past established work of EM modeling is not satisfactory and lacks in covering several essential functionalities, therefore in this survey article we discussed the background of EM and then go through the latest computational work of EM to show the existing research gaps. In Section II, the background detail and the functional objectives of episodic memory modeling in the context of intelligent machines. Section III of the article discusses the past established models. Furthermore, in Section IV, limitations and research gaps are discussed in a summarized manner. Section V presents the direction for the future computational work of EM. At last, the conclusion of the article has been drawn.

8.1.1 Background detail and applications of computational modeling of episodic memory

The section has described the essential background detail of episodic memory based on the biological and psychological research of EM. The detail would help understand the functionalities of EM and how these functionalities can help an intelligent machine do tasks of different domains.

8.1.1.1 Episodic memory and the multi-memory system

The important concept behind current neuro/psychological memory research is the idea of multiple memory systems (Atkinson & Richard, 1968; Hunsaker et al., 2008; McNaughton, 2006; Nadel, 1994; Neil, 2007; Tulving & Thomson, 1973; Tulving, 1972; Zacks & Tversky, 2001). Human memory storage is classified into long-term, short-term, and ultra-short-term memory based on the retention period of information (McNaughton, 2006; Tulving & Thomson, 1973; Yassa & Reagh, 2013) as shown in Fig. 8.1. Episodic memory (EM) is one of them which falls into the category of long-term memory which is a kind of declarative memory (Atkinson & Richard, 1968; Nadel, 1994).

In human psychology, E. Tulving first time coined the term episodic memory for the memory of daily lives events and differentiated it from semantic memory (Tulving, 1972; Zacks & Tversky, 2001), which can store as well as recall the event memory details like the location (Burgess et al., 2002; Dikshit et al., 2022; Morris & Murphy, 1990; Yassa & Reagh, 2013), time of occurrence, persons present in the event, and activities of the event (Tulving & Markowitsch, 1998), etc. Therefore, the EM is said to be highly contextualized in nature (Tulving, 1972). For example, recalling a place where the car was last parked, will require passing the context "car parking" to the EM

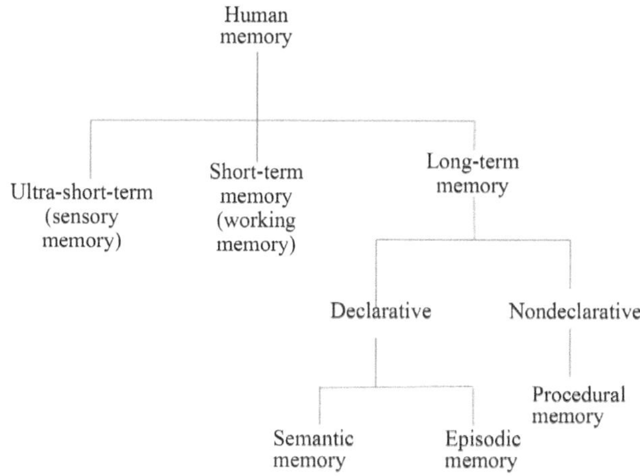

FIGURE 8.1

Multi-memory system.

to recall the event detail i.e. the place where the event has occurred. To recall an event a cue is always required. A cue can be either externally or internally generated that acts as a unique context in which the events get occur (Rifkin, 1985).

In the biological brain research of EM, a significant breakthrough was achieved when the data of several pieces of research suggested that the hippocampus (a region in a brain) and their neighboring cortical areas are involved in the encoding and recall of events (Brom, 2007; Carpenter et al., 1991a, 1991b; Tan et al., 2007; Tecuci & Porter, 2007; Wang & Wenwen, 2012).

Moreover, in the applications, robbers on distant planets take instructions for each action and send the outcome back to earth. The transmission of the signal requires a lot of energy in transmission. Due to the loss of energy, robbers cannot survive for long. Here again, we need an EM-like higher-level intelligence in robbers that can use lower-level sensory detections to construct meaningful information. The robber would then take the action based on the learned knowledge, current meaningful detail of an event, and the predictions of upcoming events.

8.1.2 Event encoding

The critical and very first step after the sensory perception of an event is encoding. An EM stores the high-level details of an event, like "Ram gave a book to Sita". Here transformation is required from the multi-domain sensory perception to the higher-level details. Although, in the field of image and video processing several computational advancements are done. But a question arises in which structure the activated higher-level detail of an event will be recorded in EM.

Knowing about the mental representation of an event or the event structure through psychological research can reveal several secrets of -

- How event activities would be organized in-memory storage as the organization decides how knowledge will be constructed from events.

- How the structural unit of an event would cover all the different contexts of the event because contextually related events make an episode.
- How the mental representation of an event deal with the action planning, inference, and goals.

Brain psychology broadly characterises the events by the taxonomy and the partonomies features (Tulving & Markowitsch, 1998). The partonomy says, like objects, events are subdivided into subparts (Baddeley, 2001; Forbus et al., 1995; Porter et al., 1990; Rolls, 2010). A car has subparts door, windows, and an engine these subparts, in turn, can be divided into subparts. This hierarchical relationship builds a partonomy. Here the event of a smaller time scale would be identified by the physical features, whereas the even the goals would identify the events of a large time scales how the events can be organized in relational hierarchies which in turn helps in knowledge building to use in inference, planning and event recognition (Hintzman, 1984).

In the psychological question answering task, on asking the participant to name the stories on seeing the event activities they tended to use the basic level names, except when the subordinate level name is required to distinguish between stories. Even the time required to answer the basic-level name category is less compared to the subordinate level which shows the event gets characterized in the hierarchical fashion of taxonomy in the human brain (Levenshtein, 1966; Pelachaud, 2007; Yeh et al., 2003).

8.1.3 Pattern-separation and completion

A person records his daily life experiences, many of which repeat themselves with small differences in their activities, for example, doing breakfast daily. In experimental brain research of the hippocampus (i.e. human's EM), almost different activation patterns of neurons are observed corresponding to two very similar events (Shastri, 1999) as shown in Fig. 8.2. The figure is showing that corresponds to two similar events E1 and E2, the activation pattern in the entorhinal cortex is highly overlapped (outer region of human episodic memory), and then the activation pattern gets projected to the hippocampus (Human's EM) for the further processing.

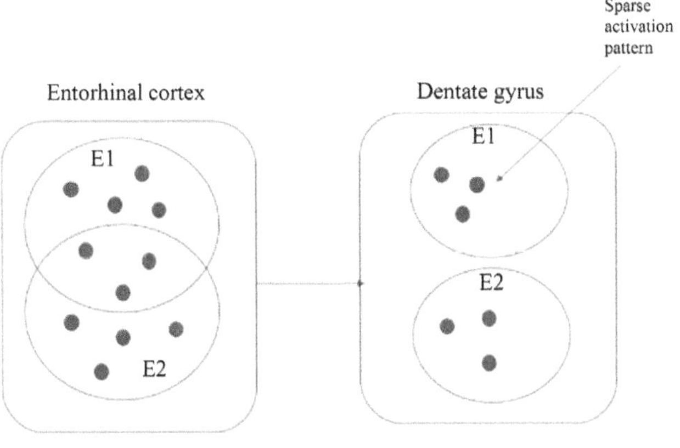

FIGURE 8.2

Pattern separation.

8.2 Applications of computational modeling of episodic memory

The integration of computational modeling of episodic memory with Industry 4.0 has the potential to revolutionize various domains and enhance human-computer interactions. Some notable applications include:

8.2.1 Smart manufacturing and process optimization

In the context of Industry 4.0, computational models of episodic memory can be utilized to improve manufacturing processes. Intelligent systems equipped with episodic memory capabilities can efficiently capture and recall past experiences, facilitating optimized decision-making, predictive maintenance, and quality control.

8.2.2 Intelligent surveillance and security

Continuous surveillance in critical environments, such as airports and borders, requires robust and attentive agents. Computational modeling of episodic memory enables intelligent machines to encode and store high-level information from visual experiences. This facilitates efficient event recognition, retrieval of relevant information, and real-time decision-making in security and surveillance tasks.

8.2.3 Human-robot collaboration

Episodic memory modeling can enhance collaboration and communication between humans and robotic agents in various industrial settings. By enabling robots to store and retrieve past experiences, they can provide valuable assistance to human workers, contribute to knowledge sharing, and improve task execution efficiency.

8.3 Merging computational modeling of episodic memory with industry 4.0

The merging of computational modeling of episodic memory with the principles of Industry 4.0 enables the development of intelligent systems capable of leveraging big data, advanced analytics, and automation. This integration empowers machines to make informed decisions, adapt to changing circumstances, and enhance overall operational efficiency.

8.3.1 Sequence learning

EM can bind the related events in sequential order as an episode. Using an episode an intelligent agent can travel in time in the space of target events that can help in making cognitive decisions like making predictions of upcoming events and recalling the detail of related events. The contextual feature for binding may include the time which drifts very slowly but may also include other stable features like space or any other event details (Shrivastava & Tripathi, 2018; Tulving & Thomson, 1973).

8.3.2 Event consolidation into knowledge

As per the competitive trace theory, at the beginning of the event encoding, the structure of the event will have all details of the event. For example: If a party event occurs in a college, then after some days some event detail would detach from the event like, what songs were played at the party.

The competitive trace theory says, at the time of event exposition or the encoding the neocortex neurons get activated which are corresponding to the event activities, and corresponding to each activation pattern of the cortex an index gets recruited in the hippocampus which represents an event (Shrivastava & Tripathi, 2019). And then during each recall and the reactivation of the event, these memory traces in the neocortex gets compete with each other to get activated. As a result of this, some of the traces get silent (forget from the events), some of the traces get activated in each further recalling's and get strongly associated with other coactive traces and constitute knowledge of the event memory (Jain et al., 2022) as shown in Fig. 8.3.

8.3.3 Ebbinghaus forgetting and the primacy effect

A forgetting system is just as important for memory storage as encoding and recall because it makes memory storage efficient by forgetting events that have no value for the agent. A theory on forgetting was proposed by Ebbinghaus proposed in 1971. As per the theory, the memory strength of memory elements decays with time at a certain rate. At the initial of encoding the memory strength of memory elements will be highest and then decays with time exponentially if the event is not recalled. Furthermore, in theory, a recalling factor is considered that says the decay rate can be reduced with a higher frequency of recalling and vice versa, as shown in Fig. 8.4. In the figure, a transformation in the decay rate is shown by using forgetting curves, where the exponential decay rate is transformed to the logarithmic rate on a higher frequency of recalling's (Jain et al., 2022).

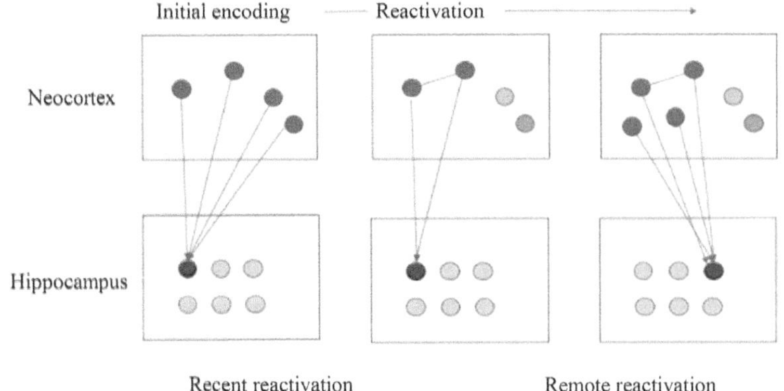

FIGURE 8.3

Competitive trace theory.

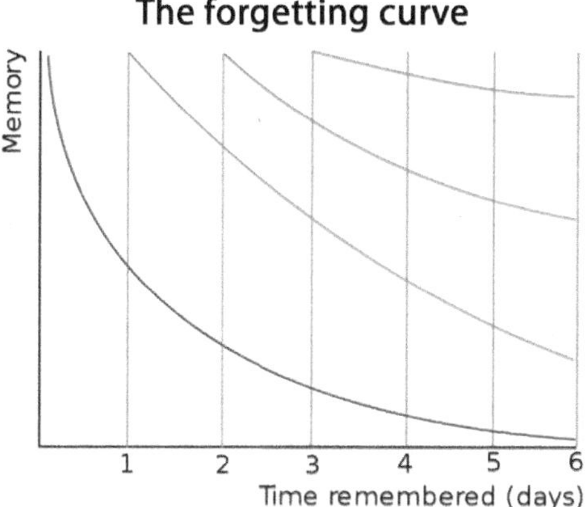

FIGURE 8.4

Ebbinghaus forgetting curve.

Many equations have since been proposed to approximate forgetting. Perhaps the simplest is an exponential curve described by the Eq. (8.1) (Jain et al., 2022).

$$R = a \times e^{(-bt)} \tag{8.1}$$

Where R is the remembrance of the event trace, t is the elapsed time, a is the initial probability of remembering something, and b is the forgetting constant, deciding how fast the event would forget.

The primacy effect puts some constraints on Ebbinghaus forgetting, according to the primacy and recency effect, memory traces that are participants in only a few events are nonvulnerable to forgetting and their decay rate even on no recalling would be lesser compared to the even traces which are the participants in several events (Jain & Jain, 2022).

8.3.4 Spatial memory in the episodic memory

Right from the beginning, it has been said by the scientific community that the EM is highly contextualized in nature, where one of the essential contexts is the place of the event. Using a spatial context one can recall where he has attended any particular party. Even in biological brain research, the hippocampus and the entorhinal cortex (both regions are involved in the episodic memory) region, place, and grid neurons are observed that enable a human to move towards the recalled place (Jain & Jain, 2023; Jain & Prasad, 2021). A hippocampal place neuron always points out a unique place in an environment that works as an object- place memory and recalls the place of a particular object or an activity (Jain & Jain, 2023; Jain & Prasad, 2021) in the memory of an event. The several grid neurons together constitute a kind of grid code that a place neuron learns through the forward connection as shown in Fig. 8.5. The recalled grid code can act as a code of recalled place and a human can reach the recalled place by traversing the current and the goal grid code (to get more information see paper (Jain & Prasad, 2020); Kumar et al., 2022).

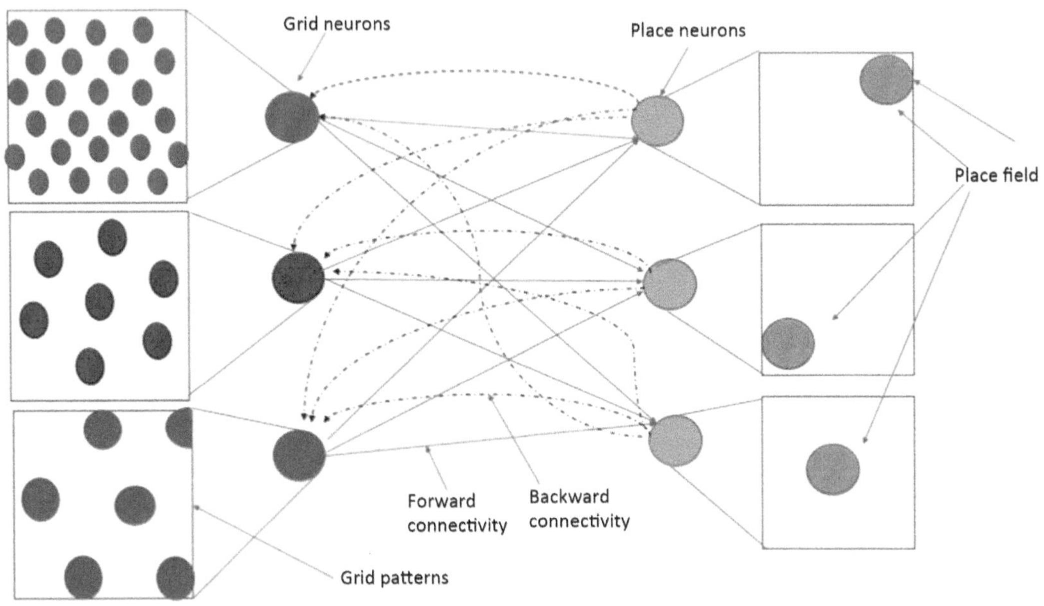

FIGURE 8.5

Interaction system of place and the grid neurons.

8.3.5 Event significance signal

Emotions are having a special place in an event memory as it represents the significance of an event. Each event can have a different significance level to different persons, which is dependent on the aroused emotions, motivations of the person, and attention at the time of encoding. Since the hippocampus takes some additional input from several other cortical subsystems like the amygdala, about which the researchers have hypothesized that this additional input is a significant signal which has a graded impact on the number of recruited cells of the events, where the cells in less number will be more prone to forgetting.

8.4 Ingredients of a healthcare system in the era of advanced technologies

8.4.1 Internet of things (IoT)

The term Internet of Things (IoT) encompasses devices with network access. Modern devices, objects, networks, and systems are equipped with sensors, software, and network capabilities, compiling and processing data arrays through internet protocols.

The impact of 5G on IoT technology is significant, providing enhanced connectivity and functionality. Key 5G technology drivers include superfast broadband, ultra-reliable low-latency communication, massive machine-type communications, high reliability/availability, and efficient energy usage.

8.4.2 Artificial intelligence (AI)

Artificial intelligence (AI) empowers computers to learn from experience, adapt to predefined parameters, and execute tasks previously exclusive to humans.

8.4.3 Big data analytics (BDA)

Big data analytics (BDA) is a crucial component of Industry 4.0, dealing with large datasets to derive information relevant for rapid decision-making. The extracted data is transformed into goal-oriented knowledge, fostering agility in problem-solving.

8.5 Digital manufacturing and advanced materials processing

Advancements in digital manufacturing yield outcomes such as 3D printing technology, also known as additive manufacturing (AM). AM facilitates the processing of polymers, ceramics, glass, and metallic alloys. Design strategies like Design for Additive Manufacturing (DfAM) and Materials Design by Additive Manufacturing (MaDe-by-AM) enable the production of novel materials with tailored compositions, structural nuances, and functional gradients. This technology allows the creation of intricate porous materials and metamaterials based on shape and composition complexity.

8.5.1 Green aspects of industry 4.0 and 5.0

The environmental dimensions of Industry 4.0, particularly in the food-water-energy nexus, merit special attention:

- The survival of humanity hinges on addressing critical concerns in the upcoming years, including a global energy shortage and depletion of raw materials (energy crisis), reduction of arable land, decrease in soil fertility, and food shortage (food crisis), depleting availability of clean water, and the catastrophic state of the environment (ecological crisis).
- Essential spheres of life, encompassing industry, transport, the fuel and energy complex, the economy, public administration, and security, are undergoing transformations due to the integration of digital technologies into everyday life and the advancement of alternative energy and electric vehicles.
- Efficient re-use and recycling procedures have become imperative for modern industrial development. Integrating cutting-edge insights from various sources, we explore the transformative journey of healthcare in the age of Industry 4.0 technologies as shown in Fig. 8.6 evolution of Healthcare industry with time.

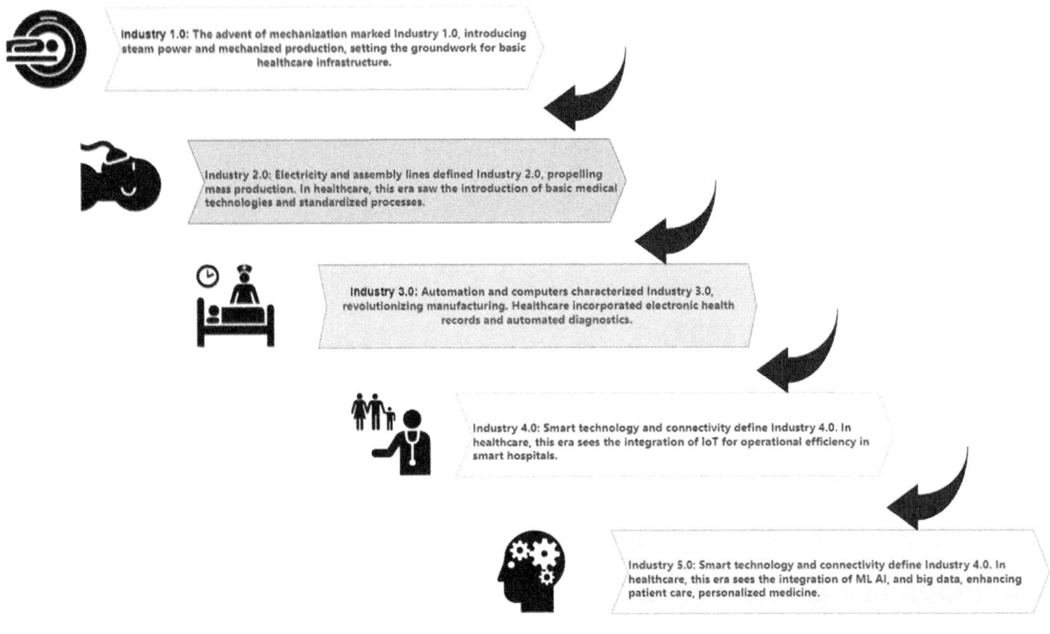

FIGURE 8.6

Evolution of Healthcare industrial developments over time.

8.6 Transformative frontiers: exploring the spectrum of robotics in healthcare

8.6.1 Robot receptionists

The incorporation of robot receptionists signals a profound transformation in healthcare administration. These automated human assistants play a pivotal role in streamlining administrative tasks, efficiently managing appointment schedules, disseminating information, and ultimately elevating patient satisfaction levels. Within the chapter, an in-depth analysis is conducted to understand the far-reaching impact of robot receptionists on healthcare facility efficiency.

8.6.2 Telemedicine robots

Robotic applications in telemedicine stand as pioneers in enhancing healthcare accessibility. This segment delves into their pivotal role in facilitating virtual consultations, establishing remote connections between patients and healthcare providers, and ensuring prompt medical care, particularly in remote or underserved regions. The chapter scrutinizes technological advancements, explores the benefits, and navigates the challenges associated with the integration of telemedicine robots, promising a transformative shift in the delivery of healthcare services.

8.6.3 Medical robots: surgical robots

A groundbreaking advancement in modern medicine lies in the realm of surgical robots. This chapter segment focuses on the transformative role of surgical robots within the operating room. Unveiling a new era in surgical practices, these robots redefine conventional techniques with their precision and minimally invasive capabilities, offering the potential for expedited recovery times and improved outcomes. The section meticulously explores the nature of surgical robots, their applications, and anticipates their profound impact on the future landscape of surgical procedures.

8.6.4 Service robots

Service robots play a pivotal role in optimizing operational efficiency within healthcare facilities. This segment delves into their crucial contributions to logistics, cleaning, and maintenance operations. By automating non-medical tasks, service robots strategically alleviate human workers from routine responsibilities, allowing them to channel their efforts towards patient-focused activities.

8.6.5 Exoskeleton robots

The incorporation of exoskeleton robots represents a significant breakthrough in the domain of physical rehabilitation. This chapter segment thoroughly investigates how these robots contribute to the restoration of movement in individuals recovering from surgeries or accidents.

8.6.6 Rehabilitation robots

Robots equipped with specialized training functions play a crucial role in delivering personalized care to patients recovering from neurological or musculoskeletal conditions. This chapter segment delves into the diverse applications, advantages, and challenges associated with rehabilitation robots. Emphasizing their significant contribution to improved patient outcomes, the exploration underscores the role of rehabilitation robots in enabling a more tailored and individualized approach to the rehabilitation process.

8.6.7 Social robots

The integration of social robots into the healthcare setting introduces a distinctly human element. This chapter segment thoroughly explores how the companionship and mental health care offered by social robots contribute to enhancing patients' overall well-being.

In conclusion, the comprehensive exploration of diverse robotic applications in healthcare highlights their collective potential to revolutionize patient care, enhance operational efficiency, and shape the evolving landscape of healthcare protocols.

8.7 Social robotics revolutionizing healthcare: navigating from industrial roots to affordable and accessible services

Within the healthcare system, robots serve a myriad of purposes, providing significant assistance in telemedicine, social interaction, rehabilitation, surgical support, companionship, and entertainment (Dikshit et al., 2022). Social robots, characterized by theories based on self-attributed attributes, error compartmentalization, and a focus on warmth and humane contact, are designed to offer cost-effective home-based, personalized, and telemedicine technologies for both preventive and curative care (Jain et al., 2022; Shrivastava & Tripathi, 2018, 2019). Surgical robots play a pivotal role in both in-person and remote surgical procedures, ushering in minimally invasive treatments characterized by heightened precision, improved vision for operators, and increased safety for both patients and healthcare workers (Atkinson & Richard, 1968).

Rehabilitation robots play a crucial role in assisting individuals with disabilities through the provision of physical and cognitive therapy. Studies consistently demonstrate the positive outcomes of human-robot interaction in therapeutic settings, notably impacting groups such as children with autism spectrum disorder (ASD) (Jain et al., 2022; Tulving & Markowitsch, 1998). Additionally, companion robots contribute significantly to improving the health and well-being of individuals, particularly the elderly and those in poor health, by offering companionship and stress reduction. Entertainment robots in healthcare engage with patients using diverse media, including games, music, films, and audio, all while seamlessly integrating medical treatment (Jain & Jain, 2022, 2023; Jain et al., 2022).

The landscape of robotics is swiftly transitioning from industrial applications, where it primarily served production and hazardous roles, to the utilization of social robots capable of interpersonal communication in specific environments. Heightened challenges, such as the limited access to healthcare services affecting 28.6 million Americans, equivalent to 9.1% of the population, have propelled the integration of social robots within the healthcare industry (Pelachaud, 2007).

8.8 Survey of computational episodic memory models

Earlier, several models have been published on EM modeling, where each one has covered a small subset of EM functionalities. The survey has discussed mechanisms of these past established works to show their contributions and research gaps. The overall objective of any EM model is to mimic the functionalities of episodic memory, therefore the survey is presented functionality-wise. Detailed information on each functionality is already been given in Section II of the paper. The survey is as follows.

8.8.1 Event encoding through computational modeling

Here, the computational encoding of an episodic event is discussed concerning the used structure and content, which are as follows.

8.8.1.1 When or what to encode in the event of episodic memory

In brain psychology, it has already been proven that the human eye captures every detail given in a picture, but its attention which is gets derived from the motivation allows only the selective part from a picture to get into the further higher-level processing (i.e., SM and the EM). This way a human memory solves the problem of enormous space requirements. Similarly, the point has been addressed but partially in extending cognitive architecture (ECA). The extending cognitive architecture demonstrated the incorporation of episodic memory in the SOAR cognitive architecture to increase its general intelligence.

The full episodic memory (FEM) did encoding in some real manner compared to the ECA. In the model, the attention is only given to only those objects that come into the agent's perception by its sensory input and the object has higher saliency. The saliency is derivable from the current activity and goals. If the object under attention is necessary for the ongoing tasks and the goal then the object will have a high saliency value (e.g. a pre-active goal of "eating" can increase the saliency of the eatable objects). The model is having both short and long-term memory as shown in Fig. 8.7.

Along with the task field, in the STM the model is having the "others task field" that contains the activities of the task which are performed by the others and observed by the agent. Each task and object is associated with a memory strength that decays with time. The decay can be slowed down by looking at the object repeatedly, or rehearsal. Similarly, tasks in the task field decay have not been used for a long time. The tasks or their associated objects on accomplishment get vanishes from the PF and the TF and get recorded into the LTM, i.e. EM. The long-term memory of the model is explained below in the section.

In this section, we delve into the event structures employed in computational models of episodic memory and explore their relevance in the context of Industry 4.0. Event structures refer to the representation and organization of individual experiences or events within the memory system.

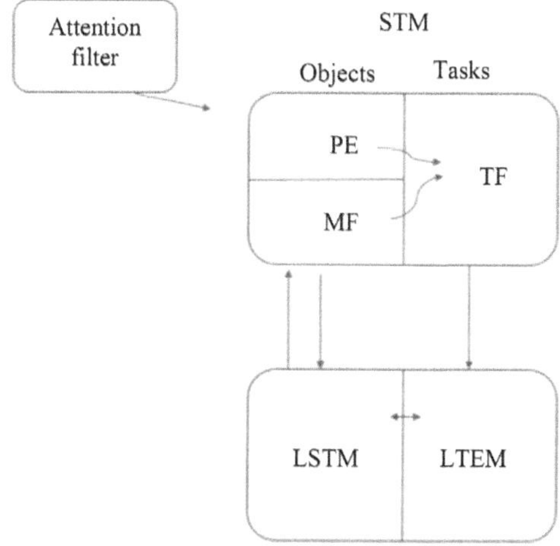

FIGURE 8.7

Architecture of full episodic memory.

8.8.1.2 Temporal event sequences

Computational models often represent episodic memories as sequences of events ordered in time. These event sequences capture the temporal relationships between experiences and enable the reconstruction of past events. In the context of Industry 4.0, temporal event sequences can be leveraged for various applications. For instance, in manufacturing processes, capturing and analyzing the temporal order of events can aid in identifying patterns, detecting anomalies, and optimizing production workflows.

8.8.1.3 Causal event networks

Some EM models utilize causal event networks to represent the causal relationships between events. These networks capture the cause-and-effect associations among experiences, allowing for the understanding of how events influence each other. In Industry 4.0, causal event networks can be valuable for analyzing the impact of different factors on production outcomes. By modeling and analyzing causal relationships between events, intelligent systems can identify critical factors affecting manufacturing quality, efficiency, and reliability.

8.8.1.4 Semantic event graphs

Semantic event graphs represent events as nodes interconnected by semantic relationships. These graphs capture the semantic associations and similarities between experiences, enabling more nuanced retrieval and pattern recognition. In the context of Industry 4.0, semantic event graphs can enhance intelligent systems' ability to analyze and interpret complex manufacturing data. By leveraging semantic associations between events, machines can make more informed decisions, detect patterns, and adapt to dynamic production environments.

8.8.1.5 Hierarchical event structures

Hierarchical event structures organize events in a hierarchical manner, allowing for the representation of events at different levels of abstraction. By capturing and organizing events hierarchically, intelligent systems can learn from past experiences and improve overall operational efficiency. The HTN, in contrast to the SOAR and the FEM has described when an agent would start encoding and how the agent would draw a boundary between the details of the event.

8.8.2 Event structures used in computational models

Event structure decides the content of an event, the structure of the event activities, context i.e. place and time, goal, outcomes of the event, and many more. Next, in the event encoding section, the models have been broadly categorized based on the event structure used in the models, which are relational, binding-based, and feature-vector-based models as shown in Fig. 8.8.

8.8.3 Event forgetting in computational EM models

In a real-world scenario, the same event does not occur, some activities are different in events, and even similar events are stored with different time references or locations. In the future, humanoids or robots will face such events daily, which can result in many events gathering in EM, which can

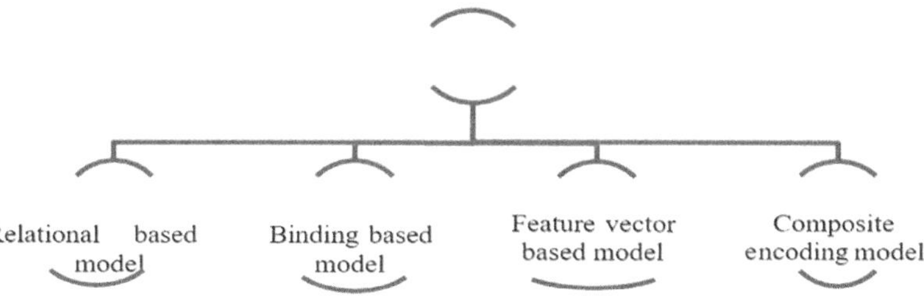

FIGURE 8.8

Categorization based on encoding.

lead to space shortages. Therefore, models for the EM must be incorporated with some kind of forgetting mechanism or can, say, dynamic event mechanism in which stored events get forgotten with the new event encodings.

To make any model space-efficient, sharing is very much required between the event space, which can be incorporated in models, by the sharing of activities among the different events. Such a mechanism is used by the CARD model, where event activities are shared between the events through a weighted link as described earlier. The weight of the link is called participation strength which is not static, it changes with every newly occurred cross-talked event according to Eq. 8.2.

In contrast to card-based EM, ART EM forgets both implicitly and explicitly. The EM ART adaption is implicit forgetting. In explicit forgetting, an event gets forgotten based on the recalling and reactivation of the events as shown in Eq. 8.2.

$$\begin{aligned} Aj^{(new)} &= A_{init,} \text{at the time of creation} \\ Aj^{(new)} &= Aj^{(old)} + \left(1\text{-}Aj^{(old)}\right)r, \text{ if reactivated} \\ Aj^{(new)} &= Aj^{(old)}(1\text{-}\mu), \text{ otherwise} \end{aligned} \tag{8.2}$$

where, A_{init} is the activation value allotted at the time of the event creation, r is the reinforcement rate by which the activation of an event increases with each reactivation, otherwise, it decreases with a decay rate μ. In contrast with the CARD, it does not forget the individual captured features of an event instead of that it forgets either the all or nothing.

As a further improvement of EM ART, a hierarchical emotional episodic memory has been proposed with the purpose to include the emotional factor to derive the retention of events. So that the high emotional events can retain over a longer period and the emotional weak events can forget fast. The model has included the emotional field in the EM ART which can detect the facial expression to detect the emotions of the event. Here, four types of emotions are used which are sorrow, anger, joy, and surprise. The emotion vector would be like [0.0,0.9, 0.1,0.2] where anger is high, slightly surprised, and other emotions are low. This input vector will be the same as other input fields of the EM ART. Like deep episodic memory. Here to find the impact of a non-emotional event on an emotional event the temporal difference is used which says that the non-emotional event having a higher difference with an emotional event will have a lower impact and vice versa, as it is calculated in Eq. 8.3.

$$\text{Temporal\_difference} = |t_e\text{-}t_n| \tag{8.3}$$

where, Temporal_difference is the impact of the kth event, t_n is the temporal activation of the kth event representing the distance from the currently occurring emotional event, and t_e is the intensity of ith emotion in the emotional input field (e) of the model.

The parameters which are considered for memory consolidation are memory strength, reinforcement rate, decay rate, learning rate, and vigilance parameter. The consolidation of events is done in the given below equations (Eq. 8.4).

Furthermore, the model did the anticipation of episodes based on the similarity between the event sequence of the cue with the episode's event sequence and based on the episode's template matching as done in Eqs. 14,15,1,6,17,18 & 19. If the anticipation value of an episode is high then the memory of the episode will be strengthened.

The model has done normalization using the difference between the length of the episode and the cue which is formulated according to Eq. 8.4.

$$\text{Cue\_normalized} = \text{Cue} \times (\text{Length\_of\_episode-Length\_of\_cue}) \tag{8.4}$$

where, Cue is the normalized activation value of the event sequence, d is the decay factor used in the episode encoding, is the length of the target episode and is the length of the cue. Also, cue normalization is only required if the cue length is smaller than the episode length.

Another problem with the episode matching is with the calculation of the match score. Since, in an episode learning, at every new event activation, the temporal activation of the past event of the episode decays by multiplying with a decay factor d. Thus, partial activation of the cue which comes in a target episode in the earlier position will have a very low match score compared to the complete cue. Therefore, the model has used log transformation which has changed the evaluation of the matching score as given in Eq. 8.5.

$$\text{Match\_score} = \log(\text{Cue\_normalized} + 1) \tag{8.5}$$

Also, the model then calculated the Levenshtein distance to evaluate the similarity between the cue and the episode's event sequence so that the episode can be anticipated to strengthen the memory [86]. The distance is the number of substitutions, deletions, and the insertion to transform the cue into the episodic event sequence, which is calculated according to Eq. 8.7.

$$D_{cue,p} = d \tag{8.6}$$

where, $D_{cue,p}$ is the distance between the given cue and the pth episode's event sequence. As the similarity greatly affects when the difference between the length of the cue and the episode changes, therefore, a length similarity factor is also considered to calculate the overall similarity factor.

$$\text{Length\_similarity\_factor} = (\text{Length\_of\_cue} + \text{Length\_of\_episode})/2 \tag{8.7}$$

where, Length_similarity_factor is the length similarity factor, which is min (Length_similarity_factor, 1).

The overall significance of an episode has considered the similarity factor, and match score both, as calculated in Eq. 8.8.

$$\text{Significance}^{P} = \text{match\_score} \times (1\text{-}C(1\text{-MS}_p) \tag{8.8}$$

where MS_p is the memory strength of the pth episode, and C is the constant that represents the maximum effect of the memory strength.

Apart from all these techniques, a probabilistic approach can be used which calculates the probability of being recalled based on various factors. As such technique is used by the HTN that calculates the probability of the event being recalled· However, the model applied the decay function to only the emotional events whose recalling probability is calculated as per Eq. 8.9, 8.10 and 8.11.

$$P_i \in [0, 1], t \geq 0, A \in [0, 1], N \in [-1, 1] \tag{8.9}$$

$$A = (N + 1)/2 \tag{8.10}$$

$$P_i = \text{if } A > 0 \text{ e} - t/A \tag{8.11}$$

Else 0. where, P_i is the probability of recalling an ith episode and t is the elapsed time since this event happened. The variable A is calculated using the factor neuroticism N which is a personality factor, based on the fact that mood affects memory retrieval and people tend to remember bad things when they are in a bad mood (Carpenter et al., 1991a).

For the models in which events are associated with time pointers having info on the day and time of event encoding like FEM (discussed in the encoding section), the event gets forgotten according to Eq. 8.11.

$$i = e \cdot 1/h \cdot 1/d^{1/2} \tag{8.12}$$

where, h is the layer of the LTM structure that represents the temporal event number on a particular day, d number of days passed from the episode, and e is either the emotional relevance of a task. However, none of the models yet not performed the calculation of the emotion factor. The forgetting used in the FEM has not considered the recalling factor as considered in the CARD, the Eq. 8.12 can add a recalling factor so that the life of recalled events can be increased.

8.9 Summary of the survey

The survey, we have looked at several biological as well as computational research on EM. In the past decade, several abstract EM models have been devised as agent architecture to enhance the performance of the agent. The functionality offered by the models is tabulated in Table 8.1. The very popular approach proposed for episodic memory is the family of ART-based neural networks of EM. Since the ART-based models encode the activities of an event as numeric values of some numeric parameters, and thus, it is not able to encode real-life concepts. The SMRITI is the first of his category which introduced the binding-based encoding to capture the complex and wide variety of real-life events. The CARD (Consolidation, Inference, and Ebbinghaus' Forgetting in Event-based Episodic Memory) model has addressed several crucial functionalities that were previously uncovered. It incorporates consolidation, inference, and Ebbinghaus' forgetting mechanisms. Additionally, the model draws inspiration from SMRITI, which is based on the concept of role entity bindings. The CARD model meets the demands outlined by competitive trace theory, enabling the learning of semantic knowledge from a set of independent events. The model employs a network of weighted synapses, utilizing events to establish bindings and provides an inference mechanism to plan a sequence of actions to achieve current goals.

Table 8.1 Table of comparison.

S. No.	Model	Event dynamics	Pattern separation	Ebbinghaus forgetting	Event consolidation	Sequence learning	Object place memory	Retrieval complexity
1.	Extending cognitive architecture with episodic memory Tan et al. (2007)	Static	Not present	Not present	Not present	Not present	Not present	Linear
2.	Generic episodic memory Baddeley (2001)	Static	Not present	Not present	Not present	Not present	Not present	Logarithmic
3.	Full episodic memory Levenshtein (1966)	Dynamic	Not present	Not present	Not present	Not present	Not present	Linear
4.	HTN Levenshtein (1966)	Dynamic	Not present	Not present	Not present	Not present	Not present	Linear
5.	SMRITI Shrivastava and Tripathi (2019)	Static	Not present	Not present	Not present	Not present	Not present	Linear
6.	EM-ART Morris and Murphy (1990)	Dynamic	Not present	Not present	Not present	Present	Not present	Linear
7.	Emotional deep ART Corballis (2013)	Dynamic	Not present	Not present	Present	Present	Not present	Linear
8.	DEEP ART Smith and Mizumori (2006)	Dynamic	Not present	Not present	Present	Present	Not present	Linear
9.	CARD model Wang and Wenwen (2012)	Dynamic	Present	Present	Present	Not present	Not present	Linear
10.	Complementary learning system Jain and Jain (2023)	Dynamic	Not present	Not present	Not present	Not present	Not present	Linear
11.	Minerva Jain and Prasad (2020)	Static	Not present	Not present	Not present	Not present	Not present	Linear

8.10 Research gaps and future directions

In the survey, we have seen the use of emotional factors for forgetting. The idea is appreciable, but its realization would require a computational mechanism to learn the semantics of events in the context of emotions and their level. That can be one of the future research directions in EM modeling.

There are several such scenarios where the agents are needed to answer queries related to past events. Answering like a human needs another computational mechanism that can convert a natural language query sentence into the form of a structure that the event follows. For example, in the SMRITI model, to make the model talkative there is a need for a computational mechanism that can convert the query into the form of role entity bindings. Using the converted cue match operation can be done between the cue and the episodic events. Moreover, another mechanism is needed to convert the outcome into a form of a natural language sentence. Using such functionalities, the agent can send the message in a natural language to report the detail of any target event.

Survey of past established works of EM modeling, we have seen that the main models have given weightage to just encoding and recalling. Particularly in recalling only SMRITI and CARD have focused on the encoding of real-life concepts in an event. With a poor encoding scheme i.e. relational tuple-based, numeric feature vector-based encoding schemes, the intelligent agent cannot expect. To act in real-life environments, it is very much necessary to encode real-life concepts, as done in SMRITI. To realize the SMRTI's encoding, there is a need for several computational mechanisms that can learn to identify the roles and their respective fillers in an event. The mechanism would learn the semantics of actions, and interaction with an object, for example: in the event "Ram gives a book to Sita", the agent must be able to identify the concept of "GIVER", "TAKER" and the "Given OBJECT" based on learned semantics of actions.

8.11 Conclusion

In conclusion, this survey has provided an overview of previously established modelling work on episodic memory, with a focus on its implications for future intelligent machines. By drawing from psychological and biological brain research, the survey identified key modeling objectives for episodic memory and compared the mechanisms employed in existing models to achieve these objectives. Through this analysis, various research gaps and crucial issues in the modeling of episodic memory were identified. In the context of Industry 4.0, the findings of this survey have significant relevance. Industry 4.0 represents a paradigm shift in manufacturing, where intelligent machines and systems play a central role. Episodic memory, with its ability to capture, store, and recall detailed event-based information, can greatly enhance the capabilities of intelligent systems in this context. The outlined research gaps provide valuable directions for computational researchers interested in modeling episodic memory for Industry 4.0 applications. These directions include incorporating emotion detection, dynamic forgetting mechanisms, navigation abilities, and the integration of place and grid neurons. By addressing these gaps, researchers can develop more comprehensive and realistic models that can contribute to the advancement of intelligent systems in Industry 4.0 environments. Overall, this survey serves as a valuable resource for researchers and practitioners in the field of computational modeling, highlighting the significance of episodic memory and offering insights into its potential applications in the context of Industry 4.0. By considering the outlined research gaps and directions, computational researchers can make substantial contributions to the development of intelligent machines with enhanced memory capabilities, leading to more efficient, adaptive, and intelligent systems in Industry 4.0 manufacturing scenarios.

References

Atkinson, R. C., & Richard, M. S. (1968). *Human memory: A proposed system and its control processes. Psychology of learning and motivation* (Vol. 2, pp. 89–195). Academic Press.

Baddeley, A. (2001). The concept of episodic memory. *Philosophical Transactions of the Royal Society of London. Series B: Biological Sciences, 356*(1413), 1345–1350.

Brom, C. (2007). *KláraPešková, and JiříLukavský. "What does your actor remember? towards characters with a full episodic memory. International conference on virtual storytelling*. Berlin, Heidelberg: Springer.

Burgess, N., Maguire, E. A., & O'Keefe., J. (2002). The human hippocampus and spatial and episodic memory. *Neuron, 35*(4), 625–641.

Carpenter, G. A., Grossberg, S., & Rosen, D. B. (1991a). Fuzzy ART: Fast stable learning and categorization of analog patterns by an adaptive resonance system. *Neural networks, 4*(6), 759–771.

Carpenter, G. A., Grossberg, S., & Rosen, D. B. Fuzzy ART: An adaptive resonance algorithm for rapid, stable classification of analog patterns. IJCNN-91-Seattle International Joint Conference on Neural Networks. Vol. 2. IEEE, 1991b.

Corballis, M. C. (2013). Mental time travel: a case for evolutionary continuity. *Trends in Cognitive Sciences, 17*(1), 5–6.

Dikshit, G., Chouhan, P. S., et al. (2022). Detecting of Brain Responses from EEG (Electroencephalography) Signals using Deep Learning and Analysis of Amalgamation of Energy Resources. *Gongcheng Kexue Yu Jishu/Advanced Engi-neering Science (International Journal), Volume 54*(2).

Forbus, K. D., Gentner, D., & Law, K. (1995). MAC/FAC: A model of similarity-based retrieval. *Cognitive Science, 19*(2), 141–205.

Hintzman, D. L. (1984). MINERVA 2: A simulation model of human memory. *Behavior Research Methods, Instruments, & Computers, 16*(2), 96–101.

Hunsaker, M. R., Lee, B., & Kesner, R. P. (2008). Evaluating the temporal context of episodic memory: the role of CA3 and CA1. *Behavioural Brain Research, 188*(2), 310–315.

Jain, G., & Jain, A. (2022). Applications of AI, IoT, and Robotics in Healthcare Service Based on Several Aspects. In M. Ab-del-Basset, A. Fahmy, & A. E. Hassanien (Eds.), *Blockchain Technology in Healthcare Applications* (2022, pp. 87–114). CRC Press.

Jain, G., & Jain, A. (2023). Applications of Internet of Robotic Things in Industry 4.0 Based on Several Aspects. In M. Khari, A. Garg, & V. Kumar (Eds.), *Artificial Intelligence Techniques in Human Resource Management* (2023, pp. 127–152). CRC Press.

Jain, G., & Prasad, R. R. (2021). Multi-antenna communication security with deep learning network and internet of things. In D. Mishra, A. Kumar, A. Kumar, L. Boubchir, & M. Elhoseny (Eds.), *Blockchain Technology for Data Privacy Management* (2021, pp. 61–80). CRC Press.

Jain, G., & Prasad, R. R. (2020). IoT Enabled Multi-Antenna Communication Channel with Deep Learning Network. Proceedings of the International Conference on Recent Advances in Computational Techniques (IC-RACT), 2020.

Jain, G., Shukla, G., Saini, P., Gaur, A., Mishra, D., & Akashe, S. (2022). Secure COVID-19 Treatment with Blockchain and IoT-Based Framework. In A. K. Nagar, D. S. Jat, G. Marín-Raventós, & D. K. Mishra

(Eds.), *Intelligent Sustainable Systems. Lecture Notes in Networks and Systems* (334). Singapore: Springer. Available from https://doi.org/10.1007/978-981-16-6369-7_70.

Kumar, A., Jain, G., Suraj., Jindal, P., Mishra, V., & Akashe, S. (2022). Design of a CPW-Fed Microstrip Elliptical Patch UWB Range Antenna for 5G Communication Application. In A. K. Nagar, D. S. Jat, G. Marín-Raventós, & D. K. Mishra (Eds.), *Intelligent Sustainable Systems. Lecture Notes in Networks and Systems* (334). Singapore: Springer. Available from https://doi.org/10.1007/978-981-16-6369-7_71.

Levenshtein, V. I. (1966). Binary codes capable of correcting deletions, insertions and reversals. *Soviet Physics Doklady*, *10*, 707.

McNaughton, B. L., et al. (2006). Path integration and the neural basis of the 'cognitive map'. *Nature Reviews Neuro-science*, *7*(8), 663.

Morris, M. W., & Murphy, G. L. (1990). Converging operations on a basic level in event taxonomies. *Memory & Cognition*, *18*(4), 407–418.

Nadel, L. (1994). Multiple memory systems: What and why, an update. *Memory systems 1994*, 39–63.

Neil, B. (2007). *Computational models of the spatial and mnemonic functions of the hippocampus.*

Pelachaud, C., et al., eds. Intelligent Virtual Agents: 7th International Working Conference, IVA 2007, Paris, France, September 17-19, 2007, Proceedings. Vol. 4722. Springer, 2007.

Porter, B. W., Bareiss, R., & Holte, R. C. (1990). Concept learning and heuristic classification in weak-theory domains. *Artificial Intelligence*, *45*(1-2), 229–263.

Rifkin, A. (1985). Evidence for a basic level in event taxonomies. *Memory & Cognition*, *13*(6), 538–556.

Rolls, E. T. (2010). A computational theory of episodic memory formation in the hippocampus. *Behavioural Brain Research*, *215*(2), 180–196.

Shastri, L. (1999). Advances in Shruti—A neurally motivated model of relational knowledge representation and rapid infer-ence using temporal synchrony. *Applied Intelligence*, *11*(1), 79–108.

Shrivastava, R., & Tripathi, S. Computational Model of Episodic Memory Formation, Recalling, and Forgetting. Proceedings of International Conference on Recent Advancement on Computer and Communication. Springer, Singapore, 2018.

Shrivastava, R., & Tripathi, S. (2019). *A New Approach of Learning Based on Episodic Memory Model. Progress in Advanced Computing and Intelligent Engineering* (pp. 129–138). Singapore: Springer.

Smith, D. M., & Mizumori, S. J. Y. (2006). Hippocampal place cells, context, and episodic memory. *Hippocampus*, *16*(9), 716–729.

Tan, A.-H., Carpenter, G. A., & Grossberg, S. Intelligence through interaction: Toward a unified theory for learning," in Proc. ISNN, vol. 1. 2007, pp. 1094–1103.

Tecuci, D. G., & Porter, B. W. (2007). *A generic memory module for events*, *68*(No. 09).

Tulving, E. (1972). Episodic and semantic memory. *Organization of memory*, *1*, 381–403.

Tulving, E., & Markowitsch, H. J. (1998). Episodic and declarative memory: role of the hippocampus. *Hippocampus*, *8*(3), 198–204.

Tulving, E., & Thomson, D. M. (1973). Encoding specificity and retrieval processes in episodic memory. *Psychological Review*, *80*(5), 352.

Wang., Wenwen., et al. (2012). Neural modeling of episodic memory: Encoding, retrieval, and forgetting. *IEEE transactions on neural networks and learning systems*, *23*(10), 1574–1586.

Yassa, M. A., & Reagh, Z. M. (2013). Competitive trace theory: a role for the hippocampus in contextual inter-ference during retrieval. *Frontiers in behavioral neuroscience*, *7*, 107.

Yeh, P. Z., Porter, B., & Barker, K. (2003). *Using transformations to improve semantic matching. Proceedings of the 2nd international conference on Knowledge capture* (pp. 180–189). ACM.

Zacks, J. M., & Tversky, B. (2001). Event structure in perception and conception. *Psychological Bulletin*, *127* (1), 3.

CHAPTER

Advancing electronic medical data protection through blockchain innovation

9

Atul B. Kathole[1], Amit Sanjiv Mirge[2] and Avinash P. Jadhao[3]

[1]*Department of Computer Engineering, Dr. D. Y. Patil Institute of Technology, Pune, Maharashtra, India*
[2]*Information Technology Department, Pimpri Chinchwad College of Engineering, Pune, Maharashtra, India*
[3]*Department of Computer Science & Engineering, DRGIT&R, Amravati, Maharashtra, India*

9.1 Introduction

The use of electronic health records (EHRs) and other health information technology is driving a revolutionary movement in the healthcare industry toward digitization. While these improvements have many advantages, they also raise concerns about the security and privacy of sensitive medical data (Patil et al., 2024). Cybersecurity concerns, data breaches, and unauthorized access all pose major hazards to patient confidentiality and integrity (Taherdoost, 2023) (Fig. 9.1).

Blockchain technology offers a viable answer to these issues by establishing a decentralized, secure, and transparent framework for managing medical data as shown in Fig. 9.1. This strategy not only improves patient record security, but also provides data integrity, traceability, and patient-centered control over their health information (Esposito et al., 2023).

Healthcare has advanced significantly in the digital age, particularly in the management and use of EMRs. These records contain detailed patient information, including clinical histories, diagnostic information, treatment plans, and personal health metrics. The transition from paper-based records to digital formats has resulted in various benefits, including greater accessibility, care coordination, and the facilitation of large-scale medical research. However, digitalization creates significant obstacles, the most important of which is the security and privacy of sensitive medical data (Zhang et al., 2023). The healthcare business has become a popular target for hackers due to the enormous value of medical information on the black market. Data breaches jeopardize patient privacy, weaken faith in healthcare systems, and result in severe financial losses as mention in Table 9.1.

Current methods for securing electronic medical data, while robust, sometimes fail to keep up with the changing spectrum of cyber threats. Traditional security architectures rely mainly on centralized databases, which, despite broad use, have single points of failure (Sharma et al., 2022). A breach in a centralized system can result in the exposing of massive amounts of data, making it an appealing target for hostile actors. Furthermore, challenges like data integrity, unauthorized access, and compliance with demanding regulatory standards (such as HIPAA in the United States and GDPR in Europe) complicate medical record security (Gupta et al., 2023).

Blockchain and Digital Twin for Smart Hospitals. DOI: https://doi.org/10.1016/B978-0-443-34226-4.00010-1

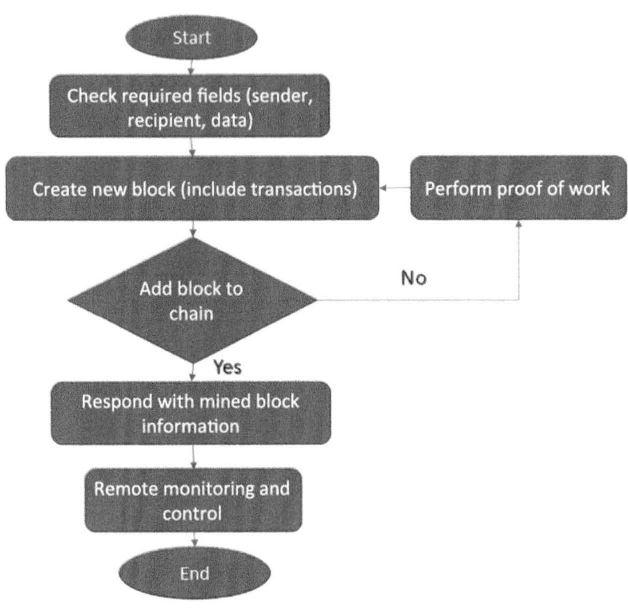

FIGURE 9.1

Flow of proposed approach.

Given these problems, blockchain technology has emerged as a possible alternative to transform the way electronic medical data is protected. Blockchain, the fundamental technology that powers cryptocurrencies like Bitcoin, is essentially a decentralized ledger that records transactions across a network of computers in a safe, transparent, and immutable fashion. Decentralization decreases the chance of a single point of failure by distributing data over several nodes, making it substantially more resistant to attacks. Furthermore, blockchain's cryptographic capabilities ensure that once data has been recorded, it cannot be changed or tampered with, ensuring data integrity and validity (Kumar, Goyal, et al., 2023).

The use of blockchain in healthcare can address a number of crucial challenges related to medical data privacy. For starters, it improves security by using its decentralized structure to disseminate data over a network, making unauthorized access much more difficult. Second, blockchain can enhance data privacy using smart contracts, which automate and enforce privacy rules, ensuring that only authorized parties have access to specific information. This is especially useful for managing patient consent and maintaining compliance with regulatory standards. Third, blockchain's openness and traceability allow for more effective audits and monitoring of data access and usage, reducing the risk of data misuse (Patel, Pandya, et al., 2022).

Several innovative projects and pilot programmed have already started to investigate the use of blockchain in healthcare. Initiatives such as MedRec, a decentralized record management system, seek to provide people authority over their own medical information while maintaining smooth access for authorized healthcare practitioners. Similarly, systems like the blockchain-based Health Information Exchange (HIE) are being created to allow for the secure and efficient sharing of medical data across several healthcare organizations, improving interoperability and patient outcomes (Nguyen et al., 2022).

Table 9.1 Literature review for health chain (blockchain-based medical data-sharing security).

Focus area	Key contributions	Challenges addressed	Unique features	References
Security and Privacy	Dynamic access control using smart contracts	Data-sharing security	Automated patient consent management	Esposito et al. (2023)
Data Management	Tamper-proof data handling with encryption	Data privacy	Decentralized management system	Zhang et al. (2023)
Privacy	Advanced cryptographic techniques for data privacy	Data-sharing security	Privacy-preserving mechanisms	Sharma et al. (2022)
Data Integrity	Immutable ledger for data integrity and authenticity	Data tampering	Reliable audit trails	Gupta et al. (2023)
Data Auditing	Secure and transparent auditing system	Compliance	Immutable logging of data access and modifications	Kumar et al. (2023a)
Data Integrity	Immutable record of transactions and modifications	Data integrity	Enhanced trust and reliability	Patel et al. (2022a)
Interoperability	Blockchain-based architecture for data sharing	System interoperability	Seamless data sharing	Nguyen et al. (2022)
Interoperability	Review of blockchain-enabled HIE solutions	Data-sharing security	Case studies and pilot projects	Patel et al. (2022a)
Interoperability	Secure data exchange between providers	Data confidentiality	Interoperable framework	Al Hadhrami et al. (2023)
Consent Management	Automating patient consent with smart contracts	Regulatory compliance	Real-time consent management	Liu et al. (2023)
Access Control	Secure data permissions management using smart contracts	Data privacy	Authorized access only	Sharma et al. (2023)
Consent Management	Immutable recording of patient consent	Consent verification	Easy verification of consent	Zhang et al. (2022)
Scalability	Solutions like sharding and off-chain transactions	Scalability issues	Layer-two protocols	Tang et al. (2022)
Integration	Strategies for hybrid architecture	System integration	Combining blockchain with traditional databases	Mohammed et al. (2023)

Despite blockchain's intriguing promise, its use in healthcare is not without hurdles. Scalability, interoperability with existing systems, and the requirement for a thorough regulatory framework are all critical issues to overcome (Patel, Agrawal, et al., 2022). Furthermore, integrating blockchain technology involves major infrastructure investment as well as a shift in the healthcare sector's existing data management paradigms. Nonetheless, continued research and development, combined with a growing realization of blockchain's merits, is propelling its application.

The key components of a blockchain-based approach are as follows:

- *Decentralized data storage*: Minimize the risk of a single point of failure and unauthorized access (Zhang et al., 2023).
- *Immutable record keeping*: Ensure the integrity and auditability of medical data (Sharma et al., 2022).
- *Patient-controlled access and consent*: Empower patients with control over their health information (Gupta et al., 2023).

- *Interoperability and data exchange*: Facilitate seamless and secure sharing of medical data between healthcare providers (Kumar, Goyal, et al., 2023).
- *Secure identity management*: Prevent identity theft and unauthorized access to patient records (Patel, Pandya, et al., 2022).
- *Auditable access logs*: Enhance accountability and traceability of data access (Nguyen et al., 2022).
- *The advantages of blockchain technology in the electronic medical data protection are below*:
- Implement blockchain to provide an immutable and tamper-proof ledger for storing medical data (Patel, Agrawal, et al., 2022).
- Ensure that once medical data is recorded on the blockchain, it cannot be altered or deleted, maintaining the integrity of patient records.
- Utilize smart contracts to establish access controls that allow patients to control who can access their medical records (Al Hadhrami et al., 2023).
- Empower patients to grant or revoke access permissions, ensuring that only authorized healthcare providers can view specific aspects of their health information.
- Enable healthcare organizations and regulatory bodies to audit and trace access to patient records, ensuring accountability and aiding in investigations.
- Implement monitoring tools and processes to continuously assess the security posture of the blockchain-based medical data system (Liu et al., 2023).
- Proactively identify and address potential security vulnerabilities, ensuring ongoing improvement and adaptability to emerging threats.

By defining and pursuing these objectives, a blockchain-based approach to ensuring the security of medical data can effectively address key challenges, empower patients, and create a resilient and trustworthy healthcare information ecosystem (Sharma et al., 2023).

9.2 Related work

The interoperability, privacy, and data integrity issues plaguing healthcare systems have sparked interest in a blockchain-based solution to the problem of medical data security. Here are some synopsis of relevant studies and works in this field:

The authors in Patil et al. (2024) explain the comprehensive review delves into various applications of blockchain in healthcare. It discusses how blockchain enhances security by ensuring data integrity, promoting patient-centric care, and addressing interoperability challenges. The paper also explores existing challenges and suggests future research directions.

In Taherdoost (2023), authors focus on securing EHRs through blockchain technology. It emphasizes the immutability and transparency features of blockchain to enhance the security and integrity of patient data. The paper discusses how a blockchain-based system can be resistant to tampering and unauthorized access.

The work in Esposito et al. (2023) presents a blockchain-based approach for secure and privacy-preserving sharing of EHRs. The authors leverage smart contracts to manage access controls, allowing patients to have more control over who can access their health information. The work emphasizes the importance of ensuring data privacy in healthcare systems.

Focusing on the pharmaceutical supply chain, this research explores how blockchain can be used to detect falsified drugs. The study emphasizes the potential of blockchain to ensure the authenticity and safety of pharmaceuticals by providing a transparent and traceable supply chain (Zhang et al., 2023).

In Sharma et al. (2022), the authors systematically review security issues and propose solutions related to the application of blockchain in healthcare. It covers a wide range of topics, including data privacy, access control, and network security. This work provides insights into the current challenges and potential solutions for securing medical data using blockchain.

The case study in Kumar, Goyal, et al. (2023) explores the implementation of a blockchain-based EHR system using smart contracts. The authors discuss how smart contracts can be utilized to enhance transparency, security, and patient control in managing health records. Their works collectively contribute to the understanding of how blockchain technology can be effectively applied to secure medical data. They address issues related to data integrity, patient privacy, and system transparency, showcasing the potential of blockchain in revolutionizing healthcare information management (Patel, Pandya, et al., 2022).

The comparative analysis of recent research papers highlights the significant advancements in using blockchain technology to protect electronic medical data (Zhang et al., 2022). Blockchain's ability to enhance security, privacy, data integrity, and interoperability positions it as a transformative technology for healthcare. Despite challenges related to scalability, integration, and regulatory compliance, ongoing research and pilot projects indicate a promising future for blockchain in creating a more secure and efficient healthcare ecosystem.

9.3 Proposed workflow

9.3.1 Main phases of the planned process

Each step of the planned process for improving the security of electronic medical data via blockchain innovation deals with a different facet of incorporating blockchain technology into healthcare data management systems (Tang et al., 2022). To ensure a strong and efficient system that satisfies the varied demands of all parties participating in the healthcare ecosystem, this all-encompassing plan aims to use blockchain's inherent characteristics to improve the privacy, interoperability, and security of medical data.

9.3.1.1 Phase 1: initial setup and system design

9.3.1.1.1 Stakeholder identification and requirements gathering

The first phase involves identifying all stakeholders within the healthcare data ecosystem, including patients, healthcare providers (such as hospitals and clinics), insurance companies, regulatory bodies, and researchers. Understanding the unique data protection needs of each stakeholder is critical (Mohammed et al., 2023). This phase includes thorough requirements analysis to determine data security and privacy needs, compliance with regulatory standards (such as GDPR and HIPAA), interoperability requirements, and specific needs for consent management and auditability.

9.3.1.1.2 Blockchain network selection

Once stakeholder needs are understood, the next step is selecting an appropriate blockchain framework. The choice of blockchain network will depend on factors such as the consensus mechanism (e.g., proof of work, proof of stake, practical Byzantine fault tolerance), scalability and performance requirements, and whether a public or private blockchain is more suitable given the privacy and permissioning needs (Johnson et al., 2023).

9.3.1.2 Phase 2: system architecture design

9.3.1.2.1 Data storage layer design

In this phase, a hybrid data storage system is designed. On-chain storage will be used for critical metadata and audit logs, ensuring immutability and transparency, while off-chain storage will handle large medical files using distributed storage solutions like Interplanetary File System (IPFS) (Ekblaw et al., 2022). This hybrid approach balances the benefits of blockchain's immutability with the need for efficient data handling.

9.3.1.2.2 Smart contract development

Smart contracts form the backbone of the proposed system, automating key processes such as access control policies, consent management, data-sharing agreements, and compliance checks. These contracts will be developed and tested to ensure they operate correctly and securely, facilitating automated and transparent interactions among stakeholders.

9.3.1.2.3 Interoperability layer implementation

To ensure seamless data exchange between disparate healthcare systems, interoperability protocols will be implemented. This includes using standards such as HL7 FHIR for data formats and developing application programming interface (APIs) for integration with existing EHR systems. The goal is to create a system where data can be shared and accessed securely across different platforms.

9.3.1.3 Phase 3: implementation phase

9.3.1.3.1 Blockchain network deployment

Deploying the blockchain network involves setting up nodes in a distributed manner among stakeholders to ensure decentralization and security. Proper network security measures, such as encryption and node authentication, will be implemented to protect against unauthorized access and tampering.

9.3.1.3.2 Smart contract deployment

Smart contracts developed in the previous phase will be deployed on the blockchain network. Rigorous testing will be conducted to verify their correctness and security. This ensures that all stakeholders can interact with the contracts as intended, maintaining the integrity and security of the data management processes.

9.3.1.3.3 Data migration

Existing medical records will be migrated to the new system. This involves implementing data validation and cleansing processes to ensure that the migrated data is accurate and complete. Care will be taken to maintain the integrity of historical data, ensuring that past records are preserved accurately (Kumar, Sharma, et al., 2023).

9.3.1.4 Phase 4: data protection and security mechanisms

9.3.1.4.1 Data encryption

Data security is paramount, and all data stored both on-chain and off-chain will be encrypted. Advanced encryption standards (AES) will be used for data at rest, while end-to-end encryption will protect data in transit. This ensures that sensitive medical data is protected against unauthorized access and breaches.

9.3.1.4.2 Access control

Role-based and attribute-based access control mechanisms will be implemented using smart contracts. These controls will define access levels for different stakeholders and automate access permissions based on predefined policies. This ensures that only authorized individuals can access sensitive data, enhancing privacy and security.

9.3.1.4.3 Consent management

Patient consent management will be automated through smart contracts. Patient consent will be recorded on the blockchain, allowing patients to dynamically grant or revoke access to their data. This system ensures that patient consent is always up to date and verifiable, enhancing trust and transparency.

9.3.1.4.4 Auditability and transparency

An immutable audit trail will be maintained for all transactions on the blockchain. This includes recording all access, modifications (Ali et al., 2023), and data-sharing events. Real-time auditability ensures transparency and accountability, allowing for easy tracking and verification of data usage.

9.3.1.5 Phase 5: scalability and performance optimization

9.3.1.5.1 Sharding and layer-2 solutions

Scalability solutions such as sharding and layer-2 protocols will be implemented to enhance the performance of the blockchain network. Sharding distributes the load across multiple chains, while layer-2 solutions like state channels or sidechains offload transactions from the main chain, increasing throughput and reducing latency.

9.3.1.5.2 Performance monitoring

Continuous monitoring of the blockchain network's performance will be conducted to identify and address bottlenecks. Performance metrics will be used to optimize smart contract execution and data retrieval processes, ensuring that the system remains efficient and responsive.

9.3.1.6 Phase 6: compliance and regulatory adherence

9.3.1.6.1 Compliance framework

Ensuring compliance with regulatory standards such as GDPR and HIPAA is crucial. Compliance measures will be integrated into smart contracts to automate compliance checks and reporting. This framework ensures that the system operates within legal and ethical boundaries, protecting patient rights and data privacy (Patel, Joshi, et al., 2022).

9.3.1.6.2 Regular audits

Regular audits will be conducted to validate the system's compliance with regulations. External auditors will be engaged to provide independent verification, while self-auditing mechanisms within the blockchain network will ensure ongoing adherence to compliance requirements.

9.3.1.7 Phase 7: user interface and experience

9.3.1.7.1 User-friendly interfaces

Intuitive user interfaces will be developed for different stakeholders. Patients will have access to portals for managing consent and accessing their data, healthcare providers will have dashboards for data sharing and retrieval, and researchers will have interfaces for accessing anonymized datasets. These interfaces will be designed to be user-friendly and accessible, ensuring ease of use for all stakeholders.

9.3.1.7.2 Mobile access

Mobile accessibility is critical in today's digital age. Mobile apps will be developed for patients and providers, ensuring secure and convenient access to the blockchain network. These apps will incorporate robust security features to protect data integrity and privacy.

9.3.1.8 Phase 8: testing and validation

9.3.1.8.1 Pilot testing

Pilot tests will be conducted with a small group of stakeholders to validate the system's functionality and performance. Feedback from these tests will be used to make necessary adjustments and improvements, ensuring that the system meets user needs and expectations.

9.3.1.8.2 Full-scale deployment

Once pilot testing is successfully completed, the system will be rolled out to all stakeholders. This transition will be carefully managed to ensure a smooth deployment. Training and support will be provided to all users to facilitate the adoption and effective use of the system.

9.3.1.9 Phase 9: continuous improvement

9.3.1.9.1 Feedback mechanism

A continuous feedback mechanism will be established to collect and analyze feedback from all stakeholders. This feedback will be used to implement iterative improvements, ensuring that the system evolves to meet changing needs and challenges.

9.3.1.9.2 Technology upgradation

The system will stay updated with advancements in blockchain technology. Regular updates will incorporate new features and security improvements, and emerging technologies such as quantum-resistant cryptography will be explored to future-proof the system.

9.3.2 Basic steps of the planned process

Assuring the security of medical data using a blockchain-based approach can be better understood by drawing out a flowchart of the system's phases and interactions (Smith et al., 2022). The suggested method is illustrated by the following simple flowchart:

This flowchart outlines the main steps in the process:

- Start the process.
- Receive a new transaction (sender, recipient, data).
- Check if the required fields are present in the transaction.
- Create a new block, including the transaction.
- Perform proof of work to find a new proof.
- Add the new block to the blockchain.
- Respond with information about the mined block.
- Optionally, view the entire blockchain.
- End the process.

Keep in mind that this is a simplified flowchart for educational purposes. In a real-world scenario (Nguyen et al., 2022), additional considerations, such as security measures, encryption, and compliance with healthcare regulations, would need to be incorporated into the design.

9.4 Discussion and flow of implementation

Implementing a blockchain-based approach to ensure the security of medical data involves creating a blockchain system, securing data through encryption, and utilizing smart contracts for access control (Patel, Agrawal, et al., 2022). Below is a simplified outline of a proposed approach using Python. Note that this is a basic illustration, and in a real-world scenario, a more robust and specialized implementation would be required (Kathole and Chaudhari, 2019).

Step 1: Install Required Libraries

```
pip install Flask
pip install Flask-SocketIO
pip install cryptography
```

Step 2: Blockchain Class

Step 3: Interacting with the Blockchain

```
curl -X GET http://localhost:5000/mine
curl -X GET http://localhost:5000/chain
```

For a production system, additional considerations such as data encryption, access controls, and compliance with healthcare regulations need to be taken into account (Al Hadhrami et al., 2023).

Also, consider using more sophisticated frameworks like Flask-RESTful and Flask-RESTful-reqparse for handling API requests.

9.5 Application of working approach

A blockchain-based approach to ensuring the security of medical data can be applied across various healthcare use cases (Liu et al., 2023). Here are some specific applications of blockchain in securing medical data:

- Storing patient health records on a blockchain ensures immutability, transparency, and secure sharing. Patients can control access to their data through smart contracts, enhancing privacy and security (Kathole et al., 2019).
- Using blockchain to record the journey of drugs from manufacturing to distribution ensures authenticity and prevents the entry of counterfeit drugs. Each transaction is recorded on the blockchain, providing a transparent and tamper-proof history (Kumar, Goyal, et al., 2023).
- Storing research data on a blockchain ensures data integrity and prevents manipulation. Smart contracts can facilitate transparent and automated processes for data sharing and consent management among research collaborators (Patel, Pandya, et al., 2022).
- Integrating blockchain for secure device communication and data exchange. Each device interaction is recorded on the blockchain, reducing the risk of unauthorized access or manipulation of health-related data.
- Issuing and managing cryptographic identities on the blockchain enhances security. Smart contracts control access permissions, ensuring that only authorized entities can access sensitive medical data (Sharma et al., 2022).
- Utilizing blockchain to record and verify patient data collected through remote monitoring devices. Smart contracts can facilitate secure and transparent data sharing between healthcare providers and patients.
- Recording epidemiological data, vaccination records, and health statistics on a blockchain ensures accuracy and transparency. This can improve the efficiency of public health surveillance efforts (Gupta et al., 2023).
- Storing genomic data on a blockchain ensures the integrity and privacy of sensitive genetic information. Patients can control access to their genomic data through blockchain-based identity management systems.

These applications demonstrate how a blockchain-based approach can enhance the security, privacy, and transparency of medical data across various aspects of the healthcare ecosystem. Implementation should consider the specific requirements and regulatory considerations of each use case (Kumar, Goyal, et al., 2023).

9.6 Advantages and disadvantages of proposed system

Immutability, decentralization, transparency, and better security through cryptographic techniques are the main benefits of a blockchain-based approach to medical data protection. Immutability is a built-in characteristic of blockchain technology that guarantees patient information cannot be updated or removed once entered. This includes medical data. Decentralization improves system availability and resilience by doing away with the requirement for a central authority, spreading control, and decreasing the likelihood of a single point of failure. Because the entire blockchain is visible to all network participants, transparency is a major advantage that fosters accountability and confidence. To prevent unauthorized parties from accessing sensitive medical information, cryptographic techniques are used to secure data storage and transfer (Zhang et al., 2023).

Additionally, the incorporation of smart contracts in a blockchain-based healthcare system facilitates automated and enforceable access controls. This means that only authorized entities, as defined by smart contracts, can access specific medical data, providing granular control over data privacy and security. The traceability feature of blockchain ensures an auditable and traceable history of medical data transactions, supporting applications such as drug traceability to ensure the authenticity and safety of pharmaceuticals. Moreover, the implementation of consent mechanisms allows patients to have more control over their data, granting or revoking access as needed (Sharma et al., 2022).

The regulatory uncertainty, particularly in the evolving landscape of healthcare and blockchain technology, poses challenges that require adaptability to comply with emerging regulations. Integrating blockchain with existing healthcare IT systems is a complex process that demands careful planning and consideration of interoperability solutions. Ensuring data privacy is crucial, and addressing this concern may involve implementing encryption and privacy-preserving techniques (Patel, Pandya, et al., 2022). The lack of standardized protocols in healthcare blockchains can hinder interoperability, emphasizing the need for collaborative efforts and standardization within the industry. Finally, user education is essential, as healthcare professionals and patients may require increased awareness and understanding of blockchain technology and its implications. In summary, while a blockchain-based approach presents promising solutions for securing medical data, addressing these challenges is crucial for successful implementation in the healthcare ecosystem (Baars et al., 2018).

9.6.1 Advantages

- All participants in the network have visibility into the entire blockchain, promoting transparency.
- Each transaction is linked to the previous one, creating an auditable and traceable history of medical data.
- Patients have more control over their data and can grant or revoke access through consent mechanisms.

9.6.2 Disadvantages

- As the size of the blockchain grows, scalability becomes a concern, leading to potential performance issues.
- Proof of work consensus mechanisms, as used in many blockchains, can be energy-intensive.
- Integrating blockchain with existing healthcare IT systems can be complex.

- Lack of standardized protocols and frameworks for healthcare blockchains can hinder interoperability.
- Users, including healthcare professionals and patients, may need education on blockchain technology and its implications.

It is important to note that the advantages and challenges may vary depending on the specific implementation and use case. Addressing these challenges requires careful planning (Patel, Agrawal, et al., 2022), collaboration, and ongoing technological advancements in the field of blockchain and healthcare (Kathole and Chaudhari, 2019).

9.7 Conclusion

In conclusion, a blockchain-based approach to ensuring the security of medical data holds significant promise for revolutionizing the healthcare industry. The immutability, decentralization, transparency, and security features inherent in blockchain technology address critical challenges related to data integrity, privacy, and interoperability in healthcare systems. By leveraging cryptographic techniques and smart contracts, this approach provides a robust framework for securing sensitive medical information, granting patients greater control over their data, and automating access controls.

The advantages of blockchain technology, such as traceability and the ability to create a tamper-proof and auditable history of medical transactions, offer tangible benefits for applications like drug traceability and patient record management. The potential to streamline processes, enhance data accuracy, and reduce fraud in healthcare operations makes blockchain a compelling solution.

However, it is crucial to acknowledge the challenges and considerations associated with implementing blockchain in healthcare. Scalability concerns, environmental implications of energy-intensive consensus mechanisms, regulatory uncertainties, and the need for interoperability with existing systems pose notable hurdles. Overcoming these challenges requires a collaborative effort from industry stakeholders, policymakers, and technologists.

In navigating the path toward a blockchain-based healthcare system, it is imperative to prioritize user education, ensuring that healthcare professionals and patients alike understand the technology and its implications. Additionally, adherence to evolving regulatory frameworks and the development of standardized protocols are essential for the successful integration of blockchain into the healthcare ecosystem.

In essence, while a blockchain-based approach introduces innovative solutions to enhance the security and integrity of medical data, its effective implementation requires a holistic and adaptive strategy. As the healthcare industry continues to evolve, embracing emerging technologies like blockchain can pave the way for a more secure, transparent, and patient-centric healthcare landscape.

References

Al Hadhrami, M., Al Ghafri, M., & Al Farsi, R. (2023). Blockchain for interoperable and secure healthcare data exchange. *Journal of Healthcare Engineering*, *2023*, 9846231.

Ali, M., Malik, S. B., & Khan, N. A. (2023). Blockchain for pharmaceutical supply chain management. *International Journal of Pharmaceutical Sciences*, *2023*, 123–135.

Baars, M. L. R., et al. (2018). Blockchain-based electronic health record: A case study of smart contracts. *Studies in Health Technology and Informatics*.

Ekblaw, A., Azaria, A., Halamka, J. D., & Lippman, A. (2022). MedRec: A blockchain-based medical record management system. *Blockchain in Healthcare Today*, *5*, 100043.

Esposito, G., Minutolo, L., Otoom, A. M., & Martinelli, F. (2023). Blockchain-based access control framework for secure data sharing. *Journal of Blockchain Technology in Healthcare*, *15*(2), 120–135.

Gupta, M., Bajpai, J., & Mahajan, V. (2023). Ensuring data integrity and authenticity in healthcare information systems with blockchain. *IEEE Transactions on Healthcare Informatics*, *27*(3), 561–575.

Johnson, A., Lee, E., & Chen, P. (2023). Overcoming regulatory and compliance challenges in blockchain for healthcare. *Regulatory and Ethical Aspects of Blockchain in Healthcare*, *19*(2), 203–215.

Kathole, A. B., & Chaudhari, D. D. N. (2019). Pros & Cons of machine learning and security methods. *JGRS*, *21*(4). ISSN: 0374-8588. http://gujaratresearchsociety.in/index.php/

Kathole, A. B., Halgaonkar, D. P. S., & Nikhade, A. (July 2019). Machine learning & its classification techniques. *International Journal of Innovative Technology and Exploring Engineering (IJITEE)*, *8*(9S3). ISSN: 2278-3075.

Kumar, R., Goyal, S. K., & Singh, M. (2023). Blockchain for secure and transparent medical data auditing. *Computer Methods and Programs in Biomedicine*, *224*, 107049.

Kumar, S., Sharma, R., & Jain, T. (2023). Blockchain-based health information exchange in rural healthcare. *Journal of Rural Health*, *39*(1), 100–110.

Liu, L., Chen, K., & Wang, Q. (2023). Smart contracts for automated patient consent in healthcare. *Computer Networks*, *229*, 108992.

Mohammed, N. A., Alotaibi, F., & Alzahrani, M. (2023). Integrating blockchain with existing healthcare IT infrastructure. *Journal of Medical Systems*, *47*(1), 156.

Nguyen, T., Chau, P. C., & Lee, M. (2022). Interoperable health information systems with blockchain technology. *Journal of Biomedical Informatics*, *127*, 104051.

Patel, D., Joshi, H., & Shah, A. (2022). Blockchain-based telemedicine platform for secure and efficient healthcare delivery. *Journal of Telemedicine and Telecare*, *28*(6), 453–465.

Patel, N., Pandya, R., & Bhavsar, S. (2022). A blockchain-based framework for ensuring data integrity in healthcare. *Healthcare Technology Letters*, *9*(4), 123–129.

Patel, S., Agrawal, A., & Mohanty, R. P. (2022). Blockchain-enabled Health Information Exchange: A Survey. *Health Informatics Journal*, *28*(3), 183–198.

Patil, S. D., Kathole, A. B., Kumbhare, S., & Vhatkar, K. (2024). A blockchain-based approach to ensuring the security of electronic data. *International Journal of Intelligent Systems and Applications in Engineering*.

Sharma, A., Singh, M., & Gupta, N. (2023). Blockchain and smart contracts for secure patient data access control. *Future Generation Computer Systems*, *131*, 493–503.

Sharma, S., Sharma, P., & Singhal, M. (2022). Privacy-preserving blockchain-based system for healthcare data. *Journal of Medical Systems*, *46*(5), 879–896.

Smith, E., Brown, J., & Thompson, K. (2022). Blockchain applications in clinical trials and research. *Journal of Clinical Research and Bioethics*, *13*(4), 245–256.

Taherdoost, H. (2023). Blockchain-based internet of medical things. *Applied Science*, *13*, 1287.

Tang, J., Luo, H., & Zhang, X. (2022). Scalability solutions for blockchain in healthcare. *Journal of Network and Computer Applications*, *201*, 103353.

Zhang, H., Wang, Z., Zhao, Y., & Gao, Y. (2023). Decentralized medical data management using blockchain. *International Journal of Medical Informatics*, *162*, 104872.

Zhang, J., Liu, Y., & Zhang, S. (2022). A blockchain-based approach for patient consent management. *IEEE Access*, *10*, 75908–75918.

CHAPTER

Efficient and provably secure framework for authenticating internet of medical things in smart hospitals

10

Vincent Omollo Nyangaresi[1,2]

[1]*Jaramogi Oginga Odinga University of Science & Technology, Bondo, Kenya* [2]*Department of Applied Electronics, Saveetha School of Engineering, SIMATS, Chennai, Tamilnadu, India*

10.1 Introduction

In the conventional healthcare setup, hospitalized patients are physically and continuously monitored by medical professionals. However, with the increase in patient population, this physical monitoring presents some difficulties especially for patients at critical conditions (Sureshkumar et al., 2019). To alleviate this problem, electronic and mobile healthcare technologies have been developed. The Wireless Body Area Networks (WBANs) are typical applications of electronic health (e-health) in which patient health status monitoring is accomplished using sensors. The components of WBANs are normally lightweight smart devices which are characterized with limited battery life, storage space, transmission range and computation power (Deebak et al., 2021; Ever, 2018; Nyangaresi, 2022a). As pointed out in (Sobin, 2020), WBANs can potentially enhance the quality of services offered to patients. This is due to their abilities to permit the collection and transmission of real-time patient data which can facilitate timely emergency response (Kadhim et al., 2020). As a vital building block of Healthcare 4.0, WBANs deploy sensors that are implanted or placed on the human body to monitor the health status in real-time. Some of the physiological parameters that can be monitored this way include electromyography (EMG), body temperature, electrocardiogram (ECG), blood pressure, electroencephalogram (EEG) and heart rate (Pu et al., 2022; Roshini & Kiran, 2022). It is also possible for the WBAN sensors to monitor the patient surrounding environmental parameters such as winds speed, humidity and ambient temperature (Li & Xu, 2022).

Any abnormalities in the values of these parameters are communicated to the remote medical professionals through the internet, which can trigger some corrective reactions (Chen et al., 2022). By providing healthcare to anyone, anywhere and at any time, WBANs in smart hospitals promote pervasive healthcare in which location and time constraints are eliminated (Vijayalakshmi et al., 2021). The data from the wearable and implantable sensors are typically forwarded wirelessly to the nearby controller node, such as a smartphone (Hajar et al., 2021; Kim et al., 2022; Nyangaresi, 2022e). This node may in turn transmit the information to the cloud servers or directly to the

Blockchain and Digital Twin for Smart Hospitals. DOI: https://doi.org/10.1016/B978-0-443-34226-4.00011-3

hospital medical servers. At these endpoints, the data is stored and processed to facilitate medical diagnosis and appropriate response. Although WBANs bring forth convenience, many security and privacy issues in these networks are yet to be solved. For instance, there are some risks of the patient's private information being leaked during data transfer over wireless public channels (Li & Xu, 2022). This can be attributed to the mobility, signal noise and openness of the communication process (Arfaoui et al., 2018). It is therefore possible for attackers to eavesdrop, intercept, forge and modify the transmitted information (Hussain et al., 2022). Although many sophisticated cryptographic procedures have been developed to address some of these problems, they are not appropriate for deployment in WBAN sensors due to their limited energy, storage, CPU capabilities and communication abilities.

It is evident that WBANs in smart hospitals convey critical patient data that is highly secret and sensitive. Any compromise of this data can endanger the lives of the patients, leading to overdoses that can cause deaths. Consequently, security and privacy protection is paramount but challenging (Chandrakar & Om, 2018). As explained in (Nyangaresi & Ma, 2022), authentication and confidentiality are key WBAN issues that require immediate attention. The authors in (Pu et al., 2022) point out that the difficulties in the design of secure and efficient security protocols is the main cause of the challenges encountered in securing information access. For instance, although many of the current schemes allow for mutual authentication and session key negotiation between the WBAN client and Access Point (AP), the client's identities are exchanged in plaintext (Alzahrani et al., 2020). It is therefore feasible for the adversary to discern information emanating from different clients (Li & Xu, 2022) and hence un-traceability is not upheld.

10.1.1 Motivation

Sensitive and private patient information is exchanged between WBAN medical intelligent sensors and the remote medical professionals. The utilization of the public channels for message exchanges exposes it to a myriad of privacy and security attacks. It is therefore paramount that secure authentication protocols be developed to boost people's confidence in these smart health applications. Although many protocols have been developed for this purpose, the provision of perfect security and privacy at low computation and communication complexities is still a mirage. This is because of the many vulnerabilities that still exist in the current protocols. In addition, most of these protocols are based on techniques such as Rivest-Shamir-Adleman (RSA), bilinear pairing, blockchain and Advanced Encryption Standard (AES) which are inefficient for the battery powered WBAN sensors. To reduce communication overheads, long-term permanent security keys can be pre-loaded on the sensors and the controller node can then utilize the common master key to communicate with these sensors. However, the disclosure of these keys will compromise the entire WBAN network. Moreover, forward key secrecy is largely ignored in most of the current authentication protocols. As such, a formally validated secure and privacy preserving protocol is developed in this paper to address some of these issues.

10.1.2 Contributions

Based on the shortcomings noted in most of the conventional WBAN authentication protocols, this paper makes the following contributions:

- Lightweight cryptographic primitives are deployed to authenticate the WBAN intelligent medical sensors and medical professionals in smart hospitals. This helps address inefficiencies in most of the RSA, blockchain, bilinear pairing, AES and public key infrastructure based protocols.
- The freshness checks of all the exchanged messages are accomplished via random nonces, which help alleviate clock syncronization challenges in timestamp-based protocols.
- Transient pseudo-identities are deployed to presever anonymity and untraceability of the WBAN entities during the exchange of sensitive medical information.
- Rigorous formal security verification is executed using both ROR model and BAN logic to demonstrate the strength of the negotiated session key.
- Extensive informal security analysis is carried out to show the robustness of the proposed protocol against typical WBAN attack vectors such as stolen verifier, body sensor unit capture, spoofing, physical capture, offline password guessing, eavesdropping, man-in-the-middle, packet replay, de-synchronization, session hijacking, impersonation, forgery, privileged insider, stolen smart card, and known session-specific temporary information attacks. It is also shown to offer anonymity, untraceability, strong mutual authentication, perfect backward and forward key secrecy.
- Comparative performance analysis is carried out to demonstrate that the proposed protocol offers the highest number of salient security and privacy features at the lowest computation and communication overheads.

10.1.3 Adversarial model

The Dolev-Yao (D-Y) and Canetti-Krawczyk (C-K) models are the most popular threat models that have been heavily deployed in the analysis of authentication protocols. Considering adversary $\tilde{A}$, the D-Y model assumes that $\tilde{A}$ can eavesdrop, intercept, impersonate, modify and delete the exchanged messages. In addition, $\tilde{A}$ can physically capture the sensors and retrieve all security tokens stored in their memories. The adversary in the C-K model has all the capabilities of the D-Y model, and can additionally capture the session states and session keys negotiated among the communicating partics.

10.1.4 Security requirements

To provide strong security and privacy protection that will counter the adversaries with all the capabilities of the D-Y and C-K threat models, the authentication protocol should uphold the following properties:

Anonymity: It should be cumbersome for the adversary to discern the actual identities of the communicating parties from the exchanged messages.

Untraceability: The adversary should find it difficult to associate any communication session to a particular network entity.

Strong mutual authentication: Before the onset of message exchanges, all the involved parties should verify the legitimacy of each other.

Perfect backward and forward key secrecy: Once the attacker has captured the session key used in the current communication process, it should be hard for past and future session keys to be computed from the captured keys.

Robustness againt attacks: The security protocol should withstand stolen verifier, body sensor unit capture, spoofing, physical capture, offline password guessing, eavesdropping, man-in-the-middle, packet replay, de-synchronization, session hijacking, impersonation, forgery, privileged insider, stolen smart card,and known session-specific temporary information attacks.

The rest of this paper is organized as follows: Section discuses some of the related work while Section 10.3 presents the proposed protocol. On the other hand, Section 10.4 details the security analysis of this scheme while Section 10.6 presents its performance evaluation. Finally, Section 10.6 concludes this paper and provides some future work.

10.2 Related work

Many protocols have been presented in literature to provide protection for the information exchanged in WBANs. For instance, authors in (Iqbal et al., 2019; Lu et al., 2018; Prameela, 2018; Vijayakumar et al., 2019; Xiong et al., 2021) have presented bilinear pairing based schemes. Although these protocols provide some levels of security, bilinear pairing operations are computationally extensive (Nyangaresi, 2022b). Similarly, the identity-based signcryption techniques in (Li, Xu, et al., 2019; Shen et al., 2022; Wang & Zhao, 2019) incur excessive computation overheads (Li & Xu, 2022). To solve these performance issues, a lightweight user authentication protocol is developed in (Amin et al., 2018). However, this scheme is susceptible to password guessing and forgery attacks (Ali et al., 2018; Wu et al., 2018). To offer forward key secrecy, an identity-based anonymous authentication protocol is developed in (He et al., 2016). Although this approach is demonstrated to resist many attacks, it cannot provide anonymity and is still vulnerable to key replacement attacks (Kumar, 2020). This challenge is addressed by the anonymous identity-based scheme introduced in (Kumar & Chand, 2020). However, this approach cannot uphold forward key secrecy and malicious user revocation (Pu et al., 2022). On the other hand, a Public Key Infrastructure (PKI) based scheme is developed in (Saeed et al., 2018a). Unfortunately, this protocol faces difficulties in certificate revocation, secret key distribution and certificate management (Nyangaresi et al., 2022).

Based on pseudonyms and hash functions, three-factor authentication techniques are presented in (Ali et al., 2018) and (Shuai et al., 2019). However, these two schemes are susceptible to offline dictionary guessing and privileged insider attacks (Mo et al., 2020). Therefore, a biometrics-based protocol is introduced in (Wan et al., 2021). However, any significant variations of the physiological parameters render this approach unfeasible (Pu et al., 2022). Although the three-factor scheme in (Li, Peng, et al., 2019) can address this issue, it cannot provide anonymity and has high computation overheads. In addition, it is not robust against man-in-the-middle (MitM), privileged insider and packet replays. To offer anonymous authentication, a signature-based scheme is developed in (Saeed et al., 2018b). However, this authentication technique is vulnerable to forgery attacks (Liao et al., 2019). On the other hand, a blockchain based security protocol is developed in (Mwitende et al., 2020). Although this scheme improves the security posture of WBANs, it incurs high storage and computation costs (Nyangaresi, 2022c). Similarly, the scheme in (Gao et al., 2019) exhibits high computation and communication complexities (Hussain et al., 2022). The Elliptic Curve Cryptography (ECC) based user authentication protocol in (Rangwani & Om, 2021) is fairly lightweight and hence may solve the issues in (Mwitende et al., 2020). Unfortunately, the approach in (Rangwani & Om, 2021) fails to offer un-traceability as well as backward and forward key secrecy. In addition, it cannot protect against privileged insider attacks (Yuanbing et al., 2021).

Using digital certificates, a security protocol is presented in (Ullah et al., 2019). Unfortunately, certificate management in networks with large number of devices presents some challenges. In addition, this protocol fails to provide anonymity and mutual authentication (Hussain et al., 2022). Therefore, an anonymous mutual authentication and key negotiation approach is introduced in (Gupta, Tripathi, et al., 2020). Similarly, a privacy preserving mutual authentication technique in (Khatoon et al., 2019) can solve the issues in (Ullah et al., 2019). However, the scheme in (Gupta, Tripathi, et al., 2020) incurs large computation and communication complexities (Nyangaresi, 2022d) while the protocol in (Khatoon et al., 2019) is vulnerable to de-synchronization and privileged insider attacks. The scheme in (Wu et al., 2018) is lightweight and hence might address inefficiencies in (Gupta, Tripathi, et al., 2020). Unfortunately, this scheme cannot offer forward key security (Li et al., 2018) and fails to prevent replay attacks (Chandrakar & Om, 2018). Therefore, the forward key security preserving scheme in (Xiong & Qin, 2015) can address the issues in (Wu et al., 2018). Although this scheme offers anonymity and compromised keys revocation, it cannot withstand sender impersonation (Shim, 2018). To further solve the certificate management challenges in (Ullah et al., 2019), a certificate-less hyper-elliptic curve based protocol is developed in (Noor et al., 2021). Unfortunately, the informal and formal support of the acclaimed security requirements is missing (Hussain et al., 2022). Although the scheme in (Liu et al., 2019) provides security proofs, it cannot offer un-traceability and anonymity (Hsu et al., 2020).

It is clear from the above discussion that security and privacy preservation in WBANs is still a challenging issue. For instance, it has been shown that PKI-based techniques requires the Certificate Authority (CA) to generate, sign, distribute and revoke the certificates (Chen et al., 2020; Gupta, Islam, et al., 2020; Watanabe et al., 2021). Therefore, the CA presents a single point of failure and can become the network bottleneck (Babu et al., 2022; Khezr et al., 2022; Nyangaresi, 2021). In addition, certificate management is cumbersome and inefficient for resource-constrained WBAN intelligent medical sensors (Li & Xu, 2022). On the other hand, it has been shown that bilinear pairing based protocols are time-consuming and hence inapplicable in battery powered WBAN sensors. In addition, majority of the existing schemes have been demonstrated to lack forward key secrecy. It is also possible for the Public Key Generators (PKGs) in PKI-based schemes to have access to private keys belonging to other communicating entities. Therefore, the security of the exchanged messages can be compromised by privileged insiders.

10.3 Proposed protocol

The communicating entities in the proposed protocol include the Medical Professional (*MP*), Gateway Node (*GWN*) and the patient Body Sensor Unit (*BSU*). As shown in Fig. 10.1, the body sensor units are implanted or placed on the patient body and collect vital physiological parameters.

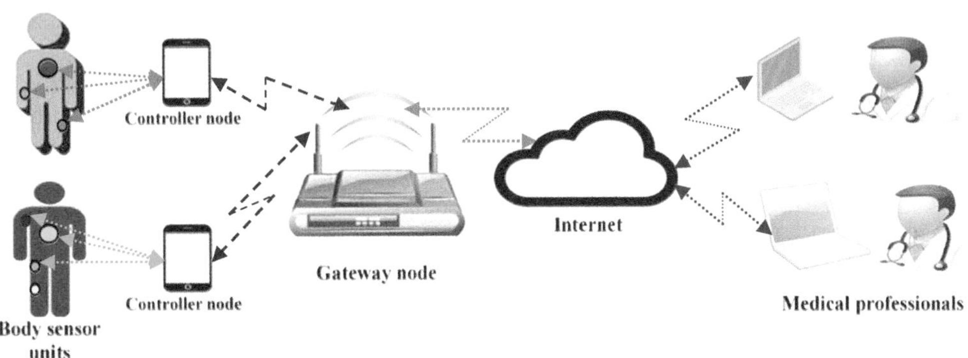

FIGURE 10.1

Proposed protocol with Medical Professional (MP), Gateway Node (GWN) and the patient Body Sensor Unit (BSU).

Table 10.1 Symbols.

Symbol	Description
BSU_i	Body sensor unit *i*
MP_i	Medical expert *i*
GWN	Gateway node
BID_j	*BSU* real identity
MK_{GWN}	Master key of the GWN
MID_i	MP_i real identity
A_3	MP_i masked identity
A_4	MP_i pseudo-identity
PW_M	MP_i password
$\tilde{A}$	Polynomial time adversary
ψ	Session key
$h(.)$	One-way hashing function
$\|\|$	Concatenation operation
$\oplus$	XOR operation
R_i	Random nonces

On the other hand, the controller nodes amalgamate the collected data from the various body sensor units before forwarding them to the *GWN*.

Thereafter, the *GWN* forwards the collected sensor data to the remote medical professionals over the insecure public internet. During these transfers, the adversary can launch numerous security and privacy attacks which can endanger the observed patients. Table 10.1 shows the symbols used in the proposed protocol.

In most cases, the battery powered body sensor units are implented in the body and hence presents some challenges in battery replacement. As such, the proposed protocol uses only light cryptographic primitives such as one-way hashing and exclusive-or (XOR) functions. The four phases that characterize this protocol include body sensor unit registration, medial professional registration, login and mutual authentication, and password update.

10.3.1 Body sensor unit registration

In this phase, the BSU_i must send registration request to the GWN before its actual deployment. Upon receiving this request, the GWN derives some secret tokens for the BSU_i. These private security parameters are then forwarded to the BSU_i for storage in its memory. The steps below describe this registration process in some great details.

Step 1: The BSU_i chooses its real identity BID_j and generates random nonce R_1. This is followed by the computation of $A_1 = h\ (BID_j||R_1)$. Next, it composes registration request message $RQ_1 = \{BID_j, A_1\}$ that is forwarded to the GWN over some private channels as shown in Fig. 10.2.

Step 2: Upon receiving message RQ_1 from the BSU_i, the GWN computes $A_2 = h\ (h\ (BID_j||R_1)||MK_{GWN})$. The GWN then stores parameter set $\{BID_j, A_1\}$ in its database.

Next, it constructs registration response message $RQ_2 = \{A_2\}$ that it transmits to the BSU_i over secured channels.

Step 3: After getting message RQ_2, the BSU_i stores $\{BID_j, A_2\}$ in its memory.

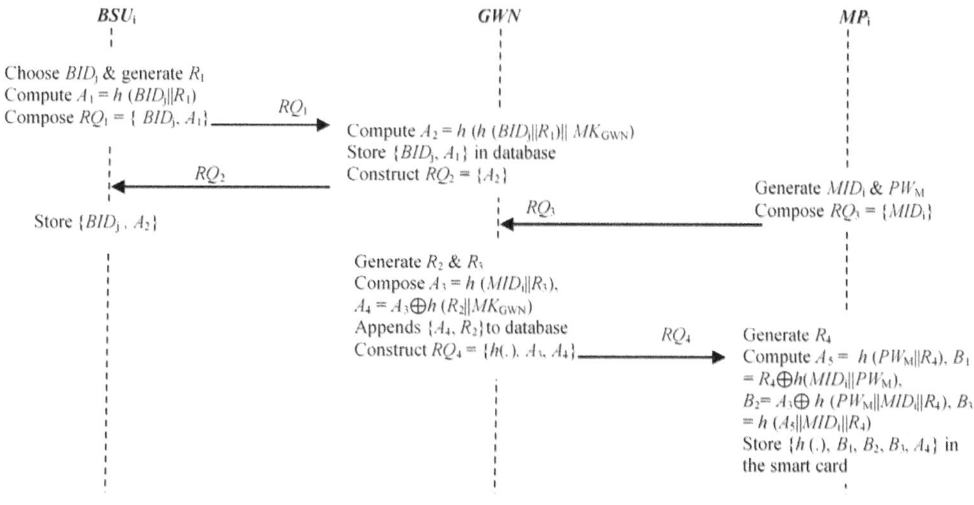

FIGURE 10.2

Registration phase.

10.3.2 Medical professional registration

In this phase, the medical professional MP_i begins by sending registration request to the GWN. Afterwards, the GWN proceeds to derive some private values for the MP_i and issues smart card as described in the following steps.

Step 1: The MP_i generates unique real identity MID_i and some high entropy password PW_M. Next, registration request $RQ_3 = \{MID_i\}$ is composed and sent to the GWN over private channels.

Step 2: On receiving message RQ_3, the GWN generates random nonces R_2 and R_3. This is followed by the computation of $A_3 = h\ (MID_i||R_3)$ and $A_4 = A_3 \oplus h\ (R_2||MK_{GWN})$. Afterwards, the GWN appends value set $\{A_4, R_2\}$ to its database. Finally, it composes registration response message $RQ_4 = \{h(.), A_3, A_4\}$ that it forwards to the MP_i over secured channels as shown in Fig. 10.2.

Step 3: After getting message RQ_4 from the GWN, the MP_i generates random nonce R_4 that it uses to compute parameters $A_5 = h\ (PW_M||R_4)$, $B_1 = R_4 \oplus h(MID_i||PW_M)$, $B_2 = A_3 \oplus\ h\ (PW_M||MID_i|| R_4)$ and $B_3 = h\ (A_5||MID_i||R_4)$. At the end, the MP_i stores value set $\{h\ (.), B_1, B_2, B_3, A_4\}$ in the smart card.

10.3.3 Login and mutual authentication

This phase is executed whenever the MP_i wishes to have access to some patient data held at the BSU_i. To accomplish this, MP_i sends a login request to the GWN which then triggers the steps described below.

Step 1: The MP_i inserts the smart card into its reader and inputs MID_i as well as PW_M. Thereafter, the smart card derives $R_4{}^* = B_1 \oplus h(MID_i||PW_M)$, $A_5{}^* = h\ (PW_M||R_4)$ and $B_3{}^* = h\ (A_5{}^*|| MID_i||R_4{}^*)$. Next, the smart card retrieves B_3 and checks if $B_3{}^* \stackrel{?}{=} B_3$. Upon successful verification, the smart card generates nonce R_5 and computes $A_3 = B_2 \oplus h\ (PW_M||MID_i||R_4)$, $B_4 = BID_j \oplus h(A_4|| A_3)$, $B_5 = R_5 \oplus h\ (A_3||A_4)$ and $C_1 = h\ (BID_j||A_4||R_5||A_3)$. Finally, it constructs authentication message $AUT_1 = \{A_4, B_4, B_5, C_1\}$ and transmits it to the GWN over insecure communication channels as shown in Fig. 10.3.

Step 2: Upon receipt of message AUT_1 from MP_i, the GWN extracts A_4 and nonce R_2 from its database and derives $A_3{}^* = A_4 \oplus h\ (R_2||MK_{GWN})$, $BID_j{}^* = B_4 \oplus h(A_4||A_3{}^*)$, $R_5{}^* = B_5 \oplus h\ (A_3{}^*||A_4)$ and $C_1{}^* = h\ (BID_j{}^*||A_4||R_5{}^*||A_3{}^*)$. Next, it confirms if $C_1{}^* \stackrel{?}{=} C_1$ such that the login request is rejected and the session is aborted if this verification flops. Otherwise, parameters BID_j and $A_1 = h\ (BID_j||R_1)$ are retrieved from the database.

Step 3: The GWN generates nonce R_6 and calculates $A_2 = h\ (h\ (BID_j||R_1)||MK_{GWN})$, $C_2 = h\ (R_6|| A_3) \oplus h\ (A_2||A_4)$, $C_3 = R_5 \oplus\ h(h(R_6||A_3)||A_2)$ and $C_4 = h\ (A_4||BID_j||h(R_6||A_3)||R_5)$. Finally, it composes authentication message $AUT_2 = \{A_4, C_2, C_3, C_4\}$ that is forwarded to the BSU_i over some public channels.

Step 4: When the BSU_i receives message AUT_2 from the GWN, it computes $h\ (R_6||A_3)^* = C_2 \oplus h\ (A_2||A_4)$, $R_5{}^* = C_3 \oplus\ h(h(R_6||A_3)^*||A_2)$ and $C_4{}^* = h\ (A_4||BID_j||h(R_6||A_3)||R_5{}^*)$. Thereafter, it checks if $C_4{}^* \stackrel{?}{=} C_4$. Provided that this validation succeeds, the BSU_i generates random nonce R_7 and derives the session key $\psi = h(h(R_6||A_3)||R_7||R_5)$, $C_5 = R_7 \oplus\ h\ (A_2||R_6)$ and $D_1 = h\ (\psi||R_7||BID_j)$. At last, the BSU_i constructs authentication message $AUT_3 = \{C_5, D_1\}$ that it transmits to the GWN across insecure public channels.

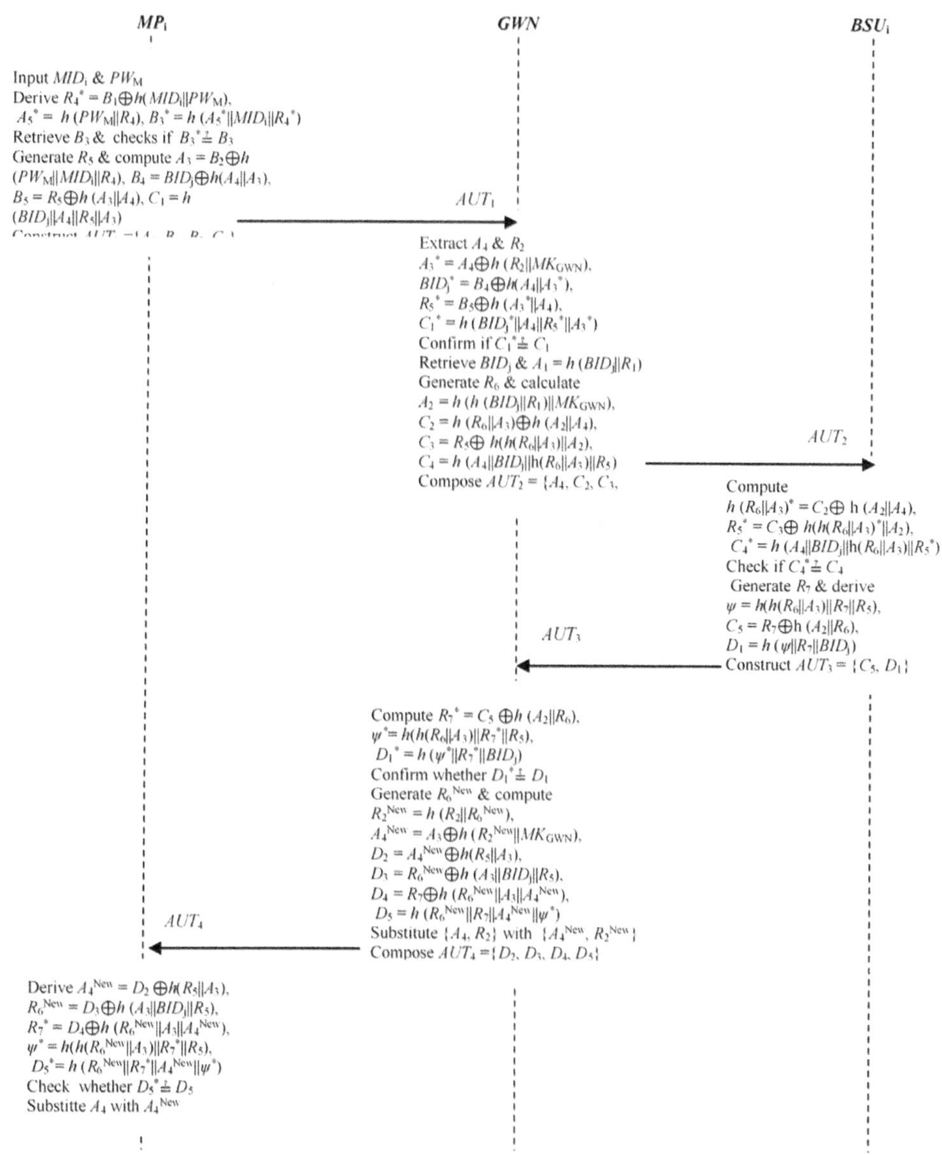

FIGURE 10.3

Login and mutual authentication phase.

Step 5: After getting message AUT_3 from the BSU_j, the GWN computes $R_7^* = C_5 \oplus h\ (A_2||R_6)$, $\psi^* = h(h(R_6||A_3)||R_7^*||R_5)$ and $D_1^* = h\ (\psi^*||R_7^*||BID_j)$. Afterwards, it confirms whether $D_1^* \stackrel{?}{=} D_1$. If this validation is successful, the GWN generates random number R_6^{New}, and computes $R_2^{New} = h$

$(R_2||R_6^{New})$, $A_4^{New} = A_3 \oplus h\ (R_2^{New}||MK_{GWN})$, $D_2 = A_4^{New} \oplus h(R_5||A_3)$, $D_3 = R_6^{New} \oplus h\ (A_3||BID_j||R_5)$, $D_4 = R_7 \oplus h\ (R_6^{New}||A_3||A_4^{New})$ and $D_5 = h\ (R_6^{New}||R_7||A_4^{New}||\psi^*)$. Finally, it composes authentication message $AUT_4 = \{D_2, D_3, D_4, D_5\}$ that is forwarded to the MP_i. Meanwhile the *GWN* substitutes values $\{A_4, R_2\}$ with their updated versions $\{A_4^{New}, R_2^{New}\}$ in its database.

Step 6: On receiving message AUT_4 from the *GWN*, the MP_i derives $A_4^{New} = D_2 \oplus h(R_5||A_3)$, $R_6^{New} = D_3 \oplus h\ (A_3||BID_j||R_5)$, $R_7^* = D_4 \oplus h\ (R_6^{New}||A_3||A_4^{New})$, $\psi^* = h(h(R_6^{New}||A_3)||R_7^*||R_5)$ and $D_5^* = h\ (R_6^{New}||R_7^*||A_4^{New}||\psi^*)$. Next, it checks whether $D_5^* \stackrel{?}{=} D_5$. Provided that this verification is successful, the MP_i substitutes value A_4 with its updated version A_4^{New} in the smart card.

10.3.4 Password change phase

This phase may be triggered when the password belonging to MP_i is compromised. This is a two-step process as described below.

Step 1: The MP_i inserts the smart card into its reader and inputs the current MID_i as well as PW_M. Afterwards, the smart card derives $R_4^* = B_1 \oplus h(MID_i||PW_M)$, $A_5^* = h\ (PW_M||R_4)$ and $B_3^* = h\ (A_5||MID_i||R_4^*)$. It then checks whether $B_3^* \stackrel{?}{=} B_3$. If this validation is succesful, the smart card requests MP_i to input new password.

Step 2: The MP_i generates new password PW_M^* and inputs it to the smart card. Thereafter, the smart card generate random nonce R_4^{New} and derives $A_5^{New} = h\ (PW_M^*||R_4^{New})$, $B_1^{New} = R_4^{New} \oplus (MID_i\ ||PW_M^*)$, $B_2^{New} = A_3 \oplus\ h\ (PW_M^*||MID_i||R_4^{New})$ and $B_3^{New} = h\ (A_5^{New}||MID_i||R_4^{New})$. At last, the smart card stores parameter set $\{h\ (.), B_1^{New}, B_2^{New}, B_3^{New}, A_4\}$.

10.4 Security analysis

In this section, both formal and informal security analyzes of the proposed protocol are described.

10.4.1 Formal security analysis

In this section, both the BAN logic and Real-Or-Random (ROR) model are utilized to prove the security of the derived session key. The choice of these two models is informed by their prevalence during the formal verification of majority of the security schemes.

10.4.1.1 ROR Model-based formal analysis

In the proposed protocol, three participants are involved in the Authentication and Key Agreeement (AKA) procedures. These entities are the MP_i, *GWN* and BSU_i. In this threat model, it is assumed that the WBAN is under active attack by adversary $\tilde{A}$. Here, $\tilde{A}$ can eavesdrop the communication channel and capture the exchanged parameters. Thereafter, packet insertion and deletion can be carried out by $\tilde{A}$. To accomplish this, the five queries in Table 10.2 are executed.

Essentially, if $\tilde{A}$ obtains $f_c = 1$ or $f_c = 0$, it means that ψ is fresh, or not fresh respectively. Otherwise a NULL value is obtained by $\tilde{A}$. The security of ψ is upheld when $\tilde{A}$ is unable to differentiate the result value between ψ and a random nonce. As such, the security proof proceeds as follows.

Table 10.2 Adversarial queries.

Query	Description
Send ()	$\tilde{A}$ sends some message to the network entities upon which it receives some response. It represents an active attack
Reveal ()	Adversary $\tilde{A}$ discloses session key ψ
Execute ()	This is a passive attack in which $\tilde{A}$ eavesdrops exchanged messages
Corrupt ()	$\tilde{A}$ can compromise the security tokens stored in the smart card *SC* or memory
Test ()	Before the onset of the game, $\tilde{A}$ gets access to a flipped unbiased coin f_c.

Hypothesis: Suppose that $Adv_{\tilde{A}}(\check{T})$ is the advantage that $\tilde{A}$ has in breaking session key ψ in polynomial time $\check{T}$. In addition, let $\check{n}_h$ be the number of *Hash* queries, $\check{n}_s$ be the number of *Send* queries and $\hat{H}$ be the range space of the hash function. Morever, let z'_{p_1} and z'_{p_2} denote Zipf's parameters. With these notations, the following holds:

$$Adv_{\tilde{A}}(\check{T}) \leq \frac{\check{n}_h^2}{|\hat{H}|} + 2\left\{ z'_{p_2} \check{n}_s^{z'_{p_1}} \right\}$$

To proof this hypothesis, four games $Game_n^{\tilde{A}}$ are simulated, where $n \in [0, 3]$. Here, the event that adversary $\tilde{A}$ guesses a correct bit f_c in game $Game_n^{\tilde{A}}$ is given by $S_{\tilde{A}}, Game_n^{\tilde{A}}$. The corresponding probability of $S_{\tilde{A}}, Game_n^{\tilde{A}}$ is denoted by $Pr\ [S_{\tilde{A}}, Game_n^{\tilde{A}}]$. Thereafter, these four games are simulated as follows.

$Game_0^{\tilde{A}}$: This game mimics the actual attack of $\tilde{A}$ on the proposed protocol under the *ROR* model. Before the start of the game, random bit f_c is selected. In accordance with the *Hypothesis* above:

$$Adv_{\tilde{A}}(\check{T}) = |2P_r\left[S_{\tilde{A}}, Game_0^{\tilde{A}}\right] - 1| \tag{10.1}$$

$Game_1^{\tilde{A}}$: In this game, $\tilde{A}$ uses the *Execute* query to obtain all the exchanged messages $AUT_1 = \{A_4, B_4, B_5, C_1\}$, $AUT_2 = \{A_4, C_2, C_3, C_4\}$, $AUT_3 = \{C_5, D_1\}$ and $AUT_4 = \{D_2, D_3, D_4, D_5\}$. Thereafter, *Test* and *Reveal* queries are performed to obtain session key $\psi = h(h(R_6||A_3)||R_7||R_5)$. To accomplish this, $\tilde{A}$ has to get nonces R_5, R_6 and R_7, as well as A_3. Therefore, $\tilde{A}$ is unable to derive session key ψ. Consequently, $Game_0^{\tilde{A}}$ and $Game_1^{\tilde{A}}$ are indistinguishable and hence:

$$P_r[S_{\tilde{A}}, Game_1^{\tilde{A}}] = P_r\ [S_{\tilde{A}}, Game_0^{\tilde{A}}] \tag{10.2}$$

$Game_2^{\tilde{A}}$: This is an active attack in which $\tilde{A}$ performs the *Send* query using the captured messages $AUT_1 = \{A_4, B_4, B_5, C_1\}$, $AUT_2 = \{A_4, C_2, C_3, C_4\}$, $AUT_3 = \{C_5, D_1\}$ and $AUT_4 = \{D_2, D_3, D_4, D_5\}$. The goal of $\tilde{A}$ in this game is to obtain session key ψ. Here, $A_4 = A_3 \oplus h\ (R_2||MK_{GWN})$, $B_4 = BID_j \oplus h(A_4||A_3)$, $B_5 = R_5 \oplus h\ (A_3||A_4)$ and $C_1 = h\ (BID_j||A_4||R_5||A_3)$, $C_2 = h\ (R_6||A_3) \oplus h\ (A_2||A_4)$, $C_3 = R_5 \oplus\ h(h(R_6||A_3)||A_2)$, $C_4 = h\ (A_4||BID_j||h(R_6||A_3)||R_5)$, $C_5 = R_7 \oplus\ h\ (A_2||R_6)$, $D_1 = h\ (\psi||R_7||BID_j)$, $D_2 = A_4^{New} \oplus h(R_5||A_3)$, $D_3 = R_6^{New} \oplus h(A_3||BID_j||R_5)$, $D_4 = R_7 \oplus h(R_6^{New}||A_3||A_4^{New})$ and $D_5 = h\ (R_6^{New}||R_7||A_4^{New}||\psi^*)$. Evidently, values C_1, C_2, C_4, D_1 and D_5 are masked by the *Hash* query. On the other hand, parameters A_4, B_5, C_3, C_5, D_2, D_3 and D_4 incorporate random nonces R_2,

R_5, R_6 and R_7. These nonces are deployed to avert collisions from other authentication sessions. Based on the birthday paradox, the following relation holds:

$$|P_r\left[S_{\tilde{A}}, Game_2^{\tilde{A}}\right] - P_r\left[S_{\tilde{A}}, Game_1^{\tilde{A}}\right]| \leq \frac{\check{n}_h^2}{|\hat{H}|} \tag{10.3}$$

Game$_3^{\tilde{A}}$: In this game, the adversary $\tilde{A}$ executes the *Corrupt* (*SC*) query that helps obtain the security tokens stored in the smart card. These values include $\{h\ (.), B_1, B_2, B_3, A_4\}$ and are obtained using power analysis techniques. Here, $B_1 = R_4 \oplus h(MID_i||PW_M)$, $B_2 = A_3 \oplus\ h\ (PW_M||MID_i||R_4)$, $B_3 = h\ (A_5|| MID_i||R_4)$, $A_3 = h\ (MID_i||R_3)$, $R_4{}^* = B_1 \oplus h(MID_i||PW_M)$ and $A_4 = A_3 \oplus h\ (R_2||MK_{GWN})$. For the $\tilde{A}$ to obtain R_4 and A_3, the MP_i's real identity MID_i and password PW_M have to be computed. Provided that it is computationally infeasible to guess PW_M, an adversary $\tilde{A}$ is unable to distinguish between $Game_2^{\tilde{A}}$ and $Game_3^{\tilde{A}}$. Therefore, using the Zipf's law, the following result is obtained:

$$|P_r[S_{\tilde{A}}, Game_3^{\tilde{A}}] - P_r\ [S_{\tilde{A}}, Game_2^{\tilde{A}}]| \leq z'_{p_2} \check{n}_s^{z'_{p_1}} \tag{10.4}$$

Since all the four games have been played, adversary $\tilde{A}$ gets the guessed bit f_c with the following probability:

$$P_r\left[S_{\tilde{A}}, Game_3^{\tilde{A}}\right] = \frac{1}{2} \tag{10.5}$$

By using (1) and (2), the following result is obtained:

$$\begin{aligned} \frac{1}{2} Adv_{\tilde{A}}(\check{T}) &= |P_r\left[S_{\tilde{A}}, Game_0^{\tilde{A}}\right] - \frac{1}{2}| \\ &= |P_r\left[S_{\tilde{A}}, Game_1^{\tilde{A}}\right] - \frac{1}{2}| \end{aligned} \tag{10.6}$$

On the other hand, relations (5) and (6) are utilized to get the following:

$$\frac{1}{2} Adv_{\tilde{A}}(\check{T}) = |P_r\left[S_{\tilde{A}}, Game_1^{\tilde{A}}\right] - P_r\left[S_{\tilde{A}}, Game_3^{\tilde{A}}\right]| \tag{10.7}$$

Using the triangular inequality, the following is obtained:

$$\begin{aligned} \frac{1}{2} Adv_{\tilde{A}}(\check{T}) &= |P_r\left[S_{\tilde{A}}, Game_1^{\tilde{A}}\right] - P_r\left[S_{\tilde{A}}, Game_3^{\tilde{A}}\right]| \\ &\leq |P_r\left[S_{\tilde{A}}, Game_1^{\tilde{A}}\right] - P_r\left[S_{\tilde{A}}, Game_2^{\tilde{A}}\right]| \\ &+ |P_r\left[S_{\tilde{A}}, Game_2^{\tilde{A}}\right] - P_r\left[S_{\tilde{A}}, Game_3^{\tilde{A}}\right]| \\ &\leq \frac{\check{n}_h^2}{2|\hat{H}|} + z'_{p_2} \check{n}_s^{z'_{p_1}} \end{aligned} \tag{10.8}$$

The multiplication of (8) by 2 results in the following relation:

$$Adv_{\tilde{A}}(\check{T}) \leq \frac{\check{n}_h^2}{|\hat{H}|} + 2\left\{z'_{p_2} \check{n}_s^{z'_{p_1}}\right\} \tag{10.9}$$

Relation (9) above completes the proof of the formulated hypothesis.

10.4.1.2 BAN logic-based formal analysis

In this sub-section, the mutual authentication among the *GWN*, MP_i and BSU_i is proved. The choice of BAN logic is due to its wide application in the analysis of mutual authentication in numerous authentication protocols. In the proposed protocol, the communicating entities negotiate a session key ψ after succesfully authenticating each other. Table 10.3 details the various BAN logic notations used in this proof.

During this proof, the BAN logic rules in Table 10.4 are deployed.

In the proposed protocol, the main objectives of the BAN logic include successful mutual authentication and session key negotiation among all the principals. The eight goals in Table 10.5 are formulated as a proof of the mutual authentication executed among the communicating entities.

During the AKA procedures, the four messages exchanged include $AUT_1 = \{A_4, B_4, B_5, C_1\}$, $AUT_2 = \{A_4, C_2, C_3, C_4\}$, $AUT_3 = \{C_5, D_1\}$and $AUT_4 = \{D_2, D_3, D_4, D_5\}$. By eliminating other parameters that cannot efficiently offer the logical properties of BAN, these messages are transformed into idealized format (IDF) as follows:

AUT_1: $MP_i \rightarrow GWN$: $\{A_4, B_4, B_5, C_1\}$
IDF: $\{R_5, BID_j\}_{A_3}$
AUT_2: $GWN \rightarrow BSU_i$: $\{A_4, C_2, C_3, C_4\}$
IDF: $\{h(R_6|(A_3), R_5\}_{A_2}$
AUT_3: $BSU_i \rightarrow GWN$: $\{C_5, D_1\}$
IDF: $\{R_7\}_{A_2}$
AUT_4: $GWN \rightarrow MP_i$: $\{D_2, D_3, D_4, D_5\}$
IDF: $\{R_6, R_7\}_{A_3}$

After every successful AKA procedures, each communicating entity trusts that it has secret keys shared among other entities as well. In addition, each party believes that the generated pseudo-identities and random nonces are fresh. Moreover, all the entities trust that each legitimate entity is in control of its parameters. During the BAN logic proofs, the following assumptions (AS_k) are made:

AS_1: $GWN| \equiv \#(R_5)$
AS_2: $GWN| \equiv \#(R_7)$
AS_3: $BSU_i| \equiv \#(h(R_6||A_3))$
AS_4: $MP_i| \equiv \#(R_6)$
AS_5: $MP_i| \equiv GWN \Rightarrow (MP_i \leftrightarrow^{\psi} GWN)$
AS_6: $GWN| \equiv MP_i \Rightarrow (MP_i \leftrightarrow^{\psi} GWN)$

Table 10.3 BAN logic notations.

Notation	Description
$S| \equiv Q$	Principal *S* believes statement *Q*
$\{Q\}_K$	Statement *Q* is enciphered with *K*
$S| \sim Q$	Principal *S* once said statement *Q*
$\# Q$	Statement *Q* is fresh
$S \Rightarrow Q$	Principal *S* controls *Q*
$S \leftrightarrow Q$	*S* receives statement *Q*
$S \leftrightarrow^{\psi} M$	Principals *S* and *M* share key ψ

Table 10.4 BAN logic rules.

Rule	Description
$\frac{S\vert\equiv M \Rightarrow Q, S\vert\equiv M\vert\equiv Q}{S\vert\equiv Q}$	Jurisdiction rule (JR)
$\frac{S\vert\equiv\#(Q)}{S\vert\equiv\#(Q,N)}$	Freshness rule (FR)
$\frac{S\vert\equiv S \leftrightarrow^{\psi} M, S \lhd \{Q\}_{\psi}}{S\vert\equiv M\vert\sim Q}$	Message-meaning rule (MMR)
$\frac{S\vert\equiv\#(Q), S\vert\equiv M\vert\sim Q}{S\vert\equiv M\vert\equiv Q}$	Nonce verification rule (NVR)
$\frac{S\vert\equiv(Q,N)}{S\vert\equiv Q}$	Believe rule (BR)

Table 10.5 Mutual authentication goals.

Goal (G)	Denotation
G_1	$MP_i\vert\equiv MP_i \leftrightarrow^{\psi} GWN$
G_2	$MP_i\vert\equiv GWN\vert\equiv MP_i \leftrightarrow^{\psi} GWN$
G_3	$GWN\vert\equiv MP_i \leftrightarrow^{\psi} GWN$
G_4	$GWN\vert\equiv MP_i \vert\equiv MPi \leftrightarrow^{\psi} \mathrm{GWN}$
G_5	$BSU_i\vert\equiv BSU_i \leftrightarrow^{\psi} GWN$
G_6	$BSU_i\vert\equiv GWN\vert\equiv BSU_i \leftrightarrow^{\psi} GWN$
G_7	$GWN\vert\equiv BSU_i \leftrightarrow^{\psi} GWN$
G_8	$GWN\vert\equiv BSU_i\vert\equiv BSU_i \leftrightarrow^{\psi} GWN$

AS_7: $BSU_i|\equiv GWN \Rightarrow \left(BSU_i \leftrightarrow^{\psi} GWN\right)$
AS_8: $GWN|\equiv BSU_i \Rightarrow \left(BSU_i \leftrightarrow^{\psi} GWN\right)$
AS_9: $MP_i|\equiv \left(MP_i \leftrightarrow^{A_3} GWN\right)$
AS_{10}: $GWN|\equiv \left(MP_i \leftrightarrow^{A_3} GWN\right)$
AS_{11}: $BSU_i|\equiv \left(BSU_i \leftrightarrow^{A_2} GWN\right)$
AS_{12}: $GWN|\equiv \left(BSU_i \leftrightarrow^{A_2} GWN\right)$

The BAN logic analysis of the proposed protocol then proceeds as follows:

Based on AUT_1, B_1 is obtained.

$\boldsymbol{B_1}$: $\mathrm{GWN} \lhd \{R_5, BID_j\}_{A_3}$

The application of *MMR* on both B_1 and AS_{10} yields B_2.

$\boldsymbol{B_2}$: $GWN|\equiv MP_i|\sim (R_5, BID_j)$

On the other hand, B_3 is obtained by applying *FR* on AS_1 and B_2.

$\boldsymbol{B_3}$: $\mathrm{GWN}|\equiv \# (\mathrm{R}_5, BID_j)$

To get B_4, *NVR* is applied on B_2 and B_3.

$\boldsymbol{B_4}$: $GWN|\equiv MP_i \mid\equiv (R_5, BID_j)$

However, B_5 is induced by the application of *BR* on B_4.

$\boldsymbol{B_5}$: $GWN|\equiv MP_i \mid\equiv (R_5)$

From AUT_2, B_6 is obtained as follows.

$\boldsymbol{B_6}$: $BSU_i \lhd \{h(R_6|(A_3), R_5\}_{A_2}$

On the other hand, using *MMR* on both B_6 and AS_{13} yields B_7.

B_7: $BSU_i|\equiv GWN| \sim \{h(R_6||A_3), R_5)$

To obtain B_8, *FR* is used on B_7 and AS_3.

B_8: $BSU_i| \equiv \# \{h(R_6||A_3), R_5)$

However, B_9 is induced by the application of *NVR* on B_7 and B_8 as follows.

B_9: $BSU_i| \equiv GWN| \equiv \{h(R_6||A_3), R_5)$

From AUT_3, B_9 is obtained as follows.

B_{10}: GWN $\lhd\{R_7\}_{A_2}$

By using *MMR* on B_8 and AS_5, B_{11} is yielded.

B_{11}: $GWN|\equiv BSU_i| \sim (R_7)$

On the other hand, using the *NVR* on B_9 and B_{10} yields B_{12}

B_{12}: $GWN| \equiv BSU_i| \equiv (R_7)$

In the proposed protocol, BSU_i and *GWN* negotiate session key $\psi = h(h(R_6||A_3)||R_7||R_5)$. Hence, both B_{13} and B_{14} can be induced from B_9 and B_{12} as follows.

B_{13}: $GWN| \equiv BSU_i| \equiv \left(BSU_i \leftrightarrow^{\psi} GWN\right)$, and thus $\boldsymbol{G_8}$ is achieved.

B_{14}: $BSU_i| \equiv GWN| \equiv \left(BSU_i \leftrightarrow^{\psi} GWN\right)$ and hence $\boldsymbol{G_6}$ is attained.

On the other hand, using *JR* on B_{13} and AS_8 yields B_{15}.

B_{15}: $GWN| \equiv \left(BSU_i \leftrightarrow^{\psi} GWN\right)$, effectively fulfilling $\boldsymbol{G_7}$.

The usage of *JR* on B_{14} and AS_7 results in B_{16}.

B_{16}: $BSU_i| \equiv \left(BSU_i \leftrightarrow^{\psi} GWN\right)$, thus $\boldsymbol{G_5}$ is satisfied.

From AUT_4, B_{17} is obtained as follows.

B_{17}: $MP_i \lhd\{R_6, R_7\}_{A_3}$

To get B_{18}, *MMR* is used on both AS_9 and B_{17}.

B_{18}: $MP_i |\equiv GWN| \sim (R_6, R_7)$

However, using *FR* on B_{18} and AS_4 induces B_{19} as follows.

B_{19}: $MP_i |\equiv \# (R_6, R_7)$

Using *NVR* on B_{16} and B_{17} results in B_{20}.

B_{20}: $MP_i |\equiv GWN |\equiv (R_6, R_7)$

During the AKA procedures, the MP_i and *GWN* negotiate session key $\psi^* = h(h(R_6||A_3)||R_7^*||R_5)$. Therefore, both B_{21} and B_{22} can be induced from B_5 and B_{18}.

B_{21}: $MP_i| \equiv GWN| \equiv \left(MP_i \leftrightarrow^{\psi} GWN\right)$, effectively attaining $\boldsymbol{G_2}$.

B_{22}: $GWN| \equiv MP_i| \equiv \left(MP_i \leftrightarrow^{\psi} GWN\right)$, and hence $\boldsymbol{G_4}$ is realized.

On the other hand, the application of *JR* on B_{21} and AS_5 results in B_{23}.

B_{23}: $MP_i| \equiv \left(MP_i \leftrightarrow^{\psi} GWN\right)$, and therefore $\boldsymbol{G_1}$ is satisfied.

Finally, B_{24} is realized by using *JR* on B_{22} and AS_6 as follows.

B_{24}: $GWN| \equiv \left(MP_i \leftrightarrow^{\psi} GWN\right)$, attaining $\boldsymbol{G_3}$.

The successful realization of all the formulated BAN logic goals demonstrate the existence of strong mutual authentication and session key agreement among MP_i, *GWN* and BSU_i.

10.4.2 Informal security analysis

In this sub-section, it is shown that the proposed protocol is secure under all the assumptions of Dolev-Yao and Canetti-Krawczyk threat models. To achieve this, the following theorems are formulated and proofed.

Theorem 10.1: This protocol offer strong mutual authentication.

Proof: All the three entities involved in information exchange have to mutually verify the legitimacy of each other before exchanging the collected data. For instance, the *GWN* authenticates the MP_i by confirming whether $C_1^* \stackrel{?}{=} C_1$, while the the BSU_i authenticates the *GWN* by checking if $C_4^* \stackrel{?}{=} C_4$. On the other hand, the the MP_i authenticates the *GWN* through the confirmation of whether $D_5^* \stackrel{?}{=} D_5$. As such, at the end of the login and authentication phase, each of the entities is assured that it is communicating with a legitimate party.

Theorem 10.2: Impersonation and forgery attacks are prevented.

Proof: The assumption made in these attacks is that the adversary $\tilde{A}$ is interested in authenticating to the *GWN* and BSU_i. It is also assumed that $\tilde{A}$ has captured messages $AUT_2 = \{A_4, C_2, C_3, C_4\}$, $AUT_3 = \{C_5, D_1\}$ and $AUT_4 = \{D_2, D_3, D_4, D_5\}$. Using these parameters, $\tilde{A}$ tries to compute $h(h(R_6\|A_3)\|A_2) = C_3 \oplus R_5$ and $h(A_2\|A_4) = C_2 \oplus h(R_6\|A_3)$ in an effort to compromise other legitimate user's sessions. To accomplish this, $\tilde{A}$ needs to derive valid session keys $\psi = h(h(R_6\|A_3)\|R_7\|R_5)$ and $\psi^* = h(h(R_6\|A_3)\|R_7^*\|R_5)$. Here, $A_3 = h(MID_i\|R_3)$, $A_4 = A_3 \oplus h(R_2\|MK_{GWN})$, $C_2 = h(R_6\|A_3) \oplus h(A_2\|A_4)$, $C_3 = R_5 \oplus h(h(R_6\|A_3)\|A_2)$, $C_4 = h(A_4\|BID_j\|h(R_6\|A_3)\|R_5)$, $C_5 = R_7 \oplus h(A_2\|R_6)$, $D_1 = h(\psi\|R_7\|BID_j)$, $D_2 = A_4^{New} \oplus h(R_5\|A_3)$, $D_3 = R_6^{New} \oplus h(A_3\|BID_j\|R_5)$, $D_4 = R_7 \oplus h(R_6^{New}\|A_3\|A_4^{New})$ and $D_5 = h(R_6^{New}\|R_7\|A_4^{New}\|\psi^*)$. Evidently, none of the captured parameters will assist $\tilde{A}$ in discerning random nonces R_3, R_5, R_6 and R_7 needed to compute ψ and ψ^*. The one-way hashing function deployed to mask these nonces and A_3 implies that it is computationally impossible to reverse this function. Therefore, the derivation of ψ flops and so does impersonation and forgery attacks.

Theorem 10.3: This scheme is robust against physical capture and offline password guessing attacks.

Proof: Suppose that adversary $\tilde{A}$ is successful in physically capturing the MP_i's smart card. Next, all the security values $\{h(.), B_1, B_2, B_3, A_4\}$ in the smart card are extracted. Thereafter, $\tilde{A}$ tries to derive MP_i's password PW_M. In this protocol, PW_M is incorporated in parameters $A_5 = h(PW_M\|R_4)$, $B_1 = R_4 \oplus h(MID_i\|PW_M)$ and $B_2 = A_3 \oplus h(PW_M\|MID_i\|R_4)$. Any efforts towards the recovery of PW_M from these parameters will require the reversing of the one-way hashing functions. However, this is computationally infeasible and none of the values retrieved from the smart card can help $\tilde{A}$ to compute PW_M. As such, both offline guessing and physical capture attacks flop.

Theorem 10.4: Perfect backward and forward key secrecy are provided.

Proof: The assumption made in this attack is that $\tilde{A}$ has access to the *GWN*'s master key MK_{GWN}. Using this key, $\tilde{A}$ tries to compute session keys used in the previous and subsequent communication sessions. In this protocol, $\psi = h(h(R_6\|A_3)\|R_7\|R_5)$, where $A_3 = h(MID_i\|R_3)$. Here, random nonce R_3 and R_6 are generated at the *GWN*, while R_5 is generated at the smart card. On the other hand, the BSU_i generates random nonce R_7. The independent generation and session-specific nature of these random nonces implies that they are cumbersome for $\tilde{A}$ to correctly and simultaneously guess them. Therefore, the secrecy of past and future session keys is upheld.

Theorem 10.5: This protocol protects against stolen smart card attacks.

Proof: Based on the premises of Theorem 10.3, an adversary $\tilde{A}$ can capture MP_i's smart card and utilize power analysis to extract $\{h\ (.), B_1, B_2, B_3, A_4\}$ stored in it. Next, $\tilde{A}$ tries to authenticate itself to the GWN and BSU_i. To succeed, authentication messages $AUT_1 = \{A_4, B_4, B_5, C_1\}$, $AUT_2 = \{A_4, C_2, C_3, C_4\}$ and $AUT_3 = \{C_5, D_1\}$ must be constructed. Here, $A_4 = A_3 \oplus h\ (R_2 || MK_{GWN})$, $B_4 = BID_j \oplus h(A_4 || A_3)$, $A_3 = h\ (MID_i || R_3)$, $B_5 = R_5 \oplus h\ (A_3 || A_4)$, $C_1 = h\ (BID_j || A_4 || R_5 || A_3)$, $C_2 = h\ (R_6 || A_3) \oplus h\ (A_2 || A_4)$, $A_2 = h\ (h\ (BID_j || R_1) || MK_{GWN})$, $C_3 = R_5 \oplus\ h(h(R_6 || A_3) || A_2)$, $C_4 = h\ (A_4 || BID_j || h(R_6 || A_3) || R_5)$, $C_5 = R_7 \oplus$ h $(A_2 || R_6)$ and $D_1 = h\ (\psi || R_7 || BID_j)$. It is clear that although $\tilde{A}$ has access to A_4, parameter set $\{B_4, B_5, C_1, C_2, C_3, C_4, C_5, D_1\}$ is still required and which cannot be obtained from the smart card. To compute these parameters, $\tilde{A}$ needs BSU's real identity BID_j, MP_i's real ident;ty MID_i, and GWN's master key MK_{GWN}. Since these parameters are never transmitted in plaintext over the insecure public channels, $\tilde{A}$ cannot obtain them. As such, stolen smart card attacks against this scheme fail.

Theorem 10.6: Known session-specific temporary information (KSSTI) attacks are prevented.

Proof: Suppose that adversary $\tilde{A}$ has captured all the random nonces utilized during the login and mutual authentication phase. The next goal is to use these nonces to derive the session key $\psi = h(h\ (R_6 || A_3) || R_7 || R_5)$ as well as the authentication parameters B_3^*, C_1^*, C_4^*, D_1^* and D_5^*. Here, $B_3^* = h\ (A_5^* || MID_i || R_4^*)$, $A_5^* = h\ (PW_M || R_4)$, $C_1^* = h\ (BID_j^* || A_4 || R_5^* || A_3^*)$, $A_4 = A_3 \oplus h\ (R_2 || MK_{GWN})$, $C_4^* = h\ (A_4 || BID_j || h(R_6 || A_3) || R_5^*)$, $A_3 = h\ (MID_i || R_3)$, $D_1^* = h\ (^{\psi *} || R_7^* || BID_j)$ and $D_5^* = h\ (R_6^{New} || R_7^* || A_4^{New} || ^{\psi *})$. Evidently, this requires knowledge of MP_i's password PW_M, real identity MID_i, BSU_i's actual identity BID_j as well GWN's master key, MK_{GWN}. According to Theorem 10.3, PW_M is computationally infeasible to recover. In addition, Theorem 10.5 demonstrates the difficulty of obtaining BID_j, MID_i and MK_{GWN}. As such, the proposed scheme is robust against *KSSTI* attack.

Theorem 10.7: This scheme can withstand session hijacking and privileged insider attacks.

Proof: Suppose that privileged insiders such as system adminsitrators manage to capture MP_i's registration message $RQ_3 = \{MID_i\}$and the BSU_i's registration message $RQ_1 = \{BID_j, A_1\}$. Here, $A_1 = h\ (BID_j || R_1)$. The goal here is to use these parameters to hijack the BSU_i and MP_i communication sessions. This requires that MP_i's authentication value C_1, the BSU_i session key $\psi = h(h(R_6 || A_3) || R_7 || R_5)$ and authenticating value D_1 be computed. However, according to Theorem 10.6, C_1 and D_1 cannot be derived by the adversary. In addition, Theorems 10.2 and 10.4 details the difficulty of adversarial derivation of sesion key ψ. During the login and authentication phase, the MP_i constructs message $AUT_1 = \{A_4, B_4, B_5, C_1\}$ while the BSU_i composes message $AUT_3 = \{C_5, D_1\}$. Suppose that $\tilde{A}$ wants to compose these messages and attempts to hijack BSU_i and MP_i sessions. According to Theorem 10.5, it is cumbersome for $\tilde{A}$ to construct these authentication messages. Therefore, both session hijacking and privileged insider attacks are thwarted.

Theorem 10.8: Packet replay and de-synchronization attacks are thwarted.

Proof: In these attacks, it is assumed that adversary $\tilde{A}$ has intercepted authentication messages $AUT_1 = \{A_4, B_4, B_5, C_1\}$, $AUT_2 = \{A_4, C_2, C_3, C_4\}$, $AUT_3 = \{C_5, D_1\}$and $AUT_4 = \{D_2, D_3, D_4, D_5\}$.

Here, $A_4 = A_3 \oplus h\ (R_2||MK_{GWN})$, $A_3 = h\ (MID_i||R_3)$, $B_4 = BID_j \oplus h(A_4||A_3)$, $B_5 = R_5 \oplus h\ (A_3||A_4)$, $C_1 = h\ (BID_j||A_4||R_5||A_3)$, $C_2 = h\ (R_6||A_3) \oplus h\ (A_2||A_4)$, $C_3 = R_5 \oplus\ h(h(R_6||A_3)||A_2)$, $C_4 = h\ (A_4||BID_j||h(R_6||A_3)||R_5)$, $C_5 = R_7 \oplus$ h $(A_2||R_6)$ and $D_1 = h\ (\psi||R_7||BID_j)$. On receiving message AUT_1 from MP_i, the GWN derives $C_1{}^* = h\ (BID_j{}^*|A_4||R_5{}^*||A_3{}^*)$ and confirms if $C_1{}^* \stackrel{?}{=} C_1$. On the other hand, after getting message AUT_2 from the GWN, the BSU_i computes $C_4{}^* = h\ (A_4||BID_j||h(R_6||A_3)||R_5{}^*)$ and checks if $C_4{}^* \stackrel{?}{=} C_4$. Similarly, on obtaining message AUT_3 from the BSU_i, the GWN computes $D_1{}^* = h\ (\psi^*||R_7{}^*||BID_j)$ and confirms whether $D_1{}^* \stackrel{?}{=} D_1$. Therefore, the freshness of the random nonces in all the exchanged messages is validated at the receiver end, hence thwarting replay attacks. However, in most schemes, timestamps are used to verify the freshness of the received messages. This renders these schemes susceptible to clock de-synchronization attacks. Since the proposed protocol confirms freshness of received messages devoid of timestamps, clock syncronization challenges are eliminated.

Theorem 10.9: This protocol is resilient against eavesdropping and man-in-the-middle attacks.

Proof: To login to the the GWN, the MP_i constructs message $AUT_1 = \{A_4, B_4, B_5, C_1\}$ and forwards it to the GWN over public channels. Suppose that $\tilde{A}$ eavesdrops the public channel and captures values A_4, B_4, B_5 and C_1. Thereafter, $\tilde{A}$ derives $A_3{}^{\tilde{A}} = h\ (MID_i{}^{\tilde{A}}||R_3{}^{\tilde{A}})$, $B_4{}^{\tilde{A}} = BID_j{}^{\tilde{A}} \oplus h(A_4{}^{\tilde{A}}||A_3{}^{\tilde{A}})$ and composes bogus login message $AUT_1{}^{\tilde{A}} = \{A_4{}^{\tilde{A}}, B_4{}^{\tilde{A}}, B_5{}^{\tilde{A}}, C_1{}^{\tilde{A}}\}$ that it transmits to GWN. Upon receiving message $AUT_1{}^{\tilde{A}}$ from $\tilde{A}$, the GWN extracts A_4 and nonce R_2 from its database and derives $A_3{}^* = A_4 \oplus h\ (R_2||MK_{GWN})$, $BID_j{}^* = B_4 \oplus h(A_4|A_3{}^*)$, $R_5{}^* = B_5 \oplus h\ (A_3{}^*||A_4)$ and $C_1{}^* = h\ (BID_j{}^*||A_4|R_5{}^*|A_3{}^*)$. This is followed by the confirmation of whether $C_1{}^* \stackrel{?}{=} C_1$. Since $A_4{}^{\tilde{A}} \neq A_4$, it follows that $C_1{}^{\tilde{A}} = h\ (BID_j{}^{\tilde{A}}|A_4{}^{\tilde{A}}|R_5{}^{\tilde{A}}|A_3{}^{\tilde{A}}) \neq C_1{}^*$. When this happens, the login request is rejected and the session is aborted. Therefore, both eavesdropping and man-in-the-middle attacks are prevented.

Theorem 10.10: Body sensor unit (BSU) capture and spoofing attacks are prevented.

Proof: In WBANs, some body sensor units are implanted in the patient body while others are placed on the patient's skin or in the vicinity of the patients. The assumption made here is that $\tilde{A}$ has captured the BSU_i placed in the vicinity of the patient. This is followed by the extraction of values $\{BID_j, A_2\}$ stored in its memory via power analysis techniques. Next, $\tilde{A}$ attempts to authentiate with the GWN. This requires that messages $AUT_3 = \{C_5, D_1\}$ be constructed, where $C_5 = R_7 \oplus h\ (A_2||R_6)$, $D_1 = h\ (\psi||R_7||BID_j)$, $\psi = h(h(R_6||A_3)||R_7||R_5)$ and $A_3 = h\ (MID_i||R_3)$. Although $\tilde{A}$ has successfully obtained keying materials BID_j and A_2, it still requires random nonces R_3, R_5, R_6 and R_7. In addition, it still needs MP_i real identity MID_i. In accordance with Theorem 10.5, it is difficult for $\tilde{A}$ to obtain MID_i. In addition, Theorem 10.4 describes the difficulty of deriving random nonces. As such, this scheme effectively prevents BSU_i capture and spoofing attacks.

Theorem 10.11: This protocol is robust against stolen verifier attacks.

Proof: Suppose that $\tilde{A}$ manages to steal the GWN database and hence captures parameter set $\{BID_j, A_1\}$,$\{A_4, R_2\}$ stored in it. Thereafter, it tries to derive the GWN's session key $\psi^* = h(h(R_6||A_3)||R_7{}^*||R_5)$. Here, $R_7{}^* = C_5 \oplus h\ (A_2||R_6)$, $A_3 = h\ (MID_i||R_3)$ and $A_2 = h\ (h\ (BID_j||R_1)||MK_{GWN})$. It is clear that although $\tilde{A}$ has values A_1, A_4, R_2 and BID_j, it cannot derive ψ^*. This is because it still requires parameter set $\{MID_i, MK_{GWN}, R_1, R_3, R_5, R_6, R_7^*\}$. In accordance with Theorem 10.4, it is difficult for $\tilde{A}$ to compute nonces R_1, R_3, R_5, R_6, R_7^*. Similarly, by Theorem 10.5, it cannot obtain MID_i and MK_{GWN}. Consequently, the proposed scheme can withstand stolen verifier attacks.

Theorem 10.12: Anonymity and untraceability are upheld.

Proof:During the login, authentication and key negotiation phase, messages $AUT_1 = \{A_4, B_4, B_5, C_1\}$, $AUT_2 = \{A_4, C_2, C_3, C_4\}$, $AUT_3 = \{C_5, D_1\}$ and $AUT_4 = \{D_2, D_3, D_4, D_5\}$ are exchanged among the GWN, BSU_i and MP_i. Here, $A_4 = A_3 \oplus h\ (R_2 || MK_{GWN})$, $B_4 = BID_j \oplus h(A_4 || A_3)$, $A_3 = h\ (MID_i || R_3)$, $B_5 = R_5 \oplus h\ (A_3 || A_4)$, $C_1 = h\ (BID_j || A_4 || R_5 || A_3)$, $C_2 = h\ (R_6 || A_3) \oplus h\ (A_2 || A_4)$, $A_2 = h\ (h\ (BID_j || R_1) || MK_{GWN})$, $C_3 = R_5 \oplus\ h(h(R_6 || A_3) || A_2)$, $C_4 = h\ (A_4 || BID_j || h(R_6 || A_3) || R_5)$, $C_5 = R_7 \oplus\ h\ (A_2 || R_6)$ and $D_1 = h\ (\psi || R_7 || BID_j)$. Evidently, none of these messages contain the plaintext identities BID_j and MID_i. It is clear that in messages AUT_1 and AUT_2, only the MP_i pseudo-identity A_4 is exchanged. It is therefore cumbersome for the adversary to discern the real identities BID_j and MID_i from these four messages. In addition, it is unfeasible for the attacker to associate any communication sessions to particular BSU_i and MP_i.

10.5 Performance evaluation

In this section, computation overheads, communication overheads and offered security features are deployed to show the superiority of the proposed protocol in comparison with other related state of the art schemes. The choice of these three metrics is due to their prevalence in comparative evaluations of majority of the security schemes. Towards the end of this section, the implementation details of the proposed protocol are provided.

10.5.1 Computation overheads

During the login, mutual authentication and key agreement procedures, the MP_i executes 13 one-way hashing operations while the GWN performs 18 one −way hashing operations. On its part, the BSU_i executes only 6 hashing operations. As such, a total of 37 one-way hashing operations are performed in the proposed protocol during the AKA phase. The practical implementation of the proposed protocol is accomplished in an HP Core i7 laptop with 8 G of RAM and 4.7 GHz processor. The operating system is Ubuntu 22.10 while the programming language employed is Python. Specifically, PyCrypto library is instrumental in the execution of the various cryptographic primitives in the proposed protocol. Table 10.6 details the execution time for the various cryptographic operations.

Table 10.7 presents the derivation of the time complexities of the various cryptographic operations executed in the proposed scheme as well as other related state of the art protocols. As shown in Fig. 10.4, the scheme in (Sureshkumar et al., 2019) incurs the highest execution time of 9.478 ms.

This is followed by the protocols in (Khatoon et al., 2019; Li, Peng, et al., 2019; Liu et al., 2019; Rangwani & Om, 2021; Yuanbing et al., 2021) with execution durations of 4.623 ms, 4.603 ms, 4.357 ms, 4.193 ms and 3.990 ms respectively. On the other hand, the proposed protocol has the least execution time of only 2.775 ms. It is therefore lightweight when compared with the rest of the other schemes.

Table 10.6 Cryptographic execution time.

Cryptographic operation	Time (ms)
One-way hashing function (T_H)	0.075
ECC point multiplication (T_{PM})	0.508
ECC point addition (T_{PA})	0.028
Symmetric encryption/decryption (T_{ED})	0.096
Fuzzy extractor operation (T_{FE})	0.508

Table 10.7 Computation overheads comparisons.

Scheme	Time complexities	Total (ms)
Sureshkumar et al (Sureshkumar et al., 2019).	18 T_H + 16T_{PM}	9.478
Li et al (Li, Peng, et al., 2019).	21 T_H + 6T_{PM}	4.623
Rangwani et al (Rangwani & Om, 2021).	17 T_H + 6T_{PM} + 10T_{PA}	4.603
Yuanbing et al (Yuanbing et al., 2021).	31 T_H + 4T_{PM}	4.357
Khatoon et al (Khatoon et al., 2019).	10 T_H + 2T_{ED} + 6 T_{PM}	3.990
Liu et al (Liu et al., 2019).	7 T_H + 6T_{PM} + 4T_{PA} + T_{FE}	4.193
Proposed	37 T_H	2.775

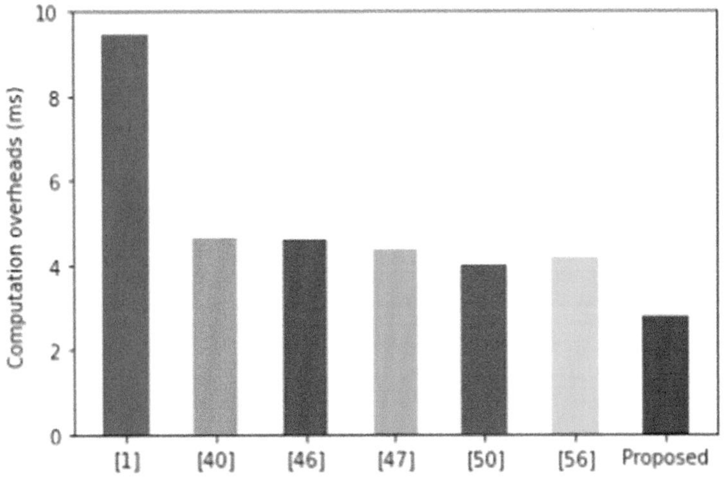

FIGURE 10.4

Computation overheads comparisons.

This renders it as the most suitable for deployment in battery powered and hence power constrained body sensor units. The deployment of the scheme in (Sureshkumar et al., 2019) in body sensor units can easily drain their battery. As such, it cannot be employed in implanted body sensor units whose battery replacement is cumbersome and tedious. Using the scheme in (Khatoon et al., 2019) as the basis, the proposed scheme yields a 30.45% reduction in the computation overheads.

10.5.2 Communication overheads

In the proposed protocol, four messages $AUT_1 = \{A_4, B_4, B_5, C_1\}$, $AUT_2 = \{A_4, C_2, C_3, C_4\}$, $AUT_3 = \{C_5, D_1\}$and $AUT_4 = \{D_2, D_3, D_4, D_5\}$ are exchanged during the login, authentication and key agreement phase. Here, $A_4 = A_3 \oplus h\ (R_2 || MK_{GWN})$, $B_4 = BID_j \oplus h(A_4 || A_3)$, $B_5 = R_5 \oplus h\ (A_3 || A_4)$, $C_1 = h\ (BID_j || A_4 || R_5 || A_3)$, $C_2 = h\ (R_6 || A_3) \oplus h\ (A_2 || A_4)$, $C_3 = R_5 \oplus\ h(h(R_6 || A_3) || A_2)$, $C_4 = h\ (A_4 || BID_j || \mathrm{h}\ (R_6 || A_3) || R_5)$, $C_5 = R_7 \oplus\ \mathrm{h}\ (A_2 || R_6)$, $D_1 = h\ (\psi || R_7 || BID_j)$, $D_2 = A_4^{New} \oplus h(R_5 || A_3)$, $D_3 = R_6^{New} \oplus h\ (A_3 || BID_j || R_5)$, $D_4 = R_7 \oplus h\ (R_6^{New} || A_3 || A_4^{New})$ and $D_5 = h\ (R_6^{New} || R_7 || A_4^{New} || \psi^*)$. Based on the values in (Hsu et al., 2020), Table 10.8 presents the output sizes of the various cryptographic operations.

Using the values in Table 10.8, the communication costs of the message exchanged in the proposed protocol are derived as follows:

$AUT_1 = \{A_4, B_4, B_5, C_1\}$: $A_4 = B_4 = B_5 = C_1 = 160$ bits
$AUT_2 = \{A_4, C_2, C_3, C_4\}$: $A_4 = C_2 = C_3 = C_4 = 160$ bits
$AUT_3 = \{C_5, D_1\}$: $C_5 = D_1 = 160$ bits
$AUT_4 = \{D_2, D_3, D_4, D_5\}$: $D_2 = D_3 = D_4 = D_5 = 160$ bits

Therefore, the overall communication overhead in the proposed scheme is 2240 bits. Table 10.9 presents the communication overheads of other related state of the art protocols. It is evident from

Table 10.8 Cryptographic execution time.

Parameter	Size (bits)
Symmetric encryption/encryption	256
Timestamp	32
One-way hash function	160
Identity	128
Random nonce	160
ECC point multiplication	320

Table 10.9 Communication overheads comparisons.

Scheme	Size (bits)
Sureshkumar et al (Sureshkumar et al., 2019).	5088
Li et al (Li, Peng, et al., 2019).	6080
Rangwani et al (Rangwani & Om, 2021).	4608
Yuanbing et al (Yuanbing et al., 2021).	8192
Khatoon et al (Khatoon et al., 2019).	3296
Liu et al (Liu et al., 2019).	2912
Proposed	2240

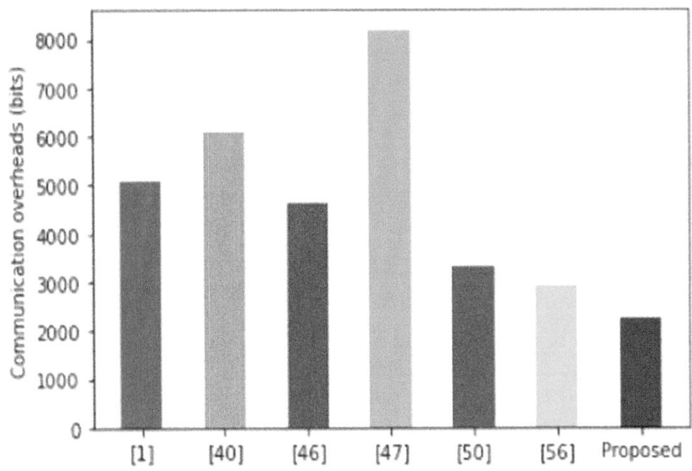

FIGURE 10.5

Communication overheads comparisons.

Fig. 10.5 that the scheme in (Yuanbing et al., 2021) has the highest communication costs of 8192 bits. This is followed by the schemes in (Khatoon et al., 2019; Li, Peng, et al., 2019; Liu et al., 2019; Rangwani & Om, 2021; Sureshkumar et al., 2019) with 6080 bits, 5088 bits, 4608 bits, 3296 bits and 2912 bits respectively.

Deploying the protocol in (Yuanbing et al., 2021) in implanted body sensor units implies that these sensors will be sending huge bits of information during the authentication and key agreement phase.

As such, energy consumption will be high and hence the sensor battery will be drained very fast. On the other hand, the proposed protocol has the lowest communication overheads of 2240 bits only. Using the protocol in (Liu et al., 2019) as the baseline, the proposed protocol results in a 23.07 reduction in the communication overheads. It is therefore power efficient compared with other related approaches.

10.5.3 Security features

To appraise the security features provided by the proposed protocol, comparisons are made against the other state of the art schemes as shown in Table 10.10. It is clear that the scheme in (Khatoon et al., 2019) provides only 4 security features and is therefore the most insecure. This is followed by the protocols in (Li, Peng, et al., 2019; Liu et al., 2019; Rangwani & Om, 2021; Sureshkumar et al., 2019; Yuanbing et al., 2021) with 7, 8, 8,12 and 13 security features respectively.

On the other hand, the proposed protocol offers all the 21 security features and hence is the most secure. It is important to note that the design of the other schemes do not consider attack vectors such as session-hijacking, forgery, eavesdropping, sensor capture and spoofing. It is also clear that very few schemes consider impersonation, de-synchronization and stolen verifier attacks. In overal, the proposed protocol has been demonstrated to have the least execution time and

Table 10.10 Security features comparisons.

Security features	(Sureshkumar et al., 2019)	(Li, Peng, et al., 2019)	(Rangwani & Om, 2021)	(Yuanbing et al., 2021)	(Khatoon et al., 2019)	(Liu et al., 2019)	Proposed
Mutual authentication	√	√	√	√	√	√	√
Session key agreement	√	√	√	√	√	√	√
Anonymity	√	×	√	√	×	×	√
Untraceability	√	√	×	√	-	×	√
Forward key secrecy	×	√	×	√	-	√	√
Backward key secrecy	×	√	×	√	-	√	√
Attacks Resilience							
Session-hijacking	-	-	-		-	-	√
Privileged insider	×	×	×	√	×	√	√
Impersonation	-	-	-	-	√	√	√
Forgery	-	-	-	-	-	-	√
Physical capture	-	-	-	-	-	√	√
Offline password guessing	√	√	√	√	-	√	√
Stolen smart card	√	√	√	√	√	√	√
De-synchronization	-	-	-		×	√	√
KSSTI	×	√	√	√	-	-	√
MitM	×	×	√	√	-	√	√
Eavesdropping	-	-	-	-	-	-	√
Sensor capture	-	-	-	-	-	-	√
Spoofing	-	-	-	-	-	-	√
Stolen verifier	-	-	-	-	-	√	√
Replays	√	×	√	√	-	√	√

√ Supported; × Not supported; - Not considered.

communication overheads. In addition, it has been demonstrated to offer the highest number of security features and attacks prevention. This projects it as the most ideal for deployment in WBAN where highly private data is being transmitted between the body sensor units and the remote medical professionals.

10.5.4 Simulations

To analyze the strength of the proposed protocol under diverse conditions, simulations are executed in Matlab R2023b. Table 10.11 presents the simulation settings deployed. In the first instance, latency characteristics of this protocol are investigated against varying number of body sensor units. In the second instance, the Packet Delivery Ratio (PDR) of this protocol is studied against varying number of body sensor units and number of authentication requests.

In each case, three scenarios are investigated. The first scenario involves 10 authentication requests while the second scenario involves 20 authentication requests. Finally, the third case involves some 30 authentication requests.

10.5.4.1 Latency characteristics

The latency measures the total time that is needed for a packet to be successfully received at the destination terminal. To investigate the latency characteristics of the proposed protocol, the number of *BSUs* is increased steadily from the initial value of 10 to 100 as shown in Fig. 10.6.

It is evident from Fig. 10.6 that different number of authentication requests resulted in varied latencies. Considering a particular number of authentication requests, there is a general increment in latencies as the number of body sensor units is increased. Among the three scenarios considered, scenario 3 resulted in the longest latencies at all *BSU* numbers. This is attributed to the high processing that must be accomplished at the *GWN* as the number of authentication requests and body sensor units increases. It is important to note that the graphs are not linear due to other transmission impairements such as packet drops and re-transmissions.

10.5.4.2 Packet delivery ratio characteristics

The PDR represents the ratio of the number of transmitted packets to the number of packets that are successfully received. To investigate the PDR characteristics of the proposed protocol, the

Table 10.11 Simulation settings.

Parameter	Value
Simulation runtime	1000 seconds
Number of sensors	800
Transmission range	300 meters
Data rate	1 Mbps
Radio propagation	Two-ray ground
Edge serves	5–50
Antenna type	Omni-directional

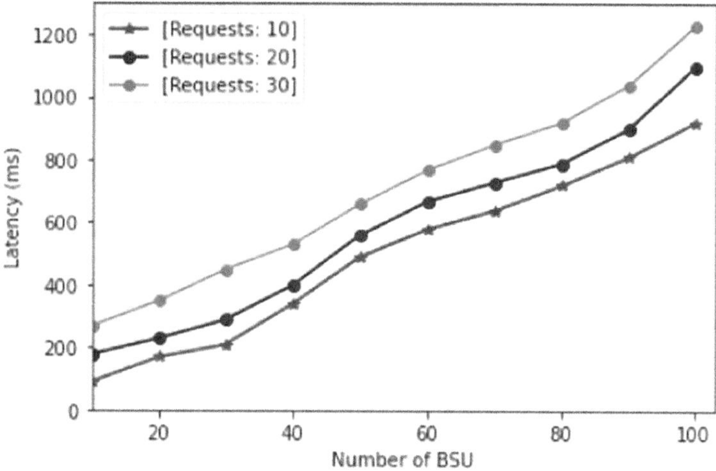

FIGURE 10.6

Latency variations.

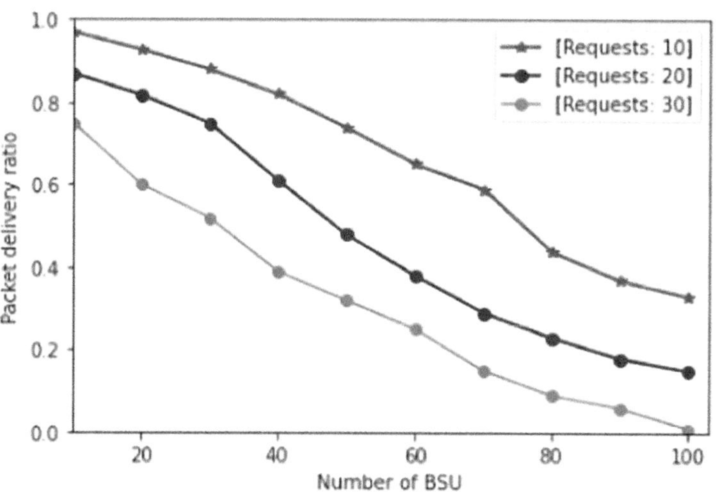

FIGURE 10.7

Packet delivery ratio variations.

number of body sensor units is incremented from 10 to a maximum of 100 under the 10, 20 and 30 authentication requests scenarios as shown in Fig. 10.7 below.

Based on the values in Fig. 10.7, it is clear that there is a general drop in PDR as the number of body sensor units and authentication requests are increased. Among the three scenarios of authentication requests, the one with 30 requests experiences a sudden drop of PDR. This is because at this level, the *GWN* is overwhelmed by the surging requests. As such, some of these requests are dropped. However, in a scenario with only 10 authentication requests, the PDR experiences a slight drop as the number of body sensor units are increased.

10.6 Conclusion

Smart health applications such as WBANs have the potential of enhancing the quality of life of the patients. However, the many security and privacy threats, vulnerabilities and attacks can potentially limit the trust of the patients and hence reduce the levels of adoption of WBANs. To address these issues, previous research works have introduced numerous security and privacy preservation techniques. Unfortunately, majority of these schemes have been demonstrated to have many security, performance and privacy challenges. Considering that many of the intelligent medical sensors are battery powered, they may not execute the computationally extensive operations required by most of the conventional protocols. As such, a lightweight authentication protocol is presented in this paper. To demonstrate that the derived session key is provably secure, BAN logic and ROR model are utilized. In addition, various theorems are formulated and proved to show its robustness under all the assumptions of the D-Y and C-K threat models. Moreover, comparative evaluation shows that the proposed protocol offers the highest number of security features at the lowest computation and communication costs. It is therefore truly lightweight and most suitable for the battery −powered WBAN sensors. Future work will involve the evaluation of this protocol using the metrics that were not within the scope of the current work.

Abbreviations

BAN Burrows−Abadi−Needham
WBANs Wireless Body Area Networks
e-health electronic health
EMG electromyography
ECG electrocardiogram
EEG electroencephalogram
RSA Rivest-Shamir-Adleman
AES Advanced Encryption Standard
ROR Real-Or-Random
D-Y Dolev-Yao
C-K Canetti-Krawczyk
PKI Public Key Infrastructure
MitM Man-in-the-Middle
ECC Elliptic Curve Cryptography
CA Certificate Authority
PKGs Public Key Generators
MP Medical Professional
GWN Gateway Node

BSU	Body Sensor Unit
XOR	exclusive-Or
AKA	Authentication and Key Agreeement
IDF	Idealized Format
JR	Jurisdiction Rule
FR	Freshness Rule
MMR	Message-Meaning Rule
NVR	Nonce Verification Rule
BR	Believe Rule
KSSTI	Known session-specific temporary information
PDR	Packet Delivery Ratio

References

Ali, R., Pal, A. K., Kumari, S., Sangaiah, A. K., Li, X., & Wu, F. (2018). An enhanced three factor based authentication protocol using wireless medical sensor networks for healthcare monitoring. *Journal of Ambient Intelligence and Humanized Computing*, 1–22.

Alzahrani, B. A., Irshad, A., Albeshri, A., Alsubhi, K., & Shafiq, M. (2020). An improved lightweight authentication protocol for wireless body area networks. *IEEE Access*, *8*, 190855–190872.

Amin, R., Islam, S. H., Biswas, G. P., Khan, M. K., & Kumar, N. (2018). A robust and anonymous patient monitoring system using wireless medical sensor networks. *Future Generation Computer Systems*, *80*, 483–495.

Arfaoui, A., Kribèche, A., Boudia, O.R. M., Letaifa, A.B., Senouci, S.M., & Hamdi, M. (2018, May). Context-aware authorization and anonymous authentication in wireless body area networks. In 2018 IEEE International Conference on Communications (ICC) (pp. 1-7). IEEE.

Babu, E. S., Dadi, A. K., Singh, K. K., Nayak, S. R., Bhoi, A. K., & Singh, A. (2022). A distributed identity-based authentication scheme for internet of things devices using permissioned blockchain system. *Expert Systems*, e12941.

Chandrakar, P., & Om, H. (2018). An extended ECC-based anonymity-preserving 3-factor remote authentication scheme usable in TMIS. *International Journal of Communication Systems*, *31*(8), e3540.

Chen, K., Lu, X., Chen, R., & Liu, J. (2022). Wireless wearable biosensor smart physiological monitoring system for risk avoidance and rescue. *Mathematical Biosciences and Engineering: MBE*, *19*, 1496–1514.

Chen, L., Li, J., Lu, Y., & Zhang, Y. (2020). Adaptively secure certificate-based broadcast encryption and its application to cloud storage service. *Information Sciences*, *538*, 273–289.

Deebak, B. D., Al-Turjman, F., & Nayyar, A. (2021). Chaotic-map based authenticated security framework with privacy preservation for remote point-of-care. *Multimedia Tools and Applications*, *80*(11), 17103–17128.

Ever, Y. K. (2018). Secure-anonymous user authentication scheme for e-healthcare application using wireless medical sensor networks. *IEEE Systems Journal*, *13*(1), 456–467.

Gao, G., Peng, X., & Jin, L. (2019). Efficient Access Control Scheme with Certificateless Signcryption for Wireless Body Area Networks. *International Journal of Networking and Security*, *21*(3), 428–437.

Gupta, A., Tripathi, M., & Sharma, A. (2020). A provably secure and efficient anonymous mutual authentication and key agreement protocol for wearable devices in WBAN. *Computer Communications*, *160*, 311–325.

Gupta, D. S., Islam, S. H., Obaidat, M. S., Vijayakumar, P., Kumar, N., & Park, Y. (2020). A provably secure and lightweight identity-based two-party authenticated key agreement protocol for IIoT environments. *IEEE Systems Journal*, *15*(2), 1732–1741.

Hajar, M. S., Al-Kadri, M. O., & Kalutarage, H. K. (2021). A survey on wireless body area networks: Architecture, security challenges and research opportunities. *Computers & Security*, *104*, 102211.

He, D., Zeadally, S., Kumar, N., & Lee, J. H. (2016). Anonymous authentication for wireless body area networks with provable security. *IEEE Systems Journal*, *11*(4), 2590–2601.

Hsu, C. L., Le, T. V., Hsieh, M. C., Tsai, K. Y., Lu, C. F., & Lin, T. W. (2020). Three-factor UCSSO scheme with fast authentication and privacy protection for telecare medicine information systems. *IEEE Access*, *8*, 196553–196566.

Hussain, S., Ullah, S. S., Uddin, M., Iqbal, J., & Chen, C. L. (2022). A comprehensive survey on signcryption security mechanisms in wireless body area networks. *Sensors*, *22*(3), 1072.

Iqbal, J., Umar, A. I., Amin, N., & Waheed, A. (2019). Efficient and secure attribute-based heterogeneous online/offline signcryption for body sensor networks based on blockchain. *International Journal of Distributed Sensor Networks*, *15*(9), 1550147719875654.

Kadhim, K. T., Alsahlany, A. M., Wadi, S. M., & Kadhum, H. T. (2020). An overview of patient's health status monitoring system based on Internet of Things (IoT). *Wireless Personal Communications*, *114*(3), 2235–2262.

Khatoon, S., Rahman, S. M. M., Alrubaian, M., & Alamri, A. (2019). Privacy-preserved, provable secure, mutually authenticated key agreement protocol for healthcare in a smart city environment. *IEEE access*, *7*, 47962–47971.

Khezr, S., Yassine, A., Benlamri, R., & Hossain, M. S. (2022). An Edge Intelligent Blockchain-based Reputation System for IIoT Data Ecosystem. *IEEE Transactions on Industrial Informatics*, *18*(11), 8346–8355.

Kim, B. S., Shah, B., He, T., & Kim, K. I. (2022). A survey on analytical models for dynamic resource management in wireless body area networks. *Ad Hoc Networks*, *135*, 102936.

Kumar, M. (2020). Cryptanalysis and improvement of anonymous authentication for wireless body area networks with provable security. *Cryptology ePrint Archive*, *2020*, 936.

Kumar, M., & Chand, S. (2020). A lightweight cloud-assisted identity-based anonymous authentication and key agreement protocol for secure wireless body area network. *IEEE Systems Journal*, *15*(2), 2779–2786.

Li, C., & Xu, C. (2022). Efficient Anonymous Authentication for Wireless Body Area Networks. *IEEE Access*, *10*, 80015–80026.

Li, C., Xu, C., Zhao, Y., Chen, K., & Zhang, X. (2019, December). Certificateless identity-concealed authenticated encryption under multi-KGC. In International Conference on Information Security and Cryptology (pp. 397-415). Springer, Cham.

Li, W., Li, B., Zhao, Y., Wang, P., & Wei, F. (2018). Cryptanalysis and security enhancement of three authentication schemes in wireless sensor networks. *Wireless Communications and Mobile Computing*, *2018*, 1–11.

Li, X., Peng, J., Obaidat, M. S., Wu, F., Khan, M. K., & Chen, C. (2019). A secure three-factor user authentication protocol with forward secrecy for wireless medical sensor network systems. *IEEE Systems Journal*, *14*(1), 39–50.

Liao, Y., Liu, Y., Liang, Y., Wu, Y., & Nie, X. (2019). Revisit of certificateless signature scheme used to remote authentication schemes for wireless body area networks. *IEEE Internet of Things Journal*, *7*(3), 2160–2168.

Liu, W., Wang, X., Peng, W., & Xing, Q. (2019). Center-less single sign-on with privacy-preserving remote biometric-based ID-MAKA scheme for mobile cloud computing services. *IEEE Access*, *7*, 137770–137783.

Lu, Y., Wang, X., Hu, C., Li, H., & Huo, Y. (2018). A traceable threshold attribute-based signcryption for mHealthcare social network. *Int. J. Sens. Networks*, *26*(1), 43–53.

Mo, J., Hu, Z., & Lin, Y. (2020). Cryptanalysis and security improvement of two authentication schemes for healthcare systems using wireless medical sensor networks. *Security and Communication Networks*, *2020*, 1–11.

Mwitende, G., Ali, I., Eltayieb, N., Wang, B., & Li, F. (2020). Authenticated key agreement for blockchain-based WBAN. *Telecommunication Systems*, *74*(3), 347–365.

Noor, F., Kordy, T. A., Alkhodre, A. B., Benrhouma, O., Nadeem, A., & Alzahrani, A. (2021). Securing Wireless Body Area Network with Efficient Secure Channel Free and Anonymous Certificateless Signcryption. *Wireless Communications and Mobile Computing*, *2021*, 1–14.

Nyangaresi, V. O. (2021, August). Hardware assisted protocol for attacks prevention in ad hoc networks. In International Conference for Emerging Technologies in Computing (pp. 3-20). Springer, Cham.

Nyangaresi, V. O. (2022a). Lightweight anonymous authentication protocol for resource-constrained smart home devices based on elliptic curve cryptography. *Journal of Systems Architecture*, *133*, 102763.

Nyangaresi, V. O. (2022b). A Formally Validated Authentication Algorithm for Secure Message Forwarding in Smart Home Networks. *SN Computer Science*, *3*(5), 1–16.

Nyangaresi, V. O. (2022c). Terminal independent security token derivation scheme for ultra-dense IoT networks. *Array*, *15*, 100210.

Nyangaresi, V. O. (2022d, June). Masked Symmetric Key Encrypted Verification Codes for Secure Authentication in Smart Grid Networks. In 2022 4th Global Power, Energy and Communication Conference (GPECOM) (pp. 427-432). IEEE.

Nyangaresi, V. O. (2022e, July). Provably Secure Pseudonyms based Authentication Protocol for Wearable Ubiquitous Computing Environment. In 2022 International Conference on Inventive Computation Technologies (ICICT) (pp. 1-6). IEEE.

Nyangaresi, V. O., Ahmad, M., Alkhayyat, A., & Feng, W. (2022). Artificial neural network and symmetric key cryptography based verification protocol for 5G enabled Internet of Things. *Expert Systems*, e13126.

Nyangaresi, V. O., & Ma, J. (2022, June). A Formally Verified Message Validation Protocol for Intelligent IoT E-Health Systems. In 2022 IEEE World Conference on Applied Intelligence and Computing (AIC) (pp. 416-422). IEEE.

Prameela, P. (2018). Enhanced Certificateless Security Improved Anonymous Access Control with Obfuscated QualityAware Confidential Data Discovery and Dissemination Protocol in WBAN. *International Journal of Pure and Applied Mathematics*, *118*, 2627–2635.

Pu, C., Zerkle, H., Wall, A., Lim, S., Choo, K. K. R., & Ahmed, I. (2022). A Lightweight and Anonymous Authentication and Key Agreement Protocol for Wireless Body Area Networks. *IEEE Internet of Things Journal*.

Rangwani, D., & Om, H. (2021). A secure user authentication protocol based on ECC for cloud computing environment. *Arabian Journal for Science and Engineering*, *46*(4), 3865–3888.

Roshini, A., & Kiran, K. V. D. (2022). Hierarchical energy efficient secure routing protocol for optimal route selection in wireless body area networks. *International Journal of Intelligent Networks*, 1–19.

Saeed, M. E. S., Liu, Q., Tian, G., Gao, B., & Li, F. (2018a). HOOSC: heterogeneous online/offline signcryption for the internet of things. *Wireless Networks*, *24*(8), 3141–3160.

Saeed, M. E. S., Liu, Q. Y., Tian, G., Gao, B., & Li, F. (2018b). Remote authentication schemes for wireless body area networks based on the Internet of Things. *IEEE Internet of Things Journal*, *5*(6), 4926–4944.

Shen, S., Wang, H., & Zhao, Y. (2022). Identity-based authenticated encryption with identity confidentiality. *Theoretical Computer Science*, *901*, 1–18.

Shim, K. A. (2018). Comments on "Revocable and scalable certificateless remote authentication protocol with anonymity for wireless body area networks". *IEEE Transactions on Information Forensics and Security*, *15*, 81–82.

Shuai, M., Liu, B., Yu, N., & Xiong, L. (2019). Lightweight and secure three-factor authentication scheme for remote patient monitoring using on-body wireless networks. *Security and Communication Networks*, *2019*, 1–14.

Sobin, C. C. (2020). A survey on architecture, protocols and challenges in IoT. *Wireless Personal Communications*, *112*(3), 1383–1429.

Sureshkumar, V., Amin, R., Vijaykumar, V. R., & Sekar, S. R. (2019). Robust secure communication protocol for smart healthcare system with FPGA implementation. *Future Generation Computer Systems, 100*, 938–951.

Ullah, I., Alomari, A., Ul Amin, N., Khan, M. A., & Khattak, H. (2019). An energy efficient and formally secured certificate-based signcryption for wireless body area networks with the internet of things. *Electronics*, *8*(10), 1171.

Vijayakumar, P., Obaidat, M. S., Azees, M., Islam, S. H., & Kumar, N. (2019). Efficient and secure anonymous authentication with location privacy for IoT-based WBANs. *IEEE Transactions on Industrial Informatics*, *16*(4), 2603–2611.

Vijayalakshmi, A., Jose, D. V., & Unnisa, S. (2021). *Wearable Sensors for Pervasive and Personalized Health Care. IoT in Healthcare and Ambient Assisted Living* (pp. 123–143). Singapore: Springer.

Wan, T., Wang, L., Liao, W., & Yue, S. (2021). A lightweight continuous authentication scheme for medical wireless body area networks. *Peer-to-Peer Networking and Applications*, *14*(6), 3473–3487.

Wang, H., & Zhao, Y. (2019). Identity-Based Higncryption. *Cryptology ePrint Archive*, *2019*, 106.

Watanabe, Y., Yanai, N., & Shikata, J. (2021, May). Anonymous broadcast authentication for securely remote-controlling IoT devices. In International Conference on Advanced Information Networking and Applications (pp. 679-690). Springer, Cham.

Wu, F., Li, X., Sangaiah, A. K., Xu, L., Kumari, S., Wu, L., & Shen, J. (2018). A lightweight and robust two-factor authentication scheme for personalized healthcare systems using wireless medical sensor networks. *Future Generation Computer Systems*, *82*, 727–737.

Xiong, H., Hou, Y., Huang, X., Zhao, Y., & Chen, C. M. (2021). Heterogeneous signcryption scheme from IBC to PKI with equality test for WBANs. *IEEE Systems Journal*, *1*, 10.

Xiong, H., & Qin, Z. (2015). Revocable and scalable certificateless remote authentication protocol with anonymity for wireless body area networks. *IEEE transactions on information forensics and security*, *10*(7), 1442–1455.

Yuanbing, W., Wanrong, L., & Bin, L. (2021). An Improved Authentication Protocol for Smart Healthcare System Using Wireless Medical Sensor Network. *IEEE Access*, *9*, 105101–105117.

CHAPTER

Telemedicine for pain management 11

Marco Cascella[1], Federica Monaco[2] and Ornella Piazza[2]

[1]*Anesthesia and Pain Medicine, Department of Medicine, Surgery and Dentistry "Scuola Medica Salernitana", University of Salerno, Baronissi, Italy* [2]*Anesthesia and Pain Medicine, ASL Napoli 1, Napoli, Italy*

11.1 Introduction

Digital health solutions encompass a range of technologies leveraging data digitalization to enhance various aspects of healthcare, including prevention, diagnosis, treatment, monitoring of diseases, research, innovation, training, management, and evaluation of healthcare services (Mayol, 2023). These technologies span from information and communication technologies (IT) such as mobile applications, telemedicine, and social media, to wearable devices, artificial intelligence (AI), Big Data, virtual and augmented reality, and blockchain. Central to all these technologies is the collection, management, analysis, and presentation of data in formats that facilitate decision-making for administrators, healthcare professionals, and patients alike (Tagde et al., 2021).

According to the World Health Organization, telemedicine is "The delivery of health care services, where distance is a critical factor, by all healthcare professionals using information and communication technologies for the exchange of valid information for diagnosis, treatment and prevention of disease and injuries, research and evaluation, and for the continuing education of health care providers, all in the interests of advancing the health of individuals and their communities" (Telemedicine: Opportunities and developments in Member States: Report on the second global survey on eHealth, 2009). The applications of telemedicine through synchronous, asynchronous, and remote patient-monitoring modalities encompass a wide array of medical disciplines and specialties, reaching into virtually every aspect of healthcare delivery. From primary care to specialized fields such as oncology, cardiology, neurology, psychiatry, and beyond, telemedicine offers versatile solutions for diagnosis, treatment, monitoring, and patient care management (Cuomo et al., 2022).

Notably, telemedicine has surfaced as a promising solution in the realm of pain medicine, particularly in addressing the intricate needs of patients suffering from cancer-related pain (Jafarzadeh et al., 2022) as well as nononcological pain conditions (Zou et al., 2024). It presents a convenient and accessible avenue for delivering healthcare services, offering significant advantages to patients who encounter barriers in accessing specialized care due to factors such as geographic distance or physical limitations. Importantly, patients can access expert care without the need for frequent, time-consuming visits to healthcare facilities, thereby reducing the logistical challenges of travel

Blockchain and Digital Twin for Smart Hospitals. DOI: https://doi.org/10.1016/B978-0-443-34226-4.00012-5

and associated costs. Furthermore, telemedicine provides enhanced flexibility in scheduling appointments, streamlining access to timely care and support for patients (Perez et al., 2021).

In this scenario, research is probably the most interesting aspect. More properly, research must inevitably offer insights into care pathways tailored to patients' needs and available resources. Crucially, other aspects needing clarification include the structure of usage platforms, especially concerning privacy assurances and data management. Moreover, while remote monitoring processes are becoming increasingly imperative, defining the applicable criteria and procedures is essential. Telemedicine can also represent a fruitful and effective method of data collection aimed at investigating pain mechanisms.

11.2 Research perspectives and applications

11.2.1 Tailored models of care

In pain management, the existing literature delineates the implementation of telemedicine across a spectrum of technological and logistical support levels. Nevertheless, in the setting of cancer patients, clinical experience of telemedicine-based processes is currently limited, hindering the ability to establish an optimal treatment pathway (Cascella et al., 2021; Emerick et al., 2020; Gersch et al., 2021). For these vulnerable patients, there is a critical need to establish a protocol ensuring swift hospital access for diagnosis or the implementation of nonpharmacological pain relief techniques (Shih et al., 2024). Additionally, this care model must be equipped to manage emergent situations during treatment that demand immediate in-person assessment and care. For instance, sudden exacerbations of pain accompanied by new symptoms (e.g., from a bone lesion) or medication side effects may necessitate prompt clinical evaluation in person. Consequently, telemedicine models must ensure lower costs and optimal efficiency by reducing missed appointments and achieving high satisfaction rates among both patients and healthcare workers.

Telemedicine models typically encompass standard visits with on-site support, standard visits without on-site support, and structured/integrated pain management programs (Hill-Oliva et al., 2023). Notably, direct comparisons of outcomes among these approaches are lacking, necessitating the selection of a model based on specific goals and available resources. Initially at the Istituto Tumori in Naples (Fondazione Pascale, Italy) and later at the University of Salerno (Department of Medicine, Italy), we introduced a "hybrid" care pathway. This model typically begins with an initial in-person visit. This visit addresses legal and regulatory matters such as consent acquisition, clinical data collection, and patient/caregiver education. The preparatory step is crucial for fostering a collaborative relationship with the patient, for both diagnostic and therapeutic purposes, and for ensuring patient proficiency with the technology being used. During remote consultations, pain physicians interact with patients and caregivers, assess clinical conditions, and review laboratory and imaging data. Multidisciplinary consultations involving other healthcare professionals can also be facilitated. In the event of unexpected hospital readmissions, prompt assistance can be guaranteed. Although remote follow-ups are scheduled, patients may require additional remote or face-to-face consultations as needed. We analyzed the results of the data collection (226 patients and 489 visits) and found that the average age of patients was 63.4 years (SD = 12.4 years), with no observed differences based on sex. About 55% of patients had an ECOG-PS ≤ 2, and 87% had metastatic disease. Furthermore, more than half of the patients received high doses of opioids. Interestingly, following this hybrid pathway, on average, each patient had two remote visits, and half of them had multiple telehealth consultations (Cascella, Schiavo, Grizzuti, et al., 2023).

Therefore research must focus on the development of telemedicine care models that are not only tailored to the resources available but also aligned with the specific needs and circumstances of the local context. To achieve this, it is recommended to incorporate process indicators and insights derived from qualitative studies (Brenner et al., 2022). These studies can offer valuable qualitative data, shedding light on the preferences, experiences, and challenges faced by both healthcare providers and patients in the telemedicine setting. Additionally, analyzing patient satisfaction through comprehensive assessments can provide essential feedback on the effectiveness and acceptability of telemedicine interventions, guiding the refinement and optimization of care models (Cascella, Coluccia, Grizzuti, et al., 2022; Flodgren et al., 2015; Irgens et al., 2024; Sten-Gahmberg et al., 2024).

11.2.2 Digital health platforms, blockchain technology, and E-health extends

Using a remote consultation platform enables patients, clinicians, and medical institutions to share multimedia information seamlessly, encompassing textual data, images, audio, and video. Several digital health platforms and mobile applications have been specifically designed for pain management. These platforms may include features such as symptom tracking, medication reminders, educational resources, and virtual support groups (Tuckson, Edmunds, and Hodgkins, 2017). Studies assessed the usability, acceptability, and effectiveness of these platforms in improving pain outcomes and patient engagement (Van Staalduinen, 2021).

A standard IT infrastructure should facilitate the management of regulatory processes, such as scheduling appointments, generating links, and sending them for visits. Additionally, the platform should be designated for data collection (e.g., imaging, laboratory tests, clinical findings, etc.), storage, and security. It should also serve as a valuable tool for both descriptive and predictive analyses (Cascella, Coluccia, Monaco, et al., 2022). The booking system grants access to the hospital portal, where an operator manages reservation calls and arranges visits. Once a connection is established, patients can submit necessary clinical data, which is then uploaded into the platform. Data entry is restricted to authorized operators, as secure login credentials are mandatory for acccssing the platform.

Ensuring patient data privacy, accuracy, consistency, and traceability during the collection process is essential for facilitating efficient information exchange in telemedicine. This, in turn, significantly influences the quality of remote consultations. Various methodologies have been proposed to achieve this objective. Blockchain technology, for instance, has garnered significant interest in telemedicine due to its potential to address various challenges related to data security, privacy, and interoperability. By leveraging blockchain's decentralized and tamper-resistant nature, telemedicine platforms can ensure the integrity and confidentiality of patient data, facilitating secure sharing among healthcare providers while maintaining patient privacy. Additionally, blockchain can streamline administrative processes, such as medical credentialing and billing, by creating transparent and immutable records. Moreover, smart contracts enabled by blockchain technology can automate and enforce agreements between patients, healthcare providers, and insurers, leading to more efficient and transparent healthcare transactions. Concerning examples of clinical application, one study introduced an efficient and secure medical data sharing scheme (i.e., MedBlock) based on medical blockchain technology, along with a trusted cloud medical data sharing example (Fan et al., 2018). Another investigation explored a privacy-protected sharing mode for electronic medical records (Liu et al., 2018). Moreover, other researchers proposed a blockchain-based electronic medical record-sharing model, leveraging the distributed and tamper-proof properties of blockchain technology (Zhang et al., 2021). Other approaches focused on the integration of smart contracts with blockchain technology-enabled remote automatic monitoring of patients in a bid to reduce electronic medical record costs (Griggs et al., 2018). Following the same strategy, a blockchain platform was developed to support clinical trials and precision medicine, highlighting challenges in blockchain technology utilization (Shae & Tsai, 2017). A model combining blockchain and smart contracts within the context of the Internet of Things (IoT) was constructed, exploring the integration of blockchain and Big Data (Hu et al., 2023; Jamil et al., 2021). The application of blockchain in supply chain management was also demonstrated in a bibliometric investigation (Cascella, Monaco, et al., 2024; Moosavi et al., 2021; Vittori et al., 2022). Interestingly, blockchain security managers for federated cloud systems in an IoT environment were introduced (Alshudukhi et al., 2023). A novel remote medical service model was proposed by integrating remote real-time interactive functions with electronic medical records containing relevant examination materials (Liao et al., 2011). Communication technologies in telemedicine systems were analyzed and corresponding module functions in multimedia were restructured to enhance communication efficiency and bandwidth utilization (Zhou et al., 2009). Additionally, the potential benefits of telemedicine in improving medical and healthcare service capabilities were elaborated upon by Chen et al. (2014).

The platform could be developed to integrate with E-health programs. E-health presents promising opportunities for pain management and healthcare services, driven by the rapid advancement of computer programming and technology. This aspect of telehealth is a rapidly evolving research field that involves utilizing digital platforms such as computers and smartphones to support or deliver health interventions. In brief, E-health programs can offer numerous advantages, including enhanced accuracy of processes, convenience for patients in terms of time and privacy, and the ability for patients to avoid face-to-face interactions. The versatility of E-health extends to its ability to cater to diverse demographics through various media formats. Concerning its applications, E-health interventions range from simple text-based programs to complex multimedia and interactive systems such as virtual reality (VR) (Law et al., 2011). It is a cutting-edge technology that immerses users in simulated environments created through computer-generated sensory inputs. These environments are experienced using head-mounted displays (HMDs), specialized goggles, or projected images onto a screen. Interaction within VR environments is enabled by hand-held devices (HHDs) and motion-tracking systems. This rapidly evolving technology has the potential to significantly enhance the remote management of pain conditions, improving pain-related outcomes (Cerda et al., 2024; Matthie et al., 2022). For instance, VR-based E-health interventions rely on distraction techniques to alleviate pain in children, incorporating interactive games, musicals, storybooks, and toys (Cascella, Cascella, et al., 2023; Fleming et al., 2014). Furthermore, VR systems may incorporate biofeedback programs utilizing sensors like galvanic skin response and heart rate variability to detect and manage stress-related physiological changes, along with relaxation training programs (Amon & Campbell, 2008). Haptic technology refers to technology that engages the sense of touch by applying forces, vibrations, or motions to the user. Interestingly, haptic technology can be implemented into VR processes, for example, to develop rehabilitation programs or facilitate remote clinical evaluation. The haptic bioholograms are an artificial intelligence (AI)-based innovative approach that involves the creation of haptic representations of biological structures or medical conditions within virtual environments. Therefore it can enable clinicians to remotely assess patients' conditions with a heightened sense of realism and detail. Thanks to haptic feedback, clinicians can interact with virtual models of anatomical structures or physiological processes, palpating, probing, and manipulating virtual tissues or organs as if they were physically present. This tactile immersion allows for more intuitive and accurate assessments, particularly in scenarios where physical proximity is limited, such as telemedicine consultations or remote diagnostic procedures (Cerda et al., 2024).

Other AI-based strategies include agent-based systems. They offer solutions for both simple and complex problems (Chakraborty & Gupta, 2014), for example, by implementing multiagent systems (MASs) (Ahmed Kamal et al., 2023). MASs in telemedicine are sophisticated approaches where multiple intelligent agents collaborate to facilitate various aspects of healthcare delivery remotely. These agents, which can be software entities or components, interact with each other and with human users to accomplish specific tasks within the telemedicine framework. In particular, MAS can be applied for appointment scheduling, considering factors such as time zones, preferences, and urgency; for remote monitoring, collecting, analyzing, and interpreting data from wearable devices or sensors, providing continuous monitoring of patients' vital signs, symptoms, and adherence to treatment plans. Moreover, agents can assist healthcare providers in clinical decision-making by aggregating and analyzing patient data, medical literature, and treatment guidelines to offer personalized recommendations. This aspect is also crucial for optimizing resource allocation (Vorenkamp et al., 2022).

11.2.3 Remote patient monitoring

Remote patient monitoring (RPM) or telemonitoring is a rapidly evolving approach to healthcare delivery that enables healthcare providers to monitor patients' health status and vital signs from a distance using various technological devices and platforms (Farias et al., 2020). Through RPM, patients can conveniently track their health metrics, such as blood pressure, heart rate, blood glucose levels, and activity levels, from the comfort of their homes. These data are then transmitted in real time or at scheduled intervals to healthcare professionals, who can remotely monitor patients' conditions and intervene promptly if any abnormalities or concerning trends are detected. RPM is particularly beneficial for managing chronic conditions, such as diabetes, hypertension, heart failure, and chronic obstructive pulmonary disease (Murphie et al., 2019), as well as for postsurgical or postacute care monitoring (Chu et al., 2024). By enabling proactive and personalized care, RPM can help prevent complications, reduce hospital readmissions, and improve overall patient outcomes and quality of life (Cracchiolo et al., 2024). As technology continues to advance and healthcare delivery models evolve, RPM is poised to play an increasingly integral role in modern healthcare, offering greater convenience, accessibility, and efficiency in patient care. Significantly, applications of RPM can be embedded with AI processes for enhancing decision-making processes in different fields (Feinstein et al., 2024).

In cancer patients, RPM is implemented for assessing the potential occurrence of chemotherapy-related toxicity (Alibhai et al., 2024). However, research has also been conducted for the diagnosis and characterization of oncological pain phenomena such as breakthrough cancer pain

(BTCP) (Homdee et al., 2024), a transient exacerbation of pain that occurs despite baseline analgesic therapy in patients with cancer (Cascella et al., 2022; Cascella, Monaco, et al., 2022). In pain medicine, further attempts at RPM have been made for real-time monitoring through an encrypted video conferencing platform to assess the effect of transcranial stimulation treatments for phantom limb pain (Pacheco-Barrios et al., 2024), to address migraine (Niiberg-Pikksööt et al., 2024), and to assess pain and functionality (Fu et al., 2024). In the realm of cancer pain management, researchers have created a mobile health application designed to provide cognitive behavioral therapy for pain, remote symptom monitoring, and pharmacological support, particularly in the context of opioid therapy (Azizoddin et al., 2024).

11.2.4 Automatic pain assessment

Telemedicine and RPM can be implemented for research in the field of automatic pain assessment (APA). APA refers to the process of quantifying and evaluating pain experiences using technology-driven methods without relying solely on subjective reports from individuals (Cascella, Schiavo, Cuomo, et al., 2023; Nagireddi Meng et al., 2022). This approach typically involves the use of various sensors and devices to collect objective data related to physiological responses (Moscato et al., 2022), such as changes in heart rate, skin conductance (Cascella, Vitale, D'Antò, Cuomo, et al., 2023), facial expressions (Cascella, Vitale, Mariani, Iuorio, et al., 2023), or movement patterns (Walsh et al., 2014), which are indicative of pain. Different APA modalities can be also combined to develop multimodal strategies (Benavent-Lledo et al., 2023; Gkikas et al., 2024).

To achieve the objective of accurate and reliable APA, digital IoT instruments can be deployed to monitor a range of physiological indicators. By analyzing these biosignals and employing AI-based strategies, APA systems can detect, monitor, and even predict pain levels in real time (Posada-Quintero et al., 2021; Pouromran et al., 2021). This technology has the potential to revolutionize pain management by providing healthcare providers with objective metrics for assessing pain, enabling earlier interventions, optimizing treatment strategies, and improving overall patient care, particularly for individuals with chronic pain conditions where subjective reporting may be unreliable or inconsistent. Additionally, APA holds promise for enhancing clinical research, facilitating remote monitoring, and advancing personalized medicine approaches in pain management (Cascella, Montomoli, Bellini, & Bignami, 2023).

11.2.5 Other research topics

Research must tackle additional topics. For example, ethical aspects represent a topic of debate (Cascella, Laudani, et al., 2024). Telemedicine consultations should maintain the same standard of care as in-person visits, with healthcare providers adhering to professional standards and guidelines (Dantas et al., 2020). Furthermore, ethical considerations must include ensuring that telemedicine platforms support accurate diagnosis, appropriate treatment recommendations, and effective communication between patients and providers. Ethics must also address potential disparities in access to pain management services among underserved populations, including rural communities, minority groups, and individuals with limited mobility or resources, or inadequate technological literacy (Seroussi & Zablit, 2024). The internet and technology are rapidly becoming ubiquitous, with around two-thirds of Europe and America now connected. Technology is also becoming more portable. This widespread availability and mobility are crucial for scaling digital health solutions. However, many emerging economies still lack such access, maintaining barriers to healthcare (Hadjiat & Arendt-Nielsen, 2023). Similarly, within developed economies, diverse communities face disparities in accessing digital health services (Equity within digital health technology within the WHO European region: A scoping review, 2022). Therefore research in this area should focus on identifying barriers to telemedicine adoption, customizing interventions to diverse patient populations, and promoting equitable access to quality pain care.

Finally, patient education is another challenge to be addressed. Dedicated tools and programs for evaluating telemedicine-based educational interventions and self-management processes are required to empower cancer patients to understand and manage their pain symptoms (Kouijzer et al., 2023; Zavagli, 2021). This key step includes providing information on pain medications (Cascella, Capuozzo, et al., 2024), coping strategies, and lifestyle modifications through the available telehealth platforms (Bramanti et al., 2024; Improta et al., 2020; Tramontano, 2021).

11.3 Conclusion

The dynamic realm of telemedicine offers unprecedented potential for revolutionizing the management of cancer-related pain. Through the utilization of remote communication technologies and cutting-edge digital health platforms, telemedicine provides a versatile toolkit for diagnosing, evaluating, monitoring, and treating pain in this clinical setting. However, key considerations surrounding the implementation of telemedicine strategies, including synchronous, asynchronous, and remote monitoring approaches, demand scrutiny and ongoing research efforts. It is essential to develop tailored models of care that cater to the distinct needs and resources of cancer patients, alongside the creation of specialized digital platforms and mobile applications dedicated to pain management. Moreover, the promise of remote monitoring technologies in delivering valuable insights into patients' pain experiences and facilitating timely interventions highlights the critical importance of continued exploration in this domain. Finally, in pain medicine, the convergence of telemedicine, AI strategies, and blockchain technology heralds a new era of patient-centered care delivery. Through remote monitoring, APA, and intelligent data analysis, healthcare providers can tailor treatment plans to individual patient needs, optimize resource allocation, and ultimately improve healthcare outcomes.

References

Ahmed Kamal, M., Ismail, Z., Shehata, I. M., Djirar, S., Talbot, N. C., Ahmadzadeh, S., Shekoohi, S., Cornett, E. M., Fox, C. J., & Kaye, A. D. (2023). Telemedicine, E-health, and multi-agent systems for chronic pain management. *Clinics and Practice*, *13*(2), 470–482. Available from https://doi.org/10.3390/clinpract13020042, https://www.mdpi.com/journal/clinpract/about.

Alibhai, S. M. H., Puts, M., Jin, R., Godhwani, K., Antonio, M., Abdallah, S., Feng, G., Krzyzanowska, M. K., Soto-Perez-de-Celis, E., Papadopoulos, E., Mach, C., Nasiri, F., Sridhar, S. S., Glicksman, R., Moody, L., Bender, J., Clarke, H., Matthew, A., McIntosh, D., . . . Emmenegger, U. (2024). Toward a comprehensive supportive care intervention for older men with metastatic prostate cancer (TOPCOP3): A pilot randomized controlled trial and process evaluation. *Journal of Geriatric Oncology*. Available from https://doi.org/10.1016/j.jgo.2024.101750, https://www.sciencedirect.com/science/journal/18794068.

Alshudukhi, K. S., Khemakhem, M. A., Eassa, F. E., & Jambi, K. M. (2023). An interoperable blockchain security frameworks based on microservices and smart contract in IoT environment. *Electronics*, *12*(3), 776. Available from https://doi.org/10.3390/electronics12030776.

Amon, K. L., & Campbell, A. (2008). Can children with AD/HD learn relaxation and breathing techniques through biofeedback video games? *Australian Journal of Educational and Developmental Psychology*, *8*, 72–84. Available from http://www.newcastle.edu.au/group/ajedp/Archive/Volume_8/v8-amon-campbell.pdf, Australia.

Azizoddin, D. R., DeForge, S. M., Baltazar, A., Edwards, R. R., Allsop, M., Tulsky, J. A., Businelle, M. S., Schreiber, K. L., & Enzinger, A. C. (2024). Development and pre-pilot testing of STAMP + CBT: an mHealth app combining pain cognitive behavioral therapy and opioid support for patients with advanced cancer and pain. *Supportive Care in Cancer*, *32*(2). Available from https://doi.org/10.1007/s00520-024-08307-7, https://www.springer.com/journal/520.

Benavent-Lledo, M., Mulero-Pérez, D., Ortiz-Perez, D., Rodriguez-Juan, J., Berenguer-Agullo, A., Psarrou, A., & Garcia-Rodriguez, J. (2023). A comprehensive study on pain assessment from multimodal sensor data. *Sensors*, *23*(24), 9675. Available from https://doi.org/10.3390/s23249675.

Bramanti, A., Ciurleo, R., Vecchione, C., Turolla, A., Piramide, N., Ciccarelli, M., Piramide, E., & Garofano, M. (2024). Telerehabilitation: a solution for patients after hip fracture? *Translational Medicine @ UniSa*, *26*(1). Available from https://doi.org/10.37825/2239-9747.1048.

Brenner, B., Brancolini, S., Eshraghi, Y., Guirguis, M., Durbhakula, S., Provenzano, D., Vorenkamp, K., Shah, S., Darden, M., & Kohan, L. (2022). Telemedicine implementation in pain medicine: A survey evaluation of pain medicine practices in spring 2020. *American Society of Interventional Pain Physicians, United States Pain Physician*, *25*(5), 387–390. Available from https://www.painphysicianjournal.com/current/pdf?article = NzUwNw%3D%3D.

Cascella, M., Cascella, A., Monaco, F., & Shariff, M. N. (2023). Envisioning gamification in anesthesia, pain management, and critical care: basic principles, integration of artificial intelligence, and simulation strategies. *Journal of Anesthesia, Analgesia and Critical Care*, *3*(1). Available from https://doi.org/10.1186/s44158-023-00118-2, https://link.springer.com/journal/44158.

Cascella, M., Coluccia, S., Grizzuti, M., Romano, M. C., Esposito, G., Crispo, A., & Cuomo, A. (2022). Satisfaction with telemedicine for cancer pain management: A model of care and cross-sectional patient satisfaction study. *Current Oncology*, *29*(8), 5566–5578. Available from https://doi.org/10.3390/curroncol29080439, https://www.mdpi.com/journal/curroncol.

Cascella, M., Coluccia, S., Monaco, F., Schiavo, D., Nocerino, D., Grizzuti, M., Romano, M. C., & Cuomo, A. (2022). Different machine learning approaches for implementing telehealth-based cancer pain management strategies. *Journal of Clinical Medicine*, *11*(18). Available from https://doi.org/10.3390/jcm11185484, https://www.mdpi.com/journal/jcm.

Cascella, M., Laudani, A., Scarpati, G., & Piazza, O. (2024). Ethical issues in pain and palliation. *Current Opinion in Anaesthesiology*, *37*(2), 199–204. Available from https://doi.org/10.1097/ACO.0000000000001345, http://journals.lww.com/co-anesthesiology/pages/default.aspx.

Cascella, M., Monaco, F., Nocerino, D., Chinè, E., Carpenedo, R., Picerno, P., Migliaccio, L., Armignacco, A., Franceschini, G., Coluccia, S., Gennaro, P. D., Tracey, M. C., Forte, C. A., Tafuri, M., Crispo, A., Cutugno, F., Vittori, A., Natoli, S., & Cuomo, A. (2022). Bibliometric network analysis on rapid-onset opioids for breakthrough cancer pain treatment. *Journal of Pain and Symptom Management*, *63*(6), 1041–1050. Available from https://doi.org/10.1016/j.jpainsymman.2022.01.023, http://www.elsevier.com/locate/jpainsymman.

Cascella, M., Schiavo, D., Cuomo, A., Ottaiano, A., Perri, F., Patrone, R., Migliarelli, S., Bignami, E. G., Vittori, A., & Cutugno, F. (2023). Artificial Intelligence for automatic pain assessment: Research methods and perspectives. *Pain Research and Management, 2023*. Available from https://doi.org/10.1155/2023/6018736, https://www.hindawi.com/journals/prm/.

Cascella, M., Schiavo, D., Grizzuti, M., Romano, M. C., Coluccia, S., Bimonte, S., & Cuomo, A. (2023). Implementation of a hybrid care model for telemedicine-based cancer pain management at the cancer center of Naples, Italy: A cohort study. *In Vivo (Athens, Greece)*, *37*(1), 385–392. Available from https://doi.org/10.21873/invivo.13090, https://iv.iiarjournals.org/content/37/1/385.

Cascella, M., Capuozzo, M., Ferrara, F., Ottaiano, A., Perri, F., Sabbatino, F., Conti, V., Santoriello, V., Ponsiglione, A. M., Romano, M., Amato, F., & Piazza, O. (2024). Two-year opioid prescription trends in local sanitary agency Naples 3 South, campania region, Italy. Descriptive analyses and AI-based translational perspectives. *Translational Medicine @ UniSa*, *26*(1). Available from https://doi.org/10.37825/2239-9747.1047.

Cascella, M., Marinangeli, F., Vittori, A., Scala, C., Piccinini, M., Braga, A., Miceli, L., & Vellucci, R. (2021). Open issues and practical suggestions for telemedicine in chronic pain. *International Journal of Environmental Research and Public Health*, *18*(23), 12416. Available from https://doi.org/10.3390/ijerph182312416.

Cascella, M., Monaco, F., Vittori, A., Elshazly, M., Carlucci, A., & Piazza, O. (2024). Bridging knowledge gaps: a bibliometric analysis of non-invasive ventilation in palliative care studies. *Journal of Anesthesia, Analgesia and Critical Care*, *4*(1). Available from https://doi.org/10.1186/s44158-024-00140-y.

Cascella, M., Montomoli, J., Bellini, V., & Bignami, E. G. (2023). Integrating data science and neural architecture techniques for automatic pain assessment in critically ill patients. *Anaesthesia Critical Care & Pain Medicine*, *42*(4)101220. Available from https://doi.org/10.1016/j.accpm.2023.101220.

Cascella, M., Racca, E., Nappi, A., Coluccia, S., Maione, S., Luongo, L., Guida, F., Avallone, A., & Cuomo, A. (2022). Bayesian network analysis for prediction of unplanned hospital readmissions of cancer patients with breakthrough cancer pain and complex care needs. *Healthcare*, *10*(10), 1853. Available from https://doi.org/10.3390/healthcare10101853.

Cascella, M., Vitale, V. N., D'Antò, M., Cuomo, A., Amato, F., Romano, M., & Ponsiglione, A. M. (2023). Exploring biosignals for quantitative pain assessment in cancer patients: A proof of concept. *Electronics*, *12*(17), 3716. Available from https://doi.org/10.3390/electronics12173716.

Cascella, M., Vitale, V. N., Mariani, F., Iuorio, M., & Cutugno, F. (2023). Development of a binary classifier model from extended facial codes toward video-based pain recognition in cancer patients. *Scandinavian Journal of Pain*, *23*(4), 638–645. Available from https://doi.org/10.1515/sjpain-2023-0011.

Cerda, I. H., Therond, A., Moreau, S., Studer, K., Donjow, A. R., Crowther, J. E., Mazzolenis, M. E., Lang, M., Tolba, R., Gilligan, C., Ashina, S., Kaye, A. D., Yong, R. J., Schatman, M. E., & Robinson, C. L. (2024). Telehealth and virtual reality technologies in chronic pain management: A narrative review. *Current Pain and Headache Reports*, *28*(3), 83–94. Available from https://doi.org/10.1007/s11916-023-01205-3, https://www.springer.com/journal/11916.

Chakraborty, S., & Gupta. (2014). Medical application using multi agent system—A literature survey. *International Journal of Engineering Research and Applications.*, *4*, 528–546.

Chen, Y., Zhang, X., Zou, X., Ye, Q., & Nie, L. (2014). Effect of telemedicine on improving medical service capacity in the county. *Chinese Journal of Hospital Administration.*, *30*. Available from https://doi.org/10.3760/cma.j.issn.1000-6672.2014.06.003.

Chu, J. J., Tadros, A. B., Vingan, P. S., Assel, M. J., McCready, T. M., Vickers, A. J., Carlsson, S., Morrow, M., Mehrara, B. J., Stern, C. S., Pusic, A. L., & Nelson, J. A. (2024). Remote symptom monitoring with clinical alerts following mastectomy: Do early symptoms predict 30-day surgical complications. *Annals of Surgical Oncology*, *31*(5), 3377–3386. Available from https://doi.org/10.1245/s10434-024-15031-3, https://www.springer.com/journal/10434.

Cracchiolo, J. R., Tin, A. L., Assel, M., McCready, T. M., Stabile, C., Simon, B., Carlsson, S. V., Vickers, A. J., & Laudone, V. (2024). Electronic patient-reported symptoms after ambulatory cancer surgery. *JAMA Surgery*, *159*(5), 554–561. Available from https://doi.org/10.1001/jamasurg.2024.0133, http://archsurg.jamanetwork.com/issues.aspx.

Cuomo, A., Cascella, M., Vittori, A., Baciarello, M., Badino, M., & Bignam, E. (2022). Telemedicine for managing cancer pain. A great opportunity to be exploited for clinical and research purposes. *Pain Physician*, *25*(6), E886. Available from http://www.painphysicianjournal.com/.

Dantas, C., Machado, N., Ortet, S., Leandro, F., Burnard, M., Grünloh, C., Grguric, A., Hörmann, V., Fiorini, L., Cavallo, F., Rovini, E., Scano, R., & Pocs, M. (2020). The iterative model of ethical analysis for large-scale implementation of ICT solutions. *Translational Medicine @ UniSa*, *23*, 1–9. Available from https://doi.org/10.37825/2239-9747.1023.

Emerick, T., Alter, B., Jarquin, S., Brancolini, S., Bernstein, C., Luong, K., Morrissey, S., & Wasan, A. (2020). Telemedicine for chronic pain in the COVID-19 era and beyond. *Pain Medicine*, *21*(9), 1743–1748. Available from https://doi.org/10.1093/pm/pnaa220.

Equity within digital health technology within the WHO European region: a scoping review. (2022). 20–20.

Fan, K., Wang, S., Ren, Y., Li, H., & Yang, Y. (2018). MedBlock: Efficient and secure medical data sharing via blockchain. *Journal of Medical Systems*, *42*(8). Available from https://doi.org/10.1007/s10916-018-0993-7.

Farias, F. A. C. D., Dagostini, C. M., Bicca, Y. D. A., Falavigna, V. F., & Falavigna, A. (2020). Remote patient monitoring: A systematic review. *Telemedicine and e-Health*, *26*(5), 576–583. Available from https://doi.org/10.1089/tmj.2019.0066.

Feinstein, M., Katz, D., Demaria, S., & Hofer, I. S. (2024). Remote monitoring and artificial intelligence: Outlook for 2050. *Anesthesia and Analgesia*, *138*(2), 350–357. Available from https://doi.org/10.1213/ANE.0000000000006712, http://journals.lww.com/anesthesia-analgesia/toc/publishahead.

Fleming, T. M., Cheek, C., Merry, S. N., Thabrew, H., Bridgman, H., Stasiak, K., Shepherd, M., Perry, Y., & Hetrick, S. (2014). Serious games for the treatment or prevention of depression: A systematic review. *Revista de Psicopatologia y Psicologia Clinica*, *19*(3), 227–242. Available from https://doi.org/10.5944/rppc.vol.19.num.3.2014.13904, http://www.aepcp.net/arc/08_2014_n3_varios.pdf.

Flodgren, G., Rachas, A., Farmer, A. J., Inzitari, M., & Shepperd, S. (2015). Interactive telemedicine: Effects on professional practice and health care outcomes. *Cochrane Database of Systematic Reviews*, *2015*(9). Available from https://doi.org/10.1002/14651858.CD002098.pub2, https://www.cochranelibrary.com/cdsr/table-of-contents.

Fu, M., Shen, J., Gu, C., Oliveira, E., Shinchuk, E., Isaac, H., Isaac, Z., Sarno, D. L., Kurz, J. L., Silbersweig, D. A., Onnela, J. P., & Barron, D. S. (2024). The Pain Intervention & Digital Research Program: an operational report on combining digital research with outpatient chronic disease management. *Frontiers in Pain Research*, *5*. Available from https://doi.org/10.3389/fpain.2024.1327859, https://www.frontiersin.org/journals/pain-research.

Gersch, W. D., Delate, T., Bergquist, K. M., & Smith, K. (2021). Clinical effectiveness of an outpatient multidisciplinary chronic pain management telementoring service. *Clinical Journal of Pain*, *37*(10), 740–746. Available from https://doi.org/10.1097/AJP.0000000000000967, http://www.clinicalpain.com.

Gkikas, S., Tachos, N. S., Andreadis, S., Pezoulas, V. C., Zaridis, D., Gkois, G., Matonaki, A., Stavropoulos, T. G., & Fotiadis, D. I. (2024). Multimodal automatic assessment of acute pain through facial videos and heart rate signals utilizing transformer-based architectures. *Frontiers in Pain Research*, *5*. Available from https://doi.org/10.3389/fpain.2024.1372814, https://www.frontiersin.org/journals/pain-research.

Griggs, K. N., Ossipova, O., Kohlios, C. P., Baccarini, A. N., Howson, E. A., & Hayajneh, T. (2018). Healthcare Blockchain system using smart contracts for secure automated remote patient monitoring. *Journal of Medical Systems*, *42*(7). Available from https://doi.org/10.1007/s10916-018-0982-x, http://www.wkap.nl/journalhome.htm/0148-5598.

Hadjiat, Y., & Arendt-Nielsen, L. (2023). Digital health in pain assessment, diagnosis, and management: Overview and perspectives. *Frontiers in Pain Research*, *4*. Available from https://doi.org/10.3389/fpain.2023.1097379.

Hill-Oliva, M., Ampem-Darko, K. K., Shekane, P., Walsh, S., Demaria, S., Gal, J., & Patel, A. (2023). The use of telemedicine in outpatient pain management: A scoping review. *Pain Physician*, *26*(7), 535–548. Available from https://www.painphysicianjournal.com/current/pdf?article = Nzc1OA%3D%3D.

Homdee, N., Lach, J., Blackhall, L., & LeBaron, V. (2024). The influence of ambient environmental factors on breakthrough cancer pain: Insights from remote health home monitoring and a proposed data analytic approach. *BMC Palliative Care*, *23*(1). Available from https://doi.org/10.1186/s12904-024-01392-9.

Hu, T., Yang, S., Wang, Y., Li, G., Wang, Y., Wang, G., & Yin, M. (2023). N-accesses: A blockchain-based access control framework for secure IoT data management. *Sensors*, *23*(20), 8535. Available from https://doi.org/10.3390/s23208535.

Improta, G., Luca, D., Illario, V., & Triassi, M. (2020). Digital innovation in healthcare: A device with a method for monitoring, managing and preventing the risk of chronic polypathological patients. *Translational Medicine @ UniSa*, *21*, 61–64.

Irgens, I., Kleven, L., Midelfart-Hoff, J., Jelnes, R., Alexander, M., Stanghelle, J. K., & Rekand, T. (2024). Cost-utility analysis and impact on the environment of videoconference in pressure injury. A randomized controlled trial in individuals with spinal cord injury. *Spinal Cord Series and Cases*, *10*(1). Available from https://doi.org/10.1038/s41394-024-00621-w, https://www.nature.com/scsandc/.

Jafarzadeh, F., Rahmani, F., Azadmehr, F., Falaki, M., & Nazari, M. (2022). Different applications of telemedicine - assessing the challenges, barriers, and opportunities- a narrative review. *Journal of Family Medicine and Primary Care*, *11*(3), 879. Available from https://doi.org/10.4103/jfmpc.jfmpc_1638_21.

Jamil, F., Kahng, H. K., Kim, S., & Kim, D.-H. (2021). Towards secure fitness framework based on IoT-enabled blockchain network integrated with machine learning algorithms. *Sensors*, *21*(5), 1640. Available from https://doi.org/10.3390/s21051640.

Kouijzer, M. M. T. E., Kip, H., Bouman, Y. H. A., & Kelders, S. M. (2023). Implementation of virtual reality in healthcare: a scoping review on the implementation process of virtual reality in various healthcare settings. *Implementation Science Communications*, *4*(1). Available from https://doi.org/10.1186/s43058-023-00442-2, https://www.springer.com/journal/43058.

Law, E. F., Dahlquist, L. M., Sil, S., Weiss, K. E., Herbert, L. J., Wohlheiter, K., & Horn, S. B. (2011). Videogame distraction using virtual reality technology for children experiencing cold pressor pain: The role of cognitive processing. *Journal of Pediatric Psychology*, *36*(1), 84–94. Available from https://doi.org/10.1093/jpepsy/jsq063.

Liao, J., Yang, J., Zhu, W., Cai, L., Han, L., & Wang, H. (2011). Design and application of telemedicine consultation system. *Practice Journal of Clinical Medicine.*, *8*, 206–208.

Liu, J., Li, X., Ye, L., Zhang, H., Du, X., & Guizani, M. (2018). BPDS: a blockchain-based privacy-preserving data sharing for electronic medical records. In *2018 IEEE global communications conference (GLOBECOM)* (pp. 1–6). doi: 10.1109/glocom.2018.8647713.

Matthie, N. S., Giordano, N. A., Jenerette, C. M., Magwood, G. S., Leslie, S. L., Northey, E. E., Webster, C. I., & Sil, S. (2022). Use and efficacy of virtual, augmented, or mixed reality technology for chronic pain: a systematic review. *Pain Management*, *12*(7), 859–878. Available from https://doi.org/10.2217/pmt-2022-0030, http://www.futuremedicine.com/loi/pmt.

Mayol, J. (2023). Digital solutions and health sciences. *Cirugía Española (English Edition)*. doi: 10.1016/j.cireng.2023.11.011.

Moosavi, J., Naeni, L. M., Fathollahi-Fard, A. M., & Fiore, U. (2021). Blockchain in supply chain management: a review, bibliometric, and network analysis. *Environmental Science and Pollution Research*. Available from https://doi.org/10.1007/s11356-021-13094-3, https://link.springer.com/journal/11356.

Moscato, S., Orlandi, S., Giannelli, A., Ostan, R., & Chiari, L. (2022). Automatic pain assessment on cancer patients using physiological signals recorded in real-world contexts. In *Proceedings of the annual international conference of the IEEE engineering in medicine and biology society, EMBS* (pp. 1931–1934). doi: 10.1109/EMBC48229.2022.9871990.

Murphie, P., Little, S., McKinstry, B., & Pinnock, H. (2019). Remote consulting with telemonitoring of continuous positive airway pressure usage data for the routine review of people with obstructive sleep apnoea hypopnoea syndrome: A systematic review. *Journal of Telemedicine and Telecare, 25*(1), 17–25. Available from https://doi.org/10.1177/1357633x17735618.

Nagireddi Meng, J. N., Vyas, A. K., Sanapati, M. R., Soin, A., & Manchikanti, L. (2022). The analysis of pain research through the lens of artificial intelligence and machine learning. *Pain Physician, 25*(2), E211. Available from https://www.painphysicianjournal.com/current/pdf?article = NzQyOQ%3D%3D.

Niiberg-Pikksööt, T., Laas, K., Aluoja, A., Braschinsky, M., & Ayatollahi, H. (2024). Implementing a digital solution for patients with migraine—Developing a methodology for comparing digitally delivered treatment with conventional treatment: A study protocol. *PLOS Digital Health, 3*(2), e0000295. Available from https://doi.org/10.1371/journal.pdig.0000295.

Pacheco-Barrios, K., Martinez-Magallanes, D., Naqui, C. X., Daibes, M., Pichardo, E., Cardenas-Rojas, A., Crandell, D., Dua, A., Datta, A., Caumo, W., & Fregni, F. (2024). Using home-based, remotely supervised, transcranial direct current stimulation for phantom limb pain. *Journal of Visualized Experiments, 2024* (205). Available from https://doi.org/10.3791/66006, https://api.jove.com/api/article/pdf/66006.

Perez, J., Niburski, K., Stoopler, M., & Ingelmob, P. (2021). Telehealth and chronic pain management from rapid adaptation to long-term implementation in pain medicine: A narrative review. *Pain Reports, 6*(1). Available from https://doi.org/10.1097/PR9.0000000000000912, journals.lww.com/painrpts/Pages/default.aspx.

Posada-Quintero, H. F., Kong, Y., & Chon, K. H. (2021). Objective pain stimulation intensity and pain sensation assessment using machine learning classification and regression based on electrodermal activity. *American Journal of Physiology - Regulatory Integrative and Comparative Physiology, 321*(2), R186. Available from https://doi.org/10.1152/ajpregu.00094.2021, https://journals.physiology.org/doi/full/10.1152/ajpregu.00094.2021.

Pouromran, F., Radhakrishnan, S., Kamarthi, S., & Le, K. N. Q. (2021). Exploration of physiological sensors, features, and machine learning models for pain intensity estimation. *PLoS One, 16*(7), e0254108. Available from https://doi.org/10.1371/journal.pone.0254108.

Seroussi, B., & Zablit, I. (2024). Implementation of digital health ethics: A first step with the adoption of 16 European ethical principles for digital health. In *Studies in health technology and informatics* (Vol. 310, pp. 1588–1592). doi: 10.3233/SHTI231331. http://www.iospress.nl/bookserie/studies-in-health-technology-and-informatics/.

Shae, Z., & Tsai, J.J. P. (2017). On the design of a blockchain platform for clinical trial and precision medicine. In *Proceedings - International conference on distributed computing systems* (pp. 1972–1980). https://doi.org/10.1109/ICDCS.2017.61.

Shih, K. K., Arechiga, A. B., Chen, X., Urbauer, D. L., De Moraes, A. R., Rodriguez, A. J., Thomas, L., Stanton, P. A., Bruera, E., & Hui, D. (2024). Telehealth preferences among patients with advanced cancer in the post COVID-19 vaccine era. *Journal of Pain and Symptom Management, 67*(6), 525. Available from https://doi.org/10.1016/j.jpainsymman.2024.02.572.

Sten-Gahmberg, S., Pedersen, K., Harsheim, I. G., Løyland, H. I., & Abelsen, B. (2024). Experiences with telemedicine-based follow-up of chronic conditions: The views of patients and health personnel enrolled in a pragmatic randomized controlled trial. BioMed Central Ltd, Norway. *BMC Health Services Research, 24*(1). Available from https://doi.org/10.1186/s12913-024-10732-7, https://bmchealthservres.biomedcentral.com/.

Tagde, P., Tagde, S., Bhattacharya, T., Tagde, P., Chopra, H., Akter, R., Kaushik, D., & Rahman, M. H. (2021). Blockchain and artificial intelligence technology in e-Health. *Environmental Science and Pollution*

Research, *28*(38), 52810–52831. Available from https://doi.org/10.1007/s11356-021-16223-0, https://link.springer.com/journal/11356.

Telemedicine: Opportunities and developments in Member States: Report on the second global survey on eHealth. (2009).

Tramontano, D. (2021). Go for it! Exercising makes you happy and strong. *Translational Medicine @ UniSa*, *23*(4). Available from https://doi.org/10.37825/2239-9747.1019.

Tuckson, R. V., Edmunds, M., & Hodgkins, M. L. (2017). Telehealth. massachussetts medical society, United States. *New England Journal of Medicine*, *377*(16), 1585–1592. Available from https://doi.org/10.1056/NEJMsr1503323, http://www.nejm.org/doi/pdf/10.1056/NEJMsr1503323.

Van Staalduinen, W. (2021). Learning to implement smart healthy age-friendly environments. *Translational Medicine @ UniSa*, *23*(4). Available from https://doi.org/10.37825/2239-9747.1021.

Vittori, A., Cascella, M., Leonardi, M., Monaco, F., Nocerino, D., Cuomo, A., Ottaiano, A., Perri, F., Mascilini, I., Francia, E., Petrucci, E., Marinangeli, F., & Picardo, S. G. (2022). VOSviewer-Based Bibliometric Network Analysis for Evaluating Research on Juvenile Primary Fibromyalgia Syndrome (JPFS). *Children*, *9*(5), 637. Available from https://doi.org/10.3390/children9050637.

Vorenkamp, K. E., Kochat, S., Breckner, F., & Dimon, C. (2022). Challenges in utilizing telehealth for chronic pain. *Current Pain and Headache Reports*, *26*(8), 617–622. Available from https://doi.org/10.1007/s11916-022-01067-1, http://www.springerlink.com/content/1531-3433/.

Walsh, J., Eccleston, C., & Keogh, E. (2014). Pain communication through body posture: The development and validation of a stimulus set. *Pain*, *155*(11), 2282–2290. Available from https://doi.org/10.1016/j.pain.2014.08.019.

Zavagli, V. (2021). The ANT home care model in palliative and end-of-life care. An investigation on family caregivers' satisfaction with the services provided. *Translational Medicine @ UniSa*, *23*(4). Available from https://doi.org/10.37825/2239-9747.1022.

Zhang, J., Xia, Q., & Zhao, Y. (2021). Research on electronic medical record data storage system based on blockchain technology. *China Medical Devices*, *36*, 106–109. Available from https://doi.org/10.3969/j.issn.1674-1633.2021.07.024.

Zhou, Y., Lin, H., Geng, Q., & Zhang. (2009). Constitution and new development of remote medical system. *China Digital Medicine*, *4*, 21–23.

Zou, H., Lu, Z., Zhao, P., Wang, J., & Wang, R. (2024). Efficacy of telerehabilitation in patients with nonspecific neck pain: A meta-analysis. *Journal of Telemedicine and Telecare*. Available from https://doi.org/10.1177/1357633x241235982.

CHAPTER

Telemedicine/telehealth in smart hospital care

12

Malgorzata Witkowska-Zimny
Department of Human Anatomy, Medical University of Warsaw, Warsaw, Poland

12.1 Introduction

The concept of telemedicine, the provision of medical services remotely, is not new. Back in antiquity, messengers or carrier pigeons were used to provide medical advice at a distance Fig. 12.1. With the industrial revolution in the mid-19th century and advancements in remote information

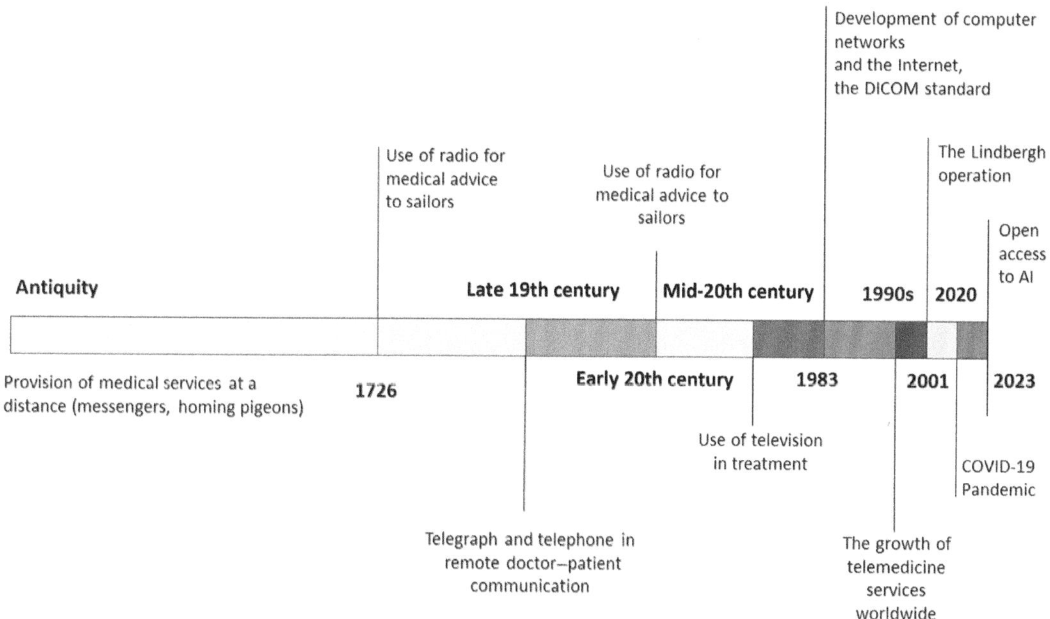

FIGURE 12.1

Selected aspects of the history of telemedicine. Telemedicine is the provision of medical and healthcare services at a distance. The history of the development of telemedicine can be divided into an era before and after the development of digital transmission tools and techniques. The diagram shows the milestones in the development of telemedicine.

Blockchain and Digital Twin for Smart Hospitals. DOI: https://doi.org/10.1016/B978-0-443-34226-4.00013-7

exchange, technology started facilitating medical services in areas lacking immediate and direct access to medical care. It was in the 1960s that space agencies made a major contribution to the development of telemedicine with the use of satellite telecommunication networks for medical care and health monitoring of astronauts. Throughout the late 1980s and early 1990s, the rapid expansion of computer networks and the Internet accelerated the development of telemedicine. Over time, more and more data were collected and better systems were developed to transmit text, voice, and visual messages. On September 7, 2001, the first remote surgical operation was performed, marking an important milestone in the development of telemedicine. Known as the Lindbergh operation, it involved the remote removal of a gallbladder. While the operator of the surgical instruments was in New York, the patient was in Strasbourg (Marescaux et al., 2002). At that time, well-developed countries with large areas and low population densities, such as Canada and Australia, and developing countries, such as Nigeria and Thailand, were interested in developing telemedicine to reach large numbers of patients at a low cost. Yet, due to a lack of economic incentives, few doctors and health systems pursued such services as they required investment in expensive telehealth technology. There is no doubt that it was the COVID-19 pandemic that marked a breakthrough in the development, but also in the general acceptance and use of telemedicine/telehealth by the public. During the pandemic, telemedicine proved a viable and safe way to deliver healthcare. Successful coordination of telemedicine services can optimize cost-effectiveness while maintaining quality care and ensuring patient satisfaction in healthcare systems constantly facing resource constraints. With the spread of smartphones, the increased availability of high-speed wireless networks, the improvement of streaming video applications, and the ubiquitous use of teleconferencing, concerns about the regulatory, liability, and funding aspects of Information Communication Technology (ICT)–enabled health services have been suppressed out of necessity. Globally, a paradigm shift in healthcare delivery has been driven by the shortage of medical staff, the need to reduce face-to-face contact, or a random combination of the above factors. Since the outbreak of the pandemic, there has also been a surge in telemedicine research and publications that address the specific needs of different patient subgroups, medical specialties, countries, and regions. As a result, we have gained better insights into the determinants of access to healthcare to better address inequalities embedded in current healthcare systems. Widespread access to artificial intelligence (AI) tools is another innovative technology with the potential to revolutionize telehealth/telemedicine practices. Emerging technologies such as digital twins, blockchain, the Internet of Things (IoT), large multimodal models (LMMs), and AI also play a key role in the technological revolution in healthcare (Healthcare 4.0). This implies the development of digital caregivers to advise patients and assist doctors, and we are beginning to talk to machines as we do to other humans. Dedicated chatbots will offer advice, answer inquiries, and monitor health, delivering services whose scope we cannot yet fully anticipate. This will entail a departure from mobile apps focused on tasks like tracking sleep quality, promoting healthy eating, and managing diabetes, which often require manual input. Remarkably, AI and other cutting-edge technologies are being adopted faster than any other consumer application in history. In its 2022 Recommendations, the WHO provided a list of technical requirements that telehealth platforms need to meet, focusing on making services accessible to those with special needs (WHO, 2022). The WHO also published comprehensive guidelines on how to ethically use and manage artificial intelligence in healthcare. These were updated in 2024 to identify both the potential benefits and potential risks of using artificial intelligence in healthcare. For various parties, such as governments, public agencies, researchers, businesses, as well as healthcare professionals and patients, the development and implementation of AI solutions in healthcare, should be guided by the following key principles: (1) protect autonomy; (2) promote human well-being, human safety and the public interest; (3) ensure transparency and intelligibility; (4) promote responsibility and accountability; (5) ensure inclusiveness and equity; and (6) promote artificial intelligence that is responsive and sustainable (WHO, 2024). The need to promote telemedicine is driven by the increasing demand for this type of healthcare services. The evolving roles of healthcare professionals and patients are essential factors in the advancement of telehealth/telemedicine. For the alpha generation, the merging of the digital with the everyday is inevitable, as they were born in the digital age, with access to technology from a young age and they communicate and socialize mainly online. As the world is constantly changing, it becomes critical to adapt to the rapid development of digital services, new technologies, big data, and AI. At the heart of the idea of Society 5.0 is the aspect of harnessing digital technologies and artificial intelligence while respecting the environment and planetary resources. The assumptions of Society 5.0 also include achieving long life through significant use of robotic and computerized medical/nursing care. New technologies and digitalization can make it easier for patients to access medical care, choose the most effective treatment methods, or reduce the burden on medical staff by automating administrative processes in hospitals and medical facilities, allowing healthcare professionals to spend more time with patients.

12.2 Telehealth and telemedicine

After an extensive introduction to the dynamics of telehealth/telemedicine, it is necessary to clarify what exactly telehealth and telemedicine entail. As a combination of medicine and technology, often used interchangeably, telemedicine and telehealth were not originally intended to be the same. Telemedicine is the delivery of health services at a distance using ICT. The term telehealth is a broader concept encompassing all health-related information, including preventive, diagnostic, and nonclinical services such as health campaigns, health education for patients and their families, training for health professionals, and management or monitoring of health systems. For a better understanding of the distinction between the two, consider this conclusion: "All telemedicine is telehealth, but not all telehealth is telemedicine." The WHO defines telemedicine as follows: "The delivery of health care services, where distance is a critical factor, by all health care professionals using information and communication technologies for the exchange of valid information for diagnosis, treatment and prevention of disease and injuries, research and evaluation, and for the continuing education of health care providers, all in the interests of advancing the health of individuals and their communities" (WHO, 2010). In turn, the American Telemedicine Association (ATA) defines telemedicine as the exchange of medical information between two or more users via electronic communication for the improvement of patient health. What should be emphasized is that telemedicine is constantly evolving and changing to reflect new technological developments as well as health needs and the social context.

As both telemedicine and telehealth apply to the healthcare sector, and as their objectives are interrelated and address the holistic care and well-being of patients, the fundamental differences between the two concepts have become blurred and it is increasingly accepted that telemedicine and telehealth are synonymous and can be used interchangeably. This is also assumed for the purposes of this publication. Other names are also used to refer to identical services, for example, mobile health, m-health, e-health, digital health, and virtual healthcare.

There are several key components to telemedicine/telehealth: providing clinical support, overcoming barriers (geography, armed conflict), using different types of information and communication technologies, and, most importantly, improving health outcomes. Telehealth can offer a more personalized approach to healthcare, focusing on delivering services in a way that is relevant to recipients, and tailored to their needs, preferences, and personal circumstances. This is especially true for chronic diseases and long-term health problems. Telehealth can address inequalities in access to healthcare services, as it allows individuals unable or unwilling to interact with healthcare professionals in person to access digital health information and tools to manage their health and care. However, when designing telehealth services, it is important to recognize that not all services can be successfully provided using telehealth solutions and that teleconsultation is not suitable for all patients.

The term telemedicine covers a wide range of services. The most common services include teleconsultation, teletriage, telemonitoring, teleeducation, telerehabilitation, teleradiology, telepathology, teledermatology, telesurgery, and teleophthalmology. In addition, the scope of services may include patient service centers, online patient information centers, e-appointments or videoconferencing between healthcare professionals, lifelong learning, patient education, monitoring and management of individual patient and hospital network health data, overall health system management, health system(s) integration, asset identification, and allocation. A better quality of life both for individuals and society, in general, is closely linked to modern technologies. They link the virtual (cyberspace) and the real world into a single integrated network. When analyzing the different classifications of telemedicine services, we should distinguish communication modes: (1) real-time—"live" contact (most commonly used in telepsychiatry, telecardiology, teleconsultation, telesurgery, telemonitoring); (2) store and forward—digital data in the form of images, video, and sound files are captured and stored on a computer, mobile device, or in the cloud (cloud storage) and transmitted via a secure link for further study or analysis (most commonly used in teleradiology, teledermatology, and telepathology); (3) remote monitoring—the patient is monitored via a system that gathers data from monitoring devices and sends it to an external control room from where the health status of the patient is monitored (most commonly used for chronic diseases such as diabetes, asthma, heart diseases, or telerehabilitation).

12.3 Telehealth/telemedicine in smart hospital care

Telemedicine offers a wide range of possibilities, including remote monitoring (telemonitoring, telediagnosis), remote health education for the chronically ill, teleconsultations/telehealth appointments, transmission of images and test results, telerehabilitation, e-prescribing and e-diagnosis, 24-hour monitoring, personal assistance, and counseling. Apart from a wide range of possibilities for the diagnosis, treatment, or supervision of patients, remote healthcare focuses primarily on reducing the need for face-to-face appointments between the patient and medical staff. This chapter will mainly consider the use of telehealth in the context of hospital medicine. Within the field of hospital medicine, the following will be discussed: teletriage, telediagnosis, telesurgery, telemonitoring in intensive care units (tele-ICU systems with audio and visual virtual solutions), and post-hospital patient monitoring with aspects of remote education.

12.3.1 Teletriage

Early proactive triage can have a significant impact on positive patient health outcomes. Traditional triage involves triage nurses/paramedics prioritizing ambulance/emergency calls based on the patient's clinical history and/or images of injuries. The use of telemedicine, particularly in the provision of prehospital and emergency department (ED) care during the COVID-19 pandemic, reduced the transmission of the SARS-Cov-2 virus and protected medical staff situations of limited resources (Witkowska-Zimny & Nieradko-Iwanicka, 2022). The early transfer of a patient to the most appropriate hospital or specialized center not only improves the outcome of an injury/burn/emergency but also reduces the cost to the healthcare provider and the healthcare system. In the case of teletriage, it is also possible to implement a specialized virtual assistant/chatbot service that suggests the best prehospital or hospital care option based on collected information, relevant algorithms, and up-to-date data from medical facilities. Teletriage with access to big data can handle emergency calls faster and more efficiently, and, importantly, multiple calls can be handled simultaneously without a language barrier, as properly configured tools allow artificial intelligence to be used in multiple languages without the need for additional personnel. The use of modern technology also allows for better resource allocation. A properly configured chatbot can not only handle the call but also appropriately filter calls that require human intervention. This allows for optimized staffing, high 24/7 availability regardless of holidays/vacations, more efficient administration, and automated triage of incoming calls. As the patient does not have to wait for help at an early stage, this also leads to higher patient satisfaction. The implementation of reliable triage can optimize existing clinical resources, particularly in the event of an unexpected incident, war, terrorism, or other mass casualty events. Teletriage can be provided either directly to the patient or through medical personnel on-site. In emergency medicine, during mass casualty events (disasters or terrorist attacks), primary triage is used to prioritize treatment and transport to save as many casualties as possible, optimizing the use of on-scene medical personnel, equipment, and logistical support. Primary triage can be supported by the use of modern technology for the assessment of the size of the incident, the area in need of medical assistance, the most common injuries, or the coordination of actions. Teletriage can be used for secondary triage at the scene of an incident to avoid disorderly transport of patients requiring urgent medical attention from the scene of the incident to the hospital. Decision-making based on continuously updated information on the availability of medical staff, free beds in medical facilities, or teleconsultation between emergency medical services and specialists in a given medical discipline, allows the selection of the optimal transport route (land, air, water) depending on the status of the casualties and the available means of transport, to arrange transport in such a way to provide the best possible care to the maximum number of casualties. A systematic evaluation examined the applications, opportunities, and challenges of triage, transfer, and referral in the most common uses of telemedicine, in managing burns (38.9%) (Hayavi-Haghighi & Alipour, 2023).

The initial assessment of the depth of burn injury during triage serves as the basis for determining the course of the clinical treatment plan. This can be done on the basis of noninvasive assessment of burn wound severity using measurement data analyzed in artificial intelligence models with machine learning algorithms (Khani et al., 2023). The significant capacity of telemedicine and new technologies to assist in the triage of acute cases and the increasing use of such consultations also provide evidence of the cost-effectiveness of such an investment. Research shows that telemedicine interventions reduce unnecessary medical appointments, improve clinical outcomes, reduce mortality and complications from injury, increase patient satisfaction, reduce provider workload, improve access to primary and specialist care, and increase patient safety and satisfaction.

In conclusion, telemedicine can improve the quality of prehospital emergency services by streamlining prehospital consultations, patient triage, and transport, thereby reducing the number of patients in emergency departments, which are always overburdened. The use of telemedicine services can contribute to the coordination of emergency systems and thus to the improvement of the overall functioning of the healthcare system.

12.3.2 Telediagnostics

Initially, telediagnosis involved only the direct transmission of test results from medical devices located in one place to another center for interpreting, diagnosing, or consulting between specialists (teleconsultation). Teleradiology, which involves the transmission of images (X-ray, ultrasound, tomography, mammography, etc.) from centers without professional radiologists, is the oldest (since the 1970s) and most widely used telediagnostic service. The service significantly speeds up the reporting process and also reduces the costs associated with the maintenance of a diagnostic imaging unit. Furthermore, it now guarantees continuous access for patients and medical staff to securely store test results. Telediagnosis also facilitates the establishment of partnerships between local healthcare providers and tele-specialists from different disciplines or remote locations. As a result, the patient can be diagnosed or even receive a treatment plan in a shorter period of time, based on the exchange of information and the views of a multidisciplinary team, even in the case of rare specialties, thus increasing the availability of health services and removing restrictions on access to specialists (La Valle et al., 2022).

Telediagnostics has broadened the range of services provided. In addition to teleradiology, it often includes telepathology (examination of specimens using a microscope or by staff located in a remote specialized center), tele-endoscopy (transmission of endoscopic images via a telecommunications network), and telecardiology (transmission of electrocardiogram (ECG) results to a remote cardiological diagnostic center). Even a simple teleconsultation does not have to be based solely on taking the patient's medical history. Increasingly, it can be supplemented by the patient's own physical examination, for example, examination of the throat or ear, auscultation of the lungs for respiratory infections, or assessment of skin lesions. A large number of medical devices/telediagnostic tools/biosensors are being developed specifically for telemedicine—including blood glucose meters, ECG machines, spirometers (breathing monitors), hearing and vision assessment devices, electronic stethoscopes, and pulse and blood pressure monitors. These devices are equipped with electronic sensors and can transmit the results of the test to monitoring centers via telephone lines, integrated services digital network (ISDN), the Internet, or mobile phones (Naceri et al., 2022). Moreover, these small devices, which can be used by the patient at home to perform the test and transmit the medical data to the doctor as images (of the throat or the inside of the ear) and sounds (auscultation of the lungs or the heart), come with an application that tells the patient which parameters to test and notifies him or her whether the test is being performed properly. Thus it is expected that telediagnostic tools will become increasingly important. More and more medical service providers are considering their implementation. There is also a growing need for specialists to be able to carry out robotic-assisted diagnostic tests such as ultrasound and Doppler scans remotely. With the latest advances in robotics, teleoperation, and improved telecommunications infrastructure, limited access to specialists in geographically remote areas can be addressed. A new generation of robots is being developed, with promising projects like RAUS (Robotic Ultrasound) in the preclinical phase, offering a solution to the shortage of health professionals in remote locations (Hidalgo et al., 2023).

Breakthroughs in telediagnostics are also being brought about by the development of AI. Advanced diagnostic tools, telediagnostic devices, and AI algorithms allow for more accurate diagnoses to be delivered faster, which is important for patients in areas with difficult access to healthcare services and advanced diagnostics. This has been made possible thanks to the collection of data from advanced examinations in many populations, in geographical locations outside large clinical centers. AI is also helping to reduce the time to diagnosis, start treatment earlier, and improve the accuracy of predicting treatment effectiveness, taking into account the heterogeneity of the population, predicting the duration of surgical procedures, and thus optimizing the availability of resources. This improves automation and efficiency and helps to overcome geographical barriers. By reducing the number of patient appointments, medical centers can operate more efficiently, ensuring that those with urgent needs can consult a specialist. Patients will have the opportunity to improve the quality of their personal and professional lives through a reduction in the number of routine medical appointments and through a sense of continuity in their treatment.

In short, telediagnostics can be described as a technology that allows a doctor to examine and diagnose a patient remotely. The benefits for both patients and healthcare professionals are numerous. A medical center can expand the range and scope of patient care, streamline and reduce the duration of the diagnostic process, and reduce costs while providing the highest level of service.

12.3.3 Telesurgery

Telesurgery is a type of surgery or medical procedure that is performed using a remotely controlled surgical robot. This most technologically advanced type of telemedicine service combines elements of surgery, telecommunications, information science, and robotics. Medical robots are playing an increasingly important role in modern surgery. Since their introduction in the 1980s, there have been significant advances in this field. Above all, robotic surgery prioritizes efficiency, precision, and repeatability in surgical procedures, resulting in less invasive operations. The devices used in surgery are usually remote manipulators, which means that all decisions are made by the operator of the robot—the medical doctor. Telesurgery does not have to be associated with a large distance between the operator and the patient—procedures performed without physical contact with the patient, not directly by the surgeon but through a controlled robot, separated by a distance of a few meters, also qualify as remote. The benefits of such procedures include increased accuracy, reduced invasiveness, visualization of the operated organ surpassing the naked eye (thanks to cameras on the manipulators), and, for the patient, less pain, less scarring, and shorter time in the ICU. On the disadvantage side, we should mention the high cost of purchasing, maintaining, and servicing the device, the need for highly specialized staff training, and the lack of direct sensory experience of the patient's tissue by the operator. As of today, the da Vinci robot is the most popular surgical robot used in hospitals around the world to perform minimally invasive procedures where high precision is required. In total, more than 170 types of procedures are performed worldwide using the da Vinci robot in the following areas: cardiac surgery (repair of the bicuspid valve), proctology (colectomy), general surgery (treatment of gallbladder disease, bariatric surgery), gynecology (hysterectomy), and urology (prostatectomy, cystectomy, partial nephrectomy).

The da Vinci robot allows to perform surgical procedures at a distance using ICT. The world's first remote surgery (the Lindbergh operation) using a medical robot was a cholecystectomy performed on September 7, 2001. The operating surgeon was Professor Jacques Marescaux, who directed the procedure from New York, while the patient was located in Strasbourg. The procedure for remote gallbladder removal lasted 54 minutes.

Remote operations allow to expand the group of patients for whom effective surgical intervention is possible, without the need for a specialist to be present at the patient's location. In the case of procedures involving the administration of radioisotope contrast medium, for example, remote robotic angiography, the isolation of the operator also limits his or her exposure to harmful radiation. However, remote surgeries are not currently a commonly used technology in hospitals due to the high cost, complexity, and size of telesurgery systems. They still remain in the realm of research and tests by academic centers and medical corporations. For telesurgery to become more widespread, steps must be taken to standardize systems present on the market and ensure their compatibility. There are also some legal concerns regarding the performance of telesurgery. The issue of liability for performing remote procedures needs to be regulated, as in many countries; the law does not stipulate who is responsible for the operation—the surgeon at the patient's location, monitoring the patient's condition, or the doctor who controls the telemedicine system remotely. It is also unclear who should take responsibility if the operation fails. Moreover, in the case of international telesurgery, we need to determine which legal system to use. The question of liability in the case of telementoring (remote assistance during surgery) is also being scrutinized. Furthermore, there are no clearly defined procedures in the event of communication breakdown. The security of virtual private network (VPN) connections used in remote operations is also questionable since appropriate encryption algorithms capable of protecting against cyber security attacks are necessary. However, it can be expected that the use of medical robots and the performance of telesurgery will increase in the next few years and that the development of nanomedicine/nanoscale medicine and single-cell procedures will promote their wider use in the future.

It is worth noting that telesurgery can also be part of remote education of specialists. Procedures performed with a medical robot can be observed by doctors who are up to several thousand kilometers away from the operating theater. In this way, it is possible to provide remote guidance to the team operating the robot, allowing the operator's skills to be honed and the knowledge and experience of the best specialists to be used during advanced operations without them being present at the operating table (telementoring) (Marcos-Pablos & García-Peñalvo, 2022).

Telemedicine has revolutionized the field of surgery, and telemonitoring and telesurgery are two of its most promising applications that could change the way surgery is performed. Digital applications can enable surgeons to perform operations by assisting others or supervising them in the mode of mentoring them from another location (telementoring). Despite the potential benefits of telemedicine and telementoring, there are still challenges to overcome before they can be widely used in clinical practice. For example, data latency can constitute a problem in telemedicine, as even a small delay in data transmission can affect the accuracy of surgery. Additionally, a sophisticated and expensive technological infrastructure is required, which may limit the use of telesurgery in some clinical settings. Although we need to work on its development technologically, ethically, and legally, it is a promising tool.

12.3.4 Hospital and out-of-hospital telemonitoring

Telemonitoring is the constant monitoring of a patient's health by means of telemedicine devices that monitor and analyze the patient's condition mainly by measuring basic vital functions. Thanks to telemonitoring, the patient's health status is always under control, and, in the event of any abnormalities, the medical staff can react immediately. Depending on the needs and the model of care, data collected during the examination is sent directly to the doctors/nurses/dieticians or to specialized centers analyzing the records from the devices. Despite high costs, there is a steadily growing interest in remote patient monitoring in the hospital setting especially in intensive care units. Remote ICU systems, with virtual audio and visual solutions, enriched with risk prediction algorithms, intelligent alarm systems, and machine learning tools, have been developed in response to the growing demand for intensive care services and shortages of specialized medical staff (Khurrum et al., 2021). New, more efficient service models and telemedicine tools for monitoring intensive care patients became more widely available during the COVID-19 pandemic, for example, the hub-and-spoke model to connect new "spokes": the 2-step activation characteristics of the hub-and-spoke infrastructure and the 6-step activation process for arranging telemedicine intensivist consultations. The pandemic has also brought about a change in the ways in which telemedicine services are reimbursed and has influenced the development and refinement of predictive analytics related to the monitoring and provision of ICU patient services (Cucchi et al., 2022). Implementing remote ICU services requires significant upfront investment and consideration of high ongoing maintenance costs. This can be challenging for hospitals with low budgets. Hence, the importance of further research into more effective strategies for integrating and implementing e-ICU services. Undoubtedly, however, the implementation of remote ICU offers many benefits and makes the delivery of intensive care more efficient for large numbers of patients, as was the case in the COVID-19 pandemic or in emergencies such as mass events (disasters, assaults) (Boustany et al., 2023).

In the out-of-hospital setting, telemonitoring makes it possible to prolong patient care by remote patient monitoring (RPM) at home or in long-term care facilities, monitoring medication adherence and early detection of disease exacerbations or conditions that may adversely affect the course of the disease or treatment. Available telemedicine tools enable the assessment of medication adherence and lifestyle modifications. This is possible either by monitoring the status of the medication (s) or by assessing indicators of treatment effectiveness, for example, vital signs, such as blood pressure, heart rate, or body weight. Telecare usually complements direct medical care, and teleeducation is an indispensable element meant to involve the patient in the therapeutic process. Telecare provides comfort and safety for patients while relieving the burden on medical facilities. Such a model is supported by telerehabilitation and is complemented by patient education on self-care or by instructions for taking correct measurements. It also offers the possibility to virtually control the operation and even change the settings of a device that has been implanted in the patient, for example, a cochlear implant or a pacemaker (telefitting) (Takano et al., 2021).

The remote care model is particularly important in the case of the elderly, lonely people, and people with limited cognitive abilities or mobility because it allows 24-hour observation and recording of the required parameters while limiting the number of visits to medical facilities to the necessary minimum, which reduces the overall occupancy of medical staff/facilities and gives more opportunity for people who urgently need to see a specialist. The collected medical data (multimedia in digital, textual, visual, and audio form) sent by means of ICT networks to specialists who can describe and interpret it leads to faster and more accurate diagnosis, but also allows for the assessment of the effectiveness of the ordered therapy in the conditions of the patient's everyday life (pharmacological telemonitoring). Awareness of ongoing care gives patients the opportunity to improve their quality of private and professional life. Telemonitoring is commonly used in cardiology, in the form of implantable cardiac monitoring devices. With these, an ECG can be performed without leaving home and the tracings are sent to an analysis center.

Studies show that telemonitoring can be a useful tool to support clinical practice during the patient's stay in the hospital but even more so after discharge, especially for long-term/chronic conditions. The main barriers to the increasing implementation of telemonitoring are mainly related to the use of the device (e.g., difficulties in using the device) (Creber et al., 2023). Further research is needed to assess the benefits of different device technologies for long-term condition management and patient engagement. Appropriate education and tailoring of interventions (e.g., type of technology used, frequency of measurements, intensity of support) to patient's needs/requirements may be necessary. In addition, attention should be given to building user-friendly interfaces for these devices, which may reduce potential barriers to using the technology (especially for older patients). It is also important to identify the most appropriate member of the medical staff to act as the main point of contact for the patient in regard to telemonitoring.

12.4 Telehealthcare service delivery companies

The provision of telehealth/telemedicine services is inextricably linked to the activity and development of a sector of companies that are market leaders in telemedicine services or providers of telemedicine technology. IBM has been developing medical software to create comprehensive patient data records since the 1960s. Microsoft has created AI-powered virtual assistants, chatbots, and cloud-based data-sharing tools, and Google is refining the use of artificial intelligence to diagnose cancer and predict the effectiveness of disease treatment.

Interestingly, however, the majority of new solutions in telehealth are being developed in innovative small telehealth start-ups(Iakovleva et al., 2021), which are evolving to meet the needs of digital healthcare and play a significant role in teleconsultation, telemonitoring, patient teleeducation, or providing electronic health record solutions. More recently, their focus has shifted toward personalized care based on artificial intelligence, including digital therapeutic agents. The global telehealth market is developing and changing, with a compound annual growth rate (CAGR) of 15% until 2022; it is expected to reach $390.7 billion in 2024. Telehealth start-ups are estimated to have generated a profit of $17 billion in 2020. Yet, after an analysis of funding trends, following an upward trend with a peak in 2021 due to investment in health technology during the COVID-19 pandemic, a continuation of the downward trend initiated in 2023 has been noted. Existing telehealth start-ups have established a significant position in the digital healthcare market. In addition to online and e-consultation, telehealth start-ups are expanding in the area of specialized services such as tele-orthopedics, teledermatology, and telepsychiatry services, but also the creation of new digital therapeutic devices, portable health monitoring devices, and personalized care based on artificial intelligence (Chakraborty et al., 2023). Smartphones, being the most efficient communication channel, enable the provision of many telehealth services. However, new technological, financial, and legal challenges are constantly emerging and hinder the innovation and commercialization of dedicated digital healthcare solutions created by startups. Undoubtedly, the 4.0 industrial revolution is significantly influencing the functioning and integration of care and health services that no longer take place only in the medical setting, between specialists, but also in the patient's home environment. Society 5.0 are people who are aware of the challenges, but also ready to take advantage of technological solutions in the area of health to make healthcare highly personalized. Medical robots are also a growing industry, estimated to be worth $12.7 billion by 2025. Surgical robots and rehabilitation robots are the two main markets for robotics—an industry driven by an aging population. In medicine, however, robots are also increasingly used in medical education and not only in training surgeons in robotic surgery but especially in training medical personnel in medical procedures with the use of high-fidelity simulators. Robots are increasingly being used in healthcare. The use of robots during the COVID-19 pandemic provided important examples of the clinical utility of this technology. With the advent of a new generation of robots, new high-speed low-latency satellite Internet communications, mobile broadband networks, and touch technology, the opportunities for the deployment of robots in healthcare services are increasing. Furthermore, the adoption of artificial intelligence in healthcare and diagnostic imaging is changing the way diseases are identified, treated, and prevented. The combination of robotics, artificial intelligence, and telecommunications has the potential to revolutionize healthcare service delivery in the future, so MedTech companies are bound to grow and offer an ever-widening spectrum of innovative and unique products and services that are of high quality and compliant with the principles required in the healthcare sector.

12.5 Benefits and limitations involved in telemedicine/telehealth

Telemedicine/telehealth is a completely new space for the exchange of information and the contact and delivery of services in the healthcare system. It is already an integral part of healthcare systems today, enabling resources, including human resources, to be used more fully with the help of appropriate technology. For this reason, any medical specialty can employ telemedicine solutions and adapt them for more efficient patient care (e.g., telecardiology, telepulmonology, teleradiology, etc.). From a patient pathway perspective, telemedicine care provides an additional type of communication channel with the medical professional, which promotes accessibility, convenience, cost-effectiveness, and better patient outcomes. When used well, telemedicine can provide the patient with earlier contact with the healthcare system and eliminate geographic and logistical barriers, and, most importantly, tailor the diagnosis and treatment pathway to the individual patient's needs in line with the concept of patient-tailored therapy. Understanding this is key from the perspective of the potential advantages of telemedicine. Although telemedicine offers many benefits, it also has some limitations and issues (Table 12.1) that need to be considered when it comes to planning.

Table 12.1 The most important benefits and limitations of telemedicine.

Benefits	Limitations
Better access to care. Telemedicine crosses geographical and logistical boundaries, enabling patients from remote or poorly developed areas to access healthcare services. It eliminates the necessity to travel long distances and provides easy access to specialists and healthcare providers.	*Limited physical examination.* One of the major challenges telemedicine needs to face is the inability to perform a comprehensive physical examination remotely. The medical team may not have access to vital signs or physical touch and cannot perform certain diagnostic tests, which may impede the process of making an accurate diagnosis and administering treatment.
Greater convenience. Telemedicine provides elasticity and convenience, enabling patients to book appointments at times and places that they prefer. Patients may consult healthcare providers at their own homes, which reduces travel and waiting time.	*Technological limitations.* Reliable and safe Internet connection is key to the success of remote appointments. In areas where access to the Internet is limited or unstable, telemedicine may not be possible or may cause low-quality sound or vision, impeding successful communication.
Timely care and reduced waiting time. Telemedicine enables patients to receive care at the right moment, reducing waiting time. Teleconsultations offer quick access to doctors, facilitating earlier diagnosis and treatment.	*Lack of personal contact.* Telemedicine may lack personal contact and face-to-face interaction, which is possible only during traditional visits to the doctor. Some patients may feel more comfortable sharing sensitive information or building rapport with the healthcare provider during in-person appointments.
Continuity of care. Telemedicine promotes continuity of care, allowing for smooth communication between the patient and the service provider. It offers remote monitoring of chronic conditions, managing medication and follow-up visits, ensuring constant support and care as well as easier access to medical records. Test results and medical history may be available for the patient and the medical team on a daily basis.	*Concerns regarding privacy and security.* Telemedicine involves the transmission of sensitive information about the patient via digital platforms, which raises concerns about data security and privacy breaches. Provision of secure transmission channels and implementing solid data security measures are key to maintaining patient confidentiality.
Greater patient involvement. Telemedicine enables patients to actively participate in healthcare, as they can access health records, view test results and cooperate with healthcare providers in the process of decision-making; it promotes a patient-centered approach and includes the patient in the therapeutic process.	*Regulatory and legal considerations.* Practice of telemedicine is subject to specific legal and regulatory requirements, which may differ depending on region or country. Issues related to licensing, reimbursement, and liability may constitute challenges for healthcare providers willing to offer telemedicine services across national boundaries.
Cost reduction. Telemedicine may lead to significant cost reductions for the patient. By eliminating travel costs and reducing the need for in-person appointments, patients may save on transport costs, parking fees, and accommodation. This increases the availability of medical services.	*Diagnostic limitations.* Some conditions may require complex diagnostic procedures, specialized equipment, or imaging studies, which cannot be performed remotely. In such cases, patients may still require appointments in healthcare settings for further studies or evaluation, which decreases the overall convenience and benefits of telemedicine.
Efficient use of healthcare resources. Telemedicine optimizes the use of healthcare resources enabling healthcare providers to serve a greater group of patients. It allows for enhanced allocation of resources, reduces overcrowding in healthcare settings, and enables healthcare providers to effectively serve more patients.	*Differences in availability.* Socioeconomic disproportions, reduced access to and lower familiarity with digital technology may limit the availability and role of telemedicine, particularly in populations that have limited access to services or in rural areas.

Undoubtedly, as technology continues to advance, telemedicine/telehealth will play an even more prominent role in the future of healthcare. However, it is important to remember that a patient may not want to use the services offered by telemedicine/telehealth and has every right to do so. One of the key values is patient autonomy, which is expressed through making informed decisions related to the protection of one's own health. Every patient should be educated about the nature of such a service, its benefits, and its limitations before using teleconsultation or any other form of telemedicine service. He or she should use telemedicine consciously, in addition to services provided in a traditional, in-person manner, and not, for example, because this form of assistance is imposed on them by a doctor or a medical facility.

12.6 Conclusion

Telemedicine/telehealth is a whole set of activities aimed at the effective, economical, and secure use of information and telecommunication technologies to support all healthcare activities, including the provision of healthcare services (consultation, care, diagnostics, therapy, patient monitoring, health education), systems for observing health-related fields, medical information technology, health information management, and information and communication technologies in healthcare, but also the development of professional literature and knowledge, as well as scientific research. Unlimited access to information may seem like a positive element in healthcare. However, we already receive more information than we can process and use. It is important to remember that medical data is by its nature always uncertain and incomplete. Synthesizing medical knowledge is becoming increasingly difficult and labor-intensive at both population and individual patient levels. Therefore artificial intelligence and the associated development of telemedicine/telehealth services may be a response to the needs of modern medicine but, at the same time, must remain in line with the philosophy of evidence-based medicine (EBM).

References

Boustany, A., Hencel, H., Svoboda, O., Fungcap, S., & Abi Fadel, F. (2023). Integration strategy for e-intensive care unit: A narrative review and implementation plan. *Telemedicine and e-Health*, *29*(3), 361–365. Available from https://doi.org/10.1089/tmj.2021.0579.

Chakraborty, I., Edirippulige, S., & Ilavarasan, P. V. (2023). The role of telehealth startups in healthcare service delivery: A systematic review. *International Journal of Medical Informatics*, *174*, 105048. Available from https://doi.org/10.1016/j.ijmedinf.2023.105048.

Creber, A., Leo, D. G., Buckley, B. J. R., Chowdhury, M., Harrison, S. L., Isanejad, M., & Lane, D. A. (2023). Use of telemonitoring in patient self-management of chronic disease: A qualitative meta-synthesis. *BMC Cardiovascular Disorders*, *23*(1). Available from https://doi.org/10.1186/s12872-023-03486-3, https://bmccardiovascdisord.biomedcentral.com/.

Cucchi, E. W., Kopec, S. E., & Lilly, C. W. (2022). COVID-19 and the Transformation of Intensive Care Unit Telemedicine. *Clinics in Chest Medicine*, *43*(3), 529–538. Available from https://doi.org/10.1016/j.ccm.2022.05.007.

Hayavi-Haghighi, M. H., & Alipour, J. (2023). Applications, opportunities, and challenges in using Telehealth for burn injury management: A systematic review. *Burns*, *49*(6), 1237–1248. Available from https://doi.org/10.1016/j.burns.2023.07.001, http://www.elsevier.com/locate/burns.

Hidalgo, E. M., Wright, L., Isaksson, M., Lambert, G., & Marwick, T. H. (2023). Current applications of robot-assisted ultrasound examination. *JACC: Cardiovascular Imaging*, *16*(2), 239–247. Available from https://doi.org/10.1016/j.jcmg.2022.07.018, http://www.elsevier.com.

Iakovleva, T., Oftedal, E., & Bessant, J. (2021). Changing role of users—innovating responsibly in digital health. *Sustainability*, *13*(4), 1616. Available from https://doi.org/10.3390/su13041616.

Khani, M. E., Harris, Z. B., Osman, O. B., Singer, A. J., & Arbab, M. H. (2023). Triage of *in vivo* burn injuries and prediction of wound healing outcome using neural networks and modeling of the terahertz permittivity based on the double Debye dielectric parameters. *Biomedical Optics Express*, *14*(2), 918–931. Available from https://doi.org/10.1364/BOE.479567.

Khurrum, M., Asmar, S., & Joseph, B. (2021). Telemedicine in the ICU: Innovation in the critical care process. *Journal of Intensive Care Medicine*, *36*(12), 1377–1384. Available from https://doi.org/10.1177/0885066620968518.

La Valle, C., Johnston, J., & Tager-Flusberg, H. (2022). A systematic review of the use of telehealth to facilitate a diagnosis for children with developmental concerns. *Research in Developmental Disabilities*, *127*, 104269. Available from https://doi.org/10.1016/j.ridd.2022.104269.

Marcos-Pablos, S., & García-Peñalvo, F. J. (2022). More than surgical tools: a systematic review of robots as didactic tools for the education of professionals in health sciences. *Advances in Health Sciences Education: Theory and Practice*, *27*, 1139–1176. Available from https://doi.org/10.1007/s10459-022-10118-6.

Marescaux, J., Leroy, J., Rubino, F., Smith, M., Vix, M., Simone, M., & Mutter, D. (2002). Transcontinental robot-assisted remote telesurgery: Feasibility and potential applications. *Annals of Surgery*, *235*(4), 487–492. Available from https://doi.org/10.1097/00000658-200204000-00005.

Naceri, A., Elsner, J., Trobinger, M., Sadeghian, H., Johannsmeier, L., Voigt, F., Chen, X., Macari, D., Jahne, C., Berlet, M., Fuchtmann, J., Figueredo, L., Feusner, H., Wilhelm, D., & Haddadin, S. (2022). Tactile robotic telemedicine for safe remote diagnostics in times of Corona: System design, feasibility and usability study. *IEEE Robotics and Automation Letters*, *7*(4), 10296–10303. Available from https://doi.org/10.1109/lra.2022.3191563.

Takano, K., Kaizaki, A., Kimura, A., Nomura, K., Yamazaki, N., Shintani, T., & Himi, T. (2021). Telefitting of nucleus cochlear implants: A feasibility study. *American Journal of Audiology*, *30*(1), 16–21. Available from https://doi.org/10.1044/2020_aja-20-00041.

WHO. (2010). World Health Organization, 2010. WHO Global Observatory for eHealth. Telemedicine: opportunities and developments in Member States: report on the second global survey on eHealth. *Report on the second global survey on eHealth*. Available from https://iris.who.int/bitstream/handle/10665/44497/9789241564144_eng.pdf?sequence = 1.

WHO. World Health Organization and International Telecommunication Union, 2022. WHO-ITU global standard for accessibility of telehealth services. Geneva: Licence: CC BY-NC-SA 3.0 IGO. Available from https://iris.who.int/bitstream/handle/10665/356160/9789240050464-eng.pdf?sequence = 1&isAllowed = y.

WHO. World Health Organization, 2024. WHO Ethics and governance of artificial intelligence for health. Guidance on large multi-modal models. Geneva: Licence: CC BY-NC-SA 3.0 IGO. Available from https://iris.who.int/bitstream/handle/10665/375579/9789240084759-eng.pdf?sequence = 1.

Witkowska-Zimny, M., & Nieradko-Iwanicka, B. (2022). Telemedicine in emergency medicine in the COVID-19 pandemic—experiences and prospects—A narrative review. *International Journal of Environmental Research and Public Health*, *19*(13), 8216. Available from https://doi.org/10.3390/ijerph19138216.

CHAPTER

Digital twin application in healthcare facilities management 13

David Ojimaojo Ebiloma[1], Clinton Ohis Aigbavboa[1] and Chimay Anumba[2]

[1]CIDB Centre of Excellence and Sustainable Human Settlement and Construction Research Centre, Faculty of Engineering and the Built Environment, University of Johannesburg, Johannesburg, South Africa [2]College of Design, Construction and Planning, University of Florida, FL, United States

13.1 Introduction

This chapter presents the application and applicability of digital twins (DTs) to healthcare facilities management. It considers the framing synopsis of hospital buildings, and theoretical perceptions for hospital facilities research. The chapter also presents the theoretical frameworks that have been recognized and identified for hospital facilities studies. The overview of DT technology and its application within the healthcare sector was also considered in this chapter. A Delphi study report on the barriers and critical success factors to DT maintenance management of healthcare facilities in developing countries was discussed in this chapter.

The use of digital information technologies is important in successfully controlling and managing building facilities, particularly in enhancing communication and coordination among participants. Maintenance information systems enable any corporation to increase its asset capacity by maintaining current fixed costs. To ensure that facilities are available, that services are of high quality, that deliveries are made on time, and that prices are competitive, it is crucial to integrate and employ information tools like DT technology with corporate strategies. Adopting DT in building facilities is crucial for the productivity and sustainability of maintenance operations, as well as for decision-making and planning. This is especially true for the maintenance management of the healthcare industry. In addition to helping to attain a robust level of routine maintenance activities that enable more efficient and effective use of staff resources in healthcare institutions, the study is significant from the perspective that when the DT is adopted, impending problems will be detected before failure occurs resulting in less failures and users' complaints.

13.2 Overview of healthcare facilities

Healthcare facilities are seen as a country's level of accessibility and care quality in both qualitative and quantitative criteria (Okafor & Ugwuibe, 2019). It is assessed based on the caliber of the physical, technological, and human resources that are readily available at a certain time. While technology refers to the equipment designed expressly for hospital use, including procedures,

Blockchain and Digital Twin for Smart Hospitals. DOI: https://doi.org/10.1016/B978-0-443-34226-4.00014-9

physical structure refers to the buildings and other fixed structures, like pipe-borne water, adequate access roads, and electricity, within the healthcare surroundings (Erinosho, 2006). Additionally, this includes computer hardware and supplies, whereas human resources refer to the workforce in the healthcare industry, which includes physicians, pharmacists, nurses, midwives, laboratory techs, administrators, accountants, and other varying employees. All of them taken together make up the framework for healthcare delivery in any society and the elements that determine its infrastructure. According to Adebanjo and Oladeji (2006), the idea of the healthcare system includes the healthcare policy, budgetary allocation, implementation, and monitoring. In terms of diagnosis, treatment, and compliance, this is more comprehensive and expansive in concept than a combination of facilities and medical consultation. Additionally, various elements related to or supplemental to the delivery of healthcare, including healthcare consumers, are involved.

The hospital project differs in several ways from the more typical projects of homes, workplaces, or services. When the user and the client in a common building are not the same, determining the needs is not difficult because most residents will share them. The project team is typically engaged in designing a facility that comprises various locations and a variety of users, including doctors, nurses, patients, visitors, cleaning staff, administrators, and others (Castro et al., 2012). In the case of hospital buildings, this is not the truth. In this regard, it is crucial to integrate various spatial requirements, which are always changing throughout their time of use as a result of new features, innovations, expanding needs, and new therapeutic approaches (Figueiredo, 2008). With the development of such structures, it appears that the patient is taking up a central position in all worries and attention. The patient should be viewed as the final consumer of these structures, and there should be a paradigm shift in the way these buildings are constructed (Castro et al., 2012). After the construction of the hospitals, there is a need to develop and adopt efficient maintenance policies for the smart and adequate management of the facilities. This is the niche for the innovative technology known as DT technology.

13.3 Definitions of digital twin

According to Opoku et al. (2021), the definition of digital twin is based on the fact that it can be applied to any field without regard to industry. DT, on the other hand, updates continuously during a physical entity's life cycle and reflects its behavior rules. According to Borth et al. (2019), DT is a synchronized, connected digital representation of physical assets that captures both the elements and the dynamics of how systems and devices interact with their surroundings and live out their lives. Schluse and Rossmann's definition of DT as virtual replicas of actual objects from 2016 defines DT as smart objects that operate as intelligent nodes in the Internet of Things and services. Smart objects are made up of virtual representations and communication capabilities. Canedo (2016) added the definition of DT as a digital depiction of an actual object that emphasizes the genuine thing. Additionally, DT was defined by Gabor et al. (2016) as the simulation of the actual physical item to forecast future system states. The fundamental components of DTs are the data that links the physical and digital worlds, as well as the dynamic bidirectional interaction between real-world items and virtual representations (Tao et al., 2019). Additionally, distinct categories of DTs are distinguished by the degree of data integration (Borgo, 2014). Digital models without self-driven data contact between the physical thing and the digital object are an example of this; DTs are fully integrated bidirectional data integrations between the current physical object and the digital object, whereas digital shadows are self-driven unidirectional data flows between the physical and digital objects (Kritzinger et al., 2018).

According to Rosen's definition of the idea, it consists of two identical spaces—one physical and the other virtual—that may be mirrored to examine the conditions that arise throughout the object's life cycle (Rosen et al., 2015). Then, Boschert and Rosen explained that a DT includes every piece of important physical and functional information about a component, product, or system (Boschert & Rosen, 2016). Both authors concur that DTs are algorithms that explain behavior and decide on actions in production, in addition to being data. According to Errandonea et al. (2020), Glaessgen and Stargel's definition of DT is the most widely used; their definition of a DT was given as follows: "An integrated multiphysics, multiscale, probabilistic simulation of a vehicle or system that uses the best available physical models, sensor updates, fleet history, and so forth, to mirror the life of its flying twin" (Glaessgen & Stargel, 2012). They stipulated that a DT consists of three parts: the physical product, the virtual product, and the communication between them. According to Tharma et al. (2018), "the digital twin of a real distributed product is a virtual mirror, which can deliver and receive product information" and "the digital twin of a real distributed product is a virtual mirror, which can describe the comprehensive physical and functional properties of the product throughout its life cycle." In a study, DT was described as a duplicate of a physical asset, procedure, or system utilized for control and decision-making (Vatn, 2018). The idea and concept of DT, "which contains mainly real-time data acquisition technology, data mapping technology, and data-based prediction technology, can make the convergence between the physical product and virtual space a reality" (Liu et al., 2019). One of the skills of the DT is to predict the system's reaction to an unexpected event before it happens, according to Schleich et al. (2017). The analysis of these occurrences and the present response can be compared to forecasts of behavior to make predictions of this kind. A sufficiently full DT instance can be obtained, depending on the capabilities of data sharing and collecting as well as the thoroughness of the simulations utilized.

13.4 Digital twin application in the healthcare industry

In manufacturing and other industries, DT solutions are frequently used. There are countless ways that DT technology can be used in the healthcare sector (Attaran & Celik, 2023). The COVID-19 epidemic compelled the healthcare and life sciences sector to quicken its attempts to change into a digital enterprise (Global Market Insight, 2022). To enable the widespread transition to the pandemic, digital healthcare practices must become more effective. The life sciences sector is looking into ways to increase efficiency and cut expenses, just like any other sector. The burden to digitally alter and adjust to rising patient expectations is now on providers. Because of this, there is growing interest in using technology like DT in the biological sciences (Research and markets, 2022). Drug discovery and development are finding increased use of the technology (Kpmg, 2021). An experimental DT of the human heart, for instance, was created by the software company "Dassault." The "Living Heart" software developed by the business converts a 2D scan of a person into a precise, three-dimensional representation of that person's heart. This accurate simulation of a human organ takes into account electricity, mechanics, and blood flow. The Living Heart model is currently being used on a global scale to develop fresh approaches to the design and testing of novel tools and pharmaceutical therapies (Dassault Systems, 2022). Additionally, DT solutions are used to build digital replicas of people, healthcare facilities, and medical equipment. Monitoring, analyzing, and forecasting concerns including individualized healthcare delivery, proactive maintenance of healthcare facilities, and rising R&D costs are the goals (FutureBridge, 2021). The following list of DT applications for the healthcare industry, as recognized by Attaran and Celik (2023), is provided.

Diagnosis and therapy: By creating DTs of a single cell, genome, or organ, researchers are investigating the use of DTs to increase understanding of the human body. With the aid of DTs, researchers can monitor patients' health, identify ailments, and create preventative care plans (Kpmg, 2021). For instance, surgeons can plan a surgical treatment using a virtual digital reproduction of a patient, identify the dangers involved, or perhaps prevent the need for surgery altogether (Gahlot et al., 2019; FutureBridge, 2021). The National Institutes of Health (NIH) DT models, which were developed to forecast athletes' concussion-related trauma from brain traumas, are one implementation of this technology (Attaran & Celik, 2023).

Drug development: The effectiveness and safety of novel medications can be tested using DT technology. Massive amounts of data are generated at every stage of the drug development process and must be controlled. These facts are used by DT to build a model (Subramanian, 2020). Since fewer patients need to be chosen to participate in clinical trials, they can proceed more quickly (Forbs, 2021). As a result, DT helps speed up clinical trials in drug research. By assisting researchers in choosing the optimal antigen to employ, where the development process may also be carried out electronically, DT will also play a significant part in the development and production of new vaccines.

Clinical research: Clinical research techniques could undergo a transformation thanks to DT technologies. Without endangering the patient's life, DTs can be utilized to forecast how experimental treatments will affect a patient, receive more accurate answers, and generate useful insights (FutureBridge, 2021). Additionally, the technology aids medical experts in analyzing the data from infected patients for next research, executing treatment simulations, and selecting the most promising avenues for additional human research (Global Market Insight, 2022). For instance, a Swedish University developed a DT of rheumatoid arthritis-affected mice to study treatment effectiveness and develop a substitute for human clinical trials (FutureBridge, 2021).

Personalized medicine: Accessible DT solutions are changing how the healthcare sector improves the lives of the people it serves. For instance, the promise of personalized medicine can be realized globally by using DT technologies (De Benedictis et al., 2022). With the use of technology, doctors can use clinical decision-support tools supported by digital care and possibly hundreds of variables to intelligently model a patient's optimum course of therapy. To speed up trial times and better comprehend the available treatments for diseases like multiple sclerosis and Alzheimer's, DT technologies are also helpful in research. Finally, DT technology can simulate new therapies and speed up the release of life-saving discoveries. For instance, researchers from Oklahoma State University tested out a DT of the respiratory system and simulated drug administration using aerosolized drug particle movements to enhance lung cancer treatment (FutureBridge, 2021). Siemens created a DT of the human heart utilizing millions of photos and reports to help predict disease or other health problems and to provide a deeper understanding of cardiac ailments.

To enable surgeons to choose different patient operating instruments based on the DT study, a French business created a DT of the aneurysm and nearby blood vessels (FutureBridge, 2021).

Facility and maintenance management: DT solutions have the ability to minimize expenses and enhance the patient experience as hospitals fight to cut operating costs and stay competitive (Ross, 2016). Healthcare firms can benefit from using DTs to optimize the workforce, workflows, hospitals, and other aspects of care delivery (El Saddik, 2018). For instance, DT's improved predictive analytics based on merging internal and external data-tracking patient flow internally and projecting future spikes using external data can offset the effects of erroneous bed occupancy projections (Ross, 2016). To improve patient care, operational effectiveness, and financial success, healthcare providers should leverage the data from DT solutions to think more strategically about capacity and resources based on better forecasting. To increase productivity and save costs, DTs can also be utilized to model personalized and intelligent medical devices and other equipment (El Saddik, 2018; Ross, 2016). To acquire data regarding the configuration and maintenance history of the equipment, DT uses data collected by IoT sensors implanted in the device. This section exemplifies the fact that DT technology can be used for the management of constructed facilities in the healthcare sector, apart from other health-centered areas.

13.5 Theoretical frameworks in hospital facilities research

This section presents a few developed and recognized theoretical frameworks and models that are domiciled within healthcare research in the body of knowledge. They are as follows: the sustainability of innovation (SOI) framework, the normalization process theory, and the dynamic sustainability framework (DSF). The need for the review of these existing models is to conceptualize this present study to the generality of the body of knowledge within healthcare research. After the assessment of these frameworks that underpin hospital facilities research, the SOI framework was selected as the best fit to underpin this chapter.

13.5.1 Dynamic sustainability framework

The DSF, proposed by Chambers et al. (2013), challenges the idea that sustainability is an endpoint and proposes a framework that entails ongoing adaptation as a result of learning, problem-solving, and evolution. The only constant, according to Heraclitus, is change. The DSF was created as a result of a cumulative experience conducting and advancing implementation science, where it was seen that failure to pay attention to ongoing change has a negative impact on the ability to sustain adopted interventions over time in challenging clinical and community contexts (Chambers et al., 2013). There is no doubt that the maintenance management of healthcare facilities has not been experiencing developmental changes through innovative systems; hence, the criticality of this model. The DSF as depicted in Fig. 13.1 highlights how the characteristics of practice settings, the usage of interventions throughout time, and the larger system that sets the framework for healthcare delivery are all subject to change. The change affects how effectively and sustainably health interventions can be used over time, as classical thought beautifully illustrates (Chambers et al., 2013). As evidenced by the ongoing practice surveillance systems that track the effects of interventions, as

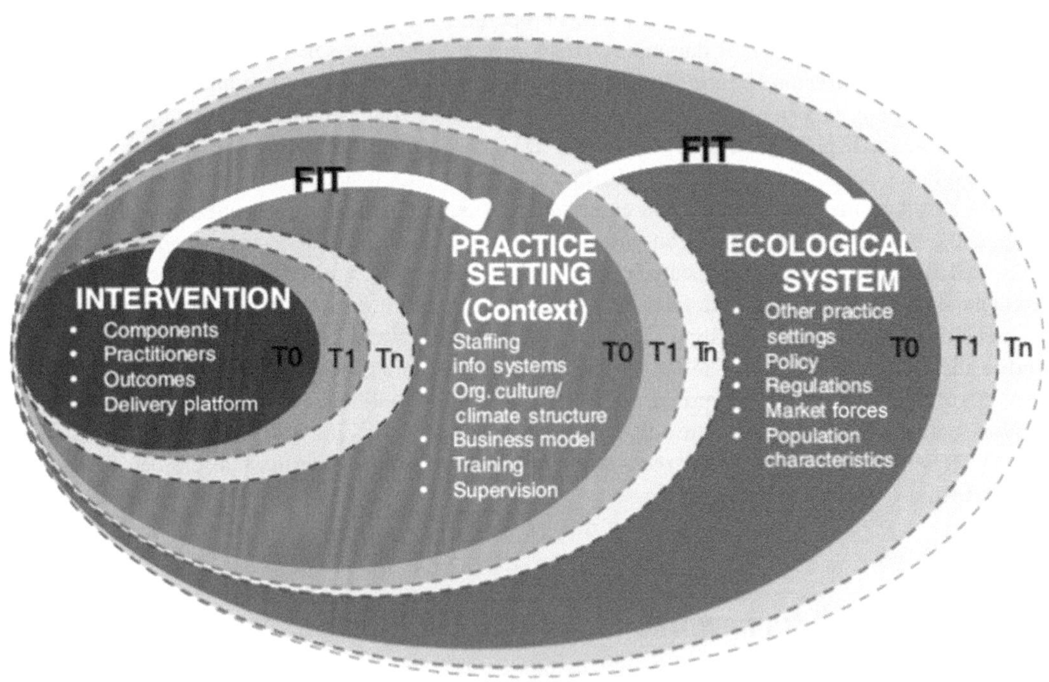

FIGURE 13.1

The dynamic sustainability framework (DSF).

From Chambers et al. (2013).

well as the steady stream of new academic journal publications that add to the body of knowledge about their efficacy, this dynamism is present in the evidence base for interventions that connect causal factors to healthcare outcomes.

The evidence-based therapies are flexible and allow for spontaneous adaptation and experimentation. Additionally, whether it is an organization, town, county, state, or nation, it is integral to the clinical or community environment and the larger healthcare system (McLaughlin & Kaluzny, 2004). Additionally, it takes place in a dynamic, multilevel setting. The DSF, like many other implementation models, focuses on three key elements: the intervention, the context in which it is delivered, and the larger ecological system within which the practicing settings exist and function. In contrast to other models, this model takes these factors into account throughout time. The intervention, as depicted in the figure, frequently consists of a number of discrete elements selected for their potential to alter behavior or biochemistry, a set of presumptive qualities defining the delivery of the intervention, and the intervention's intended, patient-centered outcomes that the intrusion should produce as a consequence of its practice, and a conveyance platform (e.g., face-to-face, telephonic, web-based, mobile health app, to mention). Supplementary constructs may also explain the intervention. The DSF grounds the intervention's ultimate benefits in terms of how well it can be implemented in a certain practice environment, generally a clinical or community setting. This environment possesses a unique collection of traits, including people and financial resources, informational systems, organizational culture, climate, and structure, as well as procedures for employee training and management. The DSF, in line with previous models, contends that these practice traits will directly affect the intervention's capacity to reach the patient population that could benefit. As a result, measuring these contextual factors is critical to determining fit (Chambers et al., 2013). It is obvious that the maintenance management of healthcare facilities has not been experiencing developmental changes through innovative systems like the DT technology; hence, the criticality of this model.

The ecological system is recognized by the DSF as a third-level driver of an intervention's successful implementation and sustainability. The legislative and regulatory environment, the features of local, regional, state, and national markets, and the characteristics of the general population are all components of the ecological system that influence those attempting to implement a specific intervention. Changes to the available interventions and practice contexts have an impact on the ecological system, which in turn has an impact on them. The dotted lines in Fig. 13.1 emphasize the DSF's expectation that change is constant at each of these levels (and ripples over several levels). Therefore the longevity of an intervention depends on how effectively it integrates into a specific environment and how that setting integrates into a wider ecological system. According to the DSF, characteristics of the intervention, practice environment, and ecological system must be regularly examined using valid, reliable, and applicable measurements to attain optimal fit. The DSF also expects that therapies, practice environments, and the ecological system will evolve over time, especially in situations where data can propose changes for each to better suit the requirements of patients, the capacity and assets available, and the larger setting.

The DSF is intended to provide a new paradigm for thinking about the long-term usage and continual refinement of treatments to reduce the risks of "program drift" and "voltage drop" (Chambers et al., 2013). It achieves this by recognizing the limitations of the evidence base developed through efficacy and effectiveness trials and by allowing that ongoing exposure of the intervention to new populations, new contexts, and new innovations may lead to a continuous improvement of the resulting outcomes. The DSF asserts that the ultimate purpose of interventions is continual quality improvement rather than quality assurance. Chambers et al. (2013) noted that it is crucial to make sure that this occurs across all healthcare systems to give clear judgments of a sufficient level of treatment. The DSF contends that quality improvement approaches centered on intervention optimization are ultimately more pertinent to accomplishing sustainment as a result of its recognition of the limits of intervention data derived only from clinical trials.

13.5.2 Normalization process theory

Between 2000 and 2009, May and other authors established the normalization process theory (NPT) (May et al., 2009). The challenge of implementing and integrating novel treatment modalities and methods of organizing care in healthcare service settings was the main issue it was designed to solve. To comprehend and explain the social processes by which new or modified ways of thinking, acting, and organizing work are operationalized in institutional settings such as healthcare, NPT offers a set of sociological tools. The theory is particularly interested in three fundamental issues: implementation is the social arrangement required to put a practice or set of practices into effect; embedding is the process through which a practice or practices are systematically incorporated into the work that people and groups conduct on a daily basis, or not; and integration refers to the procedures used to reproduce and maintain a practice or practices within the social matrices of an institution or organization. The theory posits, in brief, that practices become routinely embedded—or normalized—in social contexts as a result of people working both individually and collectively to put them into practice. The work of putting a practice into practice is promoted or inhibited through the operation of generative mechanisms (coherence, cognitive participation, collective action, reflexive monitoring) through which human agency is expressed; and the creation and dissemination of a practice necessitate ongoing agents' investment in ensembles of action that are transmitted over time and space.

The theory's premise is that to comprehend how a practice is embedded, there is a need to first understand what people actually do and how they function (May et al., 2009). This is the reason the level to which maintenance management information technologies are used in developing countries, was assessed as presented in the previous Chapter. It is an action theory. This sets it apart from other theories, such as (i) cultural transmission of innovations/ the diffusion of innovations (DOI) theory (Rogers, 1995; Coleman et al., 1966), (ii) theories of collective and individual learning and expertise (Wenger, 1998), and (iii) theories of the relationships between individual attitudes, intentions and behavioral outcomes (Ajzen & Fishbein, 1980). The emphasis on human agency and the explanatory focus of the theory distinguishes it from sociological theories of actor networks (Latour, 2005), which use ethnographic case studies as their main method (Geels, 2007) and mistakenly attribute agency to both people and things and expressly prefer description to explanation (Ajzen & Fishbein, 1980). In contrast to the latter, the goal of the study was to develop a set of sociological tools to examine social shaping as action and to do so in a way that allowed organized comparative investigation prospectively using a range of approaches. In summary, the goal of this theory was to discover and explain the variables that encouraged or hindered group action that resulted in the routine integration of sophisticated healthcare interventions into service. Interactional workability, relational integration, skill-set workability, and contextual integration were the four variables.

13.5.3 Sustainability of innovation framework

The SOI concept was formulated and developed in a study by Fox et al. (2014). The study presented that the concept is linked to Rogers' diffusion of innovation theory—a theory that is well accepted and influential in various research domains and expertise. The authors also asserted that this concept had been influenced by the normalization process theory and the dynamic sustainability framework. Any healthcare information can be examined for sustainability using the SOI framework. Political, financial, workforce, organizational, and innovation-specific considerations are the five components of the framework. A political focus on one particular policy has been shown to have a significant impact on the sustainability of an innovation related to that policy, and innovations that are closely linked to regional healthcare planning and national policy directions are more likely to become routine (Greenhalgh et al., 2004; Sibthorpe et al., 2005). Along with the change in government, these policies' funding arrangements also change. When senior management personnel and organizational culture embrace innovation, political sustainability is thought to be improved (Sibthorpe et al., 2005; Stirman et al., 2012). Therefore the political segment's main focus is on issues related to alignment, connections, and staff participation.

According to studies on organizational characteristics (Greenhalgh et al., 2004; Rogers, 2004; Stirman et al., 2012), flexibility and adaptation of the innovation to the local context and organization boost innovation sustainability. According to Chambers et al. (2013), innovation's sustainability is increased when ongoing adjustments are made to tailor it to the specific situation. Sustainability will be improved by coordinated operational governance inside an organization (May & Finch, 2009), and efficient departmental and cross-departmental communication (Sibthorpe et al., 2005). The same author emphasized that a lack of meetings and teamwork has resulted in poor sustainability and a lack of support for innovation. As a result, assessing current communication and networking tactics is a key focus of the framework's organizational aspects. The availability of money and budgetary planning for continued human and consumable resources, as well as evidence of the innovation's cost-effectiveness, are the financial elements that affect sustainability. Research on programs and projects has frequently found that after outside financing stopped, sustainability suffered. Due to the short-term funding involved with trials, innovations that are launched as projects or trials are frequently not sustained over time (Considine & Fielding, 2010). An innovation is more likely to become routine in the organization if it has dedicated, continuing, and appropriate funding to address the needs (Greenhalgh et al., 2004). Innovations are frequently vulnerable due to a lack of studies examining their economic value and cost-effectiveness (Sibthorpe et al., 2005). As a result, the financial aspects of the theoretical framework determine the innovation's funding sources, planning, and evaluation methodologies.

Based on an evaluation of workforce factors, it has been discovered that timely staff training with the use of high-quality training materials, minimum staff and role changes, and staff training support the sustainability of an invention (Greenhalgh et al., 2004). Employee views of the value of an invention have a significant impact on routinization and are more likely to be accepted when they are congruent with the values and needs of the workforce (Considine & Fielding, 2010; Sibthorpe et al., 2005). Sustainability is threatened by a lack of continuity or by having insufficient people to put an invention into practice (Sibthorpe et al., 2005). The ability to satisfy demand proved challenging for single staff member service models, and employee turnover, parental leave, and annual leave made innovations vulnerable, especially when succession planning had not been started (Considine & Fielding, 2010). Routine is improved by routinely giving workers feedback and putting mechanisms in place to check the innovation's quality and results (Greenhalgh et al., 2004). Key workforce aspects in the theoretical framework include employee attrition, continuity, employment models, staff attitudes, and views of the quality of the innovation.

Innovators' nature and methods will influence sustainability. Fluidity and flexibility to changes in finance and service requirements depending on local decision-making and demands are important characteristics of an invention (Greenhalgh et al., 2004; Sibthorpe et al., 2005). According to recent research, innovations are continually changing to meet context-specific needs. This shift is necessary for sustainability (Considine & Fielding, 2010). Sustainability is intimately related to the stakeholders' perception of the innovation's acceptability, quality, and safety. Continuous assessment of an innovation's quality using metrics important to stakeholders is essential. The innovation-specific aspects therefore concentrate on finding support for and obstacles to the innovation as well as assessment methods for the invention itself. To examine the mechanisms determining the sustainability of healthcare service innovation, the five elements can be operationalized and used as a research framework. The factors are a group of dynamic, interconnected features rather than discrete, isolated areas. As stated by Chambers et al. (2013), the framework captures the dynamic aspect of sustainability. Innovation is optimized within the pertinent context to promote rather than inhibit sustainability. There is no doubt that the maintenance management of healthcare facilities has not been experiencing developmental changes through innovative systems; hence, the criticality of this model. This model supports the continuous development and maturity of maintenance organizations and the sustainability of innovative systems like the DT technology (Fig. 13.2).

The reviews of these frameworks that are domiciled within hospital buildings research are critical, as they present a significant correlation with the study in focus. The dynamic sustainability framework, normalization process theory, and the SOI framework present the required concepts that can underpin this study. However, the sustainability of the innovation framework gives a best fit as it considers a holistic approach to supporting innovations like the DT technology for healthcare facilities management.

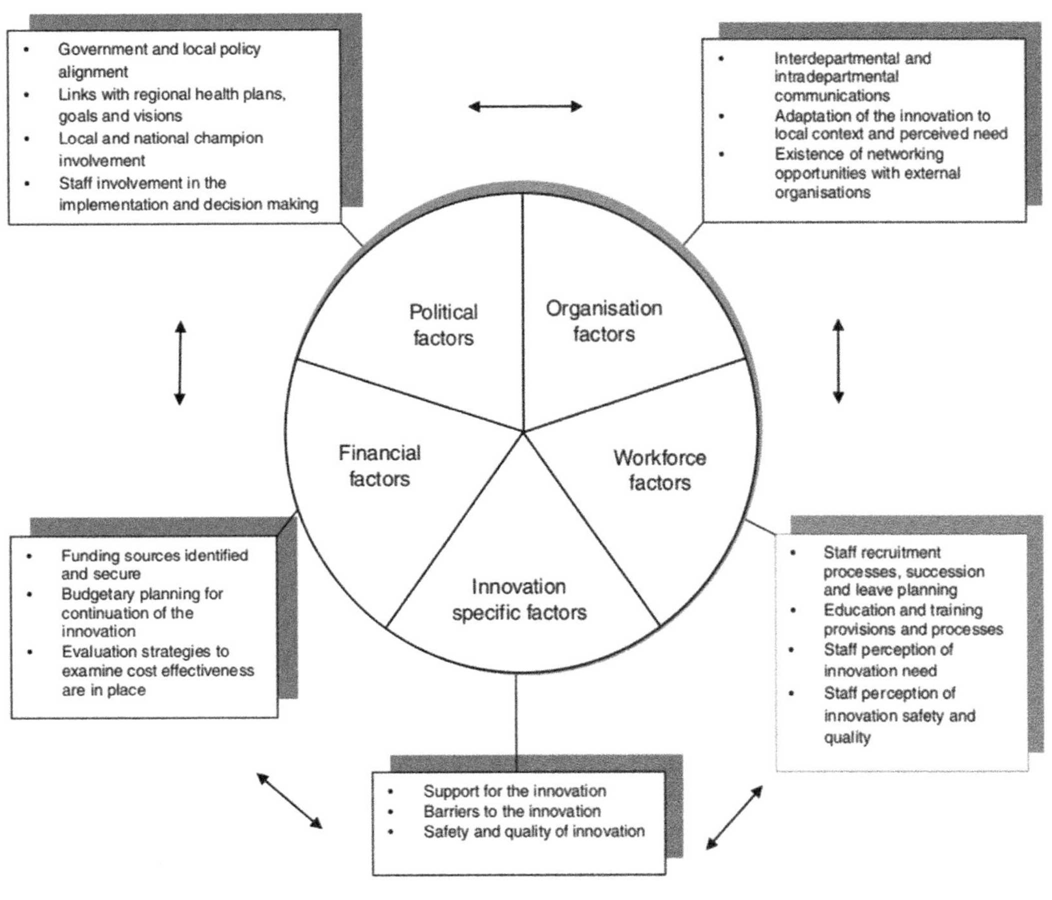

FIGURE 13.2

The sustainability of innovations (SOI) framework.

From Fox et al. (2014)

13.6 Challenges and strategies to digital twin maintenance management of healthcare facilities in developing countries

A Delphi study was carried out in developing countries, using Nigeria as a case study, to evaluate and ascertain the barriers and critical success factors to the adoption of DT for the maintenance of healthcare facilities. In the first round of the Delphi method, a group of eleven (11) experts participated. They remained involved in the study's second and third rounds as well. A high level of academic and/or practical expertise in the field of maintenance management and digital technologies in constructed facilities was given special consideration while choosing the panel of experts; all the chosen specialists possessed these qualities. These were regarded as being extremely important since professionals needed to have an extensive knowledge of maintenance management and the application of digital technologies in constructed facilities. The panelists were chosen to ensure an even distribution between operators and scholars on the subject of maintenance management and digital technologies in constructed facilities, particularly with regard to public hospital facilities. Based on the experts' responses obtained from the preceding round(s) of the Delphi study, a questionnaire was created for every round of the Delphi survey. However, a summary of the results of the thorough literature review served as the basis for the design of the round one questionnaire of the Delphi study. The Delphi survey's initial questionnaire was constructed using the reviewed literature variables, in a structurally sound manner. The goal of the first round of the Delphi study was to generate a list of factual variables that determine the DT maintenance management (DTMM) of public hospital buildings (PHBs) in Nigeria. In this round, both open-ended and closed-ended questions were used. The questions were then examined, and the findings served as the foundation for the survey instruments used in the second and third rounds of the Delphi study. The degree of agreement attained among survey participants on the survey's components was assessed using descriptive statistics. To "minimize redundancy" in the responses to the open questions, the content analysis methodology was also used (Aigbavboa, 2014).

The objective of the second phase of the Delphi study was to give the experts the opportunity to review and comment on the factors that affect PHBs' DTMM as well as other concerns regarding the efficient management of PHBs in Nigeria that had been put forth by the experts who had taken part in round one of the Delphi study. In the second phase, participants' responses indicating agreement, disagreement, or clarification regarding the postulated features that influence the DTMM of PHBs in Nigeria were examined using closed questions. The Delphi participants' responses were stimulated by the closed-ended questions' specificity. The second round's results largely indicated that the distinguished panelists agreed with each other. As a result, round two of the Delphi survey was revised in round three of the study. The statistical data derived from the second round was presented to each expert in the third round. The experts were once more requested to respond to the question using the specified grading scale. The conversation was successfully developed in round three to the point where distinct areas of agreement or disagreement could be identified. There was no need for a fourth round as a result. The mean, median, percentages, standard deviation, and interquartile deviation (IQD) scores for each question were determined using descriptive statistics. The expert panelists were asked to explain their responses in cases where the score deviated by two points from the median score. The goal of the Delphi research technique was to iterate the questions until the expert panel came to an agreement. The results of the median from the previous round of questionnaires were provided to the experts before each round of questions. When all participants agree, there has been a consensus. However, according to Stitt-Gohdes and Crews (2004) and Aigbavboa (2014), common consent is regarded when two-thirds of the participants agree (Stitt-Gohdes & Crews, 2004; Aigbavboa, 2014). Therefore ordinary consent is equally appropriate in this investigation. When 60.0% of the experts concurred on each assertion or query, there was general agreement. There was a consensus check on each individual assertion. After each round of questionnaires, the findings were statistically examined. Based on the scales supplied for each question or statement, this helped determine whether consensus had been reached for each statement or question. Additionally, if agreement was reached before the last round, that question or statement might not be necessary in the following rounds. After the third round of the Delphi survey, agreement was reached on most of the factors that affect PHBs' DTMM as well as other aspects of the Nigerian healthcare sector's effective maintenance management.

The study identified the barriers to efficient maintenance management and determined its relative impact on attaining the DTMM of PHBs in the Nigerian healthcare sector. The analysis of the experts' responses indicated that of the fourteen (14) factors that critically affect the efficient maintenance management of PHBs in the Nigerian healthcare sector, thirteen (13) of the items had a very high impact (VHI: 9.00–10.00) in determining DTMM of PHBs in Nigeria, while one (1) variable had a high impact (HI: 7.00–8.99). Hence, none was found to have had an impact on the determination of PHBs DTMM. In addition, the IQD results demonstrated that a solid consensus was reached for thirteen (13) of the items as they received scores ranging from 0.00 to 1.00. The fact that their individual standard deviations (σx) were at most (1) further demonstrated the uniformity of the experts' responses. One (1) item, though, had a good consensus, and scores ranged from 1.10 to 2.00. The item's standard deviation (σx) value suggested inconsistent and varied responses from the experts because the corresponding (σx) value was greater than one (1); hence, faulty architectural design was not agreed upon by the experts to be a barrier to the DTMM of PHBs. The factors that were foremost among the variables with a very high impact are insufficient funding for maintenance, lack of discernible maintenance culture, and issues from political decisions, all with mean values of 10. This outcome supports the view advanced by Adenuga et al. (2007), Ogunmakinde et al. (2013), Talib et al. (2014) Ebekozien (2020), and Ogunbayo et al. (2022). Other barriers that were agreed by the professionals to have a very high impact on the DT maintenance management of PHBs in the Nigerian healthcare sector are inadequate planned maintenance, use of poor-quality service components, nonavailability of materials, budget allocation not systematically done, and corruption, all with mean values of 9.82. This outcome is in agreement with the studies by Ofori et al. (2015) Olayinka and Owolabi (2015), and Okosun and Olagunju (2017) (Table 13.1).

In conclusion, all the factors that were identified from existing literature as having affected the efficient maintenance management of constructed facilities in other studies were found to affect the DT maintenance management of PHBs in Nigeria. Furthermore, although none of the factors had any impact among the factors affecting efficient maintenance management, insufficient funding for maintenance, lack of discernible maintenance culture, issues from political decisions, inadequately planned maintenance, use of poor-quality service components, nonavailability of materials, budget allocation not systematically done, corruption, insufficient research, inadequate skill and work experience, inadequate training and development, improper planning and scheduling, and lack of collaboration among team members or professionals were seen to be critical among the factors that affect the DT maintenance management of PHBs in Nigeria.

Table 13.1 Barriers to the digital twin maintenance management of public hospital buildings.

Barriers	Median (M)	Mean ($\bar{x}$)	Standard deviation (σx)	Interquartile deviation (IQD)	Mean scores ranking (R)
Inadequate skill and work experience	9	9.09	0.30	0.00	10
Inadequate training and development	9	8.82	0.60	0.50	12
Improper planning and scheduling	9	8.64	0.92	0.50	13
Lack of collaboration among team members or professionals	9	9.09	0.30	0.00	10
Inadequate planned maintenance	10	9.82	0.40	0.00	4
Faulty architectural design	7	7.82	1.47	2.00	14
Use of poor-quality service components	10	9.82	0.40	0.00	4
Nonavailability of materials	10	9.82	0.40	0.00	4
Budget allocation not systematically done	10	9.82	0.40	0.00	4
Insufficient funding for maintenance	10	10.00	0.00	0.00	1
Lack of discernible maintenance culture	10	10.00	0.00	0.00	1
Issues from political decisions	10	10.00	0.00	0.00	1
Insufficient research	10	9.55	0.82	0.50	9
Corruption	10	9.82	0.60	0.00	4

The third objective of the Delphi survey sought to identify the critical success factors for effective maintenance management and to ascertain their influence in attaining the DTMM of PHBs in Nigeria. From the analysis, the experts' responses indicated that out of the 15 listed variables, all of the items had a very high impact (VHI: 9.00–10.00) in determining the DTMM of PHBs in Nigeria. Hence, none was found to have had an impact on the determination of PHBs DTMM. In addition, the IQD results showed that a significant consensus was reached for the fifteen (15) items, as they received scores between 0.00 and 1.00. The fact that their individual standard deviations (σx) were at most (1) further demonstrated the uniformity of the experts' responses. The factors that were foremost and with a very high impact are as follows: provide sufficient funds, provide training workshops for personnel, engage professionals in maintenance, provide support for maintenance staffers and functional maintenance units, adopt good maintenance management practices, engage stakeholders in maintenance, and use high-quality materials during work, all with mean values of 10. This outcome supports the view advanced by Adenuga et al. (2007), Ogunmakinde et al. (2013), Talib et al. (2014), and Ebekozien (2020) (Table 13.2).

In conclusion, all the factors that were identified from existing literature that could lead to the efficient maintenance management of constructed facilities in other studies were found to be the factors that will lead to the attainment of DT maintenance management of buildings in the Nigerian

Table 13.2 Critical success factors to the digital twin maintenance management of public hospital buildings.

CSFs	Median (*M*)	Mean ($\bar{x}$)	Standard deviation (σx)	Interquartile deviation (IQD)	Mean scores ranking (*R*)
Provide training workshops for personnel	10	10.00	0.00	0.00	1
Development of a national maintenance policy	10	9.82	0.60	0.00	11
Engage professionals in maintenance	10	10.00	0.00	0.00	1
Provide support for maintenance staffers	10	10.00	0.00	0.00	1
Functional maintenance units	10	10.00	0.00	0.00	1
Adopt good maintenance mgt. practices	10	10.00	0.00	0.00	1
Engage stakeholders in maintenance	10	10.00	0.00	0.00	1
Use high-quality materials during work	10	10.00	0.00	0.00	1
Adopt green building technologies	10	9.45	0.93	1.00	13
Adopt maintenance software	9	8.91	0.54	0.00	14
Budget determined systematically	10	9.91	0.30	0.00	9
Planning to relocate resources effectively	10	9.91	0.30	0.00	9
Provide sufficient funds	10	10.00	0.00	0.00	1
Stricter measures to correct handling	9	8.91	0.30	0.00	14
Accountability and transparency	10	9.82	0.60	0.00	11

healthcare sector. Furthermore, although none of the factors had any impact on the success factors for efficient maintenance management, provide sufficient funds, provide training workshops for personnel, engage professionals in maintenance, provide support for maintenance staffers and functional maintenance units, adopt good maintenance management practices, engage stakeholders in maintenance, and use high-quality materials during work were seen to be the foremost critical success factors that will lead to the DT maintenance management of PHBs in Nigeria.

13.7 Conclusion

This chapter has considered the application and applicability of DT to healthcare facilities management. It reviewed the framing synopsis of hospital buildings and theoretical perceptions for hospital facilities research. The chapter also presented the theoretical frameworks that have been recognized and identified for hospital facilities studies. The overview of DT technology and its application within the healthcare sector was also considered in this chapter. A Delphi study report on the barriers and critical success factors to DT maintenance management of healthcare facilities in developing countries was discussed in this chapter. There is no doubt that the healthcare sector will greatly benefit from the DT technology when it is applied in the management of their constructed facilities. However, the challenges to the DT adoption for healthcare facilities must be surmounted, through the application of the ascertained and recommended strategies.

References

Adebanjo, A. A., & Oladeji, S. I. (2006). *Traditional and modern health systems in Nigeria. Health human capital condition: Analysis of the determinants in Nigeria* (pp. 381–398). Africa World Press.

Adenuga, A. O., Iyagba, O. R., Odusami, T. K., & Ogunsanmi, E. O. (2007). Appraisal of maintenance management strategies in public hospital buildings in Lagos State. *Nigeria Construction Research Journal, 1*, 76–86.

Aigbavboa, C.O. (2014). An integrated beneficiary centered satisfaction model for publicly funded housing schemes in South Africa. Doctorate Thesis, University of Johanessburg.

Ajzen, I., & Fishbein, M. (1980). *Understanding attitudes and predicting social behavior*. Prentice-Hall.

Attaran, M., & Celik, B. G. (2023). Digital twin: Benefits, use cases, challenges, and opportunities. *Decision Analytics Journal, 6*, 100165. Available from https://doi.org/10.1016/j.dajour.2023.100165.

De Benedictis, A., Mazzocca, N., Somma, A., Strigaro, C. (2022). Digital twins in healthcare: an architectural proposal and its application in a social distancing case study, *IEEE Journal of Biomedical and Health Informatics*, *27*(10), 5143–5154. Available from https://ieeexplore.ieee.org/stamp/stamp.jsp?arnumber = 9882337.

Borgo, S. (2014). An ontological approach for reliable data integration in the industrial domain. *Computers in Industry*, *65*(9), 1242–1252. Available from https://doi.org/10.1016/j.compind.2013.12.010.

Borth, M., Verriet, J. & Muller, G. (2019). Digital twin strategies for SoS: 4 challenges and 4 architecture setups for digital twins of SoS. SoSE In: 2019 14th Annual Conference System of Systems Engineering, 2019.

Boschert, S., & Rosen, R. (2016). *Digital twin-the simulation aspect. Mechatronic futures: Challenges and solutions for mechatronic systems and their designers* (pp. 59–74). Germany: Springer International Publishing. Available from http://doi.org/10.1007/978-3-319-32156-1, 10.1007/978-3-319-32156-1_5.

Canedo A. (2016). Industrial IoT lifecycle via digital twins. In *Proceedings of the 11th IEEE/ACM/IFIP international conference on hardware/software codesign and system synthesis, CODES 2016*. Available from http://doi.org/10.1145/2968456.2974007.

Castro, M. F., Mateus, R., & Bragança, L. (2012). Building sustainability assessment: the case of hospital buildings. In proceedings book of Workshop em Construção e Reabilitação Sustentáveis - Soluções Eficientes para um Mercado em Crise. (pp. 161–172).

Chambers, D. A., Glasgow, R. E., & Stange, K. C. (2013). The dynamic sustainability framework: addressing the paradox of sustainment amid ongoing change. *Implementation Science*, *8*, 117. Available from http://www.implementationscience.com/content/8/1/117.

Coleman, J. S., Katz, E., & Menzel, H. (1966). *Medical innovation: a diffusion study,* Indianapolis: Bobbs-Merrill; 1966.

Considine, J., & Fielding, K. (2010). Sustainable workforce reform: Case study of Victorian nurse practitioner roles. *Australian Health Review*, *34*(3), 297–303. Available from https://doi.org/10.1071/AH08727, http://www.publish.csiro.au/nid/270.htm.

Dassault Systems (2022). The living heart project, Available from https://www.3ds.com/products-services/simulia/solutions/life-sciences-healthcare/the-living-heartproject/.

Ebekozien, A. (2020). Maintenance practices in Nigeria's public health-care buildings: a systematic review of issues and feasible solutions. *Journal of Facilities Management*, *19*(1), 32–52. Available from https://doi.org/10.1108/jfm-08-2020-0052.

El Saddik, A. (2018). Digital twins: The convergence of multimedia technologies. *IEEE MultiMedia*, *25*(2), 87–92. Available from https://doi.org/10.1109/mmul.2018.023121167.

Forbs (2021). Meet your digital twin: The coming revolution in drug development. Available from https://www.forbes.com/sites/ganeskesari/2021/09/29/meet-your-digital-twin-the-coming-revolution-in-drug-development/?sh = 67679144745f.

FutureBridge (2021). Digital twin simulating the bright future of healthcare. Available from https://www.futurebridge.com/industry/perspectives-lifesciences/digital-twin-simulating-the-bright-future-of-healthcare/.

Erinosho, O. A. (2006). *Health Sociology for Universities Colleges and Health Related Institutions*. Abuja: Bulwark Consult.

Errandonea, I., Beltrán, S., & Arrizabalaga, S. (2020). Digital Twin for maintenance: a literature review. *Computers in Industry*, *123*, 103316. Available from https://doi.org/10.1016/j.compind.2020.103316.

Figueiredo, A. (2008). *Gestão do projecto de edifícios hospitalares [Tese de mestrado]*. Universidade de São Paulo.

Fox, A., Gardner, G., & Osborne, S. (2014). A theoretical framework to support research of health service innovation. *Australian Health Review*. Available from https://doi.org/10.1071/AH14031.

Gabor, T., Belzner, L., Kiermeier, M., Beck, M.T., & Neitz, A. (2016). A simulation-based architecture for smart cyber-physical systems. In *Proceedings - 2016 IEEE international conference on autonomic computing, ICAC 2016* (pp. 374–379). doi: 10.1109/ICAC.2016.29.

Gahlot, S., Reddy, S. R. N., & Kumar, D. (2019). Review of smart health monitoring approaches with survey analysis and proposed framework. *IEEE Internet of Things Journal*, *6*(2), 2116–2127.

Geels, F. W. (2007). Feelings of discontent and the promise of middle range theory for STS: Examples from technology dynamics. *Science Technology and Human Values*, *32*(6), 627–651. Available from https://doi.org/10.1177/0162243907303597.

Glaessgen, E. H., & Stargel, D. S. (2012). The digital twin paradigm for future NASA and U.S. air force vehicles. In *53rd AIAA/ASME/ASCE/AHS/ASC structures, structural dynamics and materials conference 2012*.

Global Market Insight (2022). Digital twin market. Available from https://www.gminsights.com/industry-analysis/digital-twin-market.

Greenhalgh, T., Robert, G., Macfarlane, F., Bate, P., & Kyriakidou, O. (2004). Diffusion of innovations in service organizations: Systematic review and recommendations. *The Milbank Quarterly*, *82*(4), 581–629. Available from https://doi.org/10.1111/j.0887-378x.2004.00325.x.

Kpmg. (2021). The AI-enabled digital twin for life sciences.

Kritzinger, W., Karner, M., Traar, G., Henjes, J., & Sihn, W. (2018). Digital twin in manufacturing: A categorical literature review and classification. *IFAC-PapersOnLine*, *51*(11), 1016–1022. Available from https://doi.org/10.1016/j.ifacol.2018.08.474.

Latour, B. (2005). *Reassembling the social: An introduction to actor network theory oxford*. Oxford University Press.

Liu, Z., Lu, Y., & Peh, L. C. (2019). A Review and Scientometric Analysis of Global Building Information Modelling (BIM) Research in the Architecture, Engineering and Construction (AEC) Industry. *Buildings*, *9*(10), 210.

May, C., & Finch, T. (2009). Implementing, embedding, and integrating practices: An outline of normalization process theory. *Sociology*, *43*(3), 535–554. Available from https://doi.org/10.1177/0038038509103208, https://journals.sagepub.com/home/SOC.

May, C. R., Mair, F., Finch, T., MacFarlane, A., Dowrick, C., Treweek, S., Rapley, T., Ballini, L., Ong, B. N., Rogers, A., Murray, E., Elwyn, G., Légaré, F., Gunn, J., & Montori, V. M. (2009). Development of a theory of implementation and integration: Normalization process theory. *Implementation Science*, *4*(1). Available from https://doi.org/10.1186/1748-5908-4-29.

McLaughlin, C. P., & Kaluzny, A. D. (2004). *Continuous quality improvement in healthcare, the United States of America*. Jones and Bartlett.

Ofori, I., Duodu, P., & Bonney, S. (2015). Establishing factors influencing building maintenance practices: Ghanaian perspective. *Journal of Economics and Sustainable Development*, *6*(24), 184–193.

Ogunbayo, B. F., Aigbavboa, C. O., Thwala, W., Akinradewo, O., Ikuabe, M., & Adekunle, S. A. (2022). Review of culture in maintenance management of public buildings in developing countries. *Buildings*, *12* (5). Available from https://doi.org/10.3390/buildings12050677, https://www.mdpi.com/2075-5309/12/5/677/pdf?version = 1652948544.

Ogunmakinde, O. E., Akinola, A. A., & Siyanbola, A. B. (2013). Analysis of the factors affecting building maintenance in government residential estates in Akure, Ondo State, Nigeria. *Journal of Environmental Sciences and Resources Management*, *5*(2), 89–103.

Okafor, S. O., & Ugwuibe, C. O. (2019). The ageing population and the challenges of health management: A study of retirees of public institutions in South East Nigeria. *World Journal of Social Science*, *7*(1), 31. Available from https://doi.org/10.5430/wjss.v7n1p31.

Okosun, B. O., & Olagunju, R. E. (2017). Assessment of factors contributing to maintenance problems in higher institutions in Niger state. *Journal of Building Performance*, *8*(1), 47–57.

Olayinka, A., & Owolabi, O. (2015). Evaluation of the factors affecting housing maintenance and its probable solutions. *International Journal of Latest Research in Engineering and Technology*, *1*(4), 59–64.

Opoku, D. G. J., Perera, S., Osei-Kyei, R., & Rashidi, M. (2021). Digital twin application in the construction industry: A literature review. *Journal of Building Engineering*, *40*. Available from https://doi.org/10.1016/j.jobe.2021.102726, http://www.journals.elsevier.com/journal-of-building-engineering/.

Research and markets (2022). Digital twins market by technology, twinning type, cyber-to-physical solutions, use cases and applications in industry verticals 2022–2027, Available from https://www.researchandmarkets.com/reports/5308850/digitaltwins-market-by-technology-twinning?utm_source = dynamic&utm_medium = CI&utm_code = 6q68tb&utm_campaign = 1366076 + the + Future + of + the + Digital + Twins + Industry + to + 2025 + in + Manufacturing%2c + Smart + Cities%2c + Automotive%2c + Healthcare + and + Transport&utm_exec = joca220cid.

Rogers, E. M. (2004). A prospective and retrospective look at the diffusion model. *Journal of Health Communication*, *9*(Sup1), 13–19. Available from https://doi.org/10.1080/10810730490271449.

Rogers, E. M. (1995). *The diffusion of innovations*. Free Press.

Rosen, R., Von Wichert, G., Lo, G., & Bettenhausen, K. D. (2015). About the importance of autonomy and digital twins for the future of manufacturing. *IFAC-PapersOnLine*, *28*(3), 567–572. Available from https://doi.org/10.1016/j.ifacol.2015.06.141, http://www.journals.elsevier.com/ifac-papersonline/.

Ross, D. (2016). Digital twinning. *Institution of Engineering and Technology*, *11*(4), 44–45. Available from https://doi.org/10.1049/et.2016.0403, https://eandt.theiet.org/.

Schleich, B., Anwer, N., Mathieu, L., & Wartzack, S. (2017). Shaping the digital twin for design and production engineering. *CIRP Annals*, *66*(1), 141–144. Available from https://doi.org/10.1016/j.cirp.2017.04.040.

Sibthorpe, B., Glascow, N., & Wells, R. (2005). Emergent themes in the sustainability of primary health care innovation. *Medical Journal of Australia*, *183*, 77–80.

Stirman, S. W., Kimberly, J., Cook, N., Calloway, A., Castro, F., & Charns, M. (2012). The sustainability of new programs and innovations: a review of the empirical literature and recommendations for future research. *Implementation Science*, *7*, 17.

Stitt-Gohdes, W. L., & Crews, T. B. (2004). The Delphi technique: A research strategy for career and technical education. *Journal of Career and Technical Education*, *20*(2). Available from https://doi.org/10.21061/jcte.v20i2.636.

Subramanian, K. (2020). Digital twin for drug discovery and development—The virtual liver. *Journal of the Indian Institute of Science*, *100*(4), 653–662. Available from https://doi.org/10.1007/s41745-020-00185-2.

Talib, R., Ahmad, A., Zakaria, N., & Sulieman, M. (2014). Assessment of factors affecting building maintenance and defects of public buildings in Penang. *Malaysia. Architecture Research.*, *4*(2), 48–53.

Tao, F., Sui, F., Liu, A., Qi, Q., Zhang, M., Song, B., Guo, Z., Lu, S. C. Y., & Nee, A. Y. C. (2019). Digital twin-driven product design framework. *International Journal of Production Research*, *57*(12), 3935–3953. Available from https://doi.org/10.1080/00207543.2018.1443229, http://www.tandfonline.com/toc/tprs20/current.

Tharma, R., Winter, R., & Eigner, M. (2018). An approach for the implementation of the digital twin in the automotive wiring harness field. Proceedings of International Design Conference, DESIGN, 6., pp. 3023–3032.

Vatn, J. (2018). Industry 4.0 and real-time synchronization of operation and maintenance. In *Safety and reliability - Safe societies in a changing world - Proceedings of the 28th international European safety and reliability conference, ESREL 2018* (pp. 681–686).

Wenger, E. (1998). *Communities of practice: Learning, meaning and identity*. Cambridge University Press.

CHAPTER

14 Revolutionizing healthcare: harnessing the power of integrated blockchain and digital twins in smart hospitals

Bilal Manzoor[1] **and Amna Riaz**[2]

[1]*Department of Building and Real Estate, The Hong Kong Polytechnic University, Hung Hom, Hong Kong, P.R. China* [2]*Department of Oral and Maxillofacial Surgery, De'Montmorency College of Dentistry Punjab Dental Hospital, Lahore, Pakistan*

14.1 Introduction

In the dynamic field of healthcare, the quest for cutting-edge solutions to improve patient care, streamline operations, and safeguard data has become of utmost importance. In the midst of this endeavor, the integration of two advanced technologies—blockchain and digital twins (DTs)—has arisen as a powerful force that has the potential to completely change the way healthcare is provided and organized (Lu et al., 2023; Raj, 2021). This chapter examines the integration of these technologies in the context of smart hospitals, where the incorporation of sophisticated technology and data-driven methods is transforming the future of the healthcare industry. The healthcare industry is currently experiencing a digital revolution, with smart hospitals leading the way in this process of change. The integration of blockchain technology with DTs signifies an innovative method for overseeing healthcare data and processes (Sahal et al., 2022). In addition, smart hospitals are leading the way in transforming the delivery of healthcare services by integrating advanced technologies. Smart hospitals embody a fundamental change in healthcare, where networked technology, real-time data analytics, and intelligent automation come together to form a patient-centered ecosystem (Chen et al., 2023).

Blockchain technology presents exceptional prospects for enhancing data security, integrity, and interoperability. Furthermore, blockchain technology, initially created as the foundational structure for digital currencies such as Bitcoin, is a distributed and unchangeable system for recording transactions (Nofer et al., 2017). It facilitates the secure, transparent, and unalterable recording of transactions across a decentralized network of computers. The transactions are organized into blocks, connected through cryptographic links, and systematically appended to the chain, resulting in a permanent and verifiable record of data exchanges. In addition, blockchain technology shows great potential in the healthcare industry, where ensuring the security, accuracy, and compatibility of data is of utmost importance (Gamage et al., 2020). Moreover, blockchain technology has the potential to revolutionize healthcare by offering a secure and decentralized platform for managing

Blockchain and Digital Twin for Smart Hospitals. DOI: https://doi.org/10.1016/B978-0-443-34226-4.00015-0

electronic health records (EHRs), optimizing medical supply chains, ensuring drug traceability, and facilitating secure data sharing and collaboration (Islam et al., 2020). In the realm of smart hospitals, where networked technologies and data-driven approaches are enhancing efficiency and fostering innovation, blockchain technology appears as a fundamental cornerstone. The capacity to safeguard confidential patient information, promote compatibility across different healthcare systems, and optimize administrative procedures is in complete harmony with the goals of smart hospital projects (Komalavalli et al., 2020).

DTs, on the other hand, give virtual representations of actual assets, processes, and systems, enabling predictive analytics, optimization, and simulation. DTs are virtual duplicates of actual assets, processes, or systems that are generated utilizing real-time data, sensors, and advanced analytics (Liu et al., 2021). Within the healthcare industry, DTs provide a comprehensive and ever-changing depiction of patients, medical equipment, treatment procedures, and even complete hospital systems (Haag & Anderl, 2018). DTs assist healthcare practitioners by replicating real-world scenarios and providing predictive analytics. This allows them to streamline clinical procedures, personalize patient care, and enhance operational efficiency. Moreover, in the realm of smart hospitals, where the integration of technology, data, and networking is revolutionizing the healthcare industry, DTs play a crucial role in fostering innovation and enhancing results (Tuan Anh Nguyen, 2023, Tuan Anh Nguyen, 2024; VanDerHorn & Mahadevan, 2021). DTs have a wide range of applications in healthcare, including patient monitoring, predictive analytics, asset management, and facility optimization. These applications have the potential to greatly transform the delivery and experience of healthcare (Tao et al., 2018). This chapter examines specific applications of blockchain and DT technologies in healthcare and smart hospitals, demonstrating its capacity to revolutionize patient care, enhance operational efficiency, and foster ongoing innovation. In addition, this chapter presents the concept of smart hospitals and examines the crucial role of the Internet of Medical Things (IoMT) in healthcare.

14.2 Applications of blockchain technology in healthcare

This section offers a comprehensive explanation of the basic principles of blockchain technology and its significance in ensuring the security and accuracy of healthcare data. The section explores essential characteristics such as decentralization, immutability, and transparency, and their potential to improve patient privacy and foster confidence in healthcare systems. Here are some key applications of blockchain technology in healthcare.

14.2.1 Secure and interoperable electronic health records

Blockchain has the potential to transform the management of EHRs by offering a secure and decentralized ledger for storing and exchanging patient data (Reegu et al., 2022). The blockchain can keep the medical history, treatment records, and diagnostic findings of each patient, allowing authorized healthcare providers to access them instantly. This guarantees the consistency and accuracy of data, removes the necessity for centralized data repositories that are susceptible to cyberattacks, and improves the capacity of different healthcare systems to work together (Martens et al., 2024).

14.2.2 Patient data management and consent

Blockchain empowers patients to have greater authority over their health data by endowing them with ownership and permission rights. Patients have the ability to securely authorize or withdraw access to their medical records by utilizing smart contracts, which are agreements that automatically execute and are kept on the blockchain. This guarantees the confidentiality of patients, streamlines the exchange of data with healthcare professionals and researchers, and strengthens the bond of trust between patients and hospitals (Jamil et al., 2019).

14.2.3 Clinical trials and research

Blockchain technology has the potential to optimize the process of conducting clinical trials and securely sharing research data. Smart contracts have the capability to automate and enforce agreements among researchers, participants, and regulatory agencies, thereby guaranteeing adherence to protocols and ethical norms. In addition, platforms that utilize blockchain technology can enable the secure exchange of de-identified medical data for research, while upholding patient privacy and confidentiality (Dawson et al., 2024).

14.2.4 Healthcare payments and billing

Blockchain technology has the potential to optimize healthcare payment and billing procedures by minimizing instances of fraud, errors, and administrative costs (Ranjan et al., 2018). Smart contracts enable the automation of payment arrangements among payers, providers, and patients, guaranteeing prompt and transparent compensation for services provided. Furthermore, systems based on blockchain technology have the capability to facilitate small transactions, enhance cross-border payments, and optimize revenue cycle management in the healthcare industry (Mahmood et al., 2014; Uslu et al., 2020).

14.2.5 Healthcare Internet of Things data security

With the widespread use of Internet of Things (IoT) devices in healthcare, it is crucial to prioritize the protection and confidentiality of the data produced by these devices (Almotairi, 2023). Blockchain technology can bolster the security of IoT data by employing encryption and decentralization for data storage, facilitating secure authentication and access management, and guaranteeing immutable audit trails. This enhances the robustness of healthcare IoT ecosystems and safeguards against data breaches and cyberattacks (Abouzakhar et al., 2017; Rizk et al., 2022).

14.3 Applications of DT technology in healthcare

The utilization of DT technology, which was initially created for the manufacturing and industrial domains, is progressively expanding into the healthcare field. DTs are a computer-generated model that replicates a physical object, such as a patient, medical gadget, or healthcare institution, with high fidelity in a digital environment. DTs utilize real-time data, sensors, and advanced analytics to facilitate predictive modeling, simulation, and improvement of healthcare processes and systems. Here are some key applications of DT technology in healthcare:

14.3.1 Personalized patient care

Healthcare providers utilize DTs to construct customized and dynamic representations of individual patients, amalgamating information from EHRs, wearable devices, genetic profiles, and other data sources (Kwon et al., 2022). Through the examination of this extensive dataset, healthcare providers can acquire valuable knowledge regarding the health condition of patients, forecast the advancement of diseases, and customize treatment strategies to cater to the distinct requirements of individual patients. DTs also enable remote monitoring and preventive interventions, enhancing patient outcomes and decreasing hospital readmissions (Holzinger et al., 2015).

14.3.2 Healthcare education and training

DTs are highly effective instructional tools for healthcare professionals, facilitating immersive, interactive, and experiential learning opportunities. Medical students, residents, and practicing physicians have the opportunity to engage with virtual patient situations, hone their clinical skills, and simulate surgical operations in a secure and regulated setting. DTs facilitate interdisciplinary collaboration and knowledge sharing among healthcare workers, promoting ongoing learning and professional growth (Pérez-Roman et al., 2020).

14.3.3 Medical device monitoring and optimization

DTs offer virtual duplicates of medical equipment, such as ventilators, infusion pumps, and implanted devices, allowing for continuous monitoring, maintenance, and enhancement (Tian et al., 2019). Healthcare practitioners can ensure the dependability, safety, and efficiency of medical equipment by simulating device performance, anticipating malfunctions, and identifying maintenance needs. DTs also provide predictive maintenance procedures, thereby decreasing downtime and minimizing interruptions in patient care (Gharaei et al., 2023; Wu, 2021).

14.3.4 Public health surveillance and disease management

DTs provide the continuous monitoring and simulation of population health trends, illness outbreaks, and epidemiological patterns (Jamil et al., 2020). Through the consolidation of data from EHRs, public health databases, and environmental sensors, public health professionals have the ability to identify groups at a heightened risk, trace the paths of disease transmission, and execute focused interventions to prevent and manage infectious diseases. DTs also provide predictive analytics for disease prediction, allocation of resources, and planning for disaster preparedness (Frisch, 2014).

14.3.5 Healthcare facility design and operations

Healthcare companies can utilize DTs to generate virtual duplicates of hospitals, clinics, and other healthcare facilities, therefore enhancing their design, layout, and operational effectiveness (Ben Ida et al., 2021). Healthcare providers can increase patient experience by simulating patient flows, resource utilization, and workflow procedures to identify bottlenecks and streamline operations. DTs additionally promote facility planning, extension, and remodeling projects, allowing stakeholders to visually and analytically evaluate the effects of planned modifications before their execution (Da Costa et al., 2018; Zachariadis et al., 2018).

14.4 Integration of blockchain and DTs in healthcare

The integration of blockchain and DTs is a significant merging that has the capacity to transform healthcare delivery, patient care, and operational efficiency. By integrating the decentralized, transparent, and secure ledger system of blockchain with the dynamic, virtual representations of physical entities provided by DTs, healthcare organizations can establish a strong ecosystem that improves data integrity, interoperability, and predictive analytics. The merging of blockchain and DTs can revolutionize healthcare in several significant ways:

14.4.1 Secure and interoperable health data management

Blockchain technology offers a secure and unchangeable platform for maintaining EHRs, while DTs give dynamic virtual representations of patient data and medical gadgets (Yaqoob et al., 2022). Integrating blockchain technology with DTs allows healthcare organizations to guarantee the authenticity, confidentiality, and compatibility of health data throughout the entire healthcare process (Rana et al., 2022). The digital replica of each patient can be securely connected to their blockchain-based EHR, allowing authorized individuals to easily view, modify, and exchange patient data while maintaining the confidentiality and protection of the information (Akhter Md Hasib et al., 2022).

14.4.2 Supply chain traceability and asset management

Blockchain technology improves the capacity to track and see clearly the movement of medications, medical equipment, and supplies throughout the healthcare supply chain. DTs offer virtual representations of assets, allowing for real-time monitoring, optimization, and predictive maintenance (Khan et al., 2022). Through the integration of blockchain technology with DTs, healthcare companies can effectively monitor the entire process of asset movement, from manufacturing to delivery (Jin et al., 2019). This integration allows for the verification of asset authenticity and ensures compliance with regulatory standards. This simplifies the management of inventories, minimizes waste, and improves patient safety by reducing the chances of counterfeit products and medication errors (Azbeg et al., 2022).

14.4.3 Security and real-time monitoring

In light of the rapid adoption of IoT devices in the healthcare industry, it is of the utmost importance to safeguard the confidentiality and authenticity of IoT data (Saha et al., 2021). Blockchain technology provides a decentralized and tamper-proof framework for securely encrypting and storing IoT data, whereas DTs allow for real-time monitoring and optimization of devices and sensors (Khatoon, 2020). By integrating blockchain and DTs, healthcare companies may improve the security, stability, and interoperability of IoT ecosystems, allowing for secure authentication, access management, and data sharing while protecting patient privacy and confidentiality (Verma et al., 2021).

14.5 The Internet of Medical Things in smart hospitals

The IoMT is revolutionizing the healthcare industry, especially in the realm of smart hospitals. IoMT stands for the interconnected network of medical devices, sensors, wearables, and healthcare systems that gather, transmit, and analyze patient data instantaneously. IoMT technologies in smart hospitals facilitate the smooth integration, automation, and optimization of healthcare delivery systems, leading to a transformation in patient care, operational efficiency, and clinical outcomes.

14.5.1 Remote patient monitoring and telemedicine

IoMT devices facilitate the remote monitoring of patient vital signs, medication adherence, and illness development in nontraditional healthcare environments (Ghubaish et al., 2020). Wearable sensors, intelligent gadgets, and mobile applications gather and transmit patient data to healthcare practitioners instantly, enabling remote consultations, virtual visits, and telemedicine services (Razdan and Sharma, 2022). Healthcare personnel can use this technology to observe patients' health conditions, assess the effectiveness of treatments, and take preventive measures to prevent complications. This helps to decrease the number of hospital readmissions and enhance patient outcomes (Dwivedi et al., 2022).

14.5.2 Data-driven decision-making and continuous improvement

The use of IoMT technology allows healthcare providers to have immediate access to extensive patient data, which facilitates decision-making based on data and ongoing performance enhancement (Parvathy et al., 2021). IoMT data is utilized by analytics dashboards, predictive models, and clinical decision support systems to enhance treatment pathways, resource utilization, and quality improvement programs (Jayachitra et al., 2023). Smart hospitals utilize this capability to identify specific areas where intervention is needed, implement methods that are supported by evidence, and continuously evaluate outcomes in real time. This process leads to ongoing improvement in the quality of healthcare service and fosters innovation (Hassanien et al., 2021).

14.5.3 Enhanced patient engagement and experience

The use of IoMT devices enables patients to actively participate in the management of their health and healthcare experiences. Furthermore, applications designed for patient use, wearable gadgets, and tools for remote monitoring allow patients to monitor their health measurements, receive customized advice, and contact healthcare professionals instantly (Ashfaq et al., 2022). This promotes increased patient involvement, compliance with treatment protocols, and active participation in making decisions about their care, ultimately enhancing patient happiness and results (Shreya et al., 2022).

14.5.4 Real-time asset tracking and management

IoMT technologies facilitate the continuous monitoring and enhancement of medical equipment, supplies, and resources in intelligent healthcare facilities. Radio Frequency Identification (RFID) tags, sensors, and asset tracking systems monitor the whereabouts, utilization, and maintenance condition of assets, allowing healthcare providers to manage inventory levels, avoid shortages, and expedite supply chain operations (Kotronis et al., 2019). This optimizes resource allocation, minimizes inefficiency, and increases workflow efficiency, guaranteeing prompt availability of vital medical supplies and equipment for patient treatment (Monteiro et al., 2021; Tiwari & Sharma, 2022).

14.6 Future of integrated blockchain and DTs in healthcare

The integration of blockchain and DT technologies in healthcare has a promising future since it has the ability to completely transform the delivery, management, and experience of healthcare. As these technologies progress and develop further, they will have a growing impact on solving the intricate problems in the healthcare industry and enabling new possibilities for innovation, effectiveness, and patient-focused care (Adibi et al., 2024; Volkov et al., 2021). Future advancements are anticipated to prioritize enhancing the interoperability of diverse healthcare systems and equipment. Blockchain has the potential to function as a universal framework for sharing data, while DTs can establish a consistent format for representing health data across different platforms (Lonsdale et al., 2022). In addition, with the advancement of blockchain and DT technologies, it is probable that answers to existing scaling problems will arise. This may entail implementing more efficient consensus processes in blockchain technology and creating DT models that demand fewer computational resources. Furthermore, integrating artificial intelligence (AI) with blockchain and DTs has the potential to create advanced prediction models for patient care and hospital management (Elayan et al., 2021; Ferdousi et al., 2023). AI algorithms have the capability to examine data from digital replicas to offer immediate insights and assistance in making decisions, all while being protected by the unchangeable record of transactions provided by blockchain technology (Alazab et al., 2022).

The integration of blockchain technology with DTs will facilitate the implementation of individualized and accurate medical interventions. By creating digital replicas of patients, it becomes possible to simulate how each individual might respond to various therapies (Kamel Boulos & Zhang,

2021). This enables the development of personalized therapy regimens that are specifically customized for the unique physiology of each patient. In addition, the emergence of telemedicine has created opportunities for utilizing blockchain and DTs to provide secure and dependable remote patient monitoring (Han et al., 2023). Doctors may access real-time virtual representations of their patient's health using DTs, while blockchain technology guarantees the security and confidentiality of the data being communicated (Karakra et al., 2019). Moreover, blockchain technology has the potential to automate different healthcare operations, including insurance claims, consent management, and compliance with healthcare legislation. This automation will decrease the number of administrative tasks and decrease the likelihood of mistakes made by humans (Du et al., 2021).

The integration of blockchain and DT technologies exhibits substantial potential for the future of healthcare. These technologies have the potential to transform healthcare delivery by offering secure, precise, and real-time data management and analysis. To effectively harness the advantages of these technologies for the improvement of patient care and the effectiveness of healthcare systems globally, it is imperative for stakeholders to work together and tackle the technical, ethical, and legal challenges that occur as the industry progresses (Elangovan et al., 2020).

14.7 Conclusion

To summarize, the integration of blockchain and DT technologies in smart hospitals ushers in a new period of advancement, effectiveness, and patient-focused care provision in the healthcare industry. By using the distinct capabilities of these technologies together, healthcare companies can establish integrated systems that improve data protection, compatibility, predictive analysis, and individualized healthcare. It was found that blockchain technology offers a reliable, distributed, and unalterable system for handling confidential healthcare information, guaranteeing its accuracy, privacy, and ability to work together with other systems. In addition, DTs facilitate the development of customized representations of individual patients by amalgamating data from many sources, including EHRs, wearable devices, and genetic profiles. Blockchain and DT technologies enable healthcare professionals to enhance clinical workflows, customize patient care, and enhance operational efficiency in intelligent hospitals. Furthermore, it is clear that the future of healthcare lies in harnessing the power of integrated blockchain and DT technologies in smart hospitals. Healthcare providers can enhance their delivery of care by adopting these technological innovations, resulting in increased efficiency, security, and better alignment with patient demands. As we consider the future, it is evident that the ongoing advancement and widespread acceptance of these technologies will have a crucial impact on transforming healthcare for future generations.

References

Abouzakhar, N. S., Jones, A., & Angelopoulou, O. (2017). *Internet of Things security: A review of risks and threats to healthcare sector. 2017 IEEE international conference on Internet of Things (iThings) and IEEE green computing and communications (GreenCom) and IEEE cyber, physical and social computing (CPSCom) and IEEE smart data (SmartData)* (pp. 373–378). IEEE.

Adibi, S., Rajabifard, A., Shojaei, D., & Wickramasinghe, N. (2024). Enhancing healthcare through sensor-enabled digital twins in smart environments: A comprehensive analysis. *Sensors*, *24*, 2793.

Akhter Md Hasib, K. T., Chowdhury, I., Sakib, S., Monirujjaman Khan, M., Alsufyani, N., Alsufyani, A., & Bourouis, S. (2022). Electronic health record monitoring system and data security using blockchain technology. *Security Communication Networks*, *2022*, 1–15.

Alazab, M., Khan, L. U., Koppu, S., Ramu, S. P., Iyapparaja, M., Boobalan, P., Baker, T., Maddikunta, P. K. R., Gadekallu, T. R., & Aljuhani, A. (2022). Digital twins for healthcare 4.0—Recent advances, architecture, and open challenges. *IEEE Consumer Electronics Magazine*, *12*, 29–37.

Almotairi, K. H. (2023). Application of internet of things in healthcare domain. *Journal of Umm Al-Qura University Engineering Architecture*, *14*, 1–12.

Ashfaq, Z., Rafay, A., Mumtaz, R., Zaidi, S. M. H., Saleem, H., Zaidi, S. A. R., Mumtaz, S., & Haque, A. (2022). A review of enabling technologies for Internet of Medical Things (IoMT) Ecosystem. *Ain Shams Engineering Journal*, *13*, 101660.

Azbeg, K., Ouchetto, O., & Andaloussi, S. J. (2022). BlockMedCare: A healthcare system based on IoT, blockchain and IPFS for data management security, Egypt. *Informatics Journals*, *23*, 329–343.

Ben Ida, I., Balti, M., Chaabane, S., & Jemai, A. (2021). Adaptative vital signs monitoring system based on the early warning score approach in smart hospital context. *IET Smart Cities*, *3*, 16–28.

Chen, J., Wang, W., Fang, B., Liu, Y., Yu, K., Leung, V. C. M., & Hu, X. (2023). Digital twin empowered wireless healthcare monitoring for smart home. *IEEE Journal on Selected Areas in Communications*.

Da Costa, C. A., Pasluosta, C. F., Eskofier, B., Da Silva, D. B., & da Rosa Righi, R. (2018). Internet of health things: Toward intelligent vital signs monitoring in hospital wards. *Artificial Intelligence in Medicine*, *89*, 61–69.

Dawson, J., Phanich, K. J., & Wiese, J. (2024). Reenvisioning patient education with smart hospital patient rooms. *Proceedings of the ACM Interactive, Mobile, Wearable Ubiquitous Technology*, *7*, 1–23.

Du, X., Chen, B., Ma, M., & Zhang, Y. (2021). Research on the application of blockchain in smart healthcare: Constructing a hierarchical framework. *Journal of Healthcare Engineering*, *2021*.

Dwivedi, R., Mehrotra, D., & Chandra, S. (2022). Potential of internet of medical things (IoMT) applications in building a smart healthcare system: A systematic review. *Journal of Oral Biology Craniofacial Research*, *12*, 302–318.

Elangovan, D., Long, C. S., Bakrin, F. S., Tan, C. S., Goh, K. W., Hussain, Z., Al-Worafi, Y. M., Lee, K. S., Kassab, Y. W., & Ming, L. C. (2020). Application of blockchain technology in hospital information system. *Mathematical Modeling and Soft Computing in Epidemiology*, 231–246.

Elayan, H., Aloqaily, M., & Guizani, M. (2021). Digital twin for intelligent context-aware IoT healthcare systems. *IEEE Internet of Things Journal*, *8*, 16749–16757.

Ferdousi, R., Laamarti, F., & El Saddik, A. (2023). *Artificial intelligence models in digital twins for health and well-being. Digital twin healthcare* (pp. 121–136). Elsevier.

Frisch, P. (2014). What is an intelligent hospital?: A place where technology and design converge to enhance patient care. *IEEE Pulse*, *5*, 10–15.

Gamage, H. T. M., Weerasinghe, H. D., & Dias, N. G. J. (2020). A survey on blockchain technology concepts, applications, and issues. *SN Computer Science*, *1*, 1–15.

Gharaei, N., Al Otaibi, Y. D., Malebary, S. J., & Almagrabi, A. O. (2023). A storage optimization and energy efficiency-based edge-enabled companion-side eHealth monitoring system for IoT-based smart hospitals. *IEEE Internet of Things Journal*.

Ghubaish, A., Salman, T., Zolanvari, M., Unal, D., Al-Ali, A., & Jain, R. (2020). Recent advances in the internet-of-medical-things (IoMT) systems security. *IEEE Internet of Things Journal*, *8*, 8707–8718.

Haag, S., & Anderl, R. (2018). Digital twin—proof of concept. *Manufacturing Letters*, *15*, 64–66.

Han, Y., Li, Y., Li, Y., Yang, B., & Cao, L. (2023). Digital twinning for smart hospital operations: Framework and proof of concept. *Technology in Society*, *74*, 102317.

Hassanien, A. E., Khamparia, A., Gupta, D., Shankar, K., & Slowik, A. (2021). *Cognitive internet of medical things for smart healthcare*. Springer.

Holzinger, A., Röcker, C., & Ziefle, M. (2015). From smart health to smart hospitals. *Smart Health Open Problems and Future Challenges*, 1–20.

Islam, I., Munim, K. M., Oishwee, S. J., Islam, A. K. M. N., & Islam, M. N. (2020). A critical review of concepts, benefits, and pitfalls of blockchain technology using concept map. *IEEE Access*, *8*, 68333–68341.

Jamil, F., Ahmad, S., Iqbal, N., & Kim, D.-H. (2020). Towards a remote monitoring of patient vital signs based on IoT-based blockchain integrity management platforms in smart hospitals. *Sensors*, *20*, 2195.

Jamil, F., Hang, L., Kim, K., & Kim, D. (2019). A novel medical blockchain model for drug supply chain integrity management in a smart hospital. *Electronics*, *8*, 505.

Jayachitra, S., Prasanth, A., Hariprasath, S., Benazir Begam, R., & Madiajagan, M. (2023). *AI enabled internet of medical things in smart healthcare. AI model blockchain-based intell networks IoT system concepts, methodology tools, applying* (pp. 141–161). Springer.

Jin, H., Xu, C., Luo, Y., Li, P., Cao, Y., & Mathew, J. (2019). *Toward secure, privacy-preserving, and interoperable medical data sharing via blockchain. 2019 IEEE 25th international conference on parallel and distributed systems (ICPADS)* (pp. 852–861). IEEE.

Kamel Boulos, M. N., & Zhang, P. (2021). Digital twins: From personalised medicine to precision public health. *Journal of Personalized Medicine.*, *11*, 745.

Karakra, A., Fontanili, F., Lamine, E., & Lamothe, J. (2019). *HospiT'Win: A predictive simulation-based digital twin for patients pathways in hospital. 2019 IEEE EMBS International Conference on Biomedical and Health Informatics* (pp. 1–4). IEEE.

Khan, A. A., Laghari, A. A., Shafiq, M., Cheikhrouhou, O., Alhakami, W., Hamam, H., & Shaikh, Z. A. (2022). Healthcare ledger management: A blockchain and machine learning-enabled novel and secure architecture for medical industry. *Human-Centric Computing and Information Sciences*, *12*, 55.

Khatoon, A. (2020). A blockchain-based smart contract system for healthcare management. *Electronics*, *9*, 94.

Komalavalli, C., Saxena, D., & Laroiya, C. (2020). *Overview of blockchain technology concepts. Handbook of research on blockchain technology* (pp. 349–371). Elsevier.

Kotronis, C., Routis, I., Politi, E., Nikolaidou, M., Dimitrakopoulos, G., Anagnostopoulos, D., Amira, A., Bensaali, F., & Djelouat, H. (2019). Evaluating internet of medical things (IoMT)-based systems from a human-centric perspective. *Internet of Things*, *8*, 100125.

Kwon, H., An, S., Lee, H.-Y., Cha, W. C., Kim, S., Cho, M., & Kong, H.-J. (2022). Review of smart hospital services in real healthcare environments. *Healthcare Information Research*, *28*, 3.

Liu, M., Fang, S., Dong, H., & Xu, C. (2021). Review of digital twin about concepts, technologies, and industrial applications. *Journal of Manufacuring Systems*, *58*, 346–361.

Lonsdale, H., Gray, G. M., Ahumada, L. M., Yates, H. M., Varughese, A., & Rehman, M. A. (2022). The perioperative human digital twin. *Anesthesia and Analgesia*, *134*, 885–892.

Lu, Q., Chen, L., Xie, X., Fang, Z., Ye, Z., & Pitt, M. (2023). *Framing blockchain-integrated digital twins for emergent healthcare: A proof of concept. Proceedings of the institution of civil engineering sustainability* (pp. 228–243). Emerald Publishing Limited.

Mahmood, N., Shah, A., Waqas, A., Bhatti, Z., Abubakar, A., & Malik, H. A. M. (2014). *RFID based smart hospital management system: A conceptual framework. 5th International conference on information and communication technology for the Muslim World* (pp. 1–6). IEEE.

Martens, E., Haase, H.-U., Mastella, G., Henkel, A., Spinner, C., Hahn, F., Zou, C., Sanches, A. F., Allescher, J., & Heid, D. (2024). Smart hospital: Achieving interoperability and raw data collection from medical devices in clinical routine. *Frontiers in Digital Health*, *6*, 1341475.

Monteiro, K., Silva, É., Remigio, É., Santos, G. L., & Endo, P. T. (2021). Internet of medical things (IoMT) applications in E-health systems context: An overview and research challenges. *Emerging Technology Biomedical Engineering and Sustainable Telemedicine*, 1–12.

Nofer, M., Gomber, P., Hinz, O., & Schiereck, D. (2017). Blockchain. *Business & Information Systems Engineering*, *59*, 183–187.

Parvathy, V.S., Pothiraj, S., & Sampson, J. (2021). Automated internet of medical things (IoMT) based healthcare monitoring system. In: *Cognitive internet of medical things for smart healthcare: services and applications* (pp. 117–128).

Pérez-Roman, E., Alvarado, M., & Barrett, M. (2020). *Personalizing healthcare in smart cities. Smart cities in application: Healthcare, policy, and innovation* (pp. 3–18). Springer.

Raj, P. (2021). *Empowering digital twins with blockchain. Advanced computing* (pp. 267–283). Elsevier.

Rana, S. K., Rana, S. K., Nisar, K., Ag Ibrahim, A. A., Rana, A. K., Goyal, N., & Chawla, P. (2022). Blockchain technology and artificial intelligence based decentralized access control model to enable secure interoperability for healthcare. *Sustainability*, *14*, 9471.

Ranjan, P., Soman, S., Ateria, A. K., & Srivastava, P. K. (2018). *Streamlining payment workflows using a patient wallet for hospital information systems. 2018 IEEE 31st international symposium on the computer-based medical systems* (pp. 339–344). IEEE.

Razdan, S., & Sharma, S. (2022). Internet of medical things (IoMT): Overview, emerging technologies, and case studies. *IETE Technical Review*, *39*, 775–788.

Reegu, F. A., Abas, H., Hakami, Z., Tiwari, S., Akmam, R., Muda, I., Almashqbeh, H. A., & Jain, R. (2022). Systematic assessment of the interoperability requirements and challenges of secure blockchain-based electronic health records. *Security Communication Networks*, *2022*.

Rizk, D. K. A. A., Hosny, H. M., ElHorbety, S., & Salem, A.-B. (2022). Smart hospital management systems based on Internet of Things: Challenges, intelligent solutions and functional requirements. *International Journal of Intelligent Computing and Information Science*, *22*, 32–43.

Saha, S., Majumder, A., Bhowmik, T., Basu, A., & Choudhury, A. (2021). *A healthcare data management system on blockchain framework. 2021 International conference on smart generation computing, communication and networking (SMART GENCON)* (pp. 1–5). IEEE.

Sahal, R., Alsamhi, S. H., & Brown, K. N. (2022). Personal digital twin: A close look into the present and a step towards the future of personalised healthcare industry. *Sensors*, *22*, 5918.

Shreya, S., Chatterjee, K., & Singh, A. (2022). A smart secure healthcare monitoring system with internet of medical things. *Computers & Electrical Engineering*, *101*, 107969.

Tao, F., Zhang, H., Liu, A., & Nee, A. Y. C. (2018). Digital twin in industry: State-of-the-art. *IEEE Translation on Industrial Informatics*, *15*, 2405–2415.

Tian, S., Yang, W., Le Grange, J. M., Wang, P., Huang, W., & Ye, Z. (2019). Smart healthcare: Making medical care more intelligent. *Global Health Journal*, *3*, 62–65.

Tiwari, S., & Sharma, N. (2022). Idea, architecture, and applications of 5G enabled IoMT systems for smart health care system. *ECS Transactions*, *107*, 5499.

Tuan Anh Nguyen. (2023). Blockchain and digital twin for industry 4.0/5.0. *Kenkyu Journal of Nanotechnology & Nanoscience*, *9*, 01–05.

Tuan Anh Nguyen. (2024). Digital twin-based universe (complexiverse): Where real world and virtual/digital world are unified. *Kenkyu Journal of Nanotechnology & Nanoscience*, *10*, 01–04.

Uslu, B. Ç., Okay, E., & Dursun, E. (2020). Analysis of factors affecting IoT-based smart hospital design. *Journal of Cloud Computing*, *9*, 67.

VanDerHorn, E., & Mahadevan, S. (2021). Digital twin: Generalization, characterization and implementation. *Decision Support System.*, *145*, 113524.

Verma, G., Pathak, N., & Sharma, N. (2021). *A secure framework for health record management using blockchain in cloud environment. Journal of Physics Conference Series* (p. 12019) IOP Publishing.

Volkov, I., Radchenko, G., & Tchernykh, A. (2021). Digital twins, internet of things and mobile medicine: A review of current platforms to support smart healthcare. *Program Computer Software*, *47*, 578–590.

Wu, Q. (2021). Optimization of AI-driven communication systems for green hospitals in sustainable cities. *Sustainable Cities Society*, *72*, 103050.

Yaqoob, I., Salah, K., Jayaraman, R., & Al-Hammadi, Y. (2022). Blockchain for healthcare data management: Opportunities, challenges, and future recommendations. *Neural Computing and Applications.*, 1–16.

Zachariadis, C., Velivassaki, T. H., Zahariadis, T., Railis, K., & Leligou, H. C. (2018). *Matisse: A smart hospital ecosystem. 2018 21st Euromicro conference digital system design* (pp. 464–471). IEEE.

CHAPTER

6G and blockchain convergence in the smart industry

15

Fah Choy Chia
Department of Surveying, Universiti Tunku Abdul Rahman, Bandar Sungai Long, Selangor, Malaysia

15.1 Introduction

The construction industry, while crucial for societal progress, faces challenges with inefficiency, lack of transparency, and fragmented workflows. This chapter explores how blockchain technology, a revolutionary tool for secure and transparent data management, can address these issues and propel the industry toward a more efficient and collaborative future.

Following an introduction to blockchain technology and its core functionalities, including smart contracts (self-executing agreements), we delve into the various applications of blockchain specifically within the construction sector. We will explore how blockchain can enhance collaboration and transparency during the design phase, facilitate efficient dispute resolution, and improve safety management through integration with the Internet of Things (IoT).

Furthermore, the chapter examines how blockchain technology can streamline construction supply chains, promote sustainable procurement practices, and empower building information modeling (BIM) for improved project delivery. We will explore the powerful synergy between BIM and blockchain, highlighting their potential as a "powerful duo" and a "powerful trio" when combined with smart contracts.

Looking toward the future, the chapter delves into the potential of 6G technology and its convergence with blockchain. We will discuss the implications of 6G advancements on blockchain applications in construction, offering a glimpse into the transformative possibilities this powerful combination holds for the industry.

15.2 Introduction to blockchain technology

Satoshi Nakamoto's seminal 2009 whitepaper, A Peer-to-Peer Electronic Cash System, laid the groundwork for what we now call blockchain technology. Although the whitepaper does not use the exact term "Distributed Ledger Technology" (DLT), it proposed the use of a peer-to-peer distributed timestamp server to generate a record of the chronological order of transactions. This distributed database system is the foundation and first prominent example of what is now known as DLT.

Blockchain and Digital Twin for Smart Hospitals. DOI: https://doi.org/10.1016/B978-0-443-34226-4.00016-2

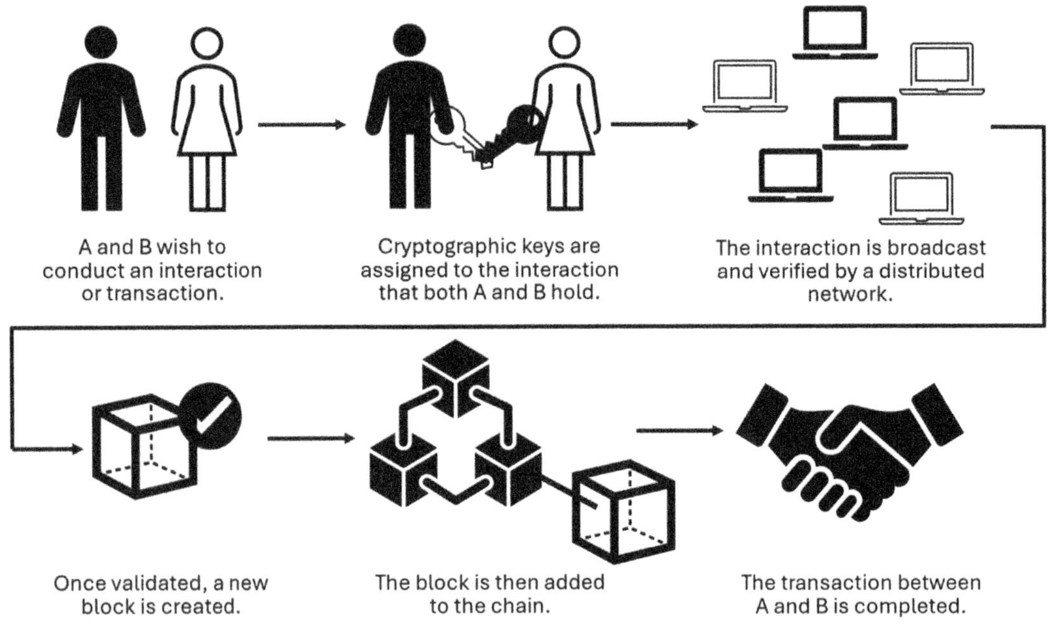
A and B wish to conduct an interaction or transaction.
Cryptographic keys are assigned to the interaction that both A and B hold.
The interaction is broadcast and verified by a distributed network.
Once validated, a new block is created.
The block is then added to the chain.
The transaction between A and B is completed.

FIGURE 15.1

Blockchain transaction flow.

Blockchain's robust network protocol and consensus mechanism enable secure information exchange without relying on third parties. This security hinges on the core structure of the blockchain itself. It acts as an append-only ledger, a continuously growing chain of fixed-sized blocks. Each block contains validated transactions and cryptographically references the one before it, creating a tamper-evident chain. Modifying a single block would require altering the entire chain, a near-impossible feat due to the decentralized nature of the network. This immutability, combined with encryption protecting individual transactions, fosters trust and transparency.

Imagine a traditional system where all transactions between parties are recorded in a single, centralized ledger. By contrast, a blockchain offers a system of distributed ledgers. Here, multiple, identical copies of the transaction history are maintained simultaneously by every participant on the network.

A typical blockchain transaction would operate as shown in Fig. 15.1.

15.3 Smart contract

Nick Szabo introduced the concept of smart contracts in his seminal work, "Formalizing and securing relationships on public networks" (1997). Unlike traditional contracts resembling Aristotelian syllogisms ("if A, then B; else C"), smart contracts incorporate user interfaces alongside protocols to formalize and secure relationships over computer networks. By using cryptographic and other security mechanisms, these contracts would automatically fulfill the conditions outlined in the agreement, eliminating the

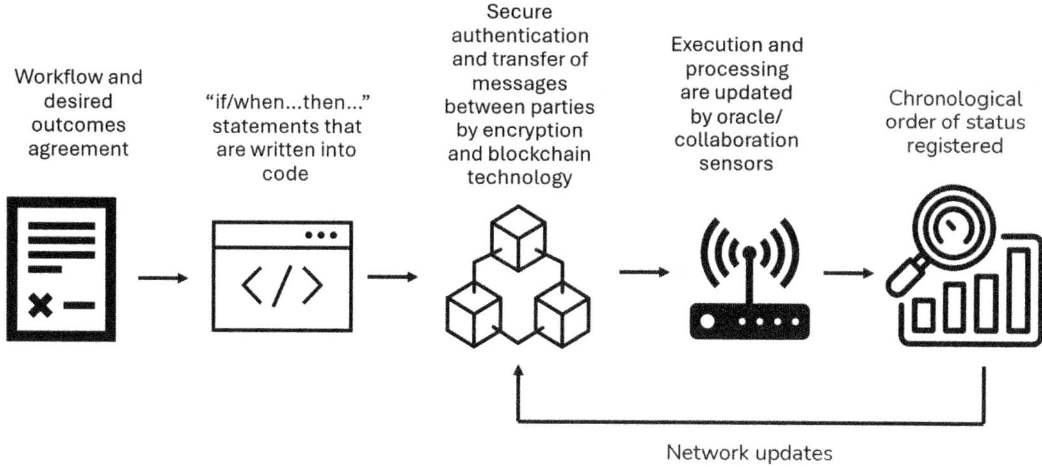

FIGURE 15.2

Smart contract flow.

need for third parties' interpretation and enforcement, and bypassing the need for arbitrators and courts to resolve disputes should issues arise. The conditions can be validated and confirmed by Remote Procedure Calls (RPC) to other smart contracts or initially to "off-chain" oracles. By using cryptographic and other security mechanisms, smart contracts can protect against breaches by designated parties (principals) and prevent unauthorized access or manipulation by third parties.

Imagine a construction contract that automatically releases payment upon completion of specific milestones. The smart contract would contain these milestones as "if/then" statements, verifying them using external data feeds when necessary, before transferring funds. This technology has the potential to revolutionize the construction industry, streamlining payments and automating material deliveries. However, thorough security checks are crucial to prevent vulnerabilities in the code.

For a detailed illustration of the smart contract flow, see Fig. 15.2.

15.4 Applicable uses of blockchain in smart industry

15.4.1 Enhancing transparency and collaboration in design phase

Consider a construction project where collaboration on the design phase is streamlined with blockchain technology. During project planning, the platform facilitates defining design packages and deliverables based on the project program. Simultaneously, the underlying blockchain platform mirrors these milestones and packages. Smart contracts are then programmed to trigger payments based on predefined conditions: worked hours and timely delivery of deliverables. These transparent and faster payments are initiated by smart contracts through a blockchain application linked to the project's bank account. Importantly, while payments remain in traditional fiat currency, the smart contract automates the initiation process.

Upon design initiation, the platform captures all essential interactions between design team members and project participants. It is crucial to note that the platform does not share the design packages themselves but rather focuses on digital signatures, approvals, and quality assurance (QA) steps for each design element. This allows the smart contracts to leverage these inputs for automatic updates on project progress. Since the system is tamper-proof, the accountability and traceability of design approvals are guaranteed. Additionally, all worked hours can be registered and shared across parties on the blockchain, eliminating the need for time-consuming administrative tasks. Smart contracts manage this administrative data and keep participants informed through the constantly updated blockchain ledger.

Upon completion of a design, the document control system notifies the smart contract of a submitted package. Designated parties are then notified to review the document. Using their registered IDs and trusted digital signatures on the blockchain, they can approve the document. All these interactions are recorded on the same platform, allowing smart contracts to initiate both payments and updates on project performance metrics.

Fig. 15.3 illustrates the design package submission through smart contract.

15.4.2 Dispute resolution through blockchain in construction

Construction projects are complex, and unforeseen issues can lead to disputes. Traditional record-keeping methods can be inadequate. Blockchain technology offers several advantages in dispute resolution, such as the following:

- *Secure, shared record-keeping*: All transactions, approvals, and payments are immutably recorded on the blockchain. This creates a transparent and accountable system for all parties involved.

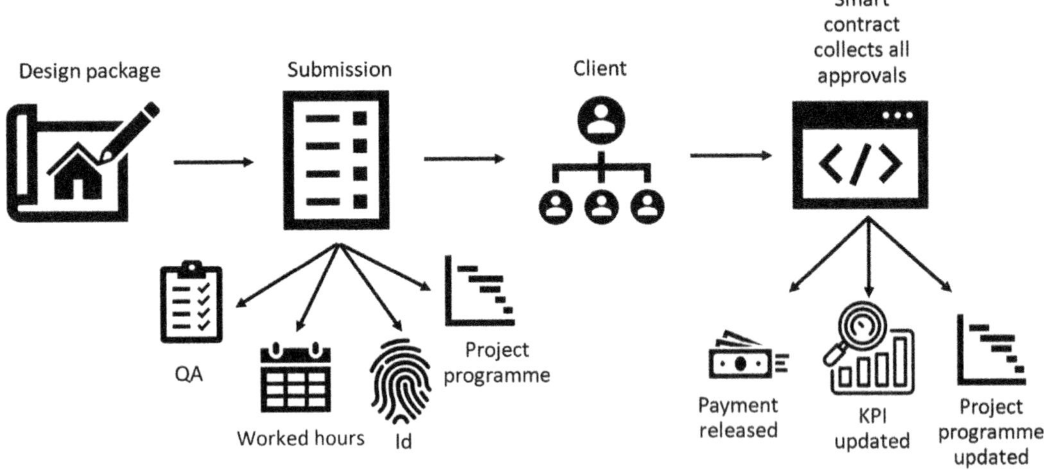

FIGURE 15.3

Design package submission through smart contract.

- *Enhanced claims assessment*: Claims based on client instructions or unforeseen events can be easily assessed against the immutable record. This facilitates fair adjustments and fosters better quality services throughout the project.
- *Transparency for industry*: Blockchain creates a permanent record of adjustments, leading to a new level of transparency in the construction industry.

15.4.3 Safety management with blockchain and IoT

Safety is paramount in construction. Blockchain, coupled with the IoT, can significantly improve health and safety (H&S) management:

- *Immutable record of H&S data*: All H&S information and incidents are meticulously logged on the blockchain, providing an immutable record for future reference and claims management.
- *Real-time risk mitigation*: The system allows for registration of H&S incidents and unsafe conditions (e.g., weather, unauthorized activity). Sensors and IoT devices provide real-time data for risk assessment.
- *Automated safety measures*: Smart contracts can process sensor data and trigger predefined safety protocols. For example, if crane sensors detect overload or extreme wind, a smart contract can automatically notify personnel and adjust the construction plan.
- *Tamper-proof data with accountability*: Sensor data is recorded on the blockchain, creating a tamper-proof record with clear accountability. This helps prevent accidents and ensures project safety.

15.4.4 Streamlining construction supply chains with blockchain technology

The construction industry grapples with a notoriously fragmented supply chain. Blockchain technology offers an innovative solution to streamline this cumbersome process. It achieves this through the following:

- *Standardized processes and transparency*: Blockchain enables the creation of a standardized procurement system with a transparent record of transactions. This provides real-time material provenance, allowing for true track-and-trace functionality.
- *Reduced waste and improved management*: By tracking materials from origin to site, blockchain minimizes waste and facilitates on-site material management. It also tackles the critical issue of material counterfeiting by verifying origin and authenticity.
- *Elimination of paperwork and automation*: A blockchain platform replaces paper-based documentation and wet signatures with tamper-proof digital approvals for goods movement. Additionally, it continuously updates and shares shipment statuses with all parties involved.
- *Smart contracts for efficiency*: The blockchain can house all documentation, allowing smart contracts to automate invoicing and payments upon fulfillment of predefined shipment terms. This fosters a cohesive document and supply chain management system, enhancing accountability.

Benefits of a blockchain-powered supply chain:

- *Faster issue resolution*: The shared, distributed ledger provides real-time visibility into transactions and procurement processes, allowing for quicker identification and resolution of issues, ultimately reducing project risk and complexity.
- *Transparency and accountability for all*: All participants benefit from high visibility into the supply chain.
- *Universal applicability*: The principles of tracking goods, registering interactions, and including crucial documentation are remarkably similar across industries. Construction can leverage these established blockchain practices for materials like flowers, steel, or prefabricated elements, making every stage transparent and accountable.

By implementing a blockchain-powered solution, the construction industry can achieve a streamlined and accountable supply chain, contributing to smoother project execution and reduced risks.

15.4.5 Blockchain for sustainable procurement

Beyond streamlining processes, blockchain technology can significantly enhance the sustainability of construction supply chains.

- *Optimizing procurement for sustainability*: Blockchain fosters a more sustainable industry by optimizing fragmented procurement and implementing material provenance. Material provenance is crucial for reusing and recycling materials based on certified specifications.
- *Whole-life-cycle considerations*: True sustainability requires considering a structure's entire life cycle. Currently, verifying material details after construction is challenging, hindering decisions on extending a structure's lifespan or designing optimal maintenance strategies.

The application of blockchain technology offers a solution to this challenge through simplified sustainability measurement. Storing and sharing material certificates and quality checks on the blockchain simplifies measuring sustainability metrics like total carbon footprint, percentage of reusable materials, and whole-life-cycle costs. This data transparency also supports mandatory initiatives like Site Waste Management Plans, which rely heavily on supply chain data.

By implementing a blockchain-powered supply chain, the construction industry can achieve greater transparency, improve sustainability practices, and make data-driven decisions throughout a structure's life cycle.

15.4.6 Building information modeling and blockchain: a powerful duo

BIM and blockchain can be a powerful duo with the potential to transform the construction industry. Both BIM and blockchain excel at creating a single source of truth. Construction projects generate massive amounts of data: design details, management decisions, and various file types. Blockchain can strengthen BIM by the following:

- *Enhanced data integrity*: Blockchain's tamper-proof nature adds a layer of accountability and transparency to BIM data.

- *Unified audit trail*: An advanced digital engineering framework can leverage BIM for core data, while the blockchain stores the audit trail of design approvals, data verification, and project management decisions. This combined source of truth eliminates the longstanding issues of fragmented information and lack of accountability.

BIM acts as a central information hub for a project's entire lifecycle, not just delivery. BIM and blockchain can work together in the following:

- *BIM benefits from blockchain data*: During construction, BIM can integrate details from the blockchain, such as supply chain information, material provenance, and payment records.
- *BIM contributes to the blockchain*: BIM can add data to the blockchain, including design decisions, data sources, and model modification orders. Smart contracts can then utilize this data to trigger actions like payments or material orders.

The benefits of the powerful duo include the following:

- *Strengthened BIM model*: This approach positions the blockchain as an underlying infrastructure, bolstering any BIM model with verifiable information.
- *Automated workflows*: Data exchange between BIM and the blockchain can be automated, with smart contracts initiating automatic payments and task orders.
- *Enhanced interoperability*: APIs can facilitate seamless information exchange between different software packages.
- *Reduced disputes and increased trust*: Every decision is immutably logged on the blockchain, fostering trust and eliminating time-consuming checks. Clear liability and accountability are established, reducing disputes.
- *Intellectual property allocation*: The comprehensive data collection on the blockchain, encompassing design decisions, content checks, procurement, and transactional data, creates a secure and immutable log for IP allocation.
- *Promoting innovation*: The blockchain serves as a record of innovative design features, encouraging their propagation across projects and potentially mitigating the fear of not receiving credit within collaborative efforts.

By merging BIM and blockchain, the construction industry can achieve a new level of transparency, accountability, and collaboration, paving the way for a more efficient and innovative future.

15.4.7 BIM, blockchain, and smart contracts: a powerful trio

BIM offers significant advantages over paper-based methods, but its full potential lies in achieving a fully digital and automated delivery process. However, trust remains a hurdle for complete automation. This is where blockchain technology and smart contracts come in.

By combining BIM with smart contracts, predefined criteria can trigger automated actions, ensuring both parties' needs are met. For example, a smart contract can perform the following:

- Enforce quality criteria based on the approved BIM model. If changes are necessary, it can initiate additional design time, update the schedule, and notify relevant parties.
- Incentivize accurate BIM updates throughout construction. For instance, payment for a precast beam placement might be contingent on a certified GPS machine verifying its position within the model.

These features foster transparency and collaboration in quality checks and ensure the model reflects reality. This paves the way for a true "digital twin" of the asset.

One of BIM's challenges is capturing construction information like structural changes and cost/time updates in the model. Blockchain solutions, as discussed earlier, can ensure material provenance is recorded, which the BIM model can retrieve. Smart contracts can further incentivize these updates.

Smart contracts can trigger subsequent actions based on BIM updates. For example, upon verifying portal framework placement, the contract could automatically order the next batch of beams (Fig. 15.4). This streamlines workflows from material production to construction.

A blockchain-enhanced BIM framework can even facilitate a circular economy throughout an asset's lifecycle. Data captured during construction can be stored for future maintenance, replacement, and eventual removal of materials and components. This allows buildings to act as material banks, significantly reducing waste.

Kamel et al. (2023) propose a framework in their paper "A framework for smart construction contracts using BIM and blockchain." This framework combines several technologies:

- *5D BIM*: Integrates cost data into the existing 3D BIM model, enabling real-time cost estimation and progress tracking.
- *Smart contracts*: Automate specific aspects of construction agreements.
- *Instant messaging (WhatsApp)*: Facilitates real-time communication and chronological record-keeping.

The framework is divided into the following six interrelated layers:

- *Data acquisition layer*: This layer collects real-time data from the construction site, including human-sourced records of work performed and engineer's decisions about completed work. This data serves as the basis for payments.
- *BIM layer*: The 5D BIM model is used to visualize the project timeline and construction costs and track progress payments. Project drawings, baseline data, and progress updates from the

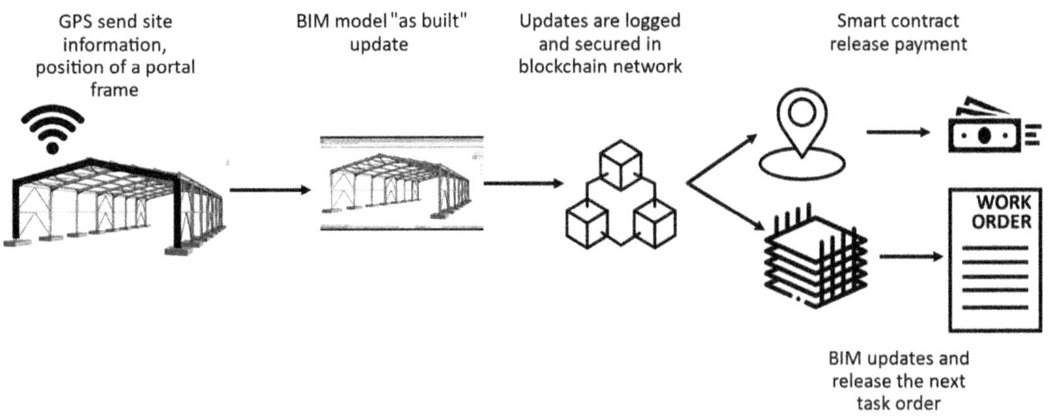

FIGURE 15.4

Smart contract triggers subsequent actions based on BIM updates.

data acquisition layer are fed into this layer to generate an updated 5D BIM model for the framework.
- *Smart contracts layer*: Contract clauses related to payments are transformed into machine-readable code and embedded into smart contracts. These contracts are triggered when the engineer certifies work completion. Based on this certification, the amount due is transferred from the updated schedule to the blockchain network layer.
- *Blockchain network layer*: This layer handles project payments. It eliminates the need for banks to facilitate payments directly through the blockchain network. Upon receiving the engineer's certificate, the employer's payment is issued to the contractor. The value and timing of payments are obtained from the smart contracts layer. Transaction data is then transferred to the communication layer via Twilio API.
- *Communication layer*: This layer is responsible for real-time communication between project parties. It transmits details like project decisions, payment statuses, and contract updates to all relevant parties.
- *Cloud service layer*: This layer stores and retrieves project data, facilitating data flow between parties and reducing the risk of data centralization. It acts as a repository for data used in real-time notifications through the WhatsApp communication application (Kamel et al., 2023).

This approach promotes automated workflows, improved data collection, and a more sustainable construction industry.

15.4.8 BIM and blockchain for smart asset management

The convergence of BIM and blockchain technology is creating a powerful force for smart asset management (SAM) through "digital twins."

Many construction projects transition into long-term operation and maintenance (O&M). SAM systems, powered by the concept of digital twins, are gaining traction to address this need. A digital twin is a virtual replica of a real-world asset, encompassing its entire lifecycle—from design and construction to decommissioning.

A robust BIM framework is crucial from the project's inception to achieve this holistic approach. The COBie standard emphasizes collecting data during design and construction to support O&M. This data can include crucial aspects like the following:

- Structural component lifespans
- Designer-specified maintenance needs
- Embedded carbon footprints of materials.

Blockchain elevates the digital twin beyond simply housing operational data. It guarantees data traceability, enabling pinpoint identification of issues. For instance, if a structural failure occurs, the digital twin can identify the responsible elements, their assembly process, and procurement parties. This translates to:

- Reduced time and cost associated with insurance disputes and warranty claims.
- Incentive for quality from all project participants due to increased accountability.

Digital twins can evolve beyond their "as built" status by incorporating real-time data streams from IoT sensors. This transforms the digital twin into a dynamic dashboard for proactive asset management.

However, the quality of insights hinges on the quality of data fed into the system. Here, blockchain plays a vital role by ensuring:

- Verification of IoT data
- Adherence to client requirements for data integrity.

This creates a secure log of O&M actions, similar to its role in design and construction. This log fosters accountability, discourages misconduct, and serves as a legal tool for enforcing quality services. Combining live data, Construction Operations Building Information Exchange (COBie parameters), and O&M action logs on the blockchain creates a valuable knowledge base within the BIM model. This data, accumulated over the asset's lifecycle, can link decisions made on the blockchain to their impact on the models and the real asset.

Analyzing such datasets can yield valuable insights, including the following:

- Optimal maintenance intervals
- Potential carbon footprint reduction strategies
- Whole-life-cycle cost optimization.

Imagine a bridge deck with sensors measuring traffic conditions. This data, linked to the central model, can provide real-time maintenance needs, which can trigger automatic repairs via smart contracts (Balint et al., 2018).

15.5 Blockchain technology and 6G

The phenomenal growth of mobile data usage and the ever-increasing demand for seamless connectivity are driving advancements in mobile communication technology. As 5G networks continue to be rolled out globally, researchers are already looking ahead to the next generation—6G. Expected to be commercially available by 2030, 6G promises significant leaps in data rates, network latency, and overall network capacity compared to its predecessors. On the other hand, blockchain technology has emerged as a revolutionary platform for secure and transparent data storage and management. However, current blockchain implementations face limitations in scalability and transaction processing speed. 6G offers several technical features that can significantly impact blockchain technology.

15.5.1 6G Flagship

The 6G Flagship program, established in 2018 by the University of Oulu in Finland, is the world's first research initiative dedicated to exploring and shaping the next generation of mobile communication networks: 6G.

6G Flagship actively defines the vision for 6G, considering user needs, the evolution of technology, and the potential societal impact of this next-generation network. This comprehensive vision serves as a guiding light for researchers and industry leaders as they explore the possibilities of 6G.

The program delves into various technical aspects of 6G, including the following:

- *Network architectures*: Research within 6G Flagship explores innovative network architectures capable of handling the exponential growth in data traffic and network demands anticipated with 6G.
- *Advanced radio access technologies*: Their research focuses on developing new and efficient methods for transmitting and receiving signals in the higher frequency bands expected for 6G.
- *Integration with emerging technologies*: Recognizing the convergence of technologies, 6G Flagship investigates how 6G can seamlessly integrate with artificial intelligence (AI), machine learning (ML), and big data analytics to create a more intelligent network ecosystem.
- *Security and privacy solutions*: As the number of connected devices and the volume of data exchange grows, robust security and privacy solutions are crucial. 6G Flagship actively explores methods to safeguard user data and ensure network security in a more interconnected world.

The program fosters collaboration between researchers, universities, and industry leaders around the world. This ensures a diverse pool of expertise contributes to the development of 6G. Additionally, 6G Flagship actively disseminates knowledge through white papers, conferences, and workshops. This global collaboration and open exchange of information are essential for preparing the industry for the future of mobile communication.

Staying at the forefront of 6G research, the 6G Flagship recently concluded the Hexa-X project, which focused on defining a comprehensive vision for 6G. Currently, the program is engaged in Hexa-X II, which aims to develop a technical system view of 6G and further explore how this technology can address societal needs in the 2030s.

By spearheading research and fostering global collaboration, the 6G Flagship program plays a vital role in shaping the future of mobile communication. Their ongoing efforts will significantly influence the technical capabilities, applications, and societal impact of 6G technology in the years to come.

The 6G Flagship program has spearheaded several key initiatives in shaping the vision for 6G. One of the most significant undertakings is the Hexa-X project. Launched in 2021, Hexa-X was a 2.5-year collaborative effort funded by the EU's Horizon 2020 ICT-52 program. It brought together a consortium of 25 key players, including industry leaders, academic institutions, and research centers.

Hexa-X played a pivotal role in the following:

Defining the 6G vision: The project actively contributed to shaping a clear and comprehensive vision for 6G. This vision emphasizes the transformation of wireless networks from simple communication tools to intelligent platforms capable of connecting the physical, digital, and human worlds.

Developing key technology enablers: The consortium focused on identifying and exploring key technology enablers that will make 6G a reality. These enablers encompass advancements in the following:

- *High-frequency radio technologies*: Exploration of new radio access technologies capable of utilizing higher frequency bands for significantly increased data rates in 6G networks.
- *High-resolution localization and sensing*: Research into advanced techniques for precise device localization and environmental sensing, enabling novel applications and services.
- *Network disaggregation and dynamic dependability*: Investigating innovative network architectures that are more flexible, scalable, and reliable to meet the diverse demands of 6G.

Legacy of Hexa-X: The successful completion of the Hexa-X project in 2023 laid a critical foundation for further research and development efforts toward 6G. It established a comprehensive vision, identified key technology enablers, and fostered collaboration within the global research community. These advancements pave the way for the ongoing Hexa-X II project, which delves deeper into the technical system view of 6G and its potential societal applications (6G Flagship, 2024).

15.5.2 6G: The Next Horizon

In their book "6G: The Next Horizon," Tong & Zhu (2021) present a compelling vision for the future of mobile communication networks. This vision emphasizes a paradigm shift—transitioning from simply connecting people and devices to achieving a state of "connected intelligence".

6G as the era of "Intelligence of Everything": Tong & Zhu (2021) argue that 6G will go beyond simple communication, transforming into a distributed neural network facilitating the fusion of physical, cyber, and biological worlds. This will usher in an era where everything is potentially connected, intelligent, and able to sense its surroundings.

Key drivers and capabilities: Tong & Zhu (2021) explore the key drivers and functionalities that will shape 6G. These include the following:

- Immersive human-centric communication with features like high-fidelity audio and video.
- Advanced sensing, localization, and imaging capabilities for richer interaction with the environment.
- Networked artificial intelligence and connected machine learning for intelligent decision-making at the network edge.
- Integration with satellite constellations for global, 3D full-Earth wireless coverage.

Impact on different sectors: Tong & Zhu (2021) discuss how 6G will revolutionize various sectors like the following:

- *Industry 4.0 and beyond*: Enabling intelligent factories and connected industrial processes.
- *Smart cities and life*: Enhancing urban infrastructure with intelligent transportation, energy management, and citizen services.

Enabling technologies: Tong & Zhu (2021) highlight the underlying technologies that will make 6G possible, including the following:

- Advanced materials for efficient high-frequency communication.
- New network architectures for ultra-reliable low-latency communication and massive machine-type communication.
- Artificial intelligence and machine learning for network optimization and automation.

Challenges and considerations: While outlining a compelling vision, Tong & Zhu (2021) acknowledge challenges that need to be addressed:

- *Standardization*: Establishing global standards for 6G technology to ensure interoperability across different networks.

- *Spectrum availability*: Identifying and allocating sufficient radio spectrum to support the high bandwidth demands of 6G.
- *Security and privacy*: Developing robust security protocols to protect sensitive data exchanged within the 6G network.

15.5.3 6G mobile networks

Building on established industrial and technological trends, Beniiche (2024) identified the following potential avenues for 6G development, underscoring the importance of continuity when considering the evolution of next-generation systems.

6G will continue to move to higher frequencies with wider system bandwidth: Reflecting a broader trend in mobile communication, 6G development focuses on leveraging higher frequencies with wider bandwidths. This approach addresses the depletion of available spectrum at lower frequencies and enables a tenfold increase in data rates for the next generation of mobile networks.

Higher frequencies and massive MIMO: With the lower frequency spectrum nearing depletion, 6G will move toward higher frequencies to unlock wider bandwidths. This shift will translate to significant increases in data rates, potentially exceeding 10 times what 5G offers. Massive MIMO, a defining technology of 5G that allows for a dramatic increase in antenna count, will remain crucial in 6G. By leveraging even more antennas, 6G aims to further enhance spectral efficiency, the ability to transmit more data within a given spectrum (Bambara & Allen, 2018).

Cloud-centric approach: The high data rates, low latency, and reduced transmission costs of 6G will pave the way for a cloud-centric approach to mobile communication. This means a substantial portion of the computational and storage tasks currently handled by smartphones will be offloaded to the cloud. This shift will free up processing power on smartphones, allowing them to focus on delivering a richer user experience for applications like virtual reality (VR), augmented reality (AR), and extended reality (XR). Additionally, the cloud-centric approach can facilitate the wider adoption of cloud-based AI services and potentially lead to the development of simpler and more affordable user terminals.

Evolving access techniques: Traditionally, cellular networks have relied on grant-based transmission, where devices require permission before transmitting data. 6G is expected to see a rise in grant-free transmissions, which could offer improved performance. Nonorthogonal multiple access (NOMA), a technology that did not gain significant traction in 5G, might find renewed interest in 6G due to its potential for shorter delays in grant-free scenarios.

mMTC and network transformation: Massive machine-type communication (mMTC), which refers to a large number of devices communicating with minimal human intervention, has been a major focus for future network design. While 5G envisioned significant growth in mMTC applications, the reality has not quite matched expectations. It is possible that mMTC will find greater success using established technologies operating in lower frequency bands, rather than waiting for a breakthrough in 6G.

Toward a computing network: Perhaps the most transformative aspect of 6G could be its evolution from a simple transmission network to a platform that integrates functionalities like computing, AI, machine learning, and big data analytics. This convergence could enable 6G to autonomously detect user intent and provide personalized services based on individual needs and desires.

15.5.4 Implications of 6G on blockchain technology

The emergence of 6G presents a unique opportunity to address current limitations and unlock new possibilities for blockchain technology. 6G offers several technical features that can significantly impact blockchain technology. Here are some key areas of potential influence:

Ultra-reliable low-latency communication: 6G ability to provide near-instantaneous communication with minimal delays can significantly enhance the security of blockchain networks. Faster data exchange translates to quicker verification of transactions and improved real-time monitoring of the network, leading to a more robust defense against cyberattacks.

Massive machine-type communication: 6G capacity to support a vast number of connected devices can contribute to the scalability of blockchain networks. By enabling a more extensive and distributed ledger system with a higher number of nodes, 6G can potentially address the scalability limitations faced by current blockchain implementations (Huawei, 2021).

Empowering decentralized applications (dApps): The low latency and increased capacity of 6G can revolutionize the development and user experience of dApps by the following:

- *Real-time dApps*: 6G low latency can pave the way for the development of real-time dApps that require fast and reliable data exchange. This opens doors for applications in diverse fields like supply chain management, secure voting systems, and real-time financial transactions.
- *Enhanced user experience*: Faster speeds and higher bandwidth offered by 6G can significantly improve the user experience of existing dApps. This can lead to faster loading times, smoother interactions, and wider adoption of blockchain-based technologies.

Synergies with emerging technologies: The convergence of 6G with other emerging technologies can further amplify the potential of blockchain:

- *AI and IoT integration*: 6G seamless integration with AI and IoT devices can create a powerful platform for blockchain applications. Imagine smart contracts automatically triggered by real-time sensor data or AI analysis, leading to a more dynamic and intelligent blockchain ecosystem.
- *Self-sovereign identity (SSI)*: 6G focus on security and privacy can empower SSI solutions. Blockchain can leverage 6G features to provide users with greater control over their digital identities, facilitating secure and private interactions in the online world.

While the potential for synergy between 6G and blockchain technology is promising, significant challenges need to be addressed:

- *Standardization and implementation*: Both 6G and blockchain technology are still evolving. Effective standardization and efficient implementation strategies are crucial for successful integration and widespread adoption.
- *Energy consumption*: The large-scale deployment of 6G and blockchain networks raises concerns about energy consumption. Research efforts are needed to develop energy-efficient protocols and hardware for both technologies (Beniiche, 2024).

The emergence of 6G presents a unique opportunity to address current limitations and unlock new possibilities for blockchain technology. By offering enhanced security, scalability, and lower latency, 6G can empower the development of real-time dApps and foster integration with AI and IoT devices.

15.5.5 A glimpse into the future: 6G and blockchain convergence in the construction industry

The convergence of two emerging technologies—6G and blockchain—has the potential to revolutionize the construction industry to create a more secure, transparent, and efficient construction ecosystem.

Enhanced security and traceability

Ultra-reliable low-latency communication: 6G's near-instantaneous communication allows for real-time verification of data within the blockchain. This can be applied to track material deliveries, verify labor hours, and ensure compliance with building codes, significantly reducing the risk of fraud and errors.

Immutable ledger: Blockchain's tamper-proof nature creates an auditable record of all transactions and activities throughout the project lifecycle. This provides greater transparency for stakeholders, improves accountability, and reduces disputes.

Streamlined supply chain management

Massive machine-type communication: 6G enables seamless communication between a vast network of connected devices like sensors, trackers, and wearables. This data can be integrated with blockchain to track materials in real time, ensuring efficient inventory management and optimized logistics.

Smart contracts: 6G's ultra-reliable low-latency communication (URLLC) facilitates real-time verification of data used by smart contracts. This allows for immediate confirmation of successful deliveries or material inspections, triggering automated payments and expediting workflows with greater efficiency and reduced risk of errors. In addition, 6G potential for seamless sensor integration enables real-time data collection from the construction site. This data can be fed directly into smart contracts, providing greater transparency and traceability regarding the execution of these automated agreements within the construction supply chain.

Improved project management and collaboration

Real-time data sharing: 6G's low latency allows for instant data exchange between project stakeholders like architects, engineers, and contractors. This facilitates real-time project monitoring, enables faster decision-making, and promotes better coordination across teams.

Decentralized data management: 6G's near-instantaneous communication allows for real-time verification of data stored on the blockchain. Construction inspectors equipped with 6G-enabled sensors that can transmit data directly to the blockchain, creating an immutable record of inspections and eliminating the risk of tampering.

Innovative applications for quality assurance

Sensor integration: 6G facilitates seamless communication with a network of sensors embedded in building materials and infrastructure. This real-time sensor data can be integrated with blockchain to create a verifiable record of a structure's health and performance throughout its lifecycle.

Automated inspections: Smart contracts can be designed to trigger automated inspections based on predefined parameters or sensor readings. This ensures timely identification of potential issues and facilitates proactive maintenance, improving construction quality and safety.

The combined potential of 6G and blockchain presents a transformative vision for the construction industry. By enhancing security, traceability, and collaboration, this technological convergence can revolutionize project management, streamline workflows, and ensure greater efficiency and quality throughout the construction lifecycle. Both 6G and blockchain are still in their early stages of development. Integrating these technologies within the construction industry requires buy-in from stakeholders and investments in infrastructure and training. While challenges remain, proactive efforts toward standardization and industry adoption can pave the way for a blockchain-based construction ecosystem.

15.6 Conclusion

This chapter has explored the transformative potential of blockchain technology within the smart industry. We have delved into the core functionalities of blockchain, including its tamper-proof ledger and smart contracts, highlighting their potential to revolutionize how the industry operates. We then explored various applications of blockchain across the construction lifecycle, including:

- Enhancing transparency and collaboration during the design phase.
- Facilitating efficient dispute resolution.
- Improving safety management through integration with the IoT.
- Streamlining construction supply chains for greater efficiency and reduced risk.
- Promoting sustainable procurement practices for a more environmentally conscious industry.
- Empowering BIM for enhanced project delivery through a "powerful duo" and "powerful trio" combination with blockchain and smart contracts.
- Revolutionizing smart asset management through the creation of secure and transparent digital twins.

This chapter has explored the transformative potential of blockchain technology within the construction industry. We have delved into the core functionalities of blockchain, including its tamper-proof ledger and smart contracts, highlighting their potential to revolutionize how the industry operates. We then explored various applications of blockchain across the construction lifecycle.

Furthermore, the chapter introduced the concept of 6G mobile networks and their potential impact on blockchain technology. We highlighted the 6G Flagship program, a pioneering initiative spearheading research and development efforts toward 6G. The program's Hexa-X project played a pivotal role in defining a comprehensive vision for 6G, emphasizing its transformation from simple communication tools to intelligent platforms capable of connecting the physical, digital, and human worlds.

Looking ahead, the convergence of 6G and blockchain holds immense potential for the construction industry, paving the way for the following:

- Unprecedented levels of efficiency and automation. 6G ultra-reliable low-latency communication and massive machine-type communication will enable real-time data exchange and seamless integration with sensors and IoT devices. This can streamline workflows, automate tasks, and optimize project management.
- Enhanced transparency and trust throughout the project lifecycle. Blockchain's immutable ledger and 6G secure communication will ensure the tamper-proof recording of data, from material deliveries and labor hours to inspections and quality control. This fosters greater transparency for stakeholders, improves accountability, and reduces disputes.

- Improved sustainability practices and a reduced environmental footprint. Real-time data from sensors integrated with blockchain can enable better monitoring of resource consumption and waste generation. This data-driven approach can promote sustainable construction practices and minimize environmental impact.
- The creation of a truly data-driven construction industry. 6G high data rates and blockchain's secure data storage will facilitate the collection, analysis, and utilization of vast amounts of data throughout the construction lifecycle. This data can be used to optimize processes, improve decision-making, and drive innovation within the industry.

While both 6G and blockchain are under development, their convergence presents a transformative vision for the construction industry. By overcoming challenges related to standardization, implementation, and energy consumption, this technological marriage can revolutionize project management, streamline workflows, and ensure greater efficiency, transparency, and quality in building the future.

This chapter serves as a springboard for further research and development efforts toward integrating blockchain technology and 6G capabilities into mainstream construction practices. By embracing these transformative technologies, the construction industry can propel itself toward a more secure, transparent, efficient, and sustainable future.

Reference

6G Flagship. (2024). 19 6G Flagship about us. https://www.6gflagship.com/.

Balint, P., Adam, K., Chris, G., Tamas, D., & Mat, C. (2018). London Institution of Civil Engineers Blockchain technology in the construction industry: Digital transformation for high productivity 2018.

Bambara, J., & Allen, P. (2018). *Blockchain: A practical guide to developing business, law, and technology solutions*. McGraw-Hill.

Beniiche, A. (2024). *6G and next-generation internet under blockchain Web3 economy*. CRC Press.

Huawei. (2021). *6G: The Next Horizon 2021*. Shenzen Huawei Technologies Co Ltd.

Kamel, M., Bakhoum, E., & Marzouk, M. (2023). A framework for smart construction contracts using BIM and blockchain. *Scientific Reports*. Available from http://doi.org/10.1038/s41598-023-37353-0.

Tong, W., & Zhu, P. (Eds.), (2021). *6G: The Next Horizonm*. UK: Cambridge University Press. Available from https://doi.org/10.1017/9781108989817.

CHAPTER

Blockchain-based digital twin management architecture for Internet of Medical Things Networks 16

Santosh Gore
Sai Info Solution, Nashik, Maharashtra, India

16.1 Introduction to IoT devices and digital twins

In the previous section, we explored the basic ideas behind digital twins as well as blockchain in addition to their integration in smart cities and wireless sensor networks. In the current section, introducing a novel idea for a way to manage Internet of Things (IoT) devices, the study will discuss the architecture of blockchain-based digital twin management. This method employs strong blockchain security in digital twin technology. The goal is to create a robust and clear idea for managing IoT devices. As IoT devices are a fundamental part of smart cities to collect data along with digital twins, it is important to implement strategies to keep data safe, ensure security, and build trust in smart city systems.

The introduction of the IoT has led to a profound transformation in data acquisition and utilization for businesses, fueling a surge in technological progress by enabling real-time data collection and analysis. Presently, there are more than 17 billion interconnected IoT devices globally in 2024, marking a monumental proliferation (Fig. 16.1). Projections indicate a potential doubling of this figure by 2030, signifying an exponential growth trajectory for IoT device deployment worldwide. This rapid expansion underscores the pervasive influence of IoT technology, emphasizing its pivotal role in shaping the future landscape of data-driven innovation and connectivity across various industries.

A rapid development of the IoT is observed in the modern world of computing. These developments have altered how we collect and interpret data from smart sensors. Digital twin (DT) technology is leading the technological advancement where the creation of virtual clones of physical IoT devices enables monitoring, data analysis, and prediction of these devices' future behavior and performance. The increase in embedded sensors providing smart services needs the development of an innovative IoT prototype capable of seamless horizontal interoperability among applications. Emerging technologies such as digital twins and microservices have gained interest in the IoT ecosystem, primarily solving common concerns like interoperability, real-time data collection, and analysis. The origins of digital twin technology may be traced back to the University of Michigan in 2002, and it has since established itself as a stable and prominent concept (Grieves, 2016). Basically, the DT includes the formation of virtual reproductions of physical IoT devices reflected on the cloud. Fig. 16.2 in the reference depicts the concept of DT as a virtual counterpart of IoT devices, allowing device-as-a-service to be provided. The capacity of digital twin to construct an abstraction layer,

Blockchain and Digital Twin for Smart Hospitals. DOI: https://doi.org/10.1016/B978-0-443-34226-4.00017-4

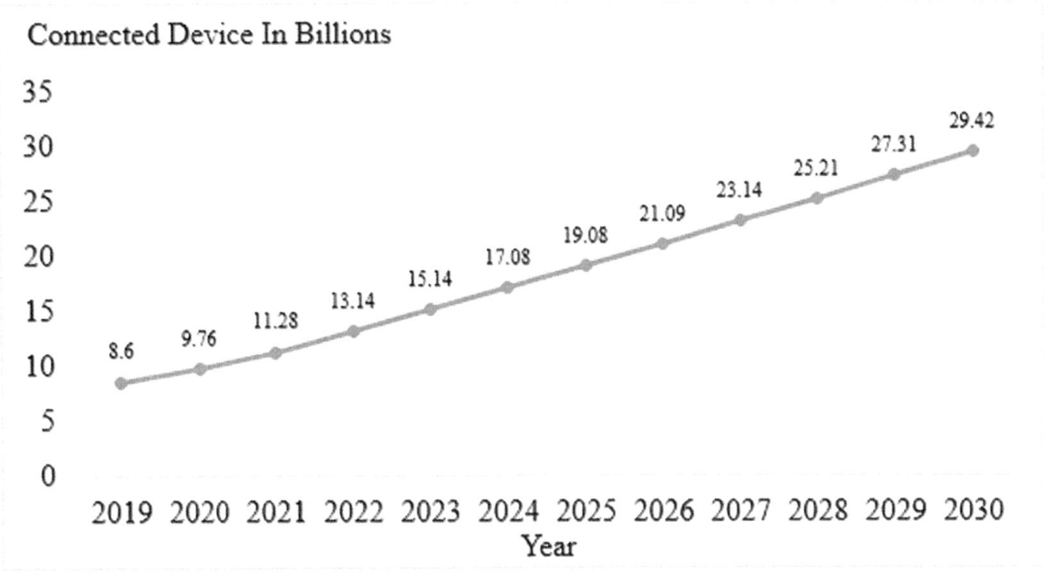

FIGURE 16.1

Global IoT device connectivity (Luchko, 2023).

ensuring continuous communication between IoT applications and devices, is a key feature. The main goal of digital twins is to manage the lifecycle and integrated data linked with the device. Device simulation throughout development, monitoring device attributes and behaviors over time, and incorporating analytics for comprehensive insights are all features of DTs. Moreover, it is observed to be more critical in enhancing the functionality, probability, as well as efficiency of IoT devices. Thus it allows their integration as well as usage in different areas such as smart cities.

The digital twin market refers to the rapidly growing sector centered around the development and utilization of digital twin technology. As the digital twin is a highly accurate virtual representation of a physical asset or process, it provides insights into its functionality and behavior. It allows stakeholders to predict, simulate, and optimize various aspects of an asset or process before investing in physical prototypes or modifications. Combining multiphysics simulations, data analytics, and artificial intelligence, digital twins can effectively showcase the impacts of design alterations, diverse usage scenarios, environmental changes, and other variables in a controlled virtual environment.

Recent research (Infopulse, 2023) indicates an impressive growth trajectory for the digital twin market. The market size was estimated to be USD 3.8 billion in 2019 and is projected to reach a substantial value of USD 35.8 billion by 2025, indicating a compound annual growth rate (CAGR) of 37.8%. This phenomenal growth is primarily attributed to the increasing adoption of cloud and IoT technologies, which play crucial roles in advancing digital twin capabilities and applications.

A survey conducted by Gartner further underscores this trend, revealing that 62% of respondents are either in the process of implementing digital twin technology or are planning to do so in the near future. The high level of interest and adoption emphasizes the significant impact and potential value of digital twins across various industries and smart city applications, driving their integration

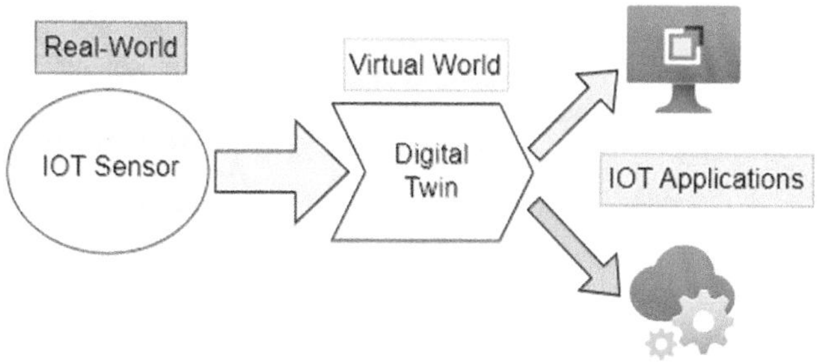

FIGURE 16.2

Concept of digital twin in IoT.

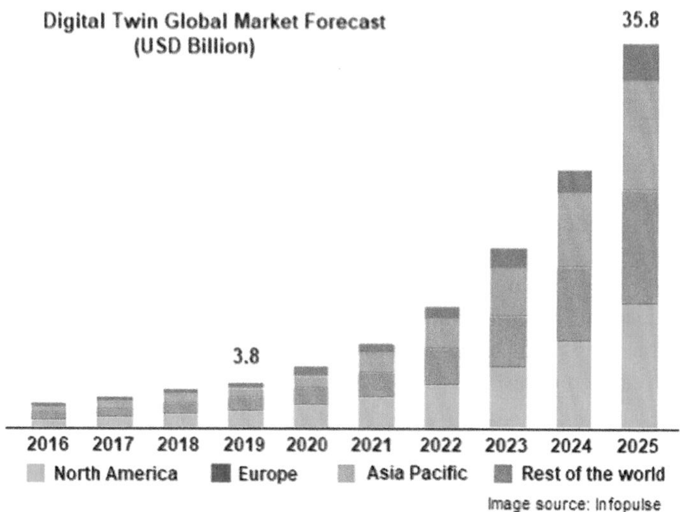

FIGURE 16.3

Digital twin market forecast worldwide by region.

Source: *Infopulse.com. (2023). How different industries exploit the digital twin technology.*

into different strategies for enhanced efficiency, innovation, and predictive capabilities as depicted in Fig. 16.3. Fig. 16.4 shows the emerging IoT-connected devices.

16.2 Integrating digital twins with IoT

The adoption of DT techniques at the network edge is critical in the environment of IoT integration in smart cities. This strategy solves issues caused by fragmented application management systems and disparate protocols used by various tools and services. The implantation of DT management in

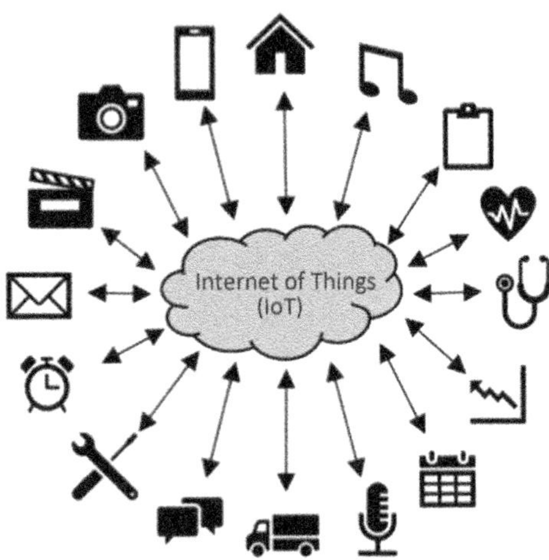

FIGURE 16.4

Internet of Things—connected devices.

IoT devices in smart cities necessitates dealing with issues such as network heterogeneity, various protocols, as well as fragmented application systems. Handling heterogeneity, managing network heterogeneity, and dynamic resource administration are all so critical. The use of DTs at the network edge addresses the variability inherent in isolated application solutions and diverse protocols from various manufacturing tools. This method assists in harmonizing these disparate parts, resulting in seamless interactions and efficient operations. Network heterogeneity is a key barrier to the effective design and deployment of DT-oriented applications. Application-driven digital twin connectivity technology serves to prevent this. It streamlines interaction between devices by allowing DTs to use IP-based protocols instead of specific protocols. This standardization improves the expressive potential of packet content by enhancing data with well-defined norms. The dynamic control of network resources is critical in edge environments. Software-defined networking (SDN), optimizes communication protocols to meet the needs of specific applications. It varies from basic IP protocols to more advanced ones according to packet content, providing data transmission versatility and effectiveness. These issues can be mitigated by employing DT techniques at the network edge as well as utilizing modern networking software allowing smooth communication and faster data transmission.

The continuous transition to Industry 4.0, the fourth technological revolution following the digital revolution (the third), is radically changing industrial production. Through the intelligent integration of equipment and processes, this approach shift emphasizes optimizing as well as automating industrial operations. Concepts such as the IoT, DT, artificial intelligence (AI), machine learning (ML), big data, and cognitive services are integral to Industry 4.0 (Jagatheesaperumal et al., 2022). Decentralized decision-making, another Industry 4.0 paradigm, is made easier by adding AI and ML into DTs to provide cognitive services. These improved DTs, known as cognitive twins (CTs), contribute to better decision-making, more automation, and higher overall productivity (D'Amico et al., 2022). In essence, the combination of IoT devices and digital twins is critical in the Industry 4.0 landscape, providing interconnection, information transparency, and sophisticated decision-making capabilities that are critical for optimizing operations and efficiency.

In the context of smart cities, the convergence of big data analytics (BDA), IoT devices, and blockchain security plays a pivotal role in advancing the implementation of DTs and fostering efficient, secure, and effective governance. The analysis of vast datasets generated by IoT devices within smart cities enables precise governance and enhances data processing efficiency and safety. Through techniques like deep learning (DL) algorithms, specifically convolutional neural networks (CNN) applied within BDA, there is a focus on distributed parallelism strategies. This approach, alongside DTs and multihop transmission technology, constructs an IoT-BDA system based on DL. Analyzing the system's performance aids in enhancing energy efficiency, reducing data transmission delays, and improving data forecasting accuracy (Selmy et al., 2024). Emphasizing the comprehensive utilization of big data, AI, and blockchain techniques is instrumental in enhancing national governance modernization, improving livelihoods, and ensuring data security within smart cities (Sharma et al., 2021). Blockchain's role lies in accelerating digital infrastructure improvement, promoting data resource integration and open sharing, and guaranteeing data security in the development and implementation of DTs in smart city environments.

DTs have evolved as an essential component in the creation of smart cities, boosting urban development while adding value to urban settings. Researchers have conducted significant investigations on the evolution of DTs in smart cities, investigating different designs with patterns of interaction. Alam and Saddik (2017), for example, presented a cloud computing-based cyber twin physical system (C2PS) DTs architectural reference model. This model clarified the fundamental characteristics of C2PS, assisting in recognizing both primary and hybrid computational interaction modalities while offering insights into varied computing connections within smart cities.

The convergence of the IoT, BDA, and DL holds major consequences for smart city DTs. Data acquired from many sources, particularly IoT devices, is increasing as urbanization increases. However, the increased data collecting causes issues due to storage capacity restrictions. A technique merging the distributed CNN parallelism approach using BDA efficiently handles the growing volume as well as the diversity of data within smart cities. This integration builds a DL-based smart city DTs IoT-BDA system. This technology optimizes data processing, allowing for more precise governance, efficient data processing, and the security of data acquired from multiple sources in smart cities. As a result, using DTs to improve urban development, streamline governance, and assure efficient and safe data processing is required, necessitating creative techniques integrating IoT, BDA, and DL strategies.

16.2.1 Smart city applications

The concept of digital twins holds significant promise for various applications within smart cities, capitalizing on the advancements in connectivity through the IoT and AI. The potential applications (Mylonas et al., 2021) and advantages of digital twins within smart cities are evolving, driven by the increasing interconnectivity and data availability facilitated by IoT sensors embedded across urban infrastructures.

- *Enhanced connectivity and data utilization*: With the spread of smart cities, the integration of IoT devices has resulted in more connected communities. This enhanced connectivity leads to increased utilization of digital twins. The data gathered from these IoT sensors embedded in various city services provides valuable insights into utility distribution and usage patterns. This data becomes instrumental in planning and developing existing smart cities, as well as aiding ongoing developments in new smart city projects.

- *Planning and future-proofing*: IoT-enabled sensors and devices offer invaluable inputs for future-proofing cities. They assist in monitoring city services and infrastructures, providing critical data for planning and development. Digital twins have the potential to simulate various scenarios, creating a virtual environment that can be used as a testbed (Mihai et al., 2022). This enables city planners to experiment, analyze changes, and learn from the environment by leveraging the data collected from sensors.
- *Energy optimization*: The utilization of digital twin technology within smart cities holds promise in the domain of energy conservation and optimization (Huang et al., 2022). By analyzing the data collected from sensors across the city, digital twins can provide insights into how utilities are distributed and consumed. This understanding facilitates more efficient energy usage and paves the way for advancements in energy-saving strategies within smart cities.
- *Data analytics and monitoring*: Digital twins offer the capability to collect vast amounts of data from various sources. Analyzing this data enables city planners and administrators to gain insights into city operations, facilitating informed decision-making. These insights aid in monitoring city services, optimizing resource allocation, and enhancing overall operational efficiency.
- *AI and continuous learning*: As the amount of usable data in smart cities increases due to IoT connectivity, the potential for digital twins to leverage advanced AI algorithms and ML grows (Rathore et al., 2021). Digital twins can learn from the environment by analyzing changes in the data collected over time. This continuous learning allows for adaptive and intelligent decision-making, improving the effectiveness of city planning and management.

Digital twins present an array of applications and opportunities within IoT-connected smart cities, offering the potential to revolutionize urban planning, energy management, data analytics, and decision-making processes. As smart cities continue to evolve and become more connected, the scope and viability of digital twins are expected to expand, contributing significantly to the efficiency and sustainability of urban environments.

16.2.2 Benefits of integrating digital twins with IoT

Integrating digital twins with IoT presents a multitude of advantages for businesses, and smart city management, especially in terms of improving monitoring and optimization capabilities (Luchko, 2023). The synergy of predictive maintenance from digital twins and real-time insights obtained through IoT sensors allows companies to optimize maintenance schedules, thus reducing costs and ensuring uninterrupted operations.

16.2.2.1 Monitoring and optimization

Digital twins in conjunction with IoT sensors enable continuous tracking of asset performance metrics like usage patterns and wear and tear. This data enhances asset management and optimizes maintenance schedules, ultimately improving operational efficiency. For instance, service operators achieve significant savings on maintenance costs by implementing IoT and digital twins, leading to reduced unexpected downtimes and smoother operations with substantial cost savings.

16.2.2.2 Risk assessment

Additionally, digital twins facilitate risk assessment by simulating processes virtually, enabling experts to preemptively identify potential risks or failures. This proactive approach allows for the formulation of mitigation strategies, reducing the likelihood of costly errors and saving time. Furthermore, the simulation of the process expedites development by enabling designers to assess multiple design options, identifying the most efficient and cost-effective ones, thus streamlining development processes and cutting down both time and expenses.

16.2.2.3 Resource optimization

Finally, the integration of digital twins and IoT sensors allows for the optimization of resource allocation and utilization. By leveraging real-time data gathered from IoT devices, digital twins can analyze factors such as utilization, energy consumption, and maintenance, identifying inefficiencies and recommending improvements. This insight enables optimizing processes, reducing waste, enhancing resource utilization, and minimizing downtime.

16.2.2.3.1 Blockchain-based digital twins for IoT

Implementing blockchain-based digital twins in smart cities demands meticulous attention to several critical factors. First, establishing a clear vision and defining key performance indicators (KPIs) are paramount to aligning stakeholders and ensuring the initiative's success. With a shared understanding of objectives and measurable outcomes, stakeholders from government, utilities, transportation, and technology sectors can collaboratively work toward enhancing city services and quality of life. Secondly, effective coordination is essential to navigate the complexity of such projects. A robust governance framework is required to prioritize use cases, allocate resources efficiently, and ensure alignment with the city's strategic goals. This framework not only facilitates decision-making but also mitigates conflicts and ensures optimal resource utilization.

Building trust among stakeholders is fundamental for the adoption of blockchain-based digital twins in smart cities. Transparency in data processes, coupled with robust security measures, fosters confidence in the digital twin ecosystem. Establishing standards and best practices for data governance, privacy protection, and cybersecurity promotes trust and facilitates data sharing. Furthermore, ensuring data quality and sufficiency is crucial for the accuracy and reliability of digital twins. Cleansing, standardizing, and continuously updating data, while respecting privacy regulations, ensures that digital twins accurately reflect real-world conditions. Overall, addressing these considerations enables smart cities to leverage blockchain-based digital twins effectively, driving innovation, improving urban planning, and enhancing service delivery for residents and businesses alike.

16.2.2.3.2 Significance of the study

The study holds paramount significance in revolutionizing IoT ecosystems. By enhancing security, ensuring data integrity, and fostering trust through decentralized control and consensus mechanisms, the research addresses critical vulnerabilities in traditional IoT architectures. Moreover, the exploration of use cases across diverse industries not only inspires innovation but also paves the way for practical applications in healthcare, supply chain management, smart cities, and beyond.

Through insights into regulatory compliance, governance frameworks, and future research directions, the study provides a comprehensive roadmap for leveraging blockchain technology to unlock the full potential of IoT deployments, thereby shaping the future of interconnected devices and systems.

16.2.2.3.3 Novelty of the work

The study introduces a pioneering approach by integrating digital twins with blockchain technology to secure IoT devices within smart cities. This innovative architecture ensures the integrity of data transfer, mitigating cyber threats prevalent in interconnected environments. By leveraging AI techniques like DL, the IDS swiftly detects and addresses intrusions, bolstering the security of digital twins and IoT networks. This novel model not only enhances the protection of sensitive data but also advances the resilience of smart city infrastructures.

16.3 Related work

16.3.1 Digital twins within smart cities

Mohammadi and Taylor (Francisco et al., 2020) underline the increasing urbanization coupled with IoT and data analytics as a motivating factor for their research. Mohammadi and Taylor focus on spatiotemporal fluctuations, utilizing digital twins and virtual reality headsets for real-time analytics, allowing predictions and monitoring of fluctuations. Similarly, leveraging IoT advancements to create smart city digital twins provides a framework that aids in urban planning, particularly in energy consumption monitoring and comparison. Emphasizing the importance of Industry 4.0 concepts, Mylonas et al. (2021) present a cloud-based digital twin monitoring system for wind farms. This system, based on technical and business parameters, facilitates the creation of a functional twin for wind farm development. Stadtmann et al. (2023) delve into wind farm energy consumption, proposing a methodology that integrates IoT sensors and data analytics within a digital twin environment to predict maintenance. Alves et al. (2023) focus on the development of a digital twin for a smart irrigation system aimed at improving water usage efficiency in agriculture. The proposed system integrates an IoT platform with a simulation model, where physical components like sensors and actuators are linked with their virtual counterparts. The IoT platform, based on FIWARE, gathers and processes soil, weather, and crop data to calculate daily irrigation prescriptions. This information is then communicated in real-time to a discrete event simulation model in Siemens Plant Simulation software, enabling the evaluation of different irrigation strategies. The study contributes to providing a framework to assess the behavior of both the IoT platform and the irrigation system before field implementation. By simulating irrigation scenarios, the system allows for the comparison of different strategies alongside current farm practices and ensures the efficacy of the proposed IoT-based irrigation system in addition to facilitating informed decision-making regarding irrigation management, ultimately leading to improved water conservation and agricultural productivity.

Table 16.1 highlights several kinds of research in the domain of digital twins within smart cities, explaining various applications with the underlying technologies utilized.

The findings related to digital twins within smart cities highlight many potential applications underscoring the need for further investigation and standardization. Some studies in digital twins for smart cities cover diverse aspects, spanning from broad city-wide digital twins to more specialized applications like traffic management (Wang et al., 2022), livestock management (Neethirajan & Kemp, 2021),

Table 16.1 Digital twin and their applications in smart cities.

Reference	Twin technology	Application area	Techniques
Francisco et al. (2020)	DT	Infrastructure analysis	Simulation, VR
Mylonas et al. (2021)	DT	Sustainable urban governance networks	Spatial cognition algorithms; virtual simulation tools
Yu et al. (2023)	DT	Smart city transformation	City information modeling (CIM); building information modeling (BIM)
Kismul et al. (2023)	DT	Smart city confidentiality	Critical analysis of current literature
Rezaei et al. (2023)	DT	Traffic controlling in smart cities	Digital twin technology; 3D Information modeling
Hemdan et al. (2023)	Blockchain DT	Blockchain-based digital twins for smart cities	Discusses the concept of blockchain digital twin (BDT) models, and need for interoperability frameworks
Glass and Serugendo (2023)	DT	Smart grids	Illustrates the process of developing cyber-physical systems
Motlagh et al. (2024)	DT	Smart spaces	Proposes a vision for adoption of digital twinning
Evangelou et al. (2022)	DT	Smart buildings	Methodology for providing digital twins of buildings
Diakite et al. (2022)	DT	Liveable cities	Development of a demonstration digital twin
Wang, Chen, et al. (2023)	DT	Smart city management	Identifying drivers, challenges, and solutions

and renewable energy (You et al., no date). These studies illustrate the multifaceted utility of digital twins in urban environments and highlight their potential to revolutionize various sectors within a city, including infrastructure, transportation, energy, and agriculture. The merger of digital twins with local infrastructure in Deng et al. (2021), utilizing 3D modeling for smart city development and maintenance, offers promising avenues for enhancing city planning, management, and operational efficiency. However, the need for standardized digital twins tailored for smart cities is imperative (Wang et al., 2022) and requires deeper investigation into data fusion techniques for seamless interaction between physical and virtual data within digital twins.

Generic models that holistically represent the various facets of a smart city would facilitate better interoperability and scalability of digital twins across diverse urban environments. Furthermore, Chen's work on traffic management showcases the integration of digital twins without the need for extensive additional developments, setting benchmarks for compatibility between smart buildings and traffic management systems. Thus the rise of digital twins in manufacturing holds promise for their expanded applications in smart cities. While ongoing research demonstrates their potential, there is a clear need for continued exploration, standardization, and advancement to harness the full capabilities of digital twins for the efficient and intelligent management of smart cities.

16.3.2 Challenges of integrating digital twins with IoT

Integrating digital twin technology with IoT systems in smart cities offers significant benefits but comes with its own set of challenges. Security and privacy concerns regarding the vast amount of IoT data collected in smart city applications are primary issues. The data generated by digital twins includes critical insights and application-specific information that are highly valuable and must be protected from both external and internal threats. A cyber-attack on a digital twin could compromise trade secrets, intellectual property, and sensitive individual data, potentially leading to reputational damage and financial losses.

Privacy is another pivotal challenge when integrating digital twins with IoT. Personal information contained in the data generated by digital twins must adhere to privacy regulations like GDPR and CCPA to prevent data breaches. Without robust privacy measures, smart cities face legal, security, and financial risks. To address these challenges, robust security and privacy policies are essential, encompassing technical safeguards like encryption and firewalls, along with training programs to raise awareness among personnel. Another challenge is the need for specialized expertise. Leveraging digital twins effectively requires a skilled team proficient in software engineering, data science, and automation. Finding the right talent and expertise is crucial for successful implementation. Scalability is also a concern. While digital twins promise operational efficiency, difficulties arise when scaling them to numerous devices. Handling the complexities of integrating diverse data collection, processing methods, and data formats from a vast array of devices becomes challenging. To overcome these issues, common standards and reference frameworks are vital, enabling streamlined data interchange and communication among devices, regardless of underlying technologies.

16.3.3 Integration of the IoT and blockchain in smart cities

The integration of the IoT and blockchain technology in smart cities has substantial implications, significantly altering the landscape of urban infrastructure and services. The IoT has revolutionized conventional processes, gathering vast amounts of data that enable sophisticated insights, leading to the creation of smart applications and services that enhance the quality of life for city dwellers.

By leveraging blockchain technology in the IoT ecosystem (Sharma et al., 2021), participants can ensure the authenticity and security of data, averting potential fraud or data risks. The ability to swiftly trace sources of data leaks through reliable data sharing can significantly reduce the search time, potentially saving data and minimizing economic repercussions on economies.

16.3.3.1 Benefits of blockchain in IoT

The integration of blockchain with the IoT presents numerous benefits and opportunities that can significantly enhance the functionality and reliability of IoT systems within smart cities. However, several research challenges need to be addressed to ensure seamless integration between these technologies. It includes decentralization and scalability along with device identification as well as confirming reliable and trusted authentication and authorization. It ensures the reliability, security, and traceability of data extracted from IoT devices in smart cities while validation by smart contracts strengthens communication security. It also enhances security in deploying and tracking updates to IoT devices, enhancing code deployment reliability and security within IoT systems.

Decentralization and scalability (Veena et al., 2015) are pivotal benefits of leveraging blockchain in IoT devices in smart cities. Transitioning from centralized architectures to peer-to-peer (P2P) distributed systems eliminates single points of failure and reduces bottlenecks, promoting fault tolerance and scalability. This shift mitigates the control applied by a few entities over vast amounts of data in a smart city environment, fostering improved fault tolerance and scalability.

The use of a common blockchain system facilitates robust device identification and data immutability, enhancing trust and security (Babu et al., 2022). Every device's data is uniquely identified and immutable, ensuring reliable and trusted authentication and authorization for smart city IoT applications. Moreover, blockchain's autonomy enables the development of smart autonomous assets, allowing devices to interact without relying on centralized servers, facilitating device-agnostic and decoupled applications.

Blockchain technology ensures the reliability, security, and traceability of IoT data. Information stored on the blockchain remains immutable over time, ensuring data authenticity and accountability. This secure, tamper-proof method of storing IoT data enhances reliability and ensures that data exchanges between devices are secure and verifiable. Furthermore, blockchain's capacity to treat device message exchanges as transactions, validated by smart contracts, strengthens communication security.

Additionally, blockchain accelerates the creation of IoT service ecosystems and data marketplaces within smart city environments by enabling secure, peer-to-peer transactions without intermediaries. This fosters an environment for microservices deployment and safe micropayments, improving IoT interconnection and access to IoT data. Consequently, leveraging blockchain's secure and immutable storage, smart cities can securely deploy and track updates to IoT devices, enhancing code deployment reliability and security within IoT systems.

16.3.3.2 Significance of blockchain in enhancing digital twin management

The integration of emerging technologies like sixth-generation (6G) mobile networks, IoT, and mobile-edge computing (MEC) has contributed significantly to developing sustainable computing networks. However, handling massive privacy-sensitive data generated in sustainable computing networks poses challenges, particularly on resource-limited IoT devices. To address this, a novel blockchain-supported hierarchical digital twin IoT (HDTIoT) framework integrates digital twins into edge networks, employing blockchain for secure real-time computation (Wang, Li, et al., 2023). This framework incorporates data and knowledge-driven learning solutions to enable real-time interaction and optimization between physical and digital realms. Leveraging proximal policy optimization (PPO)–based multiagent reinforcement learning (MARL) algorithms aids in resource allocation, enhancing the efficiency, reliability, security, and learning accuracy of the HDTIoT system.

To facilitate interaction between physical IoT assets and digital services, the rapid expansion of the IoT emphasizes the digitization of industrial processes. Incorporating digital twins into IoT networks enables real-time virtualization of physical entities, enabling efficient control, rapid maintenance, and improved decision-making (Rathore et al., 2021). However, this integration often leads to challenges in managing the substantial data generated within a digital twin-enabled IoT network, encompassing storage, processing, and security concerns.

Addressing these challenges involves the implementation of a blockchain and SDN-integrated framework within IoT networks. This framework establishes decentralized and secure data operations by incorporating packet analyzers and feature extraction modules at the SDN control layer. It utilizes an elliptic curve point technique to construct the blockchain, ensuring the authentication of IoT devices and showcasing superior performance in latency and throughput.

The integration of blockchain with digital twins for building lifecycle data management has garnered significant attention from researchers. This integration, alongside enabling technologies such as AI, ML, IoT, cloud and edge computing, and BDA, reveals the evolving nature of this field and the need for practical implementations to realize their full potential. The amalgamation of these technologies offers promising solutions to implementation challenges and presents opportunities for a unified system tailored for smart city environments.

16.4 Blockchain-based digital twin management system

16.4.1 Key components of the blockchain-based architecture

The architecture of a blockchain-based digital twin management system includes different interconnected layers such as the IoT layer, blockchain layer, and digital twin layer (Fig. 16.5). The IoT layer incorporates physical IoT devices equipped with sensors that collect real-time data for secure transmission and data analytics. Within the digital twin layer, this information is used to create and maintain digital replicas or representations of the physical devices, facilitating real-time monitoring, analysis, and decision-making. The blockchain layer, acting as the backbone, ensures secure, decentralized storage and immutability of the data exchanged between the IoT and digital twin layers, enhancing security and transparency in the entire system.

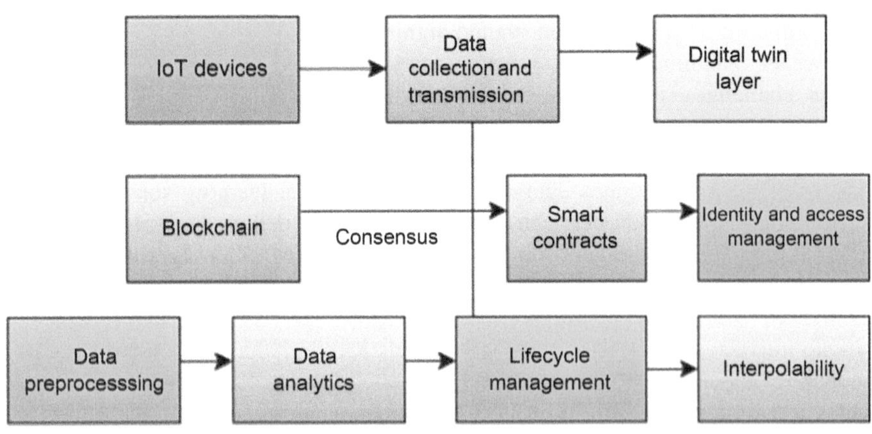

FIGURE 16.5

The architecture of blockchain-based digital twin management system for IoT devices in a smart city.

16.4.2 Layers and components in the architecture

The architecture for IoT devices in smart cities and digital twins is a comprehensive framework structured around several key components.

- *IoT devices layer*: This foundational layer consists of physical IoT devices equipped with sensors and actuators that gather real-time data from the smart city environment. These devices serve as the primary data collection points.
- *Data collection and transmission*: Collected data from IoT devices is securely transmitted to the digital twin layer using encryption methods. This guarantees the integrity and confidentiality of the data throughout its transmission process.
- *Digital twin layer*: Comprising digital replicas known as DTs, this layer mirrors the behavior, characteristics, and real-time state of the physical IoT devices. DTs play a crucial role in simulating and representing their physical counterparts.
- Blockchain: The blockchain layer provides a decentralized and immutable ledger system for securely storing DT data and transactions. It ensures transparency and prevents unauthorized alterations or tampering of data related to IoT devices in smart cities.
- Smart contracts and consensus mechanisms: Embedded within the blockchain, smart contracts automate interactions between DTs and devices. Consensus mechanisms validate and verify data accuracy before recording it onto the blockchain, ensuring data integrity.
- *Identity management and authentication*: Identity management systems authenticate IoT devices accessing their respective DTs. Access controls and authentication mechanisms prevent unauthorized access, ensuring robust security measures.
- *Data processing and analytics*: Data received from IoT devices undergoes processing, analysis, and visualization within the DTs. This step extracts valuable insights that facilitate informed decision-making processes.
- *Lifecycle management*: Tools and protocols manage the complete lifecycle of DTs in the smart city environment. This includes their creation, deployment, monitoring, updates, and retirement, ensuring comprehensive control over DTs.
- *Interoperability and integration*: Interoperability standards facilitate seamless communication between various IoT devices and their corresponding DTs. This ensures compatibility and efficient data exchange among interconnected devices in smart city applications.

This architecture integrates multiple functionalities to ensure secure, efficient, and transparent management of digital twins for IoT devices in smart cities. It prioritizes data integrity, security, and lifecycle control while enabling seamless interactions and interoperability among IoT devices and their digital representations, thereby enhancing the overall functionality and reliability of smart city applications.

16.4.3 Digital twin management

DT management in IoT-based smart cities involves a systematic, comprehensive approach aimed at efficiently handling digital twin lifecycles. It encompasses various phases, stakeholders, and tool support systems to effectively manage assets of different types and scales.

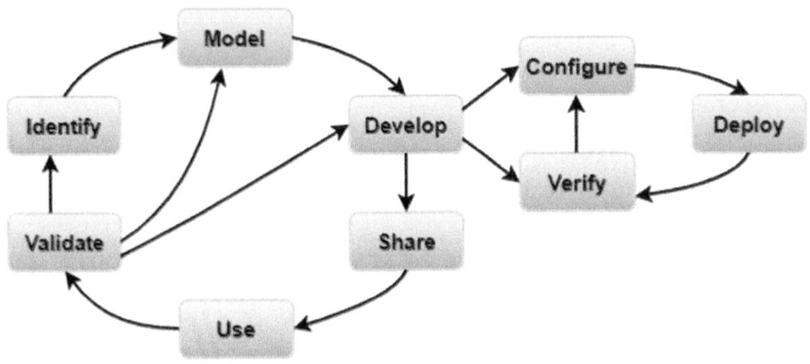

FIGURE 16.6

Digital twin life cycle.

The DT lifecycle is central to this management framework (Fig. 16.6). It comprises several interconnected phases that contribute significantly to the overall outcome of the DT. These phases involve identifying, modeling, creating, sharing, using, and refining a DT. The lifecycle is depicted as a cyclic process, signifying that the DT is continuously refined and evolved over time. A Digital Twin comprises data representing physical system attributes, models describing the system's behavior, and services utilizing the data and models. It can also reference or incorporate other DTs, especially in complex use cases.

Each phase of the DT lifecycle demands specific attention, skills, knowledge, and technological tools.

- *Identify*: This phase involves clearly defining the purpose and necessity for creating a DT, and outlining the objectives it needs to achieve.
- *Model*: In this phase, a comprehensive model representing the data and behavior of the physical system is developed.
- *Develop*: Furthermore, this phase generates a deployable software artifact based on the DT model. It involves collecting, preprocessing, and storing data, applying various models and services, and providing APIs for external access and interaction.
- *Share*: This phase stores the DT in a repository for access, reuse, and potential customization by stakeholders.
- *Use*: In this phase, the DT is implemented within a context that enables its operation, establishing data connections to the physical system and other entities, logging interactions, and collecting feedback.
- *Validate*: This phase regularly updates and reviews the DT's relevance, validity, and synchronization with the physical system. Continuous validation ensures its accuracy and alignment with intended use cases.

A well-structured approach to the entire DT lifecycle streamlines the effort required for its creation and ensures high-quality outcomes. It facilitates sharing, continuous improvement, and maintenance of DT solutions. Additionally, this approach aids in identifying bottlenecks, enhancing data collection processes, and pinpointing areas for human skill development or DT component improvements. Ultimately, a robust DT management concept fosters efficiency, reliability, and resilience in IoT-based smart city applications.

16.4.4 Proposed methodology

The efficiency of the proposed blockchain-based digital twin management framework is tested using data collected from diverse IoT devices within a smart city environment. This assessment primarily focused on reinforcing security as well as privacy within an IoT network, to enhance the performance of computational resources for simulations. The experimental setup integrated TensorFlow and Keras API to construct DL models, while Ganache and Ethereum are used for the creation of private blockchains and the execution of smart contracts. Seamless connectivity between the blockchain networks and the IoT infrastructure was achieved through the utilization of the WEB3 interface. Datasets CICIDS-2017 (D_C) (Kumar et al., 2022) and ToN-IoT (D_T), (Kumar et al., 2021) are renowned network datasets used for expediting training, preprocessing, and feature scaling procedures. These datasets were further segregated into training and testing subsets to ensure model generalization and performance evaluation.

The assessment of model performance was conducted using evaluation metrics like accuracy, precision, detection rate, F1 score, and false alarm rate. An in-depth analysis comparing the performance of the system on both the CICIDS-2017 and ToN-IoT datasets. This comparative evaluation provided valuable insights into the framework's efficacy across diverse network settings and scenarios. The findings derived from the performance analysis underscored the IDS's remarkable ability to detect intrusions, fortify security measures, and safeguard privacy within the expansive IIoT framework. By harnessing the capabilities of blockchain technology and sophisticated DL algorithms, the proposed framework exhibited robustness and efficiency in enhancing security and privacy measures within the IoT network of a smart city. Thus the performance analysis demonstrates the efficacy and reliability of the blockchain-powered digital twin framework, integrated with cutting-edge DL models, in bolstering security and privacy aspects within the dynamic landscape of a smart city's IoT infrastructure.

The proposed method tests a blockchain-based digital twin management framework using IoT data in a smart city, focusing on security and privacy enhancement. DL models and private blockchains are integrated, ensuring seamless connectivity with IoT infrastructure. Evaluation using CICIDS-2017 and ToN-IoT datasets demonstrates the framework's effectiveness in fortifying security measures within smart city IoT networks. The findings validate the framework's reliability in bolstering security and privacy, showcasing its robustness in real-world settings.

16.5 Result and discussion

16.5.1 Evaluation of blockchain within digital twin

The performance evaluation of blockchain technology within the digital twin framework for IoT devices in a smart city context focuses on ensuring robust privacy and security measures. The framework implements registration and authentication processes for IoT nodes to safeguard against potential malicious behavior within the network. Table 16.2 shows various events on different IoT devices. Table 16.3 presents the time analysis for number of transactions and storage size for varying number of transactions.

Table 16.2 Digital twin lifecycle sample events.

IoT device	Event ID	Event type	Description
1	EV 1	Registration	Device registration
2	EV 2	Data update	Sensor data update
3	EV 3	Configuration	Configuration change
1	EV 4	Maintenance	Routine maintenance
2	EV 5	Data update	Sensor data refresh

Table 16.3 Time analysis for number of transactions and storage size for varying number of transactions.

No. of IoT nodes	Registration time in ms	Number of transactions	Storage size in KB
6	7	28	3
12	24	56	6
18	48	84	10
24	52	112	13
30	69	-	-

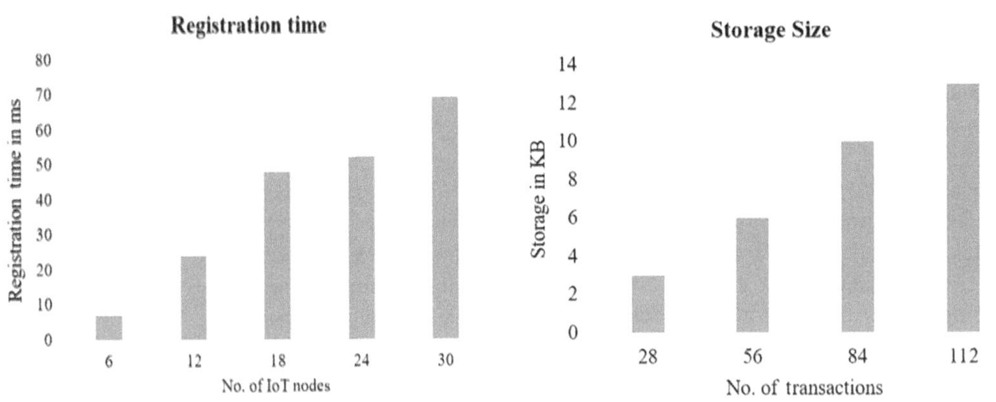

FIGURE 16.7

Analysis of blockchain scheme.

Fig. 16.7 shows blockchain analysis including registration, upload time as well as time analysis for different processes. This figure gives a visual representation of the performance evaluation of the blockchain in the proposed architecture. In Fig. 16.7, the registration process is presented, emphasizing the crucial step of authenticating IoT nodes, a pivotal aspect in maintaining the network's integrity and security.

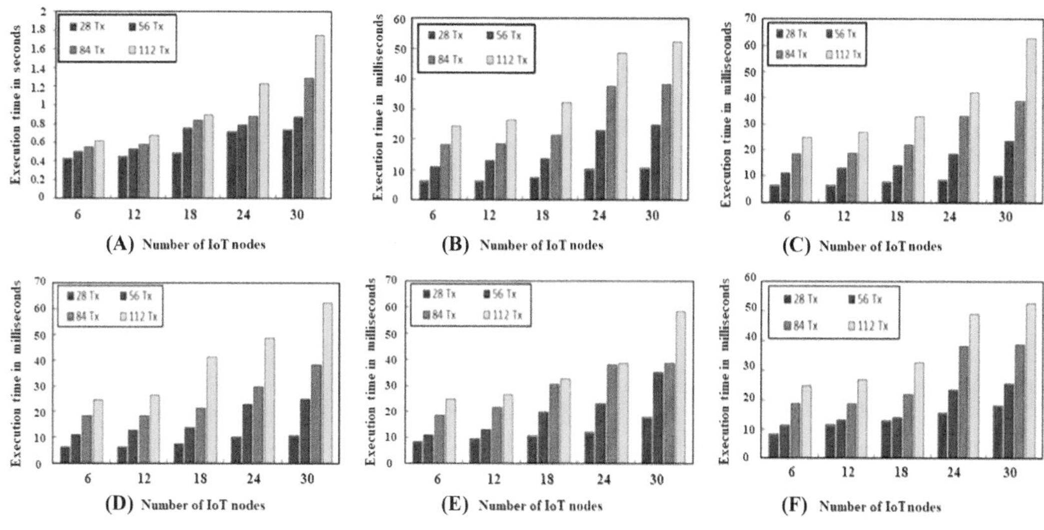

FIGURE 16.8

Blockchain time analysis for varying transactions Tx: (A) upload time in off-chain storage layer; (B) PoA-based consensus; (C) time for block creation; (D) time for block access; (E) time for contract deployment; (F) time for nonrepudiation using digital signature creation.

A significant aspect of the framework involves the actual uploading of transactions into the interplanetary file system (IPFS) storage layer, as shown in Fig. 16.8A. This figure gives an illustration of the data storage mechanism within the framework, showcasing how transactions are stored and managed within the network's decentralized storage layer. The performance analysis further delves into various operational aspects of the blockchain network. Fig. 16.8B, C, and D shows block mining, creation, and access times, respectively. These figures demonstrate that as the number of IoT nodes within the network increases, the execution time similarly increases. It shows potential scalability challenges raised with the network expansion, impacting the overall efficiency of the system. Additionally, Fig. 16.8E and F highlights the time required for digital signature generation and contract deployment. These aspects are crucial as they ensure nonrepudiation across the entire network, emphasizing the importance of timely and secure execution of such operations for maintaining network integrity. The analysis of the size of actual transactions stored within the storage layer, depicted in Fig. 16.8, shows growth in the number of transactions resulting in a corresponding increase in the storage size required. Thus scalable storage solutions are important to accommodate the expanding volume of transactions within the network effectively.

The results obtained for the blockchain-based digital twin framework offer insights into the performance characteristics of the system as well as discuss execution times, storage requirements, and critical operational processes. They also signal potential challenges related to scalability, emphasizing the need for continual optimization and scalability solutions in deploying blockchain technology within digital twins for IoT in smart city infrastructures to ensure robust security and privacy measures.

16.5.2 Evaluation of deep learning

The performance of the DL within the framework includes the outcomes and numerical results derived from the implemented intrusion detection system (IDS). The subsection dedicated to the DL scheme delves into crucial details and metrics that showcase the effectiveness and robustness of the deployed IDS model.

The relationship between accuracy and loss metrics obtained from two distinct datasets depicts a gradual increase in both training and validation accuracy, signifying a lack of variance issues within the trained model. This suggests the model's capability to effectively generalize its learnings to the testing dataset, ensuring consistent performance across different datasets. A closer inspection of the D_T dataset shows the progressive growth in training and validation accuracy and simultaneously, the loss steadily reduces. Similarly, in the case of the D_C dataset, the training and validation accuracy increase, while the loss consistently reduces.

Furthermore, Tables 16.4 and 16.5 present detailed class-wise experimental results for both attack and normal classes, measured in terms of precision, detection rate, and false alarm rate using the D_T and D_C datasets, respectively. These tables highlight that the proposed IDS model has yielded notably higher numerical values for these evaluation metrics, showcasing superior performance in accurately identifying attacks and normal behaviors. Notably, the model has effectively minimized the false alarm rate (FAR) close to 0%, indicating its proficiency in distinguishing between genuine anomalies and false alarms.

In summary, the numerical results obtained from the DL scheme's evaluation underscore the efficacy of the implemented IDS model in effectively detecting intrusions while maintaining high accuracy, precision, and low false alarm rates across various datasets. These findings affirm the reliability and robustness of the deep learning-based IDS within the context of securing IoT devices in a smart city environment.

Table 16.4 Performance of intrusion detection on dataset D_T.

Attacks	PR	Dr	FAR
Backdoor	99.91	99.84	0.00015
DDoS	98.45	95.11	0.00246
Injection	95.33	94.76	0.00198
Ransomware	98.45	99.54	0.00015
Password	98.12	97.57	0.00021

Table 16.5 Performance of intrusion detection on dataset D_C.

Attacks	PR	Dr	FAR
Backdoor	98.29	97.88	0.09581
DDoS	97.75	99.11	0.00076
Bot	98.24	44.71	0.00019
Web attack	95.63	92.18	0.00005
Benign	87.45	96.05	0.09521

16.5.3 Comparative analysis

The comparative analysis assesses the performance of a DL-based IDS in comparison to traditional ML techniques using Nave Bayes, decision tree, and random forest on datasets D_T and D_C. The evaluation includes class-wise detection rates derived from both datasets, as presented in

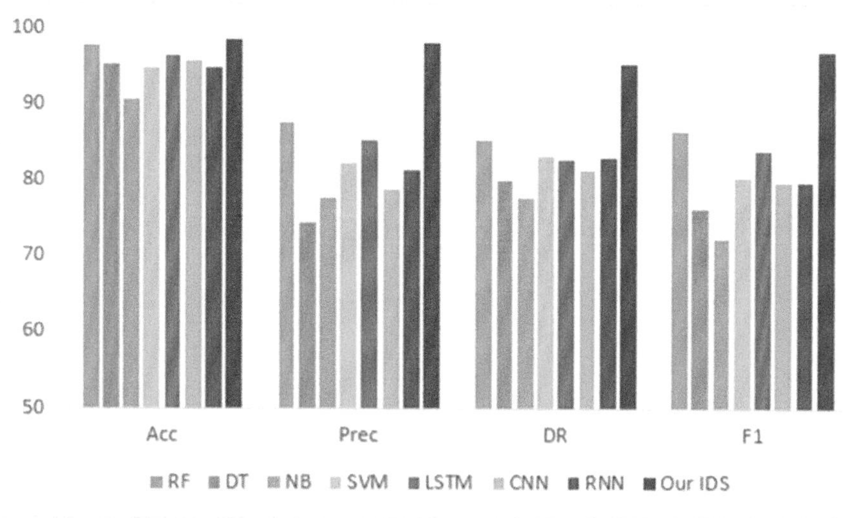

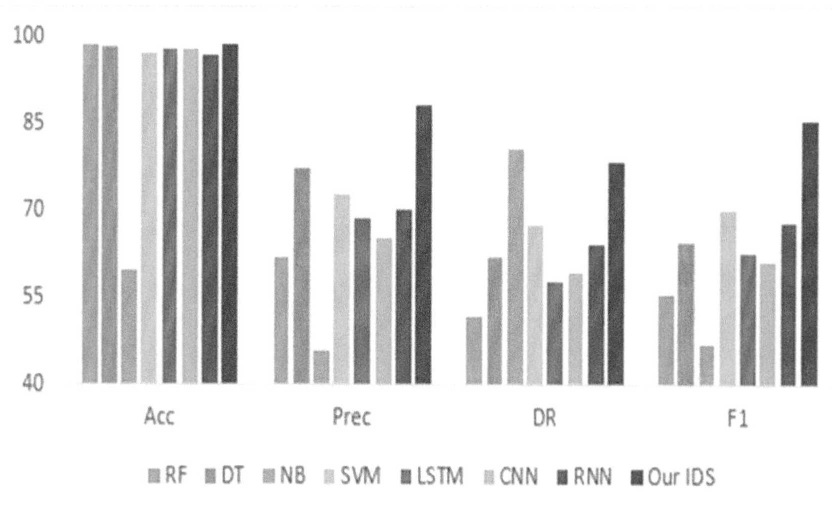

FIGURE 16.9

Comparison with different techniques.

Table 16.5, showing the efficiency of DL-based IDS than other ML techniques for most classes. Higher Dr values signify the IDS' enhanced ability to accurately detect intrusions across various classes, showcasing its efficacy in identifying anomalous behaviors within the datasets. Moreover, an efficient IDS is characterized by high values of accuracy, precision, Dr, and F1 score.

Fig. 16.9 illustrates the obtained values for these crucial parameters. It is observed that the proposed DL-based IDS achieves significantly higher values—98.56%, 98.16%, 95.23%, and 96.84% for accuracy, precision, detection rate, and F1 score for dataset D_T, while, for the D_C dataset, these values are 98.89%, 88.25%, 78.63%, and 85.44% respectively. As compared to the ML techniques (RF, DT, and NB), as well as LSTM, CNN, SVM, and RNN better performance on both datasets is achieved in the proposed deep learning-based IDS system.

This significant performance gap suggests the advantage of the DL model in accurately identifying intrusions and normal behaviors within the datasets. The robust performance of the DL model can simulate and capture complex spatial-temporal representations inherent in the IoT network data. This capability to comprehend intricate data patterns is crucial in effectively distinguishing between normal and anomalous activities within the network. Furthermore, the study underscores the integration of blockchain technology within the network, emphasizing its role in fortifying the IDS against malicious or low-quality parameters. This integration enhances the efficiency and trustworthiness of the IDS, enabling it to outperform traditional ML techniques by ensuring a more robust defense mechanism against potential threats.

Thus the comparative analysis highlights the superior performance of the DL-based IDS, substantiating its efficiency in accurately detecting intrusions within the IoT network in smart cities. The advanced DL and blockchain integration contributes significantly to the secure communication between IoT networks and digital twins with enhanced performance and reliability compared to conventional approaches.

Table 16.6 Performance of different IDS techniques on both datasets (Kumar et al., 2021, 2022).

	Dataset D_T				Dataset D_C			
Model	**Acc**	**Prec**	**Dr**	**F1**	**Acc**	**Prec**	**Dr**	**F1**
RF	97.81	87.55	85.43	86.41	98.62	62.01	51.77	55.62
DT	95.34	74.42	80.05	76.32	98.34	77.4	62.16	64.58
NB	90.69	77.68	77.7	72.43	59.57	45.75	80.65	47
SVM	94.78	82.36	83.21	80.45	97.21	72.89	67.54	70.12
LSTM	96.45	85.23	82.67	83.98	97.89	68.75	57.92	62.84
CNN	95.67	78.92	81.34	79.78	98.01	65.43	59.28	61.04
RNN	94.89	81.47	82.95	79.89	96.78	70.32	64.21	67.84
Our IDS	98.56	98.16	95.23	96.84	98.89	88.25	78.63	85.44

Acc, accuracy; Prec, precision; Dr, detection rate; F1, F1 score.

16.6 Conclusion

In the modern era of digital twins, the security of virtual twins is important to protect physical assets connected to the digital environment. IoT devices connected in smart city environments play an important role in updating digital twins that contain sensitive data. Thus DTs for IoT are more vulnerable to cyberattacks. The study provides the comprehensive structure of DT with the architecture of secure management of IoT devices. It includes a blockchain layer between the IoT layer and the DT layer to protect data transmitted among these layers. Adopting blockchain technology, digital twins are provided with immutable and transparent transaction records, where the proposed architecture ensures data integrity and authenticity. However, decentralized consensus mechanisms in blockchain provide a tamper-resistant system as well as protect the data of digital twins from unauthorized access or deceitful activities. The blockchain not only enhances trust among users but also secures data sharing. It enables traceability, offering a robust and secure digital twin for IoT devices in smart city environments. The study evaluates the blockchain system for security over a number of transactions and offers a deep learning-based IDS to provide secure data transmission from IoT devices to DT. The model is trained on two different datasets to provide robust IDS for real-time attack detection making the framework more secure. The proposed model provides better outcomes as compared to other ML techniques. Thus the study contributes to enabling the security of IoT devices in a smart city environment (Table 16.6).

References

Alam, K. M., & Saddik, A. E. (2017). C2PS: A digital twin architecture reference model for the cloud-based cyber-physical systems. *IEEE Access*, *5*, 2050–2062. Available from https://doi.org/10.1109/ACCESS.2017.2657006, http://ieeexplore.ieee.org/xpl/RecentIssue.jsp?punumber = 6287639.

Alves, R. G., Maia, R. F., & Lima, F. (2023). Development of a digital twin for smart farming: Irrigation management system for water saving. *Journal of Cleaner Production*, *388*, 135920. Available from https://doi.org/10.1016/j.jclepro.2023.135920.

Babu, E. S., Kavati, I., Cheruku, R., Nayak, S. R., & Ghosh, U. (2022). Trust-based permissioned blockchain network for identification and authentication of internet of smart devices: An E-commerce prospective. *Journal of Interconnection Networks*. Available from https://doi.org/10.1142/S0219265922430010, http://www.worldscinet.com/join/join.shtml.

D'Amico, R. D., Erkoyuncu, J. A., Addepalli, S., & Penver, S. (2022). Cognitive digital twin: An approach to improve the maintenance management. *CIRP Journal of Manufacturing Science and Technology*, *38*, 613–630. Available from https://doi.org/10.1016/j.cirpj.2022.06.004, http://www.elsevier.com/wps/find/journaldescription.cws_home/714185/description#description.

Deng, T., Zhang, K., & Shen, Z. J. (2021). A systematic review of a digital twin city: A new pattern of urban governance toward smart cities. *Journal of Management Science and Engineering*, *6*(2), 125–134. Available from https://doi.org/10.1016/j.jmse.2021.03.003, http://www.keaipublishing.com/en/journals/journal-of-management-science-and-engineering/.

Diakite, A.A., Ng, L., Barton, J., Rigby, M., Williams, K., & Barr, S. (2022). ISPRS Ann Photogramm Remote Sens Spat Inf Sci.

Evangelou, T., Gkeli, M., & Potsiou, C. (2022). Building digital twins for smart cities: A case study in Greece. *ISPRS Annals of the Photogrammetry, Remote Sensing and Spatial Information Sciences*, *X-4/W2-2022*(4), 61–68. Available from https://doi.org/10.5194/isprs-annals-x-4-w2-2022-61-2022.

Francisco, A., Mohammadi, N., & Taylor, J. E. (2020). Smart city digital twin-enabled energy management: Toward real-time urban building energy benchmarking. *Journal of Management in Engineering*, *36*(2). Available from https://doi.org/10.1061/(ASCE)ME.1943-5479.0000741, https://ascelibrary.org/journal/jmenea.

Glass, P., & Serugendo, G. D. M. (2023). Coordination model and digital twins for managing energy consumption and production in a smart grid. *Energies*, *16*(22), 7629. Available from https://doi.org/10.3390/en16227629.

Grieves, M. (2016). *Origins of the digital twin concept. NASA, Work Pap.* Florida Institute of Technology.

Hemdan, E. E. D., El-Shafai, W., & Sayed, A. (2023). Integrating digital twins with IoT-based blockchain: Concept, architecture, challenges, and future scope. *Wireless Personal Communications*, *131*(3), 2193–2216. Available from https://doi.org/10.1007/s11277-023-10538-6, https://www.springer.com/journal/11277.

Huang, W., Zhang, Y., & Zeng, W. (2022). Development and application of digital twin technology for integrated regional energy systems in smart cities. *Sustainable Computing: Informatics and Systems*, *36*, 100781. Available from https://doi.org/10.1016/j.suscom.2022.100781.

Infopulse.com. (2023). How different industries exploit the digital twin technology.

Jagatheesaperumal, S. K., Rahouti, M., Ahmad, K., Al-Fuqaha, A., & Guizani, M. (2022). The duo of artificial Intelligence and big data for Industry 4.0: Applications, techniques, challenges, and future research directions. *IEEE Internet of Things Journal*, *9*(15), 12861–12885. Available from https://doi.org/10.1109/jiot.2021.3139827.

Kismul, A., Al-Khateeb, H., & Jahankhani, H. (2023). *A critical review of digital twin confidentiality in a smart city advanced sciences and technologies for security applications* (pp. 437–450). United Kingdom: Springer. Available from https://www.springer.com/series/5540, https://doi.org/10.1007/978-3-031-20160-8_25.

Kumar, R., Kumar, P., Tripathi, R., Gupta, G. P., Gadekallu, T. R., & Srivastava, G. (2021). SP2F: A secured privacy-preserving framework for smart agricultural unmanned aerial vehicles. *Computer Networks*, *187*, 107819. Available from https://doi.org/10.1016/j.comnet.2021.107819.

Kumar, R., Kumar, P., Tripathi, R., Gupta, G. P., & Kumar, N. (2022). P2SF-IoV: A privacy-preservation-based secured framework for internet of vehicles. *IEEE Transactions on Intelligent Transportation Systems*, *23*(11), 22571–22582. Available from https://doi.org/10.1109/TITS.2021.3102581, http://ieeexplore.ieee.org/xpl/RecentIssue.jsp?punumber = 6979.

Luchko, N., tech-stack.com. (2023). The benefits & challenges of integrating digital twins with IoT.

Mihai, S., Yaqoob, M., Hung, D. V., Davis, W., Towakel, P., Raza, M., Karamanoglu, M., Barn, B., Shetve, D., Prasad, R. V., Venkataraman, H., Trestian, R., & Nguyen, H. X. (2022). Digital twins: A survey on enabling technologies, challenges, trends and future prospects. *IEEE Communications Surveys and Tutorials*, *24*(4), 2255–2291. Available from https://doi.org/10.1109/COMST.2022.3208773, http://ieeexplore.ieee.org/xpl/RecentIssue.jsp?punumber = 9739.

Motlagh, N. H., Zaidan, M. A., Lovén, L., Fung, P. L., Hänninen, T., Morabito, R., Nurmi, P., & Tarkoma, S. (2024). Digital twins for smart spaces—beyond IoT analytics. *IEEE Internet of Things Journal*, *11*(1), 573–583. Available from https://doi.org/10.1109/jiot.2023.3287032.

Mylonas, G., Kalogeras, A., Kalogeras, G., Anagnostopoulos, C., Alexakos, C., & Munoz, L. (2021). Digital twins from smart manufacturing to smart cities: A survey. *IEEE Access*, *9*, 143222–143249. Available from https://doi.org/10.1109/access.2021.3120843.

Neethirajan, S., & Kemp, B. (2021). Digital twins in livestock farming. *Animals*, *11*(4). Available from https://doi.org/10.3390/ani11041008, https://www.mdpi.com/2076-2615/11/4/1008/pdf.

Rathore, M. M., Shah, S. A., Shukla, D., Bentafat, E., & Bakiras, S. (2021). The role of AI, machine learning, and big data in digital twinning: A systematic literature review, challenges, and opportunities. *IEEE Access*, *9*, 32030–32052. Available from https://doi.org/10.1109/ACCESS.2021.3060863, http://ieeexplore.ieee.org/xpl/RecentIssue.jsp?punumber = 6287639.

Rezaei, Z., Vahidnia., Aghamohammadi., Azizi, Z., & Behzadi. (2023). Digital twins and 3D information modeling in a smart city for traffic controlling: A review. *Journal of Geography and Cartography*, *6*(1).

Selmy, H. A., Mohamed, H. K., & Medhat, W. (2024). Big data analytics deep learning techniques and applications: A survey. *Information Systems*, *120*, 102318. Available from https://doi.org/10.1016/j.is.2023.102318.

Sharma, A., Podoplelova, E., Shapovalov, G., Tselykh, A., & Tselykh, A. (2021). Sustainable smart cities: Convergence of artificial intelligence and blockchain. *Federation Sustainability (Switzerland)*, *13*(23). Available from https://doi.org/10.3390/su132313076, https://www.mdpi.com/2071-1050/13/23/13076/pdf.

Stadtmann, F., Rasheed, A., Kvamsdal, T., Johannessen, K. A., San, O., Kölle, K., Tande, J. O., Barstad, I., Benhamou, A., Brathaug, T., Christiansen, T., Firle, A.-L., Fjeldly, A., Frøyd, L., Gleim, A., Høiberget, A., Meissner, C., Nygård, G., Olsen, J., . . . Skogås, J. O. (2023). Digital twins in wind energy: Emerging technologies and industry-informed future directions. *IEEE Access*, *11*, 110762–110795. Available from https://doi.org/10.1109/access.2023.3321320.

Veena, P., Panikkar, S., & Nair, S. (2015). Brody, empowering the edge-practical insights on a decentralized internet of things. *IBM Inst Bus Value*, *17*.

Wang, D., Li, B., Song, B., Liu, Y., Muhammad, K., & Zhou, X. (2023). Dual-driven resource management for sustainable computing in the blockchain-supported digital twin IoT. *IEEE Internet of Things Journal*, *10*(8), 6549–6560. Available from https://doi.org/10.1109/JIOT.2022.3162714, http://ieeexplore.ieee.org/servlet/opac?punumber = 6488907.

Wang, H., Chen, X., Jia, F., & Cheng, X. (2023). Digital twin-supported smart city: Status, challenges and future research directions. *Expert Systems with Applications*, *217*, 119531. Available from https://doi.org/10.1016/j.eswa.2023.119531.

Wang, S. H., Tu, C. H., & Juang, J. C. (2022). Automatic traffic modelling for creating digital twins to facilitate autonomous vehicle development. *Connection Science*, *34*(1), 1018–1037. Available from https://doi.org/10.1080/09540091.2021.1997914, http://www.tandfonline.com/toc/ccos20/current.

You, Q. Wang, Sun, Castro, J. Jiang, Digital twins based day-ahead integrated energy system scheduling under load and renewable energy uncertainties.

Yu, P., Lang, H., Galang, J. I., & Xu, Y. (2023). *The role of digital twin in accelerating the digital transformation of smart cities: Case studies in China opportunities and challenges of industrial IoT in 5G and 6G networks* (pp. 155–177). China: IGI Global. Available from https://www.igi-global.com/book/opportunities-challenges-industrial-iot-networks/276938, https://doi.org/10.4018/978-1-7998-9266-3.ch008.

CHAPTER

Blockchain for secure data sharing in zero-trust human digital twin systems

17

Samuel D. Okegbile[1,2], Jun Cai[1], Jiayuan Chen[3] and Changyan Yi[3]

[1]Network Intelligence and Innovation Laboratory (NI2L), Department of Electrical and Computer Engineering, Concordia University, Montreal QC, Canada [2]School of Computing, University of the Fraser Valley, Abbotsford, BC, Canada [3]College of Computer Science and Technology, Nanjing University of Aeronautics and Astronautics, Nanjing, Jiangsu, P.R. China

17.1 Introduction

Human digital twin (HDT) is an innovative and emerging technology poised to revolutionize every human-centric system (Chen, Yi, Du, et al., 2024; Xiang et al., 2023). Its objective is to create and maintain virtual replicas of individuals, enabling optimized decision-making in the physical environment through insights gained in the virtual environment (Okegbile, Cai, Chen, et al., 2023). However, the efficacy of such a system may be compromised by malicious nodes, leading to significant performance degradation (Okegbile, Talabi, et al., 2023). Hence, it becomes imperative to integrate the zero-trust security model into the HDT framework, ensuring that no node or activity is inherently trusted and must undergo verification. Blockchain technology continues to attract considerable attention across various data-sharing applications and systems due to its capacity to ensure security, transparency, and data integrity. Originally proposed as a distributed ledger for the Bitcoin system to tackle the issue of double-spending in cryptocurrency (Nakamoto, 2008), blockchain has since garnered significant interest beyond its initial application. Researchers have increasingly explored its adoption in diverse large-scale systems and applications, including internet-of-things (IoT) (Okegbile, Cai, et al., 2022a) and edge computing (Okegbile, Cai, et al., 2022b) frameworks. By enabling trust among untrusted parties in a decentralized manner, blockchain offers a foundational architecture wherein each node contains a cryptographically secured and tamper-proof record of transactions, established through a consensus process (Mollah et al., 2021; Okegbile et al., 2022a). Consequently, blockchain has emerged as a crucial tool for enhancing security within zero-trust human digital twins (zHDT) systems (Okegbile, Cai, Niyato, et al., 2023) gaining recognition for its ability to ensure anonymity, authentication, trustworthiness, data integrity, and fairness within such zero-trust architectures.

Despite its potential to improve security in zHDT systems, blockchain technology suffers from several limitations, including high latency, low transactions per second rates, and scalability issues. Latency in blockchain-enabled systems can increase significantly with increases in data size, number of users, and consensus nodes, as these factors extend processing times due to the complexity of validation

Blockchain and Digital Twin for Smart Hospitals. DOI: https://doi.org/10.1016/B978-0-443-34226-4.00018-6

processes. Similarly, scalability challenges arise as ledger sizes expand (Yun et al., 2021). This has led to numerous studies investigating the suitability of blockchain in latency-sensitive applications (Lee et al., 2021), such as HDT which has stringent requirements (Chen, Yi, Okegbile, et al., 2024; Okegbile, Cai, Niyato, et al., 2023). Addressing these concerns necessitates a possible modification of existing blockchain architectures to mitigate existing latency, scalability, and throughput issues.

Recent efforts have introduced consensus algorithms like proof-of-stake (PoS) (Vashchuk & Shuwar, 2018), proof of model quality (Okegbile, Cai, Zheng, et al., 2023), and practical Byzantine fault tolerance (PBFT) schemes (Castro & Liskov, 1999) to reduce latency and enhance system performance, diverging from the proof-of-work (PoW) consensus algorithm. Compared to proof-based consensus protocols, BFT-based algorithms deliver deterministic execution results while achieving relatively high performance, rendering them suitable for permissioned blockchains. The BFT-based consensus protocol overcomes the limitations of proof-based consensus protocols by facilitating data exchange among a group of validators called replicas, thus achieving lower transaction latency than the PoW scheme (Fan et al., 2020). However, the frequent message transitions among validators during the consensus process entail communication costs that can hinder scalability in large-scale networks (Fan et al., 2020; Yun et al., 2021), necessitating rigorous performance evaluations. Presently, there remains a limited number of works focusing on the analysis and management of validation latency in BFT-based blockchain systems, given its difficulty (Alaslani et al., 2019).

The sharding technique offers a potential solution to scalability issues in PBFT-based blockchain systems by parallelizing transaction processing, thereby maximizing overall throughput relative to the number of shards (Luu et al., 2016). However, this technique may face challenges such as single shard takeover, when adopted in HDT, as the number of shards increases (Yun et al., 2021). Indeed, the widely discussed trilemma of blockchain systems suggests that any blockchain framework can at most satisfy two of the three features: decentralization, security, and scalability. Consequently, a trade-off often exists among these features, as maximizing one may compromise others. Finding an optimal scalability point without compromising security and decentralization is essential if blockchain must be used in HDT.

This chapter presents a shard-based blockchain-enabled data-sharing (sBeDS) framework for secure data sharing in zHDT. To address scalability, latency, and throughput issues while ensuring decentralization and security, we propose a shard-based reputation-enhanced PBFT consensus scheme with a priority-based block appending process to prevent forking attacks (Yang, Chang, et al., 2022; Ye et al., 2022). The main contributions of this chapter are summarized as follows:

- We introduce a novel blockchain-enabled data-sharing framework, called sBeDS, with parallel offloading and validation processes for zHDT systems, aiming to improve system throughput while reducing latency. To ensure security, we integrate trust-based proof-of-reputation and PBFT consensus techniques.
- We propose a priority-based block appending process using queuing theory with a priority modeling technique to prevent forking attacks within the proposed framework.
- We provide an analysis of relevant metrics and formulate the transaction offloading and computation resource allocation problem as a Markov decision process (MDP) to optimize transaction throughput while reducing both communication and computation latency.
- By employing the branching dueling Q-Network (BDQ) approach, we offer solutions capable of addressing the large dimensions of the action space in the optimization problem.

17.2 Related work

Before delving into the details of the proposed sBeDS framework, we first present relevant literature in three related areas: performance issues in data sharing, performance optimization techniques, and parallel validation methods in blockchain technology. This provides further justification for the proposed solution.

17.2.1 Performance issues in data sharing

To adopt blockchain toward secure data sharing among multiple untrusted nodes in HDT, it is important to understand how such a technology can be optimized for improved performance. Interestingly, enhancing performances in blockchain-enabled data-sharing systems has garnered significant research attention, aiming to reduce latency and maximize throughput. For instance, studies in (Sun et al., 2019a, 2019b) focused on maximizing throughput by examining the relationship between communication and blockchain within a spatiotemporal domain. Similarly, the authors in Liu, Teng, et al. (2019) and Liu, Yu, et al. (2019) maximized transaction throughput to ensure decentralization, low latency, and improved security of the blockchain system. As consensus latency significantly impacts performance, the work in Kim et al. (2022) conducted joint modeling of transmission and consensus latency.

The PBFT consensus protocol was applied in Liu, Teng, et al. (2019) and Liu, Yu, et al. (2019) to showcase its suitability in internet-of-vehicle networks (Liu, Teng, et al., 2019) and industrial IoT systems (Liu, Yu, et al., 2019). Furthermore, the work in Zhang et al. (2022) introduced a BFT protocol with graceful performance degradation, while (Chen et al., 2021) presented a BFT decentralized federated learning method with privacy preservation for autonomous vehicles. Evaluation of BFT fault tolerance under various network settings in terms of throughput and latency was conducted in Alfandi et al. (2020), whereas Gao et al. (2019) aimed to enhance PBFT performance through an Eigen trust-based approach, ensuring the selection of high-quality nodes for consensus group formation. Additionally, the authors in Kim et al. (2020) and Loveless et al. (2021) carried out performance modeling of BFT schemes to minimize consensus latency through multiblock approaches and multicore processors. Notably, none of these works (Loveless et al., 2021; Sun et al., 2019a) considered parallel validation, with only (Liu, Teng, et al., 2019; Liu, Yu, et al., 2019) incorporating latency during validation and message exchange periods in their analyses.

17.2.2 Performance optimization techniques

Recent efforts to enhance system performance in blockchain-enabled data-sharing systems employed optimization techniques, particularly deep reinforcement learning (DRL), due to its ability to optimize resources with low complexity in complex networks. For instance, the work in Liu, Teng, et al. (2019) employed a DRL-based performance optimization framework for the blockchain-enabled Internet of Vehicles, maximizing transaction throughput. Given the unreliable network connection leading to data insecurity and scalability issues, the authors in Jiang et al. (2022) integrated multiaccess edge computing and blockchain technologies into the internet of autonomous vehicles to optimize transaction throughput while reducing latency. This joint optimization problem was later modeled as an MDP using DRL and was solved using the A3C algorithm.

Similarly, the A3C algorithm was adopted in Liu et al. (2021) to solve the DRL-enabled optimization problem, employing a delegated Byzantine fault tolerance consensus mechanism with blockchain nodes deployed on edge servers. Additionally, a novel BDQ approach proposed in Tavakoli et al. (2018) enables the use of discrete-action algorithms in DRL for high-dimensional discrete or continuous action space domains, as adopted in Wei et al. (2020). Moreover, the performance of user-sharing-based caching was improved in Zhang et al. (2020) through a blockchain-incentivized device-to-device and mobile edge computing caching system. Further optimization was achieved in Feng et al. (2020) by maximizing the weighted sum of computation rate and transaction throughput through cooperative offloading decision and resource allocation, formulated as an MDP and addressed using an efficient DRL-based algorithm. Although DRL-based optimization techniques exhibit promises in enhancing the performance of blockchain-enabled data-sharing systems, the adoption of a single validation process in these works limits their performance.

17.2.3 Parallel validation methods

Parallel validation methods can significantly enhance the validation process, thereby improving overall system performance (Halgamuge et al., 2020; Huang et al., 2021). For instance, Deng et al. (2019) adopted a parallel offloading strategy in mobile edge computing to ensure task computation and processing timelines. In blockchain systems, parallel validation was initially introduced using sharding techniques in Yun et al. (2021) while a clustering-based sharded blockchain strategy was presented in Yang, Yang, et al. (2022) for collaborative computing in IoT networks. Security issues in sharding were analyzed in Huang et al. (2021) for blockchain-based fog computing networks. Sharding techniques were also explored in Gao et al. (2022), Yuan et al. (2021), where blockchain validators were clustered into different shard groups, each independently creating and validating blocks through intra-shard consensus processes. Each validated block from each shard was then merged and validated again through a final consensus process before appending such a block to the chain (Yang, Yang, et al., 2022; Yuan et al., 2021; Yun et al., 2021) following the double-layer validation method to guarantee security.

The double-layer validation method, however, may increase overall consensus latency while compromising the throughput, scalability, and decentralization of the system. Hence, this chapter proposes a single-layer validation method by integrating PBFT and trust-based proof-of-reputation consensus mechanisms to ensure security levels similar to conventional PBFT schemes, while improving scalability, decentralization, and throughput. More details on this integration are provided in the subsequent sections of this chapter.

17.3 System model

This section introduces the overall framework of the sBeDS system. We define a shard as each partition (i.e., cluster) within the blockchain system, comprising a group of validators empowered to make distinctive and independent validation decisions.

17.3.1 Network model

The zero-trust HDT framework aims to combine elements from various cybersecurity and identity management principles to enhance security and privacy within HDT. Given that HDT involves collaborations among numerous untrusted users in both physical and virtual environments, verification and authentication become imperative to minimize the attack surface and prevent unauthorized access. Therefore we propose a sBeDS-enabled zero-trust HDT system, wherein users, encompassing both physical and virtual twins, can function as either data owners (DOs) or data requesters (DRs), as illustrated in Fig. 17.1.

The validation process is parallelized to allow for the simultaneous occurrence of $K \geq 1$ validation processes. Each validation process validates only one block at any given time within each shard. We adopt a discrete-time model, where time is discretized into equal time slots $t = 1, \ldots, \infty$. Consequently, arrivals and departures (i.e., completion of validation processes) of blocks occur within the boundaries of these time slots. Departure from the system can only occur within the interval (t^{-}, t), while arrival can only occur within the interval (t, t^{+}).

Similar to the work in Feng et al. (2020), we consider the orthogonal spectrum for the transmission between users $U = \{u_1, u_2, ., u_N\}$ and the group of base stations (BSs), referred to as clients, where users offload transactions to the blockchain layer for validation. Each block is generated immediately after reaching the maximum block capacity limit B. If the block maximum capacity is not reached within any time slot interval t_{int}, all arrived transactions at the client during the interval t_{int} are packaged into a single block, ensuring that each block contains at least one transaction.

After the generation of any block, it is forwarded to an idle shard $k \in \{1, 2, \ldots, K\}$. We assume the system is stable, meaning the block generation rate is lower than the average joint validation rate, ensuring there is always at least one shard available for each generated block. As in the PBFT

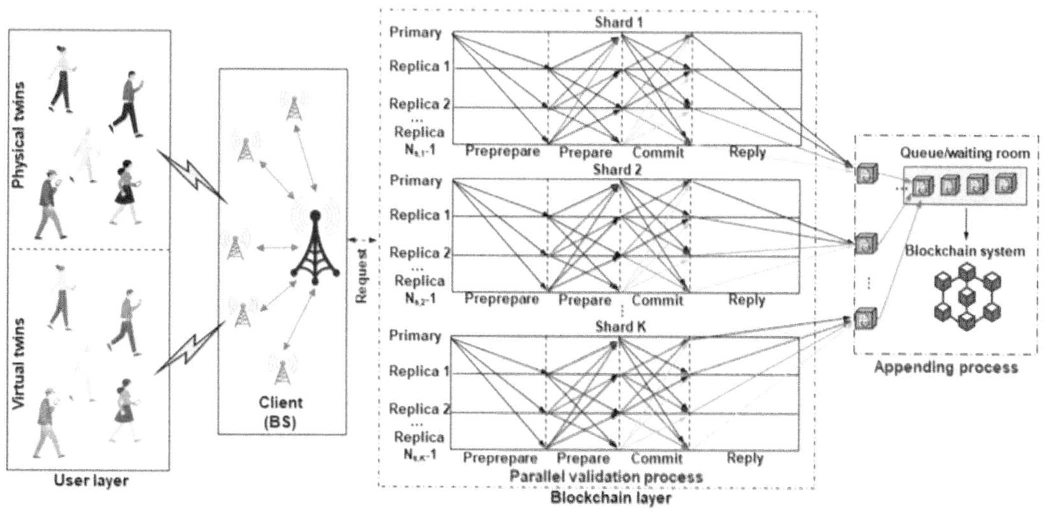

FIGURE 17.1

sBeDS framework.

consensus protocol, each data package goes through multiple stages for validation. However, such a system may be susceptible to forking attacks, particularly when the first arriving block for the appending process is not the first to be generated among the blocks currently under validation. To mitigate this issue, we propose a priority-based block appending process. Shards are categorized into different priority classes based on their reputation scores (derived from the average reputation scores of validators within each shard) and the number of currently active shards. Essentially, any idle shard with the highest reputation score receives the next priority after the currently active shards. Consequently, any newly generated block is forwarded to the idle shard with the highest priority, ensuring that the block from the shard with the highest priority is appended first to the chain. Further details regarding the shard-based validation process will be provided in Section V.

Consider a tagged user u_0 and its associated client, located at the origin 0. The achievable data rate between the user u_0 and the associated client (Okegbile, Maharaj, et al., 2022a, 2022b) can be quantified as

$$R_{u_0,o} = W\log_2\left(1 + \frac{P_{u_0,o}h_{o,o}}{\sigma^2}\right), \tag{17.1}$$

where W is the bandwidth. Given that χ is the average size of each transaction, the average offloading time of any transaction is given as

$$T^{\text{off}}_{u_i,o} = \frac{\chi}{R_{u_i,o}}. \tag{17.2}$$

At any block generation phase, let the first transaction arrive at the client during the slot $t = t_0$ and let the Bth transaction arrive during the slot $t = t_B$. The time to generate a block (TGB) is obtained as

$$\text{TGB} = \min\{t_B - t_0, t_{\text{int}}\}. \tag{17.3}$$

17.3.2 Shard formation

The formation of shards is a crucial aspect of the validation process, often posing significant complexities due to the imperative of maintaining robust security within each shard. Given the pivotal role of high data throughput in enhancing performance within PBFT-based systems, we conceptualize the shard formation process as a coalitional game with Shapley value enhancement and transferable utility. Moreover, to uphold security standards within each shard, we integrate a trust-based reputation framework. This mechanism ensures that only validators operating within the same coverage area (Okegbile & Maharaj, 2021; Okegbile et al., 2020) can collaboratively establish a shard while adhering to the constraints of the PBFT consensus protocol.

A transferable utility-based coalitional game is formulated as a pair (V, v), where $V = \{v_1, v_2, \ldots, v_N\}$ is the set of validators (i.e., players) and $v{:}2^N \rightarrow R$ is a mapping with $v(\phi) = 0$. The mapping v is generally known as the value function, such that for any subset V_k of V, $v(V_k)$ represents the value of the coalition V_k and captures the overall transferable utility that is achievable by validators in V_k without the contribution of validators $V\ V_k$. We know that the set of validators V is the grand coalition with $v(V)$ representing the value of the grand coalition. Define a function $F_d{:}X \times X \rightarrow \mathrm{K}^+ \cup \{0\}$, where $F_d(v_i, v_j)\forall v_i, v_j \in V$ indicates the distance between v_i and v_j

while $F_d(v_i, v_i) = 0$. If $\hat{f}$:$K^+ \cup \{0\} \rightarrow [0, 1)$ is a monotonically nondecreasing dissimilarity function over F_d given that $\hat{f}(0) = 0$ and f:$K^+ \cup \{0\} \rightarrow [0, 1)$ represents the corresponding similarity given that $f(.) = 1 - \hat{f}(.)$, then the shard formation through clustering approach can be seen as either grouping together validators with less dissimilarity as given by $\hat{f}$ or equivalently or validators with more similarity as in f.

At the beginning of every shard formation process, validators $v_i \in V$ with reputation values below a predefined acceptable threshold a_{th} are excluded from the blockchain system. Similarly, newly joined validators are assigned the reputation value of a_{th}. Every eligible validator interacts with other validators with the aim of maximizing its value. Let $v(\{v_i\}) = 0, \forall v_i$ such that v_i do not belong to any shard. In addition, given any shard V_k,

$$v(V_k) = \frac{1}{2} \sum_{v_i, v_j \in V; v_i \neq v_j} f\left(F_d\left(v_i, v_j\right)\right). \tag{17.4}$$

This approach captures the overall value of any shard as the sum of pairwise similarities between the validators since points within a cluster are generally similar to each other. For any two validators $v_i, v_j, \forall F_d\left(v_i, v_j\right) \leq \epsilon$ in the convex game setting where $\epsilon \rightarrow 0$, their Shapley values are almost equal (Garg et al., 2013). From this, the Shapley value-enhanced clustering is realized through the transferable utility-based coalitional game following Algorithm 17.1. Note that Algorithm 17.1 relies on the use of the similarity threshold parameter s_{tr} to assign validators with almost equal Shapley values to the same shard while the validators selected as primary validators (i.e., the center of each shard) are reasonably far apart.

Let $N \geq 3f + 1$ denote the total number of validators during any shard formation process, where f represents the total number of possible faulty or malicious validators. $N_{s,k} \leq N, (\forall k \in \{1, 2, ., K\}$ and $N \geq 3f + 1)$ captures the number of validators in shard k. Increasing $N_{s,k}$ enhances security, as a higher number of possibly malicious validators within shard $k\left(f_k \geq \frac{N_{s,k} - 1}{3}\right)$ would be needed to compromise it. However, reducing $N_{s,k}$ increases the total number of shards, improving decentralization and scalability at the expense of security. Communication overhead and latency within each

Algorithm 17.1 Shapley value-enhanced shard formation process.

Input: Set of validators $V = \{v_1, v_2, \ldots, v_N\}$; similarity threshold parameter $s_{tr} \in (0, 1]$
Output: Set of shards
For i to n do
Compute the Shapley value of each validator using$\phi_i = \frac{1}{2}\sum_{v_j \in V; i \neq j} f\left(F_d\left(v_i, v_j\right)\right)$.
End For
Initialize $Q = V; K = \{\}$
While $Q \neq \{\}$
$p = \arg\max_{i, v_i \in Q} \phi_i$
$K = K \cup \{v_p\}$
$P_p = \{v_i \in Q: f\left(F_d\left(v_p, v_j\right)\right) \geq s_{tr}\}$
$Q = Q\ P_p$
Apply k-means algorithm using K as the shard centers (primary validators) subject to PBFT constraints.

shard also increase with $N_{s,k}$ due to a larger number of messages needed for consensus, with time consumption increasing exponentially. It becomes immediately clear that if we minimize the number of possible faulty or malicious validators f_k within each shard k, we can reduce $N_{s,k}$, such that the security level remains acceptable, while the decentralization and scalability levels increase. Thus given N, it is desirable to

$$\min_{v_i \in V} f < \frac{N-1}{3}, \tag{17.5}$$

$$\text{s.t.} f_k < \frac{N_{s,k}-1}{3}, \forall k \in \{1,2,.,K\}, \tag{17.5a}$$

$$\sum_k N_{s,k} \leq N, \tag{17.5b}$$

$$\sum_k f_k \leq f. \tag{17.5c}$$

The constraints in (17.5a)–(17.5c) ensure that honest consensus is always guaranteed for each shard by enforcing a higher value of a_{th}.

17.3.3 PBFT consensus scheme

The PBFT consensus process typically comprises five phases, as depicted in Fig. 17.1: REQUEST, PRE-PREPARE, PREPARE, COMMIT, and REPLY. During the REQUEST phase, the client submits any newly generated block to a randomly selected primary validator for validation. Subsequently, the selected primary validator verifies the message authentication code (MAC) of each transaction within the received data package during the PRE-PREPARE phase. Upon successful verification, the primary broadcasts the package to $N_{s,k} - 1$ replicas for further validation.

In the PREPARE phase, each replica authenticates the received pre-prepare message and exchanges MACs with all other replicas within the corresponding shard, ensuring consistency in the received package from the primary. The validators then transition to the COMMIT phase, where the data package undergoes validation. Following validation, each validator communicates its validation outcome to the appending stage during the REPLY phase. Here, a block from each shard is appended to the chain if consensus is achieved among validators within the shard, subject to the intershard priority class. Typically, a package progresses from one phase to the next in the PBFT scheme if two-thirds of the responses from the participating nodes agree (Yun et al., 2021).

17.3.4 Reputation model

We adopt a trust-based reputation model where each validator $v_i^k \in V_k$ generates a reputation opinion or value about each validating pair $v_j^k \in V_k, j \neq i$ within the same shard k after every validation process. If the received validation decision is consistent with the majority of the received decision, the validator v_i^k updates its direct consistent value $\text{con}_{v_i^k, v_j^k}$ with validator v_j^k, otherwise, it updates its direct inconsistent reputation value, $\text{incon}_{v_i^k, v_j^k}$. These values are continually aggregated and stored in the blockchain system and are used during the replica selection process. The reputation value of each validator is calculated using both direct and indirect trust values discussed in Section IV.

Generally, the direct trust value of any validator v_i^k for another validator v_j^k is defined as trust values obtained through previous direct transactions between the pair v_i^k and v_j^k, while indirect trust values of validator v_i^k for any validator v_l^k is based on the recommendation of another validator (for instance v_j^k) based on the previous transactions between v_j^k and v_l^k.

Note that the reputation score of each validator is obtained through the accumulation of its previous transactions. Hence, the validator with a higher reputation score has a higher behavior consistency and thus higher trustworthiness (Feng et al., 2020; Gao et al., 2019; Ye et al., 2022). With this, we know that f_k depends on the reputations of selected validators within any shard k. It is worth mentioning that these reputation opinions are not only based on the actual intentions of the participating validators but are also influenced by link quality. As a result, a clustering-based shard formation technique is adopted, such that the distance between nodes within the same shard is limited, thus reducing the effect of bad link quality. To prevent misrepresentation of trust values (e.g., v_i^k generating a wrong recommendation of v_j^k to mislead other validators), we integrate recommendation reliability into the sBeDS framework to ensure validators with inconsistent recommendations are always detected and penalized.

17.3.5 Association rule model

We model the transaction-block, block-shard, and validator-shard association rules for more clarification and details. We adopt a tuple $G(S, B_l, V, K)$ to describe the presented shard-based blockchain-enabled data-sharing framework, where S is the set of transactions and B_l is the set of blocks. We can use the weight matrix $SB = [sb_{ij}]$ to represent the association relations between transactions and blocks, where $sb_{ij} = 1$ indicates that a transaction s_i is packaged into a block b_j and $sb_{ij} = 0$ otherwise. Thus a transaction can only be packaged into only one block, such that $\sum_j sb_{ij} = 1$. The transaction-block association matrix is generally of the form

$$\begin{bmatrix} sb_{11} & sb_{12} & \dots & sb_{1B} \\ sb_{21} & sb_{22} & \dots & sb_{2B} \\ \vdots & \vdots & \dots & \vdots \\ sb_{S1} & sb_{S2} & \cdots & sb_{SB} \end{bmatrix}. \tag{17.6}$$

Similarly, a block b_i can only be validated in a single shard k_j, such that the weight matrix $BK = [bk_{ij}]$, with $\sum_j kb_{ij} = 1$, while a validator v_i can only belong to one shard k_j at any observation time, with the weight matrix $VK = [vk_{ij}]$ and $\sum_j vk_{ij} = 1$. Thus the block-shard and validator-shard association matrices follow the same form as in Okegbile et al. (2022a).

17.4 Reputation-enabled PBFT consensus scheme

Next, we delve into the details of the adopted reputation-enabled PBFT consensus algorithm, with a specific focus on analyzing both direct and indirect trust values. These insights will be seamlessly integrated into the examination of critical performance metrics outlined in Section V.

17.4.1 Integrated trust-based reputation and PBFT scheme

Given N and $v_i \in V$, the number of validators in each shard $N_{s,k}$ satisfies the PBFT constraints

$$N_{s,k} \geq 3f_k + 1, \forall \sum_K N_{s,k} \leq N, k \in \{1, \ldots, K\}. \tag{17.7}$$

As mentioned in Section III, we integrate a trust-based reputation scheme with the PBFT-based validation process to minimize the number of malicious validators. Given that $d_{\text{th}} > a_{\text{th}}$ is the predefined reputation threshold, each validator v_i^k with reputation values $D^{\text{trust}}_{B,v_i^k} < d_{\text{th}}$, as evaluated by the blockchain system, is tagged as a node with a high probability of failure. The blockchain system continuously compares the reporting trust values of each node and removes nodes with inconsistent reports. The updated aggregated trust values of validators D^{trust}_{B,v_i} are stored in the blockchain to facilitate the removal of validators with low reputation values. With this, the blockchain system can estimate the reliability of received indirect trust values (i.e., recommendations) from each node and penalize nodes with malicious recommendations.

During each stage of the PBFT, each tagged validator $v_j^k \in V_k$ develops a direct trust value for every other validator $v_i^k \in V_k (\forall j \neq i, V_k \in V)$ within the same shard k. These trust values are forwarded to the trust aggregation server located in the blockchain system at the end of each observation phase via dedicated error-free communication links. Thus the blockchain system maintains a continuously updated and aggregated indirect trust value for each validator $v_i \in V$ based on the direct trust values received from other validating nodes. To capture the possible influence of bad link quality, the PBFT constraints in Nakamoto (2008) should be achieved as a function of the reputation value and the achievable data rate of each validator within the coverage region of the selected primary. Hence, we can allow the transmission data rate R_{0,v_i^k} between the center of any shard k and each validator $v_i^k \in V_k, \forall p \neq i$ to depend on the overall reputation value $D^{\text{trust}}_{v_p,v_i}$ of each validator $v_i^k \in V_k$. With this, any validator v_i^k at time t is selected to join a shard k based on Algorithm 1 if $R_{0,v_i^k}(t) \geq R_{d_{\text{th}}}$, where $R_{d_{\text{th}}}$ is the data rate threshold obtained from d_{th}.

Between any two nodes $\mathbf{v}_i^k$ and $\mathbf{v}_j^k$, let $D^{\text{trust}}_{v_i^k,v_j^k} = [0, 1]$ denote the trust value of the node $\mathbf{v}_j^k$ from node $\mathbf{v}_i^k$. The data transmission rate of node $\mathbf{v}_j^k$ received at the node $\mathbf{v}_i^k$ can be obtained as

$$R_{v_i^k,v_j^k}(t) = W D^{\text{trust}}_{v_i^k,v_j^k}(t) \log_2\left(1 + \frac{P_{v_i^k,v_j^k} h_{v_i^k,v_j^k}}{\sigma^2 + \sum_{v_l^k \in V_k \setminus v_j^k} P_{v_l^k,v_i^k} h_{v_l^k,v_i^k}}\right). \tag{17.8}$$

From Okegbile, Talabi, et al. (2023), the transmission time of any block of size S^B between any two validators $\mathbf{v}_i^k, \mathbf{v}_j^k \in \mathbf{V}_k$ is thus given as

$$\varphi_{v_i^k,v_j^k} = \frac{S^B}{R_{v_i^k,v_j^k}}, \forall R_{v_i^k,v_j^k} \neq R_{v_j^k,v_i^k}. \tag{17.9}$$

Next, we present the analysis for direct and indirect trusts between any two nodes, which helps to obtain the analysis of $D^{\text{trust}}_{v_i^k,v_j^k}$.

17.4.2 Direct trust

The direct trust between any two validators v_i^k and v_j^k is obtained following the subjective logic framework, described as a tuple $\omega_{v_i^k,v_j^k} = \left\{b_{v_i^k,v_j^k}, d_{v_i^k,v_j^k}, \nu_{v_i^k,v_j^k}\right\}$, where $b_{v_i^k,v_j^k}$ and $d_{v_i^k,v_j^k}$ are the belief and disbelief, respectively, of node v_i^k for node v_j^k, while $v_{v_i^k,v_j^k}$ is the degree of uncertainty in the belief system. These parameters satisfy the constraints

$$b_{v_i^k,v_j^k}, d_{v_i^k,v_j^k}, v_{v_i^k,v_j^k} \in [0, 1]$$

$$b_{v_i^k,v_j^k} + d_{v_i^k,v_j^k} + v_{v_i^k,v_j^k} = 1. \tag{17.10}$$

Hence, the reliability level of a validator v_j^k from any validator v_i^k can be obtained as

$$RD_{v_i^k,v_j^k} = b_{v_i^k,v_j^k} + \varepsilon v_{v_i^k,v_j^k}, \tag{17.11}$$

where $0 \leq \varepsilon \leq 1$ captures the influence of the trust uncertainty. We know that

$$b_{v_i^k,v_j^k} = \frac{\mathrm{con}_{v_i^k,v_j^k}\left(1 - v_{v_i^k,v_j^k}\right)}{\mathrm{con}_{v_i^k,v_j^k} + \mathrm{incon}_{v_i^k,v_j^k}},$$

$$d_{v_i^k,v_j^k} = \frac{\mathrm{incon}_{v_i^k,v_j^k}\left(1 - v_{v_i^k,v_j^k}\right)}{\mathrm{con}_{v_i^k,v_j^k} + \mathrm{incon}_{v_i^k,v_j^k}}, \tag{17.12}$$

$$v_{v_i^k,v_j^k} = 1 - Q_{v_i^k,v_j^k}.$$

Note that $\mathrm{con}_{v_i^k,v_j^k}$ and $\mathrm{incon}_{v_i^k,v_j^k}$ represent the overall historical number of consistent and inconsistent responses received from any v_j^k by any v_i^k, while $Q_{v_i^k,v_j^k}$ captures the quality of the validation method. Since the parameters $\mathrm{con}_{v_i^k,v_j^k}$ and $\mathrm{incon}_{v_i^k,v_j^k}$ are not only a result of malicious intentions or faulty nodes but are also influenced by unreliable communication links, the transmission error can contribute to the trust values of each node. With this,

$$\mathrm{con}_{v_i^k,v_j^k} = \mathrm{con}_{v_j^k} + p_{\mathrm{tras}}\left(\mathrm{con}_{v_j^k} + \mathrm{incon}_{v_j^k}\right),$$

$$\mathrm{incon}_{v_i^k,v_j^k} = \mathrm{incon}_{v_j^k} - p_{\mathrm{tras}}\left(con_{v_j^k} + \mathrm{incon}_{v_j^k}\right), \tag{17.13}$$

where $\mathrm{con}_{v_j^k}$ and $\mathrm{incon}_{v_j^k}$ represent the number of consistent and inconsistent validation decisions, respectively made by the validator v_j^k. The transmission error rate p_{tras} is given as

$$p_{\mathrm{tras}} = 1 - \frac{\sum_i^n \omega(i) X \omega(i)}{\sum_i^n \omega(i)}, \tag{17.14}$$

where $\omega(i)$ is the weight of the historical link-state, with $\aleph = (\omega(1), \omega(2), \ldots, \omega(n))$ representing the historical link-state record and $\omega(i) = \frac{2i}{n(n+1)}$. The average aggregated direct trust $D^{\mathrm{dir}}_{v_i^k,v_j^k}$ is thus obtained from $RD_{v_i^k,v_j^k}$ as

$$D^{dir}_{v_i^k,v_j^k} = \frac{\sum_n RD_{v_i^k,v_j^k}(n)}{n}. \tag{17.15}$$

17.4.3 Indirect trust

In the context of indirect trust values, a primary node can access the indirect trust values of other validators from the blockchain system while selecting replicas within its shard. Likewise, the blockchain system can assess the reputations of certain nodes through indirect trust metrics. As each validator forwards the trust values of their communication partners to the blockchain system after each observation period, the aggregated indirect trust value of every validator remains consistently accessible to enhance validation decisions at every observation interval. To estimate the indirect trust value, suppose $D^{\text{dir}}_{v_i^k,v_l^k}$ and $D^{\text{dir}}_{v_j^k,v_l^k}$ are, respectively, the average aggregated direct trust values of nodes v_i^k and v_j^k about node v_l^k. Then, the collective trust values of nodes v_i^k and v_j^k about node v_l^k is given as

$$D_{v_l^k}^{v_i^k,v_j^k} = D^{\text{dir}}_{v_i^k,v_l^k} \oplus D^{\text{dir}}_{v_j^k,v_l^k} = \left(b_{v_l^k}^{v_i^k,v_j^k}, d_{v_l^k}^{v_i^k,v_j^k}, v_{v_l^k}^{v_i^k,v_j^k}\right), \tag{17.16}$$

where

$$\begin{cases} b_{v_l^k}^{v_i^k,v_j^k} = \left(b_{v_i^k,v_l^k} v_{v_j^k,v_l^k} + b_{v_j^k,v_l^k} v_{v_i^k,v_l^k}\right)/q \\ d_{v_l^k}^{v_i^k,v_j^k} = \left(d_{v_i^k,v_l^k} v_{v_j^k,v_l^k} + d_{v_j^k,v_l^k} v_{v_i^k,v_l^k}\right)/q \\ v_{v_l}^{v_i,v_j} = \left(v_{v_j^k,v_l^k} v_{v_i^k,v_l^k}\right)/q \end{cases} \tag{17.17}$$

and

$$q = v_{v_j^k,v_l^k} + v_{v_i^k,v_l^k} - v_{v_j^k,v_l^k} v_{v_i^k,v_l^k}, \forall q \neq 0. \tag{17.18}$$

Similarly, given that $D^{\text{dir}}_{v_i^k,v_j^k}$ and $D^{\text{dir}}_{v_j^k,v_l^k}$ represent the direct trust values of validator v_i^k for validator v_j^k and validator v_j^k for validator v_l^k, respectively. We can obtain the indirect trust value of validator v_i^k for validator v_l^k as

$$D_{v_l^k}^{v_i^k,v_j^k} = D^{\text{dir}}_{v_i^k,v_j^k} \otimes D^{\text{dir}}_{v_j^k,v_l^k} = \left(b_{v_l^k}^{v_i^k,v_j^k}, d_{v_l^k}^{v_i^k,v_j^k}, v_{v_l^k}^{v_i^k,v_j^k}\right), \tag{17.19}$$

where

$$\begin{cases} b_{v_l^k}^{v_i^k,v_j^k} = b_{v_i^k,v_j^k} b_{v_j^k,v_l^k} \\ d_{v_l^k}^{v_i^k,v_j^k} = b_{v_i^k,v_j^k} d_{v_j^k,v_l^k} \\ v_{v_l^k}^{v_i^k,v_j^k} = d_{v_i^k,v_j^k} + v_{v_i^k,v_j^k} + b_{v_i^k,v_j^k} v_{v_j^k,v_l^k}. \end{cases} \tag{17.20}$$

The indirect trust value $D^{\text{ind}}_{v_i^k,v_l^k}$ is obtained as in Castro and Liskov (1999). To investigate the reliability of recommendations in Yang, Chang, et al. (2022), let $D^{\text{ave}}_{v_l^k}$ represent the average value of all received recommendations for v_l^k. Then we can obtain the difference between $D_{v_l^k}^{v_i^k,v_j^k}$ and $D^{\text{ave}}_{v_l^k}$. The greater the difference, the lower the reliability of the recommendation. Therefore the recommendation reliability is given as

$$\text{Rel}D_{v_l^k}^{v_i^k,v_j^k} = 1 - \left|D_{v_l^k}^{v_i^k,v_j^k} - D^{\text{ave}}_{v_l^k}\right|. \tag{17.21}$$

Finally, the reputation is obtained as a function of both direct and indirect trusts, such that

$$D^{\text{trust}}_{v_i^k, v_j^k} = \omega_{\text{dir}} D^{\text{dir}}_{v_i^k, v_j^k} + \omega_{\text{ind}} D^{\text{ind}}_{v_i^k, v_j^k}, \tag{17.22}$$

where ω_{dir} and ω_{ind} are the weights of direct and indirect trust values respectively, given that $\omega_{\text{dir}} + \omega_{\text{ind}} = 1$. As an abuse of notation, let $D^{\text{trust}}_{v_i}$ depict the average aggregate reputation value of each validator $v_i \in V$. To maintain the security level, each validator with a reputation value below $D^{\text{trust}}_{v_i} < a_{\text{th}}$ is removed from the system, such that f is defined as

$$f = \sum_{i=1}^{N} 1_{\left\{a_{\text{th}} \le D^{\text{trust}}_{v_i} < d_{\text{th}}\right\}}, \tag{17.23}$$

where $1_{[.]}$ is an indicator function that is equal to 1 if [.] is true and 0 otherwise. From this, K can be bounded as

$$K \le \frac{N}{3\left(N - \sum_{i=1}^{N} 1_{\left\{D^{\text{trust}}_{v_i} \ge d_{\text{th}}\right\}}\right) + 1}. \tag{17.24}$$

17.5 Performance analysis

We are now ready to obtain analyses for some selected performance metrics of interest.

17.5.1 Scalability

Scalability is an important metric when characterizing blockchain-enabled zHDT systems. It measures the number of transactions that can be processed per second (called transaction throughput). This transaction throughput can be improved by either increasing the block size S^B or reducing the block interval T^I, although an increase in the S^B or a decrease in T^I can impose stricter constraints on consensus latency. Hence, the choice of appropriate method, as well as the adopted consensus algorithm, should be properly considered to obtain a trade-off of blockchain scalability. The transaction throughput in the proposed framework is given as

$$T_{\text{thru}}\left(S^B, T^I\right) = \frac{K\left\lfloor S^B/\chi\right\rfloor}{T^I}, \tag{17.25}$$

where the block interval T^I represents the average time required to generate a new block. From Kim et al. (2022), an increase in S^B or K increases the number of transactions per second $T_{\text{thru}}\left(S^B, T^I\right)$.

17.5.2 Latency

Latency can be measured as the time to finality (Yuan et al., 2022), which is the time required to successfully append a block to the chain through any shard k. This is the same as the time until a transaction written in the blockchain is irreversible. This latency in the presented framework includes three main components: block generation time T^I, consensus time and block appending time. The time to finality can be obtained as

$$T_{\text{TTF}} = T^I + T^k_{\text{cons}} + T^k_{\text{app}}, \tag{17.26}$$

where T^k_{cons} and T^k_{app} are the consensus time and block appending time, respectively, for any shard k. The consensus time depends on the PBFT consensus scheme and is obtained as

$$T^k_{\text{cons}} = T^k_{\text{deliv}} + T^k_{\text{val}}, \tag{17.27}$$

where T^k_{deliv} and T^k_{val} are the message delivery and block validation times within any shard k respectively. For simplicity, we evaluate the validation time as a function of cryptographic operations computing cost similar to Liu, Teng, et al. (2019) and Liu, Yu, et al. (2019), where a block validation process includes signatures validation, generation, and validation of MACs using ζ, η, and η CPUs cycles, respectively.

In the REQUEST stage, the client v_c sends a block validation request to any available primary $v_p, \forall p \neq c$, where only one MAC verification is performed for each validation request. Each request contains one signature, which requires verification of each validator during any consensus process. During the PRE-PREPARE stage, the primary in any shard k processes a batch of M validation requests and forwards a single pre-prepare message to all replicas within shard k. In this case, the primary generates $N_{s,k} - 1$ MACs and each replica processes one MAC for verifications. Each replica then authenticates the received pre-prepare message during the PREPARE stage by generating $N_{s,k} - 1$ MACs to every other replica within shard k excluding the primary, while verifying $N_{s,k} - 2$ MACs. Next, each validator carries out block validation in the COMMIT stage, where all validators within shard k including the primary sends and receives $N_{s,k} - 1$ commit message, thereby generating and validating $N_{s,k} - 1$ MACs. Finally, each validator generates 1 MAC for each validation request to reply to the client during the REPLY stage. It becomes immediately clear that for each of M validation requests in any shard k, the primary processes $2M + 4(N_{s,k} - 1)$ MAC operations, while each replica processes $M + 4(N_{s,k} - 1)$ MAC operations. The validation time of a primary validator in any shard k is given as

$$\mathcal{O}^k_{v_p} = \frac{M\zeta + [2M + 4(N_{s,k} + f_k - 1)]\eta}{c_{v_p}}, \tag{17.28}$$

where c_{v_k} is the computation capacity of the validator v_k. Similarly, the validation time of any replica is given as

$$\mathcal{O}^k_{v_i} = \frac{M\zeta + [M + 4(N_{s,k} + f_k - 1)]\eta}{c_{v_i}}. \tag{17.29}$$

The total validation time T^k_{val} can thus be obtained as

$$T^k_{\text{val}} = \frac{1}{M} \max_{v^k_i \in V_k} \left\{ \mathcal{O}^k_{v_p}, \mathcal{O}^k_{v_i} \right\}. \tag{17.30}$$

Similarly, the message delivery time T^k_{deliv} depends on the total time to transmit a block from the client to the primary and the total message exchanging time during validation. From Okegbile, Cai, Niyato, et al. (2023), the time to transmit a block from the client to any primary is given as

$$\varphi_{v_c, v^k_p} = \frac{MS^B}{R_{v_c, v^k_p}}. \tag{17.31}$$

From Loveless et al. (2021), we can obtain the message delivery time T^k_{deliv}, given that τ is the timeout, as

$$T^k_{\text{deliv}} = \frac{1}{M}\left(T_{\text{request}} + T^k_{\text{pre-prepare}} + T^k_{\text{prepare}} + T^k_{\text{commit}} + T^k_{\text{reply}}\right)$$

$$= \frac{1}{M}\left(\min\left\{\varphi_{v_c,v_p^k},\tau\right\} + \min\left\{\max_{v_i^k \neq v_p^k, v_c}\left\{\varphi_{v_p^k,v_i^k}\right\},\tau\right\} + \min\left\{\max_{v_i^k \neq v_j^k, v_i^k, v_j^k \neq v_c}\left\{\varphi_{v_i^k,v_j^k}\right\},\tau\right\} + \min\left\{\max_{v_i^k \neq v_j^k}\left\{\varphi_{v_i^k,v_j^k}\right\},\tau\right\} + \min\left\{\max_{v_i^k \neq v_c}\left\{\varphi_{v_i^k,v_c}\right\},\tau\right\}\right). \tag{17.32}$$

From Jiang et al. (2022), the consensus time T^k_{cons} is obtained.

17.5.3 Block appending time

Since the validation process in each shard is independent of the validation process in other shards, two or more shards may complete the validation of a block at the same time slot. To ensure an efficient appending process, each shard is assigned a different priority such that the block appending process is based on the nonpreemptive priority of each shard. We hence model the block appending process as a Geo/G/1 queuing system with nonpreemptive priority, where any shard k has nonpreemptive priority over shard $k+m, 0<m\leq K-1$, such that blocks from shard $1>2>K-1>K$. The arrival of validated blocks from each shard, therefore, follows an independent Bernoulli process with a probability λ_k, while each validated block requires a general appending service with service probability μ_k. Under the considered stable condition,

$$\rho = \sum_{k=1}^{K}\frac{\lambda_k}{\mu_k} < 1. \tag{17.33}$$

Following the proposed priority-based block appending technique, the block from any shard k is appended to the chain before the block from shard $k+1$. As in real-life systems, the appending time of any block from shard 1 is not affected by the appending time of blocks from lower priority shards $k>1$, while the appending time of any block from shard 2 is only affected by the appending time of blocks from higher priority shard 1. It follows that the appending time of blocks from any shard k is only affected by the appending time of blocks from higher priority shards $m>k$. Thus the proposed block appending process can be captured for two special classes: higher priority class and lower priority class. The block appending time of a block from the highest priority shard $k=1$ at any time slot can be calculated as

$$T^1_{app} = \frac{1}{2\mu_1} + \frac{\left[\mho_{\lambda_1}\frac{1}{\mu_1} + \lambda_1^2\mho_{b_1}\right]}{2\lambda_1(1-\rho_1)} + \frac{\lambda_2\left(\mho_{b_1} + \frac{1}{\mu_2}\left(\frac{1}{\mu_2}-1\right)\right)}{2(1-\rho_1)}, \tag{17.34}$$

where $\mho_*$ is the variance of $*$, while $b_* = \frac{1}{\mu_*}$. Similarly, the block appending time of any block from any lower priority shard (say $k=2$) can be obtained following

$$T^2_{\text{app}} = \frac{1}{2\mu_2} + \frac{\mho_{\lambda_2}\frac{1}{\mu_2}}{2\lambda_2(1-\rho)} + \frac{\lambda_2\mho_{b_2}}{2(1-\rho)(1-\rho_1)} + \frac{\mho_{\lambda_1}\left(\frac{1}{\mu_1}\right)^2 + \lambda_1\mho_{b_1}}{2(1-\rho)(1-\rho_1)}. \tag{17.35}$$

The parameters λ_h and μ_h in Wei et al., (2020) capture the joint arrival and service probabilities of blocks from higher priority shards, respectively. The proof of Tavakoli et al. (2018) and Wei et al. (2020) follows from the analysis of the discrete-time single server queuing system. At any slot, the average appending time can thus be approximated as

$$T_{\text{app}}^{\text{ave}} = \frac{1}{K}\sum_{k=1}^{K} T_{\text{app}}^{k}. \tag{17.36}$$

To ensure that the latency requirements of the blockchain-enabled data-sharing system are satisfied, the total latency should be within some consecutive block intervals $\xi(\xi > 1)$, such that

$$T_{\text{TTF}} \leq \xi T^{I}, k = 1, \ldots, K. \tag{17.37}$$

17.6 Performance optimization using DRL

In this section, we employ the tool of DRL (Okegbile & Cai, 2022) to capture the dynamic nature of the proposed sBeDS system. We first formulate the problem as the MDP before adopting the BDQ algorithm to provide solutions for such a formulated problem.

17.6.1 State space

At any decision epoch $t(t \geq 1)$, the state space $\mathcal{S}^{(t)}$ is defined as the union of data achievable rate $R = \{R_{i,j}\}$, average transaction size χ, computation capacity of validators c_v, and the reputation value $D_{i,j}^{\text{trust}}$ of validators. This can be represented as

$$\mathcal{S}^{(t)} = \left[R, \chi, c_v, D_{i,j}^{\text{trust}}\right]^{(t)}. \tag{17.38}$$

17.6.1.1 Action space

The action space $\mathcal{A}^{(t)}$ at any decision epoch t includes the offloading decision $a = \{a_n\}$, $a_n \in \{0, 1\}$, block size S^B, block interval T^I, and the number of shards K^*. This is given as

$$\mathcal{A}^{(t)} = \left[a, S^B, T^I, K^*\right]^{(t)}, \tag{17.39}$$

where $a_n = 1$ when a node participates in the validation process and $a_n = 0$ otherwise. Similarly, $S^B \in \left\{0.2, 0.4, \ldots, \dot{S^B}\right\}$, $T^I \in \left\{0.5, 1, \ldots, \dot{T^I}\right\}$, and $K^* \in \left\{1, 2, \ldots, \dot{K}^*\right\}$, where $\dot{S^B}$, $\dot{T^I}$, and $\dot{K}^*$ are the block size limit, maximum block interval, and highest shard number satisfying the security constraint, respectively.

17.6.1.2 Reward function

We aim to simultaneously optimize the transaction throughput and minimize the overall latency in the proposed sBeDS solution for zHDT. The objective of the system is given as

$$O = \varpi_1 T_{\text{TTF}} - (1 - \varpi_1)\varpi_2 T_{\text{thru}}, \tag{17.40}$$

where $\varpi_1 (0 < \varpi_1 < 1)$ is a weight factor, which is useful in combining two objective functions into a single one and ϖ_2 is a mapping factor that ensures two objective functions are at the same level.

From Deng et al. (2019), the optimization problem can be formulated as

$$\min_{\mathscr{A}^{(t)}} E\left[\sum_{t=0}^{+\infty}(\varpi_1 T_{\mathrm{TTF}} - (1-\varpi_1)\varpi_2 T_{\mathrm{thru}})\right] \tag{17.41}$$

$$\text{s.t.}(\mathrm{C1}){:}T_{\mathrm{TTF}} \le \xi T^{l}$$

$$(\mathrm{C2}){:}f_k < \frac{N_{s,k}-1}{3}$$

$$(\mathrm{C3}){:}\sum_k N_{s,k} \le N$$

$$(\mathrm{C4}){:}\sum_k f_k \le f$$

$$(\mathrm{C5}){:}a_n \in \{0,1\}$$

$$(\mathrm{C6}){:}\rho < 1.$$

The reward function is thus obtained as

$$\mathscr{R}^{(t)} = \begin{cases} -O(t), \text{ifC1}-\text{C6are satisfied} \\ 0, \text{otherwise.} \end{cases} \tag{17.42}$$

To compensate for large dimensions of action space, we adopt the BDQ algorithm. BDQ is a branching variant of the dueling double deep Q-network that incorporates the action branching architecture into the deep Q-network to decrease the number of estimated actions and was first proposed in Tavakoli et al. (2018). The agent in BDQ can scale gracefully to environments with increasing action dimensionality and was shown in Tavakoli et al. (2018) to perform competitively when compared with the conventional deep deterministic policy gradient and other related algorithms. BDQ allows the adoption of discrete-action algorithms in DRL for domains with high-dimensional continuous or discrete-action spaces. For any action dimension $d \in \{1,2,\ldots,N_d\}$, each subaction has $|\mathscr{A}_d| = \vartheta$ discrete subactions. The Q-value of any branch at any state $s \in \mathscr{S}$ and subaction $a_d \in \mathscr{A}_d$ can be expressed as a function of the common state value $V(s)$ and the corresponding subaction advantage $A_d(s,a_d)$ following

$$Q_d(s,a_d) = V(s) + \left[A_d(s,a_d) - \frac{1}{\vartheta}\sum_{a_d' \in \mathscr{A}_d} A_d(s,a_d')\right], \tag{17.43}$$

such that the temporal-difference target

$$y = \mathscr{R} + \gamma \frac{1}{N_d}\sum_d \tilde{Q}_d\left(s', \operatorname*{argmax}_{a_d' \in \mathscr{A}_d} Q_d(s',a_d')\right), \tag{17.44}$$

where parameters $\tilde{Q}_d$ and γ are the branch d of the target network $\tilde{Q}$ and the learning rate, respectively. From Gao et al. (2022), the loss function can be expressed as the expected value of the mean squared temporal-difference error across the branches, given as

$$L = E_{(s,a^*,r,s')\sim\mathscr{D}}\left[\frac{1}{N_d}\sum_d (y_d - Q_d(s,a_d))^2\right], \tag{17.45}$$

where $\mathscr{D}$ is the experience replay buffer and a^* captures the joint action tuple $\left(a_1^*, a_2^*, \ldots, a_{N_d}^*\right)$. To preserve the magnitudes of the errors, the unified prioritization error can be expressed as

$$e_r\left(s, a^*, r, s'\right) = \sum_d \left|y_d - Q_d(s, a_d)\right|. \tag{17.46}$$

17.7 Numerical results

We now present the numerical results to demonstrate the performance of the proposed sBeDS solution. We carried out numerical simulations, consisting of $N = 100$ validators. Except otherwise mentioned, the parameters used for the simulations are as follows: $\chi = 200B$, $c_v \in [10, 30]$MHz, $\tau = 10$ s, $\xi = 20$, $a_{\text{th}} = 0.5$, $d_{\text{th}} = 0.6$, $W = 1$ MHz, $\sigma^2 = 10^{-9}$ W, block size limit $\dot{S}^B = 8$ MB, maximum block interval $\dot{T}^I = 10$ s, maximum allowable number of shards $\dot{K}^* = 8$. For comparison, we modified the proposed PBFT and reputation-enabled shard-based scheme to produce three baseline schemes: single shard scheme, $K = 1$; fixed block interval scheme, $T^I = 7$ s; fixed block size scheme, $S^B = 5$ MB. This allows us to investigate the performance of the proposed scheme.

The convergence performance of the proposed scheme is depicted in Fig. 17.2, where the total reward demonstrates a consistent increase throughout the learning process until the optimal blockchain parameters are attained. Our multishard scheme exhibits superior throughput and lower latency, resulting in a higher cumulative reward compared to alternative schemes. Notably, the convergence speed is relatively slower in comparison to other schemes due to the complex nature of

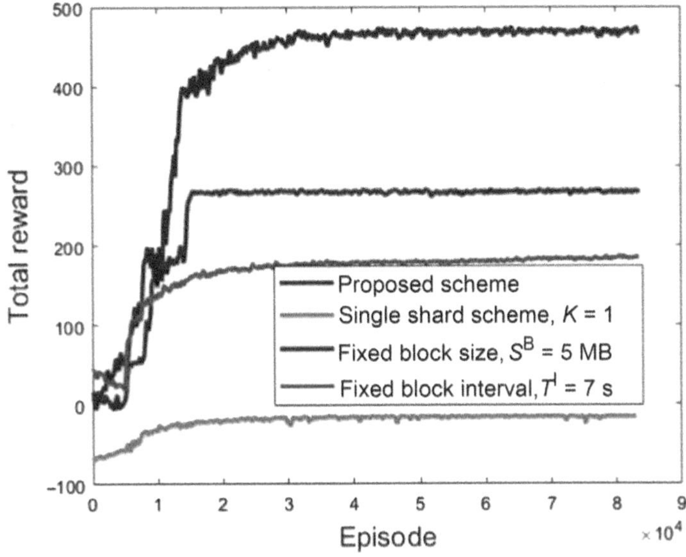

FIGURE 17.2

Convergence performances.

our adopted multishard approach, which incorporates variable block size and interval, thereby imposing a greater number of learning tasks on the agent during the initial learning phase. Despite this, our proposed multishard scheme achieves a reasonable convergence speed while delivering a higher total reward. It is important to highlight that even at $\xi = 20$, the single shard scheme continues to yield a total reward closer to zero, underscoring its inherent limitations in terms of throughput and overall latency.

We proceed by examining the impact of block intervals on the performance of the proposed approach, as illustrated in Fig. 17.3. The total reward exhibits a decrease with increasing block intervals, attributed to the increased overall latency and decreased throughput. Conversely, under the fixed block interval scheme, performance remains unaffected by changes in the block interval, thereby yielding a consistent total reward. In comparison to single shard and fixed block size schemes, the proposed scheme with variable block intervals demonstrates superior total rewards, demonstrating the efficacy of a multishard approach with variable block sizes and intervals in enhancing performance.

To investigate the impact of validator computation capacity on average throughput, Fig. 17.4 illustrates that average throughput rises with the increase in validators' computation capacity limit. This outcome is anticipated, as a higher capacity c_v enhances the validation process, thereby decreasing overall latency. Moreover, our proposed scheme demonstrates superior average throughput compared to alternative approaches. In contrast, for schemes employing a fixed block generation interval, average throughput remains constant as c_v increases. This is because in such schemes, an enhanced validation experience (i.e., reduced validation time) results in validators remaining

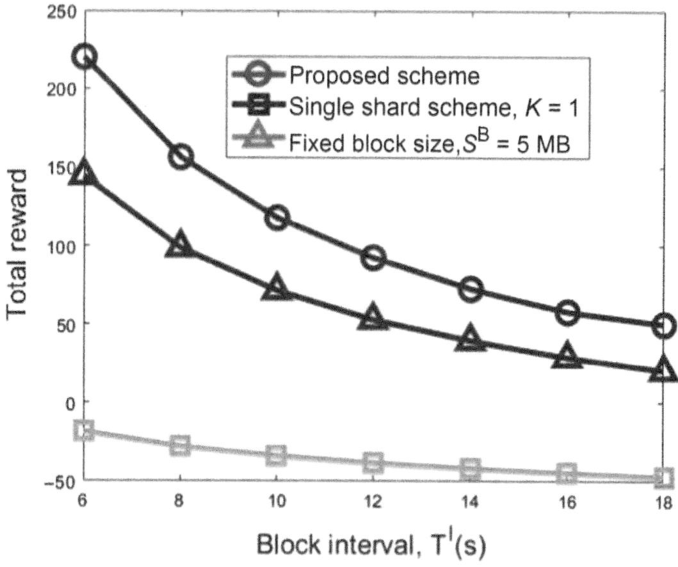

FIGURE 17.3

Impacts of block interval.

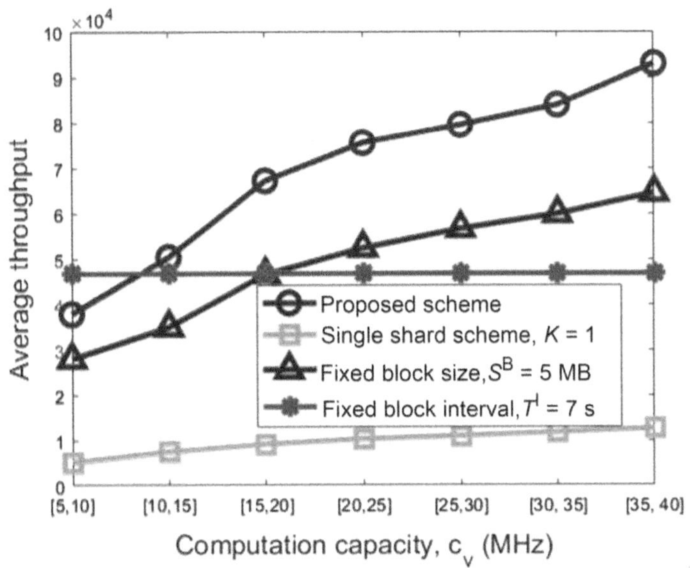

FIGURE 17.4

Average throughput performance.

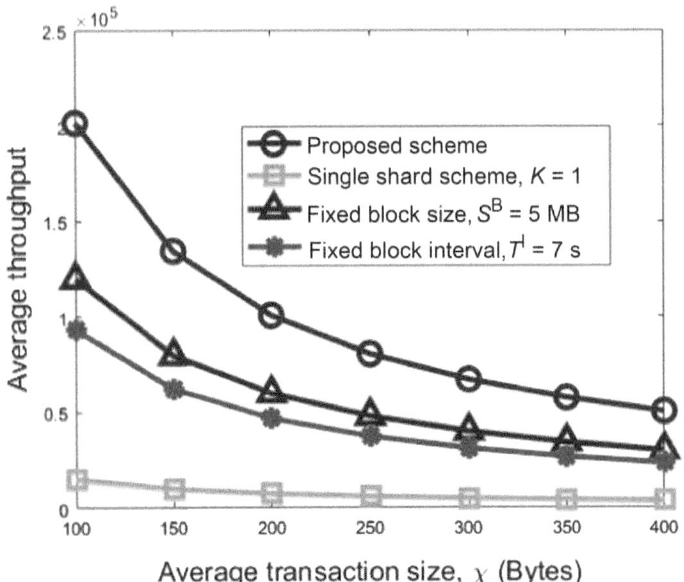

FIGURE 17.5

Impacts of transaction size on throughput.

idle for longer periods due to the fixed block interval. The fixed block interval scheme is expected to exhibit improved performance when c_v is low, as depicted in Fig. 17.4.

Finally, Fig. 17.5 illustrates the average throughput with respect to an increase in average transaction size. As transaction size increases, average throughput decreases due to the increased validation and message exchange time among validators. This, in turn, increases the overall latency. A comparison with the single shard scheme reveals that the proposed multishard scheme exhibits a better performance, further highlighting the significance of multiple validation processes in enhancing blockchain-enabled data-sharing systems.

Generally, the proposed sBeDS solution holds the potential to enhance the scalability and throughput in zHDT, while concurrently reducing overall latency as required in many latency-sensitive applications. Furthermore, the approach is decentralized while also ensuring that the security level is not compromised through the incorporation of a trust-based proof-of reputation and PBFT consensus techniques. By determining the value of f based on reputation values, only validators with acceptable historical reputations are selected during the shard formation process. This eliminates the risk of appending malicious blocks to the chain similar to the conventional PBFT schemes. As a result, this approach offers an enhanced validation experience.

17.8 Conclusions

In this chapter, we presented a PBFT and reputation-enabled shard-based framework designed to enhance the data-sharing process within zHDT systems. Our goal was to enhance scalability and throughput without compromising decentralization and security. We achieved this by integrating trust-based proof-of-reputation and PBFT consensus techniques while employing queuing theory with priority techniques to manage the block appending process. We provided analyses for key performance metrics to demonstrate the significance of parallel validation techniques in the proposed sBeDS.

To address the transaction offloading among validators and the computation resource allocation challenges, we formulated such a problem as an MDP, allowing for the optimization of transaction throughput while minimizing communication and computation latency. We leveraged the BDQ approach due to its effectiveness in handling large action spaces. Simulation results demonstrated that our proposed trust-based proof-of-reputation and PBFT-enabled parallel validation technique significantly enhance the overall data sharing experience in HDT where security must be guaranteed among untrusted nodes.

References

Alaslani, M., Nawab, F., & Shihada, B. (2019). Blockchain in IoT systems: End-to-end delay evaluation. *IEEE Internet of Things Journal*, *6*(5), 8332–8344. Available from https://doi.org/10.1109/JIOT.2019.2917226, http://ieeexplore.ieee.org/servlet/opac?punumber = 6488907.

Alfandi, O., Otoum, S., & Jararweh, Y. (2020). Emirates blockchain solution for IoT-based critical infrastructures: Byzantine fault tolerance. In *Proceedings of IEEE/IFIP network operations and management symposium 2020: Management in the age of softwarization and artificial intelligence, NOMS 2020*. http://ieeexplore.ieee.org/xpl/mostRecentIssue.jsp?punumber = 9107308. 10.1109/NOMS47738.2020.9110312.

Castro, M., & Liskov, B. (1999). Practical byzantine fault tolerance. *Operation System Design Implementation*, *99*, 173.

Chen, J., Yi, C., Du, H., Niyato, D., Kang, J., Cai, J., & Shen, X. (2024). A revolution of personalized healthcare: Enabling human digital twin with mobile AIGC. *IEEE Network*, 1. Available from https://doi.org/10.1109/MNET.2024.3366560, −1, https://ieeexplore.ieee.org/xpl/mostRecentIssue.jsp?punumber = 65.

Chen, J., Yi, C., Okegbile, S. D., Cai, J., & Shen, X. (2024). Networking architecture and key supporting technologies for human digital twin in personalized healthcare: A comprehensive survey. *IEEE Communications Surveys and Tutorials*, *26*(1), 706−746. Available from https://doi.org/10.1109/COMST.2023.3308717, http://ieeexplore.ieee.org/xpl/RecentIssue.jsp?punumber = 9739.

Chen, J. H., Chen, M. R., Zeng, G. Q., & Weng, J. S. (2021). BDFL: A byzantine-fault-tolerance decentralized federated learning method for autonomous vehicle. *IEEE Transactions on Vehicular Technology*, *70*(9), 8639−8652. Available from https://doi.org/10.1109/TVT.2021.3102121, http://ieeexplore.ieee.org/xpl/tocresult.jsp?isnumber = 8039128&punumber = 25.

Deng, Y., Chen, Z., Yao, X., Hassan, S., & Ibrahim, A. M. A. (2019). Parallel offloading in green and sustainable mobile edge computing for delay-constrained IoT system. *IEEE Transactions on Vehicular Technology*, *68*(12), 12202−12214. Available from https://doi.org/10.1109/TVT.2019.2944926, http://ieeexplore.ieee.org/xpl/tocresult.jsp?isnumber = 8039128&punumber = 25.

Fan, C., Ghaemi, S., Khazaei, H., & Musilek, P. (2020). Performance evaluation of blockchain systems: A systematic survey. *IEEE Access*, *8*, 126927−126950. Available from https://doi.org/10.1109/ACCESS.2020.3006078, http://ieeexplore.ieee.org/xpl/RecentIssue.jsp?punumber = 6287639.

Feng, J., Richard Yu, F., Pei, Q., Chu, X., Du, J., & Zhu, L. (2020). Cooperative computation offloading and resource allocation for blockchain-enabled mobile-edge computing: A deep reinforcement learning approach. *IEEE Internet of Things Journal*, *7*(7), 6214−6228. Available from https://doi.org/10.1109/JIOT.2019.2961707, http://ieeexplore.ieee.org/servlet/opac?punumber = 6488907.

Gao, N., Huo, R., Wang, S., Huang, T., & Liu, Y. (2022). Sharding-hashgraph: A high-performance blockchain-based framework for industrial internet of things with hashgraph mechanism. *IEEE Internet of Things Journal*, *9*(18), 17070−17079. Available from https://doi.org/10.1109/JIOT.2021.3126895, http://ieeexplore.ieee.org/servlet/opac?punumber = 6488907.

Gao, S., Yu, T., Zhu, J., & Cai, W. (2019). T-PBFT: An EigenTrust-based practical byzantine fault tolerance consensus algorithm. *China Communications*, *16*(12), 111−123. Available from https://doi.org/10.23919/JCC.2019.12.008, http://ieeexplore.ieee.org/search/searchresult.jsp?newsearch = true&queryText = China + Communications + &x = 54&y = 17.

Garg, V. K., Narahari, Y., & Narasimha, M. (2013). Novel biobjective clustering (BiGC) based on cooperative game theory. *IEEE Transactions on Knowledge and Data Engineering*, *25*(5), 1070−1082. Available from https://doi.org/10.1109/TKDE.2012.73.

Halgamuge, M.N., Hettikankanamge, S.C., & Mohammad, A. (2020). Trust model to minimize the influence of malicious attacks in sharding based blockchain networks. In *Proceedings - 2020 IEEE 3rd international conference on artificial intelligence and knowledge engineering, AIKE 2020* (pp. 162−167). http://ieeexplore.ieee.org/xpl/mostRecentIssue.jsp?punumber = 9355437. 10.1109/AIKE48582.2020.00032.

Huang, X., Wang, Y., Chen Q. & Zhang J. (2021). Security analyze with malicious nodes in sharding blockchain based fog computing networks. In *IEEE vehicular technology conference 2021-*. doi: 10.1109/VTC2021-Fall52928.2021.9625276.

Jiang, X., Yu, F. R., Song, T., & Leung, V. C. M. (2022). Intelligent resource allocation for video analytics in blockchain-enabled internet of autonomous vehicles with edge computing. *IEEE Internet of Things Journal*, *9*(16), 14260−14272. Available from https://doi.org/10.1109/JIOT.2020.3026354, http://ieeexplore.ieee.org/servlet/opac?punumber = 6488907.

Kim, M., Lee, S., Park, C., Lee, J., & Saad, W. (2022). Ensuring data freshness for blockchain-enabled monitoring networks. *IEEE Internet of Things Journal*, *9*(12), 9775−9788. Available from https://doi.org/10.1109/JIOT.2022.3149781, http://ieeexplore.ieee.org/servlet/opac?punumber = 6488907.

Kim, S., Lee, S., Jeong, C., & Cho, S. (2020). *Byzantine fault tolerance based multi-block consensus algorithm for throughput scalability*. In *International conference on electronics, information, and communication, ICEIC 2020*. http://ieeexplore.ieee.org/xpl/mostRecentIssue.jsp?punumber = 9040359. 10.1109/ICEIC49074.2020.9051279.

Lee, S., Kim, M., Lee, J., Hsu, R. H., & Quek, T. Q. S. (2021). Is blockchain suitable for data freshness? An age-of-information perspective. *IEEE Network*, *35*(2), 96–103. Available from https://doi.org/10.1109/MNET.011.2000044, https://ieeexplore.ieee.org/xpl/mostRecentIssue.jsp?punumber = 65.

Liu, L., Feng, J., Pei, Q., Chen, C., Ming, Y., Shang, B., & Dong, M. (2021). Blockchain-enabled secure data sharing scheme in mobile-edge computing: An asynchronous advantage actor-critic learning approach. *IEEE Internet of Things Journal*, *8*(4), 2342–2353. Available from https://doi.org/10.1109/JIOT.2020.3048345, http://ieeexplore.ieee.org/servlet/opac?punumber = 6488907.

Liu, M., Teng, Y., Yu, F.R., Leung, V.C. M., & Song, M. (2019). Deep reinforcement learning based performance optimization in blockchain-enabled internet of vehicle. In *IEEE international conference on communications 2019-*. doi: 10.1109/ICC.2019.8761206.

Liu, M., Yu, F. R., Teng, Y., Leung, V. C. M., & Song, M. (2019). Performance optimization for blockchain-enabled industrial internet of things (iiot) systems: A deep reinforcement learning approach. *IEEE Transactions on Industrial Informatics*, *15*(6), 3559–3570. Available from https://doi.org/10.1109/TII.2019.2897805, http://ieeexplore.ieee.org/xpl/RecentIssue.jsp?punumber = 9424.

Loveless, A., Dreslinski, R., Kasikci, B., & Phan, L.T. X. (2021). IGOR: Accelerating byzantine fault tolerance for real-time systems with eager execution. In *Proceedings of the IEEE real-time and embedded technology and applications symposium, RTAS 360-373 2021-*. doi: 10.1109/RTAS52030.2021.00036.

Luu, L., Narayanan, V., Zheng, C., Baweja, K., Gilbert, S., & Saxena, P. (2016). Association for computing machinery Singapore A secure sharding protocol for open blockchains. In *Proceedings of the ACM conference on computer and communications security* 17-30 24-28 10.1145/2976749.2978389.

Mollah, M. B., Zhao, J., Niyato, D., Guan, Y. L., Yuen, C., Sun, S., Lam, K.-Y., & Koh, L. H. (2021). Blockchain for the internet of vehicles towards intelligent transportation systems: A survey. *IEEE Internet of Things Journal*, *8*(6), 4157–4185. Available from https://doi.org/10.1109/jiot.2020.3028368.

Nakamoto, S. (2008). Bitcoin: A peer-to-peer electronic cash system.

Okegbile, S., & Maharaj, B. (2021). Age of information and success probability analysis in hybrid spectrum access-based massive cognitive radio networks. *Applied Sciences*, *11*(4), 1940. Available from https://doi.org/10.3390/app11041940.

Okegbile, S. D., Maharaj, B. T., & Alfa, A. S. (2020). Outage and throughput analysis of cognitive users in underlay cognitive radio networks with handover. *IEEE Access*, *8*, 208045–208057. Available from https://doi.org/10.1109/access.2020.3037787.

Okegbile, S.D., & Cai, J. (2022). Edge-assisted human-to-virtual twin connectivity scheme for human digital twin frameworks. In *IEEE vehicular technology conference 2022-*. https://doi.org/10.1109/VTC2022-Spring54318.2022.9860619.

Okegbile, S. D., Cai, J., & Alfa, A. S. (2022a). Performance analysis of blockchain-enabled data-sharing scheme in cloud-edge computing-based IoT networks. *IEEE Internet of Things Journal*, *9*(21), 21520–21536. Available from https://doi.org/10.1109/JIOT.2022.3181556, http://ieeexplore.ieee.org/servlet/opac?punumber = 6488907.

Okegbile, S. D., Cai, J., & Alfa, A. S. (2022b). Practical byzantine fault tolerance-enhanced blockchain-enabled data sharing system: Latency and age of data package analysis. *IEEE Transactions on Mobile Computing*, 1–17. Available from https://doi.org/10.1109/TMC.2022.3223306, http://ieeexplore.ieee.org/xpl/RecentIssue.jsp?puNumber = 7755.

Okegbile, S. D., Maharaj, B. T., & Alfa, A. S. (2022a). A multi-class channel access scheme for cognitive edge computing-based internet of things networks. *IEEE Transactions on Vehicular Technology*, *71*(9),

9912–9924. Available from https://doi.org/10.1109/TVT.2022.3178216, http://ieeexplore.ieee.org/xpl/tocresult.jsp?isnumber = 8039128&punumber = 25.

Okegbile, S. D., Maharaj, B. T., & Alfa, A. S. (2022b). A multi-user tasks offloading scheme for integrated edge-fog-cloud computing environments. *IEEE Transactions on Vehicular Technology*, *71*(7), 7487–7502. Available from https://doi.org/10.1109/TVT.2022.3167892, http://ieeexplore.ieee.org/xpl/tocresult.jsp?isnumber = 8039128&punumber = 25.

Okegbile,S.D., Cai,J., Chen,J., & Yi,C. (2023). A reputation-enhanced shard-based byzantine fault-tolerant scheme for secure data sharing in zero trust human digital twin systems. TechRxiv, Canada TechRxiv. https://www.techrxiv.org/, https://doi.org/10.36227/techrxiv.23511708.v2.

Okegbile, S. D., Cai, J., Niyato, D., & Yi, C. (2023). Human digital twin for personalized healthcare: Vision, architecture and future directions. *IEEE Network*, *37*(2), 262–269. Available from https://doi.org/10.1109/MNET.118.2200071, https://ieeexplore.ieee.org/xpl/mostRecentIssue.jsp?punumber = 65.

Okegbile, S. D., Cai, J., Zheng, H., Chen, J., & Yi, C. (2023). Differentially private federated multi-task learning framework for enhancing human-to-virtual connectivity in human digital twin. *IEEE Journal on Selected Areas in Communications*, *41*(11), 3533–3547. Available from https://doi.org/10.1109/JSAC.2023.3310106, http://ieeexplore.ieee.org/xpl/tocresult.jsp?isnumber = 5678773.

Okegbile,S.D., Talabi,O., Gao,H., Cai,J., & Yi,C. (2023). FLeS: A federated learning-enhanced semantic communication framework for mobile AIGC-driven human digital twins.

Sun, Y., Zhang, L., Feng, G., Yang, B., Cao, B., & Imran, M. A. (2019a). Blockchain-enabled wireless internet of things: Performance analysis and optimal communication node deployment. *IEEE Internet of Things Journal*, *6*(3), 5791–5802. Available from https://doi.org/10.1109/JIOT.2019.2905743, http://ieeexplore.ieee.org/servlet/opac?punumber = 6488907.

Sun Y. Zhang L. Feng G. Yang B. Cao B. Imran M. (2019b). Performance analysis for blockchain driven wireless IoT systems based on tempo-spatial model. In Proceedings - 2019 International conference on cyber-enabled distributed computing and knowledge discovery, CyberC 2019 (pp. 348–353). Institute of Electrical and Electronics Engineers Inc. China http://ieeexplore.ieee.org/xpl/mostRecentIssue.jsp?punumber = 8942180. 10.1109/CyberC.2019.00066.

Tavakoli, A., Pardo, F., & Kormushev, P. (2018). Action branching architectures for deep reinforcement learning. *Proceedings of the AAAI Conference on Artificial Intelligence*, *32*(1). Available from https://doi.org/10.1609/aaai.v32i1.11798.

Vashchuk, O., & Shuwar, R. (2018). Pros and cons of consensus algorithm proof of stake. Difference in the network safety in proof of work and proof of stake. *Electronics and Information Technologies*, *9*. Available from https://doi.org/10.30970/eli.9.106.

Wei, F., Feng, G., Sun, Y., Wang, Y., Qin, S., & Liang, Y. C. (2020). Network slice reconfiguration by exploiting deep reinforcement learning with large action space. *IEEE Transactions on Network and Service Management*, *17*(4), 2197–2211. Available from https://doi.org/10.1109/TNSM.2020.3019248, http://www.ieee.org/products/onlinepubs/news/0806_01.html.

Xiang, H., Wu, K., Chen, J., Yi, C., Cai,J., Niyato, D., & Shen, X. (2023). Edge computing empowered tactile Internet for human digital twin: Visions and case study. arXiv, China arXiv. https://arxiv.org, https://doi.org/10.48550/arXiv.2304.07454.

Yang, R., Chang, X., Misic, J., Misic, V. B., & Kang, H. (2022). Quantitative comparison of two chain-selection protocols under selfish mining attack. *IEEE Transactions on Network and Service Management*, *19*(2), 1142–1158. Available from https://doi.org/10.1109/TNSM.2022.3151083, http://www.ieee.org/products/onlinepubs/news/0806_01.html.

Yang, Z., Yang, R., Yu, F. R., Li, M., Zhang, Y., & Teng, Y. (2022). Sharded blockchain for collaborative computing in the internet of things: Combined of dynamic clustering and deep reinforcement learning approach. *IEEE Internet of Things Journal*, *9*(17), 16494–16509. Available from https://doi.org/10.1109/JIOT.2022.3152188, http://ieeexplore.ieee.org/servlet/opac?punumber = 6488907.

Ye, J., Kang, X., Liang, Y. C., & Sun, S. (2022). A trust-centric privacy-preserving blockchain for dynamic spectrum management in IoT networks. *IEEE Internet of Things Journal, 9*(15), 13263–13278. Available from https://doi.org/10.1109/JIOT.2022.3142989, http://ieeexplore.ieee.org/servlet/opac?punumber = 6488907.

Yuan, S., Li, J., Liang, J., Zhu, Y., Yu, X., Chen, J., & Wu, C. (2021). Sharding for blockchain-based mobile edge computing system: A deep reinforcement learning approach. In *Proceedings - IEEE global communications conference, GLOBECOM* https://ieeexplore.ieee.org/xpl/conhome/1000308/all-proceedings. 10.1109/GLOBECOM46510.2021.9685883.

Yuan, Y., Yi, C., Chen, B., Shi, Y., & Cai, J. (2022). A computation offloading game for jointly managing local pre-processing time-length and priority selection in edge computing. *IEEE Transactions on Vehicular Technology, 71*(9), 9868–9883. Available from https://doi.org/10.1109/TVT.2022.3177432, http://ieeexplore.ieee.org/xpl/tocresult.jsp?isnumber = 8039128&punumber = 25.

Yun, J., Goh, Y., & Chung, J. M. (2021). DQN-based optimization framework for secure sharded blockchain systems. *IEEE Internet of Things Journal, 8*(2), 708–722. Available from https://doi.org/10.1109/JIOT.2020.3006896, http://ieeexplore.ieee.org/servlet/opac?punumber = 6488907.

Zhang, J., Rong, Y., Cao, J., Rong, C., Bian, J., & Wu, W. (2022). DBFT: A byzantine fault tolerance protocol with graceful performance degradation. *IEEE Transactions on Dependable and Secure Computing, 19*(5), 3387–3400. Available from https://doi.org/10.1109/TDSC.2021.3095544, http://ieeexplore.ieee.org/xpl/RecentIssue.jsp?punumber = 8858.

Zhang, R., Yu, F. R., Liu, J., Huang, T., & Liu, Y. (2020). Deep reinforcement learning (DRL)-based device-to-device (D2D) caching with blockchain and mobile edge computing. *IEEE Transactions on Wireless Communications, 19*(10), 6469–6485. Available from https://doi.org/10.1109/TWC.2020.3003454, http://ieeexplore.ieee.org/xpl/RecentIssue.jsp?puNumber = 7693.

CHAPTER

Advancements and future pathway in human body digital twins 18

Xuhang Chen[1], Chenyu Tang[2], Yanning Dai[3], Cong Li[4] and Shuo Gao[4]

[1]Brain Physics Lab, The University of Cambridge, Cambridge, United Kingdom [2]Cambridge Graphene Centre, The University of Cambridge, Cambridge, United Kingdom [3]AI Initiative, KAUST, Thuwal, Saudi Arabia [4]School of Instrumentation and Optoelectronic Engineering, Beihang University, Beijing, P.R. China

18.1 Introduction

Complex mechanisms within the human body are difficult to unravel, for example, the mechanisms behind amyotrophic lateral sclerosis (Taylor et al., 2016), posing significant challenges for medical science. These challenges necessitate comprehensive monitoring, diagnostic, and therapeutic approaches that integrate technologies (e.g., artificial intelligence, wearable systems), smart hospitals, and everyday environments. Human body digital twins (DTs) offer a promising solution. These digital twins are virtual replicas of users' physiological states via various sensors (Tang, Yi, et al., 2024) that allow dynamic, data-driven models to simulate and predict physiological and pathological processes. Moreover, DTs can provide patients with assistive technologies such as neural speech (Chen et al., 2024), thereby improving their quality of life.

The implementation of human body digital twins requires support from diverse physical systems, which can be categorized into invasive and noninvasive systems. Noninvasive systems, mainly exemplified by wearable (Kim et al., 2019) technologies and essential medical technologies (e.g., computed tomography (CT), MRI, genomic sequencing), are particularly advantageous due to their ability to provide continuous monitoring without causing discomfort or requiring invasive procedures. These technologies seamlessly integrate into patients' daily lives, detecting electrical, reflective, mechanical, and chemical signals. Invasive systems (Baddour et al., 2012), are predominantly utilized in smart hospitals and can be categorized into temporary and implantable systems. Temporary means ingestible (Mundaca-Uribe et al., 2023), bioabsorbable, or removed after out-hospital (Åkerlund et al., 2024). Implantable systems involve the insertion of devices that provide continuous monitoring and therapeutic interventions, such as cardiac devices (Andreas et al., 2024). These systems offer high precision and accuracy in monitoring and can provide direct therapeutic integration.

With the booming of aforementioned human body data retrieving technologies as well as the advanced data processing techniques, including artificial intelligence (AI) and simulation modeling methods. Human body digital twin technology has seen rapid advancements (Laubenbacher et al., 2021; Laubenbacher et al., 2022), leading to the establishment of distinct levels (Tang, Yi, et al., 2024). In Fig. 18.1, DT can be divided into five progressive levels. Cross-section (real-time data),

Blockchain and Digital Twin for Smart Hospitals. DOI: https://doi.org/10.1016/B978-0-443-34226-4.00019-8

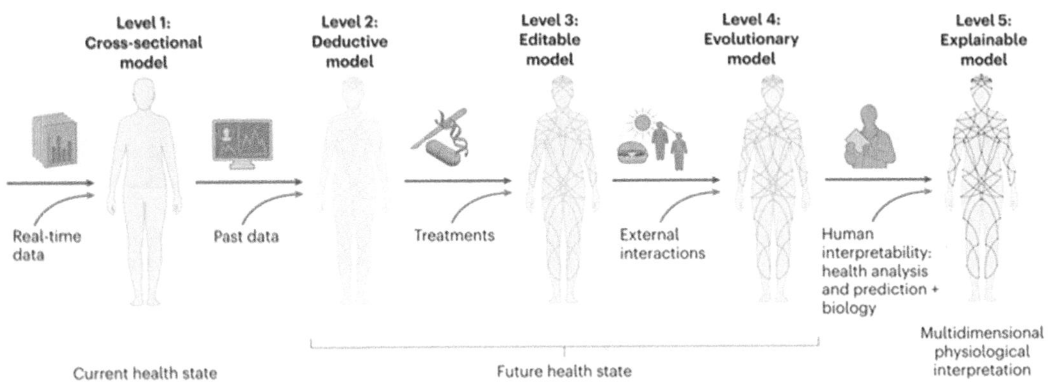

FIGURE 18.1

Five progressive digital twins models, from cross-sectional model to explainable model (Tang, Yi, et al., 2024).

deductive (real-time and past data), editable (treatments), evolutionary (external interactions), and explainable (mechanism explanations) models. These levels represent a progression from static representations of health states to more dynamic and interactive models that incorporate real-time data, historical data, interventions, and environmental interactions, finally toward a fully understandable and explainable digital human body.

These advancements and the clear roadmap for digital twin technologies have been informed by historical development and are driving the future creation of new technologies. Despite the significant progress, there remains a gap in the summary and various technologies. Few reports provide an overarching summary of the advancements and state-of-the-art applications. Therefore we seek to address this gap by summarizing the recent developments in human body digital twins and discussing potential future pathways for their evolution in the context of emerging artificial intelligence technologies.

18.2 Human body digital twins physical system

18.2.1 Noninvasive physical system

Noninvasive systems include wearables and essential medical technologies. Wearables, based on their sensor mechanisms, can be divided into four main categories: electrical, reflective, mechanical, and chemical categories (Tang, Yi, et al., 2024). Electrical sensors are designed to detect biological electrical signals within the human body, such as those measured by electrocardiogram (ECG), electroencephalogram (EEG), or electromyogram (EMG). The biological electricity is generated by cells inside the human body, primarily neurons and muscle cells. These signals are essential for communication within the nervous system and muscle control. Mechanical sensors detect physical changes within the body, including movement (Tang et al., 2022), pressure, and strain, using devices like accelerometers, strain gauges, and pressure sensors. These mechanical changes are the ultimate representation of our musculoskeletal system and can present body information

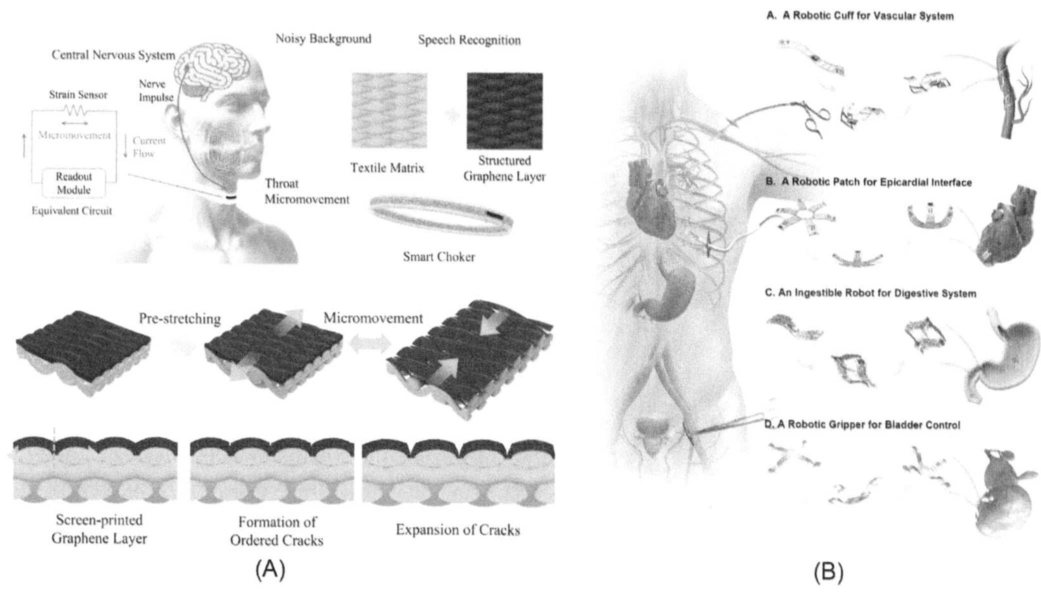

FIGURE 18.2

(A) A display of a mechanical sensor that detects strain and micromovement to capture the nuances of human silent speech (Tang et al., 2024); (B) an illustration of invasive minimal implants (part of the invasive physical system) for diagnosis, stimulation and actuator (Zhang et al., 2024).

from a holistic view (Fig. 18.2A), for example, using gait analysis, physical activity monitoring, and posture and ergonomics design. Reflective sensors (Chen et al., 2022; El-Dahshan et al., 2024) work by emitting a suitable medium, such as light or ultrasound, into the body and measuring the reflected signals to derive specific parameters. For instance, pulse oximetry (PO) (Barker & Tremper, 1987), near-infrared spectroscopy (NIRS) (Villringer et al., 1993), and photoplethysmography (PPG) (El-Dahshan et al., 2024) use light to penetrate the skin and underlying tissues. Then the device measures the absorbed and the reflected amount to analyze the oxygen saturation, oxygenated and deoxygenated hemoglobin levels, blood flow, and volume. In the case of ultrasound, the device emits high-frequency sound waves into the body and then measures the reflected wave (frequency, amplitude) bounced tissues to create the structure of a certain area and measure the flow and volume. Chemical sensors are designed to detect and measure specific chemical compounds within the body. The functions are often self-explained by their name, such as glucose, lactate, pH sensors, and various gas sensors. They can detect the chemical compounds in the human body via blood and sweat (Kim et al., 2019).

Essential medical technologies offer precise diagnostics and fundamental infrastructures for patient care, which are integral parts of creating a DT model for most patients. They involve complex physical principles and are unsuitable for wearables due to their weight, size, and stationary operation. For example, CT uses X-rays to create detailed cross-sectional images of the body, providing high-resolution images of bones, blood vessels, and soft tissues. Magnetic resonance imaging, on the other hand, employs magnetic fields and radio waves to produce detailed images of organs and tissues. Other technologies include positron emission tomography (Raichle, 1983), ultrasound imaging (Aldrich, 2007), and genomic sequencing systems (Church & Gilbert, 1984). Additionally, electronic health record (EHR) systems store comprehensive patient data, including medical histories, diagnoses, treatments, and test results. Integrating these core technologies is crucial for creating accurate digital twins of patients, enhancing diagnosis, treatment, and continuous monitoring of health conditions.

18.2.2 Invasive physical system

The rapid development of invasive devices has been hindered by technical challenges, regulatory hurdles, higher risk of complications, and patient discomfort (Blot et al., 2007). Despite these challenges, there has been an upsurge in the use of various invasive devices due to their perfect monitoring performance, with brain–computer interfaces (BCIs) such as Neuralink being one of the most popular. Invasive systems are predominantly utilized in smart hospitals and can be categorized into temporary and implantable systems. Temporary includes ingestible that can be digested in a short time (e.g., robotics pills, Mundaca-Uribe et al., 2023 or implants, Zhang et al., 2024, Fig. 18.2B and devices used temporarily during the patients in the hospital). For example, intracranial pressure monitors involve inserting an intraparenchymal probe into the brain tissue (Åkerlund et al., 2024), the same as the arterial and venous probes (Maas et al., 2022). Data collected from these physical systems can be used to construct DT models of patients. These catheters or probes would be removed when the patients recover. Besides, bioabsorbable sensors follow a similar principle. Tang, Yang, et al. (2024) presented a meta-structured hydrogel sensor that is injectable, wireless, and bioabsorbable to detect intracranial pressure, temperature, and flow rate. The size of the sensor was $2 \times 2 \times 2\ mm^3$ and can be fully degraded within 18 weeks.

Implantable systems involve the insertion of devices that provide continuous monitoring and therapeutic interventions. Cardiac devices (Andreas et al., 2024; Wang et al., 2023) as a perfect example, are implanted for heart rhythm management and tricuspid regurgitation. Besides, neurostimulators (Mao et al., 2023) can be used for spinal cord stimulation. Continuous glucose monitors (CGMs) are another example, with implantable sensors that continuously monitor blood glucose levels for diabetes management. Ingestible sensors (Mundaca-Uribe et al., 2023) are also notable, such as pills equipped with sensors to monitor conditions within the gastrointestinal tract, including pH levels, temperature, and pressure. Wang et al. (2023) demonstrated a wireless biocompatible cardiac pacemaker. Unlike the traditional cardiac devices requiring thoracotomy to implant the minimal device can be rolled to implant into intravascular. These invasive systems offer high precision and accuracy in monitoring and can provide direct therapeutic integration, although they come with risks such as infection, high costs, and complexity, necessitating their use in specialized medical areas.

18.2.3 Development pathway

Multisensory fusion (Chu et al., 2022) integrates multiple sensors to provide comprehensive information necessary for a digital twin system. Compared to traditional single devices for DT applications (Dai & Gao, 2021; Datta et al., 2020; Li et al., 2023), such as EEG for emotion recognition

(Li et al., 2022). Two main development paths emerges in current noninvasive systems. The first path involves implementing various types of sensor frontend into a versatile system (Chen et al., 2022; Chu et al., 2022; Tang et al., 2022). This benefits from the advance of flexible print circuits and textile technology. This approach benefits from advancements in flexible printed circuit and textile technologies (Tang, Xu, et al., 2024). For instance, Dai et al. (Chen et al., 2021) proposed a smart skin with polyvinylidene difluoride that can detect force (sensitivity 0.05 N), touch position (spatial resolution 0.29 mm), and humidity (responsivity 0.22%/RH%). Additionally, the development of skin technology in the general field is toward a deep penetration depth and high resolution in the human body with more sensors (Lin et al., 2022), which is aligned with the development path. Xu et al. (2023) proposed an in-ear integrated array of electrical and chemical sensors on a flexible substrate. The sensor could detect electroencephalography and lactate concentration in the sweat simultaneously.

The second path of development focuses on creating portable electronics to replace or at least shrink bulky systems (e.g., CT, ultrasound). For instance, Zhou et al. (Zhao, Ding, et al., 2024; Zhou, Gao, et al., 2024) proposed a wearable ultrasound (2 MHz) patch that performs cerebral vascular imaging and flow velocity detection. The patch, integrated with biocompatible silicone elastomer and flexible electronics, achieved comparable performance compared with traditional transcranial doppler. Additionally, Zhao et, al. (Zhao, Ding, et al., 2024; Zhou, Gao, et al., 2024) proposed the ultra-low-field whole-body MRI operating at 0.05 Tesla, resolution of $2 \times 2 \times 8\ mm^3$, and without the need for radio frequency cages, thereby reducing the size. This system uses a data-driven model pretrained on large-scale, high-resolution MRI data to enhance image quality.

Noninvasive technologies, especially wearable devices, are preferred by researchers and industries for their convenience in fabrication, and experimentation, with the potential to create ubiquitous "smart hospitals" anywhere. Meanwhile, invasive technologies are developing rapidly in multiple areas and devices, demonstrating their essential role in providing highly accurate data and therapeutic interventions. While noninvasive systems are advancing rapidly and offer numerous benefits, such as reduced risk and improved patient comfort, they are unlikely to completely replace invasive systems. Invasive systems provide unparalleled precision and real-time monitoring capabilities that are crucial for certain conditions. Both invasive and noninvasive systems have unique advantages and cannot replace each other. However, there is potential for noninvasive technologies to supplement and reduce the need for invasive systems (Blot et al., 2007), particularly as noninvasive sensors become more sophisticated and accurate, and with the assistance of artificial intelligence.

18.3 Digital twins applications in different levels

AI plays a crucial role in facilitating the large-scale application of digital twins across heterogeneous populations. A data-driven approach has proven to be an effective method for exploring the representation of different types of data that can be used in digital twins across various modalities (e.g., text and time series (Brown et al., 2020), voice (Baevski et al., 2020), image (Dosovitskiy et al., 2021), and video (Peebles & Xie, 2023)). The integration of diverse data types into sophisticated AI models has significantly advanced the capabilities and applications of digital twins

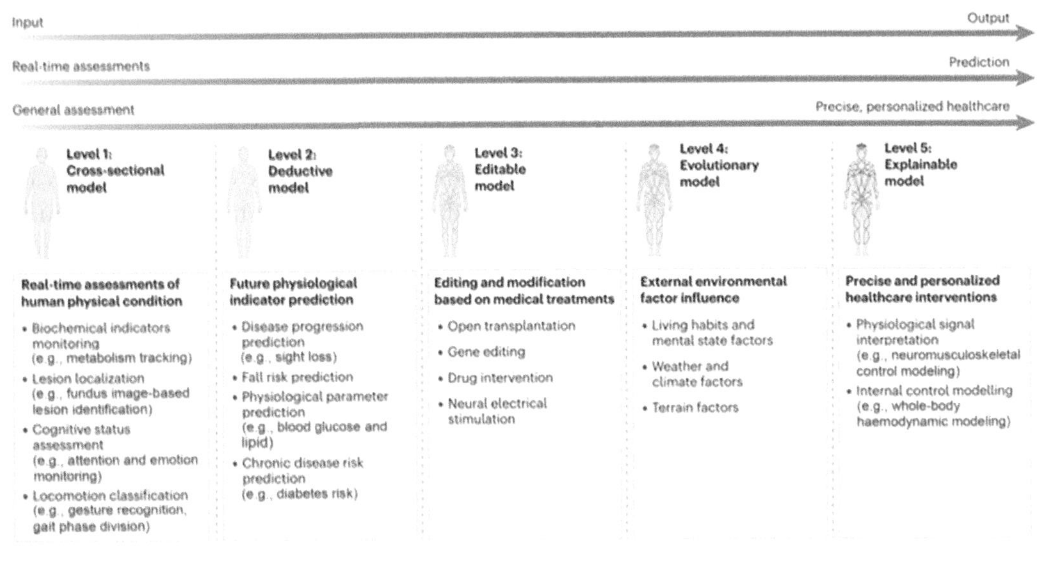

FIGURE 18.3

Applications of the five progressive models (Tang, Yi, et al., 2024).

(Fig. 18.3). In this chapter, we introduce the applications at each level of digital twins. These applications mark a significant advancement of digital twins in personalized and predictive solutions.

18.3.1 Level 1: cross-section model

The cross-sectional model involves real-time data to perform classification and prediction tasks, such as disease classification and rehabilitation classification. For example, Tang et al. proposed a wearables-based multicolumn neural network with an integrated physical system with electrical and mechanical sensors for locomotion classification, achieving 92.5% accuracy on test sets. Similarly, Zhou et al. (2023) proposed a disease prediction model with millions of unlabeled retinal images. Hence, real-time retinal photographs captured from patients can be diagnosed (i.e., classify potential diseases). Assistive technologies for patients also require real-time prediction tasks to interpret patients' motivations or combine their words. For instance, noninvasive BCI (Chen et al., 2024) are used to interpret the information, where a neural speech decoding network can translate cortex electrocorticographic signals into interpretable speech parameters, significantly improving the quality of life for patients.

18.3.2 Level 2: deductive model

The deductive model integrates historical data with real-time data to enhance predictive accuracy and understanding based on the previous level. Digital twin physical systems, especially essential medical technology, provide the reservoirs of patient history, such as previous CT scans, MRI scans, and comprehensive EHR. Then, deep learning methods are the representative algorithms to exploit the knowledge behind various historical data. For example, Liu et al. (2023) proposed to use attention-based embeddings to process more than 243,000 EHRs to predict the expected postoperative pain. They achieved an AUC value from 0.72 to 0.79 in 5 postoperation days. Similarly, long-term collected CT images can assist in pulmonary disease screening (Chaudhary et al., 2023). Historical genetic data also offer promising pathways for this level of digital twins. For example, Gribben et al. (2024) analyzed single-nucleus RNA sequencing from liver biopsies at different stages to discover new biological mechanisms and potentially open new therapeutic avenues for various chronic diseases.

18.3.3 Level 3: editable model

The editable model leverages simulation and dynamic models to customize and predict patient outcomes based on interventions. For instance, Silva et al. (2024) researched a bilingual speech neuroprosthesis driven by cortical articulatory representations shared between languages. They based on the simulation found the mechanisms of interpreting cortical signals to aid communication in multiple languages. Additionally, Chen, Prakash, et al. (2023) proposed an integrated framework combining artificial intelligence, clinical care, and continuous therapeutic monitoring. This framework, known as ClinAIOps, successfully manages conditions such as blood pressure, diabetes, and Parkinson's disease through three closed-loop feedback systems, effectively utilizing clinical and hospital resources to provide high-level care guidelines.

18.3.4 Above level 3: evolutionary and explainable models

Evolutionary models and ultimately explainable models are challenging to achieve, with few physical systems capable of long-term environmental variable monitoring. Despite the lack of mature technologies at these levels, promising developments in flexible electronics indicate potential for future applications, such as smart masks (De Fazio et al., 2023) and skin sensors (Brasier et al., 2024). However, there is a notable gap in constructing a trustworthy system that spans previous digital twin levels and integrates historical and real-time data for online computation. The application of explainable models requires a deeper understanding of complex dynamics, such as neural activity in large models, highlighting the long journey ahead in this domain.

18.4 Future pathways of human body digital twins

The future of digital twin models in healthcare is poised to integrate several key characteristics that will enhance their functionality and application. One of the primary advancements is the integration of advanced AI and machine learning. These technologies on the one hand can alleviate the artifacts in the raw data (Al-Sheikh, 2023; Chen, Feng, et al., 2023; Lee et al., 2023; Sirtoli et al., 2023) to provide more precise results. On the other hand, powerful large models (Sandmann et al., 2024) such as Generative pretrained transformer (GPT), and Large language model Meta AI (Llama) 3, can analyze vast amounts of data to support tailored therapeutic interventions. Assistive technologies, powered by AI, will improve the precision and effectiveness of treatments, ensuring that each patient receives care that is specifically designed for their unique needs.

The expansion of wearable and Internet-of-Things devices (Chen et al., 2022) will revolutionize data acquisition methods. These devices will be capable of continuously monitoring patients' health in real-time while maintaining robust interfaces with various noninvasive or other records, such as medical imaging and time-series data. This seamless integration will ensure comprehensive monitoring and data collection, which is crucial for accurate and dynamic digital twin models.

Enhanced interoperability and data integration will be crucial for the success of digital twins. Health Level Seven (HL7) (Dolin et al., 2001) and Digital Imaging and Communication in Medicine (DICOM) (Bidgood et al., 1997) are currently standard clinical exchange documents type and medical imaging type. However, a mature system should consider more than them, such as time-series data, and high-resolution data. However, a mature system should extend beyond these standards to include time-series data and high-resolution datasets for all types of data from physical systems. By incorporating diverse data sources, we can realize the transferrable and reproducible digital twin models, thereby enhancing the precision of diagnoses and the effectiveness of treatment plans.

The establishment of trustworthy data-sharing platforms will be essential for safeguarding patient privacy and security. Federated learning (FL) (Li et al., 2020) is a promising approach that enables collaborative machine learning model training across multiple healthcare centers without sharing raw patient data. This technique helps maintain data privacy and security while harnessing the collective knowledge from different institutions. Additionally, exploring other privacy-preserving methods, such as differential privacy and blockchains, can further enhance data protection (Javed et al., 2023). These platforms will ensure data is used solely for healthcare purposes, with stringent measures against unauthorized access and breaches, thereby enabling a comprehensive and secure approach to patient care.

Ethical and fair concerns (Chen, Wang, et al., 2023) will also need to be addressed to ensure that digital twin technologies are used responsibly. This includes developing ethical guidelines for data use, ensuring fair access to these technologies across different populations, and addressing any biases that may arise in AI algorithms. By prioritizing ethical considerations, the healthcare industry can ensure that digital twin technologies benefit all patients equitably and justly.

By integrating these characteristics, the future of digital twin models will be well-equipped to deliver precise, personalized, and effective healthcare, ultimately improving patient outcomes and transforming the medical landscape.

18.5 Conclusion

The development path of DTs has seen significant advancements, with multisensory fusion and robust physical systems. The five progressive levels of DT models demonstrate a clear roadmap for future research and applications. Advanced applications have emerged, symbolizing a new era for human body digital twins. However, there are still challenges to address, such as integrating artificial intelligence, enhancing physical systems, and improving data integration, privacy, and ethical standards. Future research needs to tackle these issues to fully realize the potential of DTs in personalized and predictive healthcare and medicine.

References

Åkerlund, C. A. I., Holst, A., Bhattacharyay, S., Stocchetti, N., Steyerberg, E., Smielewski, P., Menon, D. K., Ercole, A., Nelson, D. W., Åkerlund, C., Amrein, K., Andelic, N., Andreassen, L., Anke, A., Antoni, A., Audibert, G., Azouvi, P., Azzolini, M. L., Bartels, R., . . . Zoerle, T. (2024). Clinical descriptors of disease trajectories in patients with traumatic brain injury in the intensive care unit (CENTER-TBI): a multicentre observational cohort study. *The Lancet Neurology*, *23*(1), 71–80. Available from https://doi.org/10.1016/s1474-4422(23)00358-7.

Aldrich, J. E. (2007). Basic physics of ultrasound imaging. *Critical Care Medicine*, *35*(5), S131. Available from https://doi.org/10.1097/01.CCM.0000260624.99430.22.

Al-Sheikh, B. (2023). Adaptive algorithm for motion artifacts removal in wearable biomedical sensors during physical exercise. *IEEE Sensors Journal*, *23*(9), 9491–9499. Available from https://doi.org/10.1109/JSEN.2023.3256959, http://ieeexplore.ieee.org/xpl/RecentIssue.jsp?punumber = 7361.

Andreas, M., Burri, H., Praz, F., Soliman, O., Badano, L., Barreiro, M., Cavalcante, J. L., De Potter, T., Doenst, T., Friedrichs, K., Hausleiter, J., Karam, N., Kodali, S., Latib, A., Marijon, E., Mittal, S., Nickenig, G., Rinaldi, A., Rudzinski, P., . . . Leclercq, C. (2024). Tricuspid valve disease and cardiac implantable electronic devices. *European Heart Journal*, *45*(5), 346–365. Available from https://doi.org/10.1093/eurheartj/ehad783, http://eurheartj.oxfordjournals.org/.

Baddour, L. M., Cha, Y.-M., & Wilson, W. R. (2012). Infections of cardiovascular implantable electronic devices. *New England Journal of Medicine*, *367*(9), 842–849. Available from https://doi.org/10.1056/NEJMcp1107675.

Baevski, A., Zhou, H., Mohamed, A., & Auli, M. (2020). Advances in neural information processing systems. 10495258. Neural information processing systems foundation, undefined. *wav2vec 2.0: A framework for self-supervised learning of speech representations*. https://papers.nips.cc/ 2020-

Barker, S. J., & Tremper, K. K. (1987). Pulse oximetry: Applications and limitations. *International Anesthesiology Clinics*, *25*(3), 155–175. Available from https://doi.org/10.1097/00004311-198702530-00010.

Bidgood, W. D., Horii, S. C., Prior, F. W., & Van Syckle, D. E. (1997). Understanding and Using DICOM, the Data Interchange Standard for Biomedical Imaging. *Journal of the American Medical Informatics Association*, *4*(3), 199–212. Available from https://doi.org/10.1136/jamia.1997.0040199.

Blot, S. I., Peleman, R., & Vandewoude, K. H. (2007). Invasive devices: No need? No use!. *Intensive Care Medicine*, *33*(2), 209–211. Available from https://doi.org/10.1007/s00134-006-0465-2.

Brasier, N., Sempionatto, J. R., Bourke, S., Havenith, G., Schaffarczyk, D., Goldhahn, J., Lüscher, C., & Gao, W. (2024). Towards on-skin analysis of sweat for managing disorders of substance abuse. *Nature Biomedical Engineering*. Available from https://doi.org/10.1038/s41551-024-01187-6, https://www.nature.com/natbiomedeng/.

Brown, T.B., Mann, B., Ryder, N., Subbiah, M., Kaplan, J., Dhariwal, P., Neelakantan, A., Shyam, P., Sastry, G., Askell, A., Agarwal, S., Herbert-Voss, A., Krueger, G., Henighan, T., Child, R., Ramesh, A., Ziegler, D.M., Wu, J., Winter, C., . . .Amodei, D. (2020). Advances in neural information processing systems. 10495258. *Neural information processing systems foundation United States language models are few-shot learners*. https://papers.nips.cc/ 2020-.

Chaudhary, M. F. A., Hoffman, E. A., Guo, J., Comellas, A. P., Newell, J. D., Nagpal, P., Fortis, S., Christensen, G. E., Gerard, S. E., Pan, Y., Wang, D., Abtin, F., Barjaktarevic, I. Z., Barr, R. G., Bhatt, S. P., Bodduluri, S., Cooper, C. B., Gravens-Mueller, L., Han, M. L. K., . . . Reinhardt, J. M. (2023). Predicting severe chronic obstructive pulmonary disease exacerbations using quantitative CT: a retrospective model development and external validation study. *The Lancet Digital Health*, *5*(2), e83. Available from https://doi.org/10.1016/S2589-7500(22)00232-1, https://www.sciencedirect.com/journal/the-lancet-digital-health.

Chen, E., Prakash, S., Janapa Reddi, V., Kim, D., & Rajpurkar, P. (2023). A framework for integrating artificial intelligence for clinical care with continuous therapeutic monitoring. *Nature Biomedical Engineering*. Available from https://doi.org/10.1038/s41551-023-01115-0, https://www.nature.com/natbiomedeng/.

Chen, J., Zhao, Y., Lin, J., Dai, Y., Hu, B., & Gao, S. (2021). A flexible insole gait monitoring technique for the internet of health things. *IEEE Sensors Journal*, *21*(23), 26397–26405. Available from https://doi.org/10.1109/JSEN.2021.3099304, http://ieeexplore.ieee.org/xpl/RecentIssue.jsp?punumber = 7361.

Chen, R. J., Wang, J. J., Williamson, D. F. K., Chen, T. Y., Lipkova, J., Lu, M. Y., Sahai, S., & Mahmood, F. (2023). Algorithmic fairness in artificial intelligence for medicine and healthcare. *Nature Biomedical Engineering*, *7*(6), 719–742. Available from https://doi.org/10.1038/s41551-023-01056-8, https://www.nature.com/natbiomedeng/.

Chen, X., Wang, R., Khalilian-Gourtani, A., Yu, L., Dugan, P., Friedman, D., Doyle, W., Devinsky, O., Wang, Y., & Flinker, A. (2024). A neural speech decoding framework leveraging deep learning and speech synthesis. *Nature Machine Intelligence*, *6*(4), 467–480. Available from https://doi.org/10.1038/s42256-024-00824-8, https://www.nature.com/natmachintell/.

Chen, X., Fu, Z., Song, Z., Yang, L., Ndifon, A. M., Su, Z., Liu, Z., & Gao, S. (2022). An IoT and wearables-based smart home for ALS patients. *IEEE Internet of Things Journal*, *9*(21), 20945–20956. Available from https://doi.org/10.1109/JIOT.2022.3176202, http://ieeexplore.ieee.org/servlet/opac?punumber = 6488907.

Chen, Y., Feng, Y., Chen, Z., Zhou, Y., Yang, Y., Ji, Q., Xu, W., Zhou, G., Gao, T., & Li, X. (2023). A wearable physiological detection system to monitor blink from faint motion artifacts by machine learning method. *IEEE Sensors Journal*, *23*(21), 26126–26135. Available from https://doi.org/10.1109/JSEN.2023.3312975, http://ieeexplore.ieee.org/xpl/RecentIssue.jsp?punumber = 7361.

Chu, M., Cui, Z., Zhang, A., Yao, J., Tang, C., Fu, Z., Nathan, A., & Gao, S. (2022). Multisensory fusion, haptic, and visual feedback teleoperation system under IoT framework. *IEEE Internet of Things Journal*, *9*(20), 19717–19727. Available from https://doi.org/10.1109/JIOT.2022.3167920, http://ieeexplore.ieee.org/servlet/opac?punumber = 6488907.

Church, G. M., & Gilbert, W. (1984). Genomic sequencing. *Proceedings of the National Academy of Sciences*, *81*(7), 1991–1995. Available from https://doi.org/10.1073/pnas.81.7.1991.

Dai, Y., & Gao, S. (2021). A flexible multi-functional smart skin for force, touch position, proximity, and humidity sensing for humanoid robots. *IEEE Sensors Journal*, *21*(23), 26355–26363. Available from https://doi.org/10.1109/JSEN.2021.3055035, http://ieeexplore.ieee.org/xpl/RecentIssue.jsp?punumber = 7361.

Datta, S., Karmakar, C. K., Rao, A. S., Yan, B., & Palaniswami, M. (2020). Automated scoring of hemiparesis in acute stroke from measures of upper limb co-ordination using wearable accelerometry. *IEEE Transactions on Neural Systems and Rehabilitation Engineering*, *28*(4), 805–816. Available from https://doi.org/10.1109/TNSRE.2020.2972285, https://ieeexplore.ieee.org/xpl/mostRecentIssue.jsp?punumber = 7333.

De Fazio, R., Mastronardi, V. M., De Vittorio, M., & Visconti, P. (2023). Wearable sensors and smart devices to monitor rehabilitation parameters and sports performance: An overview. *Sensors*, *23*(4). Available from https://doi.org/10.3390/s23041856, http://www.mdpi.com/journal/sensors.

Dolin, R. H., Alschuler, L., Beebe, C., Biron, P. V., Boyer, S. L., Essin, D., Kimber, E., Lincoln, T., & Mattison, J. E. (2001). The HL7 clinical document architecture. *Journal of the American Medical Informatics Association*, *8*(6), 552–569. Available from https://doi.org/10.1136/jamia.2001.0080552.

Dosovitskiy, A., Beyer, L., Kolesnikov, A., Weissenborn, D., Zhai, X., Unterthiner, T., Dehghani, M., Minderer, M., Heigold, G., Gelly, S., Uszkoreit, J., & Houlsby, N. (2021). In *ICLR 2021 - 9th international conference on learning representations international conference on learning representations, ICLR*, undefined. An image is worth 16x16 words: transformers for image recognition at scale. https://iclr.cc/virtual/2021/papers.html?filter = titles

El-Dahshan, E. S. A., Bassiouni, M. M., Khare, S. K., Tan, R. S., & Rajendra Acharya, U. (2024). ExHyptNet: An explainable diagnosis of hypertension using EfficientNet with PPG signals. *Expert Systems with*

Applications, *239*. Available from https://doi.org/10.1016/j.eswa.2023.122388, https://www.journals.elsevier.com/expert-systems-with-applications.

Gribben, C., Galanakis, V., Calderwood, A., Williams, E. C., Chazarra-Gil, R., Larraz, M., Frau, C., Puengel, T., Guillot, A., Rouhani, F. J., Mahbubani, K., Godfrey, E., Davies, S. E., Athanasiadis, E., Saeb-Parsy, K., Tacke, F., Allison, M., Mohorianu, I., & Vallier, L. (2024). Acquisition of epithelial plasticity in human chronic liver disease. *Nature*, *630*(8015), 166–173. Available from https://doi.org/10.1038/s41586-024-07465-2, https://www.nature.com/nature/.

Javed, L., Anjum, A., Yakubu, B. M., Iqbal, M., Moqurrab, S. A., & Srivastava, G. (2023). ShareChain: Blockchain-enabled model for sharing patient data using federated learning and differential privacy. *Expert Systems*, *40*(5). Available from https://doi.org/10.1111/exsy.13131.

Kim, J., Campbell, A. S., de Ávila, B. E. F., & Wang, J. (2019). Wearable biosensors for healthcare monitoring. *Nature Biotechnology*, *37*(4), 389–406. Available from https://doi.org/10.1038/s41587-019-0045-y, http://www.nature.com/nbt/index.html.

Laubenbacher, R., Niarakis, A., Helikar, T., An, G., Shapiro, B., Malik-Sheriff, R. S., Sego, T. J., Knapp, A., Macklin, P., & Glazier, J. A. (2022). Building digital twins of the human immune system: Toward a roadmap. *npj Digital Medicine*, *5*(1). Available from https://doi.org/10.1038/s41746-022-00610-z.

Laubenbacher, R., Sluka, J. P., & Glazier, J. A. (2021). Using digital twins in viral infection. *Science*, *371* (6534), 1105–1106. Available from https://doi.org/10.1126/science.abf3370, https://science.sciencemag.org/content/sci/371/6534/1105.full.pdf.

Lee, S. Y., Su, P. H., Hung, Y. W., Lee, I. P., Li, S. J., & Chen, J. Y. (2023). Motion artifact reduction algorithm for wearable electrocardiogram monitoring systems. *IEEE Transactions on Consumer Electronics*, *69* (3), 533–547. Available from https://doi.org/10.1109/TCE.2023.3279258, https://ieeexplore.ieee.org/servlet/opac?punumber = 30.

Li, H., Liu, H., Li, Z., Li, C., Meng, Z., Gao, N., & Zhang, Z. (2023). Adaptive threshold-based ZUPT for single IMU-enabled wearable pedestrian localization. *IEEE Internet of Things Journal*, *10*(13), 11749–11760. Available from https://doi.org/10.1109/JIOT.2023.3243296, http://ieeexplore.ieee.org/servlet/opac?punumber = 6488907.

Li, T., Sahu, A. K., Talwalkar, A., & Smith, V. (2020). Federated learning: Challenges, methods, and future directions. *IEEE Signal Processing Magazine*, *37*(3), 50–60. Available from https://doi.org/10.1109/MSP.2020.2975749, http://ieeexplore.ieee.org/xpl/RecentIssue.jsp?punumber = 79&year = 2008.

Li, X., Zhang, Y., Tiwari, P., Song, D., Hu, B., Yang, M., Zhao, Z., Kumar, N., & Marttinen, P. (2022). EEG based emotion recognition: A tutorial and review. *ACM Computing Surveys*, *55*(4). Available from https://doi.org/10.1145/3524499, http://dl.acm.org/citation.cfm?id = J204.

Lin, M., Hu, H., Zhou, S., & Xu, S. (2022). Soft wearable devices for deep-tissue sensing. *Nature Reviews Materials*, *7*(11), 850–869. Available from https://doi.org/10.1038/s41578-022-00427-y, https://www.nature.com/natrevmats/.

Liu, R., Gutiérrez, R., Mather, R. V., Stone, T. A. D., Santa Cruz Mercado, L. A., Bharadwaj, K., Johnson, J., Das, P., Balanza, G., Uwanaka, E., Sydloski, J., Chen, A., Hagood, M., Bittner, E. A., & Purdon, P. L. (2023). Development and prospective validation of postoperative pain prediction from preoperative EHR data using attention-based set embeddings. *npj Digital Medicine*, *6*(1). Available from https://doi.org/10.1038/s41746-023-00947-z, https://www.nature.com/npjdigitalmed/.

Maas, A. I. R., Menon, D. K., Manley, G. T., Abrams, M., Åkerlund, C., Andelic, N., Aries, M., Bashford, T., Bell, M. J., Bodien, Y. G., Brett, B. L., Büki, A., Chesnut, R. M., Citerio, G., Clark, D., Clasby, B., Cooper, D. J., Czeiter, E., Czosnyka, M., … Zemek, R. (2022). Traumatic brain injury: progress and challenges in prevention, clinical care, and research. *The Lancet Neurology*, *21*(11), 1004–1060. Available from https://doi.org/10.1016/s1474-4422(22)00309-x.

Mao, G., Zhou, Z., Su, H., Chen, Y., Zhang, J., Zhang, C., Wang, Z., & Lu, X. (2023). A fully implantable and programmable epidural spinal cord stimulation system for rats with spinal cord injury. *IEEE Transactions on Neural Systems and Rehabilitation Engineering*, *31*, 818–828. Available from https://doi.org/10.1109/tnsre.2023.3234580.

Mundaca-Uribe, R., Askarinam, N., Fang, R. H., Zhang, L., & Wang, J. (2023). Towards multifunctional robotic pills. *Nature Biomedical Engineering*. Available from https://doi.org/10.1038/s41551-023-01090-6, https://www.nature.com/natbiomedeng/.

Peebles, W., & Xie, S. (2023). *Scalable diffusion models with transformers. Proceedings of the IEEE international conference on computer vision* (pp. 4172–4182). United States: Institute of Electrical and Electronics Engineers Inc. Available from http://ieeexplore.ieee.org/xpl/conhome.jsp?punumber = 1000149, 10.1109/ICCV51070.2023.00387.

Raichle, M. E. (1983). Positron emission tomography. *Annual Review of Neuroscience*, *6*, 249–267. Available from https://doi.org/10.1146/annurev.ne.06.030183.001341.

Sandmann, S., Riepenhausen, S., Plagwitz, L., & Varghese, J. (2024). Systematic analysis of ChatGPT, Google search and Llama 2 for clinical decision support tasks. *Nature Communications*, *15*(1). Available from https://doi.org/10.1038/s41467-024-46411-8, https://www.nature.com/ncomms/.

Silva, A. B., Liu, J. R., Metzger, S. L., Bhaya-Grossman, I., Dougherty, M. E., Seaton, M. P., Littlejohn, K. T., Tu-Chan, A., Ganguly, K., Moses, D. A., & Chang, E. F. (2024). A bilingual speech neuroprosthesis driven by cortical articulatory representations shared between languages. *Nature Biomedical Engineering*. Available from https://doi.org/10.1038/s41551-024-01207-5, https://www.nature.com/natbiomedeng/.

Sirtoli, V. G., Liamini, M., Lins, L. T., Lessard-Tremblay, M., Cowan, G. E. R., Zednik, R. J., & Gagnon, G. (2023). Removal of motion artifacts in capacitive electrocardiogram acquisition: A review. *IEEE Transactions on Biomedical Circuits and Systems*, *17*(3), 394–412. Available from https://doi.org/10.1109/TBCAS.2023.3270661, http://www.ieee.org/products/onlinepubs/news/0806_01.html.

Tang, C., Xu, M., Yi, W., Zhang, Z., Occhipinti, E., Dong, C., Ravenscroft, D., Jung, S. M., Lee, S., Gao, S., Kim, J. M., & Occhipinti, L. G. (2024). Ultrasensitive textile strain sensors redefine wearable silent speech interfaces with high machine learning efficiency. *npj Flexible Electronics*, *8*(1). Available from https://doi.org/10.1038/s41528-024-00315-1, https://www.nature.com/npjflexelectron/.

Tang, C., Chen, X., Gong, J., Occhipinti, L. G., & Gao, S. (2022). WMNN: Wearables-based multi-column neural network for human activity recognition. *IEEE J. Biomed. Health Inform.*, 1–11. Available from https://doi.org/10.1109/JBHI.2022.3219364.

Tang, C., Yi, W., Occhipinti, E., Dai, Y., Gao, S., & Occhipinti, L. G. (2024). A roadmap for the development of human body digital twins. *Nature Reviews Electrical Engineering*, *1*(3), 199–207. Available from https://doi.org/10.1038/s44287-024-00025-w.

Tang, H., Yang, Y., Liu, Z., Li, W., Zhang, Y., Huang, Y., Kang, T., Yu, Y., Li, N., Tian, Y., Liu, X., Cheng, Y., Yin, Z., Jiang, X., Chen, X., & Zang, J. (2024). Injectable ultrasonic sensor for wireless monitoring of intracranial signals. *Nature Research, China Nature*, *630*(8015), 84–90. Available from https://doi.org/10.1038/s41586-024-07334-y, https://www.nature.com/nature/.

Taylor, J. P., Brown, R. H., & Cleveland, D. W. (2016). Decoding ALS: From genes to mechanism. *Nature*, *539*(7628), 197–206. Available from https://doi.org/10.1038/nature20413, http://www.nature.com/nature/index.html.

Villringer, A., Planck, J., Hock, C., Schleinkofer, L., & Dirnagl, U. (1993). Near infrared spectroscopy (NIRS): A new tool to study hemodynamic changes during activation of brain function in human adults. *Neuroscience Letters*, *154*(1-2), 101–104. Available from https://doi.org/10.1016/0304-3940(93)90181-J.

Wang, S., Cui, Q., Abiri, P., Roustaei, M., Zhu, E., Li, Y. R., Wang, K., Duarte, S., Yang, L., Ebrahimi, R., Bersohn, M., Chen, J., & Hsiai, T. K. (2023). A self-assembled implantable microtubular pacemaker for wireless cardiac electrotherapy. *Science Advances*, *9*(42). Available from https://doi.org/10.1126/SCIADV.ADJ0540, https://www.science.org/doi/full/10.1126/sciadv.adj0540.

Xu, Y., De la Paz, E., Paul, A., Mahato, K., Sempionatto, J. R., Tostado, N., Lee, M., Hota, G., Lin, M., Uppal, A., Chen, W., Dua, S., Yin, L., Wuerstle, B. L., Deiss, S., Mercier, P., Xu, S., Wang, J., & Cauwenberghs, G. (2023). In-ear integrated sensor array for the continuous monitoring of brain activity and of lactate in sweat. *Nature Biomedical Engineering*, *7*(10), 1307–1320. Available from https://doi.org/10.1038/s41551-023-01095-1, https://www.nature.com/natbiomedeng/.

Zhang, L., Xing, S., Yin, H., Weisbecker, H., Tran, H. T., Guo, Z., Han, T., Wang, Y., Liu, Y., Wu, Y., Xie, W., Huang, C., Luo, W., Demaesschalck, M., McKinney, C., Hankley, S., Huang, A., Brusseau, B., Messenger, J., Zou, Y., & Bai, W. (2024). Skin-inspired, sensory robots for electronic implants. *Nature Communications*, *15*(1), 4777. Available from https://doi.org/10.1038/s41467-024-48903-z.

Zhao, Y., Ding, Y., Lau, V., Man, C., Su, S., Xiao, L., Leong, A. T. L., & Wu, E. X. (2024). Whole-body magnetic resonance imaging at 0.05 Tesla. *Science (New York, N.Y.)*, *384*(6696)eadm7168. Available from https://doi.org/10.1126/science.adm7168.

Zhou, S., Gao, X., Park, G., Yang, X., Qi, B., Lin, M., Huang, H., Bian, Y., Hu, H., Chen, X., Wu, R. S., Liu, B., Yue, W., Lu, C., Wang, R., Bheemreddy, P., Qin, S., Lam, A., Wear, K. A., . . . Xu, S. (2024). Transcranial volumetric imaging using a conformal ultrasound patch. *Nature*, *629*(8013), 810–818. Available from https://doi.org/10.1038/s41586-024-07381-5, https://www.nature.com/nature/.

Zhou, Y., Chia, M. A., Wagner, S. K., Ayhan, M. S., Williamson, D. J., Struyven, R. R., Liu, T., Xu, M., Lozano, M. G., Woodward-Court, P., Kihara, Y., Allen, N., Gallacher, J. E. J., Littlejohns, T., Aslam, T., Bishop, P., Black, G., Sergouniotis, P., Atan, D., . . . Keane, P. A. (2023). A foundation model for generalizable disease detection from retinal images. *Nature*, *622*(7981), 156–163. Available from https://doi.org/10.1038/s41586-023-06555-x, https://www.nature.com/nature/.

CHAPTER

AI-enabled IoMT for smart cancer care: plausible use cases, key challenges, and future road map

19

Partha Pratim Ray

Department of Computer Applications, Sikkim University, Gangtok, Sikkim, India

19.1 Introduction

Cancer remains a leading cause of morbidity and mortality worldwide, with an estimated 19.3 million new cases and 10 million cancer-related deaths in 2020 (Sung et al., 2021). Despite significant advancements in cancer prevention, screening, and treatment, the global burden of cancer continues to rise, driven by factors such as population aging, lifestyle changes, and environmental exposures (Bray et al., 2021). Cancer not only imposes a heavy physical and emotional toll on patients and their families but also exerts a substantial economic burden on healthcare systems and societies (Hofmarcher et al., 2020). The complex and heterogeneous nature of cancer, coupled with the increasing prevalence of comorbidities and treatment-related side effects, poses significant challenges for effective cancer management (Bluethmann et al., 2016). Therefore there is an urgent need for innovative approaches that can improve cancer prevention, early detection, personalized treatment, and survivorship care.

The IoMT refers to the network of connected medical devices, sensors, and mobile applications that enable the continuous monitoring, collection, and exchange of health-related data (Ashfaq et al., 2022). IoMT technologies encompass a wide range of devices, such as wearable sensors, smart pills, implantable devices, and remote monitoring systems, which can capture real-time data on patients' vital signs, physical activity, medication adherence, and symptom burden (Joyia et al., 2017). The integration of artificial intelligence (AI) techniques, such as ML, deep learning, and natural language processing, with IoMT data has opened up new possibilities for intelligent and personalized healthcare delivery (Ahad et al., 2019). AI algorithms can analyze vast amounts of IoMT-generated data to extract meaningful insights, predict health outcomes, and guide clinical decision-making (Jiang et al., 2017). The convergence of AI and IoMT has the potential to revolutionize various aspects of healthcare, from disease prevention and diagnosis to treatment optimization and chronic disease management (Davenport & Kalakota, 2019).

The application of AI-enabled IoMT in cancer care holds immense promise for improving patient outcomes, enhancing the quality of care, and reducing healthcare costs (Tran et al., 2019). AI-enabled IoMT technologies can enable the early detection of cancer through noninvasive, continuous monitoring of biomarkers and physiological signals (Yu et al., 2018). They can also facilitate personalized cancer treatment by capturing real-time data on patients' treatment responses, side effects, and quality of life,

Blockchain and Digital Twin for Smart Hospitals. DOI: https://doi.org/10.1016/B978-0-443-34226-4.00020-4

allowing for timely adjustments to therapy (Topol, 2019). Moreover, AI-enabled IoMT can support cancer survivorship care by monitoring patients' long-term health status, detecting recurrence, and managing the late effects of treatment (Herrmann et al., 2018). The integration of AI and IoMT can also streamline cancer clinical trials by enabling remote patient recruitment, consent management, and real-world data collection (Bender & Sartipi, 2013). Furthermore, AI-enabled IoMT can promote patient engagement and self-management by providing personalized recommendations, education, and feedback based on individual data (Kuziemsky et al., 2019).

Despite the growing interest in AI-enabled IoMT for cancer care, there are still significant challenges and opportunities that need to be addressed. The heterogeneity and complexity of cancer, the need for interoperability and standardization of IoMT devices, the ethical and legal implications of AI-based decision-making, and the integration of AI-enabled IoMT into clinical workflows are some of the key issues that require further research and discussion (Panch et al., 2018). Moreover, the rapid advancements in AI and IoMT technologies necessitate a comprehensive and up-to-date review of the state-of-the-art applications, future directions, and research challenges in this field. This chapter aims to fill this gap by providing a thorough overview of the current landscape and future prospects of AI-enabled IoMT in cancer care, with a focus on the technical, clinical, and ethical aspects.

The main objectives of this chapter are as follows:

- To provide a list of plausible use cases in AI-enabled IoMT applications for cancer care, including cancer prevention, diagnosis, treatment, and survivorship.
- To discuss the key technical, clinical, and ethical challenges and opportunities associated with the development and deployment of AI-enabled IoMT in cancer care.
- To outline the future directions for advancing the field of AI-enabled IoMT in cancer care, considering the perspectives of various stakeholders, including patients, healthcare providers, researchers, and policymakers.

The scope of this chapter encompasses the various applications of AI-enabled IoMT across the cancer care continuum, from prevention and screening to diagnosis, treatment, and survivorship. The chapter focuses on the technical aspects of AI and IoMT technologies, as well as the clinical implications and ethical considerations. The chapter also discusses the current landscape of AI-enabled IoMT in cancer care, including the available products, platforms, and research projects, as well as the future directions and research challenges. The intended audience of this chapter includes researchers, healthcare professionals, policymakers, and students interested in the intersection of AI, IoMT, and cancer care.

This chapter is organized as follows. Section 19.2 discusses the use cases of AI-enabled IoMT for cancer care. Section 19.3 identifies key challenges. Section 4 presents future directions. Section 19.4 concludes the article.

19.2 Use cases of AI-enabled IoMT for cancer care

AI and the IoMT have opened up numerous possibilities for enhancing cancer care across various aspects, from diagnosis and prognosis to treatment planning, monitoring, and survivorship. This

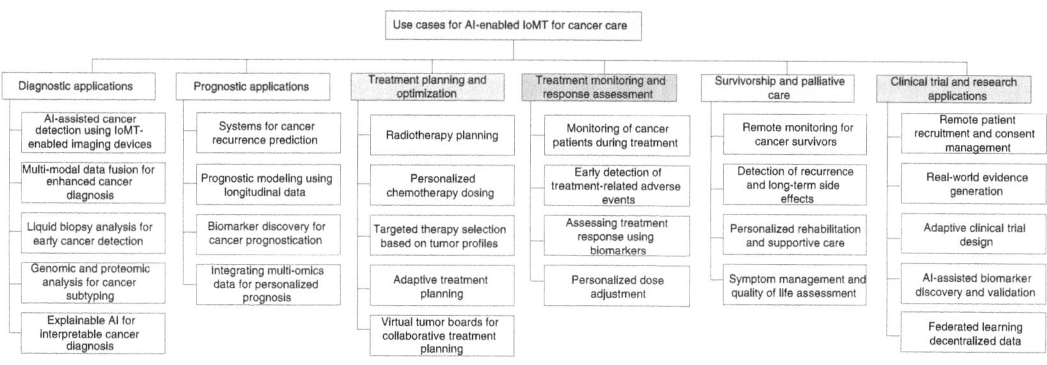

FIGURE 19.1

Taxonomy of use cases of AI-enabled IoMT for cancer care.

section delves into the key use cases of AI-enabled IoMT in cancer care, highlighting the potential of these technologies to transform the way we detect, manage, and treat cancer. Fig. 19.1 shows the classifications of use cases of AI-IoMT-based cancer care.

19.2.1 Diagnostic applications

This subsection presents various diagnostic approaches such as cancer detection using IoMT-enabled imaging devices, multimodal data fusion for enhanced cancer diagnosis, liquid biopsy analysis for early cancer detection, genomic and proteomic analysis for cancer subtyping, and explainable AI for interpretable cancer diagnosis.

19.2.1.1 Cancer detection using IoMT-enabled imaging devices

Recent advancements in IoMT-enabled imaging devices, such as smartphone-based microscopy and wearable ultrasound patches, have opened up new possibilities for AI-assisted cancer detection. These devices capture high-resolution images of suspicious lesions or abnormalities and transmit them to cloud-based AI algorithms for real-time analysis (Alkhawaldeh & Al-Dabet, 2024). Deep learning models, such as convolutional neural networks (CNNs), are trained on large datasets of annotated medical images to accurately identify and localize cancerous regions. The integration of IoMT-enabled imaging devices with AI algorithms has the potential to revolutionize cancer screening, particularly in resource-limited settings (Kaur et al., 2022). These technologies can enable low-cost, portable, and user-friendly cancer screening in remote areas, where access to traditional screening methods may be limited.

19.2.1.2 Multimodal data fusion for enhanced cancer diagnosis

Integrating multiple modalities of IoMT-collected data, such as medical imaging, biomarker measurements, and patient-reported outcomes, can significantly enhance the accuracy and robustness of cancer diagnosis. Multimodal data fusion techniques, such as deep learning-based feature extraction and decision-level fusion, leverage complementary information from different data sources to provide a comprehensive view of the patient's condition (Muhammad et al., 2021). By combining data from various IoMT devices, multimodal data fusion approaches can capture a more holistic picture of a patient's health status. These approaches can help identify subtle patterns and correlations that may not be apparent when analyzing individual data modalities in isolation, leading to the discovery of novel diagnostic biomarkers and the development of more personalized diagnostic strategies (Xu et al., 2024).

19.2.1.3 Liquid biopsy analysis for early cancer detection

Liquid biopsy, which involves the analysis of circulating tumor cells (CTCs), cell-free DNA (cfDNA), and other cancer-derived biomarkers in blood or other bodily fluids, has emerged as a promising approach for early cancer detection. IoMT-based devices, such as microfluidic chips and nanowire sensors, can capture and isolate these rare biomarkers from small volumes of liquid samples. ML algorithms, such as support vector machines (SVMs) and random forests, are then applied to the captured biomarker data to identify cancer-specific patterns and signatures (Khan et al., 2019; Soundaryaveni et al., 2022). Multimodal data fusion techniques, such as deep learning-based feature extraction and decision-level fusion, leverage the complementary information from different data sources, including medical imaging, biomarker measurements, and patient-reported outcomes, to provide a comprehensive view of the patient's condition.

19.2.1.4 Genomic and proteomic analysis for cancer subtyping

Cancer is a highly heterogeneous disease, with different molecular subtypes exhibiting distinct clinical behaviors and treatment responses. AI-driven analysis of genomic and proteomic data from IoMT-collected tumor samples can enable precise cancer subtyping and guide personalized treatment decisions (Elhoseny et al., 2019). Deep learning algorithms, such as autoencoders and graph convolutional networks, can learn latent representations of high-dimensional genomic and proteomic profiles and cluster them into clinically relevant subtypes. AI-driven analysis of genomic and proteomic data from IoMT-collected tumor samples can enable precise cancer subtyping and guide personalized treatment decisions (Judes et al., 2016).

19.2.1.5 Explainable AI for interpretable cancer diagnosis

While AI algorithms have shown remarkable performance in cancer diagnosis, their complex and opaque nature often hinders clinical adoption and trust. Explainable AI (XAI) techniques aim to provide transparent and interpretable explanations for AI-based diagnostic decisions, enabling clinicians to understand and validate the reasoning behind the predictions (Liu et al., 2023). One popular XAI approach is attention mechanisms, which highlight the most informative regions or features in the input data that contribute to the diagnostic outcome (Raza et al., 2022). XAI techniques aim to provide transparent and interpretable explanations for AI-based diagnostic decisions, enabling clinicians to understand and validate the reasoning behind the predictions.

19.2.2 Prognostic applications

We discuss four key prognostic applications such as systems for cancer recurrence prediction, prognostic modeling using longitudinal data, biomarker discovery for cancer prognostication, and integrating multiomics data for personalized prognosis in this subsection.

19.2.2.1 Systems for cancer recurrence prediction

AI-enabled IoMT systems have demonstrated significant potential in predicting cancer recurrence by continuously monitoring patients' physiological and behavioral data posttreatment (Awotunde et al., 2022; Oniani et al., 2021). These systems employ ML algorithms, such as support vector machines and random forests, to analyze IoMT-collected data, including heart rate variability, sleep patterns, and physical activity levels, to identify patterns indicative of recurrence risk. AI-enabled IoMT systems employ ML algorithms to analyze continuously monitored physiological and behavioral data posttreatment, identifying patterns indicative of recurrence risk.

19.2.2.2 Prognostic modeling using longitudinal data

IoMT devices enable the collection of longitudinal data on patients' health status, treatment response, and quality of life, which can be leveraged for prognostic modeling (Venkatesan et al., 2022). ML algorithms, such as Cox proportional hazards models and recurrent neural networks, can analyze these time-series data to predict patient outcomes, such as overall survival and progression-free survival. ML algorithms, such as Cox proportional hazards models and recurrent neural networks, can analyze time-series data collected through IoMT devices to predict patient outcomes, such as overall survival and progression-free survival (Chen et al., 2024).

19.2.2.3 Biomarker discovery for cancer prognostication

AI techniques, such as deep learning and feature selection methods, can facilitate the discovery of novel prognostic biomarkers from IoMT-collected multiomics data (Manickam et al., 2022; Yadav et al., 2021). These biomarkers can help predict patient outcomes and guide personalized treatment strategies. AI techniques, such as deep learning and feature selection methods, can facilitate the discovery of novel prognostic biomarkers from IoMT-collected multiomics data. These approaches can uncover hidden patterns and associations in complex biomedical data, such as whole-slide histopathology images, liquid biopsy samples, and multiomics profiles, leading to the identification of robust and reproducible prognostic biomarkers predictive of patient survival and treatment outcomes.

19.2.2.4 Integrating multiomics data for personalized prognosis

Integrating multiomics data, such as genomics, transcriptomics, and proteomics, from IoMT-collected tumor samples can provide a comprehensive view of cancer biology and enable personalized prognostic predictions (Lin & Wu, 2022). AI techniques, such as multiview learning and tensor factorization, can effectively integrate and analyze these high-dimensional multiomics data to identify prognostic signatures and patient subtypes. AI techniques, such as multiview learning and tensor factorization, can effectively integrate and analyze high-dimensional multiomics data from IoMT-collected tumor samples to identify prognostic signatures and patient subtypes (Parimbelli et al., 2021).

19.2.3 Treatment planning and optimization

We illustrate multiple treatment planning such as radiotherapy planning, personalized chemotherapy dosing, targeted therapy selection based on tumor profiles, adaptive treatment planning, and virtual tumor boards for collaborative treatment planning in this subsection.

19.2.3.1 Radiotherapy planning

AI-assisted radiotherapy planning leverages IoMT-collected imaging and dosimetry data to optimize the delivery of radiation to tumor targets while minimizing damage to healthy tissues (Ghantasala et al., 2021; Sebastian & Peter, 1991). Deep learning algorithms, such as convolutional neural networks and generative adversarial networks, can automatically segment tumor volumes, predict dose distributions, and generate optimal treatment plans based on IoMT-collected data. AI-assisted radiotherapy planning leverages IoMT-collected imaging and dosimetry data to optimize the delivery of radiation to tumor targets while minimizing damage to healthy tissues. Deep learning algorithms can automatically segment tumor volumes, predict dose distributions, and generate optimal treatment plans based on IoMT-collected data, such as MRI scans, CT images, and dosimetry measurements.

19.2.3.2 Personalized chemotherapy dosing

AI algorithms, combined with IoMT-collected pharmacokinetic and pharmacodynamic data, can enable personalized chemotherapy dosing for cancer patients (Garse et al., 2023). These algorithms can predict individual patients' drug responses and optimize dosing regimens based on their unique physiological and genetic profiles. AI algorithms, combined with IoMT-collected pharmacokinetic and pharmacodynamic data, can enable personalized chemotherapy dosing for cancer patients (Ponnusamy et al., 2021). ML models can analyze IoMT-collected data, such as drug concentrations, clearance rates, patient-reported symptoms, and side effects, to predict individual patients' drug responses and optimize dosing regimens.

19.2.3.3 Targeted therapy selection based on tumor profiles

AI-driven analysis of IoMT-collected tumor molecular profiles can guide the selection of targeted therapies for cancer patients. ML algorithms, such as decision trees and support vector machines, can predict patients' responsiveness to specific targeted agents based on their tumor genomic, transcriptomic, and proteomic signatures. AI-driven analysis of IoMT-collected tumor molecular profiles can guide the selection of targeted therapies for cancer patients (Chugh et al., 2024; Siddiqui et al., 2022). ML algorithms can predict patients' responsiveness to specific targeted agents based on their tumor genomic, transcriptomic, and proteomic signatures, as captured by IoMT devices.

19.2.3.4 Adaptive treatment planning

Real-time monitoring of cancer patients using IoMT devices can enable adaptive treatment planning that dynamically adjusts therapeutic strategies based on patients' evolving responses and needs (Kakhi et al., 2022). AI algorithms can analyze the continuous streams of IoMT-collected data, such as vital signs, symptoms, and biomarkers, to detect early signs of treatment failure, adverse events, or disease progression and trigger appropriate modifications to the treatment plan. Real-time monitoring of cancer patients using IoMT devices can enable adaptive treatment planning that dynamically adjusts therapeutic strategies based on patients' evolving responses and needs (Dwivedi et al., 2022).

19.2.3.5 Virtual tumor boards for collaborative treatment planning

AI-enabled virtual tumor boards leverage IoMT technologies to facilitate multidisciplinary collaboration and decision-making in cancer treatment planning (Khang et al., 2023; Ratnakar et al., 2023). These virtual platforms integrate IoMT-collected patient data, including imaging, pathology, and genomic reports, and provide AI-powered decision support tools to assist oncologists, radiologists, surgeons, and other specialists in jointly developing personalized treatment plans. AI-enabled virtual tumor boards leverage IoMT technologies to facilitate multidisciplinary collaboration and decision-making in cancer treatment planning (Nass et al., 2019). AI techniques, such as natural language processing, consensus clustering, and reinforcement learning, can extract key information from electronic health records, recommend optimal treatment strategies based on patient characteristics and preferences, and optimize the interactions among different specialists.

19.2.4 Treatment monitoring and response assessment

We discuss various forms of treatment monitoring aspects that include monitoring of cancer patients during treatment, early detection of treatment-related adverse events, assessing treatment response using biomarkers, and personalized dose adjustment in this subsection.

19.2.4.1 Monitoring of cancer patients during treatment

IoMT devices enable the remote monitoring of cancer patients during treatment, allowing for real-time assessment of their health status, treatment adherence, and side effects (Ahila et al., 2023; Shafiq et al., 2024). Wearable sensors, smart pills, and mobile apps can collect a wide range of data, including vital signs, physical activity, medication intake, and patient-reported outcomes, which can be transmitted to healthcare providers for timely intervention and support. IoMT devices enable the remote monitoring of cancer patients during treatment, allowing for real-time assessment of their health status, treatment adherence, and side effects (Asghari, 2021). Smart pill bottles and smartphone apps can be employed to track the adherence of chronic myeloid leukemia patients to oral targeted therapy, identifying patients at risk of treatment failure due to poor compliance and enabling personalized behavioral interventions.

19.2.4.2 Early detection of treatment-related adverse events

AI algorithms can analyze IoMT-collected data to identify early signs of treatment-related adverse events, such as infections, cardiotoxicity, or neurotoxicity, allowing for timely management and prevention. ML models, such as anomaly detection and time-series classification, can learn normal patterns of patient data and detect deviations indicative of adverse events (Aziz, 2007; Parimbelli et al., 2021). AI algorithms can analyze IoMT-collected data to identify early signs of treatment-related adverse events, such as infections, cardiotoxicity, or neurotoxicity, allowing for timely management and prevention. The analysis of IoMT-collected data by AI algorithms can identify early signs of treatment-related adverse events, such as infections, cardiotoxicity, or neurotoxicity, allowing for timely management and prevention.

19.2.4.3 Assessing treatment response using biomarkers

AI algorithms can analyze IoMT-collected biomarkers, such as circulating tumor DNA (ctDNA), CTCs, and immune markers, to assess patients' response to cancer treatment. These biomarkers provide real-time information on tumor burden, genetic alterations, and immune activation, which can guide treatment decisions and predict outcomes. AI algorithms can make a significant impact in assessing treatment response by analyzing IoMT-collected biomarker data (Javed et al., 2023; Ogundokun et al., 2022). Microfluidic devices can be used to isolate CTCs from the blood of prostate cancer patients undergoing chemotherapy, and deep learning models can classify the CTCs as responsive or resistant to treatment based on their morphological and molecular features.

19.2.4.4 Personalized dose adjustment

AI algorithms can leverage IoMT-collected data to guide personalized dose adjustment of cancer therapies, optimizing treatment efficacy and safety. ML models, such as reinforcement learning and Bayesian optimization, can learn from patients' individual responses to treatment and recommend optimal dosing strategies (Sinha et al., 2023). The integration of AI algorithms and IoMT-collected data can greatly benefit personalized dose adjustment in cancer treatment. Wearable devices can monitor the physical activity and toxicity symptoms of lung cancer patients receiving immunotherapy, and reinforcement learning algorithms can adaptively adjust the dose and frequency of immune checkpoint inhibitors based on each patient's individual tolerance and response (Ponnusamy et al., 2021).

19.2.5 Survivorship and palliative care

Survivorship can be harnessed in many ways. We discuss remote monitoring for cancer survivors, detection of recurrence and long-term side effects, personalized rehabilitation and supportive care, and symptom management and quality-of-life assessment herein.

19.2.5.1 Remote monitoring for cancer survivors

IoMT devices can facilitate the remote monitoring of cancer survivors, enabling the early detection of recurrence, long-term side effects, and psychosocial distress (Rani et al., 2022). Wearable sensors, mobile apps, and smart home devices can collect a wide range of data, including physical activity, sleep patterns, mood, and cognitive function, which can be analyzed by AI algorithms to identify patterns indicative of potential health issues. IoMT-enabled remote monitoring can play a vital role in improving long-term health outcomes and quality of life for cancer survivors.

19.2.5.2 Detection of recurrence and long-term side effects

AI algorithms can analyze IoMT-collected data to detect early signs of cancer recurrence and long-term treatment-related side effects, allowing for timely intervention and management. ML models, such as anomaly detection and pattern recognition, can learn normal patterns of survivor data and identify deviations indicative of potential health problems (Rodriguez et al., 2015). The early detection of recurrence and long-term side effects is crucial for improving outcomes and quality of life among cancer survivors.

19.2.5.3 Personalized rehabilitation and supportive care

AI algorithms can leverage IoMT-collected data to guide personalized rehabilitation and supportive care for cancer survivors, addressing their unique physical, psychological, and social needs (Jayachitra et al., 2023). ML models, such as decision trees and recommender systems, can analyze survivors' individual characteristics, preferences, and responses to interventions and recommend tailored rehabilitation and support strategies. Personalized rehabilitation and supportive care are essential for optimizing cancer survivors' functional outcomes and quality of life.

19.2.5.4 Symptom management and quality-of-life assessment

AI algorithms can analyze IoMT-collected data to assist in symptom management and quality-of-life assessment for cancer patients receiving palliative care. ML models, such as natural language processing and sentiment analysis, can extract meaningful information from patient-reported outcomes, such as pain, fatigue, and emotional distress, and provide insights for personalized symptom control and supportive care. Symptom management and quality-of-life assessment are crucial aspects of palliative care for cancer patients (Nigar et al., 2023).

19.2.6 Clinical trial and research applications

We discuss several clinical trials and applications in AI-enabled IoMT for cancer care in this subsection. We present the following contexts such as remote patient recruitment and consent management, real-world evidence generation, adaptive clinical trial design, AI-assisted biomarker discovery and validation, and federated learning using decentralized data.

19.2.6.1 Remote patient recruitment and consent management

IoMT technologies can streamline the recruitment and consent management of cancer clinical trial participants, overcoming geographical barriers and improving trial efficiency. Mobile apps, web-based platforms, and telemedicine tools can facilitate remote eligibility screening, informed consent, and enrollment of patients, reducing the burden of travel and in-person visits. IoMT technologies can streamline and make more accessible the recruitment and consent management of cancer clinical trial participants (Osama et al., 2023). Web-based platforms can recruit and consent prostate cancer patients for trials of personalized exercise interventions, utilizing video conferencing for remote eligibility assessment and enrollment.

19.2.6.2 Real-world evidence generation

AI algorithms can analyze IoMT-collected data from cancer patients in real-world settings to generate evidence on treatment effectiveness, safety, and patient-reported outcomes. ML models, such as causal inference and multitask learning, can leverage the rich, longitudinal data captured by IoMT devices to identify treatment effects, subgroup responses, and long-term outcomes, complementing the findings of traditional clinical trials (Prasanth et al., 2024). AI algorithms can harness the power of IoMT-collected data to generate real-world evidence that informs clinical practice and health policy.

19.2.6.3 Adaptive clinical trial design

AI algorithms can leverage IoMT-collected data to enable adaptive clinical trial designs that dynamically adjust trial parameters based on interim results and patient responses (Merabet et al., 2024). ML models, such as Bayesian optimization and reinforcement learning, can learn from the continuous stream of IoMT data to inform trial adaptations, such as sample size reassessment, treatment arm selection, and patient stratification, improving trial efficiency and ethics. AI and IoMT can be leveraged to optimize the design of adaptive clinical trials in cancer research. Wearable devices can monitor the physical activity and toxicity symptoms of breast cancer patients enrolled in phase II trials of new targeted therapies, and Bayesian optimization algorithms can adaptively adjust the dose and schedule of the therapy based on patients' individual tolerability and response, minimizing adverse events while maximizing efficacy.

19.2.6.4 AI-assisted biomarker discovery and validation

AI algorithms can assist in the discovery and validation of novel cancer biomarkers using IoMT-collected specimens, such as blood, saliva, and urine samples. ML models, such as feature selection and unsupervised learning, can identify relevant molecular signatures and patterns from high-dimensional omics data generated from these specimens, guiding the development of diagnostic, prognostic, and predictive biomarkers (Kasture & Shende, 2023). The discovery and validation of novel cancer biomarkers can be accelerated through the use of AI algorithms and IoMT-collected specimens. Microfluidic devices can collect serial blood samples from pancreatic cancer patients, and feature selection algorithms can identify panels of circulating microRNA biomarkers predictive of treatment response and survival, enabling liquid biopsy-based precision oncology.

19.2.6.5 Federated learning using decentralized data

Federated learning is an emerging AI paradigm that enables collaborative research using decentralized IoMT data, preserving patient privacy and data ownership. In federated learning, ML models are trained on distributed datasets across multiple institutions or devices, without the need for centralizing the data. Only the model parameters are shared and aggregated, while the raw data remains local (Camajori Tedeschini et al., 2022). This approach can foster large-scale, multiinstitutional research on cancer using IoMT data, overcoming the challenges of data sharing and privacy concerns. Federated learning, an emerging AI paradigm, enables collaborative research using decentralized IoMT data while preserving patient privacy and data ownership.

19.3 Key challenges

While AI-enabled IoMT holds immense promise for transforming cancer care, several key challenges need to be addressed to realize its full potential. This section discusses the main hurdles in implementing AI-enabled IoMT systems in cancer care, ranging from technical and data-related issues to ethical, regulatory, and societal considerations. Fig. 19.2 shows the key challenges of the given context.

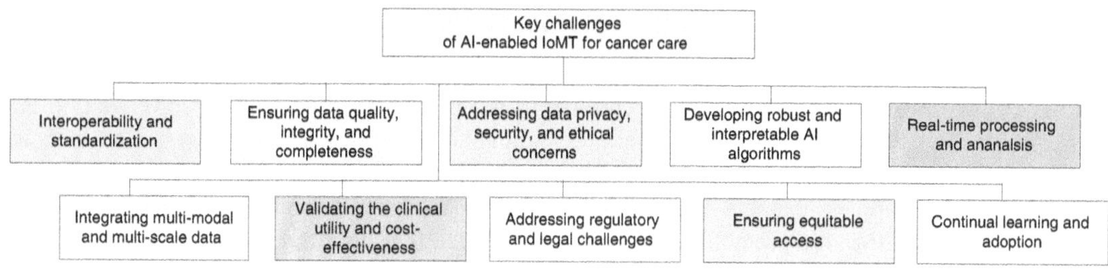

FIGURE 19.2

Classification of use cases of AI-IoMT-based cancer care.

19.3.1 Interoperability and standardization

One of the most significant challenges in implementing AI-enabled IoMT systems for cancer care is the lack of interoperability and standardization among IoMT devices and data formats. The heterogeneity of IoMT devices, communication protocols, and data structures hinders the seamless integration and exchange of information across different platforms and healthcare settings (Shafiq et al., 2024). Establishing industry-wide standards for IoMT device specifications, data formats, and communication protocols is crucial to ensure the compatibility and interoperability of AI-enabled IoMT systems. Efforts such as the development of open-source frameworks, application programming interfaces (APIs), and data exchange standards like Fast Healthcare Interoperability Resources (FHIR) can help address this challenge and promote the adoption of AI-enabled IoMT in cancer care.

19.3.2 Ensuring data quality, integrity, and completeness

The accuracy and reliability of AI-enabled IoMT systems heavily depend on the quality, integrity, and completeness of the data collected by IoMT devices. Ensuring high-quality data is challenging due to various factors, including sensor calibration issues, device malfunctions, network disruptions, and user errors (Ahmed et al., 2024). Incomplete or inconsistent data can lead to biased or inaccurate AI predictions, potentially compromising patient safety and treatment outcomes. Implementing robust data validation, cleansing, and preprocessing techniques is essential to identify and mitigate data quality issues.

19.3.3 Addressing data privacy, security, and ethical concerns

AI-enabled IoMT systems deal with highly sensitive and personal health information, raising significant concerns about data privacy, security, and ethics. Ensuring the confidentiality and integrity of patient data is crucial to prevent unauthorized access, breaches, and misuse (Imoize et al., 2023). Implementing strong encryption mechanisms, access control policies, and secure communication protocols is essential to safeguard IoMT data throughout its lifecycle. Additionally, addressing ethical concerns, such as informed consent, data ownership, and algorithmic bias, is critical to maintaining patient trust and ensuring the responsible deployment of AI-enabled IoMT systems.

19.3.4 Developing robust and interpretable AI algorithms

The heterogeneity and complexity of IoMT data pose significant challenges in developing robust and interpretable AI algorithms for cancer care applications (Sundar et al., 2024). IoMT data often comes from diverse sources, including wearables, implantables, and ambient sensors, each with its own data characteristics and formats. Integrating and analyzing such heterogeneous data requires advanced AI techniques capable of handling multimodal, multiscale, and time-series data. Moreover, ensuring the interpretability and explainability of AI algorithms is crucial for building trust and facilitating clinical decision-making.

19.3.5 Real-time processing and analysis

IoMT devices generate massive amounts of real-time data streams, presenting challenges in terms of data processing, storage, and analysis. The high volume and velocity of IoMT data require efficient and scalable computing infrastructures capable of handling the data influx and enabling real-time insights (Ahila et al., 2023). Developing distributed computing frameworks, such as edge computing and fog computing, can help process IoMT data closer to the source, reducing latency and bandwidth requirements.

19.3.6 Integrating multimodal and multiscale data

AI-enabled IoMT systems for cancer care often require the integration of multimodal and multiscale data from various IoMT sources, such as wearable sensors, medical imaging devices, and electronic health records (Muhammad et al., 2021). Integrating these diverse data types and formats into a coherent and meaningful representation is a significant challenge. Developing advanced data fusion techniques, such as multimodal deep learning and transfer learning, can help capture the complementary information from different data modalities and scales. Additionally, employing ontology-based data integration approaches can provide a semantic framework for harmonizing and linking IoMT data from disparate sources.

19.3.7 Validating the clinical utility and cost-effectiveness

Validating the clinical utility and cost-effectiveness of AI-enabled IoMT interventions is crucial for their widespread adoption in cancer care. Conducting rigorous clinical trials and real-world evaluations is necessary to assess the impact of AI-enabled IoMT systems on patient outcomes, quality of care, and healthcare costs (Sadique et al., 2024). However, designing and executing such studies can be challenging due to the complexity of IoMT systems, the variability of patient populations, and the need for long-term follow-up.

19.3.8 Addressing regulatory and legal challenges

The deployment of AI-enabled IoMT systems in cancer care faces various regulatory and legal challenges. Ensuring compliance with data protection regulations, such as HIPAA and GDPR, is essential to safeguard patient privacy and data security (Fahim et al., 2024). Additionally, obtaining regulatory approvals and certifications for AI-enabled IoMT devices and algorithms can be a lengthy and complex process, requiring extensive validation and documentation. Navigating the intellectual property landscape, including patents and licensing agreements, can also be challenging in the context of AI-enabled IoMT systems.

19.3.9 Ensuring equitable access

Ensuring equitable access and adoption of AI-enabled IoMT cancer care across diverse populations is a significant challenge. Socioeconomic disparities, digital literacy gaps, and cultural barriers can hinder the widespread adoption of AI-enabled IoMT systems, particularly in underserved and marginalized communities (Wazid et al., 2022). Addressing these disparities requires collaborative efforts to improve digital infrastructure, provide education and training, and engage communities in the design and implementation of AI-enabled IoMT solutions.

19.3.10 Continual learning and adaptation

The dynamic nature of IoMT data and the continual evolution of clinical knowledge pose challenges for the long-term performance and relevance of AI models in cancer care. As new IoMT devices, data sources, and treatment guidelines emerge, AI models need to adapt and learn continuously to maintain their accuracy and effectiveness. Developing continual learning techniques, such as incremental learning and transfer learning, can help AI models update their knowledge and adapt to new data without forgetting previously learned patterns (Aldhaen, 2022).

19.4 Future directions

The future of AI-enabled IoMT in cancer care is filled with exciting possibilities and research directions that can potentially transform the way we prevent, diagnose, treat, and manage cancer. This section explores the key future directions and research priorities in this rapidly evolving field. Fig. 19.3. shows the future road map of AI-IoMT-based cancer care.

19.4.1 Developing explainable AI techniques for transparent decision support

One of the key future directions in AI-enabled IoMT cancer care is the development of XAI techniques that provide transparent and interpretable decision support (Khamparia et al., 2023). XAI methods aim to demystify the "black box" nature of complex AI models, such as deep learning networks, by providing human-understandable explanations for their predictions and recommendations. In the context of IoMT-based cancer care, XAI techniques can help clinicians and patients understand the reasoning behind AI-generated insights, fostering trust and facilitating informed decision-making.

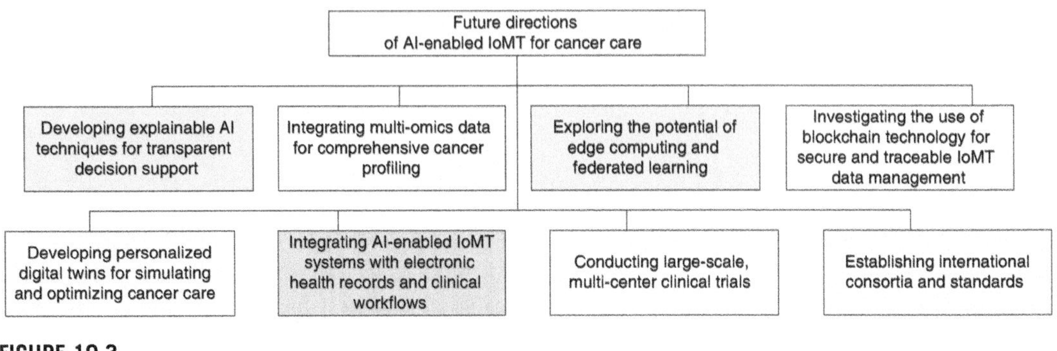

FIGURE 19.3

Future road map of AI-IoMT-based cancer care.

19.4.2 Integrating multiomics data for comprehensive cancer profiling

Integrating multiomics data, such as genomics, transcriptomics, proteomics, and metabolomics, with IoMT-collected data presents a promising avenue for comprehensive cancer profiling and personalized care. By combining the molecular-level insights from multiomics data with the real-time, longitudinal data captured by IoMT devices, AI algorithms can generate holistic patient profiles that encompass both the intrinsic tumor characteristics and the dynamic physiological responses to treatment. This integration can enable the identification of novel biomarkers, the stratification of patient subgroups, and the development of targeted therapeutic strategies (Capobianco, 2022).

19.4.3 Exploring the potential of edge computing and federated learning

Edge computing and federated learning are emerging paradigms that hold great promise for enabling decentralized and privacy-preserving AI-enabled IoMT systems in cancer care. Edge computing involves processing and analyzing IoMT data locally on devices or nearby edge servers, reducing the reliance on centralized cloud infrastructures. This approach can minimize latency, improve real-time responsiveness, and alleviate data privacy and security concerns (Ghosh & Ghosh, 2023).

19.4.4 Investigating the use of blockchain technology for secure and traceable IoMT data management

Blockchain technology has emerged as a promising solution for secure, transparent, and traceable data management in various domains, including healthcare. In the context of AI-enabled IoMT cancer care, blockchain can provide a decentralized and immutable ledger for recording and verifying IoMT data transactions, ensuring data integrity, provenance, and accountability (Polap et al., 2020). By leveraging smart contracts and consensus mechanisms, blockchain-based IoMT systems can enable automated and trustless data sharing, access control, and consent management, empowering patients with greater control over their health data.

19.4.5 Developing personalized digital twins for simulating and optimizing cancer care

Personalized digital twins, which are virtual replicas of individual patients, hold great promise for simulating and optimizing cancer care using AI and IoMT data (Tai et al., 2022). By integrating multimodal data from IoMT devices, electronic health records, and multiomics sources, digital twins can provide a holistic and dynamic representation of a patient's health status, treatment response, and disease progression. AI algorithms can leverage these digital twins to simulate various treatment scenarios, predict patient outcomes, and identify optimal personalized interventions.

19.4.6 Integrating AI-enabled IoMT systems with electronic health records and clinical workflows

Integrating AI-enabled IoMT systems with electronic health records (EHRs) and clinical workflows is essential for the seamless adoption and utilization of these technologies in cancer care (Sardjono et al., 2021). By enabling the bidirectional flow of data between IoMT devices and EHRs, clinicians can access comprehensive patient information, including real-time sensor data, treatment history, and outcomes, within a single unified platform. This integration can facilitate informed decision-making, improve care coordination, and enhance the overall efficiency of cancer care delivery.

19.4.7 Conducting large-scale, multicenter clinical trials

Conducting large-scale, multicenter clinical trials is crucial for validating the efficacy, safety, and cost-effectiveness of AI-enabled IoMT interventions in cancer care. While preliminary studies have shown promising results, rigorous clinical evidence is needed to establish the real-world impact of these technologies on patient outcomes, quality of life, and healthcare costs (Wang et al., 2023). Multicenter trials can provide the necessary statistical power, diversity of patient populations, and generalizability of findings to support the widespread adoption of AI-enabled IoMT in clinical practice.

19.4.8 Establishing international consortia and standards

Establishing international consortia and standards is essential for fostering collaborative research and development in AI-enabled IoMT cancer care. Given the global burden of cancer and the rapid advancements in AI and IoMT technologies, international collaboration is crucial to pool expertise, resources, and data from diverse populations and healthcare systems (Subramaniam et al., 2023). Consortia can provide a platform for knowledge sharing, best practice exchange, and joint research initiatives, accelerating the pace of innovation and translation in this field.

19.5 Conclusion

AI-enabled IoMT systems have the potential to enhance various aspects of cancer management, from diagnosis and prognosis to treatment planning, monitoring, and survivorship. By leveraging the vast amounts of data collected through IoMT devices and applying advanced AI algorithms, healthcare providers can deliver more personalized, precise, and effective cancer care. However, realizing the full potential of AI-enabled IoMT in cancer care requires addressing several key challenges, including interoperability, data quality, privacy, security, and regulatory issues. As we look to the future, the development of explainable AI techniques, integration of multiomics data, exploration of edge computing and federated learning, and the establishment of international consortia and standards will be crucial in shaping the landscape of AI-enabled IoMT in cancer care. Through collaborative efforts and innovative research, we can harness the power of these technologies to improve patient outcomes, enhance health equity, and ultimately, transform the way we fight against cancer.

Acknowledgment

The author used Claude 3 for the discussion about cancer and for initial drafting.

References

Ahad, A., Tahir, M., & Yau, K. L. A. (2019). 5G-based smart healthcare network: Architecture, taxonomy, challenges and future research directions. *IEEE Access*, *7*, 100747–100762. Available from https://doi.org/10.1109/ACCESS.2019.2930628, http://ieeexplore.ieee.org/xpl/RecentIssue.jsp?punumber = 6287639.

Ahila, A., Dahan, F., Alroobaea, R., Alghamdi, W. Y., Mohammed, M. K., Hajjej, F., Alsekait, D. M., & Raahemifar, K. (2023). A smart IoMT based architecture for E-healthcare patient monitoring system using artificial intelligence algorithms. *Frontiers in Physiology*, *14*. Available from https://doi.org/10.3389/fphys.2023.1125952, http://www.frontiersin.org/Physiology/archive/.

Ahmed, S. F., Alam, M. S. B., Afrin, S., Rafa, S. J., Rafa, N., & Gandomi, A. H. (2024). Insights into internet of medical things (IoMT): Data fusion, security issues and potential solutions. *Information Fusion*, *102*. Available from https://doi.org/10.1016/j.inffus.2023.102060, http://www.elsevier.com/inca/publications/store/6/2/0/8/6/2/index.htt.

Aldhaen, F. S. (2022) Study of the continuous intention to use artificial intelligence-based Internet of Medical Things (IoMT) during concurrent diffusion. The influence diffusion of innovation factors has as determinants of continuous intention to use AI-based IoMT. Doctoral dissertation, University of Bradford, https://bradscholars.brad.ac.uk/bitstream/handle/10454/19852/17018021%20Fatema%20Aldhaen%20Final%20Thesis%20Submission.pdf?sequence=1.

Alkhawaldeh, R. S., & Al-Dabet, S. (2024). Unified framework model for detecting and organizing medical cancerous images in IoMT systems. *Multimedia Tools and Applications*, *83*(13), 37743–37770. Available from https://doi.org/10.1007/s11042-023-16883-9, https://www.springer.com/journal/11042.

Asghari, P. (2021). A diagnostic prediction model for colorectal cancer in elderlies via internet of medical things. *International Journal of Information Technology*, *13*(4), 1423–1429. Available from https://doi.org/10.1007/s41870-021-00663-5.

Ashfaq, Z., Rafay, A., Mumtaz, R., Hassan Zaidi, S. M., Saleem, H., Raza Zaidi, S. A., Mumtaz, S., & Haque, A. (2022). A review of enabling technologies for internet of medical things (IoMT) ecosystem. *Ain Shams Engineering Journal*, *13*(4). Available from https://doi.org/10.1016/j.asej.2021.101660, http://www.elsevier.com/wps/find/journaldescription.cws_home/724208/description#description.

Awotunde, J. B., Folorunso, S. O., Ajagbe, S. A., Garg, J., & Ajamu, G. J. (2022). *AiIoMT: IoMT-based system-enabled artificial intelligence for enhanced smart healthcare systems. Machine learning for critical internet of medical things: Applications and use cases* (pp. 229–254). Nigeria: Springer

International Publishing. Available from https://link.springer.com/book/10.1007/978-3-030-80928-7, 10.1007/978-3-030-80928-7_10.

Aziz, N. M. (2007). Cancer survivorship research: State of knowledge, challenges and opportunities. *Acta Oncologica*, *46*(4), 417–432. Available from https://doi.org/10.1080/02841860701367878.

Bender, D., & Sartipi, K. (2013). HL7 FHIR: An agile and RESTful approach to healthcare information exchange. In *Proceedings of CBMS 2013 - 26th IEEE international symposium on computer-based medical systems* (pp. 326–331). https://doi.org/10.1109/CBMS.2013.6627810.

Bluethmann, S. M., Mariotto, A. B., & Rowland, J. H. (2016). Anticipating the "silver tsunami": Prevalence trajectories and comorbidity burden among older cancer survivors in the United States. *Cancer Epidemiology Biomarkers and Prevention.*, *25*(7), 1029–1036. Available from https://doi.org/10.1158/1055-9965.EPI-16-0133, http://cebp.aacrjournals.org/content/25/7/1029.full.pdf + html.

Bray, F., Laversanne, M., Weiderpass, E., & Soerjomataram, I. (2021). The ever-increasing importance of cancer as a leading cause of premature death worldwide. *Cancer*, *127*(16), 3029–3030. Available from https://doi.org/10.1002/cncr.33587, http://onlinelibrary.wiley.com/journal/10.1002/(ISSN)1097-0142.

Camajori Tedeschini, B., Savazzi, S., Stoklasa, R., Barbieri, L., Stathopoulos, I., Nicoli, M., & Serio, L. (2022). Decentralized federated learning for healthcare networks: A case study on tumor segmentation. *IEEE Access*, *10*, 8693–8708. Available from https://doi.org/10.1109/ACCESS.2022.3141913, http://ieeexplore.ieee.org/xpl/RecentIssue.jsp?punumber = 6287639.

Capobianco, E. (2022). High-dimensional role of AI and machine learning in cancer research. *British Journal of Cancer*, *126*(4), 523–532. Available from https://doi.org/10.1038/s41416-021-01689-z, http://www.nature.com/bjc/index.html.

Chen, X., Xie, H., Tao, X., Wang, F. L., Leng, M., & Lei, B. (2024). Artificial intelligence and multimodal data fusion for smart healthcare: Topic modeling and bibliometrics. *Artificial Intelligence Review*, *57*(4). Available from https://doi.org/10.1007/s10462-024-10712-7, https://www.springer.com/journal/10462.

Chugh, V., Basu, A., Kaushik, A., Manshu, N., Bhansali, S., & Basu, A. K. (2024). Employing nano-enabled artificial intelligence (AI)-based smart technologies for prediction, screening, and detection of cancer. *Nanoscale*, *16*(11), 5458–5486. Available from https://doi.org/10.1039/d3nr05648a, http://pubs.rsc.org/en/journals/journal/nr.

Davenport, T., & Kalakota, R. (2019). The potential for artificial intelligence in healthcare. *Future Healthcare Journal*, *6*(2), 94–98. Available from https://doi.org/10.7861/futurehosp.6-2-94.

Dwivedi, R., Mehrotra, D., & Chandra, S. (2022). Potential of internet of medical things (IoMT) applications in building a smart healthcare system: A systematic review. *Journal of Oral Biology and Craniofacial Research*, *12*(2), 302–318. Available from https://doi.org/10.1016/j.jobcr.2021.11.010, http://www.journals.elsevier.com/journal-of-oral-biology-and-craniofacial-research/.

Elhoseny, M., Bian, G. B., Lakshmanaprabu, S. K., Shankar, K., Singh, A. K., & Wu, W. (2019). Effective features to classify ovarian cancer data in internet of medical things. *Computer Networks*, *159*, 147–156. Available from https://doi.org/10.1016/j.comnet.2019.04.016, http://www.journals.elsevier.com/computer-networks/.

Fahim, K. E., Kalinaki, K., & Shafik, W. (2024). *Electronic devices in the artificial intelligence of the internet of medical things (AIoMT). Handbook of security and privacy of AI-enabled healthcare systems and internet of medical things* (pp. 41–62). CRC Press.

Garse, S., Turabi, K. S., Aich, J., Ranjan, A., Nagar, S., Basu, S., & Devarajan, S. (2023). *Cancer diagnosis using artificial intelligence (AI) and internet of things (IoT). Revolutionizing healthcare through artificial intelligence and internet of things applications* (pp. 50–71). India: IGI Global. Available from https://www.igi-global.com/book/revolutionizing-healthcare-through-artificial-intelligence/295824, https://doi.org/10.4018/978-1-6684-5422-0.ch004.

Ghantasala, G. S. P., Kumari, N. V., & Patan, R. (2021). *Cancer prediction and diagnosis hinged on HCML in IOMT environment. Machine Learning and the Internet of Medical Things in Healthcare* (pp. 179–207).

India: Elsevier. Available from https://www.sciencedirect.com/book/9780128212295, 10.1016/B978-0-12-821229-5.00004-5.

Ghosh, S., & Ghosh, S. K. (2023). FEEL: FEderated learning framework for elderly healthcare using edge-IoMT. *IEEE Transactions on Computational Social Systems*, *10*(4), 1800–1809. Available from https://doi.org/10.1109/TCSS.2022.3233300, http://ieeexplore.ieee.org/servlet/opac?punumber = 6570650.

Herrmann, M., Boehme, P., Mondritzki, T., Ehlers, J. P., Kavadias, S., & Truebel, H. (2018). Digital transformation and disruption of the health care sector: Internet-based observational study. *Journal of Medical Internet Research*, *20*(3). Available from https://doi.org/10.2196/jmir.9498, https://asset.jmir.pub/assets/66882cc0a41e6646eb77c74fc30eb2e7.pdf.

Hofmarcher, T., Lindgren, P., Wilking, N., & Jönsson, B. (2020). The cost of cancer in Europe 2018. *European Journal of Cancer*, *129*, 41–49. Available from https://doi.org/10.1016/j.ejca.2020.01.011, http://www.journals.elsevier.com/european-journal-of-cancer/.

Imoize, A. L., Balas, V. E., Solanki, V. K., Lee, C. C., & Obaidat, M. S. (2023). *Handbook of security and privacy of AI-enabled healthcare systems and internet of medical things handbook of security and privacy of AI-enabled healthcare systems and internet of medical things* (pp. 1–471). Nigeria: CRC Press. Available from http://www.tandfebooks.com/doi/book/9781000963182, https://doi.org/10.1201/9781003370321.

Javed, A. R., Saadia, A., Mughal, H., Gadekallu, T. R., Rizwan, M., Maddikunta, P. K. R., Mahmud, M., Liyanage, M., & Hussain, A. (2023). Artificial intelligence for cognitive health assessment: State-of-the-art, open challenges and future directions. *Cognitive Computation*, *15*(6), 1767–1812. Available from https://doi.org/10.1007/s12559-023-10153-4, https://www.springer.com/journal/12559.

Jayachitra, S., Prasanth, A., Hariprasath, S., Benazir Begam, R., & Madiajagan, M. (2023). *AI enabled internet of medical things in smart healthcare* (pp. 141–161). Springer Science and Business Media LLC. Available from https://doi.org/10.1007/978-3-031-31952-5_7.

Jiang, F., Jiang, Y., Zhi, H., Dong, Y., Li, H., Ma, S., Wang, Y., Dong, Q., Shen, H., & Wang, Y. (2017). Artificial intelligence in healthcare: Past, present and future. *Stroke and Vascular Neurology*, *2*(4), 230–243. Available from https://doi.org/10.1136/svn-2017-000101, svn.bmj.com.

Joyia, G. J., Liaqat, R. M., Farooq, A., & Rehman, S. (2017). Internet of medical things (IOMT): Applications, benefits and future challenges in healthcare domain. *Journal of Communications*, *12*(4), 240–247. Available from https://doi.org/10.12720/jcm.12.4.240-247, http://www.jocm.us/uploadfile/2017/0428/20170428025024260.pdf.

Judes, G., Rifaï, K., Daures, M., Dubois, L., Bignon, Y. J., Penault-Llorca, F., & Bernard-Gallon, D. (2016). High-throughput "Omics" technologies: New tools for the study of triple-negative breast cancer. *Cancer Letters*, *382* (1), 77–85. Available from https://doi.org/10.1016/j.canlet.2016.03.001, http://www.elsevier.com/locate/canlet.

Kakhi, K., Alizadehsani, R., Kabir, H. M. D., Khosravi, A., Nahavandi, S., & Acharya, U. R. (2022). The internet of medical things and artificial intelligence: Trends, challenges, and opportunities. *Biocybernetics and Biomedical Engineering*, *42*(3), 749–771. Available from https://doi.org/10.1016/j.bbe.2022.05.008, http://www.sciencedirect.com/science/journal/02085216.

Kasture, K., & Shende, P. (2023). Amalgamation of Artificial Intelligence with Nanoscience for Biomedical Applications. *Archives of Computational Methods in Engineering*, *30*(8), 4667–4685. Available from https://doi.org/10.1007/s11831-023-09948-3, https://www.springer.com/journal/11831.

Kaur, D., Singh, S., Mansoor, W., Kumar, Y., Verma, S., Dash, S., Koul, A., & Khosravi, M. R. (2022). Computational Intelligence and Metaheuristic Techniques for Brain Tumor Detection through IoMT-Enabled MRI Devices. *Wireless Communications and Mobile Computing*, *2022*, 1–20. Available from https://doi.org/10.1155/2022/1519198.

Khamparia, A., Pandey, B., Al-Turjman, F., & Podder, P. (2023). An intelligent IoMT enabled feature extraction method for early detection of knee arthritis. *Expert Systems*, *40*(4). Available from https://doi.org/10.1111/exsy.12784, http://onlinelibrary.wiley.com/journal/10.1111/(ISSN)1468-0394.

Khan, S. U., Islam, N., Jan, Z., Din, I. U., Khan, A., & Faheem, Y. (2019). An e-Health care services framework for the detection and classification of breast cancer in breast cytology images as an IoMT application. *Future Generation Computer Systems, 98*, 286–296. Available from https://doi.org/10.1016/j.future.2019.01.033.

Khang, A., Rana, G., Tailor, R. K., & Abdullayev, V. (Eds.), (2023). *Data-centric AI solutions and emerging technologies in the healthcare ecosystem*. CRC Press.

Kuziemsky, C., Maeder, A. J., John, O., Gogia, S. B., Basu, A., Meher, S., & Ito, M. (2019). Role of artificial intelligence within the telehealth domain. *Yearbook of Medical Informatics, 28*(1), 35–40. Available from https://doi.org/10.1055/s-0039-1677897.

Lin, B., & Wu, S. (2022). Digital transformation in personalized medicine with artificial intelligence and the internet of medical things. *OMICS A Journal of Integrative Biology, 26*(2), 77–81. Available from https://doi.org/10.1089/omi.2021.0037, http://www.liebertonline.com/omi.

Liu, W., Zhao, F., Shankar, A., Maple, C., Peter, J. D., Kim, B. G., Slowik, A., Parameshachari, B. D., & Lv, J. (2023). Explainable AI for medical image analysis in medical cyber-physical systems: Enhancing transparency and trustworthiness of IoMT. *IEEE Journal of Biomedical and Health Informatics*, 1–12. Available from https://doi.org/10.1109/JBHI.2023.3336721, http://ieeexplore.ieee.org/xpl/RecentIssue.jsp?punumber = 6221020.

Manickam, P., Mariappan, S. A., Murugesan, S. M., Hansda, S., Kaushik, A., Shinde, R., & Thipperudraswamy, S. P. (2022). Artificial Intelligence (AI) and internet of medical things (IoMT) assisted biomedical systems for intelligent healthcare. *Biosensors, 12*(8), 562. Available from https://doi.org/10.3390/bios12080562.

Merabet, A., Saighi, A., Laboudi, Z., & Ferradji, M. A. (2024). Multiple diseases forecast through AI and IoMT techniques: Systematic literature review. *Communications in Computer and Information Science, 1940*, 189–206. Available from https://doi.org/10.1007/978-3-031-46335-8_15, https://www.springer.com/series/7899.

Muhammad, G., Alshehri, F., Karray, F., Saddik, A. E., Alsulaiman, M., & Falk, T. H. (2021). A comprehensive survey on multimodal medical signals fusion for smart healthcare systems. *Information Fusion, 76*, 355–375. Available from https://doi.org/10.1016/j.inffus.2021.06.007, http://www.elsevier.com/inca/publications/store/6/2/0/8/6/2/index.htt.

Nass, S. J., Patlak, M., & Zevon, E. (Eds.), (2019). *Improving cancer diagnosis and care: clinical application of computational methods in precision oncology: proceedings of a workshop*. Washington, DC: The National Academies Press.

Nigar, N., Jaleel, A., Islam, S., Shahzad, M. K., & Affum, E. A. (2023). IoMT meets machine learning: From edge to cloud chronic diseases diagnosis system. *Journal of Healthcare Engineering, 2023*. Available from https://doi.org/10.1155/2023/9995292, http://www.hindawi.com/journals/jhe/contents/.

Ogundokun, R. O., Misra, S., Douglas, M., Damaševičius, R., & Maskeliūnas, R. (2022). Medical internet-of-things based breast cancer diagnosis using hyperparameter-optimized neural networks. *Future Internet, 14*(5), 153. Available from https://doi.org/10.3390/fi14050153.

Oniani, S., Marques, G., Barnovi, S., Pires, I. M., & Bhoi, A. K. (2021). Artificial intelligence for internet of things and enhanced medical systems. *Studies in Computational Intelligence, 903*, 43–59. Available from https://doi.org/10.1007/978-981-15-5495-7_3, http://www.springer.com/series/7092.

Osama, M., Ateya, A. A., Sayed, M. S., Hammad, M., Pławiak, P., Abd El-Latif, A. A., & Elsayed, R. A. (2023). Internet of medical things and healthcare 4.0: Trends, requirements, challenges, and research directions. *Sensors, 23*(17). Available from https://doi.org/10.3390/s23177435, http://www.mdpi.com/journal/sensors.

Panch, T., Szolovits, P., & Rifat, A. (2018). Artificial intelligence, machine learning and health systems. *Journal of Global Health, 8*(2). Available from https://doi.org/10.7189/jogh.08.020303.

Parimbelli, E., Wilk, S., Cornet, R., Sniatala, P., Sniatala, K., Glaser, S. L. C., Fraterman, I., Boekhout, A. H., Ottaviano, M., & Peleg, M. (2021). A review of AI and data science support for cancer management. *Artificial Intelligence in Medicine, 117*, 102111. Available from https://doi.org/10.1016/j.artmed.2021.102111.

Polap, D., Srivastava, G., Jolfaei, A., & Parizi, R.M. (2020). Blockchain technology and neural networks for the internet of medical things. In *IEEE INFOCOM 2020 - IEEE conference on computer communications workshops, INFOCOM WKSHPS 2020* (pp. 508–513). https://doi.org/10.1109/INFOCOMWKSHPS50562.2020.9162735, http://ieeexplore.ieee.org/xpl/mostRecentIssue.jsp?punumber = 9146478.

Ponnusamy, V., Christopher Clement, J., Sriharipriya, K. C., & Natarajan, S. (2021). *Smart healthcare technologies for massive internet of medical things internet of things* (pp. 71–101). India: Springer Science and Business Media Deutschland GmbH. Available from http://www.springer.com/series/11636, https://doi.org/10.1007/978-3-030-66633-0_4.

Prasanth, A., Lakshmi, D., Dhanaraj, R. K., Balusamy, B., & Sherimon, P. C. (Eds.), (2024). *Technological Advancement in Internet of Medical Things and Blockchain for Personalized Healthcare: Applications and Use Cases*. CRC Press.

Rani, S., Rajagopal, M., Kumar, N., & Shah, S. H. A. (2022). *An IoMT-based smart remote monitoring system for healthcare. IoT-enabled smart healthcare systems, services and applications* (pp. 177–198). Wiley. Available from https://doi.org/10.1002/9781119816829.ch8.

Ratnakar, N. C., Prajapati, B. R., Prajapati, B. G., & Prajapati, J. B. (2023). *Smart innovative medical devices based on artificial intelligence* (pp. 150–172). Informa UK Limited. Available from https://doi.org/10.1201/9781003346289-10.

Raza, H., Abbas., Amir, S., Arshad, K., Siddiqui, M. R., & Khan, S. I. (2022). An IoMT enabled smart healthcare model to monitor elderly people using explainable. *Artificial Intelligence (EAI). Jun, 30*(2), 16–22.

Rodriguez, J. L., Hawkins, N. A., Berkowitz, Z., & Li, C. (2015). Factors associated with health-related quality of life among colorectal cancer survivors. *American Journal of Preventive Medicine, 49*(6), S518. Available from https://doi.org/10.1016/j.amepre.2015.08.007, http://www.elsevier.com/locate/amepre.

Sadique, M. A., Yadav, S., Khan, R., & Srivastava, A. K. (2024). Engineered two-dimensional nanomaterials based diagnostics integrated with internet of medical things (IoMT) for COVID-19. *Chemical Society Reviews, 53*(8), 3774–3828. Available from https://doi.org/10.1039/d3cs00719g, http://pubs.rsc.org/en/journals/journal/cs.

Sardjono, W., Retnowardhani, A., Emil Kaburuan, R., & Rahmasari, A. (2021). Artificial intelligence and big data analysis implementation in electronic medical records. In *ACM international conference proceeding series* (pp. 231–237). https://doi.org/10.1145/3512576.3512618, http://portal.acm.org/.

Sebastian, A. M., & Peter, D. (1991). Artificial intelligence in cancer research: Trends, challenges and future directions. *Life (Chicago, Ill.: 1978), 12*.

Shafiq, M., Choi, J.-G., Cheikhrouhou, O., & Hamam, H. (2024). Advances in IoMT for healthcare systems. *Sensors, 24*(1), 10. Available from https://doi.org/10.3390/s24010010.

Siddiqui, M. F., Mouna, A., Nicolas, G., Rahat, S. A. A., Mitalipova, A., Emmanuel, N., & Tashmatova, N. (2022). Computational intelligence: A step forward in cancer biomarker discovery and therapeutic target prediction. *Studies in Computational Intelligence, 1016*, 233–250. Available from https://doi.org/10.1007/978-981-16-9221-5_14, https://www.springer.com/series/7092.

Sinha, A., Garcia, D. W., Kumar, B., & Banerjee, P. (2023). Application of big data analytics and Internet of Medical Things (IoMT) in healthcare with view of explainable artificial intelligence: A survey. *Internet of Things, 739*, 129–163. Available from https://doi.org/10.1007/978-3-031-08637-3_8, https://www.springer.com/series/11636.

Soundaryaveni, C., Prasanth, A., Lavanya, S., & Sowndarya, K. K. D. (2022). *Case studies: Cancer prediction and diagnosis in the IoMT environment* (pp. 173–198). Informa UK Limited. Available from https://doi.org/10.1201/9781003256243-9.

Subramaniam, E. V. D., Srinivasan, K., Qaisar, S. M., & Pławiak, P. (2023). Interoperable IoMT approach for remote diagnosis with privacy-preservation perspective in edge systems. *Sensors, 23*(17), 7474. Available from https://doi.org/10.3390/s23177474.

Sundar, R., Gangopadhyay, A., Gupta, T. R., Murthy, P. L. S., Gogula, S., Sharath, M. N., & Muppavaram, K. (2024). Heart health prediction and classification: An IoMT and AI collaborative model. In *MATEC Web of Conferences*. (392, p. 01142). EDP Sciences.

Sung, H., Ferlay, J., Siegel, R. L., Laversanne, M., Soerjomataram, I., Jemal, A., & Bray, F. (2021). Global cancer statistics 2020: GLOBOCAN estimates of incidence and mortality worldwide for 36 cancers in 185 countries. *Cancer Journal for Clinicians*, *71*(3), 209–249. Available from https://doi.org/10.3322/caac.21660, http://onlinelibrary.wiley.com/journal/10.3322/(ISSN)1542-4863.

Tai, Y., Zhang, L., Li, Q., Zhu, C., Chang, V., Rodrigues, J. J. P. C., & Guizani, M. (2022). Digital-twin-enabled IoMT system for surgical simulation using rAC-GAN. *IEEE Internet of Things Journal*, *9*(21), 20918–20931. Available from https://doi.org/10.1109/jiot.2022.3176300.

Topol, E. J. (2019). High-performance medicine: The convergence of human and artificial intelligence. *Nature Medicine*, *25*(1), 44–56. Available from https://doi.org/10.1038/s41591-018-0300-7, http://www.nature.com/nm/index.html.

Tran, B. X., Vu, G. T., Ha, G. H., Vuong, Q. H., Ho, M. T., Vuong, T. T., La, V. P., Ho, M. T., Nghiem, K. C. P., Nguyen, H. L. T., Latkin, C. A., Tam, W. W. S., Cheung, N. M., Nguyen, H. K. T., Ho, C. S. H., & Ho, R. C. M. (2019). Global evolution of research in artificial intelligence in health and medicine: A bibliometric study. *Journal of Clinical Medicine*, *8*(3). Available from https://doi.org/10.3390/jcm8030360, https://www.mdpi.com/2077-0383/8/3/360/pdf.

Venkatesan, D., Elangovan, A., Winster, H., Pasha, M. Y., Abraham, K. S., Satheeshkumar, J., Sivaprakash, P., Niraikulam, A., Gopalakrishnan, A. V., Narayanasamy, A., & Vellingiri, B. (2022). Diagnostic and therapeutic approach of artificial intelligence in neuro-oncological diseases. *Biosensors and Bioelectronics: X*, *11*, 100188. Available from https://doi.org/10.1016/j.biosx.2022.100188.

Wang, B., Hu, X., Zhang, J., Xu, C., & Gao, Z. (2023). Intelligent internet of things in mammography screening using multicenter transformation between unified capsules. *IEEE Internet of Things Journal*, *10*(2), 1536–1545. Available from https://doi.org/10.1109/jiot.2022.3209895.

Wazid, M., Singh, J., Das, A. K., Shetty, S., Khan, M. K., & Rodrigues, J. J. P. C. (2022). ASCP-IoMT: AI-enabled lightweight secure communication protocol for internet of medical things. *IEEE Access*, *10*, 57990–58004. Available from https://doi.org/10.1109/ACCESS.2022.3179418, http://ieeexplore.ieee.org/xpl/RecentIssue.jsp?punumber = 6287639.

Xu, X., Li, J., Zhu, Z., Zhao, L., Wang, H., Song, C., Chen, Y., Zhao, Q., Yang, J., & Pei, Y. (2024). A comprehensive review on synergy of multi-modal data and AI technologies in medical diagnosis. *Bioengineering*, *11*(3), 219. Available from https://doi.org/10.3390/bioengineering11030219.

Yadav, A. K., Verma, D., Kumar, A., Kumar, P., & Solanki, P. R. (2021). The perspectives of biomarker-based electrochemical immunosensors, artificial intelligence and the internet of medical things toward COVID-19 diagnosis and management. *Materials Today Chemistry*, *20*, 100443. Available from https://doi.org/10.1016/j.mtchem.2021.100443.

Yu, K. H., Beam, A. L., & Kohane, I. S. (2018). Artificial intelligence in healthcare. *Nature Biomedical Engineering*, *2*(10), 719–731. Available from https://doi.org/10.1038/s41551-018-0305-z, http://www.nature.com/natbiomedeng/.

CHAPTER 20

Digital twins and brain surgery: revolutionizing neurosurgical procedures through advanced simulation

Hossein Hassani[1], Benjamin Irani[2] and Saharsadat Reihaninia[2]

[1]*Research Institute of Energy Management and Planning, University of Tehran, Tehran, Iran*

[2]*Digital Team, CARE Denmark, Copenhagen, Denmark*

20.1 Introduction

This chapter delves into the groundbreaking integration of digital twin technology into the field of neurosurgery. By creating virtual replicas of patients' brains, surgeons can now simulate various surgical interventions, predict outcomes, and personalize surgical plans (Armeni et al., 2022; Sun et al., 2022, 2023). This chapter outlines the evolution of digital twins from their origins in manufacturing to their pivotal role in modern neurosurgery, highlighting their potential to transform patient care and surgical precision.

In recent years, the landscape of neurosurgery has undergone a significant transformation, heralding the advent of an era where the fusion of technology and medicine not only enhances surgical outcomes but also personalizes the patient care experience (Bahadure et al., 2018; Coorey et al., 2022; Corral-Acero et al., 2020; Ejaz et al., 2022; Eltayeb et al., 2019; Hassani et al., 2022a, 2022b; Kamel Boulos & Zhang, 2021; Malathi & Sinthia, 2018; Sarris et al., 2023; Tao & Qi, 2019; Voigt et al., 2021; Wang et al., 2022). At the heart of this transformation is the integration of digital twin technology into neurosurgical practices—a development that promises to revolutionize how brain surgeries are planned, executed, and evaluated (Coorey et al., 2022; Eltayeb et al., 2019; Kamel Boulos & Zhang, 2021; Malathi & Sinthia, 2018; Sarris et al., 2023; Voigt et al., 2021; Wang et al., 2022).

Digital twins, originally conceptualized within the manufacturing sector, are virtual replicas of physical entities, processes, or systems. Digital twin is the bridge between the real and virtual worlds (Nguyen, 2023, 2024). This technology's application in healthcare, particularly in neurosurgery, involves creating highly detailed and dynamic digital models of patients' brains (Sarris et al., 2023). These models serve as a platform for neurosurgeons to simulate various surgical interventions, assess the potential outcomes of these interventions, and devise customized surgical plans tailored to the individual needs and anatomical specifics of each patient (Malathi & Sinthia, 2018).

The journey of digital twins from industrial floors to operating rooms is a testament to the versatility and potential of this technology (Hassani et al., 2022a, 2022b). In neurosurgery, where the

Blockchain and Digital Twin for Smart Hospitals. DOI: https://doi.org/10.1016/B978-0-443-34226-4.00021-6

margin for error is minimal and the stakes are invariably high, the ability to visualize and interact with an accurate representation of the patient's brain before the actual surgery offers unprecedented opportunities for enhancing surgical precision (Coorey et al., 2022; Haleem et al., 2023; Schwartz et al., 2020; Venkatesh et al., 2022; Voigt et al., 2021). This capability is not just about avoiding risks; it is about redefining the boundaries of what is possible in neurosurgical care (Volkov et al., 2021).

The summary for Table 20.1, which details the market growth of digital twins from 2022 to 2028, shows a significant upward trajectory in both yearly and accumulated values, measured in billions of USD. Starting at 0.95 billion in 2022, the market is expected to expand to 21.1 billion by 2028. The yearly growth rate begins at 4.53% and accelerates to 40.30% by the end of the period, with the accumulated growth rate reaching 100%. This data illustrates the rapidly increasing investment and interest in digital twin technology over the estimated period.

Fig. 20.1 depicts a pyramid representing the hierarchy of digital twin applications in healthcare, specifically neurosurgery. At the base of the pyramid is the "Development and Processing of Digital Twins," indicating the foundational work in creating these complex digital models. The middle tier, labeled "Uses," includes "Clinical Trials, Hospitals and Surgical Practice; Neurosurgery," suggesting practical applications in medical settings and research. The apex of the pyramid is dedicated to "Applications," highlighting the advanced uses such as "Personalized Medicine, Surgical Planning and Patient Monitoring," which represent the ultimate goals of digital twin technology in improving patient outcomes. The geographical scope of this technology encompasses North America, Europe, and Asia-Pacific, indicating its global reach.

This chapter aims to explore the evolution of digital twins from their industrial origins to their current and potential applications in neurosurgery. It will highlight the technological underpinnings of digital twins, including the role of advanced imaging techniques and data analytics in creating and utilizing these virtual models. Furthermore, the chapter will delve into the myriad ways digital twins are set to transform neurosurgical procedures—ranging from improved presurgical planning and simulation to personalized patient care and outcomes prediction.

As we navigate through this exploration, it becomes evident that the integration of digital twin technology in neurosurgery is not merely a technological upgrade; it is a paradigm shift toward a

Table 20.1 Digital twins marketing during the estimated period (2022–28).

Year	Yearly value	Accumulated value	Yearly %	Accumulated %
2022	0.95	0.95	4.53	4.53
2023	0.64	1.6	3.06	7.58
2024	1.08	2.7	5.12	12.70
2025	1.81	4.5	8.58	21.28
2026	3.03	7.5	14.36	35.64
2027	5.07	12.6	24.06	59.70
2028	8.49	21.1	40.30	100.00
2022–28	21.1		100.0	

Unit: Billion USD.

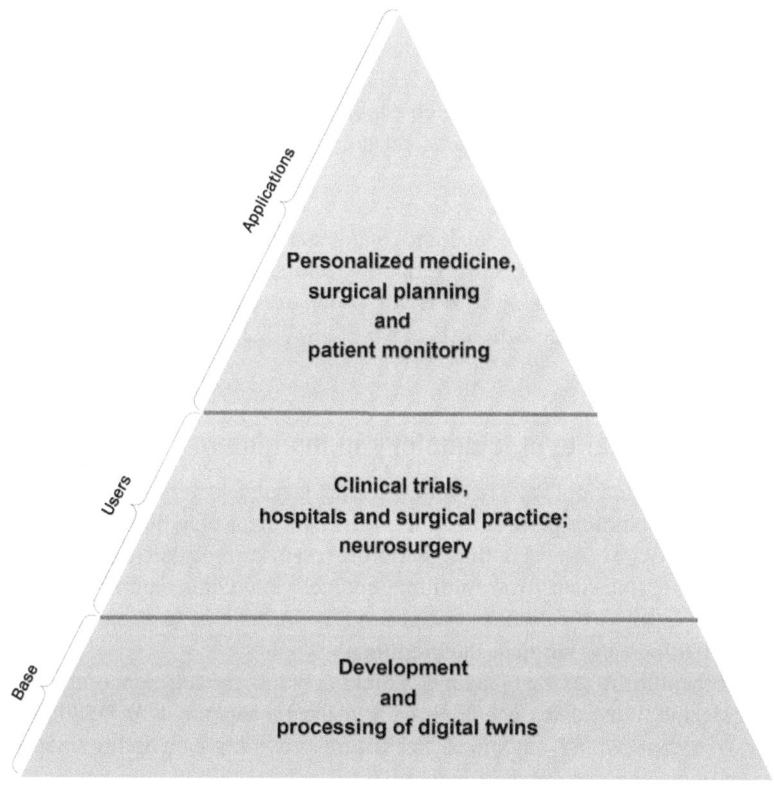

FIGURE 20.1

Hierarchy of digital twins in healthcare: development to applications.

more precise, personalized, and predictive approach to neurosurgical care (Coorey et al., 2022; Voigt et al., 2021). The potential of digital twins to enhance patient outcomes, reduce surgical risks, and streamline the surgical workflow underscores a future where technology and medicine converge to open new frontiers in healthcare (Abernethy et al., 2022; Allen et al., 2021; Elkefi & Asan, 2022; Kamel Boulos & Zhang, 2021).

20.2 The concept of digital twins

20.2.1 Definition and historical development of digital twins

The concept of digital twins represents one of the most significant technological advancements in recent history, bridging the physical and digital worlds (Hassani et al., 2022a). A digital twin is a virtual replica of a physical entity, process, or system, designed to accurately reflect its physical counterpart in real time (Hassani et al., 2022b). This concept, while having its roots in product lifecycle management and manufacturing, has evolved significantly over the years. The term "digital twin" was purportedly first coined in the early 2000s, but the idea gained substantial traction with the advent of the Internet of Things (IoT), which enabled the seamless connection between physical objects and their digital replicas through sensors and other data-gathering mechanisms (Hassani et al., 2022a).

Historically, digital twins were initially employed in complex engineering and manufacturing sectors to optimize the design, production, and maintenance of physical products and systems. NASA, in its quest for improving spacecraft reliability and safety, has been one of the pioneers in applying digital twin technologies, using it to create sophisticated simulations of spacecraft for better mission planning and anomaly detection (Hassani et al., 2022b).

20.2.2 Overview of digital twin technology in healthcare

In healthcare, digital twin technology has found fertile ground, offering transformative potential across various domains, including personalized medicine, surgical planning, and patient monitoring. In neurosurgery, digital twins allow for the creation of precise, individualized models of patients' brains. These models integrate data from multiple sources, including magnetic resonance imaging (MRI), computed tomography (CT) scans, and genomic information, to simulate and analyze complex neurological conditions and surgical interventions.

Digital twins in healthcare extend beyond patient-specific models, encompassing operational aspects of healthcare facilities, disease modeling, and the management of healthcare systems. By simulating different scenarios and outcomes, healthcare providers can optimize surgical interventions and treatment plans and even predict patient-specific risks with greater accuracy.

20.2.3 The importance of accurate data collection and real-time data synchronization

The effectiveness of a digital twin hinges on the accuracy, depth, and timeliness of the data it is built upon. In neurosurgery, where precision is paramount, the collection of detailed and accurate patient data is the foundation of creating a reliable digital twin. Advanced imaging technologies, such as MRI and CT scans, provide high-resolution insights into the unique anatomical and pathological characteristics of a patient's brain, serving as critical inputs for the digital twin (Wang et al., 2022).

Real-time data synchronization is equally crucial, ensuring that the digital twin remains an accurate reflection of the patient's current condition. This involves continuous updates from real-time monitoring devices, intraoperative imaging, and patient health records. Such synchronization not only enhances the predictive accuracy of surgical outcomes but also enables the dynamic adjustment of treatment plans in response to changing patient conditions (Schwartz et al., 2020).

The integration of digital twins into neurosurgery represents a confluence of technology, data science, and clinical expertise. By leveraging accurate data collection and real-time synchronization, digital twins offer a powerful tool for enhancing surgical precision, personalizing patient care, and ultimately, improving outcomes in one of the most complex and delicate areas of medicine (Voigt et al., 2021).

20.3 Digital twins in presurgical planning

Presurgical planning is a critical phase in neurosurgery, where the accuracy of the surgical plan directly influences the outcome. The advent of digital twins has revolutionized this phase, offering neurosurgeons a powerful tool for planning complex surgeries with increased precision and confidence.

20.3.1 How digital twins are created for neurosurgical patients

The process of creating a digital twin for neurosurgical patients begins with the collection of comprehensive medical data. This data includes detailed imaging scans, patient medical history, physiological data, and, in some cases, genetic information. Advanced software algorithms integrate this data to construct a high-fidelity, three-dimensional model of the patient's brain. This model not only replicates the anatomical structure but also simulates the functional aspects of the brain, allowing surgeons to understand the potential impacts of surgical interventions on brain functionality (Sarris et al., 2023).

20.3.2 The role of imaging techniques in building detailed brain models

Imaging techniques such as MRI and CT scans are cornerstone technologies in the creation of digital twins for neurosurgery. MRI provides unparalleled detail of soft tissues, including the brain's gray and white matter, facilitating the identification of tumors, anomalies, and other pathologies. CT scans, on the other hand, offer excellent resolution of the skull and other hard tissues, which is crucial for planning surgical entry points and trajectories (Corral-Acero et al., 2020; Voigt et al., 2021).

Advanced imaging modalities, such as functional MRI (fMRI) and Diffusion Tensor Imaging (DTI), extend these capabilities further by mapping brain activity and white matter tracts, respectively. This information is integrated into the digital twin, providing a comprehensive view of both the structural and functional landscape of the brain. Such detailed models enable surgeons to plan the surgical approach meticulously, minimizing risks to critical brain functions (Kamel Boulos & Zhang, 2021).

20.3.3 Case studies demonstrating the use of digital twins in planning complex surgeries

Several case studies highlight the transformative impact of digital twins in neurosurgical planning (Coorey et al., 2022; Corral-Acero et al., 2020; Hassani et al., 2022b; Kamel Boulos & Zhang, 2021; Voigt et al., 2021):

Tumor resection: In a case involving a complex brain tumor located near critical functional areas, the digital twin model was used to simulate various surgical approaches. This allowed the surgical team to select a path that maximized tumor removal while minimizing the risk to essential brain functions. The surgery was successful, with the patient experiencing minimal postoperative deficits.
Epilepsy surgery: For patients with drug-resistant epilepsy, pinpointing the exact location of seizure onset within the brain is crucial for successful surgical intervention. Using digital twins created from fMRI and DTI data, surgeons were able to accurately identify and resect the epileptogenic zone, significantly reducing seizure occurrence postsurgery.
Vascular abnormalities: In treating a patient with an arteriovenous malformation (AVM), a digital twin model incorporating angiographic data allowed surgeons to visualize the complex network of blood vessels involved. This facilitated the planning of a surgical strategy that effectively eliminated the AVM while preserving surrounding vascular integrity.

These case studies underscore the value of digital twins in enhancing the precision and safety of neurosurgical interventions. By allowing surgeons to visualize and simulate surgeries before stepping into the operating room, digital twins have become an indispensable tool in modern neurosurgery, paving the way for outcomes that were once deemed unattainable.

20.4 Simulation and outcome prediction

The integration of digital twins into neurosurgery has not only revolutionized presurgical planning but also introduced a new era of simulation and outcome prediction that significantly enhances surgical precision and patient safety. This section delves into the methodology behind simulations conducted using digital twins, the role of artificial intelligence (AI) and machine learning (ML) in predicting surgical outcomes, and provides examples of how predictive analytics are applied in neurosurgery (Bahadure et al., 2018; Eltayeb et al., 2019; Malathi & Sinthia, 2018; Sarris et al., 2023; Wang et al., 2022).

20.4.1 Detailed explanation of how simulations are conducted using digital twins

Simulations using digital twins in neurosurgery involve creating a dynamic, interactive model of the patient's brain that can be manipulated to predict the outcomes of various surgical interventions. These simulations are conducted through sophisticated software platforms that integrate patient-specific data, including anatomical and functional imaging, to create a comprehensive, 3D virtual replica of the patient's brain.

Surgeons can then "perform" the proposed surgical procedures on this digital twin, allowing them to visualize in real time the potential effects of their surgical decisions. These simulations consider critical factors such as the proximity to vital brain structures, the potential impact on brain function, and the most effective approach for tumor removal or alleviation of vascular anomalies, among other conditions.

20.4.2 The use of AI and machine learning algorithms for predicting surgical outcomes

AI and ML algorithms play a pivotal role in enhancing the predictive capabilities of digital twins. By analyzing vast datasets of historical surgical outcomes and patient data, these algorithms can identify patterns and correlations that may not be immediately apparent to human observers. This analysis can predict potential complications, estimate the likelihood of success, and suggest the most favorable surgical approaches.

AI models are trained to simulate and evaluate thousands of potential surgical scenarios in a fraction of the time it would take in a real-world setting. This predictive modeling allows for a more informed decision-making process, tailored to the specific nuances of each patient's condition (Bahadure et al., 2018; Ejaz et al., 2022; Malathi & Sinthia, 2018; Tao & Qi, 2019; Wang et al., 2022).

20.4.3 Examples of predictive analytics in neurosurgery

Risk assessment: Predictive analytics can assess the risk of various complications, such as postoperative neurological deficits or the likelihood of recurrence in tumor resection cases. By simulating different surgical approaches, surgeons can choose strategies that minimize these risks.

Procedural strategy optimization: For complex procedures like epilepsy surgery or the treatment of AVMs, predictive analytics help in optimizing the surgical strategy. For instance, simulations can determine the optimal resection margins for epilepsy surgery to maximize seizure control while preserving cognitive function.

Postoperative recovery prediction: AI algorithms can also predict the trajectory of patient recovery, helping healthcare teams to tailor postoperative care plans. This includes anticipating the need for rehabilitation services and setting realistic expectations for recovery milestones.

An illustrative example involves a patient with a deep-seated brain tumor near functional areas. Using the digital twin for simulations, the surgical team could predict that a particular surgical pathway would likely result in minimal disruption to critical functions while achieving maximum tumor resection. Postoperatively, the patient's recovery trajectory closely matched the predictions, allowing for a highly personalized rehabilitation plan that facilitated a quicker return to baseline function.

Through the use of digital twins, coupled with the predictive power of AI and ML, neurosurgery is witnessing unprecedented advancements in simulation and outcome prediction. These technologies not only augment the surgeon's expertise but also significantly contribute to the overall goal of achieving the best possible patient outcomes.

20.5 Personalized medicine and neurosurgery

The advent of digital twin technology in neurosurgery heralds a significant shift toward personalized medicine, where surgical interventions are tailored to the individual characteristics and needs of each patient. This section explores the critical role of digital twins in personalizing brain surgery, their impact on surgical success rates and patient recovery, and the ethical considerations surrounding the use of personal data for digital twin creation (Abernethy et al., 2022; Coorey et al., 2022; Elkefi & Asan, 2022; Kamel Boulos & Zhang, 2021; Venkatesh et al., 2022; Voigt et al., 2021; Volkov et al., 2021).

20.5.1 The role of digital twins in personalizing brain surgery

Digital twins serve as a cornerstone for personalized medicine in neurosurgery by providing a detailed, patient-specific model that reflects the unique anatomical and physiological characteristics of an individual's brain. This personalized approach allows neurosurgeons to plan and simulate surgeries with a precision that was previously unattainable, taking into account not only the structural details of the brain but also its functional aspects.

By leveraging the detailed insights offered by digital twins, surgeons can identify the most effective surgical pathways, anticipate potential challenges, and adjust their strategies to minimize risks and maximize outcomes. This level of personalization ensures that surgical interventions are not only targeted and efficient but also aligned with the patient's specific condition and overall health profile.

20.5.2 Impact of personalized simulations on surgical success rates and patient recovery

The use of personalized simulations through digital twins has shown a positive impact on surgical success rates and patient recovery. By enabling a preoperative exploration of various surgical scenarios, digital twins help surgeons choose the optimal approach, leading to improved precision during the actual surgery. This reduces the likelihood of complications, shortens surgery times, and minimizes the need for reoperations.

Furthermore, personalized simulations contribute to better postoperative outcomes and quicker recovery times. Patients benefit from surgeries that are meticulously planned to avoid critical areas and preserve brain function, resulting in fewer functional deficits and a higher quality of life post-surgery. The predictive capabilities of digital twins also allow healthcare teams to customize rehabilitation plans based on anticipated recovery trajectories, further enhancing patient outcomes.

20.5.3 Ethical considerations and patient consent in the use of personal data for digital twin creation

While the benefits of digital twins in neurosurgery are profound, they also raise important ethical considerations, particularly regarding the use of personal data. The creation of a digital twin requires the collection and integration of sensitive patient information, including medical histories, genetic data, and detailed imaging scans. Ensuring the privacy and security of this data is paramount to maintaining patient trust and upholding ethical standards.

Informed consent is a critical aspect of ethical digital twin creation. Patients must be fully informed about how their data will be used, the benefits and risks associated with digital twin technology, and their rights regarding data privacy. Transparency in the use and storage of patient data, along with strict adherence to data protection regulations, is essential to address potential ethical concerns.

Moreover, there should be an ongoing dialogue about the implications of digital twins for patient autonomy, the potential for biases in data and algorithms, and the equitable access to this advanced technology. Addressing these ethical considerations is crucial for the responsible integration of digital twins into neurosurgical practice, ensuring that the technology serves the best interests of patients while safeguarding their rights and dignity (Allen et al., 2021).

20.6 Training and education

20.6.1 The use of digital twins in neurosurgical training and education

Digital twins are revolutionizing neurosurgical training and education by providing an innovative, risk-free environment for learning and practice. By utilizing patient-specific models, trainees can engage in realistic surgical simulations, allowing them to hone their skills, understand complex neuroanatomical relationships, and anticipate potential complications before stepping into the operating room. This hands-on experience is invaluable in preparing future neurosurgeons to handle the intricacies of brain surgery with greater confidence and competence.

20.6.2 Virtual reality and augmented reality applications for immersive learning experiences

The integration of virtual reality (VR) and augmented reality (AR) technologies with digital twins creates immersive, interactive learning experiences that significantly enhance neurosurgical education. VR allows trainees to navigate through the digital twin of a patient's brain in a fully immersive 3D environment, offering a perspective that traditional methods cannot. AR, on the other hand, overlays digital information in the real world, enabling trainees to practice surgical procedures on physical models while receiving real-time guidance and feedback from the digital twin data. These technologies facilitate a deeper understanding of surgical procedures and patient anatomy, making them powerful tools for education and training.

20.6.3 Advantages of simulation-based training for young neurosurgeons

Simulation-based training using digital twins offers numerous advantages for young neurosurgeons:

- *Risk-free learning environment*: Trainees can practice surgeries in a safe, controlled setting without the risk of harming actual patients.
- *Personalized learning*: Digital twins allow for personalized training experiences, where learners can focus on areas that require additional practice.
- *Feedback and assessment*: Instant feedback during simulations helps in correcting mistakes, refining techniques, and improving decision-making skills.

- *Enhanced preoperative planning skills*: Exposure to a variety of complex cases through digital twins prepares trainees for real-life scenarios, enhancing their preoperative planning and problem-solving abilities.

20.7 Challenges and future directions

20.7.1 Technical and ethical challenges in implementing digital twin technology

While digital twins hold immense promise for neurosurgery, their implementation faces several technical and ethical challenges. Technically, creating accurate and comprehensive digital twins requires advanced computing resources and expertise in data integration, data governance, and simulation (Hassani & MacFeely, 2023). Ethically, concerns regarding patient data privacy, consent, and security need to be meticulously addressed, ensuring that the use of digital twins adheres to strict ethical standards and regulations.

20.7.2 The future of digital twins in neurosurgery

The future of digital twins in neurosurgery looks promising, with ongoing advancements in AI, ML, and imaging technologies poised to enhance their accuracy and functionality. Research areas may focus on improving the real-time updating mechanisms of digital twins, integrating genomics for personalized treatment planning, and expanding their applications in postoperative care and rehabilitation.

20.7.3 Discussion on interdisciplinary collaboration needed to advance digital twin applications in medicine

Advancing digital twin applications in medicine requires robust interdisciplinary collaboration, bringing together neurosurgeons, engineers, data scientists, ethicists, and patient advocates. This collaborative effort is crucial for addressing the technical and ethical challenges, ensuring the technology's responsible use, and exploring innovative applications that benefit patient care. Such partnerships can accelerate the development of digital twins, making them more accessible and effective in clinical practice.

In conclusion, digital twins represent a transformative tool in neurosurgical training, education, and practice. By fostering interdisciplinary collaboration and addressing the existing challenges, the future of neurosurgery with digital twins promises enhanced surgical precision, improved patient outcomes, and a new paradigm in medical education and training.

20.8 Conclusion

The exploration of digital twins within the realm of neurosurgery unveils a horizon brimming with transformative potential. This technology, emblematic of the fusion between cutting-edge computation and meticulous medical practice, has emerged as a pivotal innovation in the surgical field.

Through the meticulous crafting of virtual replicas of patients' brains, digital twins have catalyzed a paradigm shift in how neurosurgical procedures are approached—from presurgical planning and simulation to the execution of personalized surgical strategies.

The capacity of digital twins to enhance presurgical planning is unparalleled. By offering a detailed, patient-specific model, surgeons are endowed with the ability to meticulously plan and simulate surgeries, thereby significantly reducing unforeseen complications and optimizing surgical outcomes. This meticulous planning phase, supported by the rich, data-driven insights provided by digital twins, ensures that each surgical intervention is as informed and precise as possible.

Furthermore, the role of digital twins in enabling precise simulations cannot be overstated. These simulations, which leverage the latest in VR and AR technologies, provide a risk-free environment for neurosurgeons to refine their skills, explore various surgical approaches, and anticipate potential challenges. This not only enhances the surgeon's competency but also contributes significantly to patient safety and the overall success rate of neurosurgical procedures.

Perhaps most importantly, digital twins herald a new era of personalized medicine in neurosurgery. By tailoring surgical approaches to the individual characteristics of each patient, digital twins facilitate interventions that are not only effective but also minimally invasive. This personalization of surgical care underscores a commitment to patient-centered medicine, where treatments are optimized for the best possible outcomes with the least possible risk.

However, the journey toward the widespread integration of digital twins in neurosurgery is not without its challenges. Technical hurdles, such as the need for advanced computing infrastructure and sophisticated data integration techniques, must be surmounted. Moreover, the ethical implications of utilizing sensitive patient data to create digital twins demand careful consideration, ensuring that patient privacy, consent, and data security are paramount.

The future of digital twins in neurosurgery, therefore, hinges on a multifaceted approach that addresses these challenges. Interdisciplinary collaboration is essential, bringing together neurosurgeons, engineers, data scientists, ethicists, and patients to navigate the complex landscape of digital twin technology. Through such collaboration, the development and use of digital twins can be guided by ethical considerations, technical excellence, and a steadfast commitment to improving patient care.

In conclusion, digital twins represent a beacon of innovation in neurosurgery, offering a glimpse into a future where surgical precision, patient safety, and personalized care converge. As we move forward, it is imperative that the medical community embraces this technology, guided by ethical principles, interdisciplinary collaboration, and an unwavering dedication to advancing patient care. The promise of digital twins in neurosurgery is not just in their technological prowess but in their potential to fundamentally enhance the human aspect of surgical care, making a profound difference in the lives of patients around the globe.

References

Abernethy, A., Adams, L., Barrett, M., Bechtel, C., Brennan, P., Butte, A., et al. (2022). The promise of digital health: Then, now, and the future. *NAM Perspectives, 2022*. Available from https://doi.org/10.31478/202206e.

Allen, A., Siefkas, A., Pellegrini, E., Burdick, H., Barnes, G., Calvert, J., et al. (2021). A digital twins machine learning model for forecasting disease progression in stroke patients. *Applied Science*, *11*, 5576. Available from https://doi.org/10.3390/app11125576.

Armeni, P., Polat, I., De Rossi, L. M., Diaferia, L., Meregalli, S., & Gatti, A. (2022). Digital twins in healthcare: Is it the beginning of a new era of evidence-based medicine? A critical review. *Journal of Personalized Medicine*, *12*, 1255. Available from https://doi.org/10.3390/jpm12081255.

Bahadure, N. B., Ray, A. K., & Thethi, H. P. (2018). Comparative approach of MRI-based brain tumor segmentation and classification using genetic algorithm. *Journal of Digital Imaging: The Official Journal of the Society for Computer Applications in Radiology*, *31*(4), 477–489. Available from https://doi.org/10.1007/s10278-018-0050-6.

Coorey, G., Figtree, G. A., Fletcher, D. F., et al. (2022). The health digital twin to tackle cardiovascular disease—a review of an emerging interdisciplinary field. *npj Digital Medicine*, *5*, 126.

Corral-Acero, J., Margara, F., Marciniak, M., Rodero, C., Loncaric, F., Feng, Y., et al. (2020). The "digital twin" to enable the vision of precision cardiology. *European Heart Journal*, *41*, 4556–4564. Available from https://doi.org/10.1093/eurheartj/.

Ejaz, K., Mohd Rahim, M. S., Arif, M., Izdrui, D., Craciun, D. M., & Geman, O. (2022). Review on hybrid segmentation methods for identification of brain tumor in MRI. *Contrast Media & Molecular Imaging*, *2022*, 1541980. Available from https://doi.org/10.1155/2022/1541980.

Elkefi, S., & Asan, O. (2022). Digital twins for managing health care systems: Rapid literature review. *Journal of Medical Internet Research*, *24*, e37641. Available from https://doi.org/10.2196/37641.

Eltayeb, E. N., Salem, N. M., & Al-Atabany, W. (2019). Automated brain tumor segmentation from multi-slices FLAIR MRI images. *Bio-medical Materials and Engineering*, *30*(4), 449–462. Available from https://doi.org/10.3233/BME-191066.

Haleem, A., Javaid, M., Pratap Singh, R., & Suman, R. (2023). Exploring the revolution in healthcare systems through the applications of digital twin technology. *Biomedical Technology*, *4*, 28–38. Available from https://doi.org/10.1016/j.bmt.2023.02.001.

Hassani, H., Huang, X., & MacFeely, S. (2022a). Impactful digital twin in the healthcare revolution. *Big Data Cognitive Computing*, *6*, 83. Available from https://doi.org/10.3390/bdcc6030083.

Hassani, H., Huang, X., & MacFeely, S. (2022b). Enabling digital twins to support the UN SDGs. *Big Data Cognitive Computing.*, *6*, 115. Available from https://doi.org/10.3390/bdcc6040115.

Hassani, H., & MacFeely, S. (2023). Driving excellence in official statistics: Unleashing the potential of comprehensive digital data governance. *Big Data Cognitive Computing.*, *7*, 134. Available from https://doi.org/10.3390/bdcc7030134.

Kamel Boulos, M. N., & Zhang, P. (2021). Digital twins: From personalised medicine to precision public health. *Journal of Personalized Medicine*, *11*(8), 745. Available from https://doi.org/10.3390/jpm11080745.

Malathi, M., & Sinthia, P. (2018). MRI brain tumour segmentation using hybrid clustering and classification by back propagation algorithm. *Asian Pacific Journal of Cancer Prevention: APJCP*, *19*(11), 3257–3263. Available from https://doi.org/10.31557/APJCP.2018.19.11.3257.

Nguyen, T. A. (2023). Blockchain and digital twin for industry 4.0/5.0. *Kenkyu Journal of Nanotechnology & Nanoscience*, *9*, 1–5.

Nguyen, T. A. (2024). Digital twin-based universe (complexiverse): Where real world and virtual/digital world are unified. *Kenkyu Journal of Nanotechnology & Nanoscience*, *10*, 1–4.

Sarris, A. L., Sidiropoulos, E., Paraskevopoulos, E., & Bamidis, P. (2023). Towards a digital twin in human brain: Brain tumor detection using K-means. *Studies in Health Technology and Informatics*, *302*, 1052–1056. Available from https://doi.org/10.3233/SHTI230345.

Schwartz, S. M., Wildenhaus, K., Bucher, A., & Byrd, B. (2020). Digital twins and the emerging science of self: Implications for digital health experience design and "small" data. *Frontiers of Computer Science*, *2*. Available from https://www.frontiersin.org/articles/10.3389/fcomp.2020.00031.

Sun, T., He, X., & Li, Z. (2023). Digital twin in healthcare: Recent updates and challenges. *Digital Health*, *9*, 20552076221149652. Available from https://doi.org/10.1177/20552076221149651.

Sun, T., He, X., Song, X., Shu, L., & Li, Z. (2022). The digital twin in medicine: A key to the future of healthcare? *Frontiers in Medicine*, *9*, 907066. Available from https://doi.org/10.3389/fmed.2022.907066.

Tao, F., & Qi, Q. (2019). Make more digital twins. *Nature*, *573*, 490–491. Available from https://doi.org/10.1038/d41586-019-02849-1.

Venkatesh, K. P., Raza, M. M., & Kvedar, J. C. (2022). Health digital twins as tools for precision medicine: Considerations for computation, implementation, and regulation. *Npj Digital Medicine*, *5*, 1–2.

Voigt, I., Inojosa, H., Dillenseger, A., Haase, R., Akgün, K., & Ziemssen, T. (2021). Digital twins for multiple sclerosis. *Frontiers in Immunology*, *3*(12), 669811. Available from https://doi.org/10.3389/fimmu.2021.669811.

Volkov, I., Radchenko, G., & Tchernykh, A. (2021). Digital twins, internet of things and mobile medicine: A review of current platforms to support smart healthcare. *Program Computer Software*, *47*, 578–590.

Wang, H., Song, T., Wang, L., Yan, L., & Han, L. (2022). Fuzzy C-means algorithm-based ARM-Linux-embedded system combined with magnetic resonance imaging for progression prediction of brain tumors. *Computational and Mathematical Methods in Medicine*, *2022*, 4224749. Available from https://doi.org/10.1155/2022/4224749.

CHAPTER

Cloud computing- and digital twin-based monitoring framework for healthcare applications

21

Zhonghai Li and Tianze Sun

Department of Orthopedics, First Affiliated Hospital of Dalian Medical University, Dalian, Liaoning Province, P.R. China

21.1 Introduction

It is often said that "there is no disease, there is patient." Compared with other disciplines, medical treatment has its uncertainty, which makes medical practice more challenging. According to a report, medication is deemed ineffective for 38%–75% of patients with common diseases (Silver & Spring, 2013). Therefore more and more attention is paid to precision medicine, which is defined as follows (Psaty et al., 2018): An emerging approach for disease treatment and prevention that takes into account individual variability in genes, environment, and lifestyle for each person.

Cloud computing and digital twin-based health detection models are employed to achieve real-time monitoring and prediction of disease risk through the following steps. The initial step is data collection, which entails the gathering of clinical data and physiological parameters pertaining to an individual, including blood pressure, body temperature, heart rate, and electroencephalogram (EEG) signals. Thereafter, a digital twin is constructed based on the collected data, and a refined digital twin model is developed based on a specific mathematical model. The digital twin model simulates the individual's heart, lungs, liver, and other organs. The next step is to upload the individual's physiological parameter data to the cloud computing platform in real time and utilize the powerful computational processing capability of cloud computing to analyze and process this data in real time. Machine learning or deep learning models are applied to predict the potential health risks of individuals. If the model predicts potential health risks, it can be fed back to the individual for intervention, providing personalized health advice and early warning.

The development of Big Data, cloud computing, virtual reality, and the Internet of Things (IoT) lay a technical foundation for the application of digital twin (DT), which gives clinicians and researchers a more detailed dimension to study the occurrence and development of diseases, to make more precise diagnosis and treatment. DT is a living model of the physical system that constantly adjusts to variations of the online data and can predict the future of the corresponding physical counterparts (Liu et al., 2018). It has been named among the "ten most strategic emerging concepts for the coming years" and the spending on DT will be increasing for a long period.

To realize the application of DT in medicine, the first step is to build models based on physics approaches, which consist of experimental modeling and numerical modeling. Numerical modeling is

Blockchain and Digital Twin for Smart Hospitals. DOI: https://doi.org/10.1016/B978-0-443-34226-4.00022-8

widely used in various fields due to its low cost and high integrity, of which finite element models (FEMs) are the most frequently used, especially in the engineering field (DebRoy et al., 2017; Schroeder et al., 2016; Tao, Sui, et al., 2019; Tao, Zhang, et al., 2019). FEMs have also been used in medicine such as biomechanical analysis of the spine to observe the mechanical properties. For example, Kim established a FEM of the L3-L4 segment and investigated the biomechanical consequence of the facet tropism and facet orientation of the corresponding segment (Kim et al., 2013, 2015). Furthermore, the application of DT has been promoted by the development of artificial intelligence (AI), which can be seen as a data-driven model or the basis for realizing real-time estimating. A hybrid model combining AI algorithms and simulation has become more and more popular in virtue of the advantages of obtaining information based on data and knowledge (Seshadri & Krishnamurthy, 2017). But DT is more than just a digital model that is connected with a real-life twin by various emerging technologies. It is like a technological cocktail rather than a mere technology.

21.2 Concept of cloud computing

Cloud computing is a model for the delivery of computing services over the Internet. These services include servers, storage, databases, networking, software, analytics, and more (Khanna, n.d.). The primary advantage of cloud computing is that it enables users to access computing resources on an as-needed basis, rather than requiring them to own and maintain their own computing infrastructure. The fundamental components of cloud computing include servers, storage devices, databases, the Internet, and software analytics. Of these, servers are the physical devices that underpin cloud computing. They are high-performance computers that are designed to process data and requests from the Internet. In the cloud computing environment, data is stored on servers located in data centers. This can be personal data, such as documents and emails, or enterprise-level application data. Databases play a pivotal role in cloud computing (Wercelens et al., 2019). A cloud database is a database that has been optimized or constructed with the specific purpose of running in the cloud. Cloud service providers utilize sophisticated networks to ensure the secure and efficient flow of data across global networks. Cloud computing enables users to access software and applications remotely, obviating the need to install them on local devices. A multitude of cloud providers offer data analytics services, which assist users in identifying patterns and insights from their data.

21.3 Concept of DT

In 2002 Professor Michael Grieves introduced the concept of DT to describe "Product Life Management" and the preliminary meaning of the DT included three parts: physical product, virtual product, and their connections (Grieves and Vickers, 2017). The rapid development of communication technology, sensor technology, Big Data analysis, Internet of Things, and simulation technology has promoted the exponential growth of research on DT (Glaessgen & Stargel, 2012; Tuegel et al., 2011). It is initially defined by the National Aeronautics and Space Administration (NASA) as an integrated multiscale, multiphysics, high-fidelity simulation of an as-built vehicle or system to mirror the life of its corresponding flying twin (Glaessgen & Stargel, 2012). Since then, more and more research has been devoted to DT during the next few years, which is regarded as the incubation stage (Tao, Zhang & Liu, & Nee, 2019). Gabor et al. consider DT as a special simulation based on professional knowledge and real data, which realizes an accurate simulation in different scales of space and time (Gabor et al., 2016). According to Maurer, DT is a digital concept that represents the product performance and production process (Maurer, 2017). Söderberg et al. propose a concept of DT, which contains geometry representation and the function of finite element analysis to ensure the geometry in individualized production (Söderberg et al., 2017). In 2017 and 2018, DT was classified as one of the most promising technological trends in the next decade by Gartner, and it was redefined as a digital replication of living or nonliving physical entities, which opened a gateway to use DT for humans such as in the field of health and well-being (El Saddik, 2018). At the same time, the meaning of DT is becoming more and more concrete, which leads to some special concepts such as experimental digital twin (EDT) and airframe digital twin (ADT) (Schluse & Rossmann, 2016; Tuegel, 2012).

Although there are various concepts and different types, DT is identified as a definition that contains three parts: physical entity (PE) in the real world, digital model in the virtual world, and the connection between them (Lee & Fong, 2020; Rasheed et al., 2020; Tao, Zhang & Liu, & Nee, 2019). The physical entity could be a product, a system, a human body, or even a whole city. The digital model is a digital replica, which mirrors the characteristics of the entity dynamically, such as the material properties or performance. As a real-time bridge between the physical world and the virtual world, the connections interact with the entity with the corresponding digital model. Fig. 21.1

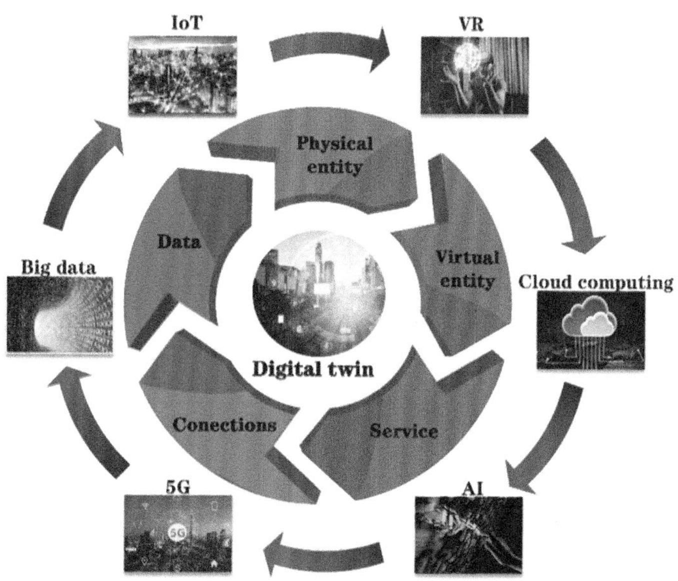

FIGURE 21.1

Basic structure and key technologies of digital twin. IoT, Internet of Things; VR, virtual reality; AI, artificial intelligence.

shows the basic structure and key technologies of digital twins, including the physical space and the digital space. At the beginning of the flow, the initial stage prepares data and models for the dynamic or steady stage. The numerical model can calculate the structural performance while the analytical model is used for structural analysis. The AI model, trained by the samples and numerical data, could obtain real-time structural performance by real-time sensor data (Agostinelli, 2020). In the dynamic stage, the reduced-order model (ROM) is used to improve the working efficiency, for which the model needs to be adjusted in time (Lai et al., 2021).

PEs are hierarchical and are generally divided into three categories according to function and structure: unit-level PE, system-level PE, and complex system-level PE (Tao, Zhang, et al., 2017). The unit-level PE is the smallest unit to realize the function and the system-level PE is a production line composed of equipment combined with configuration. The workshop composed of the production line can be regarded as a complex system-level PE, which can realize the organization, coordination, and management of the various subsystems (Tao, Liu, et al., 2018).

The digital model is formed from DT data and virtual entity. DT data include physical element data, dynamic process data, model-related simulation data, and derivative data after conversion, classification, fusion, and other processing of various data (Tao, Cheng, et al., 2017). By fusing physical live data with multispace and multidimensional data, it reflects more comprehensive and accurate information and realizes information sharing and value-added (Tao, Liu, et al., 2018).

The connection realizes the interconnection and intercommunication between the various parts of DT models (Tao, Zhang, et al., 2018). Use sensors, data acquisition cards, and so on to collect PE data in real time and then feedback on the processed data to optimize and regulate the design and operation (Tao, Liu, et al., 2018).

21.4 Cloud computing and digital twin-based healthcare monitoring

The combination of cloud computing and digital twins represents a novel technological trend that facilitates comprehensive, real-time monitoring of an individual's health status. The substantial computational processing and storage capabilities of cloud computing can be employed to process and store voluminous amounts of health detection data (Langmead & Nellore, 2018). By contrast, a digital twin is a digital model that can replicate real-world objects and processes, including the human body, in digital space. In the context of healthcare, the application of digital twins enables the construction of a fine-grained digital twin model based on the clinical data and physiological parameters of a real individual (Mrozek, 2020). This model can then be used to accurately simulate and predict an individual's health condition. For instance, a digital twin can simulate the human heart, lungs, liver, and other organs. By monitoring the physiological parameters of an individual, a cloud-based health detection model can be constructed for real-time monitoring and disease risk prediction. If potential health risks are identified in advance, it becomes possible to implement early intervention measures. The digital twin's robust predictive and simulation capabilities facilitate the implementation of personalized precision medicine (Navale et al., 2018). In the future, this cloud computing and digital twin-based health detection model may be more scalable and automated. Furthermore, the integration of advanced technologies such as Big Data analytics and artificial intelligence may enhance the precision and efficacy of health testing.

21.5 Application fields of cloud computing and DT

With the advent of INDUSTRY 4.0, the focus turned to intelligent manufacturing (Schleich et al., 2017; Tao, Zhang, et al., 2018). As precise virtual copies of systems and machines, DT is revolutionizing our society. It realizes the symbiosis of virtuality and reality through virtual-real synchronization mapping and virtual-real fusion, covering the whole life cycle of physical entities, and realizing intelligent application decision-making. With the help of data-driven sensors in real time, the computer models almost mirror every aspect of products and processes. More and more companies are using DT to improve production efficiency (Tao, Zhang, et al., 2019).

Cloud computing offers a convenient, secure, and cost-effective solution for data storage and backup. The cloud can accommodate a wide range of data types, including personal photos and documents, as well as business-critical data for organizations. Concurrently, cloud computing offers an effective and scalable solution for hosting and running websites, particularly those with fluctuating traffic demands. Furthermore, numerous software providers employ cloud computing to host their applications, which are made accessible to end users via web pages. This eliminates the need for users to concern themselves with software installation, updates, compatibility, and hardware requirements. Cloud computing provides the capacity for powerful computing capabilities, which enable the processing and analysis of large data sets. Cloud platforms permit enterprises to process and analyze vast quantities of data, thereby facilitating the acquisition of actionable insights. Cloud computing enables team members to access the same files and applications regardless of their geographical location, thus facilitating remote work and collaboration. Furthermore, the deployment of artificial intelligence and machine learning necessitates a substantial investment in computing resources. Cloud computing represents a cost-effective solution for this requirement.

DT was mainly used in the field of aerospace in the early stage. For example, NASA and the US Air Force Research Laboratory have developed aircraft health control applications based on DT to predict the life of aircraft structure (Glaessgen & Stargel, 2012; Tuegel et al., 2011). Then it is widely used in engineering and manufacturing including DT modeling, simulation, validation, verification, and accreditation; data fusion; interaction and collaboration; and service (Tao, Zhang & Liu, & Nee, 2019). Liu et al. (Weiran & TAOFei, 2020) propose the concept of a DT satellite and discuss the whole life cycle of the satellite, combining DT technology with the key scenes and key objects.

In industry, a DT of production processes contains various parameters, which are mapped to expected outcomes to predict performance. Use connected sensors and build a comprehensive virtual copy of a product or process based on massive historical data. The cost of building the best models and virtual testing in this way is much lower than experimenting on actual products. AI can detect possible maintenance needs before machine failures occur through deep learning, which opens the door to DT's real-time data collection and prediction (Burgun, 2019).

In the manufacturing field, DT can comprehensively improve the efficiency of the production process and the efficiency of the production line by simulating and predicting all aspects of product manufacturing and process cycles. In the product manufacturing process, the real-time monitoring of the production process is realized by re-engraving the processing activities to provide support for production decision-making and system optimization (Liu, Zhang, Leng, et al., 2019). Due to the lack of adequate interactions among expected and interpreted spaces in the field of production,

Tao et al. (Tao, Sui, et al., 2019) proposed a design framework to envision DT applications in product planning and detailed design, which was used in a case study on bicycle. Zhao (2020) selected cutter poster and spindle speed as the adjustable parameters and proposed a matching parameters self-adaption adjustment method to make the surface stable based on DT.

DT is also used in the efficient management of cities. The government of Singapore proposed the "Digital Singapore" plan to realize the perception, analysis, and optimization of city data through the development of a digital city management platform. In China, Xiong'an New District puts forward the concept of "digital twin city" construction, which realizes the simultaneous planning and construction of physical and virtual cities (Yu & Liu, 2018).

The workshop is the basic unit of the manufacturing industry, and realizing the digitization and intelligence of the workshop is an urgent need to realize intelligent manufacturing. Tao et al. (2017) propose the concept of a DT workshop to realize the real-time interaction and deep integration of workshop information and physical space. Driven by the fused twin data, each part of the workshop can realize iterative operation and two-way optimization, to achieve optimal workshop management, planning, and control.

21.6 Application status in medicine

DT builds a bridge between the physical world and the virtual world, and it has various research in the engineering and manufacturing fields. Similarly, it also has great application potential in the medical field. Researchers can use information about the human body to build a virtual body for research, which can be used to test new treatment options, simulate and predict the patient's response to drugs, and provide a basis for precision medicine (Lareyre et al., 2020). However, due to the inaccurate acquisition of data in vivo and ethical issues, the lack of in-depth data makes it very difficult to construct a virtual human body model. This makes the research and progress of DTs in medicine inferior to other fields.

With the improvement of engineering technology, the medical industry has also developed and gradually realized the transformation from traditional medicine to digital medicine and then to information medicine, forming today's "smart medicine" concept, which satisfied people's preventive and personalized medical needs to a greater extent. There are now two main aspects of the application of DTs in the medical field: basic research centered on building models and DT medical systems.

21.7 Basic research on DT models

Model construction is the core of basic research on DT in medicine, combining human anatomy and digital technology through image processing, digital collection processing, mathematical modeling, and other technologies. Researchers digitally process the human body's two-dimensional cross-sectional image and use three-dimensional reconstruction technology to establish an intuitive three-dimensional shape of the human body, making the body structure visualization (Madabhushi & Lee, 2016). For example, the Blue Brain Project began in 2005 as a collaboration between Ecole

Polytechnique Fédérale de Lausanne (EPFL) and International Business Machines (IBMs), which aims to model the neocortical column (Hill & Markram, 2008).

The models include mechanics modeling, mechanical network modeling, and statistical modeling. Establishing an appropriate mechanics model is possible to theoretically study the mass transmission of the human body and electrophysiological problems coupled with mechanics. The mechanical network models usually take the form of a coupled system of ordinary differential equations, which are solved to observe how the molecular concentration evolves in time when interacting and responding to network inputs. Another mechanical network model describes the interacting molecules and their concentration, rate of action, and their changes with time (Dhume & Barocas, 2019). Statistical models are complementary tools to verify the mechanic's models by finding mechanistic explanations of inductive inference (Chang et al., 2017). Similarly, data from mechanics models need to be scrutinized quantitatively for validation (Sims et al., 2018). They can predict the emergency behavior of biological systems in health and disease because they combine the interaction of biological components of the system.

However, the needs to increase validation and the lack of clinical interpretability make the DT technologies difficult to show more promising results (Winslow et al., 2012). When used on patients from different countries or centers, the models may need recalibrations and the quality of datasets needs validation before integrating them into clinical decision-making (Chang et al., 2017). To achieve clinical translation, model synergy can be used to increase clinical interpretability, verify the versatility of results, promote effective research results and testing methods, and accelerate the integration of new technologies and clinical practice (Corral-Acero et al., 2020).

21.7.1 Clinical application of DT

The purpose of building a DT diagnosis and treatment system is to realize precision medicine. The core of precision medicine is personalization and the key is patient-centric. We can use artificial intelligence and other cutting-edge technologies to accurately locate the cause of the patient's disease, clarify the treatment target, and realize personalized and precise treatment.

21.7.2 Cardiovascular disease

The application of DT in the cardiovascular system includes the establishment of DT heart models and precise treatment of cardiovascular diseases. Intel, Bayer, Hewlett-Packard Enterprise, and Pfizer are all working to build models of the cardiovascular system for research, treatment, clinical trials, and commercial purposes (Liu, Zhang, Yang, et al., 2019). Models can accurately locate the most valuable diagnostic basis and reliably infer biomarkers through noninvasive procedures. The key to DT-guided diagnosis is the personalized construction of the model, this method is used for the computation of pressure drops in flow obstruction and proved to be more accurate than that in clinical guidelines (Krittian et al., 2012). Philips developed a personalized DT model based on the unique CT images of the heart, which were obtained before the surgical procedure (Houten, 2018). The Philips HeartNavigator tool combines the CT images in a single image of the patient's heart anatomy and provides a real-time 3D insight to position the devices during surgery, which can simplify the prior procedure planning and help a surgeon select the right device.

A DT can simulate dosage effects or device response before a specific treatment to indicate whether the medical device or treatment is appropriate for patients and improve the treatment of patients with different causes. Cardiac resynchronization therapy (CRT) is widely used in patients with prolonged QRS duration, but there are still uncertainties in the decision-making in the "gray zone" (Daubert et al., 2017). Niederer et al. (2011) use mechanical models to investigate the dependence of CRT efficacy on cellular scale mechanisms and organs and identify novel patient selection criteria. Using such a model identifies the length dependence of tension as a regulator of CRT and predicts that a patient is less responsive to CRT treatment if he has cellular scale dyssynchronous electrical activation but effective length-dependent tension regulation. Another example is in the field of infarct-related ventricular tachycardia, researchers use DT to improve the ablation guidance by providing accurate identification of patient-specific optimal targets before the clinical procedure (Prakosa et al., 2018).

21.7.3 Surgery

The idea of DT in the surgical field is to create a patient model for multidisciplinary teams to plan surgery and verify the anatomy to avoid inadvertent damage to structures (Ahmed & Devoto, 2021). For example, the use of DT in cardiovascular diseases is now growing and there is an emerging interest in the application of artificial intelligence in vascular surgery (Björnsson et al., 2020; Raffort et al., 2020). The virtual model established by DT technology can develop diagnostic tools, as example, Chakshu et al. (2019) propose a semiactive DT model coupled with blood flow and head vibration to detect the severity of carotid stenosis from a video of a human face. Comparing the in vivo vibration against the virtual data and finding the best fit. Intracranial aneurysms may cause stroke and thrombosis and severe cases may immediately die. Suzuki et al. (2020) consider clinical, morphological, and hemodynamic parameters and use computational fluid dynamics to calculate hemodynamic parameters which are based on CT images. They obtain a rupture risk model by multivariate logistic regression and list age, larger length, location at a bifurcation, lower pressure loss coefficient, and presence of a bleb as risk factors. Due to the extremely high risk of surgery, doctors usually use shunts to guide the blood flow away from the aneurysm sac. This method is less invasive but the procedure is more complicated because the implant may cause additional damage to the artery. Sim and Cure uses 3D rotational angiography to create a 3D model of the aneurysm and surrounding vessels before the surgery, which is presented to the surgeon to complete the simulation process and help choose the points defining the ideal end position and the size of implants (Erol et al., 2020).

Combined with the virtual reality platforms, DT can conduct simulated practice on each patient's specific anatomy and physiological variation to improve the surgical training for residents and provide a realistic account of performance at the same time (Devoto et al., 2019).

21.7.4 Pharmacy

As human life and physiology are different, the medicine for treatment should be personal as well. DT models created by the genetic code in the DNAs can see changes in the performance of the body and help researchers obtain a more cost-effective opportunity to evaluate new compounds with more accurate results. Dassault Systèmes and the US Food and Drug Administration signed a project named The SIMULIA Living Heart in 2014, which is the first study to see the interactions of an organ with medicines by digital technology (Baillargeon et al., 2014). It is a DT model simulating human hearts and has been validated by researchers or educators in the medical field. With the help of this technology, doctors and pharmaceutical engineers could see the complex structure or the mobility of heart tissue, which will lead to personalized treatment in the future.

Takeda Pharmaceuticals has switched to DT technology in production to offer transformative therapies around the world. Creating DT models, it can shorten pharmaceutical processes and make realistic input–output predictions of biochemical reactions (Mussomeli, 2020). Atos and Siemens are also working with the pharmaceutical industry to improve the manufacturing process through physical DT models, which are created to overcome difficulties in efficiency and production (Erol et al., 2020). It is currently tested to be successful and supported by IoT, AI, and many other advanced technologies.

Modeling depends on efficient concepts for model parameters and the dynamic parameters in scale. To acquire and integrate real-time data or signals from connected bioreactors, sensors include traditional ones and newer ones such as spectroscopic sensors in process analytical technology [67]. The whole cell project models specific types of cells and organisms to understand the molecular basis of diseases [68].

21.7.5 Orthopedics

With the development of numerical simulation and wearing devices, using DT to real-time monitor and analyze lumber spines has become a cutting-edge technology in the biomechanical field and has great potential. To realize the application of DT in the field of orthopedics, it is important to develop physics-based experimental models and data-driven numerical models, which have the advantages of low cost and high integrity. Through the customized information collection of the lumbar spine bones of a specific experimenter, our team built a shape-performance integrated DT body proposed to predict the biomechanical properties of the real lumbar spine under different human postures (He, no date). The real-time motion posture and spatial position of the human body are obtained based on human motion capture technology. The lumbar posture of the corresponding human body is calculated according to the wearable VR device and a small amount of sensor data. Through the information of the inverse kinematics system, and combined with the finite element method and Gaussian process regression, a DT body of the lumbar spine is established, to realize various motion postures of the human body. In addition, the biomechanical properties of the lumbar spine were evaluated and predicted in real time. Based on the proxy model, the dynamic calculation of the mechanical properties of the DT of the lumbar spine is realized to achieve the purpose of real-time monitoring and prediction. Finally, a 3D virtual reality system is developed by Unity3D to record the real-time biomechanical performance of the lumber spine during the movement of the body, which can provide a new and effective method of warning and real-time planning in the field of orthopedic treatments, especially in spine rehabilitation.

21.7.6 COVID-19

The pandemic of COVID-19 has generated an enormous interest in the modeling and simulation of infectious diseases. The coronavirus spreads from person-to-person contact by respiratory droplets, especially when an infected patient coughs or sneezes. Zohdi (2020) builds a rapidly computable respiratory emission model and develops a combined DT and machine learning framework to optimize ventilation systems (Zohdi, 2021). It is based on a genomic algorithm and coupled with simplified equations between the particles and the fluid to ascertain the placement and flow rates of multiple ventilation units, to optimally sequester particles that are released from patients with coughs or sneezes.

During the pandemic, it is necessary to find a way to vaccinate more people in a shorter time, especially when healthcare workers are scarce. Pilati et al. (2021) developed a DT system for the vaccination process and tested it in a clinic. The system allows a real-time simulation of patients and creates a dynamic vaccination center. Running the virtual model to find problems and improve them in the real system improves the efficiency of vaccination.

21.7.7 Others

The use of DT in medicine is mainly focused on chronic disease management. For example, in neurocritical care, current digital technologies focus on interpreting EEG, monitoring intracranial pressure, and simulating the prognosis (Dang et al., 2021). It can interpret EEG by helping with annotation tracking, detecting seizures, and identifying brain activation in unresponsive patients.

In an artificial pancreas model for patients with type 1 diabetes, mathematical models of human glucose metabolism and data algorithms that simulate insulin delivery are customized into a patient-specific DT model, which can continuously calculate insulin requirements and regulate blood insulin concentrations (Brown et al., 2019; Kovatchev, 2019). Fig. 21.2 shows the connections between the physical and digital twins during the construction and application of DT. The information in the physical space is acquired by sensors and CT scans at key locations and then imported into the numerical calculation system for analysis and calculation. Human reverse dynamics and biomechanics are used to complete the fusion of various hetero-dimensional data such as human bone movement information, mechanical information, and human spatial position data. Moreover, the AI model is constructed by fused data and training data. Finally, through visualization technology, the calculation results are rendered as high-fidelity digital twins of the human musculoskeletal system. It can provide a credible digital dynamic model to show the biomechanical performance of the musculoskeletal system and provide reference data for subsequent human musculoskeletal medical studies.

21.8 Prospect of DT in medicine

With the exploration of DT and the developments in IoT, Big Data, and AI technology, the number of studies on the application of DT in medicine will increase. According to a Health Market report, the global IoT in healthcare is expected to reach USD 188.2 billion by 2025 with a growth rate of 21.0% (Jakovljevic et al., 2017). In the future, everyone will have his own DT. Combining the DT of medical equipment and the DT of medical auxiliary equipment, it will become a new platform and new experimental method for personal health management and healthcare services. Furthermore, based on DTs and Big Data processing, simulations are performed on the basis of

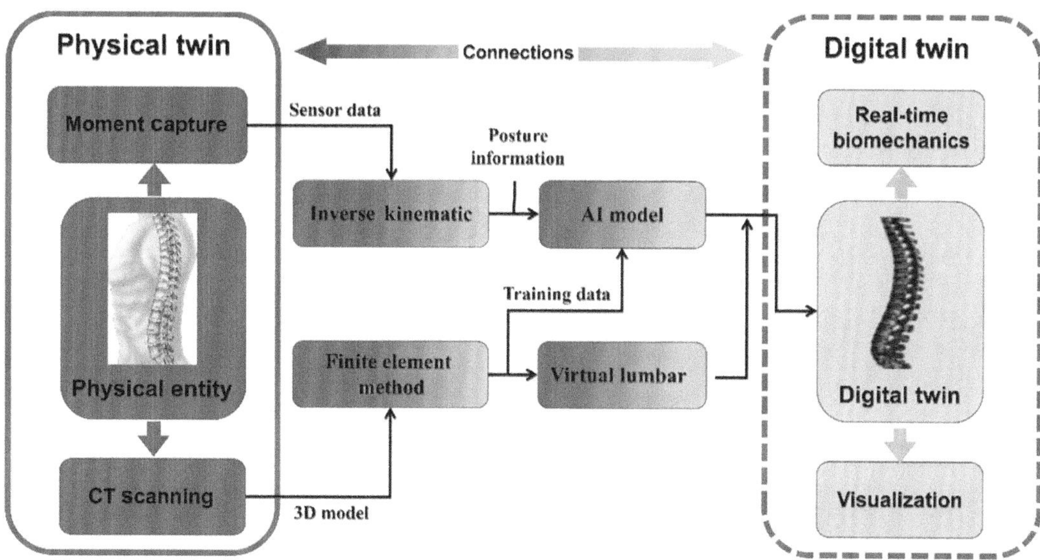

FIGURE 21.2

Connections between physical and digital twins. CT, computerized tomography; AI, artificial intelligence.

high-resolution models of patients to find accurate treatment targets and suitable drugs or treatment methods for patients to achieve precision medical treatment. Finally, establishing DT of hospitals or departments can efficiently manage medical resources and plan demand-oriented medical activities. Fig. 21.3 depicts the application process of DT in medicine and prospects its possibilities in the future.

21.8.1 Health monitoring

Generally, chronic diseases have characteristics of long duration, high incidence, and variety, which are difficult to cure. Meanwhile, the elderly have weak bodies, poor memories, and do not have enough knowledge or information about medical treatment comparatively. Hence, they need more care and community medical services, which can be effective solutions for real-time monitoring, medical guidance, and crisis warnings. The healthcare service platform can build a DT model based on the physiological parameters of the elderly and obtain real-time health data of the elderly through wearable devices or mobile phones. Then, analyze and calculate possible abnormal conditions in time to realize crisis warning. It can also transmit information on treatment methods and drugs to the model for verification to optimize the treatment plan and finally realize the early diagnosis or prevention of diseases in the elderly (Liu, Zhang, Yang, et al., 2019). DT will track each person's life journey, using data collected by wearable sensors and the lifestyle registered by people to transform clinical medicine into preventive medicine. Furthermore, DT paves the way for precision nutrition (Gkouskou, no date). Combining the information extracted from the genome with

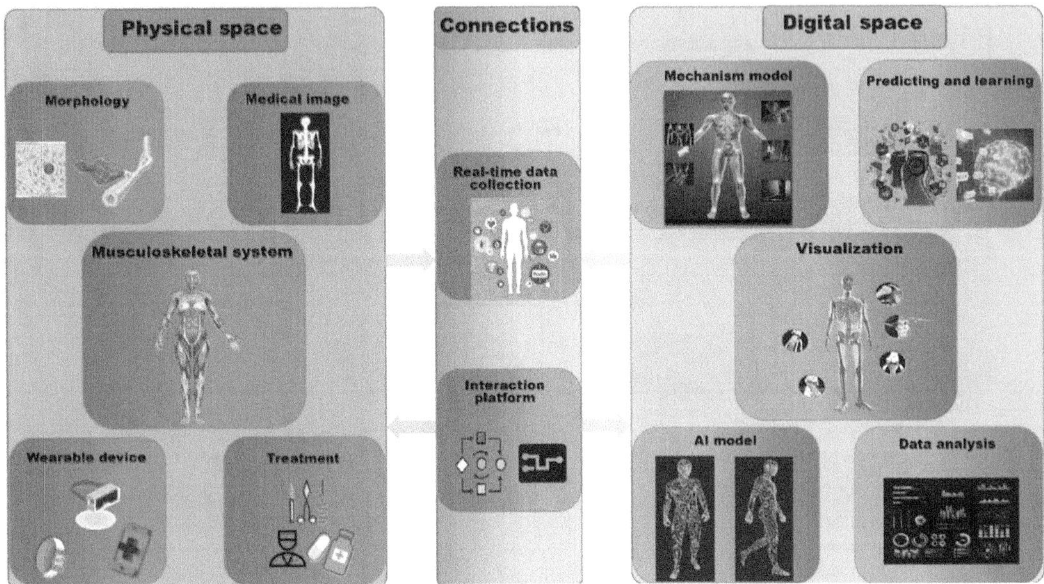

FIGURE 21.3

Digital twin of the whole musculoskeletal system for personalized diagnosis and treatment.

immune, longitudinal, and biological variables, we can improve dietary choices and provide highly individualized lifestyle recommendations.

In the future, everyone will have a full life cycle DT body, collecting data from the birth of a child to form a virtual twin, which will grow with the child and serve as a life-long health record or medical experiment object. Medical institutions can obtain data from the human body in various perceptual ways, and the real-time connection of data is the basis of a full life cycle DT body, which could ensure the accuracy of the DT model. People can get information about their physical conditions timely to predict the occurrence of risk and adjust their diet or schedule. Therefore based on the DT body and Big Data of epidemiological, the medical system can perform real-time monitoring of a patient's health status and predict the risk of disease that may occur at any time for each person. Furthermore, suggestions on lifestyle and prevention methods for each person can be given in time.

21.8.2 Precise diagnosis

The DT patient is perfectly developed by multisource data, which can be collected through various medical scanning or wearable instruments, such as CT, MRI, Emission Computed Tomography (ECT), and color ultrasound. There is also biochemical data on blood routine, urine tests, or other enzymes to simulate the microenvironment and basic vital signs, making the virtual patient more accurate. The ideal DT model should integrate all data of patients and all types of pathogenesis, to form multilayer modules (Barabási et al., 2011). Connect different data through the mapping relationship between different types of modules, such as mRNAs and proteins (Barabási et al., 2011; Zhou et al., 2014). Network tools can also link interactions between cells from different types of tissue models, thereby creating a considerable DT patient (Gustafsson et al., 2015). However, DT patients cannot be restricted to molecular profiles. We should also consider environmental factors when it comes to a patient with severe asthma, which is necessary to avoid allergens. In addition, there are historical data, medical records, health prediction data, surgical simulation data, and virtual drug test data. The collected data must be complete and made suitable for analysis, which is important in terms of modeling and decision-making (Diaz, 2013). Therefore based on the DT of the human body, the medical system can make precise diagnoses of disease.

21.8.3 Precise treatment

When a person has a disease, according to the data and models, expert doctors do not need to have face-to-face consultations but only need remote visual consultations to determine the cause or carry out disease prevention. Before the operation, the DT can assist in drawing up the surgical procedure plan and the surgeon can use the virtual display to preimplement the operation plan verification on the virtual human body. Try the operation process from multiple angles and multiple modules to verify the safety and feasibility and make improvements until you are satisfied. During the operation, DT can increase the surgical perspective, warn of the danger of blind spots, predict hidden bleeding, and help prepare or respond to the action according to circumstance (Golse et al., 2021). It can also reference the surgery to verify anatomy and avoid unnecessary damage to structures. In addition, combining virtual data at the molecular cell level to conduct virtual experiments and clinical trials of drugs can greatly reduce the development period of drugs and the side effects of drugs on the human body. In a word, DT could help enable personalized medicine including targeted intervention before the disease gets worse and making accurate predictions, accurate detections, and precise treatments.

For example, DT plays a vital role when using precision medical methods to treat malignant tumors. Using computer algorithm-based methods and principles in bioinformatics, it is possible to choose more effective treatment options for malignant tumors according to the DT model of the individual patient, thereby improving the survival rate and quality of the patient's life. Input the patient's genotype data into the calculation model for predicting the effect of anticancer drugs, the model can output the patient's sensitivity to single or multiple drugs, helping doctors screen out the most suitable therapeutic drugs for the cancer patient. All of those can help accomplish precise treatment of cancer patients.

In hospitals, resource management and clinical departments can use DT to solve the lack of resources in healthcare, especially during the COVID-19 pandemic process. For example, in the radiology department, Mater Private Hospitals created a DT to make various predictions and test many scenarios. Based on the information provided by the DT, the hospital adjusted the planning and organization of the radiology department, which reduced the waiting time of patients and improved hospital efficiency. DT will be widely used in more departments in hospitals. For example, adjust the doctor's visit time according to the flow of outpatients, predict the occurrence of failures according to the DT of the equipment, and repair them in time to reduce the error rate and the loss of the hospital. In addition, we can also use the virtual human body to train medical staff to improve medical skills, the treatment success rate, and the teaching level of the hospital.

21.8.4 Socio-ethical benefits and risks

The use of DT in medicine has promoted not only the revolution of treatment and diagnostics but also aroused discussions about its socio-ethical consequences (Bruynseels, 2020). With the critics of the traditional medical system, DT is considered to have a positive impact on individual happiness and personalized medicine, because it can allow patients to exercise a greater degree of autonomy and make the equal treatment of patients related to race or gender come true. However, there are also socio-ethical risks in DT healthcare. Privacy, which seems to be the most important socio-ethical risk, is the main reason why DT may be disadvantageous. Furthermore, the high cost of DT healthcare may lead to inequality and injustice, which could widen the existing socioeconomic gap.

It is assumed that an emerging technology is more adjustable in the early stage for the fundamental research and clinical trials have not fully begun, and the effects to society are easy to control (Popa et al., 2021). In my opinion, too little privacy is undesirable, and too much privacy is equally undesirable. There should be a privacy golden section to determine standard issues. To be sure, healthy people are more worried about their data privacy issues than patients with terminal cancer.

21.9 Conclusion

The development of DT medicine is expected to achieve a quantitative understanding of health and disease and bring about a revolution in the development of medicine. However, it is still at a marginal position compared with mainstream academic fields. As a multidisciplinary emerging discipline, its research threshold is relatively high, which usually requires the participation of mathematics experts, computer experts, and medical scholars, and the talent training cycle is long. To promote DT medicine research and talent training, the discipline construction of the Institute of DT should be emphasized and strengthened.

Existing models are still inadequate to simulate the real situation because it is still difficult to find tools that can define the connection between the virtual world and the experience world, especially the validity of the computer simulation model. With the continuous development of Big Data, IoT, genomics, and medical imaging, these will all be overcome.

To some extent, DT healthcare has problems on legal and economic. To address privacy concerns, the government and international legislatures should conduct strict supervision and establish unified, effective, and feasible standards. At the same time, more investment is needed to support the development of DT. In brief, with the application of new technologies and the improvement of government policy and public facilities, DT healthcare, as a key fusion method for future medicine, will achieve precise medicine and bring the light of personalized medicine into reality.

References

Agostinelli, S. (2020). The potential of digital twin model integrated with artificial intelligence systems. In *IEEE International conference on environment and electrical engineering and 2020.*

Ahmed, H., & Devoto, L. (2021). The potential of a digital twin in surgery. *Surgical Innovation*, *28*(4), 509–510. Available from https://doi.org/10.1177/1553350620975896.

Baillargeon, B., Rebelo, N., Fox, D. D., Taylor, R. L., & Kuhl, E. (2014). The living heart project: A robust and integrative simulator for human heart function. *European Journal of Mechanics - A/Solids*, *48*(1), 38–47. Available from https://doi.org/10.1016/j.euromechsol.2014.04.001.

Barabási, A. L., Gulbahce, N., & Loscalzo, J. (2011). Network medicine: A network-based approach to human disease. *Nature Reviews. Genetics*, *12*(1), 56–68. Available from https://doi.org/10.1038/nrg2918.

Björnsson, B., Borrebaeck, C., Elander, N., Gasslander, T., Gawel, D. R., Gustafsson, M., Jörnsten, R., Lee, E. J., Li, X., Lilja, S., Martínez-Enguita, D., Matussek, A., Sandström, P., Schäfer, S., Stenmarker, M., Sun, X. F., Sysoev, O., Zhang, H., & Benson, M. (2020). Digital twins to personalize medicine. *Genome Medicine*, *12*(1). Available from https://doi.org/10.1186/s13073-019-0701-3.

Brown, S. A., Kovatchev, B. P., Raghinaru, D., Lum, J. W., Buckingham, B. A., Kudva, Y. C., Laffel, L. M., Levy, C. J., Pinsker, J. E., Wadwa, R. P., Dassau, E., Doyle, F. J., Anderson, S. M., Church, M. M., Dadlani, V., Ekhlaspour, L., Forlenza, G. P., Isganaitis, E., Lam, D. W., ... Beck, R. W. (2019). Six-month randomized, multicenter trial of closed-loop control in type 1 diabetes. *New England Journal of Medicine*, *381*(18), 1707–1717. Available from https://doi.org/10.1056/NEJMoa1907863, http://www.nejm.org/medical-index.

Bruynseels, K. (2020). When nature goes digital: Routes for responsible innovation. *Journal of Responsible Innovation*, *7*(3), 342–360. Available from https://doi.org/10.1080/23299460.2020.1771144, http://www.tandfonline.com/action/journalInformation?show = aimsScope&journalCode = tjri20.

Burgun, A. (2019). Basis and perspectives of artificial intelligence in radiation therapy. *Cancer/Radiotherapie*, *23*(8), 913–916. Available from https://doi.org/10.1016/j.canrad.2019.08.005, http://www.elsevier.com/html/detrevue.cfm?code = CR-Modul.

Chakshu, N. K., Carson, J., Sazonov, I., & Nithiarasu, P. (2019). A semi-active human digital twin model for detecting severity of carotid stenoses from head vibration—A coupled computational mechanics and computer vision method. *International Journal for Numerical Methods in Biomedical Engineering*, *35*(5). Available from https://doi.org/10.1002/cnm.3180, http://onlinelibrary.wiley.com/journal/10.1002/(ISSN)2040-7947.

Chang, K. C., Dutta, S., Mirams, G. R., Beattie, K. A., Sheng, J., Tran, P. N., Wu, M., Wu, W. W., Colatsky, T., Strauss, D. G., & Li, Z. (2017). Uncertainty quantification reveals the importance of data variability and experimental design considerations for in silico proarrhythmia risk assessment. *Frontiers in Physiology*, *8*. Available from https://doi.org/10.3389/fphys.2017.00917, https://www.frontiersin.org/articles/10.3389/fphys.2017.00917/full.

Corral-Acero, J., Margara, F., Marciniak, M., Rodero, C., Loncaric, F., Feng, Y., Gilbert, A., Fernandes, J. F., Bukhari, H. A., Wajdan, A., Martinez, M. V., Santos, M. S., Shamohammdi, M., Luo, H., Westphal, P., Leeson, P., DiAchille, P., Gurev, V., Mayr, M., ... Lamata, P. (2020). The 'digital twin' to enable the vision of precision cardiology. *European Heart Journal*, *41*(48), 4556–4564. Available from https://doi.org/10.1093/eurheartj/ehaa159.

Dang, J., Lal, A., Flurin, L., James, A., Gajic, O., & Rabinstein, A. A. (2021). Predictive modeling in neurocritical care using causal artificial intelligence. *World Journal of Critical Care Medicine*, *10*(4), 112–119. Available from https://doi.org/10.5492/wjccm.v10.i4.112.

Daubert, C., Behar, N., Martins, R. P., Mabo, P., & Leclercq, C. (2017). Avoiding non-responders to cardiac resynchronization therapy: A practical guide. *European Heart Journal*, *38*(19), 1463–1472. Available from https://doi.org/10.1093/eurheartj/ehw270, http://eurheartj.oxfordjournals.org/.

DebRoy, T., Zhang, W., Turner, J., & Babu, S. S. (2017). Building digital twins of 3D printing machines. *Scripta Materialia*, *135*, 119–124. Available from https://doi.org/10.1016/j.scriptamat.2016.12.005.

Devoto, L., Muscroft, S., & Chand, M. (2019). Highly accurate, patient-specific, 3-dimensional mixed-reality model creation for surgical training and decision-making. *JAMA Surgery*, *154*(10), 968–969. Available from https://doi.org/10.1001/jamasurg.2019.2546, http://archsurg.jamanetwork.com/issues.aspx.

Dhume, R. Y., & Barocas, V. H. (2019). Emergent structure-dependent relaxation spectra in viscoelastic fiber networks in extension. *Acta Biomaterialia*, *87*, 245–255. Available from https://doi.org/10.1016/j.actbio.2019.01.027, http://www.journals.elsevier.com/acta-biomaterialia.

Diaz, V. (2013). Roadmap for the digital patient.

Erol, T., Mendi, A. F., & Doğan, D. (2020). *The digital twin revolution in healthcare, . 4th International Symposium on Multidisciplinary Studies and Innovative Technologies (ISMSIT)* (2020). IEEE.

Gabor, T., Belzner, L., Kiermeier, M., Beck, M.T., Neitz, A. (2016). A simulation-based architecture for smart cyber-physical systems. In *Proceedings - 2016 IEEE international conference on autonomic computing, ICAC 2016* (pp. 374–379). https://doi.org/10.1109/ICAC.2016.29.

Gkouskou K. Concept in precision nutrition, Advances in Nutrition, 1405 1413.

Glaessgen, E.H., & Stargel, D.S. (2012). The digital twin paradigm for future NASA and U.S. air force vehicles. In *53rd AIAA/ASME/ASCE/AHS/ASC structures, structural dynamics and materials conference 2012.*

Golse, N., Joly, F., Combari, P., Lewin, M., Nicolas, Q., Audebert, C., Samuel, D., Allard, M. A., Sa Cunha, A., Castaing, D., Cherqui, D., Adam, R., Vibert, E., & Vignon-Clementel, I. E. (2021). Predicting the risk of post-hepatectomy portal hypertension using a digital twin: A clinical proof of concept. *Journal of Hepatology*, *74*(3), 661–669. Available from https://doi.org/10.1016/j.jhep.2020.10.036.

Gustafsson, M., Gawel, D. R., Alfredsson, L., Baranzini, S., Björkander, J., Blomgran, R., Hellberg, S., Eklund, D., Ernerudh, J., Kockum, I., Konstantinell, A., Lahesmaa, R., Lentini, A., Liljenström, H. R. I., Mattson, L., Matussek, A., Mellergård, J., Mendez, M., Olsson, T., ... Benson, M. (2015). A validated gene regulatory network and GWAS identifies early regulators of T cell–associated diseases. *Science Translational Medicine*, *7*(313). Available from https://doi.org/10.1126/scitranslmed.aad2722.

He, X. (n.d.). Towards a shape-performance integrated digital twin for lumbar spine analysis.

Hill, S., & Markram, H. (2008). *The blue brain project. 30th Annual international conference of the IEEE engineering in medicine and biology society*. IEEE.

Houten. (2018). *How a virtual heart could save your real one-Blog| Philips.*

Jakovljevic, M., Potapchik, E., Popovich, L., Barik, D., & Getzen, T. E. (2017). Evolving health expenditure landscape of the BRICS nations and projections to 2025. *Health Economics*, *26*(7), 844–852. Available from https://doi.org/10.1002/hec.3406.

Khanna, A. (n.d.). Blockchain-cloud integration: A survey. *Sensors (Basel).*

Kim, H. J., Chun, H. J., Lee, H. M., Kang, K. T., Lee, C. K., Chang, B. S., & Yeom, J. S. (2013). The biomechanical influence of the facet joint orientation and the facet tropism in the lumbar spine. *Spine Journal*, *13*(10), 1301–1308. Available from https://doi.org/10.1016/j.spinee.2013.06.025.

Kim, H. J., Kang, K. T., Son, J., Lee, C. K., Chang, B. S., & Yeom, J. S. (2015). The influence of facet joint orientation and tropism on the stress at the adjacent segment after lumbar fusion surgery: A biomechanical analysis. *Spine Journal*, *15*(8), 1841–1847. Available from https://doi.org/10.1016/j.spinee.2015.03.038, http://www.elsevier.com/locate/spinee.

Kovatchev, B. (2019). A century of diabetes technology: Signals, models, and artificial pancreas control. *Trends in Endocrinology & Metabolism*, *30*(7), 432–444. Available from https://doi.org/10.1016/j.tem.2019.04.008.

Krittian, S. B. S., Lamata, P., Michler, C., Nordsletten, D. A., Bock, J., Bradley, C. P., Pitcher, A., Kilner, P. J., Markl, M., & Smith, N. P. (2012). A finite-element approach to the direct computation of relative cardiovascular pressure from time-resolved MR velocity data. *Medical Image Analysis*, *16*(5), 1029–1037. Available from https://doi.org/10.1016/j.media.2012.04.003.

Lai, X., Wang, S., Guo, Z., Zhang, C., Sun, W., & Song, X. (2021). Designing a shape-performance integrated digital twin based on multiple models and dynamic data: A boom crane example. *Journal of Mechanical Design*, *143*(7). Available from https://doi.org/10.1115/1.4049861, https://asmedigitalcollection.asme.org/mechanicaldesign.

Langmead, B., & Nellore, A. (2018). Cloud computing for genomic data analysis and collaboration. *Nature Reviews. Genetics*, *19*(4), 208–219. Available from https://doi.org/10.1038/nrg.2017.113, http://www.nature.com/reviews/genetics.

Lareyre, F., Adam, C., Carrier, M., & Raffort, J. (2020). Using digital twins for precision medicine in vascular surgery. *Annals of Vascular Surgery*, *67*, e577. Available from https://doi.org/10.1016/j.avsg.2020.04.042.

Lee, Y. H., & Fong, Z. H. (2020). Study on building digital-twin of face-milled hypoid gear from measured tooth surface topographical data. *Journal of Mechanical Design*, *142*(11). Available from https://doi.org/10.1115/1.4046915, https://asmedigitalcollection.asme.org/mechanicaldesign.

Liu, Q., Zhang, H., Leng, J., & Chen, X. (2019). Digital twin-driven rapid individualised designing of automated flow-shop manufacturing system. *International Journal of Production Research*, *57*(12), 3903–3919. Available from https://doi.org/10.1080/00207543.2018.1471243, http://www.tandfonline.com/toc/tprs20/current.

Liu, Y., Zhang, L., Yang, Y., Zhou, L., Ren, L., Wang, F., Liu, R., Pang, Z., & Deen, M. J. (2019). A novel cloud-based framework for the elderly healthcare services using digital twin. *IEEE Access*, *7*, 49088–49101. Available from https://doi.org/10.1109/access.2019.2909828.

Liu, Z., Meyendorf, N., & Mrad, N. (2018). The role of data fusion in predictive maintenance using digital twin. In *AIP conference proceedings* (Vol. 1949). http://scitation.aip.org/content/aip/proceeding/aipcp https://doi.org/10.1063/1.5031520.

Madabhushi, A., & Lee, G. (2016). Image analysis and machine learning in digital pathology: Challenges and opportunities. *Medical Image Analysis*, *33*, 170–175. Available from https://doi.org/10.1016/j.media.2016.06.037, http://www.elsevier.com/inca/publications/store/6/2/0/9/8/3/index.htt.

T.J.S.P.L.M.S.I. Maurer (2017). What is a digital twin.

Mrozek, D. (2020). A review of Cloud computing technologies for comprehensive microRNA analyses. *Computational Biology and Chemistry*, *88*107365. Available from https://doi.org/10.1016/j.compbiolchem.2020.107365.

A. Mussomeli. (2020). Digital twins bridging the physical and digital.

Navale, V., Bourne, P. E., & Ouellette, F. (2018). Cloud computing applications for biomedical science: A perspective. *PLoS Computational Biology*, *14*(6), e1006144. Available from https://doi.org/10.1371/journal.pcbi.1006144.

Niederer, S. A., Plank, G., Chinchapatnam, P., Ginks, M., Lamata, P., Rhode, K. S., Rinaldi, C. A., Razavi, R., & Smith, N. P. (2011). Length-dependent tension in the failing heart and the efficacy of cardiac resynchronization therapy. *Cardiovascular Research*, *89*(2), 336–343. Available from https://doi.org/10.1093/cvr/cvq318.

Pilati, F., Tronconi, R., Nollo, G., Heragu, S. S., & Zerzer, F. (2021). Digital twin of COVID-19 mass vaccination centers. *Sustainability*, *13*(13), 7396. Available from https://doi.org/10.3390/su13137396.

Popa, E. O., van Hilten, M., Oosterkamp, E., & Bogaardt, M. J. (2021). The use of digital twins in healthcare: Socio-ethical benefits and socio-ethical risks. *Life Sciences, Society and Policy*, *17*(1). Available from https://doi.org/10.1186/s40504-021-00113-x, https://lsspjournal.biomedcentral.com/.

Prakosa, A., Arevalo, H. J., Deng, D., Boyle, P. M., Nikolov, P. P., Ashikaga, H., Blauer, J. J. E., Ghafoori, E., Park, C. J., Blake, R. C., Han, F. T., MacLeod, R. S., Halperin, H. R., Callans, D. J., Ranjan, R., Chrispin, J., Nazarian, S., & Trayanova, N. A. (2018). Personalized virtual-heart technology for guiding the ablation of infarct-related ventricular tachycardia. *Nature Biomedical Engineering*, *2*(10), 732–740. Available from https://doi.org/10.1038/s41551-018-0282-2.

Psaty, B. M., Dekkers, O. M., & Cooper, R. S. (2018). Comparison of 2 treatment models precision medicine and preventive medicine. *JAMA - Journal of the American Medical Association*, *320*(8), 751–752. Available from https://doi.org/10.1001/jama.2018.8377, http://jama.jamanetwork.com/journal.aspx.

Raffort, J., Adam, C., Carrier, M., & Lareyre, F. (2020). Fundamentals in artificial intelligence for vascular surgeons. *Annals of Vascular Surgery*, *65*, 254–260. Available from https://doi.org/10.1016/j.avsg.2019.11.037.

Rasheed, A., San, O., & Kvamsdal, T. (2020). Digital twin: Values, challenges and enablers from a modeling perspective. *IEEE Access*, *8*, 21980–22012. Available from https://doi.org/10.1109/ACCESS.2020.2970143, http://ieeexplore.ieee.org/xpl/RecentIssue.jsp?punumber = 6287639.

El Saddik, A. (2018). Digital twins: The convergence of multimedia technologies. *IEEE Multimedia*, *25*(2), 87–92. Available from https://doi.org/10.1109/MMUL.2018.023121167.

Schleich, B., Anwer, N., Mathieu, L., & Wartzack, S. (2017). Shaping the digital twin for design and production engineering. *CIRP Annals*, *66*(1), 141–144. Available from https://doi.org/10.1016/j.cirp.2017.04.040.

Schluse, M., & Rossmann, J. (2016). From simulation to experimentable digital twins: Simulation-based development and operation of complex technical systems. In *ISSE 2016 - 2016 international symposium on systems engineering - Proceedings papers*. doi: 10.1109/SysEng.2016.7753162.

Schroeder, G. N., Steinmetz, C., Pereira, C. E., & Espindola, D. B. (2016). Digital twin data modeling with automation ML and a communication methodology for data exchange. *IFAC-PapersOnLine*, *49*(30), 12–17. Available from https://doi.org/10.1016/j.ifacol.2016.11.115, http://www.journals.elsevier.com/ifac-papersonline/.

Seshadri, B.R., & Krishnamurthy, T. (2017). Structural health management of damaged aircraft structures using the digital twin concept. In *25th AIAA/AHS adaptive structures conference, 2017*. doi: https://doi.org/10.2514/6.2017-1675.

Silver, & Spring,M. (2013). Paving the way for personalized medicine: FDA's role in a new era of medical product development.

Sims, C. R., Delima, L. R., Calimaran, A., Hester, R., & Pruett, W. A. (2018). Validating the physiologic model HumMod as a substitute for clinical trials involving acute normovolemic hemodilution. *Anesthesia and Analgesia*, *126*(1), 93–101. Available from https://doi.org/10.1213/ANE.0000000000002430, http://journals.lww.com/anesthesia-analgesia/toc/publishahead.

Suzuki, T., Takao, H., Rapaka, S., Fujimura, S., Ioan Nita, C., Uchiyama, Y., Ohno, H., Otani, K., Dahmani, C., Mihalef, V., Sharma, P., Mohamed, A., Redel, T., Ishibashi, T., Yamamoto, M., & Murayama, Y. (2020). Rupture risk of small unruptured untracranial aneurysms in Japanese adults. *Stroke; a Journal of Cerebral Circulation*, *51*(2), 641–643. Available from https://doi.org/10.1161/strokeaha.119.027664.

Söderberg, R., Wärmefjord, K., Carlson, J. S., & Lindkvist, L. (2017). Toward a digital twin for real-time geometry assurance in individualized production. *CIRP Annals*, *66*(1), 137–140. Available from https://doi.org/10.1016/j.cirp.2017.04.038.

Tao, F., Cheng, Y., Cheng, J., Zhang, M., Xu, W., & Qi, Q. (2017). Theories and technologies for cyber-physical fusion in digital twin shop-floor. *Jisuanji Jicheng Zhizao Xitong/Computer Integrated Manufacturing Systems, CIMS*, *23*(8), 1603–1611. Available from https://doi.org/10.13196/j.cims.2017.08.001, http://www.cims-journal.cn/CN/volumn/home.shtml.

Tao, F., Liu, W., Liu, J., Liu, X., Liu, Q., Qu, T., Hu, T., Zhang, Z., Xiang, F., Xu, W., Wang, J., Zhang, Y., Liu, Z., Li, H., Cheng, J., Qi, Q., Zhang, M., Zhang, H., Sui, F., ... Cheng, H. (2018). Digital twin and its potential application exploration. *Jisuanji Jicheng Zhizao Xitong/Computer Integrated Manufacturing Systems, CIMS*, *24*(1), 1–18. Available from https://doi.org/10.13196/j.cims.2018.01.001, http://www.cims-journal.cn/CN/volumn/home.shtml.

Tao, F., Zhang, M., Liu, Y., & Nee, A. Y. C. (2018). Digital twin driven prognostics and health management for complex equipment. *CIRP Annals*, *67*(1), 169–172. Available from https://doi.org/10.1016/j.cirp.2018.04.055.

Tao, F., Sui, F., Liu, A., Qi, Q., Zhang, M., Song, B., Guo, Z., Lu, S. C. Y., & Nee, A. Y. C. (2019). Digital twin-driven product design framework. *International Journal of Production Research*, *57*(12), 3935–3953. Available from https://doi.org/10.1080/00207543.2018.1443229, http://www.tandfonline.com/toc/tprs20/current.

Tao, F., Zhang, M., & Nee, A. Y. C. (2019). *Digital twin driven smart manufacturing digital twin driven smart manufacturing* (pp. 1–269). China: Elsevier. Available from https://www.sciencedirect.com/book/9780128176306, 10.1016/C2018-0-02206-9.

Tao, F., Zhang, H., Liu, A., & Nee, A. Y. C. (2019). Digital twin in industry: State-of-the-art. *IEEE Transactions on Industrial Informatics, 15*(4), 2405–2415. Available from https://doi.org/10.1109/tii.2018.2873186.

Tao, F., Zhang, M., Cheng, J., & Qi, Q. (2017). Digital twin workshop: A new paradigm for future workshop. *Jisuanji Jicheng Zhizao Xitong/Computer Integrated Manufacturing Systems, CIMS, 23*(1), 1–9. Available from https://doi.org/10.13196/j.cims.2017.01.001, http://www.cims-journal.cn/CN/volumn/home.shtml.

Tuegel, E. (2012). The airframe digital twin: Some challenges to realization. In *53rd AIAA/ASME/ASCE/AHS/ASC structures, structural dynamics and materials conference. 20th AIAA/ASME/AHS adaptive structures conference. 14th AIAA.*

Tuegel, E. J., Ingraffea, A. R., Eason, T. G., & Spottswood, S. M. (2011). Reengineering aircraft structural life prediction using a digital twin. *International Journal of Aerospace Engineering, 2011*, 1–14. Available from https://doi.org/10.1155/2011/154798.

Vickers, G. (2017). *Undesirable emergent behavior in complex systems. Transdisciplinary perspectives on complex systems: New findings and approaches* (pp. 85–113). Springer International Publishing.

Weiran, L. & TAOFei, C.J. C.M. (2020). Digital twin satellite: Concept, key technologies and applications.

Wercelens, P., da Silva, W., Hondo, F., Castro, K., Walter, M. E., Araújo, A., Lifschitz, S., & Holanda, M. (2019). Bioinformatics workflows with NoSQL database in cloud computing. *Evolutionary Bioinformatics, 15*. Available from https://doi.org/10.1177/1176934319889974, 117693431988997.

Winslow, R. L., Trayanova, N., Geman, D., & Miller, M. I. (2012). Computational medicine: Translating models to clinical care. *Science Translational Medicine, 4*(158). Available from https://doi.org/10.1126/scitranslmed.3003528, http://stm.sciencemag.org/content/4/158/158rv11.full.pdf.

Zhao, Z. (2020). Surface roughness stabilization method based on digital twin-driven machining parameters self-adaption adjustment: A case study in five-axis machining. 1–10.

Yu, Z., & Liu, C. (2018). The Logic and Innovation of Building a Digital Twin City in Xiong'an New District. *Urban Development Research, 25*(10), 66–73.

Zhou, I. Y., Liang, Y. X., Chan, R. W., Gao, P. P., Cheng, J. S., Hu, Y., So, K. F., & Wu, E. X. (2014). Brain resting-state functional MRI connectivity: Morphological foundation and plasticity. *Neuroimage, 84*, 1–10. Available from https://doi.org/10.1016/j.neuroimage.2013.08.037.

Zohdi, T.J. A.O. C.M. I.E. (2021). A digital-twin and machine-learning framework for ventilation system optimization for capturing infectious disease respiratory emissions. 1–13.

Zohdi, T. I. (2020). Modeling and simulation of the infection zone from a cough. *Computational Mechanics, 66*(4), 1025–1034. Available from https://doi.org/10.1007/s00466-020-01875-5.

CHAPTER

Green blockchain privacy—evidence from patients' identities management in healthcare

22

Anwar Ali Sathio[1,2], Muhammad Malook Rind[2], Shafique Ahmad Awan[1], Sameer Ali[3] and Allah Rakhio Junejo[4]

[1]*Department of CS&IT, Benazir Bhutto Shaheed University, Karachi, Sindh, Pakistan* [2]*Sindh Madressatul Islam University, Karachi, Sindh, Pakistan* [3]*Australian National University, Canberra, ACT, Australia* [4]*Government College University, Hyderabad, Sindh, Pakistan*

22.1 Introduction

22.1.1 Background

Today, the central issue of the world is data security; due to the flow of all data transactions by networks globally, the risk factors of data, such as hacking and theft of confidential data, have increased exponentially. The new evolutionary approach of data distribution ledger technology, blockchain technology, enforced through cross-border mechanisms, decentralized the implementation of health sector industries to be more at risk and rethink data security globally. The healthcare industry has been generating trillions of data—electronic health records (EHRs) daily, and the large volume of health-related data needs special care over cross-border blockchain networks. There are many challenges to pervasive healthcare data generated and stored when designed for decentralized architecture. As green blockchain technology development emerges in all fields of the world for security reasons, it ultimately opens new research horizons for unpredictable threats and challenges. Healthcare data requires more careful protection when working in a cross-border decentralized green blockchain network. We know that every healthcare data record is vital because of fear of exploitation and illegal use. We understand that the technology behind the secret of bitcoin's success is blockchain, which is architecture in a distributed manner.

By contrast, cross-border is a concept of decentralization of nodes and peer-to-peer (P2P) communication without the interference of middleman agents to invoke the cross-border green blockchain network. The cross-border network ensured the two main factors: minimizing the cost of computing and using fewer resources in minimal time to complete the process of validating the records. The cross-border concept can be understood well by financial applications such as the business-to-business (B2B) model and remittances in the business world. B2B models are invoked in the decentralized cross-border green blockchain network so that every country deals independently and separately. Conversely, the average conventional time is three to four days, which is required to validate and transact data processing to the Customer-to-Customer (C2C) model.

Some countries have more detailed responses when thinking about bitcoin, but the secret behind the success of this digital currency is a mechanism that holds lives between threats. According to the authors,

Blockchain and Digital Twin for Smart Hospitals. DOI: https://doi.org/10.1016/B978-0-443-34226-4.00023-X

"Bitcoin by blockchain processes approximately seven transactions per second, yet there were over 10 million users and 200,000 daily transactions" (Böhme et al., 2015). Previous research studies discussed and identified components of blockchain, in which the following factors (Xiong & Xiong, 2021) are critical:

- *Data block*: we keep information on transactions like a Merkle-tree structure in the data block.
- *Distributed ledger*: data mode shall be in a distributed database and float on Networks.
- *Consensus algorithm*: it makes a promise of replicas of the shared states and secures the transactions, like the proof of work (PoW) in bitcoin, which has been assumed as the consensus mechanism, whereas the byzantine-fault tolerance (BFT) is a suitable protocol, dealing fault tolerance mechanism in the distributed ledger technologies.
- *Smart contracts*: when it judges an application that is code-able with blockchain, the smart contracts solution is the emerging source of such blockchain technology and has become popular since its first release. That smart contract platform, coined as Ethereum, was released in 2015 and is sometimes called an "autonomous agent" or "self-executing engine" in the literature, respectively (Xiong & Xiong, 2021).

22.1.2 Cross-border green blockchain technology

Cross-border green blockchain technology facilitates secure and efficient cross-border transactions, particularly in international trade and finance. This technology has gained significant attention in recent years due to its potential to address issues such as inefficient payment processing, high transaction costs, and lack of transparency in cross-border transactions. Many industries, including healthcare, logistics, and finance, have explored cross-border green blockchain technology to streamline operations and improve efficiency. For example, cross-border green blockchain technology in healthcare can enable the secure sharing of medical data across different countries and healthcare providers, improving patient outcomes and reducing healthcare costs (Chelladurai & Pandian, 2022; Jadhav & Deshmukh, 2022; Nalin et al., 2019).

We define the cross-border green blockchain as an emerging tech with the following key attributes:

- A green blockchain technology mechanism.
- That communicates across the border with another green blockchain technology mechanism.
- With an independent P2P network covered.
- Wallet–wallet cross-border without a middleman or intermediary barriers—communication.
- P-2-P–TCP global network—data communication.
- An Independent Entity of one P2P to talk with another Entity of P2P networks without a middleman character.
- Cross-border data, assets, or money transfer/exchange using wallet's token-passing algorithm. between two different systems/applications by permissioned consensus algorithm of every node and authentication of Master(Full) node of two various entities.
- Digital identities security and management—transmissions between heterogeneous cross-border green blockchain network applications.

The above points summarized the definition of cross-border green blockchain technology as follows:

"Cross-border blockchain-an emerging technology, a most secured way to transfer/share data, digital identities, money, any digital assets with complete encryption methods and removing the intermediatory layer of granting permission for any transfer/share of digital assets data between two nodes, parties, networks, out of frontiers/countries in a minimum time."

22.2 Literature review

Blockchain technology is gaining popularity in the healthcare sector for its potential to improve healthcare data management efficiency, security, and privacy. The literature review of blockchain technology in healthcare shows that it can enhance various aspects of healthcare, including medical records management, drug supply chains, clinical trials, and health insurance. One of the significant applications of blockchain technology in healthcare is the management of electronic medical records (EMRs) (Song et al., 2022). Blockchain-based EMR systems can provide a secure and tamper-proof way to store and share patient data across healthcare providers. Blockchain can improve care coordination and reduce the risk of medical errors due to incomplete or inaccurate information. Blockchain technology can also address the issue of counterfeit drugs in the pharmaceutical industry by enabling the tracking and verification of medicines throughout the supply chain. Blockchain can improve drug safety and prevent the distribution of fake or substandard medications. Clinical trials can also benefit from blockchain technology by providing a secure and transparent way to manage trial data and ensure its integrity. Blockchain can enhance the reliability of trial results and accelerate the development of new treatments. Blockchain technology can also improve the efficiency and transparency of health insurance by enabling real-time claims processing, reducing administrative costs, and eliminating the need for intermediaries. In the literature, blockchain technology has the potential to transform the healthcare industry by improving data management, increasing efficiency, and enhancing security and privacy. However, the adoption of blockchain technology in healthcare is still in its early stages. Several challenges must be addressed, such as regulatory and legal issues, technical complexity, and interoperability with existing systems.

In the literature, the following essential opportunities were identified in the healthcare sector (Xiao et al., 2021):

- A distributed decentralized approach for every node
- Building trust level among all users, devices, networks
- Reduces the costs
- Cryptography makes secure communication
- Real-time interaction with data
- Strong, valid communication between devices and users.

The layer of data transaction maintains data blocks, which are classified into two types of storage as information for the blockchain transaction layer (Chenthara et al., 2020):

- On-chain
- Off-chain.

The blockchain transaction layer can access identifiable data, including digitized identities of patients and stakeholders, and medicine is treated as an integrated factor. The information extracted from the blockchain can be available to big data analytics, cognitive machine learning data sets, research institutions, and government departments. The patient is crucial in technological development because consensus is required in medical decision-making. That consensus can benefit patients' security, empower them, and improve their relationship with healthcare organizations, reflecting successful outcomes. As we learned from previous literature, the existing access control mechanisms did not emphasize engaging the patients or obtaining their consent before making decisions (Xiong & Xiong, 2021). The blockchain access policy can be determined according to licensed healthcare authorities. All attributes keep all records safe and secure from attack by converting them from the public into a private blockchain.

From the security evaluation analysis perspective concerning data flow protocols in blockchain applications (MedIC) obtain the patient's consent and counter-check them, some of these are below (Xiong & Xiong, 2021):

- *Spoofing*: In this concept, the spoof person's identity is used to get illegal access to any system and steal private and secured data.
- *Man-in-the-middle attacks (MITMs)*: In the off-chain approach, dissociative identity disorder (DID), after authentication, occurred (as long as the agents do not share keys outside of the agent pair) to get accessibility to private data and information.
- *Denial of service*: In this kind of attack, when the consensus ledger is compromised, these attacks are observed, to some extent, between blockchain nodes through the consensus mechanism.

The blockchain data authorization consensus requires entities to authorize data decryption, ensuring security as blockchain technology promises. This consensus mechanism enhances flexibility in access rights management, particularly when protocol violations occur. As indicated in Table 22.1, integrating cloud-based systems with blockchain technology can significantly improve data storage and security. The Ethereum framework is a prominent blockchain platform used for this purpose, while the Hyperledger Fabric framework is also gaining traction. These blockchain technologies streamline access control mechanisms, effectively managing access rights and ensuring high-level data security through advanced measures as part of a long-term policy process.

This study explores integrating decentralized concepts in pervasive healthcare into cross-border blockchain applications. The key factors identified for mapping the roadmap and architecture of decentralized cross-border networks include the following:

- *Enhanced security*: Blockchain technology ensures data integrity and security through cryptographic techniques, making unauthorized data decryption impossible. This security measure is critical in maintaining the confidentiality and authenticity of healthcare data across borders.

Table 22.1 A literature review of the technology used in healthcare systems.

Research study	Domain	Technology used	Methods/type	Factors
Pilares et al. (2022)	EHR	Blockchain	EHR/encryption	Transactional records
Dagher et al. (2018)	EHR	Blockchain	Access control policy algorithm	Access control policy mechanism
Xiao et al. (2021)	EHR	Blockchain	System automation framework	Automation of testing mechanisms using hospital cloud services to doctors for validation and consultation
Hussien et al. (2019)	EHR	Blockchain	EHR chain, a new framework	Dual blockchains based on Hyperledger Sawtooth to allow patient data decentralization
Madine et al. (2020)	PEHR	Blockchain	Decentralized storage of interplanetary file systems (IPFSs)	Evaluate smart contracts—two essential performance metrics
Chelladurai and Pandian (2022)	EHR	Blockchain	A smart e-health system	Cryptographic hash function

- *Access control*: The ability to revoke and modify access rights dynamically ensures compliance with international data-sharing protocols. This flexibility is essential in managing data access in a decentralized healthcare system.
- *Interoperability*: Combining cloud-based systems with blockchain enhances interoperability, allowing seamless data exchange between healthcare entities and systems. This integration is crucial for the efficient functioning of cross-border healthcare networks (Belchior et al., 2022).
- *Scalability*: Blockchain frameworks like Ethereum and Hyperledger Fabric provide scalable solutions to handle the increasing volume of healthcare data, ensuring robust performance and reliability (Androulaki et al., 2018).
- *Transparency and traceability*: Blockchain's inherent transparency and traceability features enable real-time monitoring and auditing of data transactions, which is vital for regulatory compliance and trust-building in cross-border healthcare initiatives (Yaqoob et al., 2022).
- These factors collectively form the foundation for developing a secure, interoperable, and efficient decentralized cross-border healthcare network, leveraging blockchain technology's strengths to address global healthcare data management challenges.

22.2.1 Background of security management and authentication in cross-border blockchain

Security management is a critical issue in the network when distributed architecture and open access to all nodes; blockchain makes it possible to ensure the data is transparently over the web along with the surety of data for any mutation or updating at any level without an authorized node (Neisse et al., 2020). There are many ways to implement this level of security, and some of them are mentioned below.

22.2.1.1 Self-sovereign identity and digital identity of blockchain

The self-sovereign identity (SSI) process, composed of mechanisms for authorization (authentication and verification), includes the single attributes of consolidated digital identity; still, much work is required concerning data privacy mechanisms. The authors reviewed digital identities in detail with many SSI features (Van Bokkem et al., 2019; Zhu & Badr, 2018).

22.2.1.2 Identity management approaches and actors in blockchain

The following main approaches and actors play functional roles in the blockchain.

22.2.1.2.1 Functional actors

There are some below concepts referred for identities and explored as functional actors in blockchain technology:

- User-centric identity
- User-hybrid identity
- User-distributed identity
- Centralized identity
- Federated Identity, that is, Facebook and Google

22.2.1.2.2 Players in blockchain identities

The following are the essential role players in the blockchain digital identities support the technical implementation of the system (Zhu & Badr, 2018):

- Vendors/blockchain service providers
- *Management of identities—identity service providers*: this is further subdivided into the following.

22.2.1.2.3 Authentication providers make the authorization processing a secure way

- Attribute providers
- Service providers
- Identity providers
- SSI—identity owner, this is ownership of data to use transparency and one unique digital identity to manage by the identity owner
- One central control-authority single user manages Personal Identifies Information (PII)
- Central authority: A service provider is to control all actors and monitor the issues in time. It retains supreme power in this approach by collecting the user's records or information through a prescribed authentication system
- Federated Instance authority, the federated service provider, separates entity-related matters like enrollment, authentication, and verification of users' identities in a distributed network environment (Zhu & Badr, 2018).

The degree of anonymity and linkability of personal data may be affected by personal data, which is the selective revelation of PII and personal data privacy issues. As reported, PII is a degree of identity holder concerning related information in all labels. Individual Personal Private Identity Information (PPII) is the subset of personal records with complete identity information in all attributes. General Data Protection Regulation (GDPR) is a platform to secure consumer rights through interactive information exchange between service providers and holders for their identity to ensure a fair transient policy agreement. GDPR gets complaints about digital rights with (the SSI) principle of user-centric identity in recognition, allowing an individual to manage and control her data freely.

22.2.2 User's data privacy

The current blockchain research on data privacy targets data anonymity and has provided various solutions to protect personally identifiable information. The k-anonymity approach offers a resolution of linking information and requires the input set to be indistinguishable from other $k-1$ information records. Other solutions proposed include the diversified representation and distribution of sensitive data to secure data sharing and minimalization by different researchers.

22.2.2.1 Identity proofing and attribute assurance

These service managers provide the identity attributes at best services and maintain a high level of trust by legal information for characteristics of digital identities.

22.2.2.2 Verification factors in digital identities

The following are the main factors involved in the verification of digital identities:

- The individual credential data
- Taking the biometric data
- The private key-PII generation

The two main methods were applied to get the claim of verifications:

- *Identity registry model*: This claim is stored offline through the issuer's consent.
- *Claim registry model*: this holds the identifier in the blockchain and records of attested claims.

22.2.3 Authentication approaches in blockchain technology

The way we secure the data is encrypting, and methods of authentication, which make the data secure and safe, listed below factors reviewed in the literature (Diro et al., 2024):

- Decentralized authentication-public key infrastructure (DPKI.)
  This approach is responsible for public key management and authentication of correct mapping between users and their respective keys, existing two methods for authentication under critical public infrastructure in current practice.
- Centralized authentication-public key infrastructure (CPKI.)
  In a centralized approach, the hierarchically structured central certificate authorities manage the certificate and hold the power to issue or revoke the certificate at any time to keep secure authentication streamlined. There are at least four components related to SSI in blockchain: registration identification, authentication, identity proofing, and personal data management.

22.2.4 Security challenges

As the world changes rapidly due to technological advancements, these open emerging dimensions and challenges, especially in data security when working in a distributed environment or cloud-based systems; issues reviewed in the current literature research have been appended below for further discussion (Gupta et al., 2024; Shahidinejad & Abawajy, 2024):

22.2.4.1 Accessibility in services

The node is considered a role player and hyperfoundation layer in the distributed and decentralized network environment. Researchers have found some critical issues they viewed as significant threats to blockchain identity accessibility listed below:

- DoS—denial of services
- Modification attack
- Dropping attacks
- Mining attacks

The challenges of blockchain healthcare research are subdivided into four significant obstacles: cloud-based, network-based, Internet of Things (IoT)-enabled, and industrial IoT (IIoT)-enabled.

22.2.4.2 Cloud-based challenges

In the literature, data transforming into cloud-based servers through decentralized networks, some issues were identified, which appended:

- IoT-based infrastructure 5G/6G wireless network issues
- Future applications accessibility over cloud issues
- Future application performance on cloud issues
- Device integration, transformation over cloud issues
- Scalability and integration issues.

22.2.4.3 Network-based data transactional challenges

As we discuss and focus on the distributed and decentralized systems in the local network and global healthcare in the cloudless environment, the following issues are observed in the current literature: blockchain technology.

- Performance issue
- Speed issues in wireless systems
- Accessibility and authentication issues
- Validation issues
- Data security and encryption issues
- Hacking threats.

22.2.4.4 MIoT-enabled challenges

Blockchain technology shall be very effective in MIoT-enabled systems, especially in the healthcare systems' environment; this technique makes MIoT-enabled strategies more profitable and efficient; the following significant challenges reviewed in the literature listed below (Kumar & Mallick, 2018):

- IoT devices 5G/6G coverage issues
- Wireless speed issues due to environmental effects
- Implementation (hardware/software) issues
- Resource pooling and transformation issues
- Interoperability issues.

22.2.4.5 Industrial IoT challenges

Blockchain can play a vital role in developing industrial fields, especially in healthcare, e-transporting, e-business, e-government, and e-learning. Some IoT-based challenges converting in blockchain-based systems we found in the literature have been identified and are listed below for further research:

- IoT-based heterogeneous environments, architectural, across platforms data synchronization and systems issues
- Communication protocol complexity and standard issues

- Hardware and software component's poor interoperability issues
- IoT-based resource constraints: computing, storage, bandwidth, and power supply issues
- IoT-based confidential data security to the cloud vulnerability
- Autonomy issues in interoperability
- Cyber-physical system issues
- Blockchain networks and transparency issues
- Blockchain P2P communication issues
- Decentralization issues
- Blockchain-SSI technology change and enhancement issues.

22.2.4.6 Other technical challenges

22.2.4.6.1 Technological issues

- A limitation of blockchain is that it runs in a peer-to-peer homogeneous manner quickly.
- Another uniqueness of IIoT is that it limits blockchain implementation at the industry level.

22.2.4.6.2 Computational and storage

The issue of time complexity in computing with high-level to low-level IIoT-based devices in blockchain requires extensive storage capability to refresh and update data of the nodes/devices in the network, which is another restriction in some cases of IIoT-based systems.

22.2.4.6.3 Communication, energy, and cost

In the blockchain network (peer-to-peer system), parallel nodes can communicate synchronously, even though these systems maintain transparency and exchange of data processing, which will ultimately consume extra energy compared to a typical P2P system.

22.2.4.6.4 Latency and capacity

The time required to build the blockchain is usually 10 minutes for any popular digital currency. It can be processed by transaction among all nodes across the board through the consensus protocol, although this is not a reasonable performance rate in significant global data transactions.

22.2.4.6.5 IIoT modes

In the IIoT, we observed at least two modes in literature:

- Stable network—fixed station-based
- Ad-hoc mode with no preexisting node depends on neighboring nodes; this situation may restrict the system in hybrid networks.

22.2.4.6.6 Timestamping authority

This timestamping label shows the details of blocks and transactions; in the literature we reviewed, some key issues relating to this authority have been listed below for further investigation:

- Deployment
- The consortium (permission) blockchain network issues
- Trust compromise of vehicular nodes

- Flexible operation limitations in dynamic and static operations
- Double spending elimination
- Unbalanced load distribution in the edge server
- Privacy-preserving analytics.

22.2.4.7 Pervasive healthcare digital identities and security challenges

Healthcare is a very progressive domain in pervasive computing; blockchain is now widespread and raising its practical usage in healthcare systems. In the current research, the following essential issues discussed in the literature by scholars are as follows:

- Interoperability issue
- Identities exchange of health records into SSI
- Health information exchange into blockchain information breakups
- SSI scalability and transformation issues on a chain of nodes
- Transactional scalability
- Data refinement and scope limitations
- Participation incentives and adoption
- Operation cost
- Regulatory framework and new administration policy problems
- Privacy rule, separating and encrypting identity issues
- PII and Protected Health Information (PHI) are isolated entities that can be accessed through the blockchain-based keyless signature interface (KSI) hierarchies
- Individuals' medical identity records and their privacy issues
- Sharing distinct identity attributes in health records (Jakhar et al., 2024).

The patients' data record is very sensitive; this shall be kept secure and not compromised. Blockchain technology promises data security through encryption hash methods, first through a distributed design approach with data blocks chained by cryptographic and immutability chaining mechanisms. The cross-border mechanism makes the versatile blockchain approach for emerging tech, as shown in Table 22.1, to enhance the usability of blockchain and make it feasible around the globe, irrespective of geographical boundaries (Table 22.2).

22.2.4.8 General challenging vital issues in the healthcare system

The main challenge in the healthcare system related to blockchain implementation, some fundamental issues have been reviewed in literature as follows:

- Ownership and interoperability in SSI
- Protection of digital identities
- Interface, identity proofing, evidence exchange between subject nodes, claim verifier, and issuer
- Authentication and user data privacy
- Distributed interoperability in centralized platform integration issues
- Advanced and enhanced identity issues management
- Optimization and scalability in distributed blockchain promises

Table 22.2 Literature overview of blockchain-based healthcare systems.

Research study and year	Domain	Technology used	Methods/type	Problem addressed/ factor focus
Velmurugan et al. (2024)	End—end node encryptions for EHRs	Do	Secure transmission between nodes of electronic health records (EHRs)	Do
Jakhar et al. (2024), and Sun et al. (2020)	Do	Do	Medical data protection access control—MDPAC model	Do
Ragab et al. (2024)	Do	Do	Feature vector selection (FVS) method applied	Do
Alubady et al. (2023)	Healthcare services	Do	Secure federated learning (BT-SFL-IoMT)	Do
Idrissi and Palmieri (2024)	Do	Do	Selective ring-based access control (SRAC)/some cryptography methods	Do
Chen et al. (2021)	Do	Do	Blockchain-assisted secure data management framework (BSDMF)	A dynamic approach, scalability

- Parties—attestation verifiers and trust agreement issues
- Integration issues of users' experiences.

22.3 Methodology

Conceptual model procedure—steps of digital identity in the pervasive healthcare system with a cross-border mechanism of green blockchain technology:

22.3.1 New pervasive node signup—registrations

The following are the processing included in terms of registration:

- Devices identification—certificates (physical address, virtual address, private key, public key)
- (Associative degree method and cumulative degree method)
- A hashing method by secure hash algorithm (SHA) 256 of device data
- Digital signature of the nodes—the elliptic curve digital signature method for pervasive, according to Amofa et al. (2024) includes the following:
- Cross-border network node's verification and validation after signature approval by the cross-border green blockchain networks
- Data transmission granted approved signatory nodes

- Transaction making and block chaining into green blockchain network—cross-border communication
- Adding to archive after fixed time duration—per authorities of pervasive healthcare systems.

22.3.2 Proposed mathematical model and wallet token-passing algorithm

22.3.2.1 Mathematical model explanation

A mathematical model for token passing of the digital identities of any patient data transaction between two cross borders enables green blockchain networks with two classes, associative and cumulative set rules identities in pervasive healthcare systems, which would involve several elements. First, it would apply a way to represent the digital identities of patients, which could be modeled as a set of tuples (patient_id, name, date, hash). The hash is a cryptographic representation of the data generated using a hash function such as SHA-256. Second, it would involve a way to model the token-passing process, which could be represented as a set of rules that dictate who is authorized to pass tokens to whom. Two rules that could be used are the "associative" rule, which checks if the sender and receiver have a common association, and the "cumulative" rule, which checks if the sender and receiver have a certain level of authorization or access. The associative rule could be modeled mathematically as a function f(sender, receiver) that returns a Boolean value indicating if the sender and receiver have a common association. The cumulative rule could be modeled mathematically as a function g(sender, receiver) that returns a Boolean value indicating if the sender and receiver have a specific authorization level or access. It would also involve modeling the cross-border green blockchain networks, which could be represented mathematically as a directed graph. The green nodes represent the blockchain networks, and the edges represent the transactions between them. Finally, it would involve a way to model the system's security, which could be expressed mathematically as a set of cryptographic algorithms and protocols that ensure the integrity and confidentiality of the patient data.

It is important to note that it is a general mathematical model, and the actual implementation will depend on the specific requirements of the system, the blockchain networks being used, and the security measures in place. For example, the hash of the patient data in the digital identity class is represented as shown in Fig. 22.1 (cross-border-transaction (CBT) token attributes) by a mathematical equation and algorithms that explain the procedure for token passing with data of pervasive healthcare systems as follows:

hash = SHA-256(data)
SHA-256 is a cryptographic hash function; the data is the patient's data.
The associative rule could be modeled mathematically as a function f(sender, receiver) that returns a Boolean value indicating if the sender and receiver have a common association.
f(sender, receiver) = (sender.association = = receiver.association)
The cumulative rule could be modeled mathematically as a function g(sender, receiver) that returns a Boolean value indicating if the sender and receiver have a certain authorization level or access.
g(sender, receiver) = (sender.authorization > = access_level)
It is important to note that these equations are just examples of the actual implementation; the system's specific requirements will determine the exact equations used.

Description of mathematical model:

```
# ########### (* Define a SHA-256 hash function *) ############

HashFunction[data_] := IntegerString[Hash[data, "SHA256"], 16, 64]

# (* Define the associative and cumulative set rules *)

AssociativeSetRule[sender_, receiver_] := sender["organization"] ===
receiver["organization"]
CumulativeSetRule[sender_, receiver_] := sender["authLevel"] >= receiver["authLevel"]

# (* Define the verification function *)

VerifyIdentities[sender_, receiver_] := HashFunction[sender["data"]] ===
HashFunction[receiver["data"]]

# (* Define the token passing process *)

PassToken[sender_, receiver_] := Module[{},
 If [!VerifyIdentities[sender, receiver],
  Return["Identity verification failed."]
 ];
 If[!(AssociativeSetRule[sender, receiver] && CumulativeSetRule[sender, receiver]),
  Return["Permission denied."]
 ];

 # (* Update blockchain and transfer token ownership *)

 "Token passed successfully."
]

# (* Example identities *)

sender = <|"patientID" -> "001", "name" -> "Alice", "data" -> "Patient Data Alice",
"organization" -> "Org1", "authLevel" -> 2|>;
receiver = <|"patientID" -> "002", "name" -> "Bob", "data" -> "Patient Data Alice",
"organization" -> "Org1", "authLevel" -> 2|>;

# (* Pass the token *)

PassToken[sender, receiver]
######################################
```

22.3.2.2 Algorithm 1 wallet token pass explanation

The possible wallet token-passing algorithm is a primary algorithm for implementing token passing of digital identities for patient data transactions between cross-border green blockchain networks in a pervasive healthcare system:

- Define two classes, digital identity, and token passing, to represent the digital identities and the token-passing process.
- In the digital identity class, include the patient's ID, name, data, and a hash of the data. The hash can be generated using a cryptographic hash function such as SHA-256.

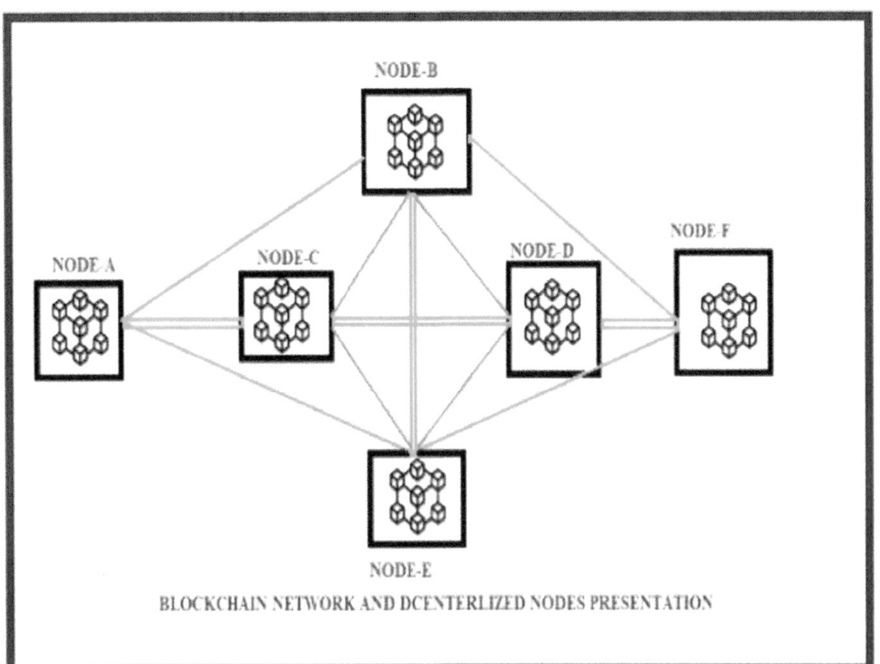

FIGURE 22.1

Concepts of decentralization blockchain mechanism.

- In the token-passing class, include a list of digital identities and methods for passing tokens between identities.
- In the pass token method, retrieve the sender and receiver identities based on the provided patient IDs from the list of identities.
- Verify that the sender and receiver identities match by comparing the data hashes. If the hashes do not match, an error will be raised.
- Check if the sender can pass the token to the receiver by implementing your logic in the check permission method. If the sender does not have permission, an error will be raised.
- If the sender and receiver identities match and the sender has permission, perform the token-passing process. That may involve updating the blockchain network, transferring token ownership, or other actions depending on the system's requirements.
- In the check permission method, use the associative and cumulative set rules defined for the system to check if the sender is authorized to pass the token to the receiver.
- The associative set rule checks that the sender and receiver have a common association, such as being members of the same healthcare organization.
- The cumulative set rule checks that the sender and receiver have a particular authorization level or access.

Pseudocode:

```
class DigitalIdentity:
  def __init__(self, patient_id, name, data):
    self.patient_id = patient_id
    self.name = name
    self.data = data
    self.data_hash = hash_function(data)

class TokenPassing:
  def __init__(self):
    self.identities = []

  def add_identity(self, identity):
    self.identities.append(identity)

  def pass_token(self, sender_id, receiver_id):
    sender = self.get_identity_by_id(sender_id)
    receiver = self.get_identity_by_id(receiver_id)

    if not self.verify_identities(sender, receiver):
      raise Error("Identity verification failed.")

    if not self.check_permission(sender, receiver):
      raise Error("Permission denied.")

    self.update_blockchain(sender, receiver)
    self.transfer_token(sender, receiver)

  def get_identity_by_id(self, patient_id):
    for identity in self.identities:
      if identity.patient_id == patient_id:
        return identity
    raise Error("Identity not found.")

  def verify_identities(self, sender, receiver):
    return sender.data_hash == receiver.data_hash

  def check_permission(self, sender, receiver):
    return self.associative_set_rule(sender, receiver) and self.cumulative_set_rule(sender, receiver)

  def associative_set_rule(self, sender, receiver):
    return sender.organization == receiver.organization

  def cumulative_set_rule(self, sender, receiver):
    return sender.auth_level >= receiver.auth_level

  def update_blockchain(self, sender, receiver):
    # Update blockchain network

      pass

    def transfer_token(self, sender, receiver):
      # Transfer token ownership
      pass

  def hash_function(data):
    # Implement SHA-256 or other cryptographic hash function
    Pass
```

Python code for Algorithm 1:

```
import hashlib

class DigitalIdentity:
  def __init__(self, patient_id, name, data, organization, auth_level):
    self.patient_id = patient_id
    self.name = name
    self.data = data
    self.organization = organization
    self.auth_level = auth_level
    self.data_hash = self.hash_function(data)

  @staticmethod
  def hash_function(data):
    return hashlib.sha256(data.encode()).hexdigest()

class TokenPassing:
  def __init__(self):
    self.identities = []

  def add_identity(self, identity):
    self.identities.append(identity)

  def pass_token(self, sender_id, receiver_id):
    sender = self.get_identity_by_id(sender_id)
    receiver = self.get_identity_by_id(receiver_id)

    if not self.verify_identities(sender, receiver):
      raise Exception("Identity verification failed.")

    if not self.check_permission(sender, receiver):
      raise Exception("Permission denied.")

    self.update_blockchain(sender, receiver)
    self.transfer_token(sender, receiver)

  def get_identity_by_id(self, patient_id):
    for identity in self.identities:
      if identity.patient_id== patient_id:
        return identity
    raise Exception("Identity not found.")

  def verify_identities(self, sender, receiver):
    return sender.data_hash == receiver.data_hash

  def check_permission(self, sender, receiver):
    return self.associative_set_rule(sender, receiver) and self.cumulative_set_rule(sender, receiver)

  def associative_set_rule(self, sender, receiver):
    return sender.organization == receiver.organization

  def cumulative_set_rule(self, sender, receiver):
    return sender.auth_level >= receiver.auth_level
```

```
    def update_blockchain(self, sender, receiver):

        # Code to update the blockchain network
        pass

    def transfer_token(self, sender, receiver):
        # Code to transfer token ownership
        pass

# Example usage

identity1 = DigitalIdentity("001", "Alice", "Patient Data Alice", "Org1", 2)
identity2 = DigitalIdentity("002", "Bob", "Patient Data Alice", "Org1", 2)

token_passing = TokenPassing()
token_passing.add_identity(identity1)
token_passing.add_identity(identity2)

try:
    token_passing.pass_token("001", "002")
    print("Token passed successfully.")
except Exception as e:
    print(e)
###################################
```

Algorithm1. Wallet Token Pass: Proposed Digital Identity token passing for Cross Border-green blockchain technology networks for pervasive healthcare systems' - Associative &Cumulative roles (D1+D2…….D9) & (D1*D2….Dn.) identities.

```
Begin
   IF Di < 10 check_Per_ID (ROLE_ON_01, xy) = true then
 return Error () ;
  ElseIF Di>9 check Per_ID (ROLE_ON_02, xy )=true then
Return error ();

   IF check Phy_Addr (PHY_ADD_Di, ab) = true then
 return Error () ;
   IF (Per_ID. type = associative) then

       IF check_Per_ID (ROLE_ON_01, xy) = true then
           return Error () ;

       end
       ElseIF check_Per_ID(ROLE_ON_02, xy) then
              IF check Logical-Add-(IP_ADD , xy) = false then

                  return Error () ;
              end
              IF (xy. C.B.T.Verify(CBT.data, xy) = failed then
                  return Error ();
               end
          end
   end
end
```

A process flow for the digital identities of any patient data transaction between two cross-border enable green blockchain networks with two classes associative and cumulative set rules identities in pervasive healthcare systems might include the following steps:

- A user initiates a request to pass a token, providing the patient's IDs for the sender and receiver.
- The system retrieves the digital identities of the sender and receiver from the blockchain network.
- The system compares the hashes of the data in the sender and receiver's digital identities to ensure they match.
- The system checks if the sender can pass the token to the receiver by applying the associative and cumulative set rules.
- The request is denied if the sender does not have permission and an error message is displayed.
- If the sender has permission, the token-passing process is performed, which may involve updating the blockchain network, transferring ownership of the token, or other actions depending on the system's specific requirements.
- The token-passing process is recorded in the blockchain network.
- A confirmation message is displayed to the user, indicating the successful token-passing process.

In the literature, it was observed that the existing technology was employed to get the original-complete data of patients in an encrypted structure and maintained the data in an "off-

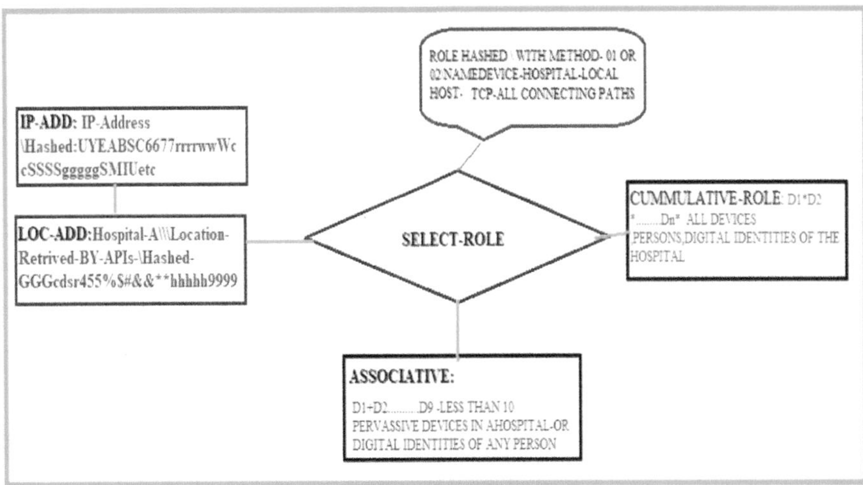

FIGURE 22.2

Describe the cross-border-transaction (CBT) token attributes.

chain" fold manner. Dagher et al. (2018) observed that blockchain-enabled technologies would provide complete and detailed information relating to all sourced data with a security encapsulation mechanism in the future. In 2016 a basic conceptual framework was introduced, and a use case was introduced by Pilares et al. (2022), as shown in Fig. 22.2. This will also be referred to for blockchain-shown enabled healthcare records have been shown in the Figs. 22.3 and 22.4.

The study devises a novel distributed digital healthcare system based on blockchain in the distributed fog cloud network. The study considered the number of base stations Fog_Hospital_Hn connecting to the patient application. All patients exploit particular base stations to access healthcare applications implemented in specific fog hospitals, such as H1, in the network. All the fog nodes, such as H1, H2, and H3 (hospital 1, 2.n), are implemented in hospitals as servers with blockchain technology implementation. For instance, D1 to Dn (Device 1, Device N). Each blockchain has different attributes such as hashing, block ID, transaction, and encryption and decryption techniques to store and share the data between hospitals. The proposed system is elastic and can implement healthcare applications based on

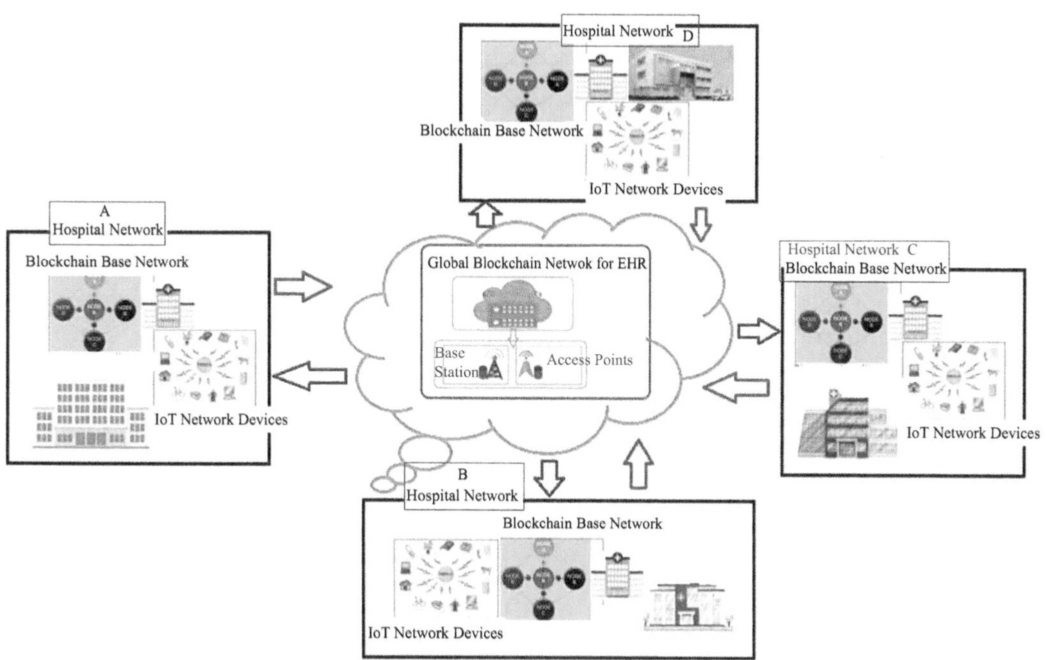

FIGURE 22.3

Cross-border blockchain mobility aware system in pervasive healthcare systems.

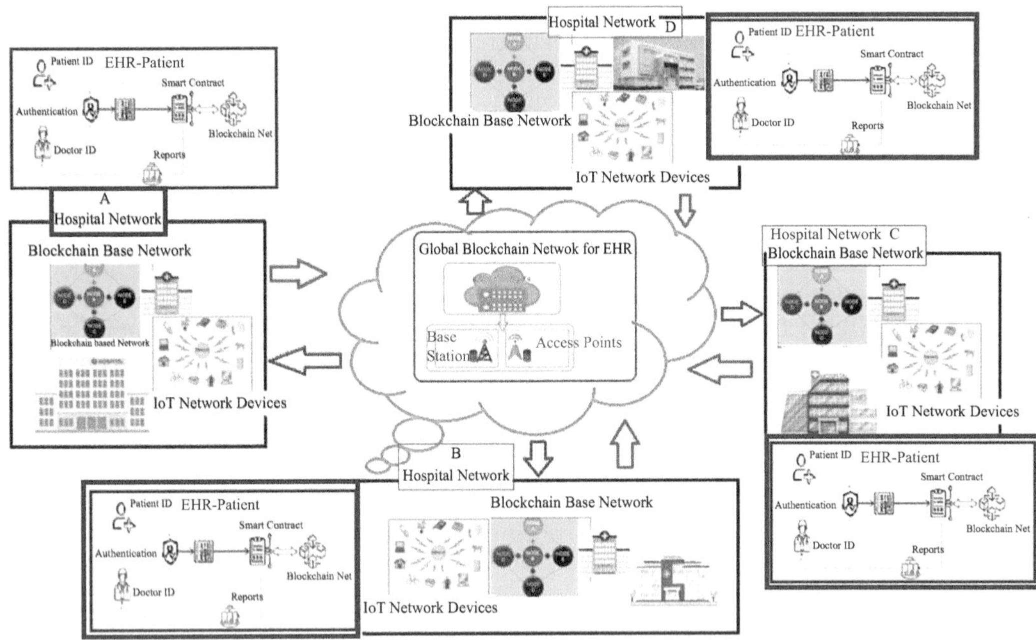

FIGURE 22.4

Processing mechanism of digital identities in pervasive healthcare networks for cross-border blockchain-enabled communications.

different servicing models. For instance, service-oriented architecture, socket programming, remote procedure call, and remote method invocation. These methods can be used to design distributed healthcare based on blockchain technology in the geographically distributed healthcare system in the network. The proposed plan can support the mobility of the services when patients move from one place to another during their business trips. However, we discuss the blockchain technology that can be implemented in the proposed system for cross-border environments.

22.4 Implementation evaluation analysis

Blockchain-oriented pervasive healthcare systems are very secure systems in the domain of cross-border transactional data of any identity; the following key factors to be considered before the implementation of green blockchain cross-border environments:

22.4.1 Approaches and methods

Different researchers suggest many existing cross-border green blockchain approaches. The methods are consensus algorithms such as proof of work, proof of stake, proof of knowledge, and fault-aware benzynes. These methods are widely designed in all systems, such as consortium and hybrid. At the same time, these studies suggested different evolutionary algorithms to deal with the methods above in the cross-border remittance firms in the systems.

22.4.2 Platforms, interfaces, networks

Many Java runtime environments, JSON-enabled platforms, were introduced to deal with cross-border remittance applications in heterogeneous environments where many nodes are connected to transfer transactions for execution. These nodes are either homogeneous or heterologous and can be flexible to work on the system's single interfaces of users' applications. Many platforms have been introduced based on Java or open-source platforms, such as Ethereum, Hyperledger, distributed ledger, and the different environments to run cross-border applications.

22.4.3 Communications

In recent technologies, the communication protocols widely suggested based on both homogeneous and heterogeneous such as Representational state transfer (REST), Application Programming Interface (API), *JavaScript* Object Notation (JSON), and Teletype Networks (Telenet). These protocols are widely validated and secure during communication using XML and yet Another Markup Language (YAML) format sliding window schemes on different platforms.

22.4.4 Transformation of legacy systems

These technologies are not new but traditional and run many remittance systems in the distributed environment. However, the current trend will change the runtime environment and node security validation. For instance, many centralized systems are converted into a divide-and-conquer strategy where many centralized nodes break down into chunks. Therefore the new technology has been designed and architected based on a decentralized system In which decisions and sharing empower all nodes. New technologies such as bitcoin, cryptocurrency, distributed ledger, blockchain, Ethereum, Hyperledger, and others are examples of new technologies compared to existing legacy distributed in the environment.

22.4.5 Implementations of digital identity transactions in cross-border networks

Sample code in Python shows the implementation of digital identity transactions below:

```
import hashlib
import json
from typing import List

Class digital identity:
  def __init__(self, patient_id: str, name: str, data: dict):
    self.patient_id = patient_id
    self.name = name
    self.data = data
    self.hash = self.generate_hash()

    def generate_hash(self):
      data = json.dumps(self.data, sort_keys=True).encode()
      return hashlib.sha256(data).hexdigest()

  Class TokenPassing:
    def __init__(self, identities: List[DigitalIdentity]):
      self.identities = identities

    def pass_token(self, sender_id: str, receiver_id: str):
      sender = next(id for id in self.identities if id.patient_id == sender_id)
      receiver = next(id for id in self.identities if id.patient_id == receiver_id)

      # Check if the sender and receiver identities match
      if sender.hash != receiver.hash:
        raise ValueError("Identity mismatch between sender and receiver")

      # Check if the sender has permission to pass the token to the receiver
      if not self.check_permission(sender, receiver):
        raise PermissionError("Sender does not have permission to pass token to
receiver")

      # Perform token passing here
      # ...

    def check_permission(self, sender: DigitalIdentity, receiver: DigitalIdentity) ->
bool:
      """
      Implement your logic to check if the sender can pass the token to the receiver.
      """
      pass

  # Example usage
  identities = [DigitalIdentity("123", "John Doe", {"age": 30, "medical_history": "..."}),
          DigitalIdentity("456", "Jane Smith", {"age": 25, "medical_history": "..."})]
  token_passing = TokenPassing(identities)
token_passing.pass_token("123", "456")
```

22.5 Conclusions

Integrating cross-border-enabled green blockchain technology into healthcare systems represents a significant advancement in managing patient identities. This technology offers a robust solution to the challenges posed by traditional centralized systems by providing a secure, decentralized ledger that enhances data security and privacy.

This chapter has thoroughly explored how green blockchain technology revolutionizes healthcare identity management by focusing on user-centric identities. This technology addresses critical issues such as data security, interoperability, and privacy. The decentralized nature of blockchain ensures that patient data remains secure and accessible only to authorized entities, mitigating the risks associated with centralized data storage.

Our analysis identified two essential rules—associative and cumulative—that govern identity data transactions within these systems. These rules are particularly effective when patient data involves fewer than 10 devices, ensuring secure and efficient data mobility. This capability is essential for managing patient data across different countries, hospital systems, and heterogeneous environments, enhancing healthcare delivery's overall efficiency and security.

Despite the promising advantages, green blockchain technology in healthcare presents complex challenges. These include the need for standardization across different systems and countries, addressing scalability issues, and ensuring compliance with diverse regulatory frameworks. Moreover, managing user-centric identities in such a dynamic and interconnected environment requires ongoing innovation and research to adapt to evolving threats and technological advancements.

Future research should address these challenges and explore new ways to enhance the scalability, interoperability, and security of green blockchain systems in healthcare. Continued innovation in this field is crucial for realizing the full potential of blockchain technology in revolutionizing healthcare identity management and ensuring secure, efficient, and privacy-preserving data transactions.

In detail, this chapter discussed the concept of digital identities in pervasive healthcare and the future of cross-border-enabled green blockchain networks, including features, functions, interoperability, and digital self-sovereign identity management concepts. Cross-border green blockchain technology is an emerging, highly transparent, and secure distributed technology that can disrupt outdated identity management practices. It ultimately promotes digital identity approaches by linking identity to personal information while addressing privacy and data security risks for cross-border pervasive healthcare systems.

The differences between various entities require identity proofing and an additional trust level for identity attributes in cross-border communications, particularly from one hospital to another, as well as in heterogeneous environments with different devices and platforms. This study discusses the proposed methodological model for digital identities in cross-border environments for pervasive healthcare systems and how to manage these systems with total security and remotely authorized wireless device control.

As suggested, the pass-card for identifying the instruments of pervasive healthcare systems could be extended to financial applications such as remittances and e-commerce payments between countries, exemplified by platforms like Alibaba.com and Online Exchange (OLX). This authentication of nodes in cross-border environments enables digital identities for cross-border mobility, ensuring data transactions with a very high level of security.

Finally, we discussed the critical challenges for transforming and implementing green blockchain in pervasive healthcare systems. In future trends, cross-border applications will likely become globally applicable, facilitating smooth interactions without significant risks or threats.

References

Alubady, R., A.shlaka, R., Diame, H. A., Abdulkareem, S. A., Hussam, R., Yassine, S., & Rajinikanth, V. (2023). Blockchain-based e-medical record and data security service management based on IoMT resource. *Journal of Intelligent Systems and Internet of Things*, *8*(2), 86–100. Available from https://doi.org/10.54216/JISIoT.080207, https://www.americaspg.com/articleinfo/18/show/2086.

Amofa, S., Xia, Q., Xia, H., Obiri, I. A., Adjei-Arthur, B., Yang, J., & Gao, J. (2024). Blockchain-secure patient digital win in healthcare using smart contracts. *PLoS ONE*, *19*(2). Available from https://doi.org/10.1371/journal.pone.0286120, https://journals.plos.org//plosone/article?id = 10.1371/journal.pone.0286120.

Androulaki, E., Barger, A., Bortnikov, V., Muralidharan, S., Cachin, C., Christidis, K., De Caro, A., Enyeart, D., Murthy, C., Ferris, C., Laventman, G., Manevich, Y., Nguyen, B., Sethi, M., Singh, G., Smith, K., Sorniotti, A., Stathakopoulou, C., Vukolić, M., … Yellick, J. (2018). *Hyperledger fabric: A Distributed operating system for permissioned blockchains. Proceedings of the 13th EuroSys Conference, EuroSys 2018*. United States: Association for Computing Machinery, Inc. Available from http://doi.org/10.1145/3190508.3190538.

Belchior, R., Vasconcelos, A., Guerreiro, S., & Correia, M. (2022). A survey on blockchain interoperability: Past, present, and future trends. *ACM Computing Surveys*, *54*(8), 1–41. Available from https://doi.org/10.1145/3471140.

Böhme, R., Christin, N., Edelman, B., & Moore, T. (2015). Bitcoin: Economics, technology, and Governance. *Journal of Economic Perspectives*, *29*(2), 213–238. Available from https://doi.org/10.1257/jep.29.2.213.

Chelladurai, U., & Pandian, S. (2022). A novel blockchain based electronic health record automation system for healthcare. *Journal of Ambient Intelligence and Humanized Computing*, *13*(1), 693–703. Available from https://doi.org/10.1007/s12652-021-03163-3.

Chen, Y., Meng, L., Zhou, H., Xue, G., & Lin, Y. (2021). A blockchain-based medical data sharing mechanism with attribute-based access control and privacy protection. *Wireless Communications and Mobile Computing*, *2021*, 1–12. Available from https://doi.org/10.1155/2021/6685762.

Chenthara, S., Ahmed, K., Wang, H., Whittaker, F., Chen, Z., & Huang, X. (2020). Healthchain: A novel framework on privacy preservation of electronic health records using blockchain technology. *PLOS ONE*, *15*(12), e0243043. Available from https://doi.org/10.1371/journal.pone.0243043.

Dagher, G. G., Mohler, J., Milojkovic, M., & Marella, P. B. (2018). *Ancile: Privacy-preserving framework for access control and interoperability of electronic health records using blockchain technology. Sustainable Cities and Society* (39, pp. 283–297). United States: Elsevier Ltd. Available from http://www.elsevier.com/wps/find/journaldescription.cws_home/724360/description#description, https://doi.org/10.1016/j.scs.2018.02.014.

Diro, A., Zhou, L., Saini, A., Kaisar, S., & Hiep, P. C. (2024). *Leveraging zero knowledge proofs for blockchain-based identity sharing: A survey of advancements, challenges and opportunities, . Journal of Information Security and Applications* (80). Australia: Elsevier Ltd. Available from https://www.sciencedirect.com/science/journal/22142126, https://doi.org/10.1016/j.jisa.2023.103678.

Gupta, M., Tanwar, S., Bhatia, T. K., Badotra, S., & Hu, Y. C. (2024). A comparative study on blockchain-based distributed public key infrastructure for IoT applications. Springer, India. *Multimedia Tools and Applications*, *83*(12), 35471–35496. Available from https://doi.org/10.1007/s11042-023-16970-x, https://www.springer.com/journal/11042.

Hussien, H. M., Yasin, S. M., Udzir, S. N. I., Zaidan, A. A., & Zaidan, B. B. (2019). A systematic review for enabling of develop a blockchain technology in healthcare application: Taxonomy, substantially analysis, motivations, challenges, recommendations and future direction. *Journal of Medical Systems*, *43*(10). Available from https://doi.org/10.1007/s10916-019-1445-8.

Idrissi, H., & Palmieri, P. (2024). Agent-based blockchain model for robust authentication and authorization in IoT-based healthcare systems. *Journal of Supercomputing*, *80*(5), 6622–6660. Available from https://doi.org/10.1007/s11227-023-05649-7, https://www.springer.com/journal/11227.

Jadhav, J. S., & Deshmukh, J. (2022). A review study of the blockchain-based healthcare supply chain. *Social Sciences and Humanities Open*, *6*(1). Available from https://doi.org/10.1016/j.ssaho.2022.100328, https://www.journals.elsevier.com/social-sciences-and-humanities-open.

Jakhar, A. K., Singh, M., Sharma, R., Viriyasitavat, W., Dhiman, G., & Goel, S. (2024). *A blockchain-based privacy-preserving and access-control framework for electronic health records management. Multimedia tools and applications*. India: Springer. Available from https://www.springer.com/journal/11042, https://doi.org/10.1007/s11042-024-18827-3.

Kumar, N. M., & Mallick, P. K. (2018). *Blockchain technology for security issues and challenges in IoT, . Procedia computer science* (132, pp. 1815–1823). Malaysia: Elsevier B.V. Available from http://doi.org/10.1016/j.procs.2018.05.140, http://www.sciencedirect.com/science/journal/18770509.

Madine, M. M., Battah, A. A., Yaqoob, I., Salah, K., Jayaraman, R., Al-Hammadi, Y., Pesic, S., & Ellahham, S. (2020). *Blockchain for giving patients control over their medical records. IEEE Access* (8, pp. 193102–193115). United Arab Emirates: Institute of Electrical and Electronics Engineers Inc. Available from http://ieeexplore.ieee.org/xpl/RecentIssue.jsp?punumber = 6287639, https://doi.org/10.1109/ACCESS.2020.3032553.

Nalin, M., Baroni, I., Faiella, G., Romano, M., Matrisciano, F., Gelenbe, E., Martinez, D. M., Dumortier, J., Natsiavas, P., Votis, K., Koutkias, V., Tzovaras, D., & Clemente, F. (2019). *The European cross-border health data exchange roadmap: Case study in the Italian setting. Journal of Biomedical Informatics* (94). Italy: Academic Press Inc. Available from http://www.elsevier.com/inca/publications/store/6/2/2/8/5/7/index.htt, https://doi.org/10.1016/j.jbi.2019.103183.

Neisse, R., Hernandez-Ramos, J. L., Matheu-Garcia, S. N., Baldini, G., Skarmeta, A., Siris, V., Lagutin, D., & Nikander, P. (2020). An interledger blockchain platform for cross-border management of cybersecurity information. *IEEE Internet Computing*, *24*(3), 19–29. Available from https://doi.org/10.1109/MIC.2020.3002423, https://ieeexplore.ieee.org/servlet/opac?punumber = 4236.

Pilares, I. C. A., Azam, S., Akbulut, S., Jonkman, M., & Shanmugam, B. (2022). Addressing the challenges of electronic health records using blockchain and IPFS. *Sensors*, *22*(11). Available from https://doi.org/10.3390/s22114032, https://www.mdpi.com/1424-8220/22/11/4032/pdf?version = 1653624944.

Ragab, M., Bahaddad, A. A., Hamed, D., Alkhayyat, A., Gupta, D., & Mansour, R. F. (2024). *Blockchain-driven privacy preserving electronic health records analysis using sine cosine algorithm with deep learning model. Human-centric computing and information sciences* (14). Saudi Arabia: Korea Information Processing Society. Available from http://hcisj.com, https://doi.org/10.22967/HCIS.2024.14.009.

Shahidinejad, A., & Abawajy, J. (2024). An all-inclusive taxonomy and critical review of blockchain-assisted authentication and session key generation Protocols for IoT. *ACM Computing Surveys*, *56*(7), 1–38. Available from https://doi.org/10.1145/3645087.

Song, Z., Wang, G., Yu, Y., Chen, T., & Bhushan, B. (2022). Digital identity verification and management system of blockchain-based verifiable certificate with the privacy protection of identity and behavior. *Security and Communication Networks*, *2022*, 1–24. Available from https://doi.org/10.1155/2022/6800938.

Sun, J., Ren, L., Wang, S., Yao, X., & Debiao, H. (2020). A blockchain-based framework for electronic medical records sharing with fine-grained access control. *PLOS ONE*, *15*(10), e0239946. Available from https://doi.org/10.1371/journal.pone.0239946.

Van Bokkem, D., Hageman, R., Koning, G., Nguyen, L., & Zarin, N. (2019). Self-sovereign identity solutions: The necessity of blockchain technology. *arXiv*. Available from https://doi.org/10.48550/arxiv.1904.12816, https://arxiv.org.

Velmurugan, S., Prakash, M., Neelakandan, S., & Martinson, E. O. (2024). *An efficient secure sharing of electronic health records using IoT-based hyperledger blockchain. International Journal of Intelligent Systems* (2024). India: Wiley-Hindawi. Available from https://www.hindawi.com/journals/ijis/, https://doi.org/10.1155/2024/6995202.

Xiao, Y., Xu, B., Jiang, W., & Wu, Y. (2021). The health chain blockchain for electronic health records: Development study. *Journal of Medical Internet Research*, *23*(1), e13556. Available from https://doi.org/10.2196/13556.

Xiong, W., & Xiong, L. (2021). Data trading certification based on consortium blockchain and smart contracts. *IEEE Access*, *9*, 3482–3496. Available from https://doi.org/10.1109/access.2020.3047398.

Yaqoob, I., Salah, K., Jayaraman, R., & Al-Hammadi, Y. (2022). Blockchain for healthcare data management: Opportunities, challenges, and future recommendations. *Neural Computing and Applications*, *34*(14), 11475–11490. Available from https://doi.org/10.1007/s00521-020-05519-w.

Zhu, X., & Badr, Y. (2018). Identity management systems for the internet of things: A survey towards blockchain solutions. *Sensors*, *18*(12), 4215. Available from https://doi.org/10.3390/s18124215.

CHAPTER

AI-enabled IoMT: transforming healthcare in smart hospitals

23

Norah Alsaeed[1] and Farrukh Nadeem[2]

[1]Department of Computer Science, The Applied College, King Khalid University, Abha, Saudi Arabia [2]Department of Information Systems, Faculty of Computing and Information Technology, King Abdulaziz University, Jeddah, Saudi Arabia

23.1 Introduction

The Internet of Medical Things (IoMT) is defined as a network of sensors, applications, and medical devices joined through the Internet. This technology framework includes an array of devices such as wearable biosensors, implanted devices, and connected monitors that gather, transmit, and analyze data to enhance patient care and operational efficiency in medical environments (Singh et al., 2023). The IoMT ecosystem offers vast improvements in healthcare services including continuous data collection, monitoring, and analysis, transforming the way healthcare is delivered and managed. IoMT has the potential to improve patient services and overall healthcare efficiency.

As the healthcare industry continues to evolve, the adoption of IoMT technology in smart hospitals is pivotal for improving clinical operations, reducing healthcare costs, and enhancing healthcare outcomes. By leveraging real-time data acquisition and analysis, IoMT facilitates proactive patient monitoring, personalized treatment plans, and optimized resource allocation that significantly transform traditional healthcare delivery models (Dimitrov, 2016). In smart hospitals, IoMT finds its application in various critical areas including remote patient monitoring, asset management, and clinical workflow optimization. Remote patient monitoring systems utilize IoMT devices to continuously track patient vitals and other health indicators to send alerts to healthcare professionals when anomalies are detected. Beyond enhancing patient safety through timely interventions, IoMT acts as a game-changer for remote areas. By enabling remote healthcare delivery, IoMT bridges the gap and extends access to quality healthcare services for geographically isolated populations (Javaid et al., 2022). Furthermore, IoMT facilitates the integration of asset management systems in hospitals, which helps in tracking and managing medical equipment. Thereby, IoMT improves operational efficiency and reduces equipment downtime. Additionally, the data-driven insights provided by IoMT devices support clinical decision-making processes, optimize hospital workflows, and contribute to the overall enhancement of patient care quality (Alloghani et al., 2020).

Traditional IoMT systems exhibit several limitations that can hinder their effectiveness in smart healthcare environments. One major limitation of IoMT is the volume of data generated by the vast number and variety of IoMT devices. This big data can overwhelm traditional data processing methods, leading to delays and inefficiencies in decision-making (Kelly et al., 2019). Effectively managing, processing, and analyzing this data stream is essential to unlock the full benefit of IoMT

Blockchain and Digital Twin for Smart Hospitals. DOI: https://doi.org/10.1016/B978-0-443-34226-4.00024-1

for healthcare insights. Moreover, these systems cannot often dynamically adapt to changing environments or patient conditions, which is crucial for personalized healthcare. The dependency on manual configuration and intervention makes these systems less efficient in real-time data analysis and response, thus potentially compromising patient care quality and operational efficiency (Zanella et al., 2014). IoMT and artificial intelligence (AI) integration is gaining traction as a powerful tool to address inherent limitations. AI technologies, such as deep learning excel at analyzing vast data generated by IoMT devices. This allows them to identify hidden patterns, predict potential health issues, and automate decision-making processes. This translates to enhanced responsiveness of IoMT systems, enabling timely interventions and improved adaptability to individual patient needs (Davenport & Kalakota, 2019; Raheem & Iqbal, 2022).

This chapter provides a comprehensive exploration of AI with IoMT within smart healthcare systems. It begins by establishing the fundamentals of AI in healthcare, setting the stage for a deeper understanding of AI's role in enhancing healthcare. Furthermore, it introduces the concept of IoMT, the components of the IoMT ecosystem, and applications of IoMT in healthcare. A focused section on the integration of AI and IoMT highlights how AI can amplify the capabilities of IoMT, followed by an explanation of the building blocks of AI-enabled IoMT which identifies the core components that facilitate AI functionalities. The chapter further delves into AI techniques for IoMT, showcasing various AI methods suitable for IoMT applications. It presents AI-powered IoMT applications, illustrating the practical benefits and efficiencies gained in healthcare settings. Moreover, this chapter discusses the impact of AI-enabled IoMT on healthcare and the transformative effects on patient care and system operations. It also introduces security, privacy, and ethical considerations that address the critical challenges of data security, patient privacy, and ethical deployment of technology. Finally, the chapter provides recommendations for ensuring responsible development and deployment of AI-enabled IoMT systems.

23.1.1 Fundamentals of AI in healthcare

AI in healthcare involves a suite of advanced technologies designed to emulate human cognitive processes within medical contexts. Among the primary AI technologies, machine learning algorithms excel at discovering patterns in healthcare data, allowing them to predict health outcomes or make autonomous decisions. This makes them invaluable in diagnostics processes. Deep learning, a more sophisticated branch of machine learning, leverages complex neural networks to interpret complex medical data. This translates to breakthroughs in areas like medical image analysis. Finally, natural language processing (NLP) enables computers to comprehend and process human language, facilitating the management of patient records and medical literature to support more informed decision-making (Esteva et al., 2019; Jiang et al., 2017).

AI significantly impacts medical diagnosis, treatment, and patient care by increasing accuracy and efficiency. In diagnosis, AI algorithms analyze complex datasets to detect anomalies that may elude human observers, such as early-stage cancer detection via imaging (Esteva et al., 2019). For treatment, AI supports personalized medicine approaches by recommending treatments based on individual patient data, potentially improving outcomes, and reducing side effects. In patient care, AI tools automate routine tasks, monitor patient stats in real time, and provide alerts, allowing healthcare providers to allocate more time to patient care and interaction, thus enhancing patient satisfaction and safety (Davenport & Kalakota, 2019). The adoption of AI in healthcare is rapidly growing, driven by technological advancements and the increasing availability of healthcare data. Thus many trends have emerged including the integration of AI in electronic health records (EHRs) to predict patient risks and outcomes, and the use of AI-powered wearable devices for continuous patient monitoring outside traditional clinical settings. During and beyond the COVID-19 pandemic, the integration of AI with IoMT has expanded capabilities in remote patient monitoring (Peyroteo et al., 2021). However, challenges remain significant. Data privacy and security are critical issues because of the highly sensitive nature of healthcare data. Additionally, there is a need for robust regulatory frameworks to manage AI implementation in healthcare, ensuring safety and efficiency. Another significant challenge is the digital divide; unequal access to AI technologies can exacerbate existing health disparities (khan et al., 2023).

23.1.2 Internet of Medical Things

IoMT is defined as a network of devices that gathers, transmits, and analyzes data in the healthcare environment (Liu et al., 2024). This concept is pivotal in modern healthcare as it leverages technology to improve the outcomes and efficiency of medical treatments and patient care. IoMT spans various devices, from simple sensors to complex machines, integrated seamlessly to support real-time, actionable healthcare insights. This integration facilitates preventive healthcare measures and personalized patient treatment plans and enhances chronic disease management (Khan et al., 2021). Fig. 23.1 illustrates the IoMT system that consists of sophisticated components that work together to improve healthcare delivery and patient management (Razdan & Sharma, 2022), they are as follows:

- Sensors are the foundational elements of the IoMT ecosystem. They are deployed to continuously monitor a wide range of parameters related to physiology, like body temperature,

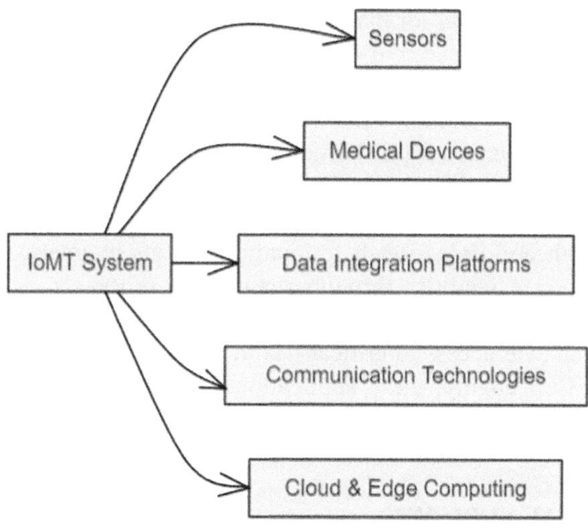

FIGURE 23.1

IoMT system components.

blood pressure, heart rate, and glucose levels. These sensors can be embedded in various devices, including wearables, implantable devices, and even medical equipment. The data collected by sensors is crucial for real-time health monitoring, enabling proactive interventions and ongoing health assessments.

- Medical devices in the IoMT system include both traditional medical equipment and newer, smart medical devices. This category encompasses a wide variety of tools, from diagnostic machines such as MRI scanners and ultrasound devices to therapeutic devices like smart inhalers and automated insulin pumps. These devices are often enhanced with smart capabilities, allowing them to operate more autonomously and interactively, improving diagnostic accuracy and therapeutic outcomes.
- Data integration platforms are essential for aggregating and analyzing the large volumes of data that IoMT devices generate. These platforms employ sophisticated algorithms, including machine learning and big data analytics, to analyze and interpret the collected data. The insights derived from this data are essential for informed clinical decision-making, personalized treatment plans, and predictive health analytics, ultimately leading to improved healthcare delivery.
- Communication technologies are what link the various components of the IoMT ecosystem, enabling the seamless transfer of data between devices and healthcare providers. Technologies like cellular networks, Wi-Fi, and Bluetooth are commonly used for data transmission.
- Cloud and edge computing infrastructures allow for scalable data storage and powerful computing capabilities at the edge of the network.
- Edge computing supports real-time data processing close to the data source, minimizing latency and bandwidth use, while cloud computing offers vast storage capabilities and advanced computational power for deeper data analysis and long-term health monitoring.

IoMT significantly transforms smart healthcare through a variety of innovative applications. Real-time health monitoring enabled by IoMT devices, such as wearable sensors, allows for continuous tracking of critical vitals, crucial for managing chronic conditions and enabling timely medical interventions. These capabilities extend into enhanced diagnostic accuracy. Additionally, IoMT supports personalized treatment plans by utilizing data to tailor treatments to individual patient needs, improving outcomes in complex conditions like cancer. Medication management is also streamlined with smart dispensers and IoT-enabled pill bottles that ensure adherence to prescribed medication schedules. Furthermore, IoMT facilitates remote patient care, expanding the availability of healthcare services, particularly in regions lacking sufficient resources, and reducing the strain on medical facilities by allowing healthcare professionals to monitor patients remotely. Operational efficiencies are achieved within healthcare facilities through streamlined processes such as patient check-ins, bed management, and inventory tracking. Moreover, in emergencies, IoMT devices can provide first responders with immediate access to critical health information, enhancing response times and potentially saving lives. Collectively, these applications underscore how IoMT enhances the efficiency, accessibility, and quality of healthcare delivery (Dwivedi et al., 2022).

23.1.3 Integration of AI and IoMT

The integration of AI with IoMT represents an evolution in the healthcare industry, particularly within smart hospital settings. This evolution aims to leverage the strengths of both domains to enhance healthcare delivery through more precise diagnostics, effective treatments, and optimized operational efficiencies. The primary rationale for integrating AI with IoMT is to increase the capability of healthcare systems to process data gathered by IoMT devices. Smart hospitals utilize numerous sensors and devices that continuously collect health data; AI algorithms can interpret this complex data stream in real time to provide actionable insights. This integration facilitates advanced patient monitoring and predictive analytics for disease prevention. Essentially, AI serves as the cognitive engine that enables IoMT systems to deliver on their potential for transforming healthcare delivery (Jiang et al., 2017).

The synergies between AI and IoMT technologies significantly reinforce data analytics, operational automation, and diagnostic and therapeutic capabilities. By applying AI techniques, IoMT devices can process health data more effectively, leading to earlier disease detection and optimized device functionality. This integration results in more effective patient monitoring and disease management systems (Amaraweera & Halgamuge, 2019). Accordingly, AI-enabled IoMT offers several benefits:

- *Improved diagnostic accuracy*: AI algorithms improve the accuracy of diagnostics by analyzing medical imaging and recognizing patterns associated with the early stages of diseases (Esteva et al., 2019).
- *Enhanced patient outcomes*: Real-time analytics support chronic disease management, reducing emergency incidents and improving overall patient care.
- *Operational efficiency*: AI predictive capabilities can optimize hospital resource management and administrative operations leading to the overall efficiency of healthcare facilities (Coravos et al., 2019).

On the other hand, implementing AI-enabled IoMT systems also presents several challenges:

- *Data security and privacy*: Ensuring the privacy and security of sensitive health data within increased connectivity is crucial.
- *Integration and interoperability*: Technical difficulties in integrating AI with existing IoMT infrastructures and achieving interoperability among diverse systems can be significant barriers.
- *Skill gaps*: The shortage of skilled professionals to manage advanced AI-IoMT systems necessitates comprehensive training programs.
- *Ethical and legal considerations*: Addressing ethical concerns and establishing clear legal frameworks for AI use in healthcare decision-making is essential (DeCamp et al., 2018; Hassan et al., 2018).

AI-powered IoMT offers significant potential for transforming smart hospitals into more efficient, effective, and patient-centered facilities. However, realizing this potential integration requires addressing the technical, regulatory, and ethical challenges associated with advanced technology deployments in healthcare (Hassan et al., 2018).

23.2 Building blocks of AI-enabled IoMT

This section focuses on the building blocks of AI-enabled IoMT, which are required to unlock the maximum potential of AI in enhancing medical devices and healthcare services. Each component plays a critical role in creating a cohesive and functional AI-enabled IoMT ecosystem.

23.2.1 AI-enabled IoMT sensors and devices

IoMT devices and sensors constitute a crucial component of AI-enabled IoMT systems. They collect and transmit vital health data required for advanced healthcare delivery. Fig. 23.2 illustrates these devices, ranging from wearables to implantable sensors, which provide the raw data necessary for AI algorithms to analyze and derive insights that inform clinical decisions and patient management (Ghubaish et al., 2020).

- *Wearable sensors*: Wearables such as fitness bands, smartwatches, and health monitors are widely adopted in IoMT ecosystems. They perform real-time, continuous monitoring of various physiological parameters, including physical activity patterns, blood oxygen saturation, and heart rate. This data is invaluable for monitoring patients' health status in real-time and detecting potential health issues before they escalate.
- *Implantable sensors*: These encapsulated electronic devices are surgically placed within a patient's body enabling real-time and continuous monitoring of internal functions. Common applications include glucose sensors for diabetes management and cardiac monitors for patients with heart conditions. These devices offer precise and continuous data from within the body, providing unique insights that external devices cannot.
- *Environmental sensors*: Beyond individual health monitoring, IoMT also includes sensors that monitor the environment. These can track room conditions in hospitals, such as temperature and cleanliness, which are critical for patient care, especially in critical settings such as intensive care units.
- *Medical devices*: Traditional medical devices, such as MRI machines, ultrasound, and X-ray equipment, are increasingly being integrated with IoMT capabilities. When enhanced with AI, these devices not only perform their primary function of imaging and diagnostics but also analyze the data they collect to aid in faster and more accurate diagnoses.

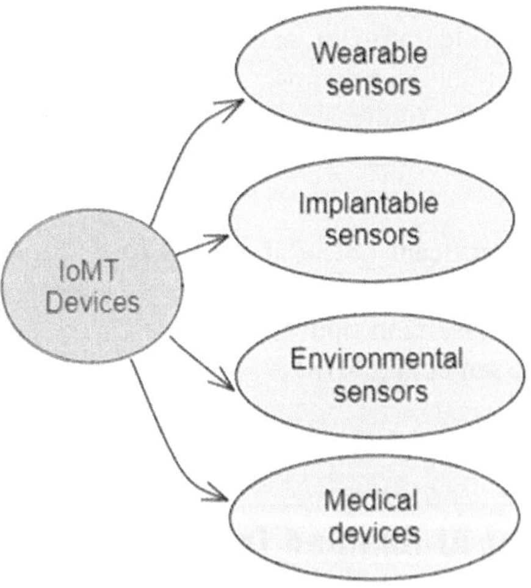

FIGURE 23.2

Different types of IoMT devices.

The integration of these devices and sensors with AI technologies transforms passive data collection into proactive healthcare management. AI algorithms can process the data gathered to detect patterns and anomalies that may indicate health issues. Furthermore, AI reinforces the functionality of these devices through adaptive learning. As the AI systems process more data, they can refine their algorithms to improve accuracy and effectiveness. Thereby, AI technologies can tailor their analyses to the specific patterns and needs of individual patients. Despite the benefits, integrating AI with IoMT devices and sensors presents many challenges. Guaranteeing privacy and security of data these devices collected is paramount. Additionally, there are technical challenges related to the interoperability of various devices and the need for robust infrastructure to support real-time data transmission and analysis (Iomt et al., 2018).

23.2.2 Data acquisition systems

Data acquisition is a fundamental component of the AI-enabled IoMT, which serves as critical infrastructure for capturing, digitizing, and transmitting data generated by IoMT devices. Data acquisition systems act as the intermediary between IoMT devices and the analytical engines that process and interpret the data. Their primary function is to ensure that data collected from various sensors and medical devices is accurately and efficiently gathered, conditioned, and transmitted for further analysis. In the context of healthcare, this data can range from simple metrics like heart rate and blood pressure to more complex information such as imaging data and real-time biometric readings. The data acquisition systems work through three main processes (Webster, 2009):

- *Signal conditioning*: Once data is captured, it often requires conditioning to ensure it is in a suitable format for digital conversion. Signal conditioning may involve amplification, filtering, and converting analog signals to digital forms. This step is vital for maintaining the accuracy and integrity of the data, which directly impacts the reliability of subsequent analyses.
- *Data conversion and digitization*: After conditioning, the data must be digitized if it isn't already in a digital format. This is typically achieved through Analog-to-digital converters (ADCs). Digitization is essential for enabling sophisticated computational processes and storage in digital databases.
- *Data transmission*: Following conversion, the data is transmitted to data centers, cloud storage, or directly to healthcare providers through secure communication channels. This transmission must be secure and efficient to protect patient data and ensure that it is available in real time for immediate medical decision-making.

Data quality and reliability are the main challenges in the data acquisition process. Poor data quality can lead to incorrect analyses and potentially harmful medical decisions. Systems must include robust validation and error-checking mechanisms to maintain high data quality. As IoMT devices proliferate, the volume of data generated grows exponentially. Data acquisition systems must scale accordingly to handle this influx efficiently without loss of performance. Data acquisition systems are integral to the functionality of AI-enabled IoMT to enable the gathering and processing of vital health data. The effectiveness of these systems is critical to the success of smart healthcare solutions, influencing everything from patient monitoring to complex diagnostic procedures. As technology evolves, these systems will continue to become more sophisticated, addressing current challenges and expanding their capabilities (Jayachitra et al., 2023).

23.2.3 Communication infrastructure

The communication infrastructure is the backbone of AI-enabled IoMT, enabling seamless and secure exchange of medical data between devices and healthcare information systems. This infrastructure ensures that medical data is transferred in real time while also upholding the privacy and integrity that are crucial in healthcare environments. Communication components include a variety of technologies and protocols, each selected based on specific needs such as data volume, speed, reliability, and security. The key communication components within an AI-enabled IoMT system are as follows (Ray, 2018):

- *Network protocols*: IoMT devices utilize specific protocols that are optimized for the constraints of healthcare applications, including power consumption, network bandwidth, and operational reliability. Message Queuing Telemetry Transport Protocol is one such example. It provides a straightforward method for network clients with limited resources to transmit telemetry data in low-bandwidth environments. Its use in IoMT raises from its effectiveness in sending messages between devices with a small code footprint and minimal network bandwidth (Ivanović et al., 2023). Constrained Application Protocol (CoAP) is designed specifically for simple electronic devices, CoAP allows them to communicate interactively over the internet. It is particularly useful in IoMT for tasks that require reliable and asynchronous transfer of data.
- *Wireless communication technologies*: Different wireless technologies are employed based on their range, data requirements, energy efficiency, and the specific medical applications they support. Bluetooth Low Energy is widely used for short-range communication and is particularly effective for wearable IoMT devices due to its low-power consumption and adequate data transfer capabilities. Zigbee is often used in hospital settings. Zigbee can create personal area networks with low-power digital radios. It is suitable for passing data through sensors in a secure and reliable manner over moderate distances. Wi-Fi offers greater range and higher data rates. Wi-Fi is commonly used for devices that are not constrained by battery life and require high throughput, such as in-hospital mobile monitoring devices. Cellular networks (LTE, 5G) are used for devices that need to operate over longer distances or outside traditional healthcare facilities. Cellular networks provide a robust solution with extensive coverage and increased data transmission capabilities, which is becoming increasingly vital with the advent of 5G technology.
- *Data security and privacy*: The communication infrastructure prioritizes the privacy and security of sensitive patient health data. It leverages advanced security protocols like Transport Layer Security (TLS) to ensure the confidentiality and integrity of data during transmission. TLS encrypts data in transit, protecting it from unauthorized access. Additionally, end-to-end encryption safeguards data throughout its entire journey, guaranteeing that only authorized recipients can decrypt it. This is critical for upholding patient confidentiality.

One of the significant challenges is ensuring that various devices and systems from different manufacturers can communicate effectively. Interoperability issues can hinder the seamless integration of technologies, impacting the overall efficacy of healthcare delivery. As the number of IoMT devices is increasing every day, the communication infrastructure must scale accordingly without compromising the performance. This requires dynamic networking solutions that can adapt to growing data volumes and connectivity demands. Recent advancements in 5G technology promise transformative changes for IoMT communication infrastructures. 5G networks offer lower latency, higher speeds, and greater capacity than their predecessors, enabling more robust and efficient IoMT applications. These networks have the capacity to support more connected IoMT devices and make it easier to use increasingly sophisticated AI algorithms for processing health data in real time (Bandyopadhyay & Sen, 2011). This translates to faster analysis and potentially deeper insights for improved healthcare decisions.

23.2.4 Data processing and analytics

Data processing and analytics are central to the functionality of AI-enabled IoMT systems. This component analyzes raw IoMT data, generating actionable insights that empower healthcare providers to enhance patient care and optimize healthcare operations (Marjani et al., 2017). Data processing in AI-enabled IoMT involves several key stages, each critical for deriving meaningful conclusions from raw data, see Fig. 23.3 (Ai et al., 2023):

- *Data cleaning and preprocessing*: The first step is to clean and prepare the data for analysis. This step is very crucial to get accurate and reliable outputs from the final analysis. It involves meticulous cleaning and preprocessing tasks, such as handling missing values, standardizing data formats, and correcting errors.
- *Data integration*: IoMT systems often collect diverse types of data from various devices, which need to be integrated into a cohesive dataset. This involves aligning data from different sources and formats, which is essential for comprehensive analytics.

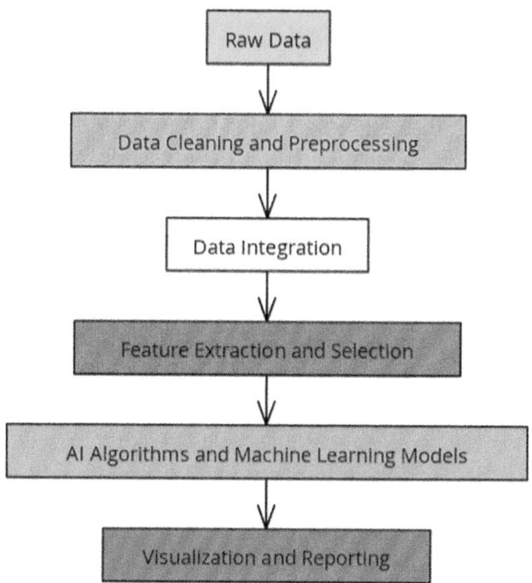

FIGURE 23.3

Data processing key stages.

- *Feature extraction and selection*: This process involves identifying the most relevant attributes of the data that are significant for the analyses. Effective feature selection enhances the machine learning models' performance by reducing the dimensionality and eliminating redundant or irrelevant data. This leads to improved accuracy, efficiency, and interpretability of the models.
- *AI algorithms and machine learning models*: At this stage, advanced algorithms analyze the processed data to identify patterns, predict outcomes, and generate insights. Techniques such as clustering, regression analysis, decision trees, and neural networks are used to forecast patient outcomes, detect early signs of diseases, and tailor treatment plans.
- *Visualization and reporting*: The final analytics output is often visualized in intuitive formats such as dashboards, graphs, and charts, which help healthcare providers quickly understand and act on the insights. Effective visualization supports better decision-making and can enhance patient care significantly.

Many healthcare applications require real-time data processing and analysis to provide timely interventions, which demands highly efficient and scalable computing resources. Advancements in AI, especially deep learning, are pushing the boundaries of what is possible in IoMT data analytics. These technologies are improving the accuracy of predictive models and enabling more personalized and preventative healthcare measures. Additionally, the integration of edge computing is seen as a promising direction to address real-time processing requirements by distributing the computational load closer to where data is collected (Marjani et al., 2017).

23.2.5 Edge, fog, and cloud computing

Edge, fog, and cloud computing are vital components in AI-enabled IoMT. They provide the necessary storage and computational resources to handle large volumes of data generated by medical devices. These computing paradigms differ in their approach to data processing and storage, but collectively they enhance the efficiency and responsiveness of IoMT systems, see Fig. 23.4 (Escamilla-Ambrosio et al., 2018).

- Cloud computing empowers healthcare providers by offering a centralized hub for data processing and storage. This enables convenient remote access to IoMT data and eliminates the need for on-site infrastructure. Additionally, healthcare providers can leverage powerful cloud-based computational resources over the Internet, facilitating complex AI model execution and large-scale data analysis, ultimately paving the way for advanced healthcare applications.
- Fog computing paradigms decentralize cloud computing functionalities by distributing processing resources closer to where data is generated (edge devices). This geographical proximity facilitates real-time or near real-time analytics on the data stream, enabling faster decision-making and reduced latency compared to traditional cloud-centric architectures. This is particularly beneficial in healthcare, where many IoMT applications require low latency to provide real-time analysis and response, such as in the monitoring of critical patient vitals or emergency medical response.

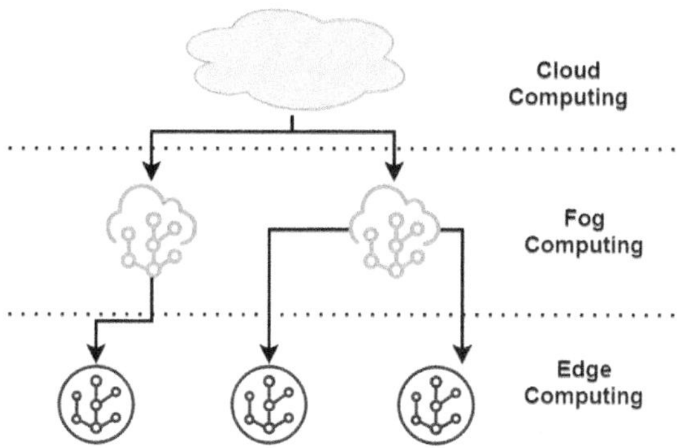

FIGURE 23.4

Cloud, fog, and edge computing.

- Edge computing involves processing data directly at or near the source of data generation, such as IoMT devices themselves or local edge servers. This approach is ideal for time-sensitive data processing in healthcare, allowing for immediate data analysis and action without the need to transmit data to distant servers (Singh et al., 2024).

The integration of cloud, fog, and edge computing creates a layered architecture that leverages the strengths of each computing paradigm. This integration ensures that AI-enabled IoMT systems can efficiently process data at different stages. Initial data processing can occur at the edge for immediate actions. More comprehensive analysis can be handled at the fog level to facilitate near real-time insights. Complex processing and long-term data storage can be managed in the cloud for deep analytics and historical comparisons. The collective use of cloud, fog, and edge computing in IoMT not only optimizes the management of healthcare data but also ensures that AI applications can operate efficiently and effectively, delivering timely healthcare interventions and improved patient care (Escamilla-Ambrosio et al., 2018).

Each of these building blocks contributes to the functionality and efficiency of AI-enabled IoMT systems and facilitates advancements in healthcare. The integration of these components requires careful planning, robust technology solutions, and ongoing management to address challenges such as data security, system compatibility, and the evolving nature of AI technologies (Verdejo Espinosa et al., 2021).

23.3 AI techniques for IoMT

AI acts as a powerful force in augmenting the capabilities of IoMT. This is achieved through a diverse set of AI techniques, including machine learning (ML), deep learning (DL), and NLP. Each technique plays a specific role in analyzing the vast amount of data generated by IoMT devices, ultimately facilitating sophisticated decision-making processes within the IoMT framework. We will now delve into a brief description of each technique.

23.3.1 Machine learning

ML techniques leverage the rich data streams generated by IoMT devices to predict, classify, and manage patient health outcomes more effectively. The various ML techniques employed in IoMT and their specific applications can be divided into three main categories:

23.3.1.1 Supervised learning

Supervised learning constitutes a fundamental paradigm within machine learning. It is characterized by the utilization of labeled datasets for training algorithms for accurate data classification and outcome prediction. It leverages labeled datasets where each training instance comprises an input vector and a corresponding label (desired output value) (Roy et al., 2022). Through this labeled data, the model learns patterns and relationships, enabling it to make predictions for unseen data. The key concept of supervised learning is illustrated in Fig. 23.5:

- *Training data*: This consists of a set of examples or samples that include both the inputs and the desired outputs. For instance, in a medical diagnosis application, the inputs could be various patient metrics, and the output would be the absence or presence of a disease.
- *Model*: This is a function that maps inputs to predicted outputs. The form of the model can vary widely, from simple linear equations to complex deep neural networks.
- *Learning algorithm*: This algorithm is essential in supervised learning, as it optimizes the model's parameters using the given training data. The goal is to minimize the error between the model's predicted outputs and the actual (ground truth) labels in the training set. This optimization process (often referred to as "training the model") typically involves iterative adjustments using well-defined loss functions that quantify the model's error.

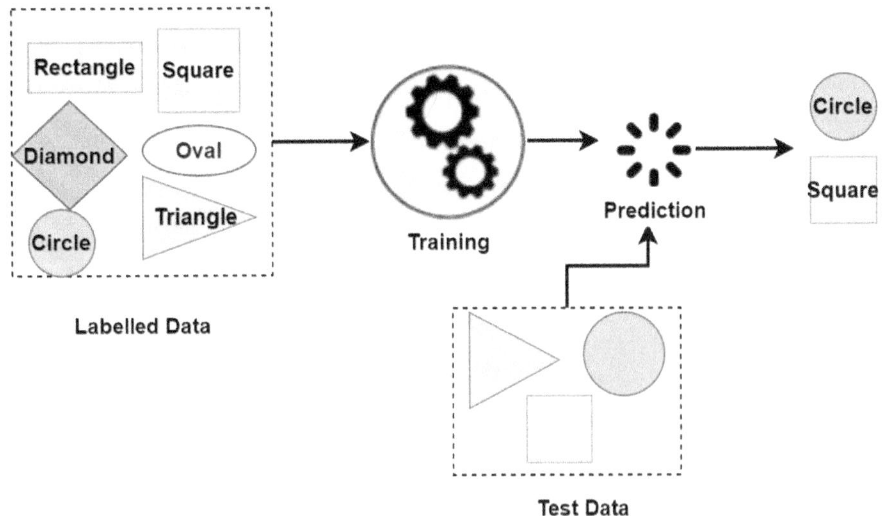

FIGURE 23.5

Supervised learning.

- *Loss function*: The loss function serves as a vital metric in supervised learning, quantifying the discrepancy between a model's predictions and the ground truth labels within the training data. Typical loss functions include mean squared error (MSE), which is commonly used for regression tasks involving the prediction of continuous values, and cross-entropy loss, which is used for classification tasks where the model predicts discrete categories.

One of the main supervised learning is classification which involves predicting a category or class label for given inputs. An example is diagnosing diseases where the outcomes could be categorical labels like "diabetes" and "no diabetes." Regression is also a primary supervised ML technique that involves predicting a continuous value for given inputs. For instance, estimating blood sugar levels from various health indicators falls under regression.

Supervised learning algorithms play a prominent role in IoMT, particularly in applications like disease diagnosis. These algorithms are trained on labeled datasets, where each data point includes an input (e.g., medical images, sensor readings) and the corresponding correct output (e.g., disease diagnosis) (Anbar, 2023). Algorithms such as support vector machines (SVMs), logistic regression, and decision trees can learn complex patterns and relationships by analyzing large volumes of historical patient data. This empowers healthcare professionals to leverage these models for accurate disease diagnosis from medical images or sensor data collected by IoMT devices. SVMs are widely used for cancer detection based on medical imaging data, where they classify images as malignant or benign based on learned patterns. Supervised learning models extend their value beyond diagnosis by predicting patient risk. This capability plays a critical role in chronic disease management, where early intervention can significantly improve patient outcomes and prevent severe complications. For example, by identifying patients at higher risk of developing specific complications, healthcare providers can proactively implement preventative measures, ultimately leading to better patient health (Rashidi et al., 2021).

23.3.1.2 Unsupervised learning

Unsupervised ML techniques, which do not rely on labeled data to learn patterns or make inferences, are crucial in the IoMT context. These techniques are particularly valuable for discovering hidden patterns, segmenting data, and detecting anomalies in vast amounts of medical data, all without the guidance of predetermined answers or outcomes. Unsupervised learning involves several key steps and methodologies. Fig. 23.6 describes the unsupervised learning (Eckhardt et al., 2023):

- *Data input*: The first step in unsupervised learning is the collection and input of data. This data is typically unstructured or unlabeled, which means that the outcomes are not known and not indicated in the dataset.
- *Exploration and preprocessing*: Like other data analysis processes, unsupervised learning starts with exploring the data to understand its structure, content, and any potential issues like missing values or outliers. Data preprocessing may include normalizing data, handling missing values, or selecting features to help improve the quality and effectiveness of the analysis.
- *Learning algorithm*: The core of unsupervised learning involves applying an algorithm to analyze the data without any preassigned labels or results. The selection of the most suitable algorithm depends heavily on the specific task and the characteristics of the data. For instance, tasks like grouping similar data points might benefit from clustering algorithms, while

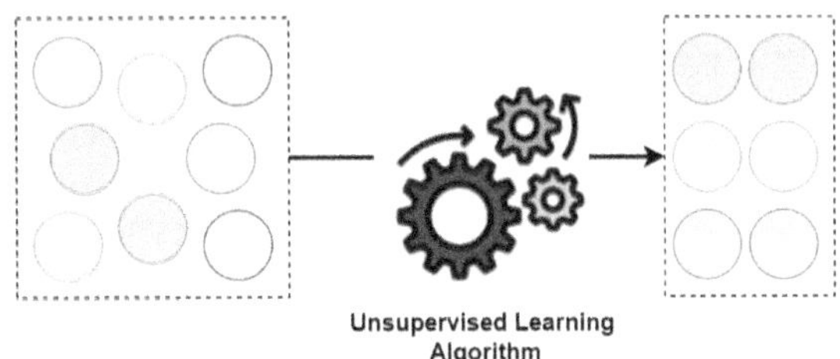

FIGURE 23.6

Unsupervised learning.

uncovering hidden relationships between variables might be better suited for association analysis techniques.

- *Pattern identification*: The algorithm identifies structures or patterns in the data, such as grouping similar data points in clustering or identifying a compact representation of data in dimensionality reduction.
- *Result interpretation and decision-making*: The output of an unsupervised learning algorithm typically requires interpretation. For instance, in clustering, the output would be the identified clusters and their characteristics. This step is crucial as it translates algorithmic outputs into actionable insights or informed decisions.

The ability of unsupervised learning to discover the underlying structure of data makes it invaluable for complex data analysis through various techniques. Clustering is unsupervised learning which groups similar data points together based on shared characteristics, without prior knowledge of group definitions. Clustering can segment patients into distinct groups based on similarities in their medical histories, behaviors, or disease markers. This helps in identifying patient cohorts that may benefit from specialized care strategies or targeted interventions. The association rule learning technique identifies interesting associations and relationships between variables in large databases. It is useful for discovering frequent co-occurring associations. Association rules can uncover relationships between different medications and patient outcomes, helping to identify potential adverse drug interactions. This can also be used to find patterns in the usage of medical tests and procedures to optimize healthcare resource management (IoMT, 2019).

Unsupervised learning techniques that identify data points, events, or observations that deviate significantly from the data set's norm can indicate critical medical incidents. In real-time patient monitoring systems, anomaly detection can alert healthcare providers to deviations from a patient's normal health parameters, signaling potential health crises. Unsupervised learning offers significant potential in exploring and understanding the vast and varied data generated within the IoMT ecosystem (IoMT, 2019).

23.3.1.3 Reinforcement learning

Reinforcement learning (RL) is a paradigm within machine learning where an intelligent agent interacts with its surrounding environment through a continuous loop of action-observation-reward. The agent learns by trial and error, aiming to maximize the cumulative reward received for its actions, ultimately leading to the development of optimal decision-making policies.

In IoMT, reinforcement learning offers significant potential to optimize healthcare processes and personalize patient treatment by learning from real-time data and continuously improving decision-making strategies based on feedback. For instance, in chronic diseases like diabetes, reinforcement learning agents can adjust insulin dosages based on continuous feedback from glucose monitoring devices, aiming to maintain optimal glucose levels without human intervention. Reinforcement learning is particularly well suited for applications in personalized medicine, where treatment plans are continuously adjusted based on individual patient responses. This includes drug dosages, therapy schedules, and other treatment parameters tailored to maximize patient health outcomes. Unlike other machine learning methods, reinforcement learning is inherently adaptive which continuously improves its policies as more data becomes available.

ML in IoMT continues to evolve, driven by advancements in algorithms, increased data availability, and improvements in computational power. The ongoing integration of ML into IoMT promises to improve predictive healthcare, personalize treatment plans, and improve overall healthcare outcomes significantly (Yu et al., 2021).

23.3.2 Deep learning

Deep learning, a subfield of machine learning leveraging artificial neural networks with multiple layers, has revolutionized the capabilities of IoMT. This powerful computational approach excels at handling the complex and vast data that IoMT devices generate, encompassing medical images, real-time sensor data, and more.

Deep learning's strength lies in extracting intricate patterns from complex data. This capability translates to significant benefits in healthcare, such as improved medical image analysis, early disease detection from sensor data, and ultimately, personalized treatment plans for better patient outcomes (Aggarwal, 2018). Deep learning is performed through various techniques as follows:

23.3.2.1 Convolutional neural networks

Convolutional neural networks (CNNs) are a specialized deep learning type architecture specifically designed to excel at processing data with a grid-like structure, commonly referred to as spatial data. Images are a prime example of spatial data, where pixels are arranged in a two-dimensional grid. CNNs leverage this inherent structure to efficiently extract features and patterns from spacial data. CNNs are particularly effective for tasks involving classification, image recognition, and analysis, leading to their extensive use in fields such as computer vision and medical imaging. The architecture of a CNN typically includes several layers that each perform different functions, Fig. 23.7 depicts CNN architecture:

- *Convolutional layers*: Convolutional layers are the fundamental building blocks of CNNs. Each convolutional layer performs a core operation known as a convolution, where a set of learnable filters (often referred to as kernels) are applied to the input data. These filters slide across the input, extracting specific features and generating a new representation called a feature map. This operation extracts basic visual features such as edges, corners, and textures.
- *Activation layer*: Following each convolution operation, a nonlinear activation function, typically the rectified linear unit (ReLU), is applied. This crucial step introduces nonlinearity into the model. Nonlinearity is essential because it allows the CNN to learn and represent

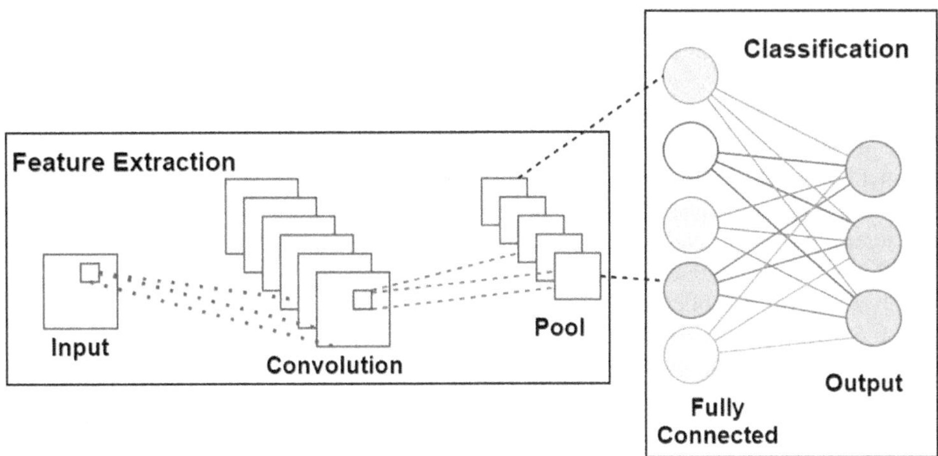

FIGURE 23.7

CNN architecture.

increasingly complex patterns within the data. Without it, the model would only be able to learn linear relationships, significantly limiting its capabilities.

- *Pooling layers*: Pooling layers serve a critical function in CNNs by downsampling the feature maps generated by the convolutional layers. This reduces the spatial dimensions (width and height) of the data, leading to a more manageable size for subsequent processing. Pooling also offers computational benefits by reducing the number of parameters and calculations required in the network. The most common pooling technique is max pooling, which selects the maximum value within a predefined window (often a 2×2 grid) across the feature map. This process retains the most prominent features while discarding less significant ones.
- *Fully connected layers*: After processing through multiple convolutional and pooling layers, the CNN transitions to fully connected layers. These layers handle the high-level reasoning within the network. Unlike convolutional layers that exploit spatial relationships, fully connected layers function similarly to regular artificial neural networks, where each neuron connects to all activations in the previous layer. This dense interconnection allows the network to process the extracted features from the convolutional layers and learn more complex, nonspatial relationships within the data. The output of each neuron in a fully connected layer is typically computed through a matrix multiplication of the input vector with the weights and then adding a bias.
- *Output layer*: The final layer of a CNN, often referred to as the output layer or classification layer, plays a critical role in transforming the processed data into a meaningful prediction. In classification tasks, this layer typically employs a softmax activation function to convert the final activation values into a set of probability distributions. These probabilities represent the likelihood of the input belonging to each possible category. For instance, in a binary classification problem (e.g., disease detection—healthy or unhealthy), the output layer would generate probabilities for each class, allowing the model to predict the class with the highest probability (Khan et al., 2020).

CNNs have emerged as a powerful tool, revolutionizing the field of medical image analysis. Their exceptional capability lies in detecting subtle and potentially disease-indicative patterns within various medical images, including X-rays and CT scans, for example, cancer, fractures, or neurological disorders, often with accuracy surpassing human experts. This capability enables CNNs to play a crucial role in computer-aided diagnosis, potentially facilitating earlier disease detection and enhancing patient outcomes (Thandapani et al., 2023).

23.3.2.2 Recurrent neural networks

Recurrent neural networks (RNNs) are a distinct category of artificial neural networks specifically designed to excel at processing sequential data. Unlike traditional ANN models that treat each input (and output) independently, RNNs can leverage their internal memory to capture temporal dependencies within the sequential data. This makes RNNs particularly well suited for applications in IoMT where time-series data is prevalent, such as in patient monitoring systems, ECG analysis, and other healthcare-related tasks where data points are interdependent. The fundamental architecture of an RNN is characterized by a series of interconnected nodes, often organized into layers. These connections form a directed acyclic graph (DAG), where information flows strictly in a forward direction along the temporal sequence of the data. This unique architecture empowers RNNs to exhibit temporal dynamic behavior. In simpler terms, RNNs can learn and exploit the inherent relationships between elements within a sequence, allowing them to process information that unfolds over time. Unlike CNNs, RNNs have loops in them, allowing information to persist.

- *Input layer*: Similar to other neural networks, the input layer in an RNN receives the initial data (often normalized) that represents the sequential input.
- *Hidden layers*: CNNs leverage multiple hidden layers, which are the workhorses of feature extraction and pattern recognition. These layers comprise interconnected neurons, where each connection possesses a learnable parameter known as a weight. During the training process, the weights within the hidden layers are iteratively adjusted to optimize the model's performance. The unique feature of RNNs is that these layers not only process data from the input layer but also receive input from themselves at the previous time step, effectively remembering previous inputs in the chain.
- *Output layer*: Depending on the application, the output could be at every timestep (many-to-many) or the end of the sequence (many-to-one), providing the final output of the network's processing (Ciaburro & Venkateswaran, 2017).

Using RNNs, deep learning can analyze time-series data from wearables and other health monitoring devices. This analysis helps in predicting health events such as heart attacks or diabetic episodes by detecting anomalies in vital signs in real time. RNNs' ability to learn from and make predictions based on time-series data offers significant opportunities for advancing patient care and healthcare operations (Idrees et al., 2023).

23.3.2.3 Generative adversarial networks

Generative adversarial networks (GANs) represent a powerful paradigm within unsupervised deep learning. They employ a unique two-network architecture where the networks are pitted against each other in an adversarial training process. This process can be conceptualized as a zero-sum game, where one network's gain corresponds to the other's loss. GANs can generate new data instances that are indistinguishable from the real data. In IoMT, GANs hold significant potential for synthesizing medical data, enhancing privacy, and augmenting datasets for training other machine learning models. GANs consist of two main components:

- *Generator network*: This network acts as the data forger, aiming to create novel data instances that closely resemble the real data distribution.
- *Discriminator network*: This network acts as the data critic, striving to accurately distinguish between the real data and the generated data produced by the generator (Alqahtani et al., 2021).

Both the generator and discriminator networks in a GAN undergo simultaneous training. During this process, the generator progressively improves its ability to create realistic synthetic samples that closely mimic the distribution of the real data. Conversely, the discriminator network refines its skill in differentiating between genuine data and the synthetic data generated by the generator. This adversarial training is typically facilitated by backpropagation and an optimization algorithm, such as stochastic gradient descent.

In the healthcare domain, acquiring vast amounts of labeled medical images can be a significant hurdle due to cost and time constraints. GANs offer a compelling solution by enabling the generation of synthetic medical images for deep learning model training. This eliminates the need for extensive real-world data collection, making GANs particularly valuable for applications involving rare diseases where real data might be scarce (Vaccari et al., 2021).

Deep learning represents a breakthrough in the ability to process and analyze visual data. In the context of IoMT, they offer the potential to significantly enhance diagnostic and monitoring capabilities, contributing to more efficient and effective healthcare solutions.

23.3.3 Natural language processing

NLP is a subfield of AI that bridges the gap between human language and computer communication. It involves various techniques that enable computers to understand, explain, and generate human language, facilitating seamless interaction between humans and machines in diverse applications, including IoMT. In healthcare, NLP is particularly crucial as it allows user interfaces to discover valuable insights from unstructured medical data, providing essential information for a wide range of tasks, including:

- *Real-time communication*: NLP can facilitate more natural and efficient communication between patients and healthcare providers by enabling features like chatbots, virtual assistants, and automated report summarization.
- *Improved data analysis*: NLP algorithms can analyze extensive amounts of unstructured medical data, such as physician notes, radiology reports, and discharge summaries, to uncover hidden patterns and trends that would be hard to detect manually. This can lead to improved clinical decision-making and research advancements.

Other applications for NLP include voice recognition systems in clinical settings, automated transcription of doctor–patient conversations, and extraction of structured information from unstructured medical records (Vaccari et al., 2021).

Voice-based interactions powered by NLP have become a transformative force in IoMT. These interactions enable more intuitive and accessible communication between healthcare systems and users, whether they are patients, doctors, or care providers. The integration of voice-based systems into IoMT devices significantly enhances user experience and accessibility, making medical technology more user-friendly and efficient (Zhang & Kamel Boulos, 2023). Some technologies which enable voice-based interactions are:

- *Automatic speech recognition* (*ASR*): This technology is at the forefront of enabling voice interactions and converting spoken language into text. ASR must be highly accurate to handle medical terminologies and patient-specific information effectively.
- *Text-to-speech* (*TTS*): TTS technologies are used to convert text data into spoken audio. In IoMT, TTS can help in delivering audible instructions or feedback to patients from their medical devices.
- *Natural language understanding* (*NLU*): NLU processes and interprets the text from ASR to understand user intents, which enables systems to generate relevant responses or actions based on user commands (Cambre & Kulkarni, 2019).

Natural language processing in IoMT is set to revolutionize the way patients and healthcare providers interact with medical technology. That makes devices not only smarter but also more accessible and responsive.

23.3.4 AI-driven solutions for IoMT challenges

To address the multifaceted challenges within IoMT, various AI techniques are strategically implemented. Deep learning and machine learning algorithms play a prominent role in this endeavor, offering powerful tools to enhance diverse aspects of IoMT functionality. The main challenges in IoMT and their AI-driven solutions are described below, see Fig. 23.8.

23.3.4.1 Data preprocessing and cleaning

These techniques are applied specifically to data preprocessing and cleaning in the IoMT context such as handling missing data. Machine learning algorithms can be deployed to impute missing values in IoMT datasets. Techniques such as k-nearest neighbors (k-NN) or more complex regression models predict missing data points based on the similarities and relationships with available

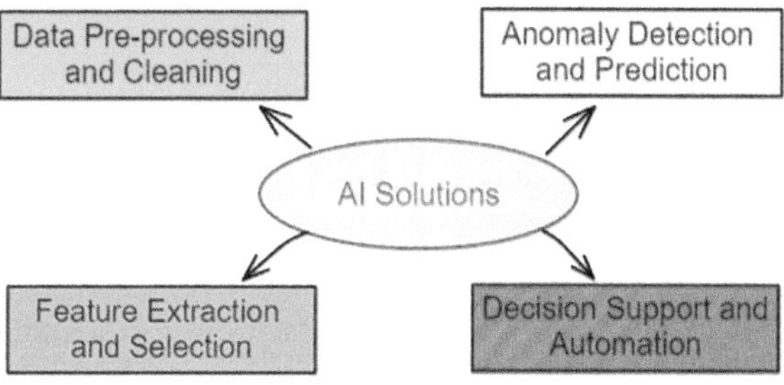

FIGURE 23.8

AI-driven solutions.

data (Turabieh et al., 2018). AI techniques play a vital role in preprocessing IoMT data by automating its transformation into a consistent format, which is essential for subsequent analysis. This preprocessing often involves data normalization or scaling to ensure all features operate on a comparable scale. Normalization techniques, such as Z-score normalization, aim to transform the data such that each feature has a mean of zero and a standard deviation of one. Alternatively, Min–Max scaling can be employed to map each feature's values to a specific range, typically between 0 and 1. These techniques mitigate potential biases introduced by varying scales in the raw data, ultimately improving the effectiveness of machine learning algorithms (Singh et al., 2024). Since the IoMT system can more effectively integrate and compare data from diverse sources. Deep learning models, especially autoencoders, are effective for detecting outliers or anomalies in IoMT data, which is crucial for maintaining the quality of the data. By learning to reconstruct the input data, autoencoders can identify data points that do not conform to the general pattern as anomalies. CNNs and denoising autoencoders are used for reducing noise from medical images or signals captured by IoMT devices. These techniques are particularly important for enhancing the quality of data before further processing or analysis (Verdejo Espinosa et al., 2021).

23.3.4.2 Feature extraction and selection

This step involves identifying the most informative and relevant features from raw data, which helps improve the efficiency and effectiveness of the subsequent learning models. NLP techniques are used to extract and normalize textual data from health records, which often contain a mix of structured and unstructured data. Techniques such as part-of-speech tagging, tokenization, and lemmatization help prepare text data for further analysis (Borjali et al., 2021). Random forest as a machine learning technique is not only a powerful classifier but also it is effective for feature selection. The importance of each feature can be measured based on how much the tree nodes, which use that feature, reduce impurity on average. In IoMT, this method is used to identify key features from complex datasets like patient health records or real-time monitoring data (Yang & Xu, 2018). Within the IoMT domain, CNNs excel at automated feature extraction, a crucial step in image analysis tasks. This inherent capability makes them particularly well suited for processing grid-like data, such as medical images commonly generated by IoMT devices. During the training process, CNNs automatically learn relevant features from the input images, alleviating the need for engineering feature manually, which can be a time-consuming and domain-specific task, for example, diagnosing diseases from X-rays or CT scans (Ghassemi et al., 2023).

23.3.4.3 Anomaly detection and prediction

Anomaly detection and prediction are critical components in IoMT. They help to ensure that the devices operate reliably and that the data they generate is accurate and actionable. By identifying outliers or unusual patterns, AI-driven anomaly detection can alert healthcare providers to potential health crises or device malfunctions before they lead to serious consequences. Dimensionality reduction techniques such as k-means and principal component analysis are used to identify data points that do not fit the normal clusters or patterns (Kalinaki et al., 2024). That is useful in cases where no prior labeling of data is available, such as identifying unusual patterns in patient behavior or sensor outputs that have not been previously encountered. Autoencoders are effective for continuous monitoring of IoMT devices, where they can continuously learn from data streams and detect anomalies in real-time, such as unexpected patterns in ECG signals (Zhou & Paffenroth, 2017). CNNs are particularly useful for medical imaging applications in IoMT, such as detecting tumors or other abnormalities in radiological images that do not conform to common patterns (Wang et al., 2022).

23.3.4.4 Decision support and automation

AI techniques play a critical role in reinforcing decision support and automation within IoMT. These AI-driven systems help healthcare providers make better data-driven decisions by analyzing large volumes of data collected from IoMT devices. AI automates administrative tasks, helping healthcare providers to assign more time to direct patient interaction and personalized care plans. Clustering and classification techniques are used to stratify patients based on their risk levels to facilitate targeted interventions for high-risk patients (Zhao et al., 2021). Natural language generation (NLG) systems use data to automatically generate textual summaries, which can be used in clinical reports. After processing medical images, AI systems can generate preliminary reports which are then reviewed or modified by healthcare professionals. That implies streamlining the reporting process (Sim et al., 2023).

By employing these advanced AI techniques, IoMT can enhance the quality and utility of the data collected, facilitating better healthcare outcomes through more informed data-driven decisions.

23.4 AI-powered IoMT applications in smart hospitals

AI significantly enhances the capabilities of IoMT devices, which in turn drives advancements in today's smart healthcare systems. AI algorithms can rapidly process and extract insights from the massive datasets generated by IoMT devices, such as vital signs, imaging data, and patient history. Machine learning models, particularly deep learning, are adept at identifying anomalies and uncommon patterns that may indicate health issues. AI acts as a transformative force, not only by augmenting the capabilities of IoMT devices but also by playing a pivotal role in shaping healthcare systems toward greater efficiency, proactivity, and patient-centered care (Manickam et al., 2022). Below are applications where AI contributes to the enforcement of IoMT in different hospital departments:

23.4.1 Remote patient monitoring and early disease detection

Remote patient monitoring involves employing various technologies to observe and collect medical data from patients in one place, and then securely transmitting this information electronically to healthcare providers in another location for evaluation and recommendations. Both patients and providers use interfaces, such as web portals or mobile apps, to interact with the remote patient monitoring system. Patients can view their data and receive notifications. Healthcare providers can monitor alerts, track patient progress, and make clinical decisions based on the data received. AI algorithms are adept at interpreting complex health data obtained from IoMT devices in the remote monitoring system (Manickam et al., 2022). Fig. 23.9 illustrates the overall remote AI-enabled patient monitoring system. For instance, AI can analyze data from a heart rate monitor to detect anomalies that may indicate cardiac issues. An example is the Apple Watch's ECG feature, which

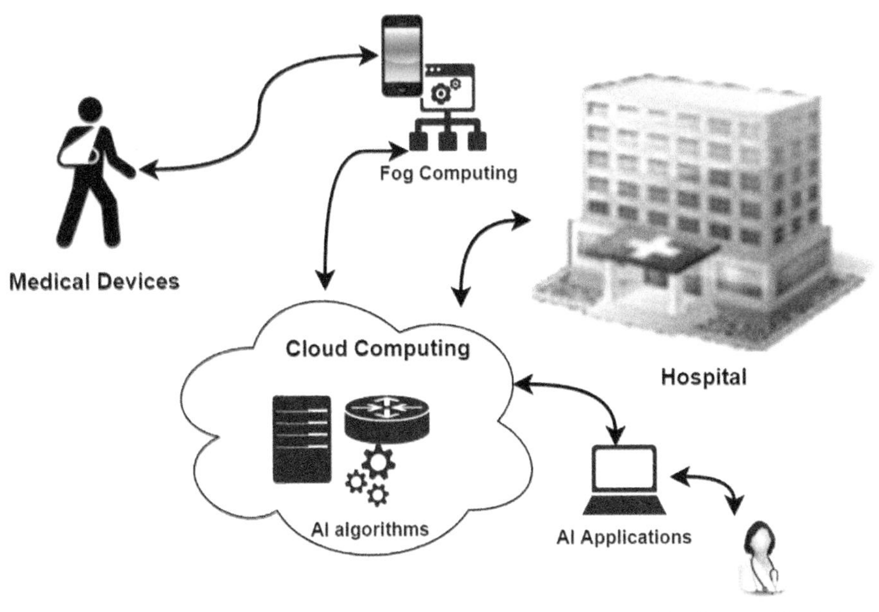

FIGURE 23.9

Remote AI-enabled patient monitoring system.

uses machine learning to identify signs of atrial fibrillation, alerting users to potential heart problems that require clinical attention (Manimurugan et al., 2022).

AI-enabled IoMT devices continuously monitor patient health status, enabling the early detection of adverse events. For example, wearable sensors equipped with AI can analyze motion and physiological parameters to predict and detect falls among elderly patients. Wearable biosensor provides notifications to clinical staff if a patient's condition deteriorates, allowing for quick intervention. AI models customize alerts based on the patient's specific health profile, enhancing the relevance and timeliness of the interventions. For instance, AI algorithms can learn from a diabetic patient's historical glucose data to predict future trends and send alerts when predictive patterns indicate a potential risk of hyperglycemia (Vettoretti et al., 2020).

AI-enabled IoMT system is utilized in detecting early signs of diseases. A notable example is Google's AI model, which helps detect breast cancer in mammography screenings with accuracy comparable to that of expert radiologists. This model analyses mammograms to identify subtle patterns that human eyes might miss, enabling earlier and potentially life-saving interventions. IoMT devices equipped with AI can provide real-time analysis of collected data to issue early warnings about potential health issues. An application of this is in the monitoring of respiratory conditions. Smart inhalers equipped with sensors and AI capabilities can track usage patterns and environmental conditions to predict and alert patients of potential exacerbations (Awotunde et al., 2022).

While AI-enabled IoMT holds great potential for revolutionizing remote patient monitoring and enabling earlier disease detection, several challenges need to be overcome to fully harness its potential. Ensuring patients consistently use IoMT devices as intended and adhere to monitoring protocols can be difficult (Hayat et al., 2022). Furthermore, ensuring the reliability and accuracy of IoMT data is critical for the effectiveness of AI-powered healthcare solutions. The reliability and accuracy of data are reduced due to sensor malfunctions, signal interference, and user errors. Furthermore, the distributed architecture of IoMT systems, while offering advantages in scalability and flexibility, also presents significant challenges in safeguarding sensitive patient data. The interconnected nature of these systems creates multiple potential entry points for cyberattacks, raising concerns about data breaches and unauthorized access. Robust cybersecurity measures are essential to mitigate these risks and ensure patient data privacy (Radanliev et al., 2018).

23.4.2 Personalized treatment plans and medication management

Personalized treatment plans involve customizing medical care to the individual characteristics of each patient. AI-enabled IoMT holds the potential for transforming personalized treatment plans and medication management. By leveraging continuous data collection, and predictive analytics, these systems provide a holistic view of the patient's health. Hence, AI-enabled IoMT systems enable more precise and tailored treatment plans and they enhance patient outcomes and adherence to treatments. Effective medication management is important for ensuring that patients adhere to their prescribed treatments and avoid adverse drug events. Wearable devices and smart bottles track whether patients take their medications as prescribed. Then, AI algorithms analyze this data to detect patterns of nonadherence (Rajkomar et al., 2019).

AI-enabled personalized treatment plans and medication management have been implemented in various healthcare settings. That demonstrates significant improvements in patient outcomes through tailored healthcare strategies. IBM Watson for Oncology is an AI system developed to assist oncologists in creating personalized cancer treatment plans. By analyzing large amounts of clinical trials, patient data, and medical literature, Watson provides evidence-based treatment recommendations tailored to individual patients. The system uses ML algorithms to identify treatment options that are more effective based on the patient's unique profile, including genetic characteristics (Zou et al., 2020). Stanford Health Care has adopted AI to provide personalized care for patients undergoing surgery, aiming to improve recovery times and reduce complications. AI models are increasingly leveraged to analyze patient data, enabling them to predict surgical outcomes and identify potential risks with greater accuracy. Based on these predictions, personalized recovery plans are developed, including tailored physiotherapy exercises, dietary recommendations, and follow-up schedules (Maddox et al., 2019).

While AI-enabled personalized treatment plans and medication management offer transformative potential for improving patient care, fragmented, inconsistent, and incomplete medical data can reduce the transformation benefits of such systems. Efforts must focus on improving data quality, ensuring ethical practices, integrating AI seamlessly into clinical workflows, and providing adequate training for healthcare providers (Chen & Decary, 2020).

23.4.3 Robotic-assisted surgery and automated drug delivery

The integration of AI with IoMT has opened new frontiers in healthcare, particularly in the domains of robotic-assisted surgery and automated drug delivery. Robotic-assisted surgery represents one of the most advanced applications of AI-enabled IoMT, combining robotics, machine learning, and real-time data analytics to perform complex surgical procedures. AI algorithms analyze real-time data from surgical instruments and patient vitals, assisting surgeons in making precise movements and decisions during surgery. This leads to reduced surgical errors, minimized tissue damage, and quicker recovery times for patients (Li et al., 2020). Robotic systems equipped with AI can perform minimally invasive procedures by making smaller incisions, which are guided by detailed preoperative planning and intraoperative imaging. Minimally invasive surgeries decrease postoperative pain and scarring and provide faster patient recovery (Rivero-Moreno et al., 2023).

Automated drug delivery systems leverage AI and IoMT to administer medications accurately and timely, improving treatment efficacy and patient adherence. AI algorithms analyze real-time physiological metrics and patient historical data to determine optimal drug dosages and schedules. These systems adjust medication delivery based on continuous monitoring and feedback. Closed-loop drug delivery is a case study of such systems. It uses real-time data from IoMT devices, such as continuous glucose monitors (CGMs) for diabetic patients, to automatically adjust insulin delivery through AI-driven insulin pumps (Boughton & Hovorka, 2019).

Despite the great promise of AI-enabled IoMT for enhancing remote surgery and automated drug delivery, there are vital challenges that need to be addressed. Robotic-assisted surgeries rely on highly sophisticated technologies, including advanced sensors, actuators, and AI algorithms. Ensuring the reliability and precision of these systems is a major challenge. High training requirements can limit the adoption of robotic-assisted surgery and may lead to skill degradation over time without adequate practice. Regulatory approval and ethical considerations are significant challenges, particularly for autonomous systems in healthcare. Integrating AI and IoMT technologies into existing healthcare infrastructures requires significant technical expertise and investment (Topol, 2019).

23.4.4 Real-time patient safety monitoring and fall prevention

Real-time patient safety monitoring and fall prevention are critical applications of AI-enabled IoMT that enhance patient care, particularly for elderly populations and individuals with mobility impairments (Alhazmi et al., 2024). By leveraging AI and interconnected medical devices, these systems can detect potential fall risks, monitor patient movements, and provide timely interventions. Thereby, such systems reduce the incidence of falls and improve overall patient safety.

AI-enabled IoMT devices provide real-time data on patient activity which allows immediate detection of unusual movements or potential falls. Smart home systems powered by cameras, motion sensors, and floor pressure sensors monitor the environment for potential hazards and track patient movements throughout the home. IoMT devices continuously collect and transmit data to centralized systems. This enables constant monitoring of patient activity and immediate detection of any anomalies. AI algorithms analyze data from sensors to detect patterns indicative of fall risks. These algorithms are trained on large datasets of patient movements to distinguish between normal activities and potential falls. When a potential fall is detected, the system automatically generates alerts to notify caregivers, family members, or medical professionals. Alerts can be sent via mobile apps, text messages, or integrated hospital systems (Izdihar et al., 2024).

Lively Mobile Plus by GreatCall's is a personal emergency response system (PERS) designed to detect falls and provide immediate assistance. It combines wearable technology with AI to monitor patient safety. AI algorithms process the sensor data to distinguish between normal activities and potential falls. Upon detecting a fall, the device automatically contacts GreatCall's emergency response center, which can dispatch emergency services if needed (Orlov, 2011). Fall guardian is another successful example of a real-time patient safety monitoring and fall prevention system. Fall guardian offers a range of fall detection devices that utilize AI and IoMT technologies to ensure the safety of elderly patients. The fall detection algorithms analyze sensor data in real time to identify falls accurately. When a fall is detected, the devices automatically alert Fall Guardian's monitoring center, which then contacts emergency responders or designated caregivers (Ferdous et al., 2021). One of the major challenges of real-time patient safety monitoring and fall prevention systems is to ensure that patients, particularly the elderly, are comfortable with and willing to use these technologies. That is essential for the effectiveness of those systems.

23.4.5 AI-driven administrative tasks and workflow optimization

For automating routine tasks, improving data management, and enhancing decision-making processes, AI-enabled IoMT can streamline such operations, reduce costs, and improve patient care. For instance, AI algorithms analyze patient data, preferences, and provider availability to automate appointment scheduling. AI models predict optimal appointment times to reduce no-shows and cancellations. This reduces administrative burdens, improves clinic utilization rates, and enhances patient satisfaction by offering more convenient scheduling options (Maleki Varnosfaderani & Forouzanfar, 2024). Moreover, AI-powered systems manage and organize EHRs by extracting and structuring data from unstructured clinical documents. NLP and machine learning models facilitate accurate and efficient data entry and retrieval. Improved EHRs management enhances data accuracy, reduces the time healthcare providers spend on documentation, and allows for better patient care through easily accessible and comprehensive health records (Wang et al., 2018).

AI algorithms can automate the medical billing and coding process by extracting relevant information from clinical notes and utilize it to assign appropriate medical codes for accurate billing purposes. AI systems can also identify discrepancies and potential errors in billing. Automation of billing and coding reduces administrative errors, speeds up the reimbursement process, and ensures compliance with regulatory standards (Davenport & Kalakota, 2019). For supply chain and inventory management, IoMT devices track the usage and stock levels of medical supplies in real time. Using AI algorithms, the demand patterns can be predicted and inventory levels can be optimized to ensure that necessary supplies are always available without overstocking. Efficient supply chain management reduces waste, lowers costs, and ensures that critical supplies are available when needed, improving overall healthcare delivery (Belhadi et al., 2021). Although the significant benefits of AI-driven administrative tasks and workflow optimization tools, integrating those solutions with existing healthcare IT infrastructure can be complex and requires seamless interoperability between various systems and devices.

23.4.6 Predictive maintenance of medical equipment

Predictive maintenance of medical equipment is an emerging application of AI-enabled IoMT that significantly reinforces the reliability and efficiency of healthcare delivery. AI-enabled IoMT can forecast failures of critical equipment before they occur and schedule timely maintenance to avoid unexpected downtimes. This proactive approach not only reduces maintenance costs but also ensures that critical medical devices are always operational. Thereby it improves patient care (Zhao et al., 2019).

IoMT collects data on parameters such as pressure, vibration, temperature, and usage patterns. Real-time data collection enables continuous monitoring of equipment health, providing valuable insights into its condition. Then, AI algorithms analyze the data collected by IoMT devices to identify patterns and anomalies that may signal potential equipment failures. These early warnings empower proactive maintenance strategies, allowing for timely interventions before critical failures occur. For instance, AI might detect abnormal vibration patterns in machinery, potentially indicative of bearing wear, or identify fluctuations in temperature readings that could suggest impending overheating. Combining real-time monitoring with historical data, AI models can predict when a device is likely to fail. Predictive analytics allows for proactive maintenance scheduling, reducing the likelihood of equipment breakdowns and extending the lifespan of medical devices.

AI-driven predictive maintenance schedules maintenance activities based on equipment conditions rather than fixed intervals. This ensures that maintenance is performed only when necessary, preventing unnecessary service interruptions. This approach minimizes downtime, ensuring that critical medical equipment is available when needed. Predictive maintenance reduces the frequency and cost of maintenance by avoiding unnecessary routine checks and focusing on equipment that shows signs of wear and tear. AI algorithms optimize resource allocation, ensuring that maintenance efforts are directed where they are most needed. This leads to significant cost savings in maintenance budgets and enhances the operational efficiency of healthcare facilities. Continuous monitoring and timely maintenance prevent minor issues from escalating into major problems, thereby extending the lifespan of medical equipment. AI algorithms can also optimize equipment performance by adjusting operational parameters based on real-time data. This ensures that medical devices operate at peak efficiency, improving the quality of patient care (Zhao et al., 2019).

On the other hand, AI-driven predictive maintenance of medical equipment brings major challenges. The accuracy and reliability of predictive maintenance algorithms depend on the quality and quantity of data collected. Ensuring that AI models are trained on comprehensive and representative datasets is essential for making accurate predictions. Integrating predictive maintenance solutions with existing healthcare IT infrastructure can be challenging. Ensuring interoperability between different systems and devices is critical for seamless operation (Elkateb et al., 2024).

23.4.7 Chatbots for patient education and symptom analysis

Chatbots powered by AI and integrated with IoMT are valuable tools for patient education and symptom analysis. These AI-driven systems provide personalized, real-time interactions that can improve patient' understanding of their health conditions and assist in preliminary diagnosis. By leveraging NLP and machine learning algorithms, chatbots can analyze symptoms, offer educational content, and recommend the next steps.

For instance, the company "Your.MD" offered an AI-driven chatbot that provides symptom-checking and personalized health information. The chatbot aims to empower users with reliable medical information and guidance based on their symptoms. Woebot is also a case study of an AI-driven chatbot that is designed to support mental health through cognitive-behavioral therapy techniques. It engages users in conversations to help them manage anxiety, depression, and other mental health issues. Ada Health developed an AI-powered chatbot that provides personalized symptom assessments and health guidance. The chatbot aims to support users in understanding their symptoms and making informed health decisions (Milne-Ives et al., 2020).

Chatbots can deliver personalized educational content based on patient queries and health records. They provide information on medications, lifestyle changes, and disease management. They empower patients by enhancing their understanding of their conditions and treatments, ultimately leading to better medication adherence and improved health outcomes. AI algorithms analyze patient-reported symptoms entered through chatbot interfaces. By comparing these symptoms with vast databases of medical knowledge, the chatbots can suggest possible conditions and recommend whether a patient should seek medical attention. Furthermore, Chatbots are available 24/7 and provide immediate responses to patient queries, eliminating the need for appointments or waiting times (Miner et al., 2017).

Data privacy, ethics, and user acceptance are among the key challenges that need to be addressed for successful implementation and widespread use of AI-driven Chatbots. Moreover, Chatbots require regular updates and maintenance to ensure they provide up-to-date and accurate information. This involves continuously updating medical knowledge databases and improving AI algorithms. Failure to address language and cultural barriers can limit the accessibility and effectiveness of chatbot technology (Miner et al., 2017).

23.5 Impact of AI-enabled IoMT on healthcare

Nowadays, smart healthcare is revolutionized by integrating advanced AI technologies with Internet-connected medical devices. This integration offers numerous benefits for healthcare stakeholders, including:

23.5.1 Potential benefits of AI-enabled IoMT for patients

One of the major benefits of AI-enabled IoMT for patients is improved health outcomes. Improved health outcomes are guaranteed by enhanced diagnostic accuracy. AI algorithms can analyze large datasets from IoMT devices to detect patterns and anomalies that may not be apparent to human clinicians. This can lead to more accurate diagnoses. Improved diagnostic accuracy helps in identifying diseases at earlier stages, leading to better prognosis and treatment outcomes (Topol, 2019). Furthermore, IoMT devices provide continuous monitoring of health metrics, enabling their real-time analysis. Continuous monitoring allows for the timely detection of health deterioration and immediate medical interventions, reducing the risk of severe complications (Li et al., 2017).

Personalized healthcare is vital for today's healthcare which is mainly based on a patient-centered approach. AI acts as a powerful tool in tailoring treatment plans to individual needs. By processing patient data from IoMT devices, AI can integrate a wealth of information, including real-time health metrics, genetic predispositions, and lifestyle factors. Personalized treatment plans improve the interventions' efficacy and patient adherence. AI algorithms further can adjust treatment protocols in real time based on continuous feedback from IoMT devices. Therefore therapies are optimized for each patient. Adaptive therapies provide a dynamic and responsive approach to patient care, improving the effectiveness of treatments and reducing side effects (Chen & Decary, 2020).

AI uses predictive analytics to forecast potential health events, such as heart attacks or diabetic complications, based on historical and real-time data from IoMT devices. Predictive analytics enables proactive interventions for chronic conditions, reducing emergency visits and hospitalizations. On the other hand, IoMT devices equipped with AI can alert healthcare providers and patients to early signs of health issues, prompting immediate action. Early intervention can prevent the progression of diseases and mitigate the severity of health problems. That reinforces the overall patient health as the main healthcare stakeholder (Bini, 2018).

Cleveland Clinic is one of the leading healthcare institutions in the United States. It implemented an AI-enabled IoMT system for remote patient monitoring to manage chronic diseases and improve patient outcomes. This institution has many successful case studies to prove the AI-enabled IoMT's impact on patient health. A 45-year-old patient with type 2 diabetes used a continuous glucose monitor integrated with the AI-enabled IoMT system. The AI algorithms analyzed the patient's glucose levels in real time and identified patterns related to diet and physical activity. Personalized recommendations were provided, including specific dietary adjustments and exercise routines. The patient's HbA1c levels improved significantly over 6 months, demonstrating better control of their diabetes (Beck et al., 2017). This case study highlights the potential of AI-enabled IoMT in delivering high-quality, patient-centered healthcare.

23.5.2 Potential benefits of AI-enabled IoMT for healthcare providers

AI-enabled IoMT solutions enable healthcare providers to make data-driven decisions, optimize clinical outcomes, and improve operational efficiency and hence reduce healthcare costs. Streamlined workflows improve the overall efficiency of care delivery, reducing patient wait times and reinforcing the quality of care. AI-enabled IoMT reduces costs by automating routine tasks, optimizing resource use, and preventing costly medical errors.

A clinical decision support system (CDSS) integrates data from various IoMT devices with EHRs and other healthcare databases. AI algorithms then analyze this comprehensive dataset to provide evidence-based recommendations. CDSS supports healthcare providers in making informed clinical decisions, reducing variability in care, and improving diagnostic and treatment accuracy. Mount Sinai Health System as a real-world settings case study deployed an AI-enabled IoMT system to enhance data-driven decision-making and improve medical services efficiency. The system integrates data from IoMT devices with EHRs to provide real-time insights. As AI and IoMT technologies continue to evolve, healthcare providers will be able to reinforce healthcare delivery efficiency and reduce healthcare costs (Beam & Kohane, 2018).

23.5.3 Potential benefits of AI-enabled IoMT for hospitals and healthcare institutions

AI-enabled IoMT is reconstructing the healthcare landscape by providing innovative solutions across the board. These innovative solutions are making medical services more efficient by automating tasks, accurate through real-time data analysis, and effective with personalized treatment plans. Hospitals and healthcare institutions are leveraging these advanced technologies to drive innovation, improve patient care, and streamline operations. AI-enabled IoMT systems collect and analyze volumes of health data, providing insights that drive medical research and innovation. Machine learning models are powerful tools capable of uncovering hidden patterns and correlations within massive datasets. These insights facilitate the discovery of new treatments, help understand disease mechanisms, and support the development of predictive models for disease outbreaks and progression. Furthermore, AI algorithms analyze patient data to identify suitable candidates for clinical trials, monitor trial progress, and ensure protocol adherence. IoMT devices provide continuous data collection from trial participants. Optimizing clinical trials accelerates the development of new treatments and medical innovations, making them available to patients more quickly and efficiently (Chen & Decary, 2020).

AI-enabled IoMT systems significantly upgrade the capacity of hospitals and healthcare institutions to innovate and improve patient care. AI optimizes resource utilization by predicting patient influx, managing bed occupancy, and streamlining supply chain logistics based on real-time data from IoMT devices. Efficient resource management ensures that healthcare facilities operate smoothly and that resources are available when needed. Moreover, AI-enabled chatbots and virtual assistants provide personalized interactions, answering patient queries, offering health advice, and scheduling appointments. Personalized patient interactions improve patient satisfaction and engagement with their health management. That implies a better patient experience (Bibault et al., 2019).

23.6 Security, privacy, and ethical considerations

Despite the positive impact of AI-driven IoMT systems in modern smart healthcare, addressing data security, patient privacy, and ethical considerations is essential for the successful implementation of AI-enabled IoMT systems in healthcare.

23.6.1 Security and privacy

The continuous collection and transmission of sensitive patient data by IoMT devices introduces inherent security vulnerabilities (Singh & Kaunert, 2024). These vulnerabilities expose patient data to potential cyberattacks (such as malware, ransomware, and hacking), data breaches, and unauthorized access, necessitating robust cybersecurity measures to safeguard patient privacy and health information.

Limited computational resources in IoMT devices pose a significant challenge to implementing robust security measures. This can leave them vulnerable to cyberattacks, potentially compromising sensitive patient data. These devices may also have vulnerabilities in their firmware or software that can be exploited by attackers. Compromised IoMT devices can be used to access patient data, manipulate device functionality, or launch further attacks on the network. Attackers can manipulate data to mislead healthcare providers, leading to incorrect diagnoses or inappropriate (Al-Turjman & Nayyar, 2022).

Compromised data integrity can undermine the reliability of AI algorithms and clinical decision support systems, leading to poor patient outcomes and loss of trust in healthcare providers. Poor interoperability and inconsistent security measures also threaten the AI-enabled IoMT systems. They can create vulnerabilities that can be exploited by attackers, compromising the overall security of the IoMT ecosystem. This vulnerability can lead to unauthorized access to sensitive patient data, potentially resulting in privacy violations if data protection measures are inadequate. Unauthorized access or sharing of patient data can occur due to weak security measures or accidental exposure. Privacy violations can lead to legal and regulatory consequences, loss of patient trust, and harm to patients if their personal health information is exposed or misused (Al-Turjman & Nayyar, 2022).

The privacy and confidentiality of IoMT data is paramount. Implementing strong encryption protocols for data at rest and in transit protects patient information from unauthorized access. Moreover, multifactor authentication and suitable access control approaches ensure that the sensitive data may be accessed by authorized personnel only. To safeguard sensitive patient data and ensure regulatory compliance, healthcare providers must prioritize robust data security practices. This entails performing routine security audits and vulnerability assessments to proactively detect and address potential threats. Additionally, implementing best practices for data anonymization, encryption, and access control creates a multilayered defense against cyberattacks and unauthorized access (Parthasarathy & Rajendran, 2016).

Data masking, a data anonymization technique, replaces sensitive data elements with fictitious or scrambled values while preserving the overall data format. Masking data fields involving personally identifiable information (PII), like names and social security numbers, is considered a best practice for anonymizing patient data. This approach protects patient privacy while allowing researchers and healthcare professionals to analyze the anonymized data for valuable insights. Differential privacy is also a best practice for data anonymization. It adds statistical noise to the data, protecting individual privacy while still enabling aggregate data analysis. This technique is particularly useful when sharing datasets for research (Parthasarathy & Rajendran, 2016).

Encryption is a critical component of data security. Encrypting data at rest is a critical security measure that safeguards sensitive information stored on devices and servers. This process utilizes robust encryption algorithms (like Rivest, Shamir, Adleman algorithm [RES] or elliptic curve cryptography [ECC]) to render the data unreadable by unauthorized users, even if they gain access to the storage location. This ensures that even if physical security is breached, the data remains protected. Encrypting data in transit is equally important, protecting data during transmission between IoMT devices and central systems. Secure communication protocols such as message queuing telemetry transport (MQTT) and CoAP are essential for this purpose. Effective key management is also crucial, involving the secure generation, storage, and management of encryption keys. End-to-end encryption provides a robust security layer by ensuring that data remains encrypted from the moment it is sent by the originator to the moment it is decrypted by the intended recipient. This additional layer of protection safeguards sensitive information throughout its entire transmission journey. This approach is particularly important for protecting sensitive patient data transmitted by IoMT devices to healthcare providers (Kalinaki et al., 2023).

Robust access control measures are essential for protecting sensitive data. To safeguard sensitive data within IoMT systems, a layered security approach is crucial. Role-based access control (RBAC) assigns permissions based on user roles, ensuring that users only have access to the data necessary for their job functions. Multifactor authentication (MFA) enhances security by requiring multiple verification steps, such as biometrics and passwords, to confirm a user's identity before granting access (Yalamati, 2024). Furthermore, the principle of least privilege ensures that users are given the minimum level of access necessary to perform their tasks, thereby reducing the potential damage from unauthorized access. Regularly reviewing and adjusting access permissions helps maintain compliance with this principle. Maintaining audit trails and monitoring access and activity related to sensitive data can help detect and investigate unauthorized access. Automated monitoring and alerting systems can enhance security by detecting suspicious activity in real time. Access control lists (ACLs) are considered an important means to define and enforce rules specifying users or system processes that have access to resources and secure sensitive data and resources (Kalinaki et al., 2023).

23.6.2 Ethical considerations

AI-enabled IoMT also raises critical ethical considerations, particularly concerning algorithm bias, fairness, and transparency. Algorithm bias occurs when AI systems produce systematically prejudiced results due to flawed training data or biased algorithms. In healthcare, this can lead to unequal treatment of different patient groups. Bias in AI can exacerbate existing health disparities, leading to misdiagnoses, inappropriate treatments, and unequal access to healthcare services.

AI algorithms trained on historical healthcare data risk perpetuating existing biases present in the medical field and wider society. These biases can lead to unequal treatment and inaccurate diagnoses, particularly for marginalized populations. For example, if a training dataset predominantly includes data from a specific demographic group, the AI may not perform well for other groups. The design and implementation of AI algorithms can introduce bias if certain features or attributes are improperly weighted or selected (Parthasarathy & Rajendran, 2016).

Diverse training data is one of the bias mitigation strategies that ensure that training datasets are representative of the entire patient population, including diverse demographic and socioeconomic groups. Bias detection and correction implements techniques to detect and correct bias in AI models, such as resampling, reweighting, and algorithmic adjustments. It is important to regularly monitor AI systems for bias and make necessary adjustments to maintain fairness (Kalinaki et al., 2023).

Fairness in AI-enabled IoMT applications involves ensuring that all patients receive equitable treatment and that AI systems do not favor one group over another. Lack of fairness can lead to unequal healthcare outcomes and loss of trust in AI technologies among patients and healthcare providers. AI systems should provide equal treatment to all patients, regardless of their background or characteristics. Furthermore, AI should aim for equitable health outcomes, recognizing that some groups may require different types of care to achieve similar health results. The development and use of metrics is an effective strategy to measure and evaluate the fairness of AI systems, such as demographic parity, equal opportunity, and disparate impact. It is important to involve diverse stakeholders, including patients from various backgrounds, in the design and testing of AI systems to ensure that different perspectives are considered (Jayachitra et al., 2023).

In AI-powered healthcare applications, transparency is paramount. It allows us to understand and explain how AI systems arrive at their decisions. Without transparency, healthcare providers and patients may develop mistrust and resistance, hindering the adoption of AI in clinical settings. Conversely, transparency fosters trust, ensures accountability, and facilitates the seamless integration of AI into routine healthcare practices. To overcome the transparency issue, interpretable models are used where possible that are developed to interpret complex models (e.g., using feature importance scores, decision trees, or rule-based systems). The explainable AI (XAI) system is an example that offers a high level of transparency for AI applications. XAI focuses on creating AI systems that offer clear explanations for their actions. This transparency in the decision-making process is crucial for building trust in AI, particularly in critical fields like healthcare. The use of XAI helps healthcare providers understand AI recommendations, which can improve clinical decision-making as well as patient trust. The comprehensive documentation of AI systems, including their design, data sources, and decision-making processes, and the communication of this information effectively to users are considered the best practices that ensure transparency. Engaging stakeholders, such as patients, healthcare providers, and regulatory bodies, promotes transparency and accountability in AI systems (Jayachitra et al., 2023). This collaborative approach ensures that AI is developed and deployed in a way that prioritizes patient well-being, ethical considerations, and responsible innovation.

23.6.3 Recommendations for ensuring responsible development and deployment of AI-enabled IoMT systems

The development and deployment of AI-enabled IoMT systems must be handled responsibly to ensure they are safe, effective, and equitable. The following recommendations help to achieve that goal:

- Ensuring compliance with privacy regulations like General Data Protection Regulation (GDPR) and Health Insurance Portability and Accountability Act (HIPAA) is paramount in the age of AI-powered healthcare. These regulations safeguard sensitive patient data and empower individuals to control their health information. Regular audits can ensure adherence to these regulations and help update policies as needed.
- It is essential to diversify training data by collecting data from diverse demographic groups and regularly updating datasets to reflect current populations. Techniques such as resampling, reweighting, and algorithmic adjustments can detect and correct bias.
- Implementing data quality checks to ensure the completeness, reliability, and accuracy of the data used for AI systems is important. Regularly validating and cleaning data can maintain high quality.
- Creating a code of ethics for AI in healthcare and ensuring adherence by all stakeholders can promote responsible use. Promoting awareness of ethical considerations in AI among developers, healthcare providers, and other stakeholders through training and resources is crucial.
- Performing comprehensive security audits to identify and address vulnerabilities in AI-enabled IoMT systems is recommended. Engaging external security experts to perform regular audits and implementing their recommendations can enhance security.
- Collaboration between healthcare providers and academic/research institutions can provide a wealth of benefits. By working together, they can stay updated on the latest advancements in AI and IoMT. This knowledge exchange fosters innovation, promotes the development of best practices, and ultimately paves the way for the future of healthcare.

23.7 Conclusion

The integration of AI and IoMT within smart healthcare systems represents a transformative leap in healthcare delivery. AI enhances the capabilities of IoMT by enabling sophisticated data analysis, predictive analytics, and real-time decision-making. This synergy leads to improved diagnostic accuracy, personalized treatment plans, and proactive patient monitoring, significantly enhancing patient outcomes and operational efficiency. However, the implementation of AI-enabled IoMT also presents challenges, including data security, patient privacy, and ethical considerations. Addressing these challenges requires robust security measures, ethical guidelines, and regulatory frameworks to ensure the safe and equitable deployment of these technologies. The potential benefits of AI-enabled IoMT for patients, healthcare providers, and institutions are immense, offering a pathway to more efficient, effective, and patient-centered healthcare. As the technology continues to evolve, ongoing research, innovation, and collaboration will be essential to fully realize its potential and address emerging challenges in the dynamic landscape of smart healthcare.

Acknowledgments

The authors acknowledge the assistance of Open AI's ChatGPT-4o in refining the language, proofreading, and enhancing the coherence of the manuscript.

References

Aggarwal, C. C. (2018). *Neural networks and deep learning*. Springer.

Alahi, E. E., Sukkuea, A., Tina, F. W., Nag, A., Kurdthongmee, W., Suwannarat, K., & Mukhopadhyay, S. C. (2023). Integration of IoT-enabled technologies and artificial intelligence (AI) for smart city scenario: Recent advancements and future trends. *Sensors*.

Alhazmi, A. K., Alanazi, M. A., Alshehry, A. H., Alshahry, S. M., Jaszek, J., Djukic, C., Brown, A., Jackson, K., & Chodavarapu, V. P. (2024). Intelligent millimeter-wave system for human activity monitoring for telemedicine. *Sensors, 24*, 268.

Alloghani, M., Al-Jumeily, D., Mustafina, J., Hussain, A., & Aljaaf, A. J. (2020). A systematic review on supervised and unsupervised machine learning algorithms for data science. In M. W. Berry, A. Mohamed, & B. W. Yap (Eds.), *Supervised unsupervised learning for data science* (pp. 3–21). Cham: Springer International Publishing. Available from https://doi.org/10.1001/jama.2017.18391.

Alqahtani, H., Kavakli-Thorne, M., & Kumar, G. (2021). Applications of generative adversarial networks (gans): An updated review. *Archives Computational Methods Engineering, 28*, 525–552.

Al-Turjman, F., & Nayyar, A. (2022). *Machine learning for critical Internet of Medical Things: Applications and use cases* (pp. 1–261). Springer International Publishing. Available from https://doi.org/10.1007/978-3-030-80928-7.

Amaraweera, S. P., & Halgamuge, M. N. (2019). *Security, privacy and trust in the IoT environment* (pp. 2–11). Cham: Springer. Available from https://doi.org/10.1007/978-3-030-18075-1.

Anbar, A. (2023). *Classification of DDoS Attack with Machine Learning Architectures and Exploratory Analysis (Master's thesis)*. Canada: The University of Western Ontario.

Awotunde, J. B., Folorunso, S. O., Ajagbe, S. A., Garg, J., & Ajamu, G. J. (2022). *AiIoMT: IoMT-based system-enabled artificial intelligence for enhanced smart healthcare systems. Machine learning critical Internet of Medical Things applied use cases* (pp. 229–254). Cham: Springer.

Bandyopadhyay, D., & Sen, J. (2011). Internet of things: Applications and challenges in technology and standardization. *Wireless Personal Communications, 58*, 49–69.

Beam, A. L., & Kohane, I. S. (2018). Big data and machine learning in health care. *JAMA: the Journal of the American Medical Association*, *319*, 1317–1318. Available from https://doi.org/10.1001/jama.2017.18391.

Beck, J., Greenwood, D. A., Blanton, L., Bollinger, S. T., Butcher, M. K., Condon, J. E., Cypress, M., Faulkner, P., Fischl, A. H., Francis, T., Kolb, L. E., Lavin-Tompkins, J. M., MacLeod, J., Maryniuk, M., Mensing, C., Orzeck, E. A., Pope, D. D., Pulizzi, J. L., Reed, A. A., ... Wang, J. (2017). 2017 National standards for diabetes self-management education and support. *Diabetes Care*, *40*, 1409–1419. Available from https://doi.org/10.2337/dci17-0025.

Belhadi, A., Mani, V., Kamble, S. S., Khan, S. A. R., & Verma, S. (2021). Artificial intelligence-driven innovation for enhancing supply chain resilience and performance under the effect of supply chain dynamism: an empirical investigation. *Annals Operation Research*, 1–26. Available from https://doi.org/10.1007/s10479-021-03956-x.

Bibault, J.-E., Chaix, B., Nectoux, P., Pienkowsky, A., Guillemasse, A., & Brouard, B. (2019). Healthcare ex Machina: Are conversational agents ready for prime time in oncology? *Clinical Translational Radiation Oncology*, *16*, 55–59. Available from https://doi.org/10.1016/j.ctro.2019.04.002.

Bini, S. A. (2018). Artificial intelligence, machine learning, deep learning, and cognitive computing: What do these terms mean and how will they impact health care? *The Journal of Arthroplasty*, *33*, 2358–2361. Available from https://doi.org/10.1016/j.arth.2018.02.067.

Borjali, A., Magnéli, M., Shin, D., Malchau, H., Muratoglu, O. K., & Varadarajan, K. M. (2021). Natural language processing with deep learning for medical adverse event detection from free-text medical narratives: A case study of detecting total hip replacement dislocation. *Computers in Biology and Medicine*, *129*, 104140.

Boughton, C. K., & Hovorka, R. (2019). Is an artificial pancreas (closed-loop system) for Type 1 diabetes effective? *Diabetic Medicine: A Journal of the British Diabetic Association*, *36*, 279–286. Available from https://doi.org/10.1111/dme.13816.

Cambre, J., & Kulkarni, C. (2019). One voice fits all? Social implications and research challenges of designing voices for smart devices. *Proceedings of the ACM Human-Computer Interaction*, *3*, 1–19.

Chen, M., & Decary, M. (2020). Artificial intelligence in healthcare: An essential guide for health leaders. *Healthcare Management Forum*, *33*, 10–18. Available from https://doi.org/10.1177/0840470419873123.

Ciaburro, G., & Venkateswaran, B. (2017). *Neural networks with R: Smart models using CNN. RNN, deep learning, and artificial intelligence principles*. Packt Publishing Ltd.

Coravos, A., Khozin, S., & Mandl, K. D. (2019). Developing and adopting safe and effective digital biomarkers to improve patient outcomes. *Npj Digital Medicine*, *2*, 1–5. Available from https://doi.org/10.1038/s41746-019-0090-4.

Davenport, T., & Kalakota, R. (2019). The potential for artificial intelligence in healthcare. *Future Healthcare Journal*, *6*, 94–102.

DeCamp, M., Pomerantz, D., Cotts, K., Dzeng, E., Farber, N., Lehmann, L., Reynolds, P. P., Sulmasy, L. S., & Tilburt, J. (2018). Ethical issues in the design and implementation of population health programs. *Journal of General Internal Medicine: Official Journal of the Society for Research and Education in Primary Care Internal Medicine*, *33*, 370–375. Available from https://doi.org/10.1007/s11606-017-4234-4.

Dimitrov, D. V. (2016). Medical Internet of Things and big data in healthcare. *Healthcare Informatics Research*, *22*, 156–163. Available from https://doi.org/10.4258/hir.2016.22.3.156.

Dwivedi, R., Mehrotra, D., & Chandra, S. (2022). Potential of Internet of Medical Things (IoMT) applications in building a smart healthcare system: A systematic review. *Journal Oral Biology and Craniofacial Research*, *12*, 302–318. Available from https://doi.org/10.1016/j.jobcr.2021.11.010.

Eckhardt, C. M., Madjarova, S. J., Williams, R. J., Ollivier, M., Karlsson, J., Pareek, A., & Nwachukwu, B. U. (2023). Unsupervised machine learning methods and emerging applications in healthcare. *Knee Surgery, Sports Traumatology Arthroscopy*, *31*, 376–381.

Elkateb, S., Métwalli, A., Shendy, A., & Abu-Elanien, A. E. B. (2024). Machine learning and IoT – Based predictive maintenance approach for industrial applications. *Alexandria Engineering Journal, 88*, 298–309. Available from https://doi.org/10.1016/j.aej.2023.12.065.

Escamilla-Ambrosio, P. J., Rodríguez-Mota, A., Aguirre-Anaya, E., Acosta-Bermejo., R., & Salinas-Rosales, M. (2018). *Distributing computing in the Internet of Things: Cloud, fog and edge computing overview. NEO 2016. Studies in computational intelligence* (pp. 87–116). Cham: Springer.

Esteva, A., Robicquet, A., Ramsundar, B., Kuleshov, V., DePristo, M., Chou, K., Cui, C., Corrado, G., Thrun, S., & Dean, J. (2019). A guide to deep learning in healthcare. *Nature Medicine, 25*, 24–29. Available from https://doi.org/10.1038/s41591-018-0316-z.

Ferdous, Z., Sakib, S., & Hashem, M. M. A. (2021). *Fall guardian: An intelligent fall detection and monitoring system for elderly. 5th International conference electronics information communication technology* (2021, pp. 1–6). IEEE.

Ghassemi, N., Shoeibi, A., Khodatars, M., Heras, J., Rahimi, A., Zare, A., Zhang, Y.-D., Pachori, R. B., & Gorriz, J. M. (2023). Automatic diagnosis of COVID-19 from CT images using CycleGAN and transfer learning. *Applied Soft Computing, 144*, 110511. Available from https://doi.org/10.1016/j.asoc.2023.110511.

Ghubaish, A., Salman, T., Zolanvari, M., Unal, D., Al-Ali, A., & Jain, R. (2020). Recent advances in the Internet of Medical Things (IoMT) systems security. *IEEE Internet of Things Journal.* Available from https://doi.org/10.1109/JIOT.2020.3045653.

Hassan, S. A., Khan, Q. F., Madani, A. U. R., (Eds.) (2018). *Internet of Things: Challenges, advances, and applications* (1st ed.), https://doi.org/10.4324/9781315155005.

Hayat, N., Salameh, A. A., Malik, H. A., & Yaacob, M. R. (2022). Exploring the adoption of wearable healthcare devices among the Pakistani adults with dual analysis techniques. *Technology in Society, 70*, 102015. Available from https://doi.org/10.1016/j.techsoc.2022.102015.

Idrees, A. K., Hasan, B. T., & Idrees, S. K. (2023). *Deep learning for combating COVID-19 pandemic in Internet of Medical Things (IOMT) networks: A comprehensive review. Advanced AI and Internet of Health Things for combating pandemics. Internet of Things* (p. 57) Cham: Springer.

IoMT, I. P. (2019). Closeness Factor Based Clustering Algorithm (CFBA) and Allied. *A Handbook of Internet of Things in Biomedical and Cyber Physical System, 165*, 191.

IoMT, M. T., Qureshi, F., & Krishnan, S. (2018). *Wearable hardware design for the Internet of Things.* https://doi.org/10.3390/s18113812.

Ivanović, D., Job, J., Puntarić, M., & Herceg, M. (2023). MQTT based monitoring and control system for remote stations in automotive industry. *Zooming innovation consumer technology conference, 2023*, 83–87. Available from https://doi.org/10.1109/ZINC58345.2023.10174189.

Izdihar, N., Amir, M., Dziyauddin, R. A., Mohamed, N., Syahidatul, N., Ismail, N., Kaidi, H. M., Ahmad, N., Azri, M., & Izhar, M. (2024). *Fall detection system using wearable sensor devices and machine learning: A review.* Authorea Prepr. Available from https://www.authorea.com/users/713479/articles/724275-fall-detection-system-using-wearable-sensor-devices-and-machine-learning-a-review.

Javaid, M., Haleem, A., Singh, R. P., Rab, S., Ul Haq, M. I., & Raina, A. (2022). Internet of Things in the global healthcare sector: Significance, applications, and barriers. *International Journal of Intelligent Networks., 3*, 165–175. Available from https://doi.org/10.1016/j.ijin.2022.10.002.

Jayachitra, S., Prasanth, A., Hariprasath, S., Benazir Begam, R., & Madiajagan, M. (2023). AI Enabled Internet of Medical Things in smart healthcare. In B. Bhushan, A. K. Sangaiah, & T. N. Nguyen (Eds.), *AI models for blockchain-based intelligent networks in IoT systems: Concepts, methodology tools, and applications* (pp. 141–161). Cham: Springer International Publishing. Available from https://doi.org/10.1007/978-3-031-31952-5_7.

Jiang, F., Jiang, Y., Zhi, H., Dong, Y., Li, H., Ma, S., Wang, Y., Dong, Q., Shen, H., & Wang, Y. (2017). Artificial intelligence in healthcare: Past, present and future. *Stroke and Vascular Neurology, 2*, 230–243. Available from https://doi.org/10.1136/svn-2017-000101.

Kalinaki, K., Acaru, S. F., Kugonza, J., & Nsubuga, R. (2024). *Towards an intelligent tomorrow: Machine learning enabling sustainable development*. Methodology from applied machine learning (pp. 66–89). IGI Global.

Kalinaki, K., Fahadi, M., Alli, A. A., Shafik, W., Yasin, M., & Mutwalibi, N. (2023). Artificial intelligence of Internet of Medical Things (AIoMT) in smart cities: A review of cybersecurity for smart healthcare. In: *Handbook security and private AI-enabled healthcare system Internet Medical Things* (pp. 271–292).

Kelly, C. J., Karthikesalingam, A., Suleyman, M., Corrado, G., & King, D. (2019). Key challenges for delivering clinical impact with artificial intelligence. *BMC Medicine*, *17*, 1–9. Available from https://doi.org/10.1186/s12916-019-1426-2.

Khan, A., Sohail, A., Zahoora, U., & Qureshi, A. S. (2020). A survey of the recent architectures of deep convolutional neural networks. *Artificial Intelligence Review*, *53*, 5455–5516.

khan, B., Fatima, H., Qureshi, A., Kumar, S., Hanan, A., Hussain, J., & Abdullah, S. (2023). Drawbacks of artificial intelligence and their potential solutions in the healthcare sector. *Biomedical Materials & Devices*, *1*, 731–738. Available from https://doi.org/10.1007/s44174-023-00063-2.

Khan, Z. A., Abbasi, U., & Kim, S. W. (2021). Machine learning and LPWAN based Internet of Things applications in healthcare sector during COVID-19 pandemic. *Electron*, *10*, 1–33. Available from https://doi.org/10.3390/electronics10141615.

Li, X., Dunn, J., Salins, D., Zhou, G., Zhou, W., Schüssler-Fiorenza Rose, S. M., Perelman, D., Colbert, E., Runge, R., Rego, S., Sonecha, R., Datta, S., McLaughlin, T., & Snyder, M. P. (2017). Digital health: Tracking physiomes and activity using wearable biosensors reveals useful health-related information. *PLoS Biology*, *15*, 1–30. Available from https://doi.org/10.1371/journal.pbio.2001402.

Li, Y., Richter, F., Lu, J., Funk, E. K., Orosco, R. K., Zhu, J., & Yip, M. C. (2020). Super: A surgical perception framework for endoscopic tissue manipulation with surgical robotics. *IEEE Robotics and Automation Letters*, *5*, 2294–2301. Available from https://doi.org/10.1109/LRA.2020.2970659.

Liu, J., Hu, H., Xu, W., & Luo, D. (2024). Internet of Things challenges and future scope for enhanced living environments. In G. Marques (Ed.), *Internet of Things: Architectures for enhanced living environment* (pp. 201–246). Elsevier. Available from https://doi.org/10.1016/bs.adcom.2023.10.007.

Maddox, T. M., Rumsfeld, J. S., & Payne, P. R. O. (2019). Questions for artificial intelligence in health care. *JAMA: the Journal of the American Medical Association*, *321*, 31–32.

Maleki Varnosfaderani, S., & Forouzanfar, M. (2024). The role of AI in hospitals and clinics: Transforming healthcare in the 21st century. *Bioeng. (Basel, Switzerland*, *11*. Available from https://doi.org/10.3390/bioengineering11040337.

Manickam, P., Mariappan, S. A., Murugesan, S. M., Hansda, S., Kaushik, A., Shinde, R., & Thipperudraswamy, S. P. (2022). Artificial intelligence (AI) and Internet of Medical Things (IoMT) assisted biomedical systems for intelligent healthcare. *Biosensors*, *12*. Available from https://doi.org/10.3390/bios12080562.

Manimurugan, S., Almutairi, S., Aborokbah, M. M., Narmatha, C., Ganesan, S., Chilamkurti, N., Alzaheb, R. A., & Almoamari, H. (2022). Two-stage classification model for the prediction of heart disease using IoMT and artificial intelligence. *Sensors*, *22*. Available from https://doi.org/10.3390/s22020476.

Marjani, M., Nasaruddin, F., Gani, A., Member, S., Karim, A., Abaker, I., Hashem, T., Siddiqa, A., & Yaqoob, I. (2017). Big IoT data analytics : Architecture, opportunities, and open research challenges. *IEEE Access*, *5*, 5247–5261. Available from https://doi.org/10.1109/ACCESS.2017.2689040.

Milne-Ives, M., de Cock, C., Lim, E., Shehadeh, M. H., de Pennington, N., Mole, G., Normando, E., & Meinert, E. (2020). The effectiveness of artificial intelligence conversational agents in health care: Systematic review. *Journal of Medical Internet Research*, *22*, e20346. Available from https://doi.org/10.2196/20346.

Miner, A. S., Milstein, A., & Hancock, J. T. (2017). Talking to machines about personal mental health problems. *JAMA: the Journal of the American Medical Association*, *318*, 1217–1218. Available from https://doi.org/10.1001/jama.2017.14151.

Orlov, L.M. (2011). Technology for aging in place 2011.

Parthasarathy, R., & Rajendran, V. D. (2016). A review: big data analytics in health care. *Indian Journal of Engineering an International Journal, 13.*

Peyroteo, M., Ferreira, I. A., Elvas, L. B., Ferreira, J. C., & Lapão, L. V. (2021). Remote monitoring systems for patients with chronic diseases in primary health care: Systematic review. *JMIR MHealth UHealth, 9,* e28285. Available from https://doi.org/10.2196/28285.

Radanliev, P., De Roure, D. C., Nicolescu, R., Huth, M., Montalvo, R. M., Cannady, S., & Burnap, P. (2018). Future developments in cyber risk assessment for the Internet of Things. *Computers in Industry, 102,* 14–22. Available from https://doi.org/10.1016/j.compind.2018.08.002.

Raheem, F., & Iqbal,N. (2022). Artificial intelligence and machine learning for the industrial Internet of Things (IIoT). https://doi.org/10.1201/9781003145004-1.

Rajkomar, A., Dean, J., & Kohane, I. S. (2019). Machine learning in medicine. *The New England Journal of Medicine, 380,* 1347–1358. Available from https://api.semanticscholar.org/CorpusID:92996321.

Rashidi, H. H., Tran, N., Albahra, S., & Dang, L. T. (2021). Machine learning in health care and laboratory medicine: General overview of supervised learning and Auto-ML. *International Journal of Laboratory Hematology, 43,* 15–22.

Ray, P. P. (2018). A survey on Internet of Things architectures. *Journal of King Saud University - Computer and Information Sciences., 30,* 291–319. Available from https://doi.org/10.1016/j.jksuci.2016.10.003.

Razdan, S., & Sharma, S. (2022). Internet of Medical Things (IoMT): Overview, emerging technologies, and case studies. *IETE Technical Review (Institution of Electronics and Telecommunication Engineers India)., 39,* 775–788. Available from https://doi.org/10.1080/02564602.2021.1927863.

Rivero-Moreno, Y., Echevarria, S., Vidal-Valderrama, C., Pianetti, L., Cordova-Guilarte, J., Navarro-Gonzalez, J., Acevedo-Rodríguez, J., Dorado-Avila, G., Osorio-Romero, L., Chavez-Campos, C., & Acero-Alvarracín, K. (2023). Robotic surgery: A comprehensive review of the literature and current trends. *Cureus, 15,* e42370. Available from https://doi.org/10.7759/cureus.42370.

Roy, S., Meena, T., & Lim, S.-J. (2022). Demystifying supervised learning in healthcare 4.0: A new reality of transforming diagnostic medicine. *Diagnostics, 12,* 2549.

Sim, J., Huang, X., Horan, M. R., Stewart, C. M., Robison, L. L., Hudson, M. M., Baker, J. N., & Huang, I.-C. (2023). Natural language processing with machine learning methods to analyze unstructured patient-reported outcomes derived from electronic health records: A systematic review. *Artificial Intelligence in Medicine,* 102701.

Singh, A. K., Sharma, A., Kumar Singh, P., Kesarwani, S., & Singh, A. P. (2024). *Internet of Things and sensor networks in Industry 5.0: Connecting devices and machines. Emerging technology digital manufacturing smart factories* (pp. 67–78). IGI Global.

Singh, B., & Kaunert, C. (2024). *Aroma of highly smart Internet of Medical Things (IoMT) and lightweight edge trust expansion medical care facilities for electronic healthcare systems: Fortified-chain architecture for remote patient monitoring and privacy protection beyond imagination. Lightweight digital trust architectures. Internet of Medical Things* (pp. 196–212). IGI Global.

Singh, B., Sharma, S., & Jain, A. (2023). Internet of things (IoT) in health care—-A review. In D. K. Yadav, & A. Gulati (Eds.), *Artificial intelligence machine learning and healthcare* (pp. 65–78). Singapore: Springer Nature Singapore. Available from https://doi.org/10.1007/978-981-99-6472-7_5.

Thandapani, S., Mahaboob, M. I., Iwendi, C., Selvaraj, D., Dumka, A., Rashid, M., & Mohan, S. (2023). IoMT with deep CNN: AI-based intelligent support system for pandemic diseases. *Electronics, 12,* 424.

Topol, E. J. (2019). High-performance medicine: the convergence of human and artificial intelligence. *Nature Medicine, 25,* 44–56. Available from https://doi.org/10.1038/s41591-018-0300-7.

Turabieh, H., Abu Salem, A., & Abu-El-Rub, N. (2018). Dynamic L-RNN recovery of missing data in IoMT applications. *Future Generation Computer Systems, 89,* 575–583. Available from https://doi.org/10.1016/j.future.2018.07.006.

Vaccari, I., Orani, V., Paglialonga, A., Cambiaso, E., & Mongelli, M. (2021). A generative adversarial network (GAN) technique for Internet of Medical Things data. *Sensors*, *21*, 3726.

Verdejo Espinosa, A., Lopez, J. L., Mata Mata, F., & Estevez, M. E. (2021). Application of IoT in healthcare: keys to implementation of the sustainable development goals. *Sensors*, *21*(7), 2330.

Vettoretti, M., Cappon, G., Facchinetti, A., & Sparacino, G. (2020). Advanced diabetes management using artificial intelligence and continuous glucose monitoring sensors. *Sensors*, *20*, 3870.

Wang, J., Jin, H., Chen, J., Tan, J., & Zhong, K. (2022). Anomaly detection in Internet of Medical Things with blockchain from the perspective of deep neural network. *Information Sciences*, *617*, 133–149. Available from https://doi.org/10.1016/j.ins.2022.10.060.

Wang, Y., Kung, L., & Byrd, T. A. (2018). Big data analytics: Understanding its capabilities and potential benefits for healthcare organizations. *Technological Forecasting and Social Change*, *126*, 3–13. Available from https://doi.org/10.1016/j.techfore.2015.12.019.

Webster, J. G. (2009). *Medical instrumentation: application and design*. John Wiley & Sons.

Yalamati, S. (2024). *Data privacy, compliance, and security in cloud computing for finance. Practical applied data processing algorithms, model* (pp. 127–144). IGI Global.

Yang, P., & Xu, L. (2018). The Internet of Things (IoT): Informatics methods for IoT-enabled health care. *Journal of Biomedical Informatics*, *87*, 154–156. Available from https://doi.org/10.1016/j.jbi.2018.10.006.

Yu, C., Liu, J., Nemati, S., & Yin, G. (2021). Reinforcement learning in healthcare: A survey. *ACM Computing Survey*, *55*, 1–36.

Zanella, A., Bui, N., Castellani, A., Vangelista, L., & Zorzi, M. (2014). Internet of Things for smart cities. *IEEE Internet Things Journal*, *1*, 22–32. Available from https://doi.org/10.1109/JIOT.2014.2306328.

Zhang, P., & Kamel Boulos, M. N. (2023). Generative AI in medicine and healthcare: Promises, opportunities and challenges. *Future Internet*, *15*, 286.

Zhao, P., Yoo, I., & Naqvi, S. H. (2021). Early prediction of unplanned 30-day hospital readmission: model development and retrospective data analysis. *JMIR Medical Informatics*, *9*, e16306.

Zhao, R., Yan, R., Chen, Z., Mao, K., Wang, P., & Gao, R. X. (2019). Deep learning and its applications to machine health monitoring. *Mechanical Systems and Signal Processing*, *115*, 213–237. Available from https://doi.org/10.1016/j.ymssp.2018.05.050.

Zhou,C., & Paffenroth,R.C. (2017). Anomaly detection with robust deep autoencoders. In: *Proceedings of the 23rd ACM SIGKDD international conference on knowledge discovery and data mining* (pp. 665–674). Association for Computing Machinery, New York, NY, USA. https://doi.org/10.1145/3097983.3098052.

Zou, F.-W., Tang, Y.-F., Liu, C.-Y., Ma, J.-A., & Hu, C.-H. (2020). Concordance study between IBM Watson for oncology and real clinical practice for cervical cancer patients in China: A retrospective analysis. *Frontiers in Genetics*, *11*, 200. Available from https://doi.org/10.3389/fgene.2020.00200.

CHAPTER

Transforming healthcare with blockchain and digital twins: innovations in IoMT for smart hospitals

24

Swati Arya[1], Shruti Aggarwal[2] and Syed Anas Ansar[1]

[1]Department of Computer Applications, Babu Banarasi Das University, Lucknow, Uttar Pradesh, India [2]Department of Computer Science and Engineering, Thapar Institute of Engineering and Technology, Patiala, Punjab, India

24.1 Introduction

Internet of Medical Things (IoMT) has revolutionized the healthcare domain; it ensures a seamless connection and data sharing among medical devices and systems to improve patient outcomes and operational efficiencies in intelligent hospitals. IoMT represents a network of medical devices and applications that can communicate with online computer networks connecting healthcare IT systems (Lodha et al., 2023). In this regard, some researchers consider this network the most significant prerequisite for building smart hospitals that work on cutting-edge technologies in health care provision. Recently, blockchain technology has emerged as an enabler for solutions to critical challenges in the health sector, such as data security, privacy, and interoperability (Samantasinghar et al., 2023). Its immutable and decentralized ledger provides a safe foundation for the administration of sensitive patient data, preventing tampering and limiting access to only authorized parties. This becomes especially crucial when you take into account the vast amounts of data that are continuously generated and shared inside IoMT systems.

Parallelly, digital twins—being virtual models of a physical object—have started to attract growing interest in the healthcare sector to simulate and monitor medical devices and systems, and even the health condition of a patient in real time (Vasiliu-Feltes et al., 2023). Digital twins, which are digital copies of actual objects, provide predictive maintenance, personalized treatment planning, and efficient resource management. Integrating digital twins with IoMT provides the path for precision and data-driven health solutions, resulting in optimal patient care and operational efficiencies.

As personalized medicine and precision health become more prevalent, it would be envisaged that the combination of blockchain technology with digital twins would lead to advancements in healthcare results (Kshetri et al., 2023). By facilitating a transparent and reliable data interchange and storage environment, blockchain technology can improve the dependability and security of digital twins. This guarantees integrity and immutability in the quality of health services through data use in digital twin simulations. Smart hospitals exemplify the use of advanced technologies to create a lean and patient-centric healthcare environment, hence standing to reap huge benefits when

Blockchain and Digital Twin for Smart Hospitals. DOI: https://doi.org/10.1016/B978-0-443-34226-4.00025-3

IoMT brings blockchain and digital twins together (Eltabakh et al., 2023). These technologies offer a practical response to problems pertaining to data management, security, and interoperability in intelligent hospitals, which will ultimately improve patient outcomes and streamline operations. This chapter delves into the potential synergies between blockchain and digital twins and their transformative impacts in the IoMT context within intelligent hospitals. Technological architecture, real application scenarios, and case studies will be undertaken to fully understand how the technologies could revolutionize health care. Further, challenges and proposed solutions are discussed, facilitating a seamless integration of blockchain and digital twins in intelligent hospitals.

24.2 Understanding the core technologies

24.2.1 Blockchain technology

While initially, blockchain technology aimed to provide only a base for cryptocurrencies, in just a couple of years, it evolved into a generic framework for securing and managing data in any field, including healthcare (Singh et al., 2023). At the crux of the definition, a blockchain is a decentralized record-keeping technology that maintains a record of transactions on many different computers while making sure that once such a transaction has been entered, it cannot change retroactively without the alteration of all subsequent blocks and gaining consensus of the network. Every transaction is recorded inside a block and linked one to another in a chain. Once added, the records become fixed, giving a clear history of transactions that cannot be tampered with. Table 24.1 presents a comparative examination of the benefits of blockchain in the healthcare industry.

Table 24.1 Comparative analysis of blockchain benefits in healthcare.

Benefit	Description	Real-world application	Impact
Security	Utilizes cryptographic techniques for data protection that prevent such data from being accessed by unauthorized individuals	Secure EHR sharing between hospitals (Sonkamble et al., 2023)	Reduces data breaches and enhances trust
Transparency	Provides a transparent history of transactions, ensuring all data is traceable and auditable	Pharmaceutical supply chain tracking (Akram et al., 2024)	Prevents counterfeit drugs
Immutability	Ensures that once data is recorded, it cannot be altered or deleted	Patient records management (Zakzouk et al., 2023)	Maintains integrity of patient data
Interoperability	Facilitates standardized and secure data sharing across different systems and entities	Integration of disparate healthcare systems (Rasel et al., 2023)	Enhances care coordination
Smart contracts	Self-executing contracts with terms directly written into code, automatically enforcing and executing agreements	Automated insurance claims processing (Karmakar et al., 2023)	Reduces administrative overhead
Cost efficiency	Reduces the need for intermediaries, lowering transaction costs	Direct payment processing (Gahlyan et al., 2023)	Lowers operational costs

24.2.2 Digital twins

A digital twin, in general, is a virtual copy of a physical object, system, or process, which reflects its real-world counterpart using real-time data (Vallée, 2023). This may be done with sensors and IoT devices added for modeling what the physical entity represents to simulate, predict, and optimize its performance. A digital replica will help with predictive maintenance, customization treatment, and resource management. In the future smart hospital, hospital digital twin might be the bridge between the real and virtual hospital. Hospital digital twin also could be the mirror that reflects the real hospital into the virtual hospital (Nguyen, 2023, 2024). Table 24.2 depicts the applications of digital twins in healthcare.

Table 24.2 Applications of digital twins in healthcare.

Application	Description	Example	Impact
Real-time monitoring	Continuous monitoring and analysis of patient health and medical devices	Remote patient monitoring systems (Aluvalu et al., 2023)	Improves patient outcomes
Predictive maintenance	Predicts failures in medical equipment, allowing for proactive maintenance and reduced downtime	Hospital equipment maintenance schedules (Gallab et al., 2024)	Enhances operational efficiency
Simulation	Simulates various scenarios to optimize hospital operations and resource allocation	Emergency response planning (Zio & Miqueles, 2024)	Improves resource management
Personalized healthcare	Creates personalized models of patients for tailored treatment plans and real-time intervention	Personalized medicine (Vallée, 2024)	Enhances treatment effectiveness

24.3 Integration of blockchain and digital twins in IoMT

24.3.1 Synergies between blockchain and digital twins

Blockchain technology dramatically enhances the potential functionality of digital twins, as it provides a very secure and transparent framework for data management (Jain et al., 2024). The immutability of the blockchain guarantees that all that is fed into the digital twin is tamper-proof and accurate. Such security is of necessity in healthcare, among other industries, where data integrity and patient privacy are priorities.

- *Data integrity:* The decentralized ledger of a blockchain gives assurance that data upon which the digital twins work cannot be tampered with and guarantees high fidelity in the simulation and analysis.
- *Security and privacy:* Blockchain has access control and strong encryption to users, thus ensuring the protection of sensitive patient information while ensuring that all regulatory

requirements for healthcare data are complied with, like Health Insurance Portability and Accountability Act (HIPAA) and the General Data Protection Regulation (GDPR).
- *Interoperability*: Blockchain ensures data interoperability in any healthcare system and IoMT devices, hence promoting the interoperability and functionality of the digital twins.

24.3.2 Technical architecture

Digital twin for IoMT with proposed blockchain integration architecture has some of the most critical components and their interactions, depicted in Fig. 24.1 The diagram outlines the interactions between sensors in the IoMT, the blockchain network, models of digital twins, storage of data, processing units, and user interfaces.

24.3.2.1 Components and their interactions

- *IoMT sensors:* The elemental things that collect data from the physical world. These may involve sensors for medical devices carried by the patient, environmental monitors, vital signs, equipment status, and environmental conditions. Data collected is then encrypted and sent to the blockchain network for safe storage.
- *Blockchain network:* A blockchain is a decentralized, secure ledger for all IoMT data. It guarantees the immutability of the data and allows data access only by authorized personnel. Each data entry is time-stamped and linked to the previous one, providing a solid audit log.

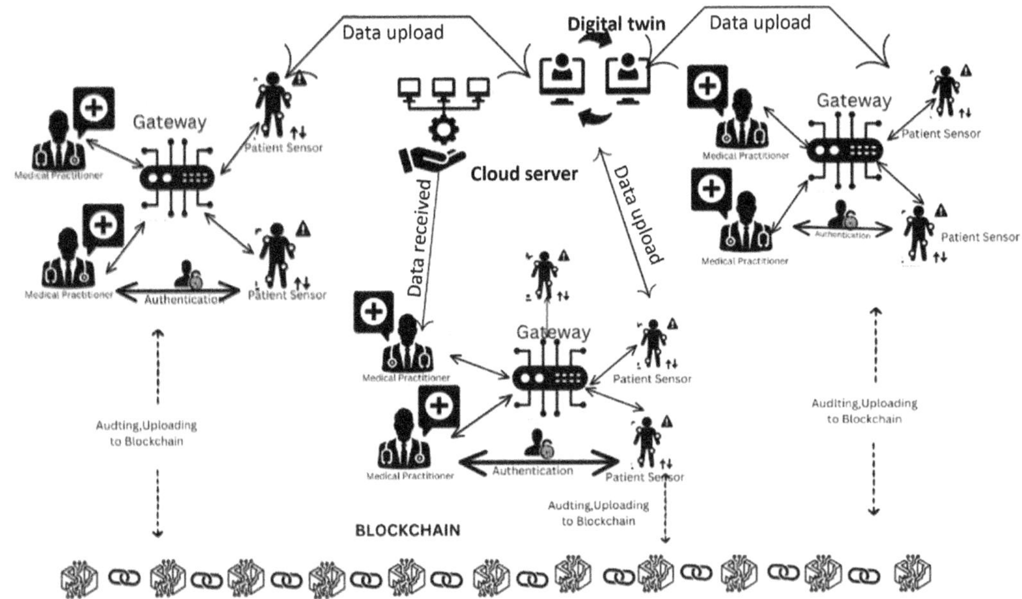

FIGURE 24.1

System architecture for integrating blockchain with digital twins in IoMT.

- *Digital twin models:* Based on the secure blockchain data, derive real-time simulations about physical entities and predict outcomes, identify anomalies, and get insights into the current state and future performances of patients and medical devices.
- *Data storage:* This additional storage service stores raw and processed data. It interacts with the blockchain to establish data integrity and with digital twins to update simulations with the latest data.
- *Processing units:* Computational resources that help in processing IoMT data and simulating the digital twins. Such units analyze the data to derive insights from it, which would be sent back to both the digital twin models and user interfaces.
- *User interfaces:* This interface allows healthcare providers to navigate digital twin models and get data stored in blockchain platforms. They provide real-time visualization, alerts, and recommendations that help the health practitioner make decisions and support patient care.

In this case, an integrated architecture of the proposed approach enables seamless data flow from the IoMT devices to the blockchain and further on to the digital twins, hence creating a compelling framework in support of advanced healthcare solutions in intelligent hospitals.

24.4 Benefits of integration

Integrating blockchain and digital twin technologies into the IoMT framework for smart hospitals has numerous benefits. These benefits include improved methods of healthcare delivery in terms of data security, operational efficiency, and patient care tailored to individual patients. These are displayed in Table 24.3, which highlights some specific contributions from blockchain and digital twins while also illustrating overall impacts on health outcomes.

24.4.1 Enhanced data security and privacy

Blockchain is one of the most efficient technologies that can be used to guarantee the security of patient data. Through cryptographic methods, blockchain ensures that once the data is written, it cannot be changed or deleted (El Azzaoui et al., 2021). In addition, it is tamper-proof and thus secure. Decentralized management by blockchain significantly reduces potential exposures to data breaches and unauthorized access. This approach also ensures more control over patients' data; hence, more privacy and compliance with the data protection regulations.

24.4.2 Improved data accuracy and reliability

Blockchain is an assurance of real-time data validation, a key ingredient to maintaining accuracy and reliability in records management within healthcare (Akash & Ferdous, 2022). Each transaction on the blockchain is validated by many nodes before being recorded, guaranteeing that only confirmed data enters the ledger. To generate simulations and predictions, digital twins require accurate and reliable data. By using blockchain, digital twins can employ tamper-proof data to ensure that their simulations and predictions are based on accurate information.

Table 24.3 Key benefits of integrating blockchain and digital twins in IoMT.

Benefit category	Description	Role of blockchain	Role of digital twins	Impact and outcome
Enhanced data security and privacy	- Ensures data integrity and security - Reduces risk of data breaches	- Secures patient data through cryptographic techniques - Decentralized data management enhances privacy (Lodha et al., 2023)	Utilizes secure data for accurate simulations and predictions (Kshetri et al., 2023)	- Protects sensitive patient information - Complies with data protection regulations
Improved data accuracy and reliability	- Validates data in real time - Ensures reliable simulations	Real-time data validation through consensus mechanisms (Vasiliu-Feltes et al., 2023)	Accurate and tamper-proof data for reliable simulations and predictions (Kshetri et al., 2023)	- Eliminates errors and inconsistencies - Enhances the reliability of patient data and medical records
Operational efficiency	- Streamlines hospital operations - Enables predictive maintenance	- Automates processes through smart contracts (Samantasinghar et al., 2023) - Tracks medical equipment and supplies (Eltabakh et al., 2023)	Predicts maintenance needs and reduces downtime (Singh et al., 2023)	- Optimizes patient monitoring and asset management - Enhances operational efficiency and reduces costs
Patient-centric care	- Enables personalized treatment plans - Continuous monitoring and feedback	Provides secure access to accurate patient data for personalization (Sonkamble et al., 2023)	Models patients for tailored treatment plans and real-time intervention (Akram et al., 2024)	- Improves patient outcomes - Provides timely interventions and enhances the precision of medical treatments

24.4.3 Operational efficiency

The union of blockchain and digital twins will significantly improve operations in hospitals by providing real-time data and automation. Continuous data collection and analysis for monitoring of patients will be used to respond in time in case of any change in a patient's situation (Lu et al., 2021). Digital twins can predict when equipment will fail so that there is ample time to organize maintenance, thus reducing downtime proactively. Digital twins, with the help of blockchain-stored data, ensure that all predictions about maintenance are based on correct and immutable records.

24.4.4 Patient-centric care

This provides an opportunity for creating personalized models of patients with digital twins that will help develop treatment matched to their real-time health data. In addition, integration with blockchain allows these models access to secure and accurate patient data to ensure the treatment plans are current and precise (Jabarulla & Lee, 2021). Monitoring through constant feedback can be an important part of patient-centered treatment. Health data acquired in real time by IoMT devices is securely saved on the blockchain and used by the digital twin to continuously monitor the patient's status. This allows healthcare providers to quickly change treatment plans, resulting in timely intervention and improved patient results.

24.5 Case studies and real-world applications

24.5.1 Case study 1: implementation of blockchain and digital twins in a smart hospital

24.5.1.1 Scenario

The smart hospital also leads in several other technology adoptions that will bring improvements to its operational efficiencies and patient care, such as blockchain and digital twin technologies.

24.5.1.1.1 Implementation

- *Blockchain:* The hospital uses blockchain to store and secure patient data to maintain the integrity and privacy of data. Every action undertaken on the patient records is traced in blockchain, which is transparent with an unchangeable audit trail.
- *Digital twins:* Real-time information from IoMT devices is used to simulate and monitor the hospital environment in modeling digital twins of the hospital infrastructure, medical equipment, and patients.
- *Integration:* The data that feeds into the digital twin is kept secure and tamper-proof due to the blockchain network. Intelligent contracts are involved in processes relating to patient admission, discharge, and billing—reduced manual intervention of resources (Hakim et al., 2023).

24.5.1.1.2 Outcome

- *Operational efficiency:* The hospital derives streamlined operations via automated workflows and minimized administrative overhead.
- *Enhanced patient care:* Real-time monitoring and predictive analytics developed by digital twins result in timely interventions and personalized treatment plans.
- *Data security:* Patients' data is also secured using blockchain technology and is compliant with data protection regulations.

24.5.2 Case study 2: IoMT devices and blockchain integration for remote patient monitoring

24.5.2.1 Scenario

A healthcare provider aims to improve the monitoring and management of chronic disease patients remotely using IoMT devices and blockchain technology.

24.5.2.1.1 Implementation

- *IoMT devices*: Patients are given prescriptions for wearable IoMT devices that continuously check their vital signs like heart rate, blood pressure, and glucose levels.
- *Blockchain:* Data created from these devices is transferred to a blockchain network, with maximum security for immutability. The data can be further ensured that it is correct and only shared with designated healthcare providers.
- *Digital twins:* Digital twins of patients are created by taking the data from IoMT devices, and by simulating the health conditions of a patient, future probable health issues are predicted (Lu et al., 2023).

24.5.2.1.2 Outcome

- *Continuous monitoring*: Patients' health is always monitored, thus any potential health concern is easily discovered in time.
- *Improved patient outcomes*: Real-time data and predictive analytics enable healthcare practitioners to tailor care to people as needed, resulting in better patient outcomes.
- *Data privacy and security*: Blockchain ensures that patient data is kept private and secure, building trust between patients and healthcare providers.

24.5.3 Case study 3: predictive analytics and digital twins in managing hospital resources

24.5.3.1 Scenario

A large hospital network aims to optimize its resource management and reduce operational costs by leveraging predictive analytics and digital twin technology.

24.5.3.1.1 Implementation

- *Digital twins:* Medical staff, facilities, and equipment are the resources that these are designed for in hospitals. These are conducted by utilizing IoMT sensor data to monitor the conditions and utilization of resources.
- *Predictive analytics:* Sophisticated analytics algorithms analyze data from digital twins to predict equipment failures, resource shortages, and other operational issues.
- *Blockchain*: Should be adopted since it ensures the security and accuracy of predictive analytics data, besides being a trusted source of information (Ahmann et al., 2022).

24.5.3.1.2 Outcome

- *Resource optimization:* The hospital network manages the resources effectively by predicting and handling unwanted situations in advance.
- *Cost reduction:* Proactive maintenance and adequate management of resources will result in substantial cost reductions.
- *Enhanced operational efficiency:* Merging predictive analytics and digital twins aids in bettering the hospital's operational effectiveness by eliminating downtime and improving service delivery.

24.6 Challenges and solutions

24.6.1 Technical challenges

24.6.1.1 Scalability issues

A significant concern in integrating blockchain and digital twins into smart hospitals is scalability. Blockchain networks may be limited in transaction throughput and latency, particularly with the increasing amount of IoMT data. The ability to process high volumes of real-time data deriving from multiple devices of the IoMT type and digital twins can overload the network with a slowing of transaction time and a fall in efficiency (Hemdan et al., 2023).

24.6.1.2 Interoperability between different systems

Another major challenge is the interoperability of health systems, including heterogeneities in technologies and applied standards. The interfacing complexity for seamless communication and data interoperability between IoMT devices, digital twins, blockchain networks, and current healthcare IT systems is thus a significant challenge. In effect, the incompatibility of data formats, protocols, and communication interfaces all too often constrains effective integration and use of such technologies.

24.6.2 Regulatory and compliance issues

24.6.2.1 Compliance with healthcare regulations (HIPAA, GDPR)

Healthcare is among the most heavily regulated industries, which adheres to requirements for privacy and security of data to the letter. It must keep in line with regulations like the HIPAA in the United States and the GDPR in Europe. Such regulations insist on ensuring patient data is protected by putting in place stringent security measures and controls that bar unauthorized access to ensure privacy (Saeed et al., 2024).

24.6.2.2 Data ownership and consent management

Data ownership and consent management are the most significant challenges associated with healthcare. Patients should be able to control personal health information by providing and retracting data-sharing consent. Being able to effectively manage consent in such decentralized environments, like a blockchain network, only adds one more dimension of complexity in ensuring that patient data is used ethically and in compliance with legal requirements.

24.6.3 Proposed solutions

24.6.3.1 Emerging standards and protocols

To address with such scalability and interoperability challenges, new emerging standards and protocols are the way. In particular, sidechains and state channels are the layer two approaches that promise superior performance by moving transactions off the chain, thereby offloading the main chain. The interoperability of different blockchain technologies can be improved using widely adopted standards in data formats and communication protocols (such as Fast Healthcare Interoperability Resources) and allowing smooth data exchange between heterogeneous systems.

24.6.3.2 Collaboration between stakeholders

Effective integration of blockchain and digital twins in healthcare is thus one that needs cooperation between healthcare providers, technology developers, and regulators. Stakeholders need to act in close correspondence with the frameworks and guidelines in place to ensure compliance with healthcare regulations, underpinned by the benefits that these technologies offer. This includes:

- *Joint development initiatives:* Collaboration-oriented projects involving various players can facilitate the best-suited solutions, which are the most acceptable and adopted. Such initiatives would be directed at developing interoperable systems, standardized protocols, and scalable blockchain solutions.
- *Regulatory sandboxes:* It would be a controlled environment where new technologies can operate, including collaborations with regulators. The very presence of regulatory sandboxes will give room for blockchain and DT solutions in health to experiment and be refined toward the meeting of regulatory requirements before being widely implemented.
- *Education and training:* Sensitizing stakeholders to the benefits and drawbacks of blockchain technology and digital twins in healthcare is crucial. Such training programs would ensure that healthcare providers and regulators are familiar with the actual application and management techniques of these technologies.

24.7 Future trends and developments

24.7.1 Advancements in blockchain technology

24.7.1.1 Emerging trends in blockchain

As blockchain technology advances, numerous developing developments are expected to enhance its capabilities and uses in the healthcare domain:

- *Quantum-resistant blockchains:* Traditional cryptographic algorithms in use in blockchain may be rendered penetrable with the advent of quantum computing. It is being developed to withstand the computational power of quantum computers to ensure long-term security and integrity in healthcare data (Thanalakshmi et al., 2023).
- *Interoperable blockchains:* There is an attempt in the direction to build interoperable blockchain networks that will be able to communicate and share data among themselves without any hindrances. This is of immense relevance in health care, as this is an area wherein information has to be transmitted between different organizations on different platforms transparently without jeopardizing data (Wang et al., 2023).
- *Scalable solutions*: The scalability of blockchain networks can be enhanced by layer 2 scaling techniques like sidechains and off-chain transactions. By lowering latency and boosting transaction throughput, these should improve blockchain's suitability for real-time healthcare applications.

24.7.1.2 Potential impact on healthcare

The general advantages that have the potential to impact healthcare are these new advancements in blockchain technology:

- *Enhancing data security and privacy:* Quantum-resistant and interoperable blockchains will ensure the security and privacy of patient data, even in a technology-changed world.
- *Improving data sharing and interoperability:* Interoperable blockchains will help overcome data sharing to ensure care coordination among health service providers and hence enhance patient outcomes.
- *Enabling real-time applications:* Real-time healthcare applications such as remote patient monitoring and predictive analytics will be supported by scalable blockchain solutions, which will add to the effectiveness of healthcare systems.

24.7.2 Evolution of digital twins

24.7.2.1 Advances in digital twin technology

Digital twin is an emerging technology, and new capabilities and applications for health care and other industry segments are quickly coming to the fore.

- *High-fidelity simulations:* Advancements in data analytics and computational modeling brought in the era where high-fidelity digital twins could be developed to run complex biological system simulations with higher precision (Du et al., 2024).
- *Integration with IoMT:* IoMT devices are rapidly being connected with digital twins to provide real-time data collecting and processing. Digital twin models get more accurate and reliable with integration (Rezaee et al., 2023).
- *Personalized medicine:* Using digital twins, it is possible to model specific individuals to create individualized treatment regimens and more accurate medical interventions.

24.7.2.2 Future applications in healthcare

The possible implementations of digital twin technology in healthcare for the future are vast and diverse, some of which include:

- *Personalized treatment plans:* Digital twins would enable the development of personalized treatment plans based on real-time IoMT data, resulting in better patient outcomes and lower healthcare costs.
- *Predictive maintenance of medical equipment:* Digital Twins can predict the moment when medical equipment is likely to fail and thereby allow proactive maintenance to be done to minimize downtime.
- *Operational efficiency:* Digital twins of hospital infrastructure and operations can help optimize resource allocation, patient flow, and overall operational efficiency within the healthcare facility.

24.7.3 Emerging IoMT innovations

24.7.3.1 New IoMT devices and their potential uses

The IoMT landscape is constantly changing with the inclusion of new devices and technologies that can change the face of health care.

- *Wearable health monitors:* Advanced wearable devices for continuous monitoring of various vital signs, activity levels, and other health metrics will relay real-time health information to healthcare providers.
- *Smart implants:* The era of sensorized implantable devices capable of monitoring and managing chronic conditions—be they related to heart disease or diabetes—from the inside of the body.
- *Remote diagnostic tools:* Portable diagnostic devices can carry out tests and analyses away from the patient. This is essential in obtaining a diagnosis and effective treatment on time in areas with the lowest possible medical services.

24.7.3.2 Integration with AI and machine learning for advanced analytics

Stated differently, new avenues for analytics in healthcare are being opened by the combination of IoMT devices with AI and machine learning.

- *Predictive analytics*: AI systems can analyze IoMT device data to discover possible problems before they become more serious and to forecast health outcomes. This can help in offering the right interventions early and yield better patient outcomes.
- *Automated decision support*: Machine learning models assist in making real-time decisions and recommendations for health care providers based on big data sets.
- *Personalized healthcare*: With AI analyzing the data from digital twins and IoMT devices, personalized healthcare plans can be developed in an exacting manner that will respond to a patient's unique needs, increasing the efficacy of treatments and cutting costs.

These advances in blockchain, digital twins, and IoMT devices, all integrated with AI and machine learning, will transform health into an efficient, individual, and secure organization.

24.8 Conclusion

The integration of blockchain with digital twins in the IoMT framework would contribute a lot to transforming smart hospitals. It will couple blockchain's strengths for ensuring data security, transparency, and interoperability with real-time simulation and predictive digital twins for innovative hospitals and, in the end, result in efficient operations, patient care, and data management in those hospitals. This chapter discusses how such technologies, applied through case studies and real-world applications, can improve data security, accuracy, and reliability, reduce hospital operations, and promote a patient-centered model of care. However, there are downsides to this in the form of scalability issues, interoperability, and conformance with regulation. All are being actively addressed through new standards, protocols, and cooperative efforts among health deliverers, technology developers, and regulators. In a similar vein, upcoming years will witness quantum-resistant blockchains and interoperable networks alongside the evolution of high-fidelity digital twins and

AI-driven IoMT innovations that will drive industry transformation. Aligning these technologies into harmony will allow much more intelligent, more efficient, and more focused healthcare systems for patients. In essence, the integration of blockchain in digital twins within the IoMT ecosystem provides enormous potential for intelligent hospitals to enable health results and foster innovation, despite existing challenges.

References

Ahmann, M., Benedikt, M., Pahl, C., & El Ioini, N. (2022). *Blockchain powered QA process management for digital twins. 2022 6th international conference on system reliability and safety (ICSRS)* (pp. 371–377). IEEE.

Akash, S. S., & Ferdous, M. S. (2022). A blockchain based system for healthcare digital twin. *IEEE Access*, *10*, 50523–50547.

Akram, W., Joshi, R., Haider, T., Sharma, P., Jain, V., Garud, N., & Narwaria, N. S. (2024). Blockchain technology: A potential tool for the management of pharma supply chain. *Research in Social and Administrative Pharmacy*.

Aluvalu, R., Mudrakola, S., Kaladevi, A. C., Sandhya, M. V. S., & Bhat, C. R. (2023). The novel emergency hospital services for patients using digital twins. *Microprocessors and Microsystems*, *98*, 104794.

Du, J., Qin, Z., Cai, X., Peng, J., Li, C., & Tai, Y. (2024). Toward Immersive and Interactive surgical training using extended reality simulator for IoMT. *International Journal of Human–Computer Interaction*, 1–18.

El Azzaoui, A., Kim, T. W., Loia, V., & Park, J. H. (2021). *Blockchain-based secure digital twin framework for smart healthy city. In advanced multimedia and ubiquitous engineering: MUE-FutureTech 2020* (pp. 107–113). Singapore: Springer.

Eltabakh, M., Nasr, M., Abdelrahman, E., & Abdelfatah, R. (2023). Blockchain for healthcare systems: Concepts, applications, challenges, and future trends. *Engineering Research Journal*. Available from https://doi.org/10.21608/erjeng.2023.227863.1207.

Gahlyan, M., Mohan, B., Kumar, V., & Mistrean, L. (2023). Block chain based identification and authorization, hospital billing along with insurance claim management. *In International Applied Social Sciences Congress*, 407–419.

Gallab, M., Ahidar, I., Zrira, N., & Ngote, N. (2024). Towards a digital predictive maintenance (DPM): Healthcare case study. *Procedia Computer Science*, *232*, 3183–3194.

Hakim, O. S., Zainuddin, M. A., Sukaridhoto, S., & Prayudi, A. (2023). Digital twin and blockchain extension in smart buildings platform as cyber-physical systems. *JUITA: Jurnal Informatika*, *11*(2), 175–183.

Hemdan, E. E. D., El-Shafai, W., & Sayed, A. (2023). Integrating digital twins with IoT-based blockchain: Concept, architecture, challenges, and future scope. *Wireless Personal Communications*, *131*(3), 2193–2216.

Jabarulla, M. Y., & Lee, H. N. (2021). A blockchain and artificial intelligence-based, patient-centric healthcare system for combating the COVID-19 pandemic: Opportunities and applications. *Healthcare*, *9*(8), 1019, Mdpi.

Jain, A., Garg, M., Gupta, A., Batra, S., & Narwal, B. (2024). Iomt-badt: a blockchain-envisioned secure architecture with a lightweight authentication scheme for the digital twin environment in the internet of medical things. *The Journal of Supercomputing*, 1–32.

Karmakar, A., Ghosh, P., Banerjee, P. S., & De, D. (2023). ChainSure: Agent free insurance system using blockchain for healthcare 4.0. *Intelligent Systems with Applications*, *17*, 200177.

Kshetri, N., Hutson, J., & Revathy, G. (2023). *HealthAIChain: Improving security and safety using blockchain technology applications in AI-based healthcare systems*. IEEE ICIMIA. Available from https://doi.org/10.1109/ICIMIA60377.2023.10426362.

Lodha, L., Baghela, V. D. S., Bhuvana, J., & Bhatt, R. (2023). A blockchain-based secured system using the internet of medical things (IoMT) network for e-healthcare monitoring. *Measurement: Sensors*. Available from https://doi.org/10.1016/j.measen.2023.100904.

Lu, Q., Chen, L., Xie, X., Fang, Z., Ye, Z., & Pitt, M. (2023). Framing blockchain-integrated digital twins for emergent healthcare management at local and city levels: A proof of concept. *Proceedings of the Institute of Civil Engineers: Engineering Sustainability*.

Lu, Q., Ye, Z., Fang, Z., Meng, J., Pitt, M., Lin, J., & Chen, L. (2021, December). Creating an inter-hospital resilient network for pandemic response based on blockchain and dynamic digital twins. In 2021 Winter simulation conference (WSC) (pp. 1-12). IEEE.

Nguyen, T. A. (2023). Blockchain and digital twin for industry 4.0/5.0. *Kenkyu Journal of Nanotechnology & Nanoscience*, *9*, 1–5.

Nguyen, T. A. (2024). Digital twin-based universe (complexiverse): Where real world and virtual/digital world are unified. *Kenkyu Journal of Nanotechnology & Nanoscience*, *10*, 1–4.

Rasel, M., Bommu, R., Shovon, R. B., & Islam, M. A. (2023). Ensuring data security in interoperable EHR systems: Exploring blockchain solutions for healthcare integration. *International Journal of Advanced Engineering Technologies and Innovations*, *1*(1), 212–232.

Rezaee, K., Khosravi, M. R., Attar, H., Menon, V. G., Khan, M. A., Issa, H., & Qi, L. (2023). IoMT-assisted medical vehicle routing based on UAV-Borne human crowd sensing and deep learning in smart cities. *IEEE Internet of Things Journal*, *10*(21), 18529–18536.

Saeed, M. M. A., Saeed, R. A., & Ahmed, Z. E. (2024). *Data security and privacy in the age of AI and digital twins. In digital twin technology and AI implementations in future-focused businesses* (pp. 99–124). IGI Global.

Samantasinghar, S., Mallick, S. R., Mishra, D., Palei, S., Lenka, R. K., & Barik, R. K. (2023). *Secure, reliable and transparent patient-centered health record management framework using blockchain technology*. IEEE CISCT. Available from https://doi.org/10.1109/CISCT57197.2023.10351279.

Singh, D., Monga, S., Tanwar, S., Hong, W. C., Sharma, R., & He, Y. L. (2023). Adoption of blockchain technology in healthcare: Challenges, solutions, and comparisons. *Applied Sciences*, *13*(4), 2380.

Sonkamble, R. G., Bongale, A. M., Phansalkar, S., Sharma, A., & Rajput, S. (2023). Secure data transmission of electronic health records using blockchain technology. *Electronics*, *12*(4), 1015.

Thanalakshmi, P., Rishikhesh, A., Marion Marceline, J., Joshi, G. P., & Cho, W. (2023). A quantum-resistant blockchain system: a comparative analysis. *Mathematics*, *11*(18), 3947.

Vallée, A. (2023). Digital twin for healthcare systems. *Frontiers in Digital Health*, *5*, 1253050.

Vallée, A. (2024). Envisioning the future of personalized medicine: Role and realities of digital twins. *Journal of Medical Internet Research*, *26*, e50204.

Vasiliu-Feltes, I.M., Mylrea, M., Yan Zhang, C., Cohen Wood, T., & Thornley, B. (2023). Impact of blockchain-digital twin technology on precision health, pharmaceutical industry, and life Sciences Conv2X 2023 Report. Blockchain in Healthcare Today. https://doi.org/10.30953/bhty.v6.281.

Wang, G., Wang, Q., & Chen, S. (2023). Exploring blockchains interoperability: A systematic survey. *ACM Computing Surveys*, *55*(13s), 1–38.

Zakzouk, A., El-Sayed, A., & Hemdan, E. E. D. (2023). A blockchain-based electronic medical records management framework in smart healthcare infrastructure. *Multimedia Tools and Applications*, *82*(23), 35419–35437.

Zio, E., & Miqueles, L. (2024). Digital twins in safety analysis, risk assessment and emergency management. *Reliability Engineering & System Safety*, 110040.

CHAPTER

25 Enhancing hospital operations efficiency through digital twin technology

Saroj Koul[1], Vinaytosh Mishra[2] and Ivan W. Taylor[3]

[1]OP Jindal Global University, Haryana, India [2]Gulf Medical University, Ajman, United Arab Emeritus
[3]Policy Dynamics Inc., Ontario, Canada

25.1 Introduction

"Digital twin (DT)" technology is a groundbreaking concept that integrates the physical and virtual worlds through ultra-fidelity models, enabling real-time interaction and data fusion. The concept of "digital twin" was initially coined by Professor Grieves of the University of Michigan in 2003, and it gained widespread recognition when NASA adopted it in 2010. DT technology has since evolved into a critical research area with significant implications across various industries (Bing et al., 2024). The core of DT lies in "its ability to create a virtual counterpart of a physical object or system," facilitating simulation, monitoring, evaluation, prediction, optimization, and control of its real-world counterpart. This is achieved by mapping real-world data to the digital domain, which can be analyzed and used to inform decisions affecting the physical entity (Yao et al., 2023).

DT technology has been employed in numerous fields, such as aerospace, transportation, industrial production, and intelligent education. Its applications range from enhancing the functionality of physical entities to optimizing their performance and extending their lifecycle. DT technology has "a strong correlation and continuity between computer-aided technology, simulation systems, extended reality, metaverse," reflecting its growing complexity and integration with correlated technologies, including "artificial intelligence (AI), the Internet of Things (IoT), and Big Data analytics" (Yao et al., 2023).

Despite its rapid advancement, DT technology faces challenges, including the need for standardized frameworks, interoperability among diverse systems, and ensuring data security. As DT continues to mature, it promises to revolutionize how we interact with and manage physical assets, driving the digital transformation of enterprises and industries (Bing et al., 2024; Yao et al., 2023).

25.1.1 Importance of operational efficiency in hospitals

Operational efficiency in hospitals is a critical factor that directly impacts patient care quality, staff satisfaction, and the financial health of healthcare institutions. It involves optimizing various processes, resources, and workflows to deliver the best healthcare services while minimizing waste

Blockchain and Digital Twin for Smart Hospitals. DOI: https://doi.org/10.1016/B978-0-443-34226-4.00026-5

and reducing costs. The following essential considerations are necessary to grasp the relevance of operational efficiency in hospitals. These include:

1. *Patient care*: Efficient operations ensure patients receive timely and quality care, which is essential for positive health outcomes. Streamlining patient flow, for example, can significantly reduce waiting times and length of hospital stays, enhancing patient satisfaction and outcomes (Al Harbi et al., 2024).
2. *Cost management*: Healthcare costs are a significant concern globally. Hospitals can reduce unnecessary expenses associated with prolonged patient stays or redundant tests by improving operational efficiency, leading to financial savings and sustainability (Al Harbi et al., 2024).
3. *Resource utilization*: Hospitals must manage their resources, including staff, equipment, and space. Operational efficiency helps maximize the use of these resources, ensuring they are available when and where needed, without overuse or underutilization (Berg et al., 2019).
4. *Staff satisfaction*: Efficient hospital operations can alleviate staff workload, prevent burnout, and improve morale. With streamlined processes, staff can focus more on patient care than administrative tasks (Berg et al., 2019).
5. *Adaptability:* In today's rapidly changing healthcare environment, operational efficiency allows hospitals to be more adaptable and responsive to new challenges, such as public health crises or technological advancements (Berg et al., 2019).
6. *Quality improvement*: Operational efficiency is often associated with quality improvement initiatives. By continuously monitoring and enhancing hospital processes, healthcare providers can maintain high standards of care and comply with regulatory requirements (Bhati et al., 2023).

As such, ultimately, operational efficiency encompasses more than simply reducing expenses. It involves establishing a hospital atmosphere that promotes excellent healthcare, guarantees the contentment of patients and staff, and sustains financial stability.

25.1.2 The potential of DTs in healthcare

DTs constitute a significant advancement in medical technology, providing a revolutionary method for patient care and system administration. Creating patient-specific models that predict individual responses to treatments and interventions allows for tailored therapies optimized for each patient's unique physiology, potentially improving outcomes and reducing adverse effects (Balasubhramanyam et al., 2024; Katsoulakis et al., 2024). DTs have the capability to replicate the impact of medications on virtual populations, thereby improving the drug development process. This can lead to a reduction in the requirement for lengthy clinical trials, resulting in time and resource savings while still ensuring the safety and effectiveness of the drugs (Katsoulakis et al., 2024; Raj, 2024). In addition, DTs can optimize workflows, resource allocation, and patient management in hospitals. By simulating different scenarios, healthcare providers can identify the most efficient processes, reducing wait times and improving patient utilization (Balasubhramanyam et al., 2024; Katsoulakis et al., 2024). They offer a secure and efficient environment for medical training. For healthcare professionals who can practice the procedures on virtual patients, gaining experience without the risk of actual patients enhances the learning process and improves medical staff quality (Katsoulakis et al., 2024; Raj, 2024). Using real-time data, DTs can predict patients' future health status or the spread of diseases within a population. This predictive capability is crucial for proactive healthcare management and preparing responses to potential health crises (Katsoulakis et al., 2024; Scott, 2024). Despite their potential, DTs in healthcare face challenges such as data privacy concerns, the need for standardization, and the integration of complex health data.

Addressing these issues is essential for successfully implementing DTs in healthcare systems (Katsoulakis et al., 2024; Scott, 2024). As such, the potential of DTs in healthcare is vast, offering opportunities for enhanced patient care, operational efficiency, and medical education. As technology matures, it is expected to become an integral part of the healthcare landscape, driving innovation and improving health outcomes.

25.2 Understanding digital twins

DT is an advanced virtual representation that precisely depicts "a physical object or system" throughout existence. The system is equipped with up-to-date information and employs sophisticated methods such as "advanced simulation, machine learning, and reasoning approaches" to support decision-making (IBM, 2024). The DT concept is crucial in various industries due to its competence in repeating and forecasting the performance of its physical counterpart, thereby enabling enhancements and innovations in product design and system operations. It is designed to reflect the physical object accurately and can evolve throughout its lifecycle through continuous learning and updating (Juarez et al., 2021). The major components of a DT can be categorized into three main elements: (1) physical object/system (ranging from a simple mechanical component to a complex industrial system or process), (2) the core of digital representation (the virtual model of the physical object generated from various sources such as "computer-aided design (CAD), product lifecycle management (PLM), and other design tools"), and (3) data and communication (relying on operational and experiential data from IoT sensors, real-world telemetry, and other data sources. Subsequently, this data undergoes processing and correlation within an information model, which presents it in a format that is easy for users to understand, such as dashboards or human–machine interfaces (HMIs). This enables the DT to mimic, evaluate, and optimize the performance of the physical entity (IBM, 2024; Juarez et al., 2021).

DTs can vary in complexity and application, ranging from simple component twins representing individual parts to complex system twins encompassing entire systems or processes. The scope of the DT depends on the application's specific requirements (IBM, 2024). DTs are utilized in numerous applications, such as manufacturing, aerospace, automotive, healthcare, and smart cities. They enable businesses and organizations to test scenarios virtually, predict outcomes, improve product quality, and enhance operational efficiency (IBM, 2024). While DTs offer immense potential, they also present challenges, such as the need for large-scale data integration, ensuring data security, and developing standardized frameworks for interoperability. DTs are expected to become increasingly prevalent as technology advances, driving innovation and efficiency across various sectors (Juarez et al., 2021).

25.2.1 Historical development and evolution of DT technology

The history and evolution of DT technology is a fascinating journey that spans several decades. The concept of a DT has its roots in practices from the 1960s. NASA employed fundamental twinning methodologies for space programming, which involved making exact replicas of systems on Earth to mirror those in space. This approach was particularly crucial during the Apollo 13 mission, where a digital twin model on Earth played a vital role in resolving the issue (Bing et al., 2024).

In 1998 the term "digital twin" was coined to refer to a digital reproduction of Alan Alda's voice. In 2002 Michael Grieves, a Professor at the University of Michigan, officially announced the notion of (DTs, which involves the integration of physical space, virtual space, and data communication (Bing et al., 2024; Grieves, 2023). DT technology originated in the mid-2010s and was primarily used for physical industrial items. It eventually grew to encompass a broad range of products and services, extending into the intangible domain of processes and abstract concepts (Grieves, 2023). DT technology is projected to grow significantly in the present decade and beyond. Based on the findings of "Accenture's Technology Trends 2022" study, the global DT market was valued at $3.21 billion in 2020 and is expected to grow to $184.5 billion by 2030 (Accenture Report 2022, 2024). Further advances and more significant uses are anticipated for the future of DT technology.

This evolution will facilitate the transition of work from the physical realm to the virtual realm, substantially impacting efficiency and effectiveness in many industries (Accenture Report 2022, 2024). The historical development of DT technology reflects its evolution from basic twinning concepts employed in space programs to a sophisticated framework that integrates with IoT and other advanced technologies. Its evolution continues to shape how industries operate, offering new opportunities for innovation and efficiency.

Some successful implementations of DT technology in healthcare:

Scientists at Johns Hopkins University have developed a unique DT that accurately depicts the anatomical structure to address heart rhythm issues of a patient's heart. This methodology has been employed to enhance prognostic diagnoses and anticipate the most effective therapeutic strategies for patients (Scott, 2024). Also, DT has been utilized to predict physiological and sociological behaviors, applying more targeted treatments and interventions for improved health outcomes (Scott, 2024). Further, hospitals have used DTs to identify bed shortages, optimize staff schedules, and manage rooms effectively, especially during events like COVID-19 cases or other emergencies (Veluvolu and Raman, 2024). DTs in hospital operations have enabled the development of virtual versions that can be utilized to evaluate and optimize different aspects of healthcare administration, such as bed management and operation room utilization (Botín-Sanabria et al., 2022). These examples highlight the practical applications of DT technology in enhancing hospital operations and patient care. Healthcare providers can create more efficient and responsive healthcare environments using real-time data and predictive analytics.

25.2.2 How DTs work: integration of IoT, AI, and data analytics

Integrating IoT, AI, and data analytics is crucial for the operation of DTs, as it allows them to efficiently handle vast quantities of data and derive insights from it to make well-informed judgments. DTs need real-time data from IoT devices to match the virtual model to reality. Sensors and IoT devices send temperature, pressure, and motion data to the DT for processing (Zayed et al., 2023). IoT data is analyzed using AI and Machine Learning algorithms to identify trends, predict outcomes, and simulate situations. These tools let DTs learn from data, improve predictions, and gain insights (Zayed et al., 2023). Data analytics analyzes data to determine its contents. Data analytics in DTs entails processing and analyzing IoT device data to understand the physical entity's status and anticipate its behavior (El-Agamy et al., 2024). These tools help DTs optimize operations and maintenance schedules, foresee failures, and test changes in a virtual environment before implementing them. This boosts efficiency, lowers downtime, and cuts costs (Luchko, 2024). Despite their potential benefits, IoT, AI, and data analytics in DTs present problems. These include data accuracy, large-scale data management, security, and system integration (Adibi et al., 2024).

As DT technology improves, IoT, AI, and data analytics will be easier to integrate, making DTs more effective. This will likely extend DT adoption across industries and spur innovation (Disrupting The Healthcare Industry Using Digital Twin Technology; Luchko, 2024). The potential benefits of this integration allow IoT, AI, and data analytics to construct accurate and predictive virtual models of physical entities.

25.3 Role of DTs in healthcare

Healthcare systems are inherently complex and challenging to manage. Moreover, healthcare systems have resource constraints and must be managed efficiently to provide quality care at an affordable cost (Balasubhramanyam et al., 2024; Berg et al., 2019; Katsoulakis et al., 2024). Digital technologies can help address the system's complexity but also help provide excellent care without increasing the cost exorbitantly. DTs is one of the digital technologies with great potential for creating operational excellence. These are digital replicas of physical systems that have been processed (Berg et al., 2019; Scott, 2024). It can be found very useful in healthcare operations management (Botín-Sanabria et al., 2022; Veluvolu and Raman, 2024). Some specific applications of the DTs in healthcare operations management are (1) remote patient monitoring, (2) precision medicine, (3) training of employees, (4) facility management and total preventive maintenance, (5) clinical trials and drug developments, and (6) emergency response and disaster management. DTs have transformative potential in improving availability, affordability, accessibility, and quality of care. DTs can also help us support advanced medical research and reduce the use of humans or animals in clinical trials. The main applications of DT are summarized in Fig. 25.1.

DTs can be built for patients, systems, processes, and policies for their continuous simulations. These digital replicas of physical systems help a care provider provide a personalized treatment plan, monitor systems and processes, and test policies before implementation. With ubiquitous technologies such as the IoT, wireless devices, wearable devices, and electronic health records (EHRs) generating data every passing second, we can sit on the plethora of unutilized data and be ready to tell us some information about the physical systems (Bruynseels et al., 2018). This data can help us create DTs for physical systems. In addition, digital biomarkers can be utilized to create a DT for the patient and can be used by doctors to customize the treatment plan. In addition, DTs of a patient can provide a realistic simulation environment, enabling surgeons to practice and refine their techniques before the surgery (Coles et al., 2010).

Similarly, DTs can be used to model and simulate hospital processes. This simulation can help hospital administrators identify bottlenecks, improve resource allocation, and enhance efficiency (Kritzinger et al., 2018). DTs can monitor systems, plan predictive maintenance, and optimize

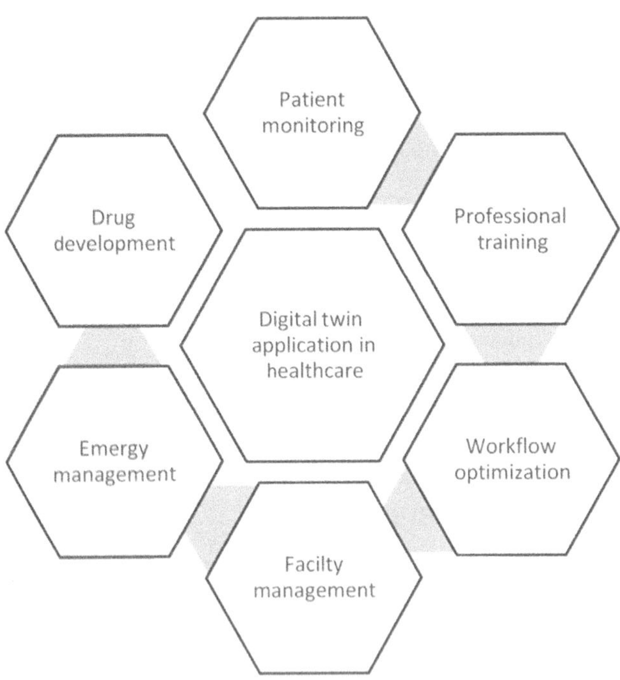

FIGURE 25.1

Application of DTs in healthcare.

resource allocation (Fuller et al., 2020). As discussed earlier, DTs can be used in simulating the effect of drugs on the patient population. This can help reduce the cost of conducting clinical trials and using humans and animals in the experiments (Björnsson et al., 2020). DTs can be utilized in emergency scenarios to simulate hospital reactions, forecast the effects of calamities, and enhance emergency preparations to guarantee prompt and efficient reactions (Negri et al., 2017).

DTs help healthcare institutions streamline procedures, enhance patient care, and save operating expenses by giving them a complete and dynamic picture of hospital operations. Next, this section discusses the implementation of DTs in a hospital and illustrates it using an example from Orion Hospital. The case study demonstrates the insight from interviews with different hospital administrators. It also depicts the transformative potential of DTs in healthcare operations management, aiming to leverage DTs for operational excellence.

Case Study: Orion Hospital (Pvt.) Ltd.

Orion Hospital is renowned for its dedication to using cutting-edge technologies to enhance patient outcomes and operational effectiveness in its daily operations. Orion Hospital started a project in 2022 to integrate DTs into all aspects of its business. Optimizing patient flow, improving resource allocation, implementing predictive maintenance for essential equipment to avoid downtime, and optimizing energy use throughout the facility were the main goals.

(Continued)

(Continued)

The first stage of the implementation consisted of merging data from several sources, such as EHRs, IoT devices, building management systems, and historical operational data. This data is necessary for the building of an accurate decision tree. Subsequently, DTs were generated for essential hospital resources and operations, including patient flow, resource allocation, and building energy models. The DTs were utilized to simulate multiple scenarios and analyze their impact on hospital operations. One such scenario involved patient flow simulations, which helped identify bottlenecks in the admissions process. Due to the connection between the DTs and real-time data streams, operational adjustments could be made dynamically and ongoing monitoring could occur. The utilization of DT predictive analytics allowed for the anticipating of equipment malfunctions and the improvement of maintenance programs.

The integration of DTs at Orion Hospital led to substantial enhancements in multiple facets of operations management. The implementation of measures to decrease patient wait times in the emergency department resulted in a 30% reduction, thereby leading to an increase in patient satisfaction. The hospital experienced a 20% surge in patient throughput, enabling them to attend to more patients efficiently. Optimal staffing levels were implemented, resulting in a 15% reduction in overtime expenses while ensuring exceptional patient care. The utilization of equipment was optimized, hence mitigating excessive usage of specific machinery and minimizing the occurrence of wear and tear. By implementing predictive maintenance, the amount of time that equipment was out of service was decreased by 25%, guaranteeing that essential devices were consistently accessible when required. Timely interventions and prevention of catastrophic equipment failures resulted in a 20% reduction in maintenance expenses. Energy use was optimized, resulting in a 10% decrease in energy expenses. During the procedure, the hospital managed to decrease its carbon footprint significantly.

Although the DTs yielded positive results, their implementation encountered numerous obstacles. Combining data from many sources necessitated substantial exertion and the implementation of robust data management methodologies. Training was necessary for the staff to adjust to new processes and technology, and it was essential to have efficient communication and training programs. The DT models required regular updates and enhancements to represent evolving hospital dynamics accurately and include new data inputs.

Note: For the case study, the authors used expert unstructured interviews with various hospitals in India.

25.3.1 Building DTs for hospital operations

Developing a DT for hospital operations involves a systematic approach to ensure accurate representation and effective integration into existing systems (Marmolejo-Saucedo, 2020; Segovia and Garcia-Alfaro, 2022; Tao and Qi, 2019). The recommended approach consists of the following six steps:

Table 25.1 outlines a six-step process for developing a DT, detailing the activities involved in each step. The first step is defining the objective and scope of the project, which includes clearly defining the goals and boundaries. The second step involves identifying data sources, collecting data, and cleaning the data for further use. The third step includes the development of the model and further validating real-world data. The fourth step provides for integrating DTs into legacy systems, which rely on real-time data feed for continuous use. The fifth step involves the simulation of DTs and analyzing the results for effective decision-making in hospital operations. The insights mainly include identifying bottlenecks and inefficiencies in the decision-making of hospital administrators. Finally, the sixth step involves reaping the benefit of DTs and continuous monitoring.

25.3.2 DT using system dynamics model

DTs can be developed using various modeling techniques, and the selection of these techniques depends on the system's complexity and desired accuracy (Ghadge et al., 2013). The breadth of

Table 25.1 Six-step process for developing a digital twin.

Steps	Description of step	Activities of steps
Step 1	Defining objective and scope	• Define the objective of the process • Define the scope of the process
Step 2	Data collection	• Identify data sources • Data acquisition • Data cleaning and preparation
Step 3	Model development	• Create baseline models • Validate models
Step 4	System integration	• Integrate with existing systems • Real-time data feeds
Step 5	Simulation and analysis	• Run simulations • Predictive analytics
Step 6	Implementation and monitoring	• Deploy the DT • Continuous monitoring

modeling techniques can span from basic linear regression to intricate agent-based simulations of the complete system. To illustrate, a basic linear regression technique can be employed to forecast the duration patients have to wait; however, to replicate the entirety of hospital operations, we want comprehensive models that incorporate several simulation methods on a wide scale. These intricate models have the ability to simulate different situations by integrating real-time data to dynamically adapt and optimize hospital operations, forecast future problems, and enhance decision-making processes. Commonly employed techniques encompass "discrete event simulation (DES), agent-based simulation (ABS), and system dynamics modeling (SDM)."

DES approach models system operations as a series of discrete events, each occurring at a particular time. This method is especially valuable for examining processes in which the time and order of occurrences are critical, such as the movement of patients through several hospital departments or the arrangement of medical treatments (Vázquez-Serrano et al., 2021). The ABS approach model focuses on modeling the interactions of individual agents, which can be patients, staff, or medical devices, within the system. This modeling approach employs a set of rules and behaviors for each agent, enabling the simulation to accurately depict intricate interactions and emergent events resulting from these interactions (Cuevas, 2020). This approach is optimal for comprehending the influence of individual activities and interactions on the overall functioning of a system, such as the transmission of infections within a hospital.

The approach discussed in this chapter for modeling the system is SDM. This approach uses differential equations to model the system's continuous feedback loops and accumulations (Liu et al., 2020). This approach is advantageous for capturing the long-term dynamics of intricate systems and comprehending the interplay between many components over time. It is highly efficient for strategic planning and policy analysis, specifically in examining the effects of resource allocation decisions on patient outcomes and hospital efficiency (Malakoane et al., 2020).

The selection of the modeling approach and level of complexity is contingent upon the objectives of the DT project, the accessible data, and the degree of precision necessary to attain reliable and valuable simulations. Hospitals can better understand their operations, pinpoint areas for enhancement, and improve overall efficiency and patient care by utilizing these sophisticated modeling tools.

Case Study: Digital Twins for Public Health.

This case study illustrates how SDM can create a DT for diabetes management (Coyle, 1997). The DT developed in this study can be used for public health decision-making. The case study utilizes the six-step process depicted in Table 25.1.

SDM is an approach that helps us understand complex systems' underlying behavior over time (Barlas, 1996; Homer and Hirsch, 2006). The main components of SDM (Senge and Forrester, 1980) include the following:

- *Stocks (levels):* These are the accumulations in the system. Examples include population, capital, and inventory.
- *Flows (rates):* These represent the rates at which stocks change over time. For example, birth and death rates change the population stock.
- *Feedback loops*: These loops can either be encouraging, also known as positive feedback, or balanced, often known as negative feedback. They play a vital role in influencing the behavior of the system.
- *Time delays*: These account for the time lag between actions and their effects on the system.

The model developer or researchers at the helm of developing DT can use established methods, such as Euler's method, for solving the system's differential equations over time, which can be represented by Eq. (25.1):

$$\text{Stock}_{\text{final}} = \text{Stock}_{\text{initial}} + \int_0^T (\text{inflow}(t) - \text{outflow}(t))dt \tag{25.1}$$

While flows are represented by the first degree of differentiation of stocks (S) given by Eq. (25.2):

$$\frac{d(S)}{d(t)} = \text{inflow}(t) - \text{outflow}(t) \tag{25.2}$$

The model can be calibrated based on the data available in different reports and publications of the International Diabetes Federation (Senge and Forrester, 1980). The steps used in SDM for DT in this case study can be summarized as follows:

1. *Problem definition*: Clearly define the problem you want to address, including its scope and boundaries.
2. *Conceptualization*: Identify the key variables and their relationships influencing the system's behavior. This usually involves creating causal loop diagrams to visualize how variables affect each other (Barlas, 1996; Homer and Hirsch, 2006).
3. *Formulating a dynamic hypothesis*: Develop hypotheses about the cause-and-effect relationships within the system (Barlas, 1996; Homer and Hirsch, 2006).
4. *Developing a simulation model*: Converts the conceptual model into a quantitative simulation model using stocks (accumulations) and flows (changes) to represent the relationships among variables over time (Barlas, 1996; Homer and Hirsch, 2006).
5. *Calibration*: Rigorously test the model to ensure it accurately represents the real system (Brailsford et al., 2009; Diabetes Atlas, 2024).
6. *Real-time data integration*: Identify data sources and integrate the model with real-time data. There should be an attempt to minimize the latency in the data so that DTs are a better representation of the real policy environment.

The model developed in this study can simulate the baseline behavior and be utilized to evaluate policy interventions before implementing them. The *stock and flow* diagram contains five stocks: the youthful population, the population without diabetes, the population with diabetes onset, and people with diagnosed and undiagnosed diabetes. The model has different auxiliary variables that affect the growth of these stocks. The model is in Fig. 25.2.

(*Continued*)

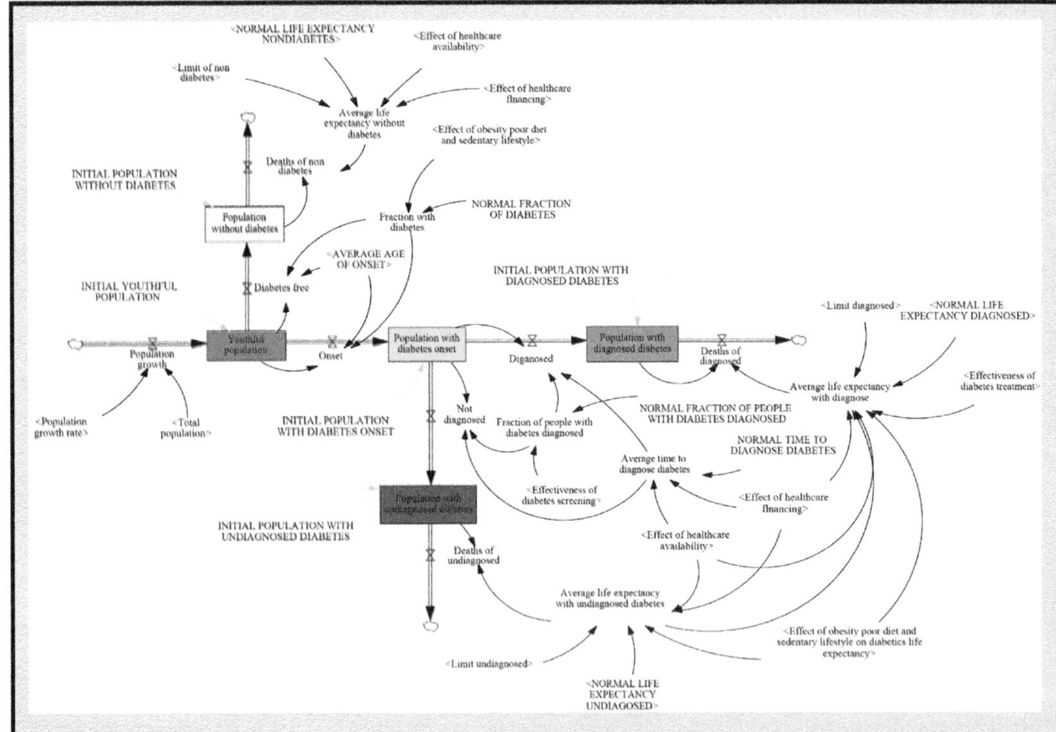

FIGURE 25.2

DTs for diabetes management using SDM.

The *stock and flow* diagram acts as DTs of the policy environment for diabetes management in India. The SDM can help decision-makers make informed decisions about public health policies. The model's accuracy depends on its complexity and the input data. A tradeoff between complexity and resources is always required to develop a DT using the SDM. After a certain level, the complexity often results in diminishing returns.

Note: The DT using SDM is based on the focus group involving practitioners and policymakers working in diabetes management.

25.4 Benefits, policies, and challenges of DTs in hospital operations

The concept of DTs, which has witnessed a recent surge in the healthcare industry, promises to transform the entire healthcare system (Katsoulakis et al., 2024). A summary of the significant benefits (Adibi et al., 2024; Armeni et al., 2022; Diabetes Atlas, 2024; Ghatti et al., 2023; Katsoulakis et al., 2024; Malakoane et al., 2020) include:

- *Patient-specific models for diagnosis and treatment planning*: These are utilized for diagnosis and treatment planning. These models can simulate the patient's health condition, forecast disease advancement, and optimize the treatment plan. This customized technique can significantly enhance patient results.

- *Optimization of resource allocation and workflow processes*: The optimization of resource allocation and workflow processes in a hospital is achieved by offering a real time, all-encompassing perspective of the operations. This enables healthcare providers to identify areas where patient flow is hindered, anticipate patient demand, and adjust staffing levels. As a result, resource allocation and workflow processes are optimized, leading to enhanced efficiency and patient care.
- *Disease detection and predicting disease spread:* To identify diseases, forecast the spread of diseases, make necessary arrangements in hospitals for anticipated outbreaks, and efficiently distribute resources.
- *Biomanufacturing and pharmaceutical industry processes*: DTs can simulate and analyze multiple scenarios to enhance the biomanufacturing and pharmaceutical industry processes, which can assist in making more informed decisions. Also, machine learning algorithms, data creation, and system modeling have the capability to evaluate vast quantities of data and offer predictive insights to facilitate decision-making.

As such, DTs in healthcare can be leveraged through various policies and strategies to optimize hospital operations. Some of the salient policies include

1. *Resource optimization:* Policies to predict demand surges in allocating adequate resources and improve bed management, staff scheduling and operation room utilization.
2. *Risk management*: DTs enable "dry runs" of new workflows, layouts, and policies without disrupting physical facilities, minimizing the risk of changing a complex system.
3. *Staff training:* High-fidelity facility replicas can conduct immersive training simulations for clinicians in various scenarios, enhancing the healthcare staff's skills and improving patient care.
4. *Enhanced decision-making and operations*: DTs can test interventions before costly infrastructural implementations, enhancing decision-making capabilities.
5. *Preparing for unusual catastrophic events*: DTs can help prepare for unusual catastrophic events by identifying flow and blockages to ensure the hospital is well-prepared for emergencies.
6. *Enterprise-wide DTs*: Organizations can create enterprise-wide DTs of healthcare facilities, resulting in significant operational benefits. For example, hospital DTs can identify bed shortages, manage staff schedules, determine the spread of germs, and more.

These policies demonstrate the capacity of DTs to increase healthcare delivery, boost patient well-being, and optimize hospital operations (Katsoulakis et al., 2024). However, it is crucial to note that these policies come with challenges and should be implemented considering the privacy concerns and data protection, which remain vital while applying DT technology in healthcare (Katsoulakis et al., 2024; Malakoane et al., 2020). As technology evolves, DTs are projected to play an increasingly important role in healthcare (Diabetes Atlas, 2024).

25.4.1 Implementation challenges and solutions

DTs have many positive implications for healthcare operations management but have technical and organizational challenges. Some of the technological difficulties include ensuring data security, addressing privacy concerns, and resolving interoperability issues. Given the sensitive nature of the information, it is important to prioritize the protection and privacy of patient data (Armeni et al., 2022). Interoperability challenges develop due to integrating diverse systems and technologies, which can be intricate and demanding regarding resources (Shahzad et al., 2022).

Organizational issues encompass staff training, change management, and stakeholder engagement. Efficient staff training programs provide healthcare workers with the expertise to employ DT technologies (Perno et al., 2022). Effective change management addresses opposition and ensures a seamless transition to new workflows and processes (Van der Aalst et al., 2021). It is crucial to involve stakeholders, such as patients, healthcare providers, and technology vendors, to achieve agreement and assistance for adopting DTs. Table 25.2 outlines the primary issues when using DTs in healthcare.

To address these technical and organizational issues, decision-makers can implement best practices and solutions that have been successfully implemented. Also, to strengthen data security and system integration, addressing technical concerns, using robust data encryption methods,

Table 25.2 Top challenges for implementing DTs in healthcare.

Top challenges	Explanation	Source
Data privacy	Integrating DT often involves using sensitive medical information, which raises concerns about data confidentiality.	Armeni et al., (2022), Katsoulakis et al. (2024)
Standards	Universal standards are necessary to ensure the seamless integration and utilization of digital technologies in the healthcare sector.	Katsoulakis et al. (2024)
Accessibility	Ensuring fair and equal access to the advantages of DT technologies is a substantial task.	Katsoulakis et al. (2024)
Technical challenges	The intricacy of healthcare data and the requirement for advanced AI applications pose technological obstacles.	Armeni et al. (2022)
Regulatory challenges	Regulatory monitoring governs the use of DTs in healthcare, presenting potential obstacles.	Bhati et al. (2023), Katsoulakis et al. (2024)
Ethical challenges	There can be ethical concerns, especially when it comes to the utilization of personal health information.	Katsoulakis et al. (2024)
Integration with AI	The successful use of DTs in healthcare is strongly dependent on the seamless integration of AI applications, which can be intricate.	Armeni et al. (2022), Zayed et al. (2023)
Data management	Effectively handling the substantial amounts of data produced by digital technologies is a notable obstacle.	Armeni et al. (2022)
Real-time analysis	DTs aim to replicate real-life systems in real time and offer anticipatory analysis, necessitating the use of sophisticated modeling, Machine Learning, and reasoning techniques.	Turab and Jamil (2023)
Interoperability	It is essential to guarantee that DTs can efficiently engage with other systems in the healthcare setting.	Iqbal et al. (2023)

conducting frequent security audits, and embracing interoperable standards are advisable (Hussain, 2023). To address organizational challenges, implementing thorough training programs, employing effective communication methods, and engaging stakeholders early in planning can help reduce resistance and foster a cooperative atmosphere (Wurm et al., 2023). To fully exploit the promise of DTs in revolutionizing healthcare operations, it is necessary to address these difficulties with specific and focused solutions.

25.5 Future trends and innovations

DTs in healthcare refer to computer-generated representations of products that replicate their information model, action, interaction processes, and products (Feng et al., 2021). They are designed to enhance healthcare organizations and address the limitations associated with this advanced technology. The primary functions of DTs in healthcare systems include overseeing health management and promoting wellness, managing operations, handling information, and ensuring safety. They have the ability to avert harm to the patient while delivering care and tackling systemic challenges presented by crises. Furthermore, DTs ensure that all parties involved have the ability to obtain up-to-date data and maintain confidentiality within the healthcare sector. They improve self-care by facilitating healthcare practices and promoting greater system efficiency, guaranteeing that healthcare facilities operate effectively and deliver high-quality care to every patient (Feng et al., 2021).

However, challenges associated with data security, accuracy, and ethical concerns must be addressed as technology evolves (Bordegoni and Ferrise, 2023). Advancements in noninvasive and high-throughput data collecting and improvements in modeling and processing capacity will play a vital role in enhancing DT systems (Veluvolu and Raman, 2024). DTs promise to transform healthcare, driving advancements in precision medicine, treatment personalization, and medical research (Bordegoni and Ferrise, 2023). As we embrace the dawn of Health 4.0, the digital transformation of healthcare, DTs will play a pivotal role (Wickramasinghe, 2022).

25.5.1 Expanding applications: from operational efficiency to patient-specific treatment plans

Operational efficiency in healthcare entails the intelligent allocation of resources and the optimization of procedures and workflows to decrease expenses, better patient outcomes, and improve the overall patient experience (Meijer et al., 2023). Integrating DTs in healthcare operations has improved patient care and operational efficiency. It can analyze complex medical imaging with a precision that rivals human experts, offering diagnostic and treatment recommendations based on patient data analysis (Kaul et al., 2023). Predictive analytics tools facilitate resource allocation and preventive healthcare planning by predicting patient admission rates, potential disease outbreaks, and the likelihood of patient readmission (Kaul et al., 2023).

The transition from operational efficiency to patient-specific treatment plans involves utilizing detailed patient data to devise personalized treatment strategies (Del Giorgio Solfa and Simonato, 2023). Through the analysis of longitudinal patient data, healthcare providers can identify individuals at a heightened risk, take preemptive measures, and customize treatment approaches to suit the specific needs of each patient. This strategy enhances patient results and decreases healthcare expenses by limiting hospital admissions (Joshi et al., 2022). The incorporation of AI into healthcare operations can have a substantial positive impact on treatment outcomes and patient satisfaction while also leading to cost reduction (Kaul et al., 2023). Technology will become increasingly crucial in transforming healthcare from operational efficiency to patient-specific treatment plans (Del Giorgio Solfa and Simonato, 2023; Joshi et al., 2022).

25.5.2 Ethical considerations and the future of digital health

The implementation of digital health technologies revolutionizes healthcare systems globally, facilitating improvements in population health outcomes. It is imperative to embrace an equitable methodology. Critical ethical considerations for the future of digital health include the following: (1) ensuring widespread digital literacy and access through the thoughtful design of digital health interventions to promote health equity among all population groups (Feng and Ali, 2024); (2) providing accurate information to end users and obtaining their fully informed consent, while upholding principles of dignity, fairness, and secure storage, access, sharing, and data ownership (Feng and Ali, 2024); (3) adopting evidence-based principles, methods, and processes to anticipate and address the ethical impacts of digital health responsibly (Johnson et al., 2022); (4) striking a balance between leveraging innovation and controlling potential adverse effects, while also understanding the challenges associated with user acceptance and the use of digital health in a novel environment (Brall et al., 2019). These examples demonstrate the intricate nature of ethical dilemmas in digital health and emphasize the necessity for continuous ethical examination as these technologies progress (Maeckelberghe et al., 2023).

25.6 Conclusion

For evidence-based management in healthcare, managers rely on historical data. In dynamic business environments, this strategy may be flawed and less effective. DTs are one of the technologies that can help us simulate the business environment and make informed decisions. The chapter discusses the role of efficiency in healthcare operations. It first introduced the DT, their evolution and factors affecting their exponential growth. The chapter further discusses the role of DTs in achieving operational excellence in healthcare.

Moreover, based on a discussion with hospital administrators taken up as a case study, the article illustrates the benefits of DTs using a hypothetical case from Orion Hospital. Next, this chapter discussed the six-step approach for developing DTs and the challenges of implementing it in a healthcare organization. The article discussed various simulation techniques helpful in creating DTs and their advantages and disadvantages. Finally, the article illustrated a DT using system dynamics modeling for public health decision-making. Finally, the article discussed future innovation in the field and ethical considerations.

This chapter has implications for theory as well as practice. First, it maps the capabilities of DTs with the excellence of operations in healthcare and provides a six-step approach for implementing DTs. Similarly, the chapter has two implications for practice. It uses a case study approach to implement DTs in a hospital and highlights its benefits using a case study. Second, this chapter illustrated the development of DTs for decision-making in diabetes management. The chapter also highlights the challenges and ethical issues of implementing DTs in healthcare settings. The findings of the chapter are helpful for healthcare administrators as well as policymakers.

SDS Model Developed in: https://vensim.com/

Calibrated SDS Model: https://github.com/vinaytosh/diabetesSDmodel

Data Availability: The model was validated using data for 2022–23 from Diabetes Atlas (n.d.), published by the International Diabetes Federation. All the data sources are listed in the reference section accessed on March 1, 2024.

References

Van der Aalst, W. M., Hinz, O., & Weinhardt, C. (2021). Resilient digital twins: Organizations need to prepare for the unexpected. *Business & Information Systems Engineering*, 1–5.

Accenture Report 2022. (April 11, 2024). Retrieved from https://www.accenture.com/us-en/insights/health/mirrored-world.

Adibi, S., Rajabifard, A., Shojaei, D., & Wickramasinghe, N. (2024). Enhancing healthcare through sensor-enabled digital twins in smart environments: A comprehensive analysis. *Sensors*, *24*(9), 2793.

Al Harbi, S., Aljohani, B., Elmasry, L., Baldovino, F. L., Raviz, K. B., Altowairqi, L., & Alshlowi, S. (2024). Streamlining patient flow and enhancing operational efficiency through case management implementation. *BMJ Open Quality*, *13*(1), e002484.

Armeni, P., Polat, I., De Rossi, L. M., Diaferia, L., Meregalli, S., & Gatti, A. (2022). Digital twins in healthcare: Is it the beginning of a new era of evidence-based medicine? A critical review. *Journal of Personalized Medicine*, *12*(8), 1255.

Balasubhramanyam, A., Ramesh, R., Sudheer, R., & Honnavalli, P.B. (2024 May 13). Revolutionizing healthcare: A review unveiling the transformative power of digital twins. IEEE Access.

Barlas, Y. (1996). Formal aspects of model validity and validation in system dynamics. *System Dynamics Review: The Journal of the System Dynamics Society*, *12*(3), 183–210.

Berg, B., Longley, G., & Dunitz, J. (2019). Improving clinic operational efficiency and utilization with RTLS. *Journal of Medical Systems*, *43*(3), 56.

Bhati, D., Deogade, M. S., & Kanyal, D. (2023). Improving patient outcomes through effective hospital administration: A comprehensive review. *Cureus*, *15*(10).

Bing, Z., Enyan, M., Amu-Darko, J. N. O., et al. (2024). Digital twin on concepts, enabling technologies, and applications. *Journal of Brazilian Society Mechanical Sciences and Engineering.*, *46*, 420. Available from https://doi.org/10.1007/s40430-024-04973-0.

Björnsson, B., Borrebaeck, C., Elander, N., Gasslander, T., Gawel, D. R., Gustafsson, M., Jörnsten, R., Lee, E. J., Li, X., Lilja, S., & Martínez-Enguita, D. (2020). Digital twins to personalize medicine. *Genome Medicine*, *12*, 1–4.

Bordegoni, M., & Ferrise, F. (2023). Exploring the intersection of metaverse, digital twins, and artificial intelligence in training and maintenance. *Journal of Computing and Information Science in Engineering*, *23*(6)060806.

Botín-Sanabria, D. M., Mihaita, A. S., Peimbert-García, R. E., Ramírez-Moreno, M. A., Ramírez-Mendoza, R. A., & Lozoya-Santos, J. D. (2022). Digital twin technology challenges and applications: A comprehensive review. *Remote Sensing*, *14*(6), 1335.

Brailsford, S. C., Harper, P. R., Patel, B., & Pitt, M. (2009). An analysis of the academic literature on simulation and modelling in health care. *Journal of Simulation* (3), 130–140.

Brall, C., Schröder-Bäck, P., & Maeckelberghe, E. (2019). Ethical aspects of digital health from a justice point of view. *European Journal of Public Health*, *29*(Supplement_3), 18–22.

Bruynseels, K., Santoni de Sio, F., & Van den Hoven, J. (2018). Digital twins in health care: Ethical implications of an emerging engineering paradigm. *Frontiers in genetics*, *9*, 320848.

Coles, T. R., Meglan, D., & John, N. W. (2010). The role of haptics in medical training simulators: A survey of the state of the art. *IEEE Transactions on Haptics*, *4*(1), 51–66.

Coyle, R. G. (1997). System dynamics modelling: A practical approach. *Journal of the Operational Research Society*, *48*(5), 544, -544.

Cuevas, E. (2020). An agent-based model to evaluate the COVID-19 transmission risks in facilities. *Computers in Biology and Medicine*, *121*103827.

Diabetes Atlas. (2024). International Diabetes Federation. Available at: <https://diabetesatlas.org/2022-reports/ > Accessed 11.04.24.

Disrupting The Healthcare Industry Using Digital Twin Technology. <https://www.challenge.org/insights/digital-twin-in-healthcare/>.

El-Agamy, R. F., Sayed, H. A., AL Akhatatneh, A. M., Aljohani, M., & Elhosseini, M. (2024). Comprehensive analysis of digital twins in smart cities: A 4200-paper bibliometric study. *Artificial Intelligence Review*, *57*(6), 154.

Feng, C., & Ali, D. A. (2024). Leveraging digital transformation and ERP for enhanced operational efficiency in manufacturing enterprises. *Journal of Law and Sustainable Development*, *12*(3), e2455.

Feng, H., Chen, D., & Lv, H. (2021). Sensible and secure IoT communication for digital, cyber, and web twins. *Internet of Things and Cyber-Physical Systems*, *1*(1), 34–44.

Fuller, A., Fan, Z., Day, C., & Barlow, C. (2020). Digital twin: Enabling technologies, challenges, and open research. *IEEE Access*, *8*, 108952–108971.

Ghadge, A., Dani, S., Chester, M., & Kalawsky, R. (2013). A systems approach for modelling supply chain risks. *Supply Chain Management: An International Journal*, *18*(5), 523–538.

Ghatti, S., Yurish, L. A., Shen, H., Rheuban, K., Enfield, K. B., Facteau, N. R., Engel, G., & Dowdell, K. (2023). Digital twins in healthcare: A survey of current methods. *Archives of Clinical and Biomedical Research*, *7*(3), 365–381.

Del Giorgio Solfa, F., & Simonato, F. R. (2023). Big data analytics in healthcare: Exploring the role of machine learning in predicting patient outcomes and improving healthcare delivery. *International Journal of Computations, Information and Manufacturing (IJCIM)*, *3*.

Grieves, M. W. (2023). *Digital twins: Past, present, and future. The digital twin* (pp. 97–121). Cham: Springer International Publishing.

Homer, J. B., & Hirsch, G. B. (2006). System dynamics modeling for public health: Background and opportunities. *American Journal of Public Health*, *96*(3), 452–458.

Hussain, R. (2023). *Towards healthcare digital twin architecture. In international conference on business informatics research* (pp. 45–60). Cham: Springer Nature Switzerland.

IBM. (April 11, 2024) What is a digital twin? Retrieved from https://www.ibm.com/topics/what-is-a-digital-twin.

Iqbal, M., Suhail, S., Matulevičius, R., & Hussain, R. (2023). *Towards healthcare digital twin architecture. InInternational conference on business informatics research* (pp. 45–60). Cham: Springer Nature Switzerland.

Johnson, M., Albizri, A., & Simsek, S. (2022). Artificial intelligence in healthcare operations to enhance treatment outcomes: A framework to predict lung cancer prognosis. *Annals of Operations Research*, *308* (1), 275–305.

Joshi, S., Sharma, M., Das, R. P., Rosak-Szyrocka, J., Żywiołek, J., Muduli, K., & Prasad, M. (2022). Modeling conceptual framework for implementing barriers of AI in public healthcare for improving operational excellence: Experiences from developing countries. *Sustainability*, *14*(18), 11698.

Juarez, M. G., Botti, V. J., & Giret, A. S. (2021). Digital twins: Review and challenges. *Journal of Computing and Information Science in Engineering*, *21*(3)030802.

Katsoulakis, E., Wang, Q., Wu, H., Shahriyari, L., Fletcher, R., Liu, J., Achenie, L., Liu, H., Jackson, P., Xiao, Y., & Syeda-Mahmood, T. (2024). Digital twins for health: A scoping review. *npj Digital Medicine*, *7*(1), 77.

Kaul, R., Ossai, C., Forkan, A. R., Jayaraman, P. P., Zelcer, J., Vaughan, S., & Wickramasinghe, N. (2023). The role of AI for developing digital twins in healthcare: The case of cancer care. *Wiley Interdisciplinary Reviews: Data Mining and Knowledge Discovery*, *13*(1)e1480.

Kritzinger, W., Karner, M., Traar, G., Henjes, J., & Sihn, W. (2018). Digital twin in manufacturing: A categorical literature review and classification. *Ifac-PapersOnline*, *51*(11), 1016–1022.

Liu, J., Liu, Y., & Wang, X. (2020). An environmental assessment model of construction and demolition waste based on: A case study in Guangzhou. *Environmental Science and Pollution Research*, *27*, 37237–37259.

Luchko, N. (April 11, 2024). The benefits & challenges of integrating digital twins with IoT. Tech-Stack. (2023 May 24). Retrieved from https://tech-stack.com/blog/the-benefits-challenges-of-integrating-digital-twins-with-iot/.

Maeckelberghe, E., Zdunek, K., Marceglia, S., Farsides, B., & Rigby, M. (2023). The ethical challenges of personalized digital health. *Frontiers in Medicine*, *10*1123863.

Malakoane, B., Heunis, J. C., Chikobvu, P., Kigozi, N. G., & Kruger, W. H. (2020). Public health system challenges in the Free State, South Africa: A situation appraisal to inform health system strengthening. *BMC Health Services Research*, *20*, 1–4.

Marmolejo-Saucedo, J. A. (2020). Design and development of digital twins: A case study in supply chains. *Mobile Networks and Applications*, *25*(6), 2141–2160.

Meijer, C., Uh, H. W., & El Bouhaddani, S. (2023). Digital twins in healthcare: Methodological challenges and opportunities. *Journal of Personalized Medicine*, *13*(10), 1522.

Negri, E., Fumagalli, L., & Macchi, M. (2017). A review of the role of digital twins in CPS-based production systems. *Procedia Manufacturing*, *11*, 939–948.

Perno, M., Hvam, L., & Haug, A. (2022). Implementation of digital twins in the process industry: A systematic literature review of enablers and barriers. *Computers in Industry*, *134*103558.

Raj, G. (2024). Unlocking the potential of digital twins in healthcare: Benefits and challenges. Retrieved from https://www.rootsanalysis.com/blog/ (April 11, 2024).

Scott, J. (2024). What are digital twins and how can they be used in healthcare? HealthTech magazine. Retrieved from https://healthtechmagazine.net/article/2024/01/what-are-digital-twins-and-how-can-they-be-used-healthcare (April 11, 2024).

Segovia, M., & Garcia-Alfaro, J. (2022). Design, modeling, and implementation of digital twins. *Sensors*, *22*(14), 5396.

Senge, P. M., & Forrester, J. W. (1980). Tests for building confidence in system dynamics models. System dynamics. *TIMS Studies in Management Sciences*, *14*, 209–228.

Shahzad, M., Shafiq, M. T., Douglas, D., & Kassem, M. (2022). Digital twins in built environments: An investigation of the characteristics, applications, and challenges. *Buildings*, *12*(2), 120.

Tao, F., & Qi, Q. (2019). Make more digital twins. *Nature*, *573*(7775), 490–491.

Turab, M., & Jamil, S. (2023). A comprehensive survey of digital twins in healthcare in the era of metaverse. *BioMedInformatics*, *3*(3), 563–584.

Veluvolu, K. C., & Raman, R. (2024). An insight in the future of healthcare: Integrating digital twin for personalized medicine. *Health and Technology*, 1–3.

Vázquez-Serrano, J. I., Peimbert-García, R. E., & Cárdenas-Barrón, L. E. (2021). Discrete-event simulation modelling in healthcare: A comprehensive review. *International Journal of Environmental Research and Public Health*, *18*(22), 12262.

Wickramasinghe, N. (2022). *The case for digital twins in healthcare. Digital disruption in healthcare* (pp. 59–65). Cham: Springer International Publishing.

Wurm, B., Becker, M., Pentland, B. T., Lyytinen, K., Weber, B., Grisold, T., Mendling, J., & Kremser, W. (2023). Digital twins of organizations: A socio-technical view on challenges and opportunities for future research. *Communications of the Association for Information Systems*, *52*(1)), 552–565.

Yao, J. F., Yang, Y., Wang, X. C., & Zhang, X. P. (2023). Systematic review of digital twin technology and applications. *Visual Computing for Industry, Biomedicine, and Art*, *6*(1), 10.

Zayed, S. M., Attiya, G. M., El-Sayed, A., & Hemdan, E. E. (2023). A review study on digital twins with artificial intelligence and internet of things: Concepts, opportunities, challenges, tools and future scope. *Multimedia Tools and Applications*, *82*(30), 47081–47107.

Index

Note: Page numbers followed by "*f*" indicate figures, "*t*" indicate tables, and "*b*" indicate boxes

B

E

F

G

H

I

S

T

Z

Printed and bound by CPI Group (UK) Ltd, Croydon, CR0 4YY
13/06/2025
01900651-0016